The rough guide to

CHINA

Researched and written by

CATHARINE SANDERS, CHRIS STEWART AND RHONDA EVANS

with
Harvey Woolfe, Alisa Joyce, Sandy Ball,
Alison Williams and Jack Holland

Contributing Editors
Kay Marles and Jackie Jones

Edited by

JOHN FISHER, MARTIN DUNFORD and MARK ELLINGHAM
with
CATHARINE SANDERS and CHRIS STEWART

Routledge & Kegan Paul
London and New York

Acknowledgments

The **editors** would like to acknowledge considerable help from Kay Marles and Jackie Jones, who consulted and contributed throughout the later stages of the book; also from Stuart Ridsdale, who provided the account of the Karakoram Highway and other North–West expeditions; Sally Thompson, for her last minute updating work; and, lastly, Danell Jones for some extremely useful background pieces.

Catharine Sanders: In China, thanks to Zi Han, professor at Shanghai's Jiaotong University, who introduced me to his native town of Shaoxing; to Colin, who taught me to ride pillion on his bicycle through Zhenjiang; to Bing Lin from Linxian, my travelling companion from Wuhan to Anyang; and to Liu Jiancheng of Xi'an. At home, thanks to Craig Clunas and others for reading chapters in their early stages and especially Kate Boyes for her suggestions, corrections and memories of Huangshan.

Chris Stewart: Special thanks to Chen Huiqing of Hohhot and to Wang Xiaoxing of Harbin.

Rhonda Evans: For her contribution to the Fuzhou section, Tsai Chu Wai.

The rough guide to

CHINA

=The= rough guides

Other Rough Guides available include
**KENYA, MOROCCO, TUNISIA, MEXICO, PERU, FRANCE,
SPAIN, PORTUGAL, GREECE, YUGOSLAVIA,
AMSTERDAM & HOLLAND, PARIS, NEW YORK**
and
HALF THE EARTH: WOMEN'S EXPERIENCES OF TRAVEL

Forthcoming:
**SCANDINAVIA, EASTERN EUROPE,
CRETE** and **BRITTANY & NORMANDY**

Series Editor
MARK ELLINGHAM

First published in 1987
Reprinted 1987 by
Routledge & Kegan Paul Ltd
11 New Fetter Lane, London EC4P 4EE

Published in the USA by
Routledge & Kegan Paul Inc.
in association with Methuen Inc.
29 West 35th Street, New York, NY 10001

Phototypeset in Linotron Helvetica and Sabon
by Input Typesetting Ltd, London
and printed in Great Britain
by Cox & Wyman Ltd
Reading, Berks

Library of Congress Cataloging in Publication Data

Sanders, Catharine
The rough guide to China.

(The rough guides)
Includes index.
1. China—Description and travel—1976- —
Guide-books. I. Stewart, Chris. II. Evans, Rhonda.
III. Series.
DS705.E94   1987   915.1'0458   86–26088

British Library CIP Data also available
ISBN 0–7102–0423–X

CONTENTS

Part one **BASICS**
1

China: where to go and when / Getting there / Red tape and visas / Maps and advance information / CITS, PSB and bureaucratic obstruction / Costs, money and banks / Health and insurance / Getting around / Sleeping / Eating and drinking / Communications – post, phones and media / Opening hours and holidays / Things to take . . . and bring back / Entertainment – acrobats, opera and festivals / Photography / Work and study / Trouble / Other things / A glossary of common Chinese terms

Part two **THE GUIDE**
35

1 Beijing and around   37
2 Dongbei: the North-East   125
3 Shaanxi and Henan   138
4 Shanghai and the East Coast   185
5 The Yangzi Basin   281
6 The South: Guangdong and Fujian   322
7 The South-West   366
8 Sichuan   408
9 The North-West   438
10 Tibet   501
11 Out of China: Hong Kong and Macau   525

Part three **CONTEXTS**
543

The historical framework   545
Monumental chronology   563
Chinese beliefs: three teachings flow into one   566
Chinese art   570
Chinese architecture   574
Books   576
Travel onwards: the Trans-Siberian Express   582
Language   585

Index   591

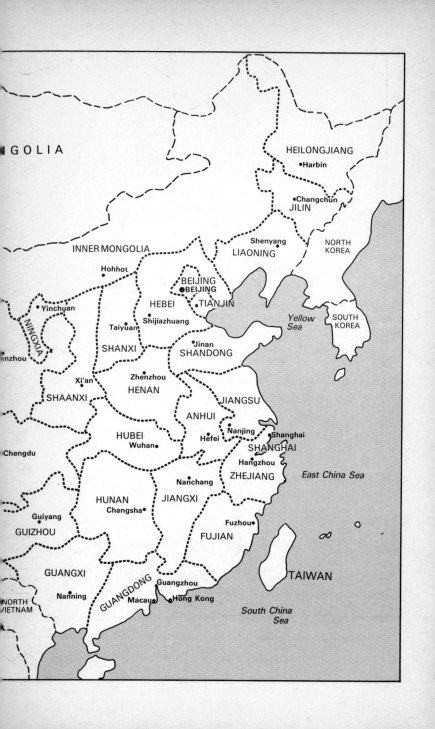

Part one
BASICS

Trans-Siberian
Soviet Train

Trans-Siberian
Chinese Train

Harbin

Urumqi

Shenyang

Hohhot BEIJING

Yantai

Yinchuan Taiyuan

Golmud Lanzhou

Zhengzhou Xuzhou

Xi'an

Nanjing

Shanghai

Wuhan

Hangzhou

Lhasa

Chengdu

Nanchang

Changsha

Guiyang

Fuzhou

Kunming

Nanning

Guangzhou

Xiamen

Hong Kong

PACIFIC OCEAN

Gulf Of
Siam

China Sea

CHINA'S RAILWAYS:
THE MAIN ROUTES

CHINA: WHERE TO GO AND WHEN

The excitement of travel in **China** – and its difference from anything else you'll have experienced – can hardly be over-estimated. Nor, however, can its diffi-culties. It sounds daunting: the third largest country on earth, barely touched by western culture, with a quarter of the world's population – only a tiny minority of whom speak any language you'll have the least familiarity with. But take confi-dence from the fact that you won't be alone. For Australasians the trip to China, or at least into Canton, is now an established part of the long-haul route to Europe, and it is becoming increasingly popular too as an individual destination. The problems lie rather in a road and rail system which is barely adequate, food and hotels which are generally rough, and above all a bureaucracy which is at times heartbreakingly frustrating.

Perhaps the most fascinating aspect right now is the sheer pace of change. In every part of Chinese life, from the economy to attitudes within the Chinese communist party and amongst the people to (most obvious to the visitor) the state of the infant independent travel industry, it can be felt. Travellers who visited China as little as two years ago are amazed to hear how much the place has opened up in the meantime and how many more liberal trends have emerged in the wake of Deng Xiaoping's free market economics. For whatever reason you are attracted to China – its history, art, culture, politics or simply its inac-cessibility – the speed at which things are changing will ensure that your trip is a unique one. Travelling independently you'll encounter innumerable aggrava-tions and occasional hardships, but these will probably be outweighed by extraordinary kindnesses on the part of the Chinese and by the sheer thrill of being somewhere where, until a very few years ago, no western foot could tread: wherever you go you'll be aware, by word of mouth from other travellers, that new towns are being opened all the time – try to get to one.

One thing which is immediately striking is the extraordinary density of **population**; central China does not have landscapes so much as peoplescapes. In the fertile plains, villages are only a mile or two apart, and the big cities are endlessly sprawling affairs with the majority of their inhabitants living in cramped shacks or in depressingly uniform dormitory blocks. It is a well-ordered society, but the myth of the Chinese as all alike really is a myth. There are many regional variations in physical type and language, and a substantial minority of the population of the People's Republic is not 'Chinese' at all but one of over 200 distinct 'Minority Peoples', ranging from the hill tribes of the south to the Muslims of the north-west.

There is also something endearingly provincial about much of China: even in Beijing (Peking – where thanks to a resident community of diplomats, students and journalists, and a high turn-over of tour groups, westerners stand out rather less) you'll find none of the sophistication of most capitals. The tallest buildings are hotels, there are no concrete flyovers or subways, and everyone travels by bike or bus, which makes for an eerie silence. After 10pm, when most people are in bed, this is almost total. Shanghai and Guangzhou (Canton), further from the central bureaucracy, are rather looser, but even here midnight is a daring hour. Since most Chinese rarely if ever have the opportunity to meet or talk with a fore-igner, you will be an object of intense curiosity wherever you go. However much you might want to, it is impossible to blend in with the crowd: you will be stared at openly and constantly, perhaps even prodded and poked, and if you can speak just a little of the language (or find someone to translate) you will be questioned endlessly. Some people find this impossible to accept, but there is no threat in it, and it can even be turned to your advantage; a smile or a greeting will be immediately returned and perhaps accompanied by offers of hospitality.

So where to go? Such a huge land-mass, well over 3000 miles from east to west and stretching from the tropics in the south to the same latitude as Hudson's Bay in the north, cannot be summarised as a single entity. For a detailed look at the geographical and cultural highlights of the different regions, see their respective chapter introductions. In general, bear in mind that there is no chance of covering more than a fraction of the places which are open and that – especially given the frustrations which often accompany making plans here – you are better off being selective and taking your time. Remember that China is not, on the whole, a country of great monuments (the Communists, like all dynasties before them, have destroyed earlier showpieces) and that her cities can seem depressingly drab and uniform. Remember, too, that this is basically a peasant country. If you stick only to the famous sights and well-known cities, you will almost inevitably be disappointed: get out into the country, or the remoter areas, and you may find quite unexpected rewards.

Entering from Hong Kong, **Guangzhou** is the obvious place to head first: very much the leader in westernising influences, this is the easiest part of the country to travel. Inevitably **Beijing** is on everyone's itinerary too (and it's possible to fly here direct) but while the Great Wall and the splendour of the Imperial City are certainly not to be missed, this is in some ways the Chinese city at its worst – vast, soulless and functional. To the south, along the **Yellow River valley** lie the Imperial capitals of old, and in particular **Xi'an**, where the celebrated **Terracotta Army** still stands guard over the tomb of emperor Qin Shihuang. The Yellow River saw the birth of Chinese civilisation, but later the focus of the empire moved south, to the **Yangzi Basin**. Here there are a whole series of beautiful cities of the middle dynasties laid out along a series of canals which centre on the **Grand Canal**, once a vital trade route linking the Yangzi and Yellow rivers. **Shanghai**, just off this network, is a relatively recent development, but now another essential visit – the largest, the most European looking, and still, in some ways, the most cosmopolitan of Chinese cities.

These are the well-known centres, and the ones for which most travellers make. Getting slightly off the beaten track you could head west from Guangzhou, staying in the sub-tropical south, through Guangxi province – where the scenery around **Guilin** is some of the most spectacularly dramatic (and most visited) in the People's Republic – to **Yunnan**, which seems closer in atmosphere and climate to neighbouring Burma and Laos than to the rest of China. North of here, **Sichuan** hides the source of both the Yangzi and Yellow rivers. There are some fine Buddhist sites here, and the trip down the Yangzi, through its gorges at the borders of Hubei, is a particularly spectacular one. Out from here, and you really are in the further-flung reaches of the Republic. The sheer scale and emptiness of the north and north-west can be a relief after the crowds in the east, but here there are vast distances between places and often hard journeys to get to them – across the plateau grasslands of **Inner Mongolia** or the high desert plains of **Xinjiang**. **Tibet**, now firmly open, still sounds the most

Average daily temperatures (°C)	Jan	Mar	May	July	Sept	Nov
Beijing	−5	2	20	26	19	4
Chongqing	7	14	20	29	24	14
Fuzhou	10	13	22	29	26	18
Guangzhou	13	18	23	28	27	20
Guilin	8	13	26	28	26	15
Harbin	−20	−5	14	23	14	−6
Hohhot	−14	0	15	22	14	−3
Kunming	8	13	19	20	18	12
Lhasa	−2	4	13	15	13	2
Shanghai	3	8	19	28	24	12
Urumqi	−15	1	19	26	17	−3
Wuhan	3	10	22	29	24	11
Xi'an	−1	8	19	27	19	6

exotic of all travel possibilities – and so in some ways it is, especially if you come across the border from Nepal or endure the real hardships of the road across the Karakoram pass from Pakistan.

About **climate** it is again almost impossible to generalise. Summers in most of China are extremely hot, which can make travel even harder work than usual, and winters bitterly cold. But the south is subtropical, still warm enough to swim in the sea in December and very rainy and humid in summer, while in the far north, and the mountains of the west, winter temperatures fall far below zero and travel is really out of the question. Tibet is ideal in mid-summer, when its mountain plateaux are pleasantly warm and dry. Overall, the best time to visit is probably spring or autumn when the weather is at its most temperate: in the spring you'd be best starting in the south and working northwards or westwards as summer approached, in the autumn start in the north and work down.

GETTING THERE

From Britain, Hong Kong and Macau
British Airways fly once a week (currently on Wednesdays) from London-Heathrow to Beijing, and charge £675 for an APEX return all year round; *CAAC* fly twice weekly from Gatwick (Thursday and Sunday) for broadly the same rates. Most people, though, fly first to Hong Kong, to which there's much better chance of picking up a cheap ticket. It's also the surest place of getting the visa without hassle and makes an interesting place in itself to hole up for a few days (see p. 526 for a rundown of what there is to do and see). Flights, if you shop around and study the classifieds in the Sunday newspapers or the London listings magazines *LAM* or *Time Out*, currently sell at around £500 return for the 17-hour haul, while a regular BA ticket (daily flights) costs £550–750 depending when you go: contact *STA Travel*, 74 Old Brompton Road, London SW7 (01 581 1022) for current best buys – they also have an agent in Hong Kong who will arrange your visa.

Once in Hong Kong, you can either enter China as most travellers do, through Guangzhou (formerly Canton) or by way of a number of other, less congested gateways. Cheapest to **Guangzhou** (though unbearably crowded at weekends) is simply to take the **MTR** (Hong Kong underground) from Hung Hom Station in Kowloon to the Chinese border station of Lo Wu, walk across the bridge to Shenzhen and from there pick up a train to Guangzhou three hours away. More comfortably, there's a twice-daily **express train** from Hung Hom which delivers you in Guangzhou in just 2½ hours. A daily **ferry** plies the route up the Pearl River to Guangzhou and costs from HK$100, depending on class and berth, for the 8-hour trip; tickets from the Pearl Steamship Co., 15–16 Connaught Road, Hong Kong, or from the China Travel Service, 1/F China Travel Building, 77 Queens Road, Hong Kong (236055). Faster, if rather less civilised, is the **hovercraft**, whose three connections a day whisk you upriver to Whampoa, Guangzhou's port, in a mere 2½ hours at a cost of about HK$150. Quicker still is the **plane**: CAAC fly three times daily to Guangzhou (35 minutes; HK$500), around five times a week to Beijing, Hangzhou and Shanghai and twice a week to Kunming and Tianjin. Cathay Pacific also fly the Hong Kong–Shanghai route.

If you want to avoid Guangzhou – or, perhaps, save it for the way back – the alternatives are numerous. One of the most popular, and luxurious, complete with bars, discos and swimming pools, is the **ferry from Hong Kong to Shanghai**: fares for this run upwards from around HK$400 (for a bed in a dormitory) and the trip takes around 60 hours (see p. 541 for more details). **Further entry-points** are **Zhuhai** in Guangdong province, to which you can take a three-times daily jetfoil (one hour); **Jiangmen**, a little way north of Zhuhai, which is connected by a sporadic ferry service; **Shantou** and **Xiamen** on the eastern coast, which are linked by a handful of erratic boats; and **Wuzhou** in Guangxi province – reachable in 11 hours every other day by early morning hovercraft from Tai Kok Tsui Wharf (cost about HK$300). This last is, if you're heading that way, probably the fastest way of reaching Guilin and the highspots of the Li Jiang River.

Getting to China **from Macau** is no

more difficult or expensive, and it makes a relatively civilised way of arriving in the People's Republic. There's a daily **bus** to Guangzhou which takes 3–4 hours, or you can take the slow **ferry** up the Pearl River, leaving Macau early evening and arriving in Guangzhou the next morning. Ferries leave from the pier just beyond the A-Ma Temple and cost HK$33 one-way (book in advance) which includes a berth. The sandy bed of the Pearl estuary has been known to play havoc with timetabling but ferries rarely arrive in Guangzhou late, and even if you are held up the views will keep you from getting bored. For some notes on the attractions of Macau itself, see p. 538.

From the USA and Canada

The best and certainly the cheapest way of getting to China **from the USA** is, again, **via Hong Kong**. Several airlines – *United* and *North West Orient* among them – fly there direct from the west coast. Direct flights into China proper, on the other hand, come expensive (well in excess of $1000 return), and usually require an overnight stop. **From Canada**, the story is much the same: direct flights to China are prohibitively expensive (roughly Can$1500 for a return to Shanghai from Vancouver) and you'll almost always do better to enter through Hong Kong, even if you're heading for somewhere in the north of China. Return fares, cheapest with *Korean Airlines*, hover around the Can$1000 mark; *Travel Cuts*, Canada's student travel organisation, is likely to have the best bargains.

From Australia and New Zealand

Once again **flights to Hong Kong** come cheapest (Apex fares from Melbourne, Sydney and Perth go for A$800–900 return) but you can, if you wish, fly direct from Melbourne and Sydney to Guangzhou and/or Beijing (and back) for not a great deal more. **From New Zealand**, Apex fares to Hong Kong (from Auckland) run from NZ$1300 to NZ$1500; there are no direct flights into China at present.

Overland routes

The cheapest way into China, at least for those who are resourceful and patient enough, is **by train from Budapest**. For some obscure reason a rail ticket from there to Beijing by way of Moscow can cost as little as £50 in hard currency. All you have to do is arm yourself with Soviet and Mongolian visas (in that order – the Mongols won't give you anything if you don't have a Soviet one) and – here's the snag – buy your ticket several weeks ahead of your intended departure. This last needn't be a problem: Budapest is easily accessible from the rest of Europe so you can always go off somewhere else in the meantime. Tickets are available from the *International Rail Ticket Agency*, 35 Nepkoztarsassag Utja and the trip takes 2 days up to Moscow, its morning arrival and evening departure giving a full day's sightseeing as a bonus; from Moscow it's a seven-day journey to Beijing. The situation regarding your Chinese visa is slightly confused: you used to have to pick up a transit visa on arrival there and then travel to Hong Kong to pick up a full one – another drawback. Now, however, you may well be able to get a visa in Budapest; check with the Chinese Embassy, for up-to-date info. A further tip for the journey: it's a good idea to do a spot of trading on the train, which is always full up with Soviet citizens. Best articles to tout around are jeans, cigarettes, cosmetics and other specifically western consumer goods; remember, though, to keep a lowish profile – the Soviet authorities take a dim view of the practice.

Less complicated, and not a great deal more expensive, is to take the **Trans-Siberian Express** from Moscow direct to Beijing. This, if you're coming from London, is around a 10-day journey (Moscow–Beijing 6 days), and although it involves a certain amount of visa-juggling and advance preparation, is well worth it at – if you buy your ticket in Berlin or Helsinki – around £150 for a third-class seat. And the trip, obviously enough, is an adventure in itself; see p. 582 for a full account.

Or, just as exciting, there's the overland route from **Kathmandu in Nepal to Tibet**. Visas for Nepal are available from the Nepalese Embassy, 12a Kensington Palace Gardens, London W8 (01 229 1594), cost £10 and are valid for a month's stay in Nepal, extendable in Kathmandu. From Kathmandu any number of operators offer tours – some by jeep – into Tibet, and you can either take one of these or make your own way. If you do decide to do this, bear in mind that the journey is difficult, and can take as much as 3 days – though due to the recent opening-up of Tibet to independent travellers, ways of doing it are changing fast, and you'll pick up the most up-to-date information in Kathmandu itself. Best way to work things for the moment is to travel by public bus from Kathmandu to the small town of Bharabise and then by lorry to the border. From here you have to walk – with the help of a porter (hirable for around RS.100) – as far as the town of Kasa, a 3 hour climb, where you can stay the night and pick up transport on to Lhasa. For an account of the journey from Lhasa to Nepal see p. 521.

A further route is now possible **from Pakistan**, up over the Pamirs, to Kashgar (or vice versa), a well-documented route tramped by such notables as Peter Fleming and Bill Tilman and by many accounts an awesome journey – though now tamed somewhat by the construction of the Karakorum Highway. *Voyages Jules Verne* (10 Glentworth Street, London NW1; 01 486 8080) will take you for about £3500, but if you want to try it alone, the road goes by way of Islamabad, Peshawar, Gilgit, Hunza, over the Khunjerab Pass to Tashkurgan and down to Kashgar. As from 1 May 1986, the pass officially opened to tourgroups and individual travellers (whatever overseas CITS offices tell you!). This means that if north-west China is your goal, it is considerably cheaper and easier to attain. You can simply fly to Islamabad and take a tour, bus, jeep or truck on from there. Be aware, however, that this is still very much an adventurers' route. The pass rises well over 6300m, the 'highway' is hardly more than a rough

track, and local tribesmen in these border areas have been known to shoot at travellers at night – just for the practice!

Inclusive tours

If it's your first time in China and there are specific number of places you want to see, you may be better off taking an **organised tour** – though be warned that most come expensive and tend to shuttle you around the country giving little chance to experience anything of China for yourself. One exception to this rule is the *Society for Anglo–Chinese Understanding* (SACU; 152 Camden High Street, London NW1; 01 482 4292) whose specialist tours – ranging from cycling trips to cooking, botanical and Buddhist tours to pre-arranged excursions on the Trans-Siberian – are very reasonably priced and attempt to give a more first-hand picture of the country. They also run language courses in London and Beijing.

Further operators are *Exodus Expeditions* (All Saints Passage, 100 Wandsworth High Street, London SW18; 01 870 0151), whose small-group cycling tours – through Tibet, Nepal and Mongolia – are pricey but consistently good; *STA Travel* (74 Old Brompton Road, London SW7; 01 582 1022), who offer a mixture of simple pre-booked accommodation and travel arrangements and fully inclusive deals; and the *UK China Travel Service* (24 Cambridge Circus, London WC2; 01 836 9911), who do a vast range of specialist and general interest tours at a vast range of prices. For the fullest rundown of the tours you can take, inquire at CITS.

RED TAPE AND VISAS

All foreign nationals need a **visa** to enter China. If you are travelling with a tour group this is a problem which need not concern you, but the position regarding visas for independent travellers seems to change almost daily. Currently FITs (Foreign Independent Tourists) are officially encouraged, so there should be no problem; watch out, though, for lightning turnarounds in policy.

At present, the simplest course is to get a **visa before you leave**. This used to be a very long-drawn-out process,

requiring you to first telex your application (and travel requirements) to Beijing and then to wait up to a month for authorisation. However, in London at least, CITS have begun issuing visas with only seven days notice – though in the summer months they request more. If you are leaving from Britain, therefore, your first call should be to the new **CITS office** at 24 Cambridge Circus, London WC2 (Tel. 01 836 9911). Elsewhere, contact your nearest Chinese embassy or consulate for details: news is that numerous international CITS offices are due to open.

The main alternative – and at the time of writing it is by far the most regular (and reliable) – is to get a **visa in Hong Kong**. This is where the first visas for independent travellers were issued and for administrative reasons the Chinese authorities continued to process most travellers through a group of authorised agents in the city. Best known among these is the *China Travel Service* (77 Queens Road or 27 Nathan Road Kowloon – see p. 528), though they tend to be unhelpful and rather expensive; better are the *Travellers Hostel* (16th floor, Chungking Mansions, Nathan Road, Kowloon), where you will have to wait between 24 hours and 3 days depending on how much you pay (standard procedure), *Wah Nam Travel* (Room 1003, Eastern Commercial Centre, 397 Hennessy Road), or the *Hong Kong Student Travel Association* (addresses p. 528). Of course, though it doesn't happen often, any one of these places might at any time be affected by directives from the People's Republic and there'll be little anyone can do about it; just keep your fingers crossed and be prepared to head off elsewhere in Asia as necessary.

The visa you'll get takes the form of a stamp in your passport, which you may well be asked to show at hotels, in banks, Public Security Bureaux (PSB) and ticket offices, so always carry it with you. Validity is unpredictable: ask for a month and you may get it, you may not; if you only get two weeks and want to stay on longer it's often easy to get an **extension** from the nearest PSB office. Again, though, this is notoriously arbitrary, and you may get a flat refusal; if so, simply move on to the next PSB office, where things could be quite different.

Entering China, you'll be asked by **customs** to fill in a form declaring all your valuable personal items – watches, walkmans, cameras, calculators,

jewellery, etc. You have to show this form when you leave – a tactic designed to prevent wealthy westerners (principally the Overseas Chinese) selling to the Chinese on the black market, so if you lose anything detailed on it best report it to the PSB; otherwise you could be in trouble. Hang on also to receipts for any major items you buy, such as jade, silk, paintings or jewellery: certain things are too old to be legally exported, and anyway, when you arrive home your own Customs may not believe your purchases were as cheap as you claim unless you have proof (duty is charged on a percentage basis). Limits on what you take in to China are, currently, 2 litres of spirits and 3 cartons of cigarettes; you may also take in as much foreign currency and travellers' cheques as you like, and bring out any you haven't used.

Once in China you'll find your visa is all you need: around 240 cities are now officially **open** (including Lhasa in Tibet) and for these and the journeys in between you don't need a permit – which should cover almost everywhere you might want to go. For more out of the way places you'll need an **alien's travel permit,** which you can pick up, usually without too much fuss, from any Public Security Bureau. This (cost ¥5 for 10 destinations) will be inspected when buying bus or train tickets and sometimes at hotels. Bear in mind, though, that distinctions between 'open' and 'closed but not forbidden' are in practice blurred, and that in some country districts the police don't seem to know whether their town is closed or not; where they are – or were at time of writing – we've indicated in the text. **Forbidden areas** tend nowadays to be only sensitive military zones, borders, penal colonies or regions of excessive poverty. Remember, though, the situation is constantly changing and you'll get by far the most reliable information from CITS or the Embassy.

MAPS AND ADVANCE INFORMATION

Offices of the **China International Travel Service** abroad are considerably more helpful than their counterparts in China (see below) and you should definitely visit one before you leave to pick

up as many free maps and leaflets as you can, as well as an up-to-date list of open cities and other information sheets.

Branches include:

LONDON: 24 Cambridge Circus, WC2 (01 836 9911)
NEW YORK: 60 E42nd St, Suite 465, NY 10165 (212 867 0271)
HONG KONG: Unit 601, Tower II, South Sea Centre, Tsimshatsui East, Kowloon (3-721 5317)

In Britain you may find the information service of **SACU** (Society for Anglo–Chinese Understanding; 152 Camden High St, London NW1) more useful still – they offer a small library and enthusiastic staff support.

The best **map** of China is the large single-sheet version produced by the Chinese Cartographic Publishing House and labelled *Zhonghua Renmin Gongheguo Ditu*. This is readily available in China and abroad and despite some eccentricities beyond the borders it marks almost everywhere of significance within China, shows main roads and rail routes with reasonable accuracy, and, most important of all, is well labelled in both Pinyin and simplified Chinese characters. There are others available which are just as good for planning routes, but most are either dated or inadequately labelled. More detailed **hiking maps** are impossible to find – either they do not exist or they are classified information.

Also available before you leave are a variety of **city maps**. These, although more often a representation of how the planners would have liked the city to be than how it actually is, are very useful, and you should get as many as you can for places you will be visiting. The best also mark bus lines. You could wait until you reached China before getting hold of a copy but the Chinese version might not feature romanised script and you may also find that a map of a particular place is available everywhere except in that place – such is the way of travel in China.

In addition to the ordinary maps, every city or tourist spot in China issues a wide range of colour brochures which feature Chinese tourists gaily disporting themselves at the facilities in question. Often they include sketch maps and a few paragraphs of information – useful, misleading and hilarious. Some are genuine collector's items.

CITS will sell some of these maps, but you'll probably find a wider selection at a specialist map shop. In London these include *Collet's Chinese Bookshop*, 40 Great Russell Street, London WC1 (01 580 7538), *Guanghwa Company*, 9 Newport Place, London WC2 (01 437 3737), *Stanfords* (12 Long Acre, WC2; 01 836 1321) and *McCarta* (122 Kings Cross Rd, WC1; 01 278 8278). SACU also have a good selection.

CITS, PSB AND BUREAUCRATIC OBSTRUCTION

Never take the initiative in making decisions – you may be held responsible for the consequences

This useful maxim, taken from an old Chinese civil service manual, sums up fairly well the attitude of modern Chinese officialdom. The Golden Rule, as everywhere, is to have as little to do with bureaucracy as possible. If you don't ask, it won't occur to anyone to say 'No'.

On this front you have two chief organisations to deal with in China, the Public Security Bureau (PSB), for permission to visit places, and the China International Travel Service (CITS), for information about them. **CITS**, known in China as *Luxingshe*, is a monolithic organisation intended partly to smooth your way around China but mainly (or so it seems) to squeeze out of you as much money as possible. For the most part they are used only to dealing with the arrangements of tour groups and show little interest in, or understanding of, the needs of independent travellers. With luck this will change over the next few years as staff numbers are increased to realistic levels and they get more used to handling individuals.

Every city in China has a CITS office, usually at one of the major hotels: the services they offer include organising tours, interpreting, guiding, and meeting and seeing off travellers. Though they are mostly obliging enough, within the limitations of their brief, you do come across cases of what appears to be deliberate obstruction, and even the best offer information which is inconsistent, dated and often plain wrong. If you use CITS booking and ticket services you may also find that you are paying well over the odds – not only the full tourist rate but also a service charge on top. In short rely on them as little as possible and never believe anything they tell you without double-checking (especially if what they tell you is that the only way of seeing something is on a CITS tour). Other travellers will usually prove a considerably more accurate and up-to-the-minute source on where you can or cannot go, which buses you can buy tickets for, and so on.

The **PSB**, known in Chinese as *Gong An Ju*, is in effect the Police, and this is the organisation you will come up against most often. They are to be seen in a variety of guises – directing traffic, keeping order in ticket queues, suppressing dissent or dealing amiably with the problems of foreigners. Uniforms consist of khaki uniforms or white jackets with armbands to denote the wearer's exact function. As a foreigner travelling independently you'll mostly come across their foreign department, a non-uniformed branch which deals with visas and travel permits. Strangely its members are not always chosen for their linguistic ability: their English varies from impeccable to none at all, but most are friendly enough and quite often a better source of information about a place than CITS. If you do come across a really unhelpful office which, for example, refuses to grant you a permit for a town which you know others have visited, it is simplest not to persist. Try somewhere else instead. The only serious trouble you are likely to get into with them is for travelling where you are not supposed to. They are empowered to arrest you, interrogate you and keep you in jail until you are escorted to the train which will take you out of their jurisdiction. In practice they are more likely simply to send you on your way, perhaps with a small fine – though expulsion from China is not unheard of.

There are a couple of other Chinese information services which you may encounter. The **China Travel Service** and **Overseas Chinese Travel Service** (CTS and OCTS) apparently fulfil the same function: handling groups of Overseas Chinese (mostly, but not exclusively from Hong Kong) who are sightseeing or visiting relatives. They don't officially deal with westerners but may occasionally be worth trying for cheaper tickets and a wider range of tours than those offered by CITS. The **China Youth Travel Service** does deal with westerners, but basically only with groups on Cultural Exchanges. In any event you are unlikely to find an office outside Beijing.

COSTS, MONEY AND BANKS

Compared to the rest of Asia China is an expensive country for travellers. Since the government opened up the country in the 1970s all foreign tourism has been controlled by the state: restrictions on where you go and stay and how you get there mean that western visitors, and to a slightly lesser extent, the Overseas Chinese, are forced to pay artificially inflated prices which bear no relation to the (state subsidised) rates paid by the Chinese themselves.

It is, however, possible to live very cheaply if you sleep only in dormitory beds, keep travel to a minimum and eat unexciting food: dormitory beds can be had for as little as £2 a night and a day's food for a pound or so. But if you want to make more of your stay than this, you'll have to dig a little deeper: a **double room** (there are few single rooms in Chinese hotels) costs between £8 and £10 a day minimum in the larger cities, and in some places it's not unusual to pay substantially more than this; everywhere hotel accommodation works out pricier than in the cheaper western countries. **Food**, too, is better and more varied if you're prepared to pay slightly more, and in a country with such a highly prized cuisine it would be stupid not to: £2–3 will get you a really decent meal, rising to around £5 in some of the smarter places.

The other major cost is **travel**. Rates paid by the Chinese are amazingly cheap, but once again visitors have to pay considerably more – close, in fact, to western levels for rail and air travel, though long-distance bus travel does come much less expensive. There are two ways of saving money on trains and planes: either by travelling third class or by buying tickets, illegally, at the Chinese rate, both of which have their drawbacks (see p. 14). There is one consolation: once you've arrived at your destination local transport and, to a lesser extent, taxis, are extremely inexpensive. One thing to avoid is the CITS guided tour, an equivalent of which you can usually find for a fraction of the price. Always remember, although CITS can be useful, their main function is to earn foreign currency rather than assist visitors.

The timing of your visit will make very little difference to your budget: there's hardly any seasonal variation in prices, though you will find, perhaps not surprisingly, that larger cities like Beijing and Shanghai work out quite a bit more expensive than remoter areas. The best way to carry the money you bring from home is in travellers' cheques, purchasable on the spot from any high street bank; credit cards are next to useless in anything but the swish upmarket joints of Canton or Shanghai. All branches of the Bank of China change money, but it's less complicated on the whole to do it in hotels – all of which change money without commission.

Chinese **currency** is the yuan, the exchange rate of which is fairly constant at just under three to the pound sterling. The yuan breaks down into 100 fen, the most common denomination of which, 10 fen, is referred to (and written) as a *jiao* or *mao* – though you'll find few enough prices in fen these days. Neither will you ever hear anyone refer to a 'yuan' in conversation: it's a written term only and the word the Chinese use is *kuai* (pronounced like *The Bridge over the River . . .*). The yuan comes in two forms: *Renminbi* (People's Money), which is the money used by the Chinese, and *Foreign Exchange Certificates* (FECs) – banknotes for foreign tourists that are designed to ease China's dependence on the west by stopping the Chinese from buying consumer goods from abroad (substantially cheaper if bought with FECs). This is what you'll receive when you change your money. In reality, though, the FEC system has been a bit of a disaster: you'll find you need to use Renminbi just as much and in many places FECs change hands on the black market at a going rate of about 140 FEC to 100 Renminbi (ironically, as tourism expands the Chinese in remoter areas are suspicious of FECs and won't accept them). Bear in mind that when you come to leave China, only FECs can be exchanged for foreign currency.

HEALTH AND INSURANCE

Travelling in China, unless you're on a well-cushioned organised tour, is no holiday. Extremes of temperature, bureaucracy and huge distances all combine to sap your strength so don't even think of going at all if you're not in reasonable health. No special **inoculations** are actually required, but typhoid and polio are recommended – something you'd be well advised to heed. There is also some small risk of contracting malaria, particularly if you go to Hainan Island, so it can be a good idea to stock up on tablets before you leave. The spread of resistant strains of malaria often makes it difficult to know which tablets are needed, so check with a reliable source before travelling, as many GPs are unaware of recent developments in foreign parts. Try the London School of Tropical Medicine. If you do decide to take tablets, plan ahead, as you're supposed to start the course well before entering the affected zone –

which in some cases means several weeks in advance.

Hepatitis is something else to watch out for, and as there's some doubt as to the effectiveness of the gammaglobulin injection against this disease it's as well to be careful (though not neurotically so) about what you eat and drink. Water should always have been boiled before you drink it (most hotels, stations and restaurants have supplies) and you should never eat raw vegetables as in China they're normally fertilised with human waste. Also be careful what you're eating *with*: liquid detergent and hot water for washing chopsticks are sometimes in short supply, and some travellers carry their own to avoid using potentially dirty ones. Also, if you're thinking of travelling through south-western China (i.e. around Kunming) during the wet seasons (spring and autumn) it may be a good idea to get vaccinated against meningitis.

Perhaps the most obvious precaution, however, is to make sure you don't get **underfed** or drastically **overtired**: hence making yourself highly vulnerable to strains of 'flu and to the common throat infections (many due to pollution in the big cities). You will probably at some stage get a **tummy upset**, best treated by eating nothing but rice and congee.

If, beyond this, you do get ill, you will find **pharmacies** are well-stocked with western and Chinese medicines but labelling is always in Chinese. If things look more serious, there are special foreigners' sections in main city **hospitals**. Elsewhere, though you'll always be treated with the utmost care and attention you should take along an interpreter to avoid language problems; these can be hired by the hour from CITS. In China's three largest cities there are foreigners' sections at: **Capital Hospital**, Dongdan Beilu, Beijing; **Shanghai Number One Hospital**, 190 Suzhou Beilu, Shanghai; **Guangzhou Number One Hospital**, Renmin Beilu, Guangzhou.

All of which means that China is one of the few countries in the world where it's not essential to take out some form of **insurance** before you leave. The medical treatment you get is free or extremely cheap and will always be excellent – sometimes even embarrassingly so – and it's highly unusual that travellers have anything ripped off by the Chinese; indeed the only people in China that are likely to steal your possessions will be fellow-foreigners. This is unlikely but could happen, or you may simply lose something valuable, so basically we'd recommend you take out at least some kind of travel insurance before you leave home. Cheapest you'll find are *ISIC* policies – available not just to students but to everyone from youth-orientated travel firms like *STA Travel* (address on p. 5).

GETTING AROUND

By train
Most of your travelling in China will probably be done by train: the Chinese rail network is vast and efficient and must be one of the most profitable outfits in the world, judging by the demand. For everyone uses the train, and carriages, particularly in the hard-seat class, are often full to bursting. Bearing this in mind, it's always a good idea to book a seat if possible – either at the station or, more expensively, through CITS or your hotel. As a foreigner, you're expected to pay about 70 per cent on top of the regular Chinese fare. With persuasion or good luck, however, you may well be able to buy ordinary tickets at ordinary Chinese prices.

There are three classes on a Chinese train. The first, *Ruanwo* or **Soft Class**, is expensive and only really within reach of party officials and foreigners. For a price very broadly equivalent to that of a second-class British rail ticket you get your own plushly appointed waiting room (a privilege well worth having in the average Chinese railway station), and on the train itself a wood-panelled four-berth compartment with soft beds with sheets, a fan and optional radio, and a choice of western and Chinese style bathroom and toilet. There's an attendant on hand too, should you desire anything out of the ordinary, and – though excellent and cheap in all classes – meals are more varied and taken separately from the other passengers. Basically, if you're going a long distance, you can afford it and your conscience will let you, Soft Class is well worth the extra money, since this way you don't have to spend a week recovering from your journey.

Yingwo or **Hard Berth** is very much cheaper than Ruanwo, and may be the one you decide to plump for – that's if you can book a seat, which is always a problem. Here you travel in a dormitory car with about 60 other passengers, stacked three-high on hardish bunks; you supply your own teacup and everyone dines together. Rates vary according to which bunk you have: the top, *Shang*, is cheapest and in my opinion best since you can sleep on it all day if you wish (everyone sits on the lower bunks during the day); more expensive are the middle (*Zhong*) and bottom (*Xia*) bunks. On entering a Yingwo compartment the attendant will take your ticket and give you a metal tag, which she will return before you leave, no matter what time of day or night. Assuming you can't book a berth from the ticket office or CITS, one way

HOW TO READ A CHINESE TIMETABLE

Name of line: 萧　甬　线

Ultimate destination (Ningbo)

More destinations: This time Shanghai (even though this timetable only runs through to Ningbo)

Left-hand annotations:
- **Train number** → (573, 571, …)
- **Specific line name** → (杭甬, 沪甬, …)
- **Train type** → (普客, 快客, …)
- **Arrival at station** → upper figure in each cell
- **Departure from station** → lower figure in each cell
- **Cumulative kilometres** (from which you can calculate your fare) → the km column
- **Stations en route** → station names

Direction →

573	571	553	551	355	353	公里	站名 / 开 往	波里	354	356	552	554	572	574
宁波	宁波	宁波	宁波	宁波	宁波	自起车次		车次自起	杭州	上海	上海	上海	杭州	杭州
杭甬	杭甬	沪甬	沪甬	杭甬	杭甬	杭公		宁公	甬杭	甬沪	甬沪	甬沪	甬杭	甬杭
普客	普客	普客	普客	快客	快客				快客	快客	普客	普客	普客	普客
14.28	– / 4.45	0.53 / 1.14	6.23 / 35	2.47 / 3.00	9.35	0	杭　州	168	14.49	18.10 / 58	10.36 / 24	46 / 33	– / 17.32	– / 20.46
37 / 40			46 / 53			3	南 星 桥	165		15 / 12	24 / 19	23 / 13	37 / 25	
52 / 54	5.02 / 05		7.05 / 07			11	钱 塘 江	157			10.01 / 59		17.01 / 08	08 / 20.05
13 / 15						15	长　河	153			50	11.03	51 / 58	58 / 56
15.06 / 11	24 / 28	51 / 56	19 / 23		10.01 / 03	21	萧　山	147	14.05 / 59	34 / 17.28	47 / 9.42	54 / 50	40 / 35	47 / 40
21 / 23			33 / 35			29	夏 家 桥	139				39 / 36	25 / 23	
36 / 38	47 / 50		48 / 51			39	钱　清	129				09 / 10.06	10 / 16.07	20 / 17
49 / 51	6.01 / 04		8.02 / 05			49	柯　桥	119			53 / 51	54 / 52	35 / 32	06 / 19.03
16.04 / 14	16 / 28	2.32 / 42	8.18 / 30	4.13 / 23	39 / 50	60	绍　兴	108	23 / 13.10	52 / 40	9.38 / 29	39 / 15.07	20 / 41	51 / 41
25 / 28	46 / 48		43 / 45			69	皋　埠	99			15 / 13	9.12	43 / 41	28 / 26
46 / 48	57 / 59		54 / 57			76	陶　堰	92			0.4 / 8.02		32 / 30	17 / 15
58 / 17.00	7.09 / 11		9.17 / 19			83	东 关 镇	85			53 / 55	57 / 18	21 / 18.03	06 / 18.03
09 / 15	20 / 25	3.13 / 18	28 / 32	52 / 5.08	11.21 / 27	89	曹　娥	79	40 / 36	11 / 16.06	41 / 35	46 / 42	09 / 14.03	54 / 50
19 / 22			36 / 38			91	上　虞	77			26 / 23		59 / 57	
31 / 34	35 / 38		47 / 49			97	驿　亭	71			14 / 12	32 / 30	48 / 46	40 / 37
47 / 49	59 / 8.01		56 / 58		41 / 43	102	(五　夫)	65			52 / 50	04 / 7.02	22 / 20	38 / 36
58 / 18.01			10.07 / 10			109	马　诸	59			53 / 50	08 / 8.05	27 / 25	13 / 17.10
14 / 24	20 / 32	48 / 58	23 / 33	38 / 51	12.02 / 21	120	余　姚	48	12.06 / 57	31 / 15.23	38 / 44	52 / 22	13.12 / 57	57 / 49
34 / 37	42 / 45					128	蜀　山	40			18 / 16			47 / 45
45 / 48	53 / 55		48 / 50			133	丈　亭	35			05 / 6.02	29 / 27	33 / 30	34 / 32
58 / 19.00			11.00 / 03			142	(叶　家)	26			51 / 49		20 / 18	
11 / 14	9.29 / 35		25 / 28	6.34 / 36		149	慈　城	19		53 / 50	38 / 7.01	03 / 12.01	04 / 14	13 / 16.11
25 / 28	47 / 49					156	洪 塘 乡	12			27 / 25	52 / 50	52 / 50	
38 / 41	56 / 59		12.02 / 05			160	庄　桥	8			18 / 16	43 / 41		59 / 56
20.05 / –	10.30 / –	5.45 / –	12.20 / –	7.25 / –	13.18 / –	168	宁　波	0	11.00	4.30	5.05	6.30	11.35	15.45

of getting one is to collar the controller (wearing a green armband) at his or her desk in car no.8 and put your name on the list; as soon as a berth becomes free the name on the top gets it – being a foreigner may give you priority. Or you can simply play the ignorant foreigner and blunder into a Yingwo carriage saying you want a bed and don't quite know how to go about it – a sneaky but, in my experience, infallible method.

For the really impecunious there's *Yingzuo*, **Hard Seat**, which is something of a trial but could well be the only alternative if Hard Berth is full up. Hard Seat is exactly what it says: your ticket gives you – if you're lucky enough to be able to book one – a hard upright seat, one of a cramped row of three, and a small table which you share with your fellow-travellers. There's barely room to get comfortable at all, let alone sleep, and on long journeys the discomfort can be excruciating, especially as the gangway is usually too crammed with travellers to get up and stretch your legs. (I spent 5 hours crammed into a washbasin on one journey, and someone else I met travelled for 56 hours on one leg – there wasn't room to put the other down). You supply your own teacup and leaves and fetch hot water from the boiler at the end of the carriage, or the attendants bring it around in a watering can. Food can be had in the dining car, or you can buy boxes of vegetable stew and rice for about 5 mao from trolleys along the train. One nice thing about travelling Hard Seat, though, is the chance it gives you to get to know the Chinese: they will forcefully insist you share their food with them and stuff you with the melons and cakes they buy at every section. The main drawback – and this applies to Hard Berth too – is the ghastly train's radio station, which continues almost incessantly from dawn till dusk, and which you can't turn off.

There are three **types of train** in China, and not all of them have all three classes on board. Express trains, identified by a number between 1 and 90 and for which you pay a small supplement, do have all three and are that much more comfortable as a rule – as are routes crossing international frontiers. Trains with a number between 100 and – roughly – 350 are marginally cheaper but make more stops and only hold soft and hard berths. Those trains numbered

400–500 stop everywhere, have seats only, and are frankly best avoided.

Local or national rail **timetables** can be bought very cheaply at any station. Once you have learned how to read them – no easy task (see the example on p. 13) – you'll find the information they contain invaluable: everything you could conceivably want to know about distances, fares, times and types of trains. Prices are cumulative, i.e. you take a fixed price over a given distance, add 70 per cent surcharge as a foreigner and the various supplements (for an express train, type of bunk, etc.), and you should have the price of your ticket.

By bus

In spite of the wide net of places served by the railway system, there are still many parts of China not reachable by train – in which case the cheapest way of getting there is by bus. Shorter journeys (5 hours or less) are best avoided as they can be nightmarishly crowded and uncomfortable, but for long distances buses can be remarkably efficient. On longer rides you'd do well to buy your ticket a day or two in advance – most easily, and only slightly more expensively, from CITS rather than from the queuebound bus station ticket offices – and on trips in excess of 12 hours in length, book a seat. Once again, like Hard Seat on the train, travelling by bus may not be luxurious but it's by far the best way of getting acquainted with the Chinese. I would recommend very strongly that you wear earplugs on bus-journeys – the air-horns are deafening.

Driving and hitching

Driving your own car isn't possible at all in China, at least for the moment. You can't bring any kind of vehicle over the border, and even if you could there isn't anywhere to buy petrol. Neither is **hitching** officially encouraged, although this is fairly laxly enforced and you may find on certain routes that it's a relatively quick way of travelling; the thing to do is scuttle into the bushes as soon as you see an official looking jeep. Lorries are the best bet for lifts and will often stop, particularly in remote spots; the best way of getting their attention is to stand in the middle of the road and flag them down. Or, if you're in a city, ask at the lorry compound (everywhere has one) between 5 and 7 am; there's nearly always someone who will take you.

By air

Those well-heeled enough and/or in a hurry can fly to most major cities. Although *CAAC* (the Chinese airline) have a reputation for being the worst airline in the world, with an appalling safety record, they are more reliable than many would care to admit. This, plus the fact that airports are currently springing up all over the place, means the service can only improve. It is expensive though – 100 per cent surcharge for tourists and about 30 per cent more than the luxury train fare – and only really worth doing for really long hops. Timetables can be obtained from CITS or CAAC, either in China itself or in London at 153 Auckland Road, Upper Norwood, London SE19 (01 771 4052). One development to look out for in the near future are the domestic flights offered by the Chinese Air Force as a rival to CAAC: at time of writing these were just starting up at fares forecast as 50 per cent cheaper.

By boat

Apart from the boat trips covered on p. 5, all of which are ways of getting into China, principally from Hong Kong, there are any number of river and sea journeys you can make once in the country itself. Most renowned is the spectacular trip through the Yangzi Gorges from Chongqing to Yichang, Wuhan and, eventually, Shanghai – a jaunt covered on pp. 432–7 – but there are quite a few other places you can reach by boat, particularly along the eastern seaboard, and even if it's not always the quickest or cheapest way of working things, a ride on board can make a wonderfully refreshing change after the gruelling trials of train and bus. Also, the wide range of classes you have to choose from on Chinese boats means there's very likely to be a berth to match your budget, and overall, unless you travel top class, boat travel can be an extremely affordable way of getting around. Another popular ride is up the Pearl River from Guangzhou to Wuzhou, which gives easy access to Guilin and Yangshou; try, too, if you have time, the lazy excursions along the Grand Canal between Suzhou and Hangzhou.

By bicycle

The bicycle is the way the Chinese get about. Bikes can be **hired** in every city for just a few yuan and, locally at least, make much the best way of travelling: few cities have many hills, and it makes a nice change from sweating it out on buses. Rental by the hour or day is the usual way of doing things, but at most places it is possible to hire a bike for longer if you wish; you'll be asked either to leave a deposit or some form of ID. There are specific areas in cities – bicycle parks – where you're supposed to leave your bike: an attendant will request a few fen in exchange for a token. One alternative to renting is to **buy a bike**: Chinese bicycles are unsophisticated machines but you can pick up a 'Flying Pigeon' for around ¥180 from a department store. Foreigners don't need a bike licence, and bikes are so popular in China that supply can't keep up with demand, so you shouldn't have any trouble getting rid of yours when you come to leave.

You can, of course, **take your own bike** into China with you. There's no problem taking it on the plane providing it's well packaged, but once you've arrived things can get complicated: best obtain a visa without mentioning the bike since there's always a chance you may be refused entry with it. Once in China, although it's normal practice to stick your bike in the luggage van on a train, the ticketry and paperwork involved can be baffling, and you may find that the bike arrives several days after you do. Better instead to travel by long distance bus, where you can simply stow your machine on the roofrack, no questions asked; or by boat, on which you can store your bike – at moderate cost – without dismantling it. Some people get over the problems by taking an inclusive tour: these, though by no means cheap, can be very good indeed, and you could always join one and spend some time travelling by yourself afterwards; for details of operators see p. 7 or contact CITS.

Local transport

City buses pack in the people like sardines. But fares are cheap and services frequent, starting up around 5 in the morning and running every few minutes until about 9pm, so you may well find yourself relying on them: most

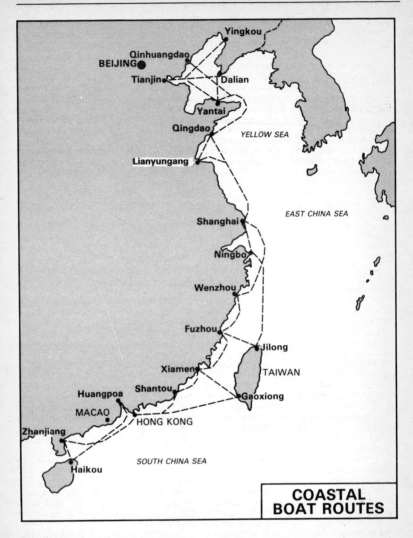

**COASTAL
BOAT ROUTES**

Chinese cities are spread out enough to defeat even the most determined walker. City maps tend to have a bus map printed on the reverse side: simple and easy to follow even if you don't read Chinese. If money's not so tight or there's a group of you, it may be worth splashing out on a **taxi**: these don't cruise the streets (except in Guangzhou) but instead can be found outside larger city hotels or at bus and railway stations.

Cheaper, and to be found congregating outside stations all over China (except, perhaps, in Beijing and hilly Chongqing), are **pedicabs** (bicycle or motorised rickshaws). Agree on a price beforehand with these – their rates are notoriously erratic. Finally, if you're heading for anywhere outside main city centres, you can usually hire a **jeep** for around ¥100 a day.

SLEEPING

Over recent years the amount of tourist and business traffic to China has more than doubled, which has left the country's network of hotels, already straining at the seams, seriously under capacity. Plans are afoot to do something about this, namely to double the number of hotel beds in China by 1990, but in the meantime accommodation options remain few and rather dated. There is little scope, either, for camping or sleeping rough, though young locals do sometimes try and get their heads down in city parks – a practice much frowned upon by the authorities. And there are, as yet, no youth hostels, though these are planned and, considering the pace at which the country is opening up, shouldn't be too long in coming. For the moment, then, the choice is mainly confined to straight hotels . . .

Other than using the listings in the Guide, the best way to find out about hotels is to ask other travellers or inquire at CITS: they'll know which ones have closed, which are now accepting foreigners and which are currently cheapest – and how to get to them. Whatever you do, though, don't slog around town hunting for that elusive hotel someone told you was cheaper than the dorms – it's just not worth it. Once at the hotel you'll find a range of rooms and prices displayed prominently at the desk, the Chinese paying least, Overseas Chinese a middle rate and ordinary foreigners top wack (though you may be able to get a reduction if you flash an ISIC card). Single rooms are few and a flat rate is charged for a double, which, if you're travelling alone, you may find yourself having to pay. In most places you should be able to find a place in a three- or four-bedded room or dormitory – though be warned that you may have to wheedle these options out of the staff who would much rather you stayed in their most expensive room: polite persistence usually pays off, or, sometimes, the waving of a receipt from a bargain hotel you stayed at before.

Most large hotels, particularly those for rich foreigners, have a wide array of facilities. There will often be a branch of CITS – good, if expensive, for buying tickets for your onward journey, and for making advance hotel reservations –

sometimes there are hairdressers and barbers, and you can almost always change money, post letters and make telephone calls. Also, hotel restaurants stay open that much later than their counterparts in town, and, if you feel so inclined, are more likely to serve western food.

Broadly speaking, the hotels you'll stay in fall into three categories. **Top of the range** are new, hi-rise, international style places modelled on western lines that are only open to foreign nationals. Inside, as well as some by Chinese standards extremely palatial bedrooms, you'll find discos, fashion shows and rooftop western-style bars, all patronised by exhausted-looking tour groups and nervous young Chinese businespeople. You may want to wander in to sample the loos or luxuriate for a night at hideous expense (minimum ¥50 a night), but all in all, unless they're the only option, these kind of places are best left alone – that is, if you want to see something of China.

Better instead to get a room at a hotel formerly reserved for foreigners – old colonial hangouts and the like but now open to the Chinese too. These are known as **Fandian** (which confusingly can also mean eating place) or **Binguan**, meaning guesthouse – often, though not always, larger and more comfortable. Much of the time they will have several wings, rooms which vary from comfortable doubles to spartan dormitories, and the standard set of hotel facilities. Most double rooms will have a couple of single beds, a TV or radio, a bathroom with shower or bath, soap and towels, mosquito nets where necessary, tea and mugs, and writing paper and slippers – all for rates from about ¥30.

Down the scale a bit, there are countless **hotels for Chinese** travellers and businesspeople, and many, as the pressure on space in 'foreigners' hotels grows, are beginning to accept overseas visitors more readily. Basically, as time goes by the rules become less and less hard and fast: time was if all the overseas hotels were full there was nowhere for a foreigner to stay; now it's quite normal for the authorities to pack budget travellers off to fleabitten hostels when peaktime demand exceeds supply. Obviously rates are that much lower (as low as ¥1–4 for a bed in out-of-the-way places) so if you're on a particularly tight shoestring a place like this can be a valuable alternative; be warned that it also usually means no post or exchange facilities, no restaurant, no one who speaks English and, sometimes, no running water or inside loo. Try also **Jiaodaisuo** – hostels for foreign students which, on production of a student card, should let you in to share a room.

At the bottom of the price range are **temples**, which you'll find in mountain areas like Emei Shan. These range in price from ¥2 to ¥10 a head, and can vary from the dirty and down-at-heel to welcoming and atmospheric places where you're woken each morning by the soft chanting of monks through the wall. If you get the chance, an experience not to be missed.

EATING AND DRINKING

Food in China is almost unbelievably varied – you'll find a never-ending range of dishes to try and of places to eat them. Yet most travellers get back to Hong Kong (or wherever) drooling at the thought of steak and chips, or a decent meal of any sort. You sometimes get the feeling that everything you are offered, whatever its name, is the same stodgily gelatinous mess, recycled and cooked in a slightly different way: and undeniably there is a bland sameness about most cheap Chinese food. Part of the problem is the structure of a Chinese meal, which assumes that you will be sampling a wide variety of dishes – perhaps 13 or 14 for a meal for 8 people. While this works reasonably well if there is a group of 4 or 5 who can share, a solitary traveller will be stuck with a single dish, which is thoroughly dull. Then there is a great gulf between the quality of the food you will get in an expensive restaurant serving Imperial style food – a veritable banquet with prices to match – and what is on offer in the average cheap eating house in a small town, which can be unspeakably bad. For the most part – unless you are planning a gourmet tour – you will be faced with the latter, enlivened only by the occasional big city treat.

Chinese cuisine has a long tradition of exotic and elaborate meals designed to please the eye as well as the palate and to achieve a subtle harmony of Yin and Yang qualities. Over 2,000 years ago, around the same time that chopsticks first get mentioned in writing, a poet wrote a lyrical description of the wonderful dishes that might call his friend's soul back from beyond the grave. But this rich and delicate cookery was always confined to the court and its wealthy entourage – a tiny minority. For the most part Chinese food has been influenced by more direct needs – the dictates of climate, geography and history and their consequences, poverty and famine. Hence the readiness – still evident – to search for everything that was edible and to eat every last bit of it: herbs, leaves and vegetables, often obscure ones, form the basis of most dishes and the Chinese have never been afraid to experiment. Bear's paw, shark fin, ducks' feet, fish lips, snake soup; all these are regarded as delicacies. On the whole, though, the impact of poverty is shown in such things as the scant quantities of meat in most Chinese food (partly, too, the influence of the Buddhist vegetarian tradition) and in cooking methods which reflect the perennial shortage of firewood: meat and vegetables would be cut into tiny pieces for quick stir frying over a short-lived blaze of twigs or straw.

In such a vast country the wide variations of climate – and thus the crops and animals which thrive – have not surprisingly produced many distinct **regional styles** of cookery. There are lots of subdivisions, but four major traditions can be defined. Grain in always the staple – indeed the Chinese word for food, literally translated, means grain – but it takes different forms. In **Beijing** (or Mandarin) cookery, and throughout the north generally, it will be wheat or millet: wheat buns, noodles, pancakes and dumpling make a solid diet to set against the cold winters. Beijing food generally is thought of as strongly flavoured – it uses a great deal of dark soya sauce and bean paste, as well as white cabbage, onions, pears, chestnuts and garlic. As the seat of the

Imperial court, Beijing also developed many of the richest delicacies, of which Peking Duck is the best known in the west. The Dowager Empress Ci Xi, who dominated China for 50 years during the final decay of the Empire, had a particular penchant for fish lips, duck feet and steamed ducks' tongues. Beijing's cooking has also been influenced over the centuries by northern neighbours and invaders: the Mongols brought their firepots and barbecue griddles and goat meat; from the Muslims came a taste for mutton and chicken.

Sichuan in the west has some of China's most fertile soil and a climate favourable enough to allow three rice crops a year. Here they can grow and eat almost anything. Sichuan food has a reputation for being very hot, with a lavish use of spices, chilli and red peppers: *Pockmarked Grandmother Chen's Bean Curd* will lift the top off your head. At the same time there are many more subtle flavourings, of which the best known is the 'home' taste – salty, hot and slightly sour, like the *Carrying-Pole Noodles* which are sold from pots slung on the end of traditional carrying poles.

In the Yangzi Basin and further south the staple grain is rice and the cookery of **Shanghai**, the lower Yangzi and the eastern seaboard reflects this. Chilly winters – though not so cold as Beijing's – give rise to sturdy rice noodles and dumplings. At the same time summers are scorchingly hot, so preserved foods – dried mushrooms or bamboo shoots and salted fish and vegetables – are also Shanghai specialities. The region is a watery one, with hundreds of rivers and lakes to supplement sea fishing, so there is a great deal of fish: usually this is cooked very lightly to preserve its flavour. A dish of tiny shrimps wrapped in ultrafine pastry would be typical.

Guangdong (**Canton** province) and the south – fertile and subtropical – boast the most cosmopolitan tastes. In AD300 there were Arab merchants in Canton and 700 years later it was the leading port for trade with the South China Seas, the Spice Islands and India. This openness is reflected in the food. When they say they will eat anything here they really mean it: anything that moves is liable to end up on the table. They eat fish maw, snake's liver, shark

fin and braised whole guineapig and have recently developed a taste for rats following a government directive to clear China of the vermin by eating them. There is an enormous range of fruit, vegetables, fish and shellfish too. Most of these are served extremely fresh and cooked simply in a wok with few sauces in order to retain the natural flavour. Perhaps Canton's greatest contribution to Chinese cookery, though, is *Dim Sum* – tiny flavoured buns, pancakes and dumplings which cater to the Chinese liking for an assortment of small dishes. Nowadays you can get Dim Sum anywhere in China, but Canton has as many as 2000 different variations, hundreds of which may be on offer in a single restaurant.

All these regional styles can be found side by side in the larger cities, but even so there's a good deal to be said for sticking to the local, which is more likely to be properly cooked with fresh ingredients. One problem you're always going to find is with the **opening hours** of restaurants, which tend to be early and short. At **breakfast** time you'll find that restaurants and canteens open early: by 6am many people are already noisily slurping their noodles and by 9 the food has usually run out. If you get up late you may have to join the first sitting for **lunch**, at 11 or 11.30, which will leave time to work up an appetite again before people start arriving for the **evening meal** around 5pm: by 6 you'll be lucky to get a table, by 7 they'll be sweeping the debris off the tables and around your ankles.

Small **noodle shops**, **foodstalls** near railway and bus stations or makeshift **eating places at tourist spots** are more flexible, their hours being limited solely by the availability of food and the need to close down to prepare more. But you may find their notions of washing up – which involve putting the chopsticks straight back on the table and dunking the bowls into a murky basin on the floor – less than appetising. Carrying your own chopsticks may help you feel better about it. These places are always cheap, while the limited selection can be a positive advantage when you have to point to what you want.

Hotel dining rooms, especially in the big cities, tend to stay open later and longer than restaurants outside. Smart hotels now invariably have expensive restaurants where a hostess in a demure cheongsam will guide you to your table and you can pay the earth for inter-national cuisine. They'll also have a café for club sandwiches and snacks. Stan-dard hotels will offer western-style breakfast of scrambled eggs, toast and coffee – often indifferent but nonetheless welcome if rice congee and pickled vegetables have lost their charm. There are other advantages to eating in hotels: some of the staff will understand English; there may well be a menu you can understand; and for single travellers a set menu – *Bao Chi* – will provide a variety of small dishes rather than the one or two standard ones you can expect elsewhere. While the food can be mass-produced and bland, some hotel restaurants are very good indeed.

As for standard **restaurants**, you will often find, especially in the larger towns, that they are divided into sections over two or three floors. The ground floor will offer a limited choice, usually scrawled illegibly on strips of paper or a board: you queue at a booth to buy chits for the dishes and then line up again at the kitchen hatch to exchange them for food. There are plastic bowls, large or small, of the local beer. In the past foreigners were discouraged from eating in these places – now you are likely to be pushed to the head of the queue. Food will be cheap, and it's easy to point at what you want. The next floor will have a wider choice, usually with waitress service and a written menu (which might be in English, though don't count on it). The final section, if there is one, will have tables for tour groups and foreigners, with side rooms for banquets and private parties. Food will be more expensive, and they may balk at accommodating a lone foreigner, but it's often worth trying. At the very least the loos will be better.

Selecting what to eat in places when you can't simply choose in the kitchen can often be problematic. Sometimes choosing blind from the menu will produce the best dish of your trip – equally you may find yourself chewing through sliced bull's penis fried with ginger. You can also wander round the tables looking for inspiration on the plates of your fellow diners, though frequently the best looking dishes turn out to taste worst. But undoubtedly the best method overall is to have things written down: then you can simply point

out what you want. We provide a few of the basics below, and any good phrase-book should have substantially more, but it is still a good idea to persuade a Chinese to write out for you the charac-ters for the different kinds of meat, fish and vegetables, for the methods of cooking, and preferably for a few of your favourite dishes.

Many travellers are reduced to the most bizarre diets simply by ignorance of what is available, or inability to ask for it. **Breakfast** is particularly difficult away from the security of the bacon and eggs, toast and marmalade, milk and cereals, provided by the fancier hotels. **Milk** is rarely available – the Chinese don't drink it and indeed consider it loathsome (it is said that their digestive systems cannot handle it, and that the only reason ours can is through long and over-indulgent habit). The Chinese themselves usually wake up to rice soup accompanied by a few plates of pickled or stir-fried vegetables and perhaps some salted peanuts. If you can't face this, a couple of **Mooncakes** (*Yue Bing*) washed down with tea make a good standby. Moon-cakes are large, flat, round pastries, their flaky cases filled with an unidentified – but pleasant – sweet substance. They are available everywhere, cheap and easy to ask for.

Dishes for **other meals** are harder to recommend because of the great regional variations. One thing you can always get is a dish of boiled white **rice** – generally dryish and coarse, but filling. **Noodles** are also served all over, in many different guises and as an accompaniment to just about anything; watch out, though for rice noodles and potato noodles, both of which are trans-lucent white and horribly slimy. Another popular accompaniment is **Beancurd** (or Tofu, *Dou Fu* here) made from fermented mashed beans – enormously variable, this can be delicious. **Steamed buns** (*Mantou*) are soft, doughy buns which tend to meld into a cloying lump in your mouth. **Jiaozi** is often translated as ravioli, which isn't far from the truth – little triangular packages of meat and vegetables, wrapped in dough. *Baozi*, **dumplings**, are larger and more formi-dable – delicious. **Bread** features only in the Muslim areas of the north-west and is virtually unavailable in the People's Republic.

Chicken and pork are the most

common forms of **meat**, followed by duck and beef. Mutton is also found in dumplings and occasionally on kebabs, while it is practically the staple diet of the Muslims of the north-west and the shepherds of Mongolia. You will find that meat is very often served cold, or luke-warm. **Fish** is consistently excellent in the areas where it comes fresh, and thanks to intensive fish-farming this is now a pretty wide area. There's rarely any indication of what type of fish it may be, it is simply *Yu. Qingcai* means **green vegetables** and gets you just that – a bowl of deep green celery, spring onions or the like fried, spicy and perhaps with little chunks of pork. **Mushrooms** are a firm favourite in China, coming in a range of varieties too wide to have names in English.

Strict **vegetarians** can find life difficult in China – many dishes have very little meat but most have some, and even apparently plain vegetables are frequently cooked in meat broth or oyster sauce. If in doubt show someone the characters for 'I am a vegetarian' (below). The one place where you will be excellently fed is in the temples, almost all of which have vegetarian canteens. If you're feeling the lack of **fresh fruit**, make the most of the large glass jars – mandarins, apples and pears especially – which you can buy in most shops: they are packed in natural juice and are delicious. Excellent, too, for taking on long bus or train journeys.

Drink in China, 90 per cent of the time, means **tea**. What they drink here, however, bears little resemblance to what we know as China tea in the west, for most of the best quality teas are exported. The first item of equipment for any Chinese is the tea-mug – travelling kit generally consists of a tin mug with a rolled-up flannel and a toothbrush inside, and a lid to keep the tea hot. Next in importance comes the pouch containing the tea-leaves; these vary enormously, from compressed bricks of coarse green leaves, through sweet-scented Jasmine teas full of flowers, to the esoteric specialist teas taken by monks as an aid to meditation. They are all much coarser in leaf than the teas we know, tending to form a thick mass of floating weed on top of the hot water in your cup. Many people dispense with the leaves altogether and just drink boiling water. Though this may seem

eccentric in the heat of a Chinese summer, it really is very refreshing. Boiling hot water is available everywhere free of charge – trains, hotels, waiting-rooms, public buildings – but you'll need to provide your own leaves (and cup). If you are fussy about tea it may be best to bring your own from home.

If you're a **coffee** addict you may have to bring some supplies with you: Chinese coffee – on the rare occasions you can find it – is execrable; jars of Nescafé can be bought in big cities (hotels).

These days **beer** is beginning to rival tea in popularity; every region has its own brewery, producing a thick, sweet, slightly fizzy lager-like solution in bottles (and just occasionally something quite good). More expensive is *Tsingtao Beer*, brewed in the German-inspired brewery at Qingdao and sold all over China; this really is good – ask for *Qingdao Pijiu*. *Sanpijiu* is a sort of draught beer brewed in huge enamel urns in the earthier restaurants; you drink this from a bowl – thick and interesting. All these beers suffer greatly from the inability of Chinese fridges to keep them cool!

One of the popular English–Chinese phrasebooks explains how to say, 'Waiter, this wine is corked, bring another bottle' and to enquire pomp-ously after the vintage. Fat hope! China rates about 789th on the list of the world's great **wine**-producing countries. In the more expensive hotels and big city restaurants you can buy *Dynasty*, red, white or rosé, the disagreeable and cloying product of a Sino-French collab-oration. This will surely improve. Other-wise there are myriad local wines which you can buy for a few jiao in soda-pop bottles. These are normally much as you'd expect, but they can be surpris-ingly delicious – ask for *Jiu*.

As for **stronger stuff**, in any restaurant you are bound to see groups of diners enthusiastically playing a drinking game, which involves a great deal of noise and the consumption of excessive quantities of a clear liquid from little porcelain cups. This is gener-ally **rice spirit** – vicious, cheap, and generally best avoided both for its taste and its after-effects. More exclusive – used for toasts at weddings and banquets but otherwise only within the reach of party officials and honoured foreign guests – is **Maotai**, a sorghum-based spirit spoken of with reverence by the masses, extremely powerful and, to most tastes, quite undrinkable.

At some stage you'll inevitably be reduced to drinking **water**. Try never to drink straight from the tap – the boiled stuff is all right, or bottled mineral water, still or fizzy, should be available in most hotels.

A CHECKLIST OF FOOD AND RESTAURANT PHRASES

I am hungry/want to eat	wǒ yào chīfàn 我要吃饭
restaurant	fàndiàn or cānguǎn 饭店或餐馆
(English) menu	(yīngwén de) càidān 英文的菜单
This is good (bad) food	hǎo (bù hǎo) chī 好（不好）吃
I am full up	wǒ chībǎole 我吃饱了
I am a vegetarian	wǒ chī sù 我吃素
I want	wǒ yào
Chinese (western)	zhōng (xī) shī zǎocān
breakfast	我要中（西）式早餐
milk	niúnǎi 牛奶
butter	huáng yóu 黄油
bread	miànbāo 面包
coffee	kāfēi 咖啡
sugar	táng 糖
jam	guǒjiàng 果酱
boiled	zhǔ 煮
scrambled	chǎo 炒
fried eggs	hébāo dàn 荷包蛋
Please bring me a bottle of	qǐng gěi wǒ yī pín 请给我一瓶
beer	píjiǔ 啤酒
mineral water	kuàng quán shuǐ 矿泉水
orange	júzi shuǐ 桔子水
Please bring me a cup of	qǐng gěi wǒ yī bēi 请给我一杯
tea	chá 茶
hot water	kāishuǐ 开水
cold water	liáng kāishuǐ 凉开水
lunch	wǔfàn 午饭
supper	wǎnfàn 晚饭
dimsum	diǎnxīn 点心
I want a bowl of	wǒ yào yī wǎn 我要一碗
soup	tāng 汤
noodles	miàn 面
rice	mǐfàn 米饭
I want a portion of	wǒ yào yī fèn 我要一份
chicken	jī 鸡
beef	niúròu 牛肉
pork	zhūròu 猪肉

fish	yǔ 鱼
mutton	yángròu 羊肉
prawns	xiā 虾
crab	pángxiè 螃蟹
duck	yā 鸭
squid	yóuyǔ 鱿鱼
beancurd	dòufù 豆腐
dumplings	jiǎozi or bāozi 饺子或包子
stir fried	kuàichǒ 快炒
baked	kǎo 烤
steamed	zhēng 蒸
boiled	zhǔ 煮
fried	zhà 炸
vegetables	shūcài 蔬菜
mushrooms	mógū 蘑菇
cabbage	báicài 白菜
beansprouts	dòuyá 豆芽
green beans	qīngdòu 青豆
bambooshoots	zhúsǔn 竹笋
soy sauce	jiàngyóu 酱油
ginger	shēngjiāng 生姜
pepper	làjiāo 辣椒
apple	pínggǔo 苹果
peach	táo 桃
orange	jǔzi 桔子
watermelon	xīguā 西瓜
knife	dāozi 刀子

COMMUNICATIONS – POST, PHONES AND MEDIA

Chinese **Post Offices** are on the whole gloomy and cavernous buildings characterised by a long table down the centre with a glue pot and brush and by even longer queues. If you can't read the signs it is easy to waste time waiting in line for the wrong desk. You'll find it much easier, wherever possible, to use the postal counter situated in most major hotels. These often sell postcards and stationery as well as (beautiful) stamps. **Airmail** to Europe, Australasia or the USA is relatively straightforward, inexpensive, and takes 5–10 days. **Parcels** are rather more complicated – decent wrapping paper is hard to find and even large envelopes seem in short supply (if

you are shopping in a Friendship Store, get them to wrap and mail the goods for you). There will be lengthy customs forms to complete, as there will for printed paper rate packages – very cheap if you want to send home books, etc., but they will insist on examining everything to ensure that nothing is hand written. Both letters and parcels can also be registered, which might be a good idea if you are sending photos back to be processed.

To receive mail you can give a **Poste Restante** address at either the main Post Office or a given hotel in any town. Given the amount which goes astray, however, and the obvious problems of language, you will be well advised to stick only to the main Post Offices of major cities or the real luxury hotels. And always make sure that letters sent to you include a 'hold until . . .' date and a return address. Your letters in and out may be opened – you are not allowed to receive such items as books and magazines.

Telephones inside any hotel will allow you to make free calls within a city. Long distance calls, whether domestic or international, are made by filling in a register slip at the service desk or through the operator. In general the system works surprisingly well, with only short delays and fairly clear lines: minimum charge is for three minutes, which to Europe should work out at around ¥30. Transfer Charge calls (which may prove cheaper) are also straightforward. If you're expecting someone to call you, make sure the hotel receptionist knows – otherwise they may be put through to the wrong room or simply cut off altogether.

Cables and telegrams, again sent from hotels or from telegraph offices in the main cities, are charged by the word – around ¥1.50 using the standard form.

As for other methods of keeping in touch, **foreign newspapers and magazines** are available from hotel shops in Beijing, Guangzhou and Shanghai, and more erratically in other cities which see large numbers of tourists. General interest periodicals can occasionally be found in foreign language bookshops. *China Daily* is an English language paper produced in China and aimed at foreign businessmen. It is a training ground for Chinese journalists and its occasionally bizarre blend of foreign news with hearty stories of peasant communes exceeding their quotas or moral tales about corruption can make interesting reading. Some hotels hand this out free, in others you have to pay. There are also English language magazines which you can often pick up in hotel lounges and the like. *Peking Daily* is a weekly political digest carrying the Party line on international and home events; *China Pictorial* and *China Reconstructs* are glossy magazines, much improved recently in lay-out and production, with articles about ethnic minorities, engineering achievements and archaeological discoveries – they

can be useful as pointers to areas recently opened to tourism. *Women in China* gives an interesting perspective. The main **Chinese newspaper** is the *Renmin Ribao* (*People's Daily*) often displayed under glass in the main street. There are also a host of local papers and news sheets which list films, operas and concerts if you can find an English-speaking Chinese to translate for you. An explosion of newsprint is one consequence of China's liberalisation, with dry technical and scientific journals now increasingly overshadowed by lurid scandal sheets (and a highly popular weekly listing of TV programmes). More traditionally, you'll still find **wall posters and public notice-boards** used as a means of getting messages across. These frequently feature moral or uplifting tales, but they may also show before and after photos of executed criminals or gory accidents.

Books are distributed throughout China by the *Xinhua* agency, which has stores in almost every town, and by the foreign language book distributor *Waiwen Shudian*. Most of what you can buy is either educational material or political tracts. There are moves to open more bookshops under different control because the present system is so cumbersome.

In more expensive hotel rooms you'll almost always find a **television**, often hidden under a chaste red chenille cover. Chinese TV is well worth watching for the news, which includes satellite material from all over the world: there's also lots of sport, including apparently endless series of fierce basketball matches against Soviet teams. The rest of the programming is also gradually being modernised, with Peking Opera and traditional or educational films giving way to repeats of old Shanghai movies or new series from Hong Kong. Depending on where you are you can get 2 or 3 channels – closedown is around 10–10.30pm. Some of the most popular programmes with the Chinese are English teaching courses like *Follow Me*.

If you carry a **short-wave radio** (you can buy tiny ones, or converters to fit a Walkman, in Hong Kong) you will also be able to pick up news broadcasts on the BBC World Service, Voice of America and others.

OPENING HOURS AND HOLIDAYS

Opening hours in China seem largely to be determined by meals. Most places open by 8 or 8.30 after an early breakfast. The midday scramble for lunch begins as early as 11.30: many public buildings and services – including museums, banks, post offices, the PSB and CITS – may close until 2 or 2.30pm, thus taking a large chunk out of your day. There is currently a drive to cut down the long lunch hour and some more popular tourist spots do now stay open straight through, which will often prove the least crowded time to visit them. The next onslaught on the restaurants (many of which shut for the rest of the afternoon) begins about 5pm. By 6 there are very few offices left open, though in larger towns many shops will stay open until 7 or even 8, especially in the main street or near the railway station.

Railway and bus station **ticket offices** tend to remain open as long as buses and trains are still running, from 5am to as late as 11pm, but the smaller ones may only sell tickets immediately before the relevant departure. **In the country-side** generally, everyone seems to be tucked up in bed by 9pm and if you arrive in out-of-the-way places after this you are likely to find the restaurants closed and local buses parked up for the night; however the dining room of your hotel, once you have reached it, should be open later. Even in the larger **cities** things are pretty dead at night: the last cinema showing will start around 8pm and the only real hope for insomniacs is to hang out in the bars and discos of the modern hotels – but take a torch to negotiate the dark streets home.

Sunday is a public holiday – most tourist attractions and temples will be open but almost everything else (except possibly CITS and the service counter in the hotel) will be shut. **Museums** close on Sundays, but this is par for the course – some shut on Mondays or Fridays too (check locally) and many close their doors quite arbitrarily when not expecting any tour groups.

Many of these places – parks, monuments, museums and some temples – make a token **admission charge**. At the most popular – the Longmen Caves or the Terracotta Army museum, for example – this may be more substantial. As a foreigner you'll often face higher charges unless you can prove you're a student.

There are nine annual **public holidays** in China, when almost everything will be closed. They are: **1 January** (standard New Year); **Chinese New Year**, usually in February, marked by a 3-day holiday when new clothes are bought, hair cut, bills paid, lucky characters pasted up everywhere and families gather for a blow-out meal which includes special dumplings and *Niangao* (rising higher every year) cakes; **8 March** (International Women's Day); **1 May** (Labour Day, a surprisingly subdued family occasion); **4 May** (Youth Day, commemorating the 1919 students' demonstration against foreign imperialism); **1 June** (Children's Day); **1 July** (anniversary of the founding of the Chinese Communist Party); **1 August** (anniversary of the founding of the PLA); and **1 October** (National Day) which commemorates the founding of the People's Republic with great meetings and demonstrations of patriotism.

THINGS TO TAKE . . . AND BRING BACK

The things you need to take with you to China are fairly predictable. Don't carry too many **clothes**; hotel laundries are quick, good and fairly cheap, while anything essential can be bought on the spot. You won't need anything formal – most Overseas Chinese visitors wear jeans or shorts. In summer light clothes are enough, though you'll need a sweater for the mountains and sturdy shoes to walk in. On arrival you can buy great sun-hats, plastic shoes or sandals and plastic raincoats or cycling capes (useful for covering a backpack). Winters can be extremely cold and though local long-johns and padded hats, coats and gloves are available, you'll need decent boots and thick socks at the least. A towel is important, and a cotton sheet sleeping bag, for some protection against mosquitoes (and dirty sheets) is also useful.

For **toilet things** you'll want to bring a small first-aid kit including insect repellent, suntan lotion, aspirin and perhaps a few basic medicines. Women should also take a supply of **tampons or sanitary towels**, which are either very crude or very expensive when you can find them in China. Soap, shampoo, washing powder, toothpaste and other basics are all widely available in China, as are all sorts of drugs – the main problem being that you can never be quite sure what you are taking. The Chinese equivalent of Tiger Balm is great for soothing tired muscles or picking you up after a long journey. For these all Chinese travellers carry with them a small **hand towel** – hanging this up on the washing line provided is an essential part of the tritual of boarding a train. Soaked in water and tied round your your head, one of these towels (sold everywhere) can go a long way towards easing the burden of summer heatwaves.

Other essentials include **books** – as many as you can carry for the endless waits and long journeys. They make a valuable currency for bartering with other voyagers, and the selection in China is poor; mostly translations of Chinese classics. A **Walkman** is another way of shutting out the world on long journeys or when you've simply had enough of *Tie A Yellow Ribbon* on the station tannoy: if you have one with a radio which will pick up the short-wave transmissions of the BBC World Service and Voice of America, so much the better. But be warned that the **batteries** sold in China are terrible. **Camera equipment** is also best brought with you, but see our section on *Photography*. You can buy imported cigarettes, spirits and some beer and soft drinks in hotel shops, Friendship Stores and a few other places which stock luxury goods, but stock up if you aim to spend your time in smaller places. Chinese drinks of all kinds are easy enough to find, but if **tea** of the sort you're used to, **coffee** or something which tastes like **milk** are important you'll have to bring those too.

Other **miscellaneous items** which will come in handy as you travel around include an umbrella, loo paper, a penknife with a tin and bottle opener, your own chopsticks, a mug and a water bottle or Thermos – all of which can easily be bought in China – and a lightweight torch and a small pack for day trips and hiking – both of which are better brought with you. A few small things you can give away as presents are useful too – foreign stamps, postcards and small denomination currency, magazines, pens, disposable lighters, and any sort of novelty item.

For everyday **shopping** the huge **department stores** or the better **markets** are your best bet – apart from anything else it is much easier where things are simply laid out so that you can point to them. The new **free markets** where people can sell their own surplus produce are also worth a look, though more out of interest than for any bargains. They mostly take place in the evening after work and often seem as much a meeting place as a market. **Friendship Stores** are more expensive as a rule – they stock goods imported from the west or which are in short supply elsewhere. Most demand payment in Foreign Exchange Certificates, and some are open only to foreigners and leading cadres – though on the whole anyone with FECs can buy. You have to remember that this is a mainly peasant economy whose industry has until recently virtually ignored consumer goods in favour of producing heavy industrial and agricultural tools. While the accumulation of possessions is no longer frowned upon – witness the ubiquitous hard-sell ads for washing machines, fridges and TVs – many of the items available to western eyes.

So buying **things to take back** is not always easy. Most of the **traditional Chinese goods** which are sold to tourists are manufactured especially for the tourist and export markets: everything from silk to ivory (which many countries will not allow you to import), jade, pottery, carpets, art works and clothes are produced for westerners at western prices and sold in the Friendship Stores. You'll find a wider choice – and perhaps better prices – at the Chinese Emporia in Hong Kong. **Antiques** are also sold in the Friendship Stores and elsewhere, but again there's little chance of a bargain. The state acts as a middleman in all these transactions: only antiques which have been cleared for export (and priced accordingly) can be taken out of the country. Items over 100 years old can be identified by a red wax seal. Perhaps the best souvenirs are the cheap **everyday items** at which no Chinese would look twice. Books, magazines and propaganda posters look particularly good once you've got them home and there are also lots of household goods to choose from: enamel bowls, lacquered wooden trays, bamboo hats, chopsticks and tea.

ENTERTAINMENT – ACROBATS, OPERA AND FESTIVALS

To an extent, China is still paying the price of the Cultural Revolution in the sphere of entertainment. Twenty years ago, even such inoffensive institutions as tea-houses, which provided a place to talk, some relief from the daily round and occasional organised entertainments, were closed down through most of China. Permitted entertainments are still largely prescribed by the state: theatre, opera, acrobatics and carefully vetted films provide the basic cultural diet. Yet in the wake of the 'Four Modernisations' things are at last beginning to change, and to do so rapidly. Wham's tour of China can be seen as one example, but on a more general plane, western culture, and greater freedom to experiment with traditional forms, is beginning to permeate every level of Chinese society.

Of the traditional entertainments, the **acrobatics** show is undoubtedly the most accessible. There is music and brilliant costume at these, but the acrobats themselves need no props, going through a routine which is almost always breathtakingly brilliant. Certainly if your experience of acrobatics ends with sequinned bikinis on trapezes you should make an effort to catch at least one Chinese performance. It's a whole new world.

Chinese **opera** is worth seeing too, even if you won't understand a word. It is a remarkably cheap and popular entertainment, with an audience which is almost as fascinating as anything going on on-stage. Here there is none of the hushed reverence for 'high art' which marks western opera; instead the workers in the crowd munch, talk and applaud appreciatively throughout. Quite what you'll see depends on the region and on the troupe. Some can be very slow moving, but costumes and make-up are always elaborately garish, and others mix drama, song and dance into a show which is almost slapstick. In any event since each performance lasts three to four hours don't be afraid of leaving if you get bored; the Chinese expect westerners to find it all totally incomprehensible.

As everywhere, traditional **festivals** are another potent source of enjoyment. These too have suffered under the Communist regime, but in the west and south – relatively safe from central control – many still flourish. As well as being enjoyable in themselves, they can be a rare opportunity for some of China's ethnic minorities to express their traditions. A couple of the bigger dates, widely celebrated across China, are the **Lantern Festival** held on the first full moon after the Chinese new year, and the **Dragon Boat Festival** on the 5th day of the 5th lunar month. At the former there are fireworks and dragon dances, while people carry weirdly shaped lanterns and eat sweet rice dumplings; the latter commemorates Qi Yuan, poet and official of the Warring States period. Dragon Boat races are held in his memory and *zongzi* – dumplings wrapped in leaves – are thrown into the water to appease the dragons who lurk beneath. But wherever you are, if you hear of a local festival, try to get to it.

The popularity of Chinese **films** must owe a great deal to the shortage of other nightlife. For while modern scripts are slightly less heavy handed than they once were, they are still very much limited to what the state regards as uplifting or morally improving. If nothing else they are usually simple to follow and make for an interesting comparison with the state of the artform in the west.

For all of these you'll find **listings** in local newspapers – assuming you can find someone to translate for you. Alternatively CITS should be prepared to book tickets, but their charge for doing so is often more than the tickets cost in the first place (rarely more than ¥3 or ¥4).

In some of the cities which are liberalising fastest – Shanghai and Guangzhou – or those far enough from central authority never to have been much affected – like Kunming – you may come across traditional **tea-houses and coffee shops**. These are once again the centres of intrigue and gossip they used to be. Elsewhere **street entertainers** go a long way to filling some of the cultural gaps, and wherever they perform they draw large, good-natured crowds. Performing monkeys are a great favourite and there are countless jugglers and acrobats too. Sometimes a travelling theatre may set up a booth in a square, by the railway station or in the market to perform favourite scenes from well-known operas or plays and these normally are accompanied by excellent musicians playing the most bizzare assortment of instruments.

For the Chinese there is still little else to do at night. The **TV news** (nightly at 7pm) is worth tuning into if you get the chance. It confirms the impression you get from talking to people that the Chinese are far more aware of the world beyond their borders than are most westerners. The rather crude adverts can be amusing too.

For tourists (and increasingly, wealthy locals) there are finally **hotel bars** – the place to hang out and meet other travellers. In Beijing everyone congregates in the Beijing Hotel; in Shanghai you head for the Peace Hotel with its legendary five-piece jazz band – all in their 70s and marvellously out of tune, these veterans of pre-war days are still hamming up the tunes they learned then. Increasingly the larger and more modern of these hotels will have **discos** too. Extremely dull if they're for westerners only, these can be rather wonderful when they allow Chinese in too: the enthusiasm is catching. In Guangzhou and Shanghai there are now said to be regular discos outside the hotels run by and for Chinese, much cheaper than the hotels. Whether you would be able to find these, though, and whether you would be welcome if you did, are matters for conjecture.

PHOTOGRAPHY

Ten years ago only a tiny minority of Chinese owned a camera. Film stock was poor stuff mainly imported from the Eastern Bloc and photographs were either tiny grainy family snaps or else ideologically sound and highly coloured magazine images of ethnic minorities or young commune workers down on the farm. Now **photography** is one of China's most popular pastimes. The benefits are manifold: you point your camera without attracting the least attention – hundreds of others will probably be doing the same thing. Nor, on the beaten track anyway, are you likely to be besieged with requests for your Polaroids.

In the main cities and tourist spots Kodak, Fuji, and other imported **films** and flash bulbs are increasingly available in ordinary shops catering for the home market. Indeed, since the Chinese are keen on doing their own processing and printing – perhaps because the service available from shops has until recently been so appalling – you will see entire shops devoted to selling solid, clumsy enlargers from Poland alongside the latest papers and chemicals from Japan. You are much more likely now to get help if you need your camera repaired or you want to buy a filter or a case. You can even get your film **processed** and printed if you wish, especially via hotels in the main cities, but I would be inclined to check up on the equipment they use first.

Most people, though, will bring cameras and film from home or else buy them in **Hong Kong**; remember to mention your camera on your Chinese Customs form. Film is good value in Hong Kong and so are cameras; but do check on your new camera by running a roll of film through and getting it processed – which only takes one hour – to make sure it is working properly before you enter China. If you run low on film your best bet is the local Friendship Store or a shop in a hotel catering for foreigners but the range and availability vary and it's better to bring at least one more roll than you think you might need.

When you come to **take pictures** you will find that in many interesting places, like the Tomb of the Terracotta Soldiers in Xi'an or the caves of Buddhist sculptures at Longmen or Datong, photography is forbidden. No doubt this is because the Chinese want to sell their own slides and postcards; it is noticeable that only the best carvings or statues are restricted and in some cases you are allowed to photograph on payment of an exorbitant fee. Some people have gone to extraordinary lengths to sidestep these restrictions; if you are really set on taking photographs inside temples or caves it's worth bringing some faster film so that you don't have to attract attention with a flash. I never heard of anyone having their film confiscated for breaking these rules. But of course you should **be careful** about taking photographs from aircraft, or photographing naval and military installations, soldiers on duty, and in some areas prisons.

As for **photographing the Chinese**, if you use a long lens no one will know what you are pointing your camera at; a standard lens requires a combination of speed and courtesy. Often the Chinese will be very happy for their children to be photographed, and may ask for a copy. Occasionally some subject may feel he is not being seen at his best; I was taking a picture of an old man in Nanjing when a complete stranger walked up and calmly did his jacket up for him. And some people – especially

the ethnic minorities – may not like having their picture taken *at all*.

The other side of the coin is that **the Chinese** are now all fanatical camera buffs: some have the SLR Japanese and German cameras now being made under licence, others have Seagulls, a solid Chinese type based on a Russian model. The rest can hire an old-fashioned box camera in parks or tourist spots; off they go with the camera and come back with a roll of film which is 'processed' on the spot with an unwieldy changing bag and a couple of buckets of murky chemicals so that they can go home trailing their record of the day's outing. You might like to hire one of these cameras for fun. The Chinese are only interested in taking photographs of each other and are often puzzled by our interest in landscape, or indeed in them. You'll often have to wait while your view empties itself of the procession of Chinese queueing up for family snaps. Stone animals at tombs are being worn away by posing tourists and often at a tourist spot you'll see an enormous exhausted papier mache tiger placed there for just this purpose. Or you can dress up in Tang costume for your picture, or poke your head through one of the many cardboard props – a medieval charger near Nanjing city wall, a Cadillac outside the Lu Xun museum in Shaoxing.

WORK AND STUDY

Work

Work opportunities in China are limited and – due to the language barrier – likely to remain so for some time to come. However, by the same token, China does have regular openings for **English language teaching** and **teacher training**.

It is possible to apply direct for teaching posts to the **Education Division** of any large Chinese embassy. They will supply you with a list of colleges and universities interested in taking on teachers – generally TEFL qualified graduates. If you get the job, you will be paid return airfares to China and a standard subsidised foreign expert salary.

Less officially – or at least arranged on the spot once you're in China – are openings in **secondary schools**. You

will be paid local wages for this work (exhausting – and breadline) but you may find yourself in a more interesting area of the country and closer in touch with local people. It is sometimes possible, too, to apply directly in China for work at a university or college (as above); don't, however, depend upon it.

Western-sponsored alternatives include **Voluntary Service Overseas (VSO)** and the **British Council**, both of whom place experienced language teachers – and also people with business or agricultural skills – in China. The British Council, on the whole, are looking for long-term (3–5 years) commitment from graduates, preferably in linguistics, with an MA in applied linguistics, London contact addresses are:

British Council, 65 Davies St, W1 (Tel. 01 499 8011)

VSO, 9 Belgrave Square, SW1 (Tel. 01 235 5191).

Other specialist bodies, which you might consider, include the **Thomson Foundation** (Regents Cottages, Inner Circle, Regents Park, London NW1; 01 486 9648), who have in the past advertised for people to work in China on newspapers, or in training Chinese journalists; the **Sino–British Trade Council** (Abford House, Wilton Rd, London SW1; 01 828 5176), for openings in the commercial or banking sectors; and the **Great Britain China Centre** (5 Belgrave Square, London SW1, Tel. 01 235 6696), an independent, government-funded body who exist to promote cultural, scientific and educational exchanges – they publish a helpful monthly newsletter.

Study

You can **study Chinese** – or other subjects (notably traditional medicine) – in China, though courses are easiest arranged on a reciprocal basis through your own college or university. For details of possibilities, write to the **Education Division** of any large Chinese Embassy. They will provide you with a list of the language – and other specialised – courses on offer at universities and institutes across China. The choice is considerable: from the prestigious Foreign Languages Institute in Beijing to courses in places like Kunming in the south-west. The financial outlay, if you are studying on your own impulse, can be considerable; it can, however, be subsidised through ad-hoc English language teaching. The British Council (see above) may also be willing to subsidise students with a first degree or equivalent and some knowledge of Chinese, who wish to further their research at a Chinese university.

SACU, the Society for Anglo–Chinese Understanding (152 Camden High St, London NW1, Tel. 01 482 4292) run a one-month summer language course in Beijing every August. The cost (about £1200) covers fares, accommodation and teaching at the People's University.

Studying Chinese **before you leave**, there are good courses on offer at the following London colleges:

Polytechnic of Central London, 309 Regents St, W1 (Tel. 01 580 2020).

Ealing College of Higher Education, St Mary's Rd, W5 (Tel. 01 579 4111).

School of Oriental and African Studies, Malet St, WC1 (Tel. 01 637 2388).

SACU (see above) also offer short, intensive Chinese courses.

TROUBLE

One of the eeriest sights in China is the poster on display outside many provincial police stations featuring small mugshots of the latest criminals condemned to death. If there is a red tick over the picture then the punishment has already been administered. Although the Chinese issue no crime statistics, executions are by no means rare, and in the border areas there are labour camps (mostly for political offenders) to go with the regular prisons elsewhere. With this in mind you could be forgiven for thinking that here is a country both threatening and dangerous. In practice, for the traveller, nothing could be further from the truth. China is as safe a place as any in the world, and if you are **attacked or robbed**, chances are it will be by a fellow foreigner.

Which is not to say that elementary precautions should not be exercised: if you leave your valuables lying around they will go. Left locked in a hotel room, however, or in the lockers or left luggage facilities which most dorms provide, they should be secure enough. Outside, on trains and in the street, the curiosity of the Chinese is such that you can feel sure that you and your things are being closely watched virtually all the time. The sort of **rip-offs** and deliberate short-changing which plague travellers elsewhere are also relatively rare here: a taxi-driver, for example, occupies a prestigious position as a state employee and is unlikely to endanger it by asking for more than the officially fixed fare.

Sexual harassment is again almost non-existent. You do hear the occasional story of western women being approached in parks or while cycling late at night, but these are the exceptions. Generally Chinese men are far too bemused by the antics of the big noses to even consider them as sexual objects. It does pay, however, to remember that

Chinese women dress very demurely and to avoid wearing anything that might appear too provocative – also to exercise more caution in the Muslim northwest, where many women cover their hair and many men have a more recognisably macho attitude.

When problems do occur they are very often the result of **insensitivity** on the part of the visitor: I once saw a tribesman pull a sword on one insistent American who was trying to take his photograph. Taking pictures of 'sensitive installations' or being caught in places where you're not supposed to be are the other most common cause of travellers having a run-in with the law, but even these rarely result in anything more than a stiff lecture and a confiscated film or order to move on.

Finally, if some crime has been committed against you, the place to go is the **PSB**. It is probably easiest to contact the foreign branch in the first place, as with luck they will act as intermediaries or translators. Don't bother with CITS, who couldn't care less. And if you get no joy, or things get serious, contact your **embassy** or consulate. But don't expect much sympathy.

OTHER THINGS

CONTRACEPTION has been an area of priority for the Chinese and local brands are reckoned to be safe and effective. Condoms are available in three sizes – and resemble rather the inner tube of a tyre than the diaphanous western item. The pill – free of charge from chemists – is also widely available, though you would certainly be wise to bring adequate supplies of your usual brand. Chemists also stock **pills for men** which they claim work. Carnality with the Big Noses, while not encouraged, does occasionally occur.

DRUGS The opium poppies which once flourished all over China are no longer cultivated but the Opium Wars and the debate that raged around them make fascinating reading – it's strange to read leading figures of the British establishment roundly asserting that the smoking of opium was beneficial to the Chinese. In any event opium is no longer openly smoked in China, if at all. Marijuana is not cultivated either, and nor is there any tradition of its use by the Chinese, but it grows in wild abundance around Kashgaria, Dunhuang, Kunming and many other places. Some of the minority peoples in these places take advantage of the cheap and plentiful supply. What the penalties would be for a westerner caught in possession we have no idea.

ELECTRICITY Throughout China it's 220V, 50Hz AC with American style two-pin plugs. Given the right adaptor, most European or Australasian appliances work fine.

EMBASSIES AND CONSULATES Just about everyone maintains an embassy in Beijing and as a rule they are far more welcoming than you'd expect. No doubt this will change as tourist numbers swell. There are also American, British and other Consulates in Shanghai and Guangzhou. For addresses, see the Listings sections for these cities.

LAUNDRY Most hotels of any size offer a reasonably good, reasonably priced laundry service – often same day. Doing your own is easy enough too, with detergent sold anywhere and some form of washing facility in most of the cheaper places to stay.

LEFT LUGGAGE All hotels and hostels will store luggage for you (whether you are staying or not) and most villages with more than two houses also seem to have somewhere to leave your bags. Bus and railway stations always have a left luggage counter too, though the queues at these are sometimes alarming. They're very cheap, so make the most of them, but be sure to check opening hours and to keep a tight hold on your receipt.

LOOS Chinese loos range from the 1920s style thrones in some Shanghai hotels to low mud or brick-walled enclosures with a hole in the ground, probably next to the pig pen. In a small village near Wuhu an old woman ushered me with great courtesy to a tub sunk in the corner of a field. Most hotels have western-style seats; some hotels have flushing squat-loos; but in the country it will more often be an earth closet, dirty, smelly and full of insects. Which doesn't deter the locals, for whom these are places to chat for hours – there's next to no privacy and a westerner may attract quite an audience, so boiler suit type clothing is not an advantage for women. Always carry a supply of paper – easily bought – and a torch for use after dusk. All human and animal excrement is used, untreated, as fertiliser: this is one of the main reasons why you have to be careful of the water, uncooked vegetables and water-based fruit like watermelons.

TIME ZONES Although China stretches some 3000 miles from east to west, passing through what in the US would be three different time zones, the whole country runs on Beijing time. This makes things very much less complicated except in the far west – Kashgar has official (Beijing) time and unofficial local time, which is one hour behind; know which you are talking about. **Hong Kong** uses daylight saving time, so is one hour different in summer.

TIPPING Don't.

WATER Drinking tap water anywhere in China is inadvisable: supplies of boiled water (often still boiling, for tea) are on hand in hotels, waiting rooms, trains and public buildings, or you can buy mineral water in most hotels and restaurants.

WEIGHTS AND MEASURES China is becoming increasingly metric, but there are some traditional Chinese measures still in use. The most common are:

Li 3 li = 1 mile; Gongli, equivalent to a kilometre, is often used now.

Mu 6 mu = 1 acre; 15 mu = 1 hectare.

Jin 1 jin = a catty, or pound; Gongjin is a kilo – for small quantities while shopping ask for *Yi Ban Jin*, half a pound.

WOMEN'S MOVEMENT Whatever the reality, as far as the Chinese are concerned women already are equal partners in the Revolution. The *All China Women's Federation* was set up in 1949 to represent women's 'deepest needs and rights': it has branches in most cities but you'd probably need a special introduction from on high to meet a representative.

A GLOSSARY OF COMMON CHINESE TERMS

APSARAS Angels in Buddhist iconography.

ARHAT See *Lohan*.

AVALOKITESVARA Sanskrit name for the Chinese GUANYIN, God of Mercy.

BEI North (Chinese use cardinal points instead of right and left when giving directions).

BINGUAN Hotel, generally a large one for tourists.

BODHIDHARMA The Indian monk who traditionally arrived in China about 520AD, founded the Ch'an (Zen) sect, and became its first head.

BODHISATTVA A disciple of the Buddha, one who has attained enlightenment but remains on earth to help others. Treated as gods and much represented in iconography.

BUDDHA Not just Buddha himself, but any one of his followers who has attained Nirvana.

CITS Tourist organisation (China International Travel Service).

DAGOBA (CHORTEN, STUPA) A shrine, shaped like an inverted vase and containing the remains of a Buddhist saint.

DA Great/big (DAJIE, main street).

DIAN Hall, Great Room.

DONG East.

FANDIAN Restaurant (or hotel).

FEC Foreign Exchange Certificate.

FEN Smallest denomination of Chinese currency – 100 to the Yuan.

FENG Peak.

GONG Palace.

GUAN Pass.

HAI Sea.

HAN The racial group which dominates China – also an early dynasty (106BC–AD220).

HE River.

HU Lake.

HUIMIN A Muslim minority people (hence Muslims in general).

HUTONG Alleyway with houses, dwelling compound.

JATAKA Illustrated story of the life of Buddha.

JIANG River.

JIAO (or MAO) 10 fen.

JIE Street (often DAJIE, avenue or main street).

JING Capital.

KMT Kuomintang: Nationalist Party founded with high ideals by Sun Yatsen – later, under Chiang Kaishek, became the main adversary of the Communists.

LAMAIC BUDDHISM Buddhism as practised in Tibet (and spread from there).
The Lamas (with the DALAI LAMA at
their head) are political as well as
secular leaders; each is believed to be
the reincarnation of his predecessor.

LOHAN (or ARHAT) Buddhist monk of
the *Iberavada* tradition who has
attained nirvana by cutting himself off
from the world.

LU Street (often preceded by BEI,
DONG, NAN or XI).

MAHAYANA The form of Buddhism
which accepts a pantheon of Buddhas
and Bodhisattvas and predominates
in China.

MAITREYA The Buddhist Messiah,
waiting in heaven to succeed
Sakyamuni.

MANDALA Mystic diagram which forms
important part of Buddhist iconography especially in Tibet.

MEN Gate.

MIAO Shrine or Temple.

NAN South.

PAGODA Multi-storeyed tower, usually
built as reliquary in Buddhist temple.

PINYIN Official method of transliterating
Chinese – superseded the old WADE-
GILES method (Beijing replaced
Peking).

PLA People's Liberation Army.

PSB Public Security Bureau – the Police.

QUAN Spring.

RENMIN The People.

RMB Renminbi – The People's money.

SAKYAMUNI The supreme and original
Buddha, often shown crosslegged on
a lotus with three fingers of the right
hand raised.

SHAN Mountain.

SHANG Top.

SHUI Water.

SI Temple.

STUPA See *Dagoba*.

SUTRA Buddhist scripture.

TA Pagoda or Dagoba.

TAI CHI Form of exercise or gentle
martial art, closely associated with
Daoism, practised by millions in
China.

TAOISM (DAOISM) Indigenous religion
of China before the arrival of
Buddhism.

TIAN Heaven/sky.

WAIGUO REN Foreigner.

XI West.

XIA Bottom.

YUAN Unit of currency, also plain or
garden.

ZHONG (ZHONG GUO) Middle/centre
(Middle Kingdom).

ZHOU Place or region.

Part two
THE GUIDE

Chapter one
BEIJING AND AROUND

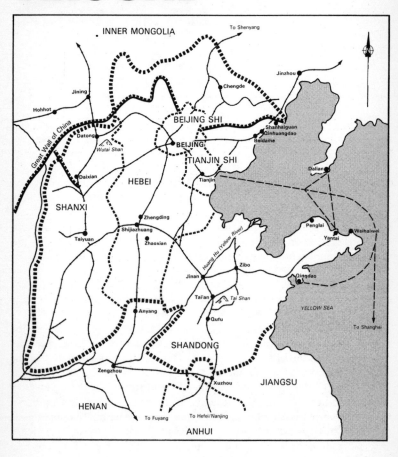

BEIJING (PEKING) SHI – TIANJIN SHI – HEBEI – SHANXI – SHANDONG

China's capital for 800 years, **Beijing** (Peking) is today one of the world's most extraordinary powerbases. Decisions made by the Communist Party here govern the lives – in just about all aspects – of over 1,000 million Chinese; while all Chinese time, from Guangdong to Tibet, runs on a single, Beijing, zone. And the city's monuments, both historic and modern, are, as you'd expect, the country's grandest: the Forbidden City, the Temple of Heaven, nearby, the Great Wall, and, at the heart of the nation, the 100 acre mass-rally Tian'anmen Square. Visiting China, whatever your interests, you will want (and most likely need) to spend some time in Beijing – to do otherwise would be wilfully perverse. Yet go prepared. Vast (on an almost ludicrous scale) and functional (to the point of tedium and beyond), Beijing is a city few travellers actually enjoy. And make no mistake, it in no way typifies the nation.

Moving out from Beijing, a comprehensive hub of transport links allow almost infinite choice, both within China and, with the start of the Trans-Siberian routes, beyond. The 'immediate' region covered in this chapter – an area getting on for the size of Northern Europe, incidentally – is not greatly visited. **Tianjin** municipality and **Hebei** province, which enclose the capital, are dominated by heavy industrial towns: though relieved, in the north, by the 18C Imperial city of **Chengde** and by **Beidahe** on the coast, a fun seaside resort to observe and join the Chinese at play. The predominantly mountainous provinces of **Shanxi** and **Shandong** – around and through which the **Huang He** (Yellow River) loops its way to the sea – offer more substantial interest. Shanxi was one of the earliest centres of Chinese Buddhist culture, a past spectacularly commemorated in the Yunggang caves at **Datong** and at numerous lesser sites. Datong, too, is worth a major detour for anyone interested in trains – it preserves what is reputed to be the world's last active steam engine plant. In Shandong, a poor province perennially flooded by the Huang He, the two main pulls are **Qufu**, birth and death place of (currently back in favour) Confucius, and the extraordinary pilgrim mountain of **Tai Shan**. The Chinese, however, are currently trying to promote more tourism around Shandong and if you've time there are worthwhile options to explore: either on your own (most of the coastal peninsula is now open with a PSB permit) or in connection with CITS, whose group tour 'themes' include living and working with rural peasant families.

A general warning on **climate**. If you can, visit Beijing and these northern heartlands in spring or autumn. Winters are biting, removing all life from the city streets; midsummer can be equally overpowering with heavy, humid heat and, in July and August especially, interminable rain.

BEIJING SHI AND TIANJIN SHI

To do any justice to **Beijing**'s monuments, you'll need about a week – at the end of which you'll probably feel more than ready to move on. As interim breaks from the capital, visits to the **Great Wall** at Badaling and the **Ming Tombs** (en route) are more or less obligatory. But keep in mind that foreigners are no longer limited to these two excursions beyond the city limits: an increasing number of places in the municipalities (*shis*) of both Beijing and Tianjin are now open, including the port city of **Tianjin** itself and the **Miyun reservoir** (which supplies all Beijing's water). These are detailed, as day trips, on p. 75 and p. 90.

BEIJING (PEKING)

Like other northern Chinese cities, **BEIJING** (PEKING) is encased in walls. Its life seems essentially private, and, as a traveller (or even a foreign resident), it can be hard to penetrate below the austere public surface of its endless geometric avenues and vast, functional official buildings. This is frustrating, of course, though fascinating too – if you want to get a feel for the size of China, and the size of the bureaucracy needed to sustain it, Beijing is the key. For an intense and immediate introduction, venture out at rush hour and watch the traffic patterns of three *million* bicyclists; stand before the Great Hall of the People in Tian'anmen square, where Mao's million-crowd rallies took place in the 1960s; and walk through the old Imperial Palace, 'the Forbidden City' of an earlier state officialdom and a good two hours non-stop from end to end.

It was in **Tian'anmen** – on 1 October 1949 – that Chiarman **Mao Zedong** hoisted the red flag to officially proclaim the foundation of the People's Republic. He told the crowds (the square could then hold only 500,000) that the Chinese had at last stood up, and defined liberation as the final culmination of a 150-year fight against foreign exploitation.

The claim, perhaps, was modest. Beijing's recorded **history** goes back a little over three millennia, to beginnings as a trading centre for Mongols, Koreans and local Chinese tribes. Its predominance, however, dates to the mid 13C, and the formation of **Mongol China** under Genghis and later Kublai Khan. It was Kublai, who took control of the city in 1264, who properly established it as capital, replacing the earlier power centres of Luoyang and Xi'an. Marco Polo visited him here, working for a while in the city, clearly impressed with the level of sophistication.

> So great a number of houses and of people, no man could tell the number ... I believe there is no place in the world to which so many merchants come, and dearer things, and of greater value and more strange, come into this town from all sides than into any city in the world ...

The wealth came from the city's path along the Silk Route: Polo described 'over a thousand carts loaded with silk' arriving 'almost each day'. And it set a precedent in terms of style and grandeur for the Khans, or emperors – Kublai built himself a palace of astonishing proportions, walled about on all sides and approached by great marble stairways.

With the accession of the **Ming** dynasty, who defeated the Mongols in 1368, the capital temporarily shifted to present-day Nanjing, but Yong Le, the second Ming emperor, returned, building around him prototypes of the city's two greatest monuments – the **Imperial Palace** and **Temple of Heaven**. It was in Yong's reign, too, that the basic cityplan took shape, rigidly symmetrical, extending in squares and rectangles from the palace and 'inner city' grid to the suburbs: much as today.

Subsequent, post-Ming history is dominated by the rise and eventual collapse of **the Manchus** – the **Qing** dynasty. Coming from their northern powerbase, the Manchus took Beijing in 1644, holding it, and power through most of China, into this century. The capital was at its most prosperous in the first half of the 18C, the period in which the Qing constructed the legendary **Summer Palace** – the world's most extraordinary royal garden, with two hundred pavilions, temples and palaces, and immense artificial lakes and hills. This, to the north of the city, was, with the central Imperial Palace, the focus of endowment and symbol of Chinese wealth and power. It does not, however, survive. In 1860 the Opium Wars brought British and French troops to the walls of the capital: the Summer Palace was first looted and then, by the British, burnt, more or less in entirety, to the ground.

But in Beijing – as throughout China – the beauty of the palaces was not, in any case, for the eyes of the people. The Imperial court lived apart, within what was essentially a separate walled city. Conditions for ordinary Chinese, in the capital's suburbs, were starkly different. Kang Youwei, a Cantonese, visited in 1895 and described this dual world:

> No matter where you look, the place is covered with beggars. The homeless and the old, the crippled and the sick with no one to care for them, fall dead on the roads. This happens everyday. And the coaches of the great officials rumble past them continuously.

The indifference, rooted according to Kang in officials throughout the province, spread from the top down. From 1884, with funds meant for the modernisation of the nation's navy, the Empress Dowager Tz'u-hsi had again turned towards the task of building a new Summer Palace of her own.

The Empress's project was really the last grand gesture of Imperial architecture and patronage – and like its model was also badly burnt by foreign troops, in another outbreak of the Opium War in 1900. By this time, with successive waves of occupation by foreign troops, the Empire and the Imperial capital were near collapse. The Manchus abdicated in 1911, leaving 'the Northern Capital' and its territory to be ruled by **warlords**; later, in 1928, by the military dictatorship of Chiang Kai-shek's **Kuomintang**; in 1939 by the **Japanese**; at the end of the Second World War, in 1945, by an alliance of Kuomintang troops and American marines.

The **Communists** took Beijing in January 1949 – nine months before Chiang Kai-shek's flight to Taiwan assured final victory. The **rebuilding** of the capital, and the erasing of symbols of the previous regimes, was an early priority. The city that Mao Zedong inherited for the Chinese people was in most ways primitive. Imperial laws had banned the building of houses higher than the official buildings and palaces – so virtually nothing was more than one storey high. The roads, although straight and uniform, were narrow and congested. There was scarcely any industry. The new plans were to reverse all except the city's sense of ordered planning, with Tian'anmen square at its heart – and initially, through the early 1950s, their inspiration was Soviet.

In retrospect, the Chinese would no doubt like to reverse much of the **early achievements**: the poor quality high-rise housing programmes, and the emphasis on heavy industry. With their new-found respect for – or at least recognition of commercial value in – historic monuments, they might too regret the speed and scale of the city's renewal. In the zest to free from the past – to create a modern, people's capital – much of 'Old Peking' was destroyed. Even the city walls and gates, relics mostly of the Ming era, were pulled down – their place taken by ring roads and avenues. And, undoubtedly, Beijing's population growth was too rapid. Official figures put the city count today at 9.3 million, but it is almost certainly higher, and long-term plans for a stabilisation at 10 million by the end of the century look ambitious. During the Cultural Revolution, upwards of half a million Beijing youths were exiled to the countryside and provinces. Most have since returned but there are said to be up to 20,000 still awaiting permission in Shanxi, and more elsewhere: in mid 1985 a demonstration was staged by several hundred of these (now not so young) exiles.

Recent **changes of policy** have, however, had some success in terms of environmental awareness. In the development plan drawn up for the capital in 1983, the authorities decided to do serious battle with industrial pollution, which in winter had become acute – blanketing the city in a pale yellow smog. Factories which couldn't be transformed were on occasions closed. The city's parkland, often reduced to bare grass, is also being revitalised, with a massive tree-planting campaign, and is to be quadrupled in extent. And to provide impetus for people to leave Beijing, there are ambitious plans for a series of satellite cities. Changing personal habits, however, is less easy. The city authorities' official campaign against spitting (which is reckoned the cause of Beijing's high rate of TB) has had minimal effect.

Orientation: arrival, rooms and getting around

There's no doubt that Beijing's culture shock (which is unavoidable) owes much to the apparent unreality of the city's **layout**. The main streets are dead straight – aligned either west–east or north–south – and extend, in a bizarre series of widening rectangles, across the whole 30 sq km 'inner' capital. And where the streets aren't vast and geometric they tend to parody the opposite extreme: in the old network of downtown *hutongs*, dark alleyways twist out from the main grid.

To get some sense of **orientation**, make fast mental notes on the more obvious and imposing **landmarks**: the **Great Hall of the People** in Tian'-anmen square; the 17-storey **Beijing Hotel** on Dongchang'an Jie (Chang'an Avenue East); the **Telegraph Office** on Xichang'an Jie (Chang'an Avenue West); further out, on the extensions of Chang'an Avenue, the **Friendship Store** and **Nationalities Cultural Palace**. **Tian'-anmen** and the **Imperial Palace** (the 'Forbidden City') mark the city's heart, with **Chan'an Avenue** running between them – changing its name, like all the major boulevards, every few kilometres along its length. The historic core of the old city, and by far the most interesting area, is south from Tian'anmen along **the Qianmen**: the lanes and hutongs below it are largely untouched by post-Liberation development.

Arriving . . .

The size of Beijing makes walking impractical for all but the shortest journeys – even Tian'anmen to the Beijing Hotel (which looks no distance on the maps) is a good 15-minute walk. So on arrival, with baggage, you need to be more than usually organised. Unless you've been told specifically otherwise, the place to make for first is **CITS** in the Chongwenmen Hotel: most of the year you *have* to arrange accommodation through them (and they in turn have an obligation to find it), and if the position has altered it's from fellow travellers in the office that you're likely to find out how things stand.

A reasonable scale **map** of the city is essential: the one we've printed overleaf isn't large enough to take in more than basic orientation detail. One of the best, especially if you can pick it up before leaving for China, is the fold-out *Falkplan*, which includes main bus and trolley routes. Once in Beijing, you can pick up reasonable English-language maps from either CITS or the major hotels: look out for the orange and green city-plan and bus map.

. . . by train

Arriving at Beijing by train should be relatively straightforward. Almost all long-distance trains pull into the main central station – **Beijing Zhan** – and from here it's only a 10-minute walk to CITS. Leaving the station, hand in your ticket at the turnstile, turn left outside and follow the main road to the Chongwenmen/Chongwenmenwai interesection – CITS are on the corner. Or get a **taxi** (tickets from the taxi depot office – a converted bus – straight in front of the station exit), or a no. **103** or **104** trolleybus.

Just possibly, if one or other rail line is under repair or reconstruction, you might come into the city at **Yongdingmen** station, 4km out from the centre. If you do, the simplest approach to CITS is probably the no. **106** trolley, which goes right the way to Chongwenmen. Alternatively, there are taxis and minibuses, with a regular shuttle service to Beijing Zhan. Or you could try your luck going straight to the *Qiao Yuan Hotel* (see below), which is in walking distance.

. . . by air

Beijing Capital Airport – which serves both international and domestic flights – is a surprisingly quiet place. You can usually clear customs and visa checks in a couple of minutes, and there's no great problem covering the 29km into the centre. Municipal bus no.**359** runs fairly regularly to the Dongzhimen bus station (about an hour's ride) and from there you can pick up a no.**44** bus to CITS. Alternatively, if you've arrived on a CAAC flight, there's a **CAAC bus** to their office at 117 Dongxie Dajie (no.104 trolley on from here to CITS). Or there are taxis – expensive (about ¥28) but an easy start to the protracted business of finding a room, below . . .

Using CITS and finding a room

Be warned. The worst part of any traveller's stay in China is **finding a hotel bed** in Beijing. The capital has a major supply problem – it is said that Tibet was initially opened up to offload a pile-up of independent travellers here – and the better hotel rooms are almost permanently occupied by foreigners or Overseas Chinese who live and work in the city. As a temporary, budget traveller, you'll find yourself at the bottom

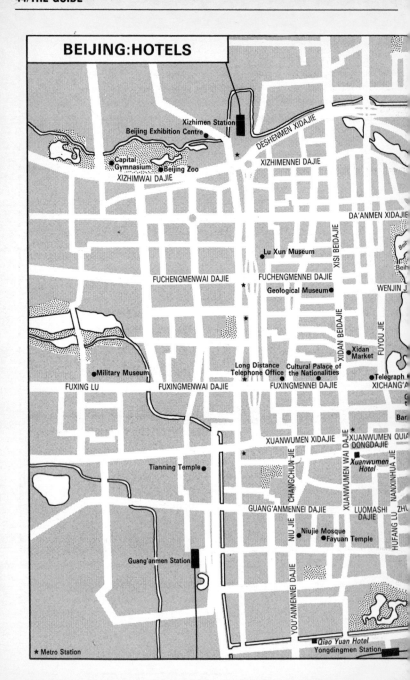

BEIJING:HOTELS

Xizhimen Station
Beijing Exhibition Centre
DESHENMEN XIDAJIE
XIZHIMENNEI DAJIE
Capital Gymnasium
Beijing Zoo
XIZHIMWAI DAJIE

DA'ANMEN XIDAJIE

Lu Xun Museum
XISI BEIDAJIE
Beih
Beih

FUCHENGMENWAI DAJIE
FUCHENGMENNEI DAJIE
WENJIN J
Geological Museum

XIDAN BEIDAJIE
FUYOU JIE
Xidan Market

Military Museum
Long Distance Telephone Office
Cultural Palace of the Nationalities
Telegraph
FUXING LU
FUXINGMENWAI DAJIE
FUXINGMENNEI DAJIE
XICHANG'A
G
t
Bar

XUANWUMEN XIDAJIE
XUANWUMEN QUIA DONGDAJIE
CHANGCHUN JIE
XUANWUMEN WAI DAJIE
Xuanwumen Hotel
NANXINHUA JIE
Tianning Temple

GUANG'ANMENNEI DAJIE
LUOMASHI DAJIE
ZHU
HUFANG LU
NIU JIE
Niujie Mosque
Fayuan Temple

Guang'anmen Station

YOU'ANMENNEI DAJIE

Qiao Yuan Hotel
Yongdingmen Station

★ Metro Station

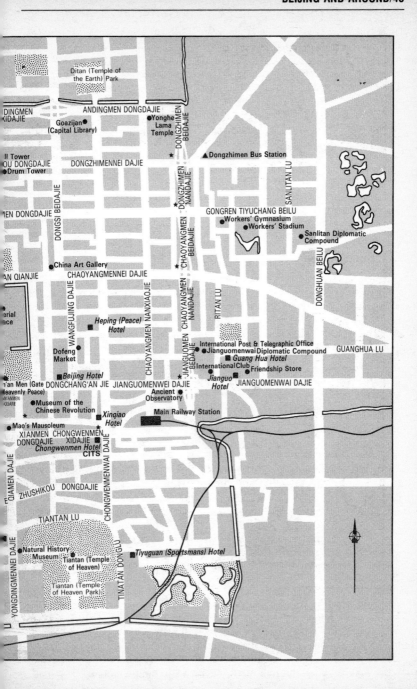

Ditan (Temple of the Earth) Park

ANDINGMEN DONGDAJIE

DINGMEN XIDAJIE

Goazijan (Capital Library)

Yonghe Lama Temple

DONGZHIMEN BEIDAJIE

▲ Dongzhimen Bus Station

SANLITAN LU

ll Tower
OU DONGDAJIE
●Drum Tower

DONGZHIMENNEI DAJIE

DONGZHIMEN NANDAJIE

GONGREN TIYUCHANG BEILU
●Workers' Gymnasium
●Workers' Stadium

DONGSI BEIDAJIE

Sanlitan Diplomatic Compound

EN DONGDAJIE

DONGHUAN BEILU

CHAOYANGMEN BEIDAJIE

●China Art Gallery

CHAOYANGMENNEI DAJIE

AN QIANJIE

CHAOYANGMEN NANXIAOJIE

CHAOYANGMEN NANDAJIE

RITAN LU

WANGFUJING DAJIE

Heping (Peace) Hotel

JIANGUOMEN BEIDAJIE

International Post & Telegraphic Office
●Jianguomenwai Diplomatic Compound
■ Guang Hua Hotel
International Club ●Friendship Store

GUANGHUA LU

●Dofeng Market

●Beijing Hotel

Jianguo Hotel

JIANGUOMENWAI DAJIE

erial
ace

n'an Men (Gate DONGCHANG'AN JIE JIANGUOMENWEI DAJIE
Heavenly Peace)
N ANMEN
SQUARE
●Museum of the Chinese Revolution

Ancient ● Observatory

●Mao's Mausoleum

Xinqiao Hotel

Main Railway Station

XIANMEN CHONGWENMEN
DONGDAJIE   XIDAJIE
Chongwenmen Hotel
CITS

CHONGWENMENWAI DAJIE

EQIAMEN DAJIE

ZHUSHIKOU DONGDAJIE

TIANTAN LU

●Natural History Museum

●Tiantan (Temple of Heaven)

Tiyuguan (Sportsmans) Hotel

Tiantan (Temple of Heaven Park)

TINTAN DONGLU

YONGDINGMENNEI DAJIE

of the heap – most probably in a dingy, poorly maintained dormitory. Just keep repeating to yourself, 'things can only get better' . . .

CITS offices tend to get better, too: Beijing's is ludicrously understaffed, consistently inaccurate and (to understate a little) very, very surly. But, on the positive front, they are not allowed to let you roam the streets looking for a bed, so they have to, in the end, find you a place – even if it's a bed in one of the city's hospitals.

The office is on the second floor of the *Chongwenmen Hotel*, at the south-west corner of the Chongwenmen/Qianmen road junction – the intersection with Chongwenmenwai Dajie. It is open on Mondays to Fridays only, from 8.30–11.30 and 1.30–5; outside these hours, you're on your own. Assuming you arrive to find them doing business, there are three main ground rules:

– Be persistent and exact about what you want: if you're told there are no available rooms, only dorm space, don't accept this as fact – tell them it's your honeymoon or you get claustrophobia in a dorm . . . anything to make your intentions clear.

– Check prices before you accept a booking; cheap hotels do exist, though CITS may have to do more work to get you in. Again be persistent.

– If you want to go to a hotel that you've heard definitely does have rooms – and CITS say it doesn't – go there after 5pm and they'll find it very hard to turn you away.

All of which accepted, you shouldn't have any real difficulties, beyond keeping your temper and telling yourself you are in the capital because you yourself decided to come. Probably the worst that can happen – and it has its own advantages – is that CITS will send you to a hostel (like Beida or the Sports College) out in the countryside suburbs. CITS charge ¥3 commission on all bookings.

Budget access to hotels in the city changes faster and more frequently in Beijing than anywhere in China. By far the most promising approach to a room is to come, after travelling a while in China, with recommendations (and a course of action) worked out from others who did the same a week before. But at the time of writing, the main choices are as follows:

Qiao Yuan Hotel, Yondingmen. Currently the cheapest option – and a big place, with 30-bed men's dorms (¥8), women's triples (¥9) and some doubles (from ¥26 up). Good western breakfast. The hotel is a 5-minute walk out of Yondingmen station – along the canal to the left of the station entrance; bus nos. 20/106 from the centre.

Guang Hua Hotel, 38 Donghuan Nanlu. Established travellers' hostel – and one CITS are fond of sending people to. Dorm beds for women and men (¥10), doubles with showers (from ¥39). To get there, ride four stops on bus no.9 from Chongwenmen to the east side of the city centre – get off just after the bus turns left on to Jianguowenmai.

Beiwei Hotel, 13 Xijing Lu (Tel. 338 631). Similar to the above but friendlier and well sited, just west of the Temple of Heaven. Doubles from ¥17 (¥26 buys a reasonable one with shower – ¥36 a triple); no dorms.

Tiyuguan (Sportsmans) Hotel, Tiyuguan Lu/Tiantan Donglu intersection (Tel. 752 831). The best of the cheapies if you can get in. Sited directly opposite the east entrance of the Temple of Heaven. Dorms (¥12), Doubles (from ¥50); negotiation possible for various permutations of room sharing – a triple with two extras on the floor, etc.

Xuan Wu Men Hotel, Qianmen Xidajie/Xuanwumen Wai intersection. A traditional Overseas Chinese hotel but brought into the foreigners' pool at times. Dorms (¥8), doubles (¥30; ¥45 with bath). Bus no.44 from CITS.

As an independent traveller, you'd find it hard to get into any of the **more upmarket** hotels – even assuming you had the money and will. All of their bookings tend to be made well in advance through official tour agencies: if you just turn up they're likely to turn you away, irrespective of whether they have space! One exception, worth a punt if you leave it late enough in the day, is the *Xinqiao Hotel*, just around the corner on Chongwenmen from CITS, opposite Maxim's Restaurant. This is a lovely, moody place which looks after various airline crews if their flights are for some reason delayed; doubles go from ¥50 (though most are more expensive) and the hotel also boasts the best western dining room in the city (see Eating and drinking, p. 77).

If you're desperate, CITS is shut, and you've exhausted the possibilities above, the best place to catch **travellers for advice** is at the *Beijing Hotel* on the corner of Dongchang'an Jie and Wangfujing Dajie. You couldn't think of staying here (doubles from ¥90–180 – all agency booked) but almost everyone finds themselves dropping in for a beer at some point in the day – the Cultural Revolution having destroyed most of the capital's tea-houses. The hotel has three sections: the central block is reserved for Chinese officials dealing with foreigners; the left, Soviet-built block for Chinese guests (though its worth walking in all the same – the roofgarden offers a fabulous and unique view over Tian'anmen square and the Imperial City); the right, rather embarrassingly, is for westerners only – no unaccompanied Chinese. But it is useful: with a left luggage service (50 fen per item per day), a post office and telegram office, bank, bookstore, pharmacy and more.

It's at the Beijing Hotel, too, that most travellers catch taxis. And if you find yourself directed by CITS to the **countryside university hostels**, the *Beida Hostel* or *Sports College*, you should certainly come here to share a ride – a hefty ¥15/17 (respectively), giving some idea of how far out you'll be staying. But once established, you could bike into the city from either hostel (about an hour's ride), sharing rides is easy to organise or there are (complicated) bus connections – see p. 48. Doubles are around ¥20 at the Beida, ¥14 at the Sports College; the latter also has dorm beds (¥7). The promised advantages are in the westward locations – well poised for biking it to the Summer Palace (see p. 68) and on into the hills.

Getting around: city transport

Public transport here must be the most over-subscribed in the world. Even though every one of the city's 140 bus services runs about once a minute, you'll find getting on (or off) often seems more like a full work-out. The idea of actually seeing anything of the city from a bus is a joke (views tend to be limited to the backs of necks), and so too is the concept of waiting to see if the next bus is less crowded (it won't be).

But **buses** are cheap and routes efficiently organised and easy to under-stand – an important factor, since stops tend to be a good kilometre apart (fight to the disembarkation point well in advance). Services generally run from 5.30am until 11pm, though some run 24hrs. Fares vary, from 3 to 20fen: you pay a conductor, who may or may not be interested in working out exactly how much – a standard 10fen always seems acceptable on all sides.

The following are the most useful **routes**:
1   West to east along Chang'an avenue.
4   East to west along Chang'an avenue from the Military Museum, turning right after the Friendship Store.
5   From Deshengmen (north-west of the city), south down the west side of the Imperial Palace and Tian'anmen to Qianmen.
20   Yongdingmen station to Tian'anmen, Beijing Hotel and the main Beijing Zhan train station. (All night.)
44   Circular route along (west) Qianmen.
103   Beijing Zhan to the Zoo, via China Art Gallery. (Trolley.)
106   Yongdingmen station to the Temple of Heaven and Chongwenmen (CITS), then up to Dongzhimennei Dajie (north-east of the city). (Trolley.)
116   Temple of Heaven to Lama Temple, via Qianmen and Dongdan. (Trolley.)
332   Beijing Zoo to the University and Summer Palace.
Other relevant routes are detailed with particular sights in the text.

Less used by tourists, perhaps because all the signs are in Chinese only, is the **metro**. This has two lines: an east-west route starting at the Beijing Zhan railway station, and a new circle line, skirting a number of important sights around the north of the city. The east-west line is essen-tially for commuters and unless you're staying in some far-flung hotel you're unlikely to find it of much use. But the circle line, just completed, offers fast and relatively uncrowded access: to the Lama Temple (*Stop 6 – Yonghegong*) and up towards the bird market and zoo (*Stop 10 –*

Xizhimen). The easiest stops to join the line are *Stop 2 – Jianguomen* (under the flyover by the Friendship Store), *Stop 17 – Qianmen* (the Qianmen railway booking office) and *Stop 1 – Beijing Zhan*. Fares are a flat 10fen; ticket offices laughably understaffed; seats quite easy to find.

Most people end up using a lot more **taxis** than they expect. They don't cruise the streets, but you can always get one at the CITS, CAAC, Friendship Store, or any of the large hotels (most obviously and centrally, the *Beijing*). If you're staying at one of the cheaper hotels, or trying to get back at night, you could phone – though it'll often be a long wait. Taxis operate *around* a standard **rate system** – about ¥3 for the first kilometre plus 80fen for each additional half-kilometre – but the charge also takes consideration of a car's age. Try and make for the old Soviet-built Warzawas, which can cost as little as half that of a new air-conditioned Nissan. Taxi-drivers are generally co-operative but, as ever, a word of warning: meal breaks are sacrosanct. Not only will it be impossible to find a car between 11–12 or 5–7 but, if you're in one, you may well be dropped wherever the driver happens to be at the start of the magic hour.

As a positive alternative to such dependencies, try, at least once, to **hire a bike.** There are two established outlets for foreigners: a blue fronted building on the north side of the (CITS) Chongwenmen intersection at 94 Chongwenmen, and another blue-fronted cycle repair hut opposite the Friendship Store on Jianguomen. Hours are 7–7 and 7–6 respectively; charge per day is around ¥2.50, with a ¥100 or passport (or whatever you have that looks suitably official) deposit. At either, test the bike out before riding out – and don't accept a machine without decent brakes. Touring around the city, you're always supposed to park your bike at an official **bike park** (there are dozens – the only problem being later recognition); if your bike falls apart, bike repair shops are equally common. In summer, getting a bike from one of these shops can be tricky – go early, or find your own outlet by just walking into a shop and trying your luck.

THE CITY

Tian'anmen Square and Qianmen

Tian'anmen is the natural – probably inevitable – place to get an initial measure of Beijing. It must rank as the greatest Square on the planet, if only through its size: 100 full acres, enlarged in 1958 from an original 27. And there is of course the Square's symbolism. Tian'anmen is the ultimate expression of the People's Republic – just as the walled and extravagant Imperial Palace was to the old Empire.

The *Tian'anmen* itself – the **Gate of Heavenly Peace** – stands at the north end of the Square, facing the Imperial Palace. If you have already spent time in China, it will feel mightily familiar – from reproductions on just about any piece of state paper or product you can imagine. It is fronted by Mao's portrait and by the two slogans: 'Long Live the People's Republic of China' and 'Long Live the Great Union between the Peoples of the World'. Heady stuff. It was from the gate that Mao delivered the liberation speech, on 1 October 1949, declaring that China had finally 'stood up'. The gate, like much in Tian'anmen square, has pilgrimage status. You won't be alone posing for photographs.

To celebrate ten years of liberation, and the Soviet-inspired enlargement of the square, the Party instituted a vast, crash building project. Ten new official buildings were built in ten months. Three of them – the Museums of Chinese History and Revolution, and the Great Hall of the People – enclose the square. In 1976 a fourth was added – Mao's mausoleum, constructed (again in ten months) by an estimated million volunteers.

The building, **Chairman Mao's Memorial Hall**, is open to visitors on Tuesday, Thursday and Saturday mornings (8.30–10.30). Access to the hall is guided and impressively ceremonial, Chinese visiting in work groups, foreigners in **CITS parties**. You will need to book a place in advance at CITS and turn up at their office at the Chongwenmen Hotel to file on to their bus (it leaves at 8.40am) to the square.* All belongings must be left on the bus and you'll spend just 10–15 minutes inside – the time it takes to file, in silence, through the chambers. Throughout the opening mornings, the space outside the mausoleum is filled with huge queues of Chinese. Much of the interest of a visit lies simply in this – the genuine (and mass) reverence of Chinese towards their former leader. But Mao's corpse, displayed within a crystal coffin, remains and intrigueing focus. It was embalmed, so the story goes, according to Russian techniques – and rumour has it that Mao's left ear fell off and had to be stitched on. (The exact symbolism of this is unclear!). Beyond the coffin hall, a wall displays one of Mao's poems, in his calligraphy, which, very, very roughly translated, reads:

> In a small globe there are a few flies with songs and sad screaming,
> The ants boast that they are strong enough to control a country but they
> can't even cut down a tree.

---

*Underground City Tour. For an inclusive ¥8, CITS offer, with Mao's mausoleum, a brief tour of the 'underground city' below Qianmen – part of a vast civil defence system constructed in the 1960s, when the Party, at least, feared Soviet invasion. The tour (which is a little over-geared to pushing souvenirs) takes in a 3km section, with dozens of tunnels off, and, shades of 1940s Fu Manchu movies, some 90 entrances/exits from neighbourhood shops. The system remains operative – you are shown the telecommunications room – but is today in largely civilian use, with a hotel (Chinese only – so far!) and warehouses for local traders.

All things should be downed efficiently as the days and nights converge
   quickly,
Ten thousand years are too long and things should be done right now.
The full seas make angry waves, the five continents start thundering,
All the harmful worms should be wiped out, leaving no enemies in the
   world.

Part of Mao's poetic licence? Perhaps you'll be able to make different sense from the original.

Taking up almost half the entire west side of the square is the **Great Hall of the People.** Great being the appropriate word. Built by 25,000 labourers, the Hall could (theoretically) contain all the buildings in the Imperial Palace put together. Public admission to the Hall follows the same hours as Mao's mausoleum (see above) though it's rather easier – tickets are sold on the spot, at the top of the steps. What you're shown, for a ¥5 charge (foreigners have to show their passports for the privilege of paying this; Chinese pay 20fen!), is a selection, usually six, of the twenty-nine reception rooms – each named after a province and filled with appropriate regional artefacts. The additional wonder, highlight and climax of scale, is the 5,000-seater banqueting hall – a neat way to intimidate world leaders, Richard M. Nixon among them on his famous 1972 presidential visit.

At the centre of the square stands another 1958 structure, the over 30-metre-high obelisk of the **Monument to the Heroes.** It commemorates, as you might expect, those who died in the struggle for liberation. On the faces are carved figures and pivotal events from the revolution, together with calligraphy by both Mao and Zhou Enlai. In 1976 the monument was the scene of an anti (Gang of Four) government demonstration – broken up, violently, by Red Guards.

Beyond, directly across from the Great Hall, are the two **museums,** housed together in a long single building and open daily (except Mondays) 8.30–3. If at all possible, visit these with someone who can interpret for you: explanatory notes in both museums are Chinese only (though you can buy an English guide of sorts to the History Museum). They are probably best attempted on separate visits. The **Museum of Chinese History** houses exhibits from Peking Man to the Opium Wars – a fair haul. The **Museum of Chinese Revolution,** which was reopened in 1978 after certain revisions, offers a confusing, but compelling, insight into how the Chinese now view their own recent history. Good ground for political debate if you *can* find a student enthusiastic to practise English.

Qianmen

The **Qianmen area,** to the south of Tian'anmen, offers a tempting respite from such monumental grandeurs – and a quick shift in scale. The lanes and hutongs here are a traditional shopping quarter, full of small, specialist stores which remain to a large extent grouped according to their particular trades. It's a part of the city to browse – and to eat, with one of the best selections of snacks available in the capital.

Entry to the quarter is easiest by way of the imposing, 15C double-arched **Qianmen Gate** on Tian'anmen. Before the city's walls were demolished, this controlled the entrance to the Inner City from the outer, suburban sector. Shops and places of entertainment were banned in Imperial days from the former, so it was in the Qianmen area that they became concentrated.

Qianmen Dajie – the quarter's big street – runs immediately south from the gate. Off, to either side, are trading streets and hutongs, with intriguing traditional chemist and herbalist shops, dozens of clothes shops (including silks) and, perhaps most important, an impressive array of sidestalls and cakeshops selling fresh food and cooked snacks. Here too you'll find some of the best city restaurants (see p. 79), perhaps the most famous the *Qianmen Roast Duck* (at no.32). Opposite the *Duck*, on the street leading west, there's a materials market with a grandly authentic pulley system for paying bills and passing on change.

Just beyond the *Duck*, heading off on the east side, is **Dazhalan Lu**, one of the oldest and most interesting of the Qianmen lanes. This was once a major theatre street, and it still has two in operation – including, about 300m down on the left, an acrobat's theatre; see p. 85 for details of access. At the end of the street, where you come upon a scattering of (Chinese-only) hotels, was the old red-light district. No such trade now, though. Among the shops along Dazhalan, look out for the musical instruments (no.104) and a number of good pottery stores. But, as elsewhere in the capital (some might add China as a whole), the pleasure is probably more in browsing than buying. The Chinese wised up to western bargain hunters, and tourist consumers, long ago. In fact, **Liulichang**, across Qianmen Dajie from Dazhalan, is exclusively devoted to such trade: a neatly reconstructed 'traditional bazaar' of antiques and curio shops, all heavily overpriced though again, fun to browse.

If you find yourself ending up eating in Qianmen, or just looking about Tian'anmen in the absence of more compelling evening's entertainment, check out the **nightmarket**. This runs from around 6.30–11pm, along Qianmen and on to Tiantan Lu (the northern perimeter of the Temple of Heaven). Nightmarkets have only re-appeared over the last decade in the People's Republic – and are particularly striking in Beijing, their brilliant lights in defiant contrast to the drabness of most of the capital's streets. The one here seems to contain a bit of everything – latest fashions brought up from Guangzhou, livestock (birds, fowl, cats, dogs . . .), furniture, hardware, plants, basketry, foodstuffs and a mass of cloth and textiles, with instant tailoring to make items up for you on the spot.*

*There are another three Beijing nightmarkets – at least; see p. 87 for a run-down.

By day this same area is host to a very large, produce-orientated **freemarket** (Ziyou Sichang), selling a vast range of vegetables and a few miscellaneous household goods.

The Temple of Heaven (Tiantan)

Most visitors – and Chinese – reckon the **Tiantan**, 'Temple of Heaven', **complex** the most beautiful in the capital. The temple itself, first built in 1420, represents the highpoint of Ming design and was for six centuries at the heart of Imperial ceremony and symbolism. And the park in which it stands is a pleasing place – the haunt of early-morning Tai Chi exercisers, and a gentle, day-long gathering and strolling point. It is open, daily, from 6.30 to 6; admission is a nominal 10fen.

The Temple was conceived and constructed for the most important ceremony of the Imperial Court calendar – the Emperor's communication with the gods, praying for the year's harvests, before the winter solstice. The proceedings took place over two days. On the first, the Emperor and his court would make their way to the park, through Tian'anmen, from the Imperial Palace. The cortège was extravagant beyond imagining – and must have seemed so to the commoners of old Peking, who were forbidden to watch, instead having to bolt their windows and remain, in silence, indoors. On arrival, the Emperor – the Son of Heaven – would meditate in the Imperial Vault, ritually conversing with the gods on the details of government, before spending the night in the Hall of Prayer of Good Harvests. The following day, amid exact and numerological ritual, he would make offerings at the ceremonial Round Altar. The rites were a sacred and serious matter, as well as an assertion of Imperial power. Their last performance, astonishingly, was just seven decades ago, in October 1915, by General Yuan Shikai, first president of the republic; he had intended reviving the Empire, and himself ascending the throne, but died the following year before doing so.

From the **south entrance**, the **Zhaohen gate**, the main pathway leads straight to the **Round Altar**, its three marble tiers representing Man, Earth and (at the summit) Heaven. The tiers themselves are composed of blocks in various multiples of nine – the highest (and cosmologically most powerful) of odd numbers, considered heavenly in ancient Chinese belief. To the east of the fountain, which was reconstructed after fire damage in 1740, are the ruins of a group of buildings used for the preparation of sacrifices.

Directly ahead is the **Imperial Vault of Heaven**, an octagonal structure made entirely of wood, with a startling roof of dark blue glazed tiles. It is preceded by the so-called **Echo Wall** – a perfect (and extraordinary) whispering gallery, if increasingly overstretched by coachloads of eagerly whispering tourists. If reminders are needed that this is a big sight, you need only walk on past row upon row of souvenir shop pavilions.

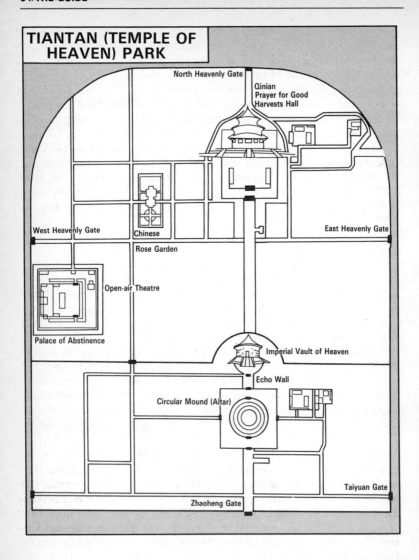

TIANTAN (TEMPLE OF HEAVEN) PARK

North Heavenly Gate

Qinian
Prayer for Good
Harvests Hall

West Heavenly Gate

Chinese

Rose Garden

East Heavenly Gate

Open-air Theatre

Palace of Abstinence

Imperial Vault of Heaven

Echo Wall

Circular Mound (Altar)

Taiyuan Gate

Zhaoheng Gate

But the principal temple structure itself – the **Hall of Prayer for Good Harvests,** at the north end of the park – ably justifies the build-up. It is, quite simply, a wonder. Made entirely of wood, without the aid of a single nail, the structure rises from a three-tiered marble terrace, four compass-point pillars supporting the vault (in representation of the seasons), enclosed in turn by twelve outer pillars (for the months of the year and the watches of the day). With its central dragon motif, the pavilion seems ultra-modern. It is actually 19C, as far as its structure goes: the original was destroyed by lightning in 1889, a fate for which thirty-two officials paid with their heads. But the reconstruction was wholly faithful to the Ming design.

Two other details in the Temple of Heaven concept, however, are not – and seem worth recording. The first is the **Palace of Abstinence**, over to the west of the park, where the Emperor originally robed; this has been adapted to an **open-air theatre**, worth keeping an eye on for signs of possible events. The second, more intrusive, is the giant **mole hill** which obscures the overall view – from Temple to Vault. It is, believe it or not, the result of the 1960s tunnelling activities for underground civil defence.

There are various **bus routes** *to Tiantan. For the south gate, take no.36 (from Tian'anmen) or no.116; for/from the north-west gate, no.106; the no.36 stops within walking distance of either gate.*

Along Chang'an – and beyond

West from Tian'anmen and along **Xichang'an Jie** – are a series of important sites: the Communist Party headquarters, the Telegraph Office and (by this time the street has changed name to Fuxingmennei Dajie) two museums – dedicated to the Chinese minorities and to the Military. **East** – along **Dongchang'an Jie** – the tone is only slightly less official, with the Friendship Store, International Club and Diplomatic Sectors. But there are interesting (and big!) shopping streets out in both directions – Xidan and Wanfujing – and back behind the Friendship Store is one of Beijing's nicest parks, Ritan, and, a block to the south, the newly opened Jesuit observatory.

West: Xichang'an Jie

The Communist Party Headquarters, the **Zhongnanhai**, is the first major building you pass – on the right – walking west from Tian'anmen. It is not hard to spot: armed sentries stand outside the gates, ensuring that only invited guests actually get inside. Which is a pity. For this is perhaps the most important and historic building in the country, base since 1949 of the Central Committee and the Central People's Government. Mao and Zhou Enlai both worked here. Before Liberation it was home to the Empress Dowager Tz'u Hsi.

At the next junction, the **Beijing Telecommunications Centre** rears above you – another of the 'ten years of liberation' building projects and suitably grandiose. It isn't, in itself, of any great interest. And nor at first sight is the length of brick walling beyond, edging Xidan avenue. This, however, is the famed **Democracy Wall** (as the West dubbed it), which in 1978 became the focus of political campaigning – the first means of publication allowed without prior permission of the state, and the first time ever in the PRC that people were permitted to openly express critical political views. They did so by pinning wall posters on to the wall, an integral form of political communication, still used today by the state. When the posters first went up the government were officially in favour, urging people to 'emancipate theirs minds' and 'search truth from facts'. Poems went up containing veiled criticisms of Mao, the first ever public criticisms of the Great Helmsmen's policies since his death, but by 1980 the authorities started to attack the wall and eventually, in December, banned all display of posters, imprisoning a number of the activists; it is said some remain jailed. During the campaign foreign correspondents living in Beijing translated and reported their contents, so that the views of Chinese dissidents were being read by millions of people worldwide. Today the wall displays advertising hoardings.

Xidan is worth exploring, at least along its initial few blocks. There's a tremendous **nightmarket**, spread along both sections of the street (north and south of Chang'an), and interesting small **shops** – not quite as esoteric as in the Qianmen area but no less capable of minor revelations. And (see Eating, p. 77) there are some well-above-average **restaurants** – notably the *Quyuan* at 133 Xidan Beidajie (north). For a little weirdness you might also step into the *Donghai Underground Restaurant*, a few blocks further on. This is another adapted part of the civil defence tunnelling, though its bizarre appeal, oddly enough, is the food – western-style Italian/French for Chinese to eat with knives and forks.

Within walking distance of the Xidan junction, the **Cultural Palace of the National Minorities** is an exhibition centre for the crafts and costumes of the nation's non Han Chinese. Reduced to statistics, these 'minorities' account only for 6% of the Chinese population, but they inhabit some 60% of the country's territory, establishing a political significance well above their numbers. The slant of the museum is, naturally enough, one of integration: all the minority regions (presented in exactly the same way) moving from a divided feudal past to a common future. It could all be a little more imaginatively and less dogmatically displayed, though the exhibits (brilliant coloured ethnic clothing, jewellery and artefacts) make a strong impression all the same, compared with the modern uniformed Beijing citizens; and the cases contrasting peasant and noble wear make their point. Upstairs a **Cultural Minorities Friendship Store** sells a range of ethnic clothing at cheapish prices. Next door, the *Minxu Hotel* has a good ground-floor restaurant.

It takes persistence to continue much beyond this point of the avenue – about to change name yet again, from Fuxingmennei to Fuxingmenwai and finally plain Fuxing Lu. But the **Military Museum** (on the latter named stretch) is more exciting than its name suggests – worth catching a bus (no.1 terminates close by) or the metro (to *Junshibowuguan*) if you've time left in the day. The exhibits stake out the history of the

People's Liberation Army, with heavy emphasis, inevitably, on the war against the Nationalists and the Japanese. Curiosities include, in the rear courtyard, a somewhat miscellaneous group of old aircraft – among them the shells of two American spy planes (with Nationalist markings) shot down in the 1950s. The museum is open 8.30–5 (last entry 4pm); no admission charge, but take your passport along.

If you want to loop back to Qianmen from here, bus no.337 offers a useful approach. It runs past the **Baiyunguan** (White Cloud) Temple, once the most influential Taoist centre in the country, recently renovated after a long spell as a military barracks. If you're on a bike, and/or a very committed temple tourist, you might continue south from Baiyunguan to the Tianningsi (Heavenly Repose) pagoda, a beautiful building stranded to great effect amidst heavy industrial plant.

East – Dongchang'an Jie

Everything on the east side of Chang'an takes bearings from the Beijing Hotel. **Wangfujing** – the city's upmarket shopping street – heads north, just as you pass the hotel's final block. Known as Morrison Street in its pre-Liberation days, this has always been the haunt of quality stores. It still is, and it is always crowded – no matter what time you're there. One of the biggest attractions, at least for Chinese, is the department store at number 390 – massive and well worth a stroll. At 289 a specialist shop sells paintings, woodcuts and calligraphy by modern artists, reasonably priced from ¥100 up. Another specialist shop, no.160, is devoted to fans. But you don't need targets – in fact the only really feasible approach is to pick your way through the crowds and look in wherever you can at whatever takes your fancy. Midway along, on the east side opposite another department store (at no.120), is **Dongfeng market**, a good workaday bazaar for general goods. Close by its north entrance is the *Donglaishun Restaurant*; at 60 Wangfujing is the *Cuhailou*; and, of course, there is the trendy and infamous *Peace Cafe*; for details/directions again see Eating, p. 77. The area also has two **nightmarkets**: one leading off the west side of Wanfujing, a block north of Chang'an; the other just east of Dongfeng on Dongdanbei Dajie.

Continuing, Dongchang'an Jie does a couple of quick name changes: to **Jianguomennei** (the street inside – now non-existent – Jianguo gate) and then **Jianguomenwai** (the street outside . . .). Just south of the avenue – where the walls used to run – is the city's **Ancient Observatory**, an unexpected survivor amid the modern avenues and recently re-opened to visitors (9–5 daily; Friday 1–5 only; 10fen). The building has an interesting history. The first observatory on this site was founded under the orders of Kublai Khan, the astronomers' commission being to reform the then faulty calendar. Later it came under Muslim control, as medieval Islamic science enjoyed pre-eminence, but, bizarrely, in the early 17C it was placed in the hands of Jesuit Christian missionaries. The Jesuits, a small group led by one Matteo Ricci, arrived in Beijing in 1601 and astonished the citizens and emperor by a series of precise astronomical forecasts. They re-equipped the Observatory (some of their instruments are displayed on the upper storey) and remained in charge through to the 1830s. The building itself is essentially a shell, of a 15C prototype, but the displays (with some English explanation) are quite imaginative, including early astronomy-influenced pottery and traditional navigational equipment.

Across the avenue, beyond a slightly mad-looking intersection, the **International Club** (no.3 bus stops from the Beijing Hotel) is the first sign that you're approaching the capital's diplomatic sector – and standing proof of China's shift in its international business policy. The club rents out small offices on its upper floors; below there are reasonable Chinese and western restaurants and (*see* nightlife) a Saturday disco; there is also a swimming pool, though you need a health certificate from Capital Hospital to use it (a neat deterrent to passing travellers).

Opposite the International Club is the newly opened **CITIC building**, a huge 36-storey skyscraper and useful landmark. Made up again of rented office and residential space, its two top floors house two of the nicest restaurants in Beijing – one Cantonese, one western – with wide-angle views right over the city. They're expensive (from around ¥50 a head) but about the best splash you could make if it's comfort and environment that you're after; both are excellent for lunch, the western restaurant serving a comprehensive buffet. On the ground floor of the building – a useful resource – is a **photographic service** which delivers prints inside the hour.

The **Friendship Store** – probably the best stocked in China – is about 350m on. This devotes its two top floors to the usual range of goods – materials, clothes, jewellery, carpets and paintings – all worth a look and with prices no higher than you'll find in most of the city's Chinese stores. You can have transportation arranged at the shipping service (which will send any goods home for you, whether or not they're bought here). Perhaps of more immediate and compelling use, however, are the Friendship Store's self-service food halls. These sell 'western' goods, as well as Chinese, including marvellous natural yoghurt and quality fruit, vegetables, wholemeal bread, cheese and pate – after a few weeks of Chinese travel it's hard to resist. There is also a laundry and dry-cleaning service, and a small café. All departments are open daily, 9–7. Taxis are available for hire at the front desk (and *China Daily* is on sale here, too).*

If you turn left off the avenue at the International Club, you'll hit **Jiangomenwai Diplomatic Compound,** the first of the two embassy complexes. This one houses the British, American and New Zealand embassies (among others – including Mongolia if you plan to take the Chinese train on the Trans-Siberian, see p. 581). The other compound, housing the Australians, Canadians, Dutch, Swedes, Soviets and, incidentally, the PLO, is way off to the north-east (bus no.110 up Dongdaqiaolu, by the Friendship Store) at **Sanlitun**. Both areas have an impressive air of unreality. The British even have their own (highly exclusive) pub, *The Bell*.

Ritan Park is just one block back north from the International Club – a five-minute walk from the avenue. As with most of the capital's parks, it is not big on grass, but it's a fun place, not much frequented by visitors though extremely popular among local Chinese, and with a really good courtyard restaurant which specialises in spring rolls and jiaozi (steamed dumplings). If you turn up around 6am you'll see groups of people of all ages engaged in an amazing spectrum of activities – painting, playing music, singing opera, practising English (one regular talks to a tree), exercising through Tai Chi. Later in the day, the park is a favourite haunt of old men, who come with their songbirds to chat and play cards, or sometimes sing operatic arias with the birds. One told me that they bring the birds – mostly larks and thrushes – to the parks to teach them to sing, picking up and imitating the sounds they hear around them. Their love of birds makes it hard to believe that not so long ago thousands of millions of birds were exterminated: the 1958 Party Congress (the Great Leap Forward) declared sparrows a pest and ordered their shooting to help protect foodstocks in the drive to self-sufficiency; later, during the Cultural Revolution, keeping birds was decreed revisionist and bourgeois and the campaign escalated to encourage the shooting of all wild birds.

[For details of the Beijing **bird market**, see p. 67].

The Imperial Palace (Forbidden City)

For the five centuries of its operation, through the reigns of twenty-four emperors of the Ming and Qing dynasties, ordinary Chinese were forbidden from even approaching the walls of the **Imperial Palace**. The complex, with its maze of eight hundred buildings and a reputed nine thousand chambers, was the symbolic and literal heart of the capital. And of the Empire too. From within, the emperors, the Sons of Heaven, issued commands with absolute authority to their millions of subjects. Very rarely did they emerge – perhaps with good reason. Their lives,

---

*The area east of the Friendship Store, towards the Jianguo Hotel, is one of the capital's main locations for **changing money** on the black market. In many Chinese cities and towns you'll be approached by someone asking to 'change money' in anything from a whisper to a yell, but in security-conscious Beijing the dealers use the same trick as their southern cousins on Hainan Island. They sell bananas – or in winter, scarves and gloves – as cover, taking in foreign currency and giving change in yuan. Hence the popular name for the currency market – the Banana Bank.

right down to the fall of the Manchu in this century, were governed by an extraordinarily developed taste for luxury and excess. It is estimated that a single meal for a Qing emperor could have fed around 5000 of his impoverished peasantry – a scale obviously appreciated by the last of the Manchus, the Empress Dowager Tz'u Hsi, who herself would commonly order preparation of one hundred or more dishes. Sex, too, provided startling statistics, with Ming dynasty harems numbering only just below five figures.

The complex is open to visitors from 9.30–5 daily, last admission at 4. Entry charge is a nominal 10fen, for which you have freedom of most of the 250 acres – though not all of the buildings. When the Manchu fell in 1911, the Forbidden City began to fall into disrepair – exacerbated by heavy looting of artefacts and jewels by the Japanese in the 1930s war and again by the Nationalists, prior to their flight to Taiwan, in 1949. A programme of restoration has been under way for decades, and it is hoped that all rooms will have been covered by around 1990, but at present large sections remain closed off. Not that this matters very greatly. The remaining extent of the two palace sections – the Ceremonial Halls and the more intimate Imperial Living Quarters – is enough to fill several separate visits. And the complex, in addition, takes in a couple of parks at its southern end. It is this sheer size (even so filled with Chinese tourists) that is extraordinary.

Although the earliest structures on the Forbidden City site began with Kublai Khan during the Mongol dynasty, the plan (and originals) of the Imperial Palace buildings are essentially **Ming**. Most date to the 15C and the ambitions of the Emperor **Yong Le,** the monarch responsible for switching the capital back to Beijing in 1403. His building programme was concentrated between 1407 and 1420, involving up to a hundred thousand artesans and perhaps a million labourers. The halls were laid out according to geomantic theories – in accordance to the yin and yang, the balance of negative and positive – and since they stood at the exact centre of Beijing, and Beijing was considered the centre of the universe, the harmony attempted was supreme. The palace complex constantly reiterates such references, alongside personal symbols of Imperial power – the Dragon and Phoenix (Emperor and Empress), the Crane and Turtle (longevity of reign), etc. What follows, inevitably, is a general guide to the site: for particular location details and explication the best policy is to tag on for a while to one of the numerous tourgroups.

On an initial visit, **Tian'anmen gate** is the most logical **entry point**. Once through, you find yourself on a long walkway between the two parks – Zhongshan and the People's Culture Park – with the moated Palace complex and massive Wumen gate directly ahead. It's at the Wumen that you buy tickets. The parks themselves, originally part of the Forbidden City, are open 6.30am–9pm. The **People's Culture Park** –

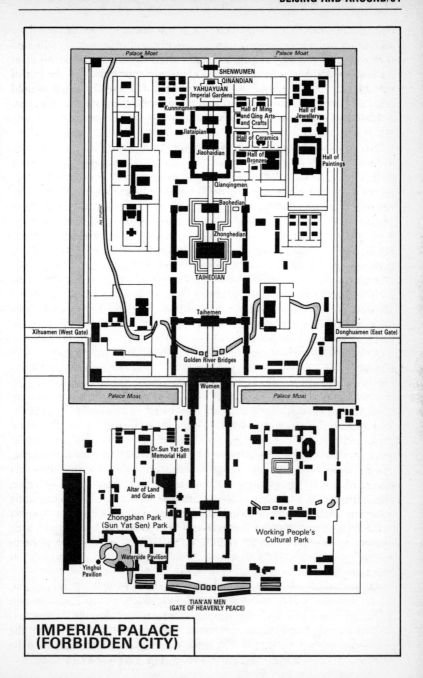

Palace Moat

Palace Moat

SHENWUMEN

QINANDIAN

YAHUAYUAN
Imperial Gardens

Kunningmen

Hall of Ming
and Qing Arts
and Crafts

Hall of
Jewellery

Jiataipian

Hall of Ceramics

Jiaohaidian

Hall of
Bronzes

Hall of
Paintings

Qianqingmen

Baohedian

Jinshui He

Zhonghedian

TAIHEDIAN

Taihemen

Xihuamen (West Gate)

Donghuamen (East Gate)

Golden River Bridges

Palace Moat

Wumen

Palace Moat

Dr. Sun Yat Sen
Memorial Hall

Altar of Land
and Grain

Zhongshan Park
(Sun Yat Sen) Park

Working People's
Cultural Park

Waterside Pavilion

Yinghui
Pavilion

TIAN'AN MEN
(GATE OF HEAVENLY PEACE)

IMPERIAL PALACE (FORBIDDEN CITY)

symbolically named in deference to the fact that only with Liberation in 1949 were ordinary Chinese allowed within this central sector of their city – has a number of modern exhibition halls (sometimes worth checking) and a scattering of original 15C structures, most of them Ming or Qing ancestral temples. **Zhongshan** (or Sun Yatsen) **Park**, boasts the remains of the Altar of Land and Grain, a biennial sacrificial site with harvest functions closely related to those of the Temple of Heaven.

The approach to the Wumen offers one of the most complete visualisations of old – Imperial – Beijing. The **walls** and **moat** remain complete about the Palace complex (the moat is used for skating when it freezes over the winter) and above the gate and at each corner of the walls are pavilions tiled in yellow – the colour reserved for Imperial use. **The Wumen** itself is the largest and grandest of the Forbidden City gates and was reserved for the Emperor's sole use. From its vantage point, the Sons of Heaven would announce the new year's calendar to their court and in times of war inspect the army. It was customary for victorious generals returning from battle to present their prisoners here for the Emperor to decide their fate. He would be flanked, at all such Imperial occasions, by a guard of elephants, the gift of Burmese subjects.

Passing through the Wumen – literally the 'Meridian Gate' – you find yourself in a vast paved court, cut east-west by the **Jinshui He**, the Golden Water Stream, with its five marble bridges. Beyond is a further ceremonial gate, the **Taihemen** Gate of Supreme Harmony, its entrance guarded by a magisterial row of lions, and beyond this a still greater courtyard where the principal Imperial audiences would be held. Within this space could be accommodated the entire court – up to a hundred thousand people. They would have made their way in through the lesser side gates – military men from the west, civilians from the east – and as the Emperor ascended his throne would wait in total silence, then with only the Imperial Guard remaining standing, prostrate themselves nine times.

The main **ceremonial halls** stand directly ahead, dominating the court. Raised on a three-tiered marble terrace is the first and most spectacular of the three, the **Taihedian**, Hall of Supreme Harmony. This was used for the most important state occasions – the Emperor's coronation or birthdays, the nomination of generals at the outset of a campaign – and last saw action in an armistice ceremony in 1918; it was proposed, though not carried through, that Parliament should sit here during the Republic. A marble pavement ramp, intricately carved with dragons and flanked by bronze incense burners, marks the path along which the Emperor's chair was carried. His golden dragon throne stands within.

Moving on, you enter the **Zhonghedian** Hall of Middle Harmony, another throne room, where the Emperor would perform ceremonies of greeting to foreigners and the address of the Imperial Offspring (products of several wives and numerous concubines – of whom more below). The hall was used too as a dressing room, for the major Taihedian events, and it was here that the Emperor examined the seed for each year's crop.

The third of the great halls, the **Baohedian** – Preserving Harmony – served for state banquets and Imperial examinations – graduates from which were appointed to positions of power in what was the first recognisably bureaucratic civil service. Its galleries, originally treasure houses, display various finds from the site, though the most spectacular, a vast block carved with dragons and clouds, stands at the rear of the hall. This is a Ming creation, reworked in the 18C, and it must be the finest carving in the palace. It is certainly the largest – a 250-ton marble transported here from well outside the city by flooding the roads to form sheets of ice.

To the north, paralleling the structure of the ceremonial halls, are the three principal palaces of the **imperial living quarters**. Again the first chamber, the **Qiangingong** – Palace of Heavenly Purity – is the most extravagant. It was originally the Imperial Bedroom – its terrace is surmounted by incense burners in the form of cranes and tortoises (symbols of immortality) – though later became a conventional state room. Beyond, echoing the Zhonghedian in the ceremonial complex, is the **Jiaotaidian** – Hall of Union – the Empress's throneroom, and finally the **Kunningong** – Palace of Earthly Tranquillity – where the Emperor and Empress traditionally spent their wedding night. This last is a bizarre seeming building, partitioned in two. On the left is a large sacrificial room with its vats ready to receive offerings (1300 pigs a year under the Ming). The wedding chamber is a small room, off to its side, painted entirely in red with 'double *xi*' decorative emblems (symbol of fertility and joy); it was last pressed into operation in 1922 for the child wedding of Pu Yi, the final Manchu emperor, who found it all 'like a melted red wax candle' and, disconcerted, 'decided that (he) preferred the Mind Nurture Palace and went back there'.

The Mind Nurture Palace, or **Yangxindiang**, is one of a group of **palaces to the west** – where the Emperors spent most of their time. Several of the palaces retain their furniture from Manchu times, most of it 18C, and in one, the **Changchundong**, is a series of paintings illustrating the Ming novel, *The Story of the Stone*. To the **east** is a similarly arranged group of palaces, adapted as **museum-galleries** for displays of **bronzes, ceramics, paintings, jewellery** and **Ming and Qing arts and crafts**: all of interest if you're not already sated with riches and detail.

But perhaps more compelling than the actual chambers is the bizarreness of the past of this Inner Court. For much of the Imperial period, it was the home of over six thousand members of the royal household – some half of their number eunuchs. The castrated male was introduced into the Imperial Court as an (obvious) means of ensuring the authenticity of the Emperor's offspring and, in daily contact with the royals, often rose to considerable power. But this was bought at the expense of their dreadfully low standing outside the confines of the court. Confucianism held that disfiguration of the body impaired the soul and eunuchs were buried apart from their ancestors in special graveyards outside the city. Rather pathetically, in the hope that they would still be buried 'whole', they kept and carried around their testicles in bags hung on their belts. They were usually recruited from the poorest families – attracted by the rare chance of amassing wealth other than by birth. Scarcely less numerous were the concubines, whose status varied from wives and consorts to basic whores. They would be delivered to the Emperor's bedchamber, wrapped in yellow cloth, and, since with feet bound they could hardly walk, carried by one of the eunuchs.

Moving away from palace chambers – and by this stage a considerable respite – the **Kunningmen** leads out from the Inner Court to the **Imperial Garden**. There are a couple of **cafés** here (and **toilets**) amid a pleasing network of ponds, walkways and pavilions, the classic elements of a Chinese garden. At the centre is the **Qinandian**, Hall of Imperial Peace, dedicated to the Taoist god of fire, Xuan Wu. Alternative **entrances and exits** to the Imperial Palace include the **Shenwumen** (which leads north, out from the Imperial Garden to Coal Hill and Beihai Park – see below) and the east and west gates, **Xihuamen** and **Donghuamen**. Useful **bus routes** are **no.3** (which runs up from Dongchang'an Jie – there is a stop near the Peking Hotel – along the west side of the Imperial Palace and Coal Hill park) and **no.5** (which takes a similar route, from Tian'anmen, around the east side of the Imperial Palace and Coal Hill park).

Coal Hill and Behai Parks – and beyond

Jingshan – Coal Hill – Park is a natural extension to visiting the Imperial Palace. An artificial mound, it was created by the digging of the palace moat and served in addition as a windbreak for the Imperial quarter of the city. It takes its popular name from a coal store once sited here. Its history, most momentously, includes the suicide of the last Ming emperor, who hung himself here from a lotus tree to escape the invading Manchu army.

But it is the views from the top that make this a really compelling target. They take in the whole extent of the Imperial Palace – a revealing perspective – and a fair swathe of the city outside, a good deal more attractive than from ground level. To the east is Beihai with its fat-snake lake; to the north the drum and bell towers; to the west the Lama Temple; all are detailed below.

Beihai Park (open 6am–9pm; 7am–8.30pm winter; 50fen) is almost half lake in extent – and a favourite skating spot in the frozen months. It was supposedly created by Kublai Khan, long before any of the Imperial

Palace structures were conceived, and its scale is suitably ambitious: the lake was man-made, an island being created in its midst with the excavated earth. Looking around is fun. On the island, which you can reach by walkways from the south and east sides, rowboats can be hired to explore the lake and its banks, or, less effort, there's a **ferry** to the nearby Nine Dragon Screen – the big attraction. 100ft long, this is a ceramic screen – finest of three famous examples in China – built to shield a (long disappeared) temple from evil spirits. Today it shields young Chinese dancegoers, who gather here in formation to practise tangoes and other steps to appropriate cassette music. A strange sight. Over to the east of the lake, if you're rowing, there are pavilions and rockeries – only recently opened to the public and a spot apparently favoured (before her arrest and trial) by Mao's widow, Jiang Qing. On the island itself the main focus is a white dagoba, built in the mid 17C to celebrate a visit by the Dalai Lama. By the boat dock is an expensive and exclusive restaurant, the *Fangshan*, with a good, accessible **snackbar** section.

For Beihai, the most direct **approach** is from Coal Hill, a few hundred metres walk. Returning to the centre, bus no.5 (from the west side of Coal Hill Park or the intersection of Beichangjie and Jingshanxijie) will take you to Tian'anmen; trolley no.103 (again from the south, near the island, on Wenjinjie) down Wangfujing Dajie; or trolley no.111 or bus no.204 (from the north end) down Dongdanbei Dajie, on to Dongchang'anjie).

Alternatively – and an interesting circuit if you've hired a bike for this trip – you could strike north to the drum and bell towers (on bus route no.5). The **Gulou** or **Drum Tower** is a 15C Ming creation, a vantage point from which, logically enough, drums were beaten to mark the hours of day and night and to call imperial officials to meetings. Some of the drums remain in situ along with the giant bell from the nearby Bell Tower; the building also hosts occasional artesania exhibitions. The **Bell Tower**, the **Zhonglou**, is visible from here – at the end of a short hutong. Originally a Ming contemporary, it was destroyed by fire and rebuilt in the 18C. More compelling, perhaps, if you find yourself looking around this area in the late afternoon, is the *Kaorouji Restaurant* at 37 Schichachai (first hutong on the right, walking south from the Drum Tower); open slightly later than usual (till 8pm), this boasts views of the Beihai lakes and a summer dining balcony. A ramshackle **farmers' market** takes place close by here, just to the south on the lakeside shore.

The most exciting sight in this part of the city, however, is undoubtedly the **Tibetan Lama Temple** (open 8.30–5.30 daily – except Tues and Thurs; 50fen). If you see no other temple in the city, this at least is worth the effort. It is not only a beautiful building – and, with its gardens, a refuge – but it also functions as an active Tibetan Buddhist centre. That it does so is in large part propaganda (China guaranteeing and respecting the religious freedoms of the Minorities) but also presumably an admission of past mistakes in policy. The history of the building is certainly interesting. Built towards the end of the 17C, it was originally a high official residence of one Count Yin Zhen. But in 1723, when the prince became the Emperor Yong Zheng and moved into the Imperial Palace, it was retiled in the Imperial yellow and restricted thereafter to religious use. It became a lamasery in 1744, housing monks from Tibet and also from Inner Mongolia, over which it had a major presiding role, supervising the election of the Mongolian Living Buddha. After the Civil War, in 1949, it was declared a national monument and for thirty years was closed to religious use. The current monastic revival, promoted and sanctioned by the state – who brought in a group of Mongolian novice monks – represents a unique and obviously welcomed shift.

Visiting, you are free to wander through the complex of prayer halls and gardens – though you should respect the temple's function (no photography, meditative quiet). The experience is largely an aesthetic one, admiring the often startling craftsmanship, the statues and the concept. Among the Buddhas, devoted to various skills and attributes, notice those of the Maitreya – the future Buddha; there is a spectacular 18m-high example in the last of the chambers, the Wanfu pavilion.

Opposite the entrance to the Lama Temple, you could, if committed, follow the hutong to the **Confucian Temple**. But it is a dry, dull place, maintained for several decades as a museum (open 9–5, closed Mons); in the courtyard are steles recording the names of those who studied here and achieved the mark of success – the civil service exams. Opposite is the old Imperial College, now the city's **National Library**.

Biking it, or bussing it, between the centre and the Lamu temple you might also look in at the **China Art Gallery**, at the top end of Wangfujing. Exhibitions here range through contemporary work by Chinese art students and amateur artists – maybe from some rural co-operative or factory – to recently held shows by major international figures, like Picasso. The interest, unless you're exceptionally lucky, is likely to be more in the general content and tone than in any particular paintings or sculptures. The state of the art here, however, is bound to tell you something about the current political atmosphere. When I last visited, flowers were back in style, along with bright colours and romantic representational scenes. Revolutionary imagery – factories and tractors – had long had its day. The gallery is open daily (except Mons) from 9–5.

Some useful **bus routes.** *From Andingmen (near the Lamu Temple) trolleys* nos. 104/108 *and buses* nos. 2/201 *run down to Wanfujing and Dongchang'anjie –* no. 2 *continuing to Tian'anmen square.*

Further out: the Zoo, University and Summer Palaces

A diverse collection of sights and sites around the north-west fringes of the city. You could, if you wanted, take them all in within a day, but by far the most pleasure to be had is in rambling about the lakeside gardens and pavilions of the **Summer Palace** – a recommended day or afternoon's escape, summer or winter.

Relevant **buses** are: to the Zoo, bus no.7 from Qianmen or trolley no.103 from the Beijing Hotel/Wangfujing. For the University* and Summer Palaces, either bus to the Zoo then bus no.332 (to stop Zhong Guan Cun for the University and Old Summer Palace; to the end of the line for the Summer Palace proper). Allow half an hour for the ride out to the zoo – more on Sundays when Beijing families descend en masse – and about the same on from there to the Summer Palace. Biking it takes only fractionally longer.

The Zoo, Exhibition Hall and Bird Market

Beijing Zoo (open daily, 7.30–6) marks the edge of the Inner City, flanked to either side by the monumental Capital Gymnasium and Soviet-built Exhibition Centre. It is the largest zoo in the country, its cages taking in some unusually rare species (snow leopards, golden monkeys) as well as the famed pandas. But it's no fun, despite massive local popularity. Conditions for the animals are squalid and uniquely unimaginative, and if China were to shift its policy even a fraction towards animal rights then it wouldn't remain open much longer.

For Chinese kids and tourists alike the Giant Pandas are the sole big attraction. You can join the queues to have your photo taken sitting aside plastic replicas. And then push your way through to glimpse the living variety – kept in their relatively palatial quarters and highly familiar through ritual diplomatic mating exchanges over the last decades.

The **Exhibition Hall**, which you reach just before the zoo on Xizh-imenwai, is worth a little inspection. It is the one Soviet-style building that really works in Beijing – an elegant low-level façade with a tapering gold spire (a clear and unusual landmark in this part of the city). Although now just one of many exhibition halls in the capital, it does have consist-ently interesting, usually international shows, details of which you'll always find in *China Daily*. It also boasts a **Russian Restaurant,** surpris-ingly good (a taste break with borscht, stroganoff, black bread . . .) and reasonably inexpensive. The restaurant is open daily, 11–1.30 and 4.30–7.30.

---

*A better **bus** for the **Beijing Languages Institute** (which is set slightly apart from the main university compound) is no.331 from the Bei Tai Ping Zhuang terminal – itself easiest reached on the no.22 from Xidan.

Close by are three large **markets**. One, at the west end of Piganli (the end of the no.204 bus route), is devoted to livestock; another, for fruit and veg. is along Beitaipingzhuang (at the end of the nos.16 or 22 bus routes). The third and most interesting is the **bird market**, on the other side of the ring road from the Zoo and Exhibition Hall off Xizhimennei. This is a treat – well worth seeking out. First off, around the entrance, there are groups of barbers, turning young boys and old men into near-skinheads. Then, to the left, are row upon row of stallholders, all of them hidden behind suspended wooden cages full of birds of every size, colour and chirp, and to the right, tropical fish stalls, equally colourful and all priced at a handful of fen. Though you may yourself be an unlikely buyer, Chinese families love to keep fish and birds and you'll see people buying and selling with an expert eye.

The University and Old Summer Palace

Beijing University (**Beida**) and **Qinghua**, the technical college, moved to their present site in 1953; originally, established and administered by Americans at the beginning of this century, they had stood on Coal Hill. Passing, en route to the Summer Palace, there is little to entice a stop. The buildings look drab, even by relative Beijing standards. But the setting is pleasant and the university, after almost schizophrenic problems in the 1970s, back at the centre of Chinese development. Strange to think, with its new contingents of foreign students from the west, that a decade or so ago it was half-deserted. The Cultural Revolution saw students and teachers alike dispersed for 'open schooling' or re-education. Later, in 1975–6, Beihai was the power base of the radical left in their campaign against Deng Xiaoping. All of which, of course, is now history.

If you stay at the university – an increasingly regular option (see p. 47) – you shouldn't find it hard to mix with the students, foreign and Chinese. The university's local quarter is Haidian, just to the south, where there are quite a number of solid, inexpensive restaurants.

Beijing's original Summer Palace – the **Yuanmingyuan** – is a halfhour's walk north of the university. But it is *very* ruined and not easy to find: best approach is to follow the road towards Qinghua and then ask someone to point you towards it. Built by the Qing Emperor K'ang-hsi in the early 18C, the palace once boasted the largest royal gardens in the world – with some two hundred pavilions and temples set around a series of lakes and natural springs. Marina Warner recreates the scene in *The Dragon Empress*:

> Scarlet and golden halls, miradors, follies and gazebos clustered around artificial hills and lakes. Tranquil tracts of water were filled with fan tailed goldfish with telescopic eyes, and covered with lotus and lily pads; a superabundance of flowering shrubs luxuriated in the gardens; antlered deer wandered through the grounds; ornamental ducks and rare birds nestled on the lakeside.

Today, however, there is little enough to hang your imagination upon. In 1860 the entire complex was burnt and destroyed by British and French troops, ordered by the Earl of Elgin to make the Imperial Court 'see reason' during one of the Opium Wars. The troops had previously spent twelve days looting the Imperial treasures, many of which found their way to the Louvre and British Museum – their return as yet undemanded.

The stone and marble remains, of fountains and columns, lie amid acres of weeds, used as grazing ground for sheep and goats. It is a popular picnic spot for foreign residents in Beijing, also for Chinese couples out to explore in relative seclusion the country's new sexual attitudes. As far as actual sights go, the only really identifiable ruins are of the Hall of Tranquillity. But there are government plans – first mooted by Zhou Enlai – to restore part of the complex, creating (at an estimated £30m cost) a national 'heritage park'. Local peasants with capital to spare from the freemarkets are said to have already invested £160,000 on restoration, in the hope of attracting tourism, and the state has allocated an initial £3m.

Yiheyuan: the 'new' Summer Palace

Yiheyuan – usually just referred to as the **Summer Palace** – is one of the loveliest spots in Beijing, a vast public park, two-thirds lake, where the latterday Imperial Court would decamp during the hottest months of the year. The site is perfect: surrounded by hills, cooled by the lake and sheltered by garden landscaping. And the place, despite another bout of European aggression in 1900, is impressive and fun, the buildings spaced out along the lakeside and connected by a suitably majestic 900-metre gallery.

There have been summer Imperial pavilions at Yiheyuan since the 11C. The present layout is essentially 18C, created by the Manchu Emperor Qian Long. But the key character associated with the palace is the Empress Dowager Tz'u Hsi (Ci Xi), who ruled over the fast-disintegrating Chinese empire from 1861 until her death in 1908. Yiheyuan was very much her pleasure ground. She rebuilt the palaces in 1888 and determinedly restored them in 1902 – her ultimate flight of fancy the construction of a magnificent marble boat from the very funds intended for the Chinese navy. Whether her misappropriations had any real effect on the Empire's path is hard to determine – but it certainly speeded the decline, with China suffering heavy naval defeats during the war with Japan.

The palaces are built to the north of the lake, on and around Wanshou Shan – Longevity Hill. In their historical interest many remain intimately linked with Tz'u Hsi – anecdotes about whom are staple fare of the numerous tourgroup guides. But to enjoy the site you need know very little. Like Beihai, the park, its lake and pavilions, are a startling array of visuals – like some traditional landscape painting brought to life.

You will probably find yourself entering through the **East Gate**, above which is the main palace compound, including the Hall of Benevolence and Longevity, the **Renshoudian**, a majestic hall where the Empress and her predecessors gave audience. It contains much of the original 19C furniture, including an imposing throne. Beyond, to the right, is the **Deheyuan**, the Palace of Virtue and Harmony, dominated by a three-storey theatre, complete with trap doors for the appearances and disappearances of the actors. Theatre was one of Tz'u Hsi's main passions and she sometimes took part in performances, dressed as Guanyin, the goddess of mercy. With a neat sense of irony, the next main building you come to, the **Yulantang** or Jade Waves Palace on the lakeside, was for ten years the prison of the Emperor Guangxu – kept in captivity here, as a minor, while Tz'u Hsi exercised his powers. Just to the west is the Dowager's own principal residence, the **Leshoutang** – Hall of Joy and Longevity.

From here to the north-west corner of the lake runs the **Long Gallery**, the 900m-covered way, painted with mythological scenes and flanked by various temples and pavilions. It is said (and you will certainly hear it being said!) that no pair of lovers can walk through without emerging betrothed. Near the west end of the gallery is the infamous **marble boat**, completed by Tz'u Hsi with the purloined naval cash and regarded by her acolytes as a suitably witty and defiant gesture.

Close by the boat – tourist focus of this site – is a jetty with **rowboats for hire**. Boating in the lake is a popular pursuit, of locals as much as foreigners, and well worth the money. You can dock again over below Longevity Hill and row out to the two **bridges** – the Jade Belt on the western side, Seventeen Arched on the east. In winter Chinese skate on the lake here – an equally spectacular sight; if you want to join them, skates are available for hire.

The Western Hills

Also known as the **Fragrant Hills**, this area is to the West of Beijing, beyond the Summer Palace. Long favoured as a restful retreat by religious men and intellectuals, because of its relative coolness at the height of summer, and its fragrance – because of the heavily wooded slopes, it is now popular with all Beijingers and the bus queues on Sundays look like Chang'an in the rush hour. Its centrepiece is a carefully landscaped park with a cable-car up to the top of **Incense Burner Peak**, from which you get, on clear days, views down towards the Summer Palace and as far as distant Beijing. *The* time to visit the Hills is in the autumn, when the leaves turn red in a massive profusion of colour, which lasts only briefly until November frosts cause the leaves to drop off.

Temples large and small are dotted around, of which the two most significant are the Wofosi and Biyunsi. The **Wofosi**, or Temple of the Reclining Buddha, is down a small road running off to the right as you approach the village at the foot of the hills, and its main hall houses a huge reclining Buddha, some 5.2 metres in length and cast in copper. The **Biyunsi**, the Temple of the Azure Clouds, stands a short way beyond the park. A striking building with distinct influences from other parts of the Buddhist world, it is dominated by a northern-Indian dagoba, its bright whiteness standing out amidst the green of the pine trees. The temple is terraced into the hillside with a gully running up behind it to the ridge. Well worth a look is the extraordinary hall of 500 Arhats, and Sun Yatsen's memorial hall.

One unexpected sight at the Fragrant Hills is the presence of Beijing's most attractive and innovative modern hotel, the *Xiangshan* (Fragrant Hills). Designed by the highly respected American/Chinese architect, I. M. Pei, it is an example of modern Chinese architecture at its best. In the landscaped gardens at the rear is Beijing's pleasantest swimming pool, open to non-residents, though at the exhorbitant price of ¥5.

Buses to the Fragrant Hills are no.333 from the Summer Palace or no.360 from the Zoo.

OUT FROM THE CITY

In 1985 Beijing officially opened its Municipal Area to foreigners. Down came all the black and white signs saying 'No Foreigners Beyond this Point' along every road leading out of the city, and for the first time it was possible to see a little more of the environs than the standard tour out to the **Great Wall** at Badaling and the **Ming Tombs** along the way.

The main advantages of this move are two. You can now visit many more spectacularly restored, and less crowded, parts of the **Great Wall**. And you can get out to the mountain areas north of Beijing, in particular to the **Miyun Reservoir** – recently linked to the capital by a fast and slightly incongruous dual carriageway. At the time of writing some of these trips are possible only by hiring a taxi (not so bad, split four ways), though with the current rate of change they may well all be linked by bus or CITS tours before very long.

The Great Wall

This is a Great Wall and only a great people with a great past could have a great wall and such a great people with such a great wall will surely have a great future.

Richard M. Nixon

The most commonly told fact about **THE GREAT WALL** – that it is the one man-made structure visible from the moon – is perhaps the most impressive. But other statistics are close rivals. The wall was begun in the 5C BC, continued until the 16C AD and stretches some 6000 kilometres across China: the remaining sections, placed end to end, would link New York with Los Angeles. Neil Armstrong's remark from space seems no less than it deserves; Nixon's hyperbole straight talking. Even at ground level, and even along the small section at Badaling that is constantly overrun by Chinese and foreign tourists, The Wall – the Wan Li Changcheng (The long wall of 10,000 li) as the Chinese call it – is clearly the PRC's most spectacular sight.

The Chinese have walled their cities since earliest times and during the Warring States period, around the 5C BC, simply extended the practice to separate rival territories. The Great Wall's origins lie in these fractured lines of fortifications and in the vision of Qin Shi Hang, who, unifying the Empire in the 3C BC, joined and extended the sections to form one continuous defence against barbarians. Under subsequent dynasties – the Han, the Wei, the Qi, the Sui – the Wall was maintained and, in response to shifting regional threats, grew. It did lose importance for a while, with Tang borders extending well to the north, then shrinking back under the Song, but with the emergence of the Ming it again became a priority – military technicians worked on its reconstruction right through the 14C to 16C.

The irony, of course, is that the 20ft high, 20ft thick Wall, with its 25,000 battlements, did not work. Successive invasions crossed its defences – Genghis Khan is supposed to have bribed the sentries – and they were in any case of little use against the sea powers of Japan and later Europe. But the Wall did have significant functions. It allowed the swift passage through the Empire of both troops and goods – there was (and is) room for five horses abreast most of the way – and, perhaps as important, it restricted the movement of the nomadic peoples in the distant, non-Han minority regions. Arguably, the Wall also served an important function as a wind-break, aiding harvests and preventing soil erosion; in recent decades the Chinese have initiated a 'great green wall' project, on a less monumental scale, along their northern frontier.

The Wall at Badaling and Qingtongqiao

If you visit the Wall from Beijing you'll probably see the restored section at **BADALING**, 70km north-west of the capital. You don't have to — there are sections within access at QINGLONGQIAO (see below) and at MUTIANYU (see p. 76), SHANHAIGUAN (p. 97), or up in the north-west — but this is where all the capital's tours go and it does need an effort of will and organisation to make your own way elsewhere.

Besides which the Wall's tourist development is itself of interest: this is the nearest the Chinese have yet got to western (almost Disneyland) overkill. You can sit astride a camel to be photographed and, whichever way you walk, are confronted by Great Wall kitsch: T-shirts, trinkets, even a totally phoney Great Wall Antique Store. The Great Wall, as Nixon might have added, is great business. If you tire of all this, and the crowds, strike west and after a while you'll come to a section that hasn't been restored, where you can see the construction technique — pounded earth on the interior with only the faces paved in stone. The footing becomes a little unsteady as you proceed but the views tremendous.

There are numerous **tours** to the Wall at Badaling, most of them offering a combined visit en route to the Ming Tombs (detailed in the following section). The cheapest is the Great Wall/Ming Tombs coach tour sold at the office opposite CITS, facing the back of the Xinqiao Hotel; aimed originally at Overseas Chinese, this at present costs ¥7. CITS's own tours are more expensive, though they do include an English-speaking guide — sometimes worthwhile. The main disadvantage, either way, is in lack of time. You only get an hour or so at the Wall itself. To overcome this you *may* want to do it yourself.

If so, options range from **local buses and trains** (around ¥3 round fare) to hiring a taxi with driver (¥80 — split up to four ways). The trains are perhaps the best independent options. The simplest is the T1 (daily except Weds; out at 8.05am, back at 12.25pm; ¥11.50 includes packed lunch) but this is basically an excursion tour — bookable only in advance through CITS who run a connecting coach on the way back at Nankou for a look at the Ming Tombs. Doing the Wall under your own steam, you've a choice between very crowded local trains to Badaling station (at 8.18am and 8.34am; again not Weds; try to book a return ticket in advance) or any of the trains running to Qinglongqiao station, west of Badaling.

QINGLONGQIAO is the station before Badaling on the line from Beijing to Hohhot or Datong. The wall is only a kilometre distant from here so you can see it at leisure as a daytrip from the capital or even as a halt en route in either direction — you can leave luggage at the station. The journey from Beijing takes just under 2hrs.

A third option — if you're pushed for time and/or flush on funds — is to take the Lido Hotel's helicopter tour. This operates daily at a cost of around ¥150 and can be booked at the Lido (which is out beyond

Sanlitun) or most of the larger downtown hotels. You set out from the Lido at 7am – by coach to the 'copter. You're then flown over a long section of the wall (hopefully not in cloud), dropped at the Ming Tombs for a conventional tour, and shuttled on by coach for a walk on the Wall at Badaling and back to Beijing around midday.

The Ming Tombs: Shisanling

Thirteen of the sixteen Ming dynasty emperors were entombed in and around the Shisanling valley, around 40km north-west of Beijing. Two of the **MING TOMBS** – Changling and Dingling – were restored in the 1950s and the latter was also excavated, yielding up various treasures to the capital's museums. They are very much on the tour circuits, conveniently placed on the way to Badaling, and if you buy a round ticket you've a pleasant scenic surprise in store. The fame of the tombs themselves, however, perhaps through the simplicity of their name, seems overstated in relation to the interest of the sights. Unless you've strong archaeological interest, this wouldn't be a trip worth making for its own sake.

Not that it isn't pleasant enough. The third Ming emperor, **Yong Le**, who shifted the capital back from Nanjing to Beijing, chose this site for its landscape – undeniably the loveliest around the capital. And the scenic appeal has already caught the eye of Beijing's tourist planners. There is a scheme to turn this whole area into a 'tourist park', with hotels poised for the capital, along with an amusement centre, swimming pools and sports centre, archery, shooting and encampments of Mongolian tents. At present only the two principal tombs have any real notice taken of them at all. The other eleven stand neglected and very beautiful amid former gardens, grass and weeds breaking through their tiled roofs and marble foundations. They make a nice place to picnic if you just feel like a break from the city and its more tangible succession of sights.

It is in fact the approach to the Ming Tombs, the 7km **Spirit Way**, that is Shisanling's most exciting feature. This commences with the *Dahongmen* – the 'Great Red Gate' – a triple-entranced Triumphal Arch, through the central opening of which only the Emperor's dead body could be carried. Beyond, the road is lined to either side with colossal stone statues of animals and men – the Ming Tombs' most famous and spectacular feature. Startlingly larger than life, the statues all date from the 15C and are among the best surviving examples of Ming sculpture. The sequence begins with groups of animals – real and mythological, including the *qilin*, a reptilian looking beast with deer's horns and a cow's tail, and the horned, feline *xiechi*. The avenue then slightly changes alignment and you are met by the first, stern human figures of military mandarins. The precise significance of the statues is unclear, however, it is assumed they were to serve the Emperors in their next lives.

Animal statuary re-appears at the entrances to various of **the tombs,** though the structures themselves are something of an anti-climax. **Changling** – Yong Le's tomb, the earliest at the site – stands at the end of the avenue. There are plans to excavate it, an exciting scheme since it is contemporary with some of the finest building of the Imperial Palace in the capital. At present the enduring impression is mainly one of scale: vast courtyards and hall buildings approached by terraced white marble. Its big feature is the Hall of Eminent Flowers, supported by huge columns of single tree trunks which it is said were imported all the way from Yenan along specially iced roads.

The main focus of the tours, however, is the **Dingling**, the underground tomb-palace of the Emperor Wan Li. Wan ascended the throne in 1573 at the age of ten and reigned for almost half a century. He began building his tomb when he was twenty-two, in line with common Ming practise, and hosted a grand party within on its completion. The mausoleum was opened in 1956 and found to be substantially intact, revealing the Emperor's coffin, flanked by those of two of his Empresses, and floors covered with the remains of scores of trunks containing Imperial robes, gold, silver, even the Imperial cookbooks. Some of the treasures are displayed in the tomb and others have been replaced by replicas. It's a cautionary sight of useless wealth accumulation, condemned in a nice line of ideology by the guides.

If you want to **make your own way to Shisanling,** take bus no.5 or no.44 to Deshengmen then no.345 to Changping; from Changping you could walk or pick up a no.314.

Miyun Reservoir, the Wall at Mutianyu and other trips

These are the less obvious tourist spots in the Beijing Municipality, at least for foreigners. **Miyun,** though, is one of the most popular day-trips for local Chinese, and easy enough to get to. Others, including the magnificent stretch of the Great Wall at **Mutianyu,** require more effort; but if you're spending any more than a few days in the capital they are certainly worthwhile.

Miyun

The town of **MIYUN** lies some 65km north-east of Beijing, at the foot of the long range of hills along which the Great Wall threads its way. Its claim to fame comes from the **reservoir** built in the flat, wide valleys behind the town. Supplying over half the capital's water, this looks as if it was built solely for pleasure and aesthetic effect. It is a huge lake, scattered with islets and bays, and backed by the mountains and the deep blue of the Beijing sky. You'd hardly believe that you were in what is for the most part a flat and dusty municipality.

The reservoir has become a favourite destination for Beijing families, who flock out here at weekends to go swimming, fishing, boating or walking. Joining them is half the fun. However, if you're here for a little solitude after the Beijing streets, it is easy enough to wander off on your own and escape the crowds. Behind the reservoir, in the hills, you'll find rockpools big enough to swim in, streams, trees, flowers and a rushing river – and on the hilltops there are outposts of the Great Wall, still in ruins.

You can get to Miyun and back to Beijing in a day, either by **bus** or by **train**. Times and prices from CITS.

The Great Wall at Mutianyu

If you have the time, the section of the **Great Wall** at **MUTIANYU** is greatly recommended. A large stretch of the wall has been restored here and you can walk right along it to the point where it becomes wilderness again. And, unlike at Badaling, you will be able to make it unharassed by T-shirt peddlers; Mutianyu is certainly on the CITS list of places to develop but as yet there's little to compete with what you have come to see. The countryside, too, is more exciting than around Badaling. From the Wall you can look for miles and miles across lush, undulating hills.

There may, by the time you reach CITS, be a regular **bus** or **tour** out to Mutianyu. I made the trip in a resident friend's car. If you go on your own, you take the same road as for Miyun, turning left at the village of Huarou; from there a narrow winding road leads up to Maiyanlu village and a path beyond leads to the Wall.

Tan Zhe Si and Jie Tai Si temples

40km south-west of Beijing, **TAN ZHE SI** occupies what must have been the most beautiful and serene temple site anywhere near Beijing. It is the largest too, and one of the oldest, first recorded in 3C as housing a thriving community of monks.

Wandering through the complex, past terraces of stupas, you reach an enormous central courtyard, at its heart an ancient and towering gingko tree. From here, you can make out other temple buildings, look round the gardens (which are still cultivated) and try out the vagaries of the coin water maze.

12km back along the road to Beijing, in complete contrast to Tan Zhe Si, is **JIE TAI SI**. Set back against the hillside, this looks more like a fortress than a temple and is surrounded by forbiddingly tall, red walls. Though badly damaged during the Cultural Revolution, it has been faithfully and extensively restored.

The **journey out** to these temples is an added bonus. Once you leave the outskirts of Beijing, the road begins a steep and winding climb up over the hills and down into the valley beyond, at the end of which lies

Tan Zhe Si. There are three possible approaches by local transport. Perhaps the easiest is to take **bus no.307** from Qianmen to the Hetan terminus, then pick up the (unnumbered) bus runs to Tan Zhe Si. The alternatives are to go by **metro** to Pinguoyan, then **bus no.336** to Hetan, then the same temple bus; or you could take **bus no.336** from Zhanglan-guan Lu (off Fuchengmenwai Dajie) to Mentougou and hitch on from there.

Lugouqiao (Marco Polo Bridge)

The original **LUGOUQIAO** – Reed Moat Bridge – was built at WANPING in 1192, its 250 grey marble balustrades emblazoned with carved lions, each of which wore a different expression. It must indeed have been a splendid piece of engineering and architecture when it was reported by Marco Polo. Today, substantially preserved, it still seems remarkable (and the elephants holding it up at either end are pleasing) although the river below has dried to a trickle and it is used, constantly, by heavy trundling lorries.

   Wanping, on the river bank, is a small back-country village, not a place you'd imagine having any real history. It was here, however, that the first shots were fired in the war between China and Japan in 1937, prompted by the illegal Japanese occupation of a railway junction nearby. After this it was only a short step to full-scale attack on Beijing.

   WANPING is linked by bus from Beijing.

THE FACTS

Eating and drinking

In terms of **food** Beijing can be both exciting and frustrating. There's a lot of variety, with most regional cuisines represented by at least one restaurant, but at the same time there aren't nearly enough actual places for the population. Being at the centre of things, Beijing has always been most directly affected by the application of ideology and the Cultural Revolution didn't ignore eating out, which was for a time deemed the epitome of bourgeois culture, resulting in the closure of most of the city's cafés and tea-rooms and a good number of restaurants. Things are changing – Beijing locals love eating out and restaurant traditions were never exactly destroyed – but getting a meal in the capital still needs a certain grasp of **tactics**. When eating hours are imminent (11–12am for lunch; dinner from 4.30–6.30pm – rarely later) be sure to find yourself in a promising area. Otherwise you'll miss out.

Restaurants

It can take a day or two of almost failing to get a meal before you finally shed western table manners and get to grips with **The System**. Try for a quicker adjustment. Get to restaurants early and size up the situation fast: if crowds aren't totally overwhelming and it looks like there'll be a table free inside half an hour then work out which one looks best and go and stand beside it – meat is served first, incidentally then rice, then soup. When you do get seated you'll usually collect your own bowl and chopsticks (better to have your own) and you'll always have to pay first.

All of which may sound daunting – and if you really want to you can screen yourself by eating in specially reserved foreigners' sections, partitioned away, sometimes on a different floor, from locals. But this is not exactly fun and for the same food you'll be paying twice, maybe three or four times, the standard price. If restaurant staff try to bludgeon you into the foreigners' section just be equally stubborn and resist – you won't be the first. Local northern **specialities**, which it's almost obligatory to try, include Beijing Duck (*Beijing Kao ya*) and Mongolian Hotpot. The first is what's served in the west as 'Fragrant Crispy Duck', small pieces of meat wrapped in pancakes filled with chopped onions and plum sauce; it's delicious and packs a fabulous cholesterol count – there's a story around the capital about a group of western businessmen going to a Beijing Duck Banquet and three of them dying from coronaries. Mongolian Hotpot is healthier, a poor man's fondue, it involves a large charcoal-heated pot of boiling stock being brought to your table – you dip in pieces of mutton, cabbage and noodle to cook, then if you're really committed drink the dregs as soup; it tends to be served with local beer, essential for washing it all down.

The more interesting **restaurants** are for the most part gathered into three areas of town: around Dongfeng market/Wangfujing, Qianmen and Xidan. There are other places to discover, of course, and you can do well just by keeping your eyes open early afternoon and then not straying too far to return. But the main areas – detailed below – do have advantages in that if one place is full there'll be other possibilities nearby. Eating with the Chinese, in almost any restaurant, should run to about ¥4 or ¥5 a head.

Around Dongfeng/Wanfujing. A good place to start – up behind the Beijing Hotel. My own favourite (among wide choice) is the *Xianshi Canting*, actually inside the Dongfeng market; it's on the right hand side as the road bends around to the left, on the second floor, and its dining area is massive enough to keep waiting to a minimum. The food is Sichuan, very hot and spicy: as always point to what you like the look of, but if you have the courage, order the beef and peanuts or the Sichuan style sweet and sour pork. At the other end of the Dongfeng market (keep following the road through the large covered area) is the *Donglaishun Fanzhuang* (Mongolian Hot Pot Restaurant) at 16 Donghuamen. Regarded as the best of its kind in town, the quality of the mutton and cabbage is excellent and the dishes come with wholemeal rolls. One floor up they serve roast duck and fried chicken dishes. Both floors have expensive foreigners' sections – beware.

Further along the street, at 60 Wanfujing, there is Shandong food at the *Cuihailou Fanzhuang*. Specialities here include sea cucumber soup, fried chicken crisp and a number of excellent seafood dishes. And just off the Wanfijing, by the Capital Hospital, is the *Wangfujing Kaoya Dian*, the so-called 'Sick Duck restaurant' a good introduction to Peking duck.
Along Qianmen Dajie. (Qianmen south: below Tian'anmen square). At 24 is the capital's most famous restaurant, the *Beijing Kaoya Dian* (Duck Factory). This is *the* place to eat Peking Duck and the posh section upstairs, which you get to via the middle of the three entrances, is where the foreign tour groups eat; the food downstairs, through the left or right entrances, is just the same, and a lot cheaper but be there at around 4.30pm. The restaurant prepares food from every part of the duck including the pancreas, liver, tongue, gizzards, feet and wings; they also have a take-away section where you can buy whole ducks for as little as ¥5. At 30 Qianonen Dajie, if you're defeated by the queues, is a reasonable *Sichuan-style* place; at 32 another duck place, the *Qianmen Kaoya Dian* (or 'Big Duck'); and at 46 a rare Shanghai restaurant, the *Laozhengxing*.
Around Xidan. (Both north and south of Xichang'an Jie.) Best known here is the *Sichuan* at 51 Rongxian: walk south from the Chang'an and turn left off Xidan at the first major traffic lights – the restaurant is just on the left. Make for the cheaper section at the back of the courtyard. Nearby, at 74 Xuanwummenai, is one of the city's few *vegetarian* restaurants.

North of Chang'an, on the right of Xidan Beidajie, is another well-known spot, the *Donghai Underground Restaurant*, announced by hoardings about 350m up the street. It's underground literally and, in a way, by reputation – run by and for Beijing's trendiest youth in pursuit of their own particular concept of western hip. The food's not so great. Carry on up though and at 133 you'll find a real gastronomic experience, the *Quyuan Hunan restaurant*. Queues can be long here but worthwhile: the cooking's better than anything I experienced in Hunan itself – mainly sweet, with a lot of dishes based on dog.
Elsewhere. Somewhat more far-flung possibilities include: by the **north gate of Ritan Park,** the *Ritan Park Restaurant* – open 4–7pm and famed for its variety of jiaozi. **Near the Lama Temple** (see p. 65 for directions), the *Bamboo Garden Restaurant*, where in summer you can eat outside in an old-style courtyard and garden. **North of Beihai Park,** the *Beijing*

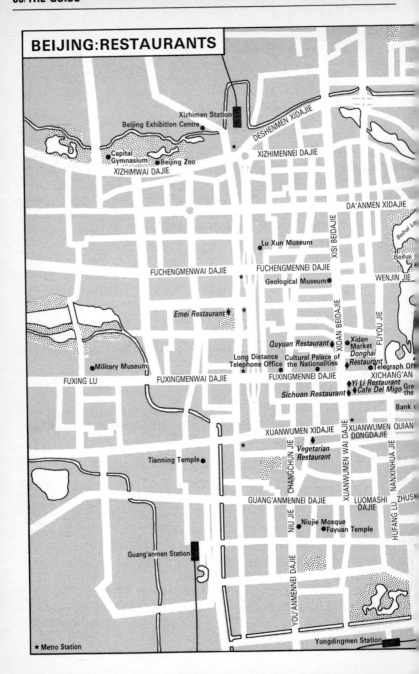

BEIJING:RESTAURANTS

Xizhimen Station

Beijing Exhibition Centre

DESHENMEN XIDAJIE

XIZHIMENNEI DAJIE

Capital
Gymnasium • Beijing Zoo

XIZHIMWAI DAJIE

DA'ANMEN XIDAJIE

Beihai La

Lu Xun Museum

XISI BEIDAJIE

Beihai

FUCHENGMENWAI DAJIE

FUCHENGMENNEI DAJIE

WENJIN JIE

Geological Museum •

Emei Restaurant

XIDAN BEIDAJIE

FUYOU JIE

Quyuan Restaurant ◆

Xidan
Market

Long Distance
Telephone Office

Cultural Palace of
the Nationalities

Donghai
Restaurant

Telegraph Off

Military Museum

FUXINGMENWAI DAJIE

FUXINGMENNEI DAJIE

XICHANG'AN

FUXING LU

◆Yi Li Restaurant

Gre
the

Sichuan Restaurant ◆ ◆Cafe Del Migo

Bank o

XUANWUMEN WAI DAJIE

XUANWUMEN QUIAN
DONGDAJIE

XUANWUMEN XIDAJIE

◆

Tianning Temple •

CHANGCHUN JIE

Vegetarian
Restaurant

NANXINHUA JIE

HUFANG LU ZHUSI

GUANG'ANMENNEI DAJIE

LUOMASHI
DAJIE

NIU JIE

Niujie Mosque
• Fayuan Temple

YOU ANMENNEI DAJIE

Guang'anmen Station

Yongdingmen Station

★ Metro Station

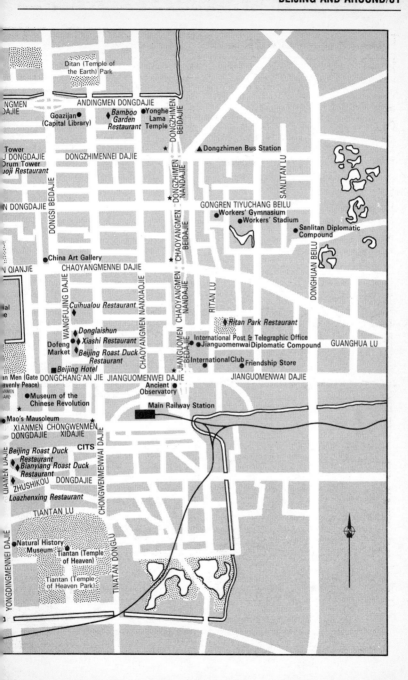

Ditan (Temple of
the Earth) Park

NGMEN
DAJIE

ANDINGMEN DONGDAJIE

Goazijan
(Capital Library)

◆ Bamboo
Garden
Restaurant

● Yonghe
Lama
Temple

DONGZHIMEN
BEIDAJIE

★

▲ Dongzhimen Bus Station

Tower
J DONGDAJIE
Drum Tower
uoji Restaurant

DONGZHIMENNEI DAJIE

DONGZHIMEN
NANDAJIE

SANLITAN LU

N DONGDAJIE

DONGSI BEIDAJIE

★

GONGREN TIYUCHANG BEILU

CHAOYANGMEN
BEIDAJIE

● Workers' Gymnasium
● Workers' Stadium

● Sanlitan Diplomatic
Compound

● China Art Gallery

N QIANJIE

CHAOYANGMENNEI DAJIE

★

CHAOYANGMEN
NANDAJIE

DONGHUAN BEILU

◆ Cuihualou Restaurant

WANGFUJING DAJIE

CHAOYANGMEN NANXIAOJIE

RITAN LU

◆ Ritan Park Restaurant

GUANGHUA LU

● Donglaishun
◆ Xiashi Restaurant
Dofeng
Market ◆ Beijing Roast Duck
Restaurant

JIANGUOMEN
BEIDAJIE

● International Post & Telegraphic Office
● Jianguomenwai Diplomatic Compound

■ Beijing Hotel

● International Club ● Friendship Store

ial
e

an Men (Gate DONGCHANG'AN JIE JIANGUOMENWEI DAJIE
venly Peace)
ANMEN
ARE

JIANGUOMENWAI DAJIE

Ancient
Observatory

● Museum of the
Chinese Revolution

Main Railway Station

★ Mao's Mausoleum

■

XIANMEN CHONGWENMEN
DONGDAJIE   XIDAJIE

CITS

CHONGWENMENNEI DAJIE

● Beijing Roast Duck
Restaurant
● Bianyiang Roast Duck
Restaurant

QIAMEN DAJIE

ZHUSHIKOU DONGDAJIE

● Loazhenxing Restaurant

TIANTAN LU

● Natural History
Museum

TINATAN DONGLU

Tiantan (Temple
of Heaven)

YONGDINGMENNEI DAJIE

Tiantan (Temple
of Heaven Park)

Kaorouii (14 Qianhaidongyan), which does a good Muslim barbecue. And finally, next to the north entrance of the **Temple of the Moon Park**, spicy Sichuan cuisine at the *Emei Canting*.

Hotels, cafés and bars
Hotel food is generally bland and expensive but there may be times when you feel the need to escape the crowds. If so, go without hesitation to the *Xinqiao Hotel* on Qianmen Dongdajie (east). Here for ¥8 a head you can eat and drink like a king, specialities including excellent curries, laid on for the Pakistani air crews who stay in the hotel between flights, and unique ice-cream sundaes. Hours are 6.30–9.30pm. Opposite the Xinqiao, just for the record, is *Maxim's*, a Beijing branch of the exclusive Paris eating chain, with set lunches for a cool ¥50 a head.

If it's simple **western food** you feel you need, the *International Club*, on Jianguomennai, is probably the best bet: set lunch for ¥8.50. The *Beijing Hotel* has nicer surroundings in its western-style restaurant but it's pricier and the food's not so great. A new alternative – more tempting than it might at first appear – is **fast food**, 'western style', at one of the two government outlets set up for tourists. Best of these is the *Yi Li* at 47 Rongxian Lu – a few doors down from the big Sichuan off the south side of Xidan, and easily recognisable from its Donald Duck logo above the entrance. Spotlessly clean, with knives and forks to confuse locals, the food here is remarkable, perhaps as good as anywhere in the city: western junk concepts taken on board and transformed to Chinese speciality. The second, newer outlet, the *Cafe del Migo*, is just west of Qianmen gate, behind the Xuan Wumen hotel's rear entrance; very popular with young Chinese, it does a neat imitation of a typical Hong Kong café. Both serve steaks and hamburgers.

This apart, **café and bar life** is still very limited – not to say virtually non-existent now that the infamous *Peace Café* has shut up shop. Most travellers, stuck for a place to while away the evening hours, tend to collect in the *Beijing Hotel*, either in one of the ground floor bars or on the roof-top café of the western block. Western residents – journalists, diplomats, businessmen – usually go to bars at the plusher hotels, like Charlie's at the *Jianguo* (beyond the Friendship Store on Jianguo Lu) or the *Great Wall* (the capital's grandest, out near Sanlitun).

Streetfood
Snacks vary greatly according to location and, to an extent, season. The best policy is probably to try anything you see – whilst remembering that locals have a very sweet tooth and many of the cakes and buns can be nauseatingly sickly (try to avoid *aiwowo*, glutinous pastries filled with sesame seed paste). Lunch-time snacks, however, are on the whole much more palatable. They include *jiaozi*, small ravioli-like pasta, popular

through the winter months and *shaomi*, traditional steamed buns stuffed with pork or chicken.

A good introduction to street snacks is to make for one of the **market** – or **nightmarket** – areas (see the listings section for a quick breakdown of addresses). Yongdingmen, along the western side of the Temple of Heaven, is particularly good. Or there's Dongfeng and the other market off to the left of Wanfujing. Or Dongso Beidajie, east of the Beijing Hotel, and around the streets in front of the main railway station. The Qianmen area is also very strong on exotic-looking snacks and takeaways.

And if you start pining for really solid, clean, healthy fare then there's always the **Friendship Store** – wholemeal bread, cheese, yoghurt and other goodies, as detailed on p. 58. The food section in the Friendship Store is on the right, as you go in, in the back supermarket section.

Entertainment

Beijing's entertainment world has never really recovered from the moral clampdown of the Liberation. The state placed a strict definition on 'culture' so out went the bourgeois decadence of bars and tea-houses and in came an artificial emphasis on **traditional and popular Chinese culture** like opera and formal theatre. The Cultural Revolution took this to the extreme. It was considered bourgeois, revisionist and counter-revolutionary even to want to enjoy yourself. Today, bourgeois pastimes like dancing still don't get much of a look in, though the government has now recognised the need for young people to have their own social pleasures and the new economic measures mean that, for the urban well-heeled, at least, there's more cash available to spend on entertainment and even travel. Another recent development is the growing interest in **foreign culture**, with both Chinese translation of western plays – like *The Mousetrap*, which was recently staged by an amateur company – and musical and operatic performances that are western in style. The **cinema** is also slowly moving away from themes of historical romanticism and political dogma, and light, western-style thrillers are now flavour of the month.

Having said that, Beijing is *the* place to see traditional entertainment. Art forms like **opera** are populist in China, with tickets cheap and moral parables relatively easy to understand. You will find details of shows in *China Daily* (or, for more local information, any of the Beijing newspapers' entertainments sections). Buying tickets for the opera and other music events, CITS are a far better bet than queueing for hours and possibly finding there are none left for the night you want; you'll only pay slightly over the odds. For cinemas and acrobatics, however, it's worth trying to get tickets yourself. And don't let CITS browbeat you into taking tickets for something you don't want to see. They regard westerners as culturally uneducated and willing to put up with anything that can be unproblematically arranged.

Opera

Jing Xi – Peking opera – is the most celebrated of the country's 350 or so regional styles – a unique combination of song, dance, acrobatics and mime, with some similarities to our pantomime. It is highly stylised and to the outsider can often seem obscure to the point of absurdity, tedious too in the end, since performances can last up to four hours, punctuated by a succession of crashing gongs and piercing, almost discordant songs. But if it bears out all CITS's prejudices it is also worth seeing – at least once – and if you can acquaint yourself with something of the plot beforehand there's a definite fascination. Most of the plots are based on historical or mythological themes – two of the most famous titles, which any Chinese will explain to you, are *The White Snake* and *The Water Margin* – and they're rigidly symbolic. Moral absolutes begin with the costumes: red signifying loyalty, yellow – slyness, blue – cruelty, white – dishonesty, black – (surprise) evil. An interesting variation on the traditions, highly instructive if you know enough to work out what's going on, are operas dealing with contemporary themes – like Mao's first wife, or the struggle of women to marry as they choose. It could be worth asking CITS if any operas of this nature are performing, or check *China Daily*.

The major **venues** are: *People's Theatre* (Hugosi Lu); *Capital Theatre* (22 Wangfu Lu); *Guanghe Theatre* (24–26 Qianmen).

Theatre and cinema

Spoken drama was only introduced into Chinese theatres this century. The **People's Art Theatre** in Beijing became its best known home and, before the Cultural Revolution, staged the kind of European plays which had a clear social message. Ibsen and Chekhov were among favourites. But in 1968 Jiang Qing, Mao's third wife, declared that 'spoken drama is dead'. The theatre, along with most of the Chinese cinemas, was closed down for almost a decade – with a corpus of just eight plays, deemed socially improving, continuing to be performed. Many of the principal actors, directors and writers were banished too, generally to rural labour.

The last years have once again seen an almost total turnabout. The People's Art Theatre, reassembled in 1979, recently had a great (perhaps surprising) success with Arthur Miller's *Death of A Salesman*. Any of its productions are worth looking out for.

Films are also shown in theatres, as well as the capital's fifty or so cinemas. Most are Chinese productions and, like some of the plays, they can still seem a bit heavy-handed – stilted romances with a solid political-moral overtone. But this itself can be interesting. Increasingly, western films are also shown – old Chaplin movies in particular are highly popular. For listings again consult CITS or *China Daily*.

Acrobatics

The most accessible and exciting of the traditional entertainments, **acrobatics** in China covers anything from gymnastics, animal tricks and juggling to plate spinning and illusion. Professional acrobats have existed in China for 2,000 years and it shows; their performances are spectacular. At one time they were regarded as gypsies but today are highly esteemed performers.

Beijing is probably the best place to see them. The place to go is the **Acrobat Rehearsal Hall** on Dazhalan, which is off Qianmen, opposite the *Roast Duck Restaurant*, about 350m south of Qianmen Gate. The theatre is about 400m up Dazhalan, on the right; the ticket office is a little further on, on the left; tickets, if you buy them yourself, are 60fen. Performances start at 7pm.

Skating and other sports

If you're in Beijing during the winter there's public **skating** on the lakes at **Beihai park** and at the **Summer Palace**. Skates are available for hire and, whatever your level of competence, it's an activity not to miss. The Chinese are obsessive about the sport and joining them on the ice is an excellent way to meet and talk.

In summer you might want to **swim** but it's something of an effort to get yourself organised. To use the pool at the International Club you need to troop up to the Capital Hospital and get yourself a public health card.

Better, perhaps, to go for spectator sport – especially if you get a chance to see a major event at the massive **Workers' Stadium** in the north-east of the city (no. 110 bus along Dongdaqiao). Chinese teams excel at **volleyball, basketball** and **gymnastics** – all played here. **Soccer** is also on the rise – though officially disgraced after an outbreak of violence (on and off the pitch) when China lost to Hong Kong in a 1985 World Cup qualifier. After the match, perhaps in imitation of the British way of things, groups of Chinese fans attacked foreigners' cars around the stadium.

Discos and other (!) nightlife

Nightlife – as you may have gathered from the *Eating and drinking* section – is not a great feature of the Chinese capital. In fact, aside from the nightmarkets (good for at least one evening) and the cultural events, it can be hard to find any signs of life at all after 7 or 8pm.

But there are a handful of **discos**. The plushest – *Juliana's* at the Lido Hotel and the *Cosmos Club* (with a Filipino band) at the Great Wall

Hotel – are for foreigners only, uninteresting and expensive. More worth-while are the shifting network of places that cater for both foreigners and Chinese. The best established of these is the disco at the *International Club* (east of Wanfujing on the corner of Dongsi Beidajie/Chaoyang-mennei Dajie; around ¥4; open from 8–11.30). Other venues change from month to month and it's hard to give any definite advice. Best ask around at the bars in the Beijing Hotel.

A more specifically Chinese alternative, and often exclusively so with Chinese-only tickets, are the **social dances** held on summer evenings in the city's parks. These are encouraged by the state to solve the very real problems of dating; it is said that Beijing has twice as many unmarried women as men in the inner city, the exact opposite proportions in the outer suburbs! The main outdoor dance venues are Beihai and Temple of Heaven parks; both host regular 'western dance nights'. Waltzing is in at present, and you'll probably see groups practising even if you don't actually make the big night itself.

Finally, in addition to the bars detailed on p. 82, there is an increasing roster of luxury **western hotels** where, if you've been travelling some time in China, you could seek a little culture shock. The *Jianguo Hotel* is a good case in point. Walking in the front door feels like entering a different country: there's a swimming pool, a delicatessen the rival of Fortnums and a cocktail bar (viciously overpriced) complete with pianist. Look in if you're curious – the staff don't seem to mind non-resident (western) guests wandering around. Still more extreme is the *Great Wall Hotel*, opened in 1984 in time for President Reagan's 300-strong entourage. With rooms upwards of ¥150 a night, it's very popular with American tourists. I overheard one once at the Great Hall of the People, commenting – 'Everything in China goes downhill once you leave the Great Wall, and I don't mean the *wall* . . .'

Listings

Airlines *CAAC* are at 117 Dongsi Xidajie (open 8–9); telephone 558 861 (enquiries), 550 497 (internal flights) and 557 319 (international flights). They also have an office at CITS (9.30–11.30 & 1.30–4). Foreign airline offices are all grouped in Building 12 of the Jianguomenwai Diplomatic Compound or at the Jianguo Hotel (*PanAm*), CITIC building (*Cathay Pacific*), Great Wall Hotel (*Thai*) or Jinglun Hotel (*Qantas*).

Antiques The best shops are on Liulichang, south-west of Tian'anmen. Good selection of calligraphy, porcelain, jade, books, seals and furniture. Expensive, but authentic, though very little over 150 years old.

Baggage Left luggage facilities at the Beijing Hotel at 50 fen per item per day.

Banks All hotels will change foreign cash and travellers' cheques. *Bank of China* at 17 Xijiaomin Xiang, open Mon–Fri 9–5, Sat 9–12.

Bicycle hire From light-blue-fronted shed opposite the Friendship Store on Jianguomennai, open 7–6, ¥2 per day plus ¥100 deposit. Or 94 Chongwenmen Dajie, open 7–7, 60 fen per hour, ¥2.50 per day, ¥100 deposit.

Black market Developing fast, but large fines have been levied on those caught. Centres are around the department store on Wanfujing and the paths off Jianguomennai between the Friendship Store and Jianguo Hotel. Current going rate is around 100FECs for 165 Renmin B.

Books *The Foreign Language Bookstore* (210 Wanfujin) stocks a wide range of English translations of Chinese classics and tourist literature. Western magazines – and *China Daily* – and novels are available from International Club and the Friendship Store. *China Travel Tourism and Press* have off-beat tourist information leaflets at CITS.

CITS 2 Chongwenmen; open 9–12.30 and 2.30–5.

Embassies are centred in two main areas: Jianguomennai, behind the Friendship Store, and Sanlitun, 6km out to the north-east near the Great Wall Hotel. *Jianguomennai embassies* include: BRITAIN (11 Guanghua Lu; tel. 521 961); IRELAND (3 Ritan Donglu; 522 691); INDIA (1 Ritan Donglu; 521 927); UNITED STATES (17 Guanghhua Lu; 522 033; also consular office near the UK embassy at 2 Xiushui Dongjie); and, for the Trans Siberian – MONGOLIA (2 Xiushui Beijie; 521 203); FINLAND (30 Guanghua Lu; 521 817); ROMANIA (523315) and POLAND (1 Ritan Lu; 521 235). At *Sanlitun* are: AUSTRALIA (15 Dongzhimenwai; 522 331); CANADA (10 Sanlitun Lu; 521 475); NETHERLANDS (10 Sanlitun Dongsijie; 521 731); NORWAY (1 Sanlitun Dongwujie; 522 261); and SWEDEN (3 Dongzhimenwai Dajie; 523 331). Also, NEPAL (12 Sanlitun Lu; 521 795); HUNGARY (12 Dongzhimenwai; 521 431); USSR (4 Dongzhiman Beizhongie, west of the main compound; 522 051). Standard hours of opening are generally from 8–12.30 and 2–5; for visas, it is usually mornings only.

Friendship Store 21 Jianguommennai (tel 593 531). Largest in China with a wide range of food, drink, clothing, jade, lacquer, artwork, carpets, silk and medicine. Also laundry, dry cleaning, postage and shipping services (¥30 per kilo by sea; ¥80 by air).

Hospital Foreigners must go to the 6th floor of Capital Hospital (553 731), a large brick building on the left going north up Dongdan Lu (which is parallel – to the east – of Wangfujing). Embassies can also give advice and addresses for local/specialist doctors.

Laundry Most major hotels run laundry services, so does the Friendship Store – though they take the best part of a fortnight.

Maps Full Cartographic series available from Cartographic Publishing House, head office at 3 Baizhifang Xijie, in the south-west of the city.

Markets/nightmarkets Best of the daytime markets are those around Qianmen/Temple of Heaven (p. 56) and Dongfeng; and to the north-east at Sanlitun, nearby the Beijing Workers Stadium. The nightmarkets operate in the summer months only, from around 6–11pm. Promising venues include: Wangfujing (at the first junction on the left – going north from the Beijing Hotel); along Qianmen, south from Tian'anmen, towards Tiantan Lu at the north end of the Temple of Heaven park; Dongdan Lu – one block east of, and parallel to, Wangfujing; Xidan – both north and south of Chang'an.

Pharmacies Useful drug selection at the Friendship Store and, if you know what you're buying, at the traditional medicine stalls in the nightmarkets.

Photography Kodak films are sold at the Friendship Store and all large hotels; film development facilities are available at the Friendship Store, Beijing Hotel, and CITIC building – the latter a 1hr-print service.

Post Office Simplest at the new International Post Office, near the International Club, or at the Beijing Hotel (Mon–Sat 7.30–7, Sun 8–4). Parcel service from shipping department of Friendship Store.

Public Security 85 Beichizi Dajie (Mon–Fri 8–11.30 & 1.30–5; tel 553 102). Friendly but not too adventurous with visas.

Shops Qianmen (see p. 52) is the most interesting shopping area, along with nearby Liulichang for antiques, and Xidan (p. 56) and Wangfujing (p. 78). Worth a look too, in addition to the main *Friendship Store*, is the *Minorities Friendship Store* in the Cultural Palace of the National Minorities (p. 56). For second-hand clothing and jewellery look in on the store at 12 Chongwenmennei. Standard shop hours – as throughout China – are around 9am–7pm, seven days a week.

Taxis Always available at CAAC and the Friendship Store, the Beijing Hotel and most other large hotels. To order by phone, dial 557 461.

Telephones You can make local calls free at most local hotels. Long-distance calls are best made at the Telegraph Office on Chang'an: hotels charge well over the odds for them.

Getting out: the ticket details

There are **trains** timetabled from Beijing to just about every city in the country – and if you can afford it, there are numerous **flights** too. A couple of points to bear in mind: **rail timetables** (which are available for study at most hotel desks) can change – don't over-rely on them if you're planning anything very esoteric; and **Chinese-rate train tickets** are harder to come by here than usual – to save money and stay sane you may find it easier to buy a short-journey ticket along the route you're planning at foreign rates, then hope for better luck over the next stage.

Train stations and ticket offices

You will almost certainly leave the capital from **Beijing Zhan**, the 'main station'. It can be chaotic, with passengers only allowed on to platforms

20 mins prior to departure (gates to platforms are usually closed again 5 mins before departure time) and trains labelled by number and not destination. So allow good time. Buses to Beijing Zhan (and **Yongdingmen**: an occasional alternative) are detailed on p. 43.

To buy tickets, you have three basic choices. You can go to CITS, to the Main Station or to one of the provincial station offices.

CITS ask for six to ten days notice of travelling (they *can* be persuaded to do it in less), charge full foreigners' rates plus a ¥3 commission, and they don't always have the tickets ready for you three days in advance, as they promise. Nor do they always get the ticket details right – checking is essential. If you do decide to use them, you'll need to take along a passport to book.

Buying tickets yourself at **Beijing Main Station** involves little more waiting than at CITS if you're straight and take your turn at the **Foreigners' Booking Office** – though be warned, there's very rarely an English speaker to be found so it's wise to have your destination written out in characters. They reserve your ticket for you up to five days in advance (a good idea if you want to be sure to get what you want); you pay for it and *must* collect it the day before you travel.

If you want to buy Chinese-rate **hard seat** tickets it is possible – but unlikely – that you'll get away with it at Beijing Zhan, by queuing at the ordinary ticket windows. Much more promising, however, are the **provincial railway offices** – at any of which you may find local Chinese willing to help you out. A problem here is in working out which office to go to – they all sell tickets for different destinations. But for short journeys, **Beixinqiao** (on Dongsi Beidajie, north of Dianmen Lu) is useful: they sell hard seats (but no sleepers) for any destination from Beijing Zhan or Yongdingmen station. For sleepers to the north-east (Shenyang, Harbin, anywhere in Chapter 2) try the office on **Dongdan** – three blocks up from Chang'an on the left-hand side of the street. For Taiyuan and on towards Shanxi, Sichuan and Ganso provinces, the **Qianmen** office (top end of Qianmen Lu). For Jinan, Nanchang and Shanghai, also for Hohhot, the **Xizhimen** station office, off to the north-west of the city.

For details of buying tickets on the Chinese and Soviet **Trans-Siberian** trains, see p. 581.

Buses
Long-distance buses are on the whole more effort than they're worth, leaving from far-flung terminals scattered near their respective routes on the periphery of the city.

Boats
Advance tickets for the **Shanghai–Hong Kong ferry** are available from CITS.

Flights

All flights leave from **Beijing Capital Airport**, 29km out from the city. To get there you're probably best off sharing a taxi (30 mins journey; around ¥28), which you can order from your hotel.

Bus alternatives are detailed on p. 43.

TIANJIN

In terms of size (6m population) and economic importance, **TIANJIN** ranks as China's third city – after Beijing and Shanghai. Directly southeast of Beijing, at the junction of the Hai river and the Grand Canal, it has long played a vital role as a port and supply point for the capital. Its main development, however, came, like Shanghai, with its status as a European treaty port in the mid-nineteenth century. At this time both its trade and industry underwent massive expansion, laying the foundations for the present mass of textile, petrochemical and metallurgy factories and for the exporting of coal from China's northern coalfields.

The city was badly hit by an earthquake in 1976, which destroyed much of its old European (and Japanese) character buildings. But Tianjin was never as glamorous as Shanghai – and it lacks Beijing's imperial grandeur. It is businessmen rather than tourists who visit. Tianjin's consumer products, often marketed under the 'Seagull' label, are available throughout the PRC, and Chinese companies here have been joined by an ever-increasing number of foreign co-producers.

If you do visit, it will probably be to catch (or more likely, leave) one of the **ferries**, which run between Tianjin (or rather, its port of Xingang, 40km east – due to the silting of the river) and Dalian (to the north) or Qingdao or Shanghai. **Travel links with Beijing** are straightforward, with regular train (and bus) departures. The journey itself is not worth taking for its own sake: a drab route across the flat, marshy countryside.

With time to fill in Tianjin, the only real interest is in **eating** (the local baozi – known as *goubuli* – are renowned) or, for serious carpet or antique buyers, in **shopping**. Tianjin's commission shops (along Heping Lu or Dongma Lu) have better prices than those in the capital, and you can also buy carpets direct from some of the factories. You might, however, be tempted to the city in April or September by its traditional **kite-flying festivals** (details from Beijing CITS).

Unless you arrive at Tianjin very late (or you are sent to one of its hotels by Beijing's CITS), there seems little reason to contemplate more than a brief stopover. There are however, several **hotels** which accept foreigners. The two most commonly used are the *Haihe* (or No.1 Hotel) at 198 Jiefang Lu, and the *Tianjin Grand*, further down the same road at 219.

HEBEI

Hebei is a somewhat anonymous province. At its heart, but outside its administration, are the municipalities of Beijing and Tianjin. About them, to the north rises bleak tableland punctuated by the Great Wall; south, poor agricultural flatlands and heavy industrial and mining towns.

The **south** is probably China at its least glamorous. **Shijiazhuang**, the provincial capital, is a case in point. As a major rail junction, you're likely to pass through. But you have to be committed to stop, whilst exploring the (admittedly spectacular) local monasteries at **Cangyan Shan** and **Zhengding**.

Northern Hebei has more promise, and en route to the former Manchurian provinces (covered in the following chapter) you should certainly try to take in either Chengde or Beidaihe. **Chengde**, set amidst the wild terrain of the Hachin Mongols, lies well north of the Great Wall – an Imperial base conceived on a grand scale by the 18C Emperor Kang Xi, and with monuments to match. **Beidaihe**, the north's most famous bathing resort, is one of the stranger experiences of contemporary Chinese travel, and to its north is **Shanhaiguan**, where the Great Wall finally meets the sea. Respectively 4hrs and 6hrs from Beijing, Chengde and Beidaihe each have enough interest to tempt a brief trip – even if you're just returning to the capital afterwards.

SOUTH: SHIJIAZHUANG AND THE MONASTERIES

At the beginning of the century **SHIJIAZHUANG** was hardly more than a village, but the building of the railway made it an important junction town, and by the 1920s it had a population of 10,000. Today it has become a major industrial centre with a highly developed textile and chemical industry, and a population of half a million. The town itself is of no real interest to travellers – the grave of Dr Norman Bethune, the Canadian much beloved by Chinese for his selfless work among the Communists in the 1930s, is a single tentative 'sight' in the Martyrs' Cemetery – but there are possible excursions to the monasteries at Cangyan Shan and to Long Xing Si at Zhengding, and to the town of Zhaoxiang with its majestic Zhaozhou bridge.

The most obvious drawback, if you do want to stay, is the cost of the city's one open **hotel**, the *Hebei Guesthouse*: rooms from ¥20 up (students from ¥14). But at least it's easy enough to find. Take bus no.6 from the railway station to the end of the line and follow the main street here, Yucai Jie, about 5 mins walk south. CITS are one block west, one block north of the guesthouse: 4th floor, no signs!

The **Martyrs' Cemetery** – if you've time to fill – is half a dozen blocks west of the railway station, just back from the main avenue, Zhongshan Lu. If you are Canadian you should definitely visit: **Dr Bethune** is more or less a household name in China and the cemetery boasts a small display on his life. It's a remarkable story – before serving with Mao in the war against Japan, Bethune had fought with the Communists in the Spanish Civil War.

Cangyan Shan
Conceived by the Sui dynasty and rebuilt by the Qing, **Cangyan Shan monastery** is one of the most amazingly sited in China. It stands, hundreds of feet up, on a single stone spanning a deep gorge. The grounds around are beautiful; the palace itself an attractive Sui type structure with a double roof.

It takes 2½hrs by bus from Shijiazhuang to Cangyan; the bus leaves at 7.30am daily from in front of the People's Department Store, returning at 2pm.

Zhengding and Long Xing Si
An easy trip out from Shijiazhuang, the town of **ZHENGDING** lies just 10km to the north-east: a 20min ride on the blue and silver *Hino* bus (which leaves Jiefang Lu, close by the railway station, at 7.30am and 1.30pm – returning around 3.30 and 9.30pm.

The town has a number of monastic buildings, of which far the most famous are the **Long Xing Si** – reputed to be the oldest surviving in China. The main temple of the complex, the Da Bei Ge, dates from the 10C; its centrepiece, a rare and magnificent example of Song dynasty craftsmanship, a 22m high statue of Guan Yin, the goddess of mercy.

Zhaouzhou bridge
The **Zhaouzhou bridge** – 3km south of the town of ZHAOXIANG – was built at the beginning of the 7C, during a period when much was done to improve communications in the recently reunited empire. Its builder, one Li Chun, had to reconcile several conflicting problems: the bridge had to be flat enough for the chariots of the Imperial army to pass, yet not so low that it would be destroyed by the frequent floods; and it had to be strong enough to withstand the military and trading convoys yet not so heavy that it would sink into the soft river banks. The result of Li's deliberations was a single flattened arch – spanning over 36m and with a rise of 7m. It is still in use, one of the undoubted masterpieces of Chinese architecture, and model for dozens of northern Chinese stone bridges.

ZHAOXIAN is some 40km south-east of Shijiazhuang; accessible by a fairly regular bus.

CHENGDE

CHENGDE – known before Liberation as JEHOL – has an interesting and clearly defined past. It was conceived and built by the Manchu Experor Kang Xi, perhaps the ablest and most enlightened of the dynasty, as a means of keeping in check and impressing the volatile northern tribes beyond the wall. Which sounds predictable enough – only Kang Xi, in contrast to his Manchu and Ming successors, was better known for his economy – 'The people are the foundation of the kingdom, if they have enough then the kingdom is rich' – than for such displays of imperial grandeur. Jehol, however, with its sumptuous **Summer Palace**, was a thoroughly pragmatic creation. Kang Xi decided it was, simply, an effective means of the Empire's defence to invite Mongol princes here, to splendid audiences and hunting parties, and to witness awe-inspiring military manoeuvres. He firmly resisted all petitions to have the Great Wall repaired, as an unnecessary burden to his people; and as a poor means of control too, no doubt, for it had posed no obstacle to the founders of his own dynasty only a few years before.

Construction of the first Jehol palaces started in 1703; by 1711 there were thirty-six palaces, temples, monasteries and pagodas set in a great walled park with ornamental pools; bridges linked the islands which were dotted with beautiful pavilions, craftsmen from all parts of China were gathered to work on the project. In its heyday, during the reign of Emperor Qian Long (1736–1796), who himself added another thirty-six Imperial buildings, it must have been an awesome spectacle.

A host of myths and legends has sprung up, loosely woven with the history of Jehol; Emperors bewitched by supernaturally beautiful concubines, blighted hopes and loves, invitations to suicide, and so on. The most important historical event was the visit of the Panchen Lama, summoned from Tibet by Qian Long for the Emperor's birthday celebrations. This was an adroit political move to impress with the devotion and good intentions of the Dragon Throne, all the followers of Lamaistic Buddhism, which included a number of prominent thorns in the Empire's side – Tibetans, Mongols, Torguts, Eleuths, Djungars, Kalmucks and a host of others. Some accounts, notably not the Chinese, tell of how Qian Long invited the Panchen Lama to sit with him on the Dragon Throne – which was taken to Jehol for the summer season. He was certainly fêted with honours and bestowed with costly gifts and titles, but the greatest impression on him and his followers must have been made by the replicas of the Potala and of his own palace, which had been constructed at Jehol to make him feel at home: a munificent gesture, and one that would not have been lost on the Lamaists. The Panchen Lama's visit ended with his succumbing to smallpox, or perhaps poison, in Beijing. His coffin was returned to Tibet with a stupendous funeral cortège and honours past description.

The first British embassy to China, under Lord McCartney, also visited Qian Long's court. Having suffered the indignity of sailing up the river to Beijing in a ship whose sails were painted with characters signifying 'Tribute-bearers from the vassal king of England', they had been somewhat disgruntled to find that the Emperor had moved court to Jehol for the summer. But they made the 150-mile journey – in European carriages, to the wonder of the populace – arriving at Jehol on 9 September 1793. They were well received by the Emperor, in spite of McCartney's refusal to *kowtow* – the humiliating ceremony of kneeling and knocking your head on the ground – and in spite of Qian's disappointment with their gifts, supplied by the opportunist East India Company. But Qian, at the height of Manchu power, was able to hold out against the British

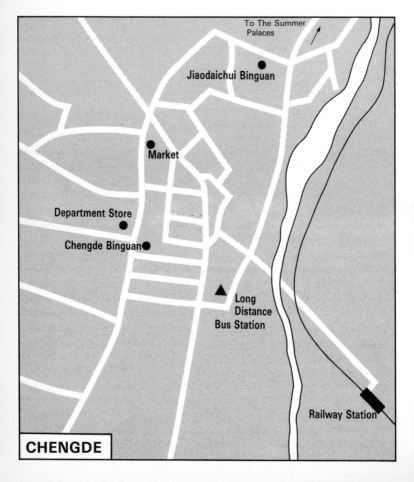

CHENGDE

demands, refusing to grant any of the treaties requested. His letter to the British monarch concluded, magnificently, 'O King – Tremblingly Obey, and Show No Negligence!'.

Jehol reached its zenith under Qian Long. His successor, Jia Qing had the misfortune to be struck by lightning in the palace. This did not augur well for the future, and under Guang Xu, the penultimate Manchu Emperor, the palaces fell into decline. By the beginning of this century, the whole place was in an advanced state of decay.

Today, there are signs of change. The palaces have been designated a National Monument and those buildings remaining are in the process of restoration. They don't at present quite match the legend but there is enough to fuel your imagination within the 15km circuit of walls that surround the park and palace complex. There is boating too, on the Imperial lake, and the landscape as a whole is pleasant enough to merit at least a couple of day's rambling exploration.

Chengde – the town

Initial appearances don't augur well for Chengde. The modern town that's grown up to the south of the old Imperial Resort is a depressed and depressing place, clouded generally in a haze of pollution. It is, however, cooler than Beijing – hence the official name Bihushanzhuang (Mountain Hamlet for Escaping the Heat) – and you will in any case spend most of your time outside, clambering about the hillside palaces and temples, or wandering up to the weirdly-eroded (and meticulously named) rock-formations that ring the town. By **rail from Beijing** it is a very pleasant 4hr journey, best made in the morning so that you get in at midday.

The resort is popular among Chinese visitors, so there are numerous **hotels** scattered around the town. Foreign visitors, however, are at present encouraged to stay either at the *Chengde Binguan*, on the main street, or the *Jiaodaichiu*, out of town close to the Imperial park. Both are reached by bus no.7 (or a tricycle ride) from the station – usually a connecting service with trains from Beijing. Rooms at either run around ¥30 for a double. Out of preference I'd probably go for the Jiaodaichiu. **Eating,** you might as well stick to the hotels – again with the Jiaodaichiu slightly ahead on quality; Chengde is not a gourmet's paradise.

Getting **from the town to the park** – which tends to be referred to as Bihushanzhuang – you'll want to use either bus no.7 (for the lower entrance) or no.6 (which runs out to the northern temples). Ideally, you'd hire a bike to cover the park and temple circuit, though when I was there none of the outlets would deal with foreigners. This may well have changed: try – and put yourself across as very persistent. Before setting out, stock up with some tea and fruit; there aren't too many refreshment places around the park.

Moving **on from Chengde** you'll probably want to backtrack to Beijing. You could, however, go on by train – or bus – into Dongbei, there is a reasonably easy connection to Shenyang (see p. 129).

Bihushanzhuang Park

There's a definite air of promise about **Bihushanzhuang park**, with its circuit of walls built to the design (and presumably in direct emulation) of the Great Wall. And though it hasn't yet been greatly restored, the remnants of grandeur are clear enough: pools and islands created to evoke the lower stretches of the Yangzi, hilly trails to scattered pavilions, and, most obviously, Qian Long's summer palace.

You enter the park compound through the **Lizhengmen** – the Gate of Splendour and Propriety – and almost immediately are confronted by the **Imperial Palace**. Chinese (rather than Manchu) in style, this bears obvious similarities to the Imperial Palace in Beijing. The scale is different, of course, but even so the idea is still to impress with size. The buildings are low, wooden halls, often with beautiful Namnu hardwood carvings. Many of the original furnishings remain, and in the **Yanbozhishuangdian** – Hall of Refreshing Mists and Waves – you can look into the Emperor's private rooms, his bedchamber, sittingroom and study. Interesting too is the **Yunshanshengdi Lou**, the last and most northerly building in the central palace section, its two storeys connected by an unusual stone spiral stairway. The 'Tower of Clouds and Mountain Resort' today houses an antique shop – well stocked but expensive.

Further to the north, beyond the palaces, a further relic of Qian Long's time is the **Wenjingge**, built in 1744 to house the complete libraries of the Four Treasuries – a 79,000 volume work on Classics, History, Philosophy and Literature. The library, sadly, is no longer at Chengde. It was sent last century to Beijing, to replace the capital's own copy, burnt with other treasures in the old Summer Palace amid the British and French destruction of 1860.

The Eight Outer Temples (Waibamiao)

Outside the park, scattered about the hilly countryside, Qian Long and Jia Qing built eleven major temples. Seven remain in recognisable form, five of which can be visited. They are constructed in Tibetan style, part of the scheme to awe and impress their wild northern visitors, most of whom were Lamaists and so would have been familiar with Tibetan architecture.

The best approach is to take bus no.6 (from the park entrance) north to the most distant temple, the **Puningsi**, a 5km ride. Set slightly apart from the rest of the group, it was built in 1755 to commemorate the 'pacification' of the Djunggars of Western Mongolia; its name means 'universal peace'. Architecturally, its main feature is the magnificent

Mahayana Hall, a huge wooden five-storey tower, roofed with gilded bronze tiles, and housing a gigantic statue of Guanyin – reputedly the largest wooden statue in the world, 23m high and a reputed 120 tons.

Five minutes walk from here, the **Putuozongshengmiao**, modelled after the Potala in Tibet, is by far the largest of the outer temples, raised by Qian to celebrate his 60th birthday and his mother's 80th. Recently renovated, it's a startling sight, set back in the hills and flanked by dagobas, sprawling in very unsymmetrical and un-Chinese fashion amidst the trees. The dominant structure, the Great Red Platform, 43m high, encloses the main hall (still dilapidated when I was there) where the religious and official ceremonies would have been held.

Just to the east is the **Ximifushoumiao**, similar in structure but smaller in size, its model was that of the Panchen Lama's monastery in Tibet. It is ten years later than its neighbour and has a greater blend of Tibetan and Chinese styles – more ordered in form. Here is another Great Red Platform, lower though still imposing; it encloses the beautiful wooden main hall, the Solemn Sumeru Hall. The roof is particularly fine with its gilded tiles and fishscale ridges, and eight magnificent gilded dragons, each one weighing one ton. This temple, built in honour of a visit by the Panchen Lama, is dedicated to the mythical Mount Sumeru, the central mountain of the Buddhist universe.

The other two visitable temples are the **Anyuan** and **Pulesi**, both across on the other side of the stream. Anyuan is said to preserve Buddhist frescoes, though it is open only sporadically. More interesting, Pulesi, recently restored, boasts a majestically ceilinged Round Pavilion.

BEIDAIHE AND SHANHAIGUAN

After a week in Beijing, **BEIDAIHE** is a very tempting target: a seaside resort, just 6hrs by train from the capital (on the SHENYANG line), and as the local literature has it 'becomes a divine spot to recuperate'. If you go you won't exactly be alone. Some 3 million Chinese daytrippers and weekend holidaymakers descend on Beidaihe between June and September each year, and with the distancing of the Cultural Revolution (seaside trips then being considered revisionist and bourgeois) figures are still rising. Which is, of course, much of the fun. This is real China-on-Sea territory: packed with beach photographers and small makeshift restaurants, summer villas for the political elite and brand new private guesthouses for the (still well-heeled, and privileged) masses. In short, Torremolinos in the making.

The Beijing **train** ride – a pleasant trip through flat, green fields of rice and maize – leaves you at Beidaihe station, 15km from the resort. There's a bus every 90mins, which more or less connects with the train services. Once at Beidaihe the **hotel** to make for is the *Xishan Guesthouse* (Tel.

2018), a series of bungalow-villas set amid gardens of conifers, which you can rent out as a group or by the bed. It's expensive, at around ¥30 a night per person, but there's a chance of bargaining down rates if you join with other travellers; getting there, initially at least (the hotel hires bikes at ¥3 a day), is easiest by taxi – the hotel's about 2km west of the bus station. Other, slightly cheaper, alternatives include the *Zhonghaitan* (Central Beach Hotel): five minutes walk from the bus station along the main road to the right. Set on the beach, with a good restaurant, this has doubles for around ¥34, though again they may let you bargain them down. They arrange train tickets and transport to the station. **Bike Hire**, if you're not staying at the Xishan, is slightly cheaper from one of the shops in the town centre (¥2 a day from by the ice-cream stall in the main square).

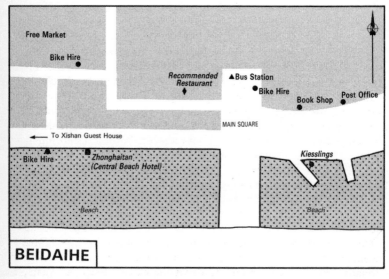

With summer temperatures steady in the 70s (F), and very swimmable water, Beidaihe has been a bathing resort since the 1890s. Its original clientele was European, diplomats and traders from the Beijing and Tianjin concessions, and the stamp of this period remains in the town's architecture: old, grand-style villas looking out to the strange formations of rock and the 10km stretch of sands. The stamp of the period also remains in Beidaihe's foremost restaurant, *Kiessling's* – established by Austrians and still serving coffee, cakes, ice cream and marvellous bread without equal in China. Kiessling's **fish** is pretty good, too. Or there are any other number of other places, many around the **free market**, where you could try the local crabs and prawns; buy them yourself and take them along to be cooked. One of the biggest and best of these restaurants (see plan) is down a small street west of the main square; they also serve delicious baozi and chicken dishes.

As for **beaches** – which is what Beidaihe is really about – you've a choice of three class structures around Bohai Bay. **Xihaitan** (west beach), flanked by a smart *International Club* complex, is reserved for foreigners – watched, in their progressive swimwear, by a shifting but constant cluster of Chinese. **Zhonghaitan** (centre beach) is the Party beach – reserved for privileged guests and Party workers, though seemingly accessible too to any foreigner who walks down. And last, liveliest and most interesting, is the regular Chinese beach, **Donghaitan**, which is where you'll find the real holidaymakers, clambering about the rocks in their long-johns and rolled up trousers and posing for photographers against a wonderfully kitsch sequence of backdrops.

Shanhaiguan

50km north of Beidaihe*, **SHANHAIGUAN** is where the Great Wall meets the sea, after its 3000km trail from the fort of Jiayuguan in the Gobi desert. The town – whose name, The Pass between Mountains and Sea, states its strategic importance – is old, walled and charming. A real rarity in northern China, it's a place to amble and, if possible, to stay. There's a cheap, spartan **hotel** by the crossroads in the old part of town, which usually accepts foreigners; an excellent base for a couple of days. The town boasts some good earthy restaurants, too, and an interesting everyday market. Access is reasonably straightforward, with daily buses around 7am from Beidaihe, a 1½hr journey.

The Wall at Shanhaiguan is far from perfectly preserved, but in many ways this is preferable to the picture-book restoration at Badaling. And you do have the chance of getting a stretch to yourself. Just outside the town is a massive **gate** built in 1639, fronted by a board announcing – 'This is the First Pass under Heaven'. Nearby is a **temple**, dedicated to a woman whose husband was press-ganged into one of the construction squads. The local tale about her is that she waited, alone, for years, then set out to search, only to find he had died long since of hunger and exhaustion. So great was her grief, that as she wept the wall crumbled – to reveal the remains of her husband and thousands of others whose tombs were the Wall itself.

---

*QINHUANGDAO – midway between Beidaihe and Shanhaiguan – is a major industrial port. It's open, and there's a **hotel** at the Seamen's Club by the port, but there's *no* reason to stop!

SHANXI

Shanxi province, with an average height of 1000m above sea level, is one huge mountain plateau. Strategically important, bounded to the north by the Great Wall, to the west and south by the Yellow River (Huang He), it was for centuries a bastion territory against the northern tribes. Today its significance is economic. Nearly a third of Chinese coal reserves are to be found in Shanxi, and around the two key towns, Datong and the capital Taiyuan, major development of the mining industry is under way.

Physically, Shanxi is dominated by the proximity of the Gobi desert. Wind and water have, over millennia, shifted sand, dust and silt – *loess* – across the province. Where irrigation is available, the loess becomes rich fertile soil, easily tilled; as a result some of the earliest Chinese civilisation started here, under the Qin, and pottery dating from 2,000 BC has been found throughout the region. But the felling of trees and the uncertainty of rainfall has left great tracts of the province fearsomely barren, with endless ranges of dusty hills cracked by fissures and gorges. (Through them too run some of the old roadways, grooved deep by use, sometimes running as much as 30m below normal land surface). The ending of the province's old isolation, and the government's increasing environmental awareness, has led to all kinds of efforts to arrest erosion and the advance of the desert: millions of trees have been planted, the land terraced and the wandering dunes even held in place by immense nets of woven straw.

As far as travel goes, Shanxi is not a big destination. **Datong**, 7hrs by train from Beijing, in the north of the province, is the only city much visited – its pull being the magnificent **Yungang cave temples**. Datong is easily taken in en route to Hohhot, if you're planning a north-western circuit. Finding time for the south of Shanxi, and the provincial capital **Taiyuan**, is a somewhat more esoteric exercise. If you do, you'll be rewarded by the famed Buddhist temple of **Jinci** – and a very drab city indeed.

One last attraction, though not yet 'open' to western travellers, is the **Wutai Shan** near Daxian – another of the country's five sacred Buddhist mountains. If you're headed for Taiyuan from Beijing, or vice versa, it may be worth seeing if you can get a permit to visit.

DATONG

The land around **DATONG** is scarred with open-cast mines and roads into the city are crowded with donkey carts and lorries, creaking under huge loads of dusty grey coal. But if this sounds unpromising, don't let it put you off. Datong, though at the heart of modern Shanxi development, offers a surprising and timeless glimpse of old China. Your first view, on arrival at the station, is of a square crowded with traditional activity: street entertainers setting up their shows, operatic and theatre companies, musicians, tinkers and trinket sellers. Many of these itinerants are Miao people from the hills of the south-west, who spend all summer camped in the square, apparently making a fair living.

From the **station**, walk a short way down the main road opposite and pick up – on the right-hand side of the street – a no.**15 bus**. This turns left at the bottom of the road – get off at the next stop and you'll find (on the left-hand side) the *Datong Binguan*, the only **hotel** in town. Rooms at the Binguan go for around ¥20 (doubles), dormitory beds from ¥6–8; some of the staff speak limited English, and there's a **CITS** (worth using here for booking train tickets – you'll queue long at the station) in the same building.

The city conforms to regular Chinese pattern. The **Old Town**, at its heart, is a rectangular grid of streets with a **Drum Tower** in the centre. Just to the east is the **Jiulongbi**, 'Nine Dragon Screen', its glazed tiles, of five colours, creating the traditional motif of dragons rising from the waves and cavorting among suns. This is the best surviving example of a form of decoration popular in the courtyards of the wealthy during the early Ming dynasty: it is a masterpiece of imaginative art. A pool of

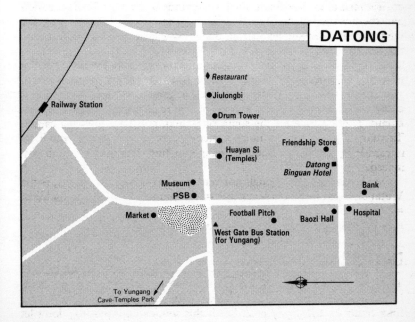

DATONG

Railway Station

Restaurant
Jiulongbi
Drum Tower

Friendship Store

Huayan Si
(Temples)

Datong
Binguan Hotel

Museum
PSB

Bank

Market

Football Pitch
Baozi Hall

Hospital

West Gate Bus Station
(for Yungang)

To Yungang
Cave-Temples Park

water at the foot of the screen reflects the dragons, and the ripples from a stone cast into the pool animate the scene, making it quite unrecognisable.

To the west of the Drum Tower are Datong's two principal temples, the upper and lower **Huayan Si**. Huayan was the name of a Tang dynasty Buddhist sect. The upper monastery was founded under the Liao, but was completely rebuilt under the Jin, in 1140. It is unusual in that it faces east rather than south, rare in China. The main building, the **Daxiong Baodian** is one of the largest Buddhist temples still standing in China. The exterior is huge and austere, devoid of almost all ornamentation, while the interior is richly decorated with sculpture – five gilded Ming Buddhas – and a vivid Qing fresco.

In the lower monastery most of the buildings are either Ming or Qing, though the **Jiaocangdian**, built to house the library of valuable Buddhist Sutras, is much earlier – 11C Liao. All the statues and frescoes and the miniature wooden houses which contain the books are original Liao work, little of which survives elsewhere in China today.

The long road **south from the Drum Tower**, though without such defined sights, is also rewarding. Like the railway station square, it's a trading centre – lined with fruit and vegetable stalls, carpentry workshops, cricket-sellers (!) and a generous scattering of small restaurants. Datong is not noted for its cooking but it's a city where there's at least no problem in finding a place to eat – and lots of simple, snack fare available – soup, baozi and noodle stalls seemingly on every corner. One of the better **restaurants** I tried is just out beyond the Jiulongbi; or, nearby the Datong Binguan (which itself does set meals for ¥9), opposite the city hospital, is a large and thriving baozi hall.

Other aspects (and possible visits) depend upon which day you find yourself in Datong. The **Steam Locomotive Factory**, an obvious highlight for railway buffs, is open to outsiders only on Tuesdays and Saturdays. Tours (¥8) are organised *exclusively* through CITS: strictly no entrance on a casual basis. What you get for your money is a morning of statistics, a wander round the works and, finally, a brief ride in one of the train cabins.

On a Sunday, there's the **People's Park market**, with a brisk trade in monkeys and racing pigeons and, in the stadium to the south, **football matches** – enthusiastically supported.

The Yungang caves

Just 45 minutes by bus from Datong, the **YUNGANG CAVE TEMPLES** are a must – fabulous and monumental in their site, substantially complete and vitally important in the development of Chinese Buddhist art. Access is straightforward: take bus no.3 from the west gate bus station (several times daily; 30fen) to the end of its route – from here it's a short walk to the caves. There are tea and snacks at the caves, no restaurant.

In all, the Yungang complex takes in 53 caves and niches, spread for over a kilometre across the Wuzhon mountainside. The earliest date from AD460, when Datong was at its peak as capital of the northern **Wei dynasty**; the last are early 6C, completed after the Wei had shifted their powerbase south to Luoyang in Hunan (see p. 301). The Wei – originally nomadic Toba tribesmen – conquered much of northern China towards the end of the 5C, fast becoming absorbed by Han Chinese influence. Initially, under Taoist influence, they persecuted the Buddhists, who had been present in small numbers in China since the 1C AD. But in 452, with the accession of the emperor Wen Chengti, there was a sudden and zealous turnabout, and over the next two hundred years Buddhism, under Wei protection and patronage, underwent an extraordinary expansion. Yungang, begun at the instigation of a monk named Tan'yao, was the first great monumental focus.

Visiting the complex, you enter through the **Old Stone Buddha Monastery,** constructed way outside the cavebuilding period, in 1652. The twenty principal caves are numbered from east to west along the cliff face. If it's just the spectacle you're after, then explore at random. To get an idea of the **changes in style**, however, and the accumulation of influences – Indian, Greek and Persian – you need to move around various groups. The caves at the east end of the cliff – 1, 2 and 3 – and the westernmost cave – 21 – were carved last. The earliest group, initiated by Wen Chengti and his successors at Datong, are numbers 16 to 20. The concept of the cave-temple spread to China from India, via Afghanistan and Central Asia. They were not built as temples, or 'chapels', as such, but essentially to house the images of the Buddhas and other divinities and figures with which they are filled, and most often crowded.

Cave 20 is a good point to start. With its roof fallen in, the Buddha here is open to view, giving a clear impression of its style (cross-legged meditational pose, deep grooved drapery; a standing Buddha to the side) and size (over 15m from base to top). This figure inevitably dominates the site, though the most impressive and best preserved of these early caves is no.18 – its central Buddha figure, standing on a lotus flower, flanked to either side by lively graceful pairs of Bodhisattvas.

Caves **7** and **8** follow chronologically, dating from the middle of the 5C. The figures are more Chinese in style – less full bodied, ponderous and round-faced, perhaps indicating the presence of craftsmen from Gansu, which the Wei conquered in 439. Note also, in the rather eroded cave 8, the blending of Indian influence – Shiva, five-headed and sitting astride an eagle, and Vishnu, three-headed riding a bull, joining the Buddha carvings. Caves **9** and **10**, slightly later, are, like 7 and 8, paired – each double chambered, their entrances richly carved with lotus flower bas reliefs. Within, there are groups of meditative Bodhisattvas and flying Apsaras (heavenly maidens), all superbly crafted; the large Buddha in cave 10 is a 'modern' addition.

Caves 5, 6 and 11 were probably the last to be completed before the Wei Imperial court transferred to Luoyang – and 6 is generally regarded as the masterpiece of Yungang. It is certainly the most extravagant, made up of an astonishing sequence of seated or standing Buddhas enclosed by Bodhisattvas, and it is the most ordered in its arrangement. The lower reliefs are used to illustrate narratives, simply but expressively carved, of episodes from the life of Sakyamuni Buddha.

Of the later caves, 13 is probably most interesting: dating from not long after the shift of the court, it introduces a diminutive four-armed Vajra figure (new to China and unique to Yungang) to support the Maitreya Buddha's arm. The remaining caves divide into two chronological groups. 4, 14 and 15, badly eroded, were added around the turn of the century. 1 and 21, with their Buddhas placed in stone pagodas, in the 5C.

Xuanggong Si

Another, longer expedition from Datong is to the **XUANGGONG SI**, a 'hanging monastery' two hours distant. This is a good trip, though expensive – the long-distance bus station at Datong won't sell tickets to foreigners for Xuanggong, so all transport has to be arranged through CITS. Which means one of two options. Either you can get a group of travellers together and hire a **minibus** and driver (around ¥160) or you can ask for a place on one of the **tour coaches** which visit most days (¥30).

If you can afford it, though, you will get to see some of the most spectacular mountain countryside in Shanxi – and the **monastery** itself, perched midway up the face of a sheer cliff, is a truly remarkable feat of engineering. Included in the cost of most trips is a lunch stop at a village nearby the monastery.

TAIYUAN

For a large industrial city – population 2m and rising, from 100,000 in 1933, twin town Newcastle – **TAIYUAN** is surprisingly pleasant; not such a bad stopover en-route to Xi'an or Zhengzhou, and with access to the superb Buddhist shrine at Jinci. Historically, it has always been a frontier town guarding the Shanxi plains to its south. It served as a capital for the Northern Qi, the Tang and the Northern Han, as well as a brief spell outside the Chinese empire in the 12C. Most recently, in line with Shanxi's independent-minded tradition, it was the base of the warlord Yan Xishan, who held control throughout the province from the collapse of the Manchus in 1911 until 1949. According to Carl Crow's contemporary *Handbook for China*, Xishan's city was a reform-minded place, 'well known for its suppression of the growing and use of opium, its schools and anti-foot binding movement'. It is today the factories that you notice, belching from all corners, processing the coal and mineral deposits from roundabout.

Practicalities are fairly straightforward. Walking out of the train station you'll find yourself facing a long main street – Yingze Lu. Walk down this for about 10 minutes and, on your left, you'll come to the large, Soviet-style *Yingze Binguan* and, a few doors on, the *Bingzhou Fandian*. Both these **hotels** are expensive – rooms around ¥35 (split two or three ways, if there's anyone else in town) – but they are the only foreign options. The Yingze is preferable, for rooms and also for a rare slice of Taiyuan action – it holds **dances** (all welcome) on Saturday and Sunday evenings. The best of a sad bunch of **restaurants** is right outside. On the way down to the Yingze, you'll pass (on the same side) the city's **Friendship Store** (with a Bank of China). **CITS** maintain an office at the Yingze hotel and hand out very reasonable maps.

The **Jinci Temple** – detailed below – stands some 25km south-west of the city; it's on a regular bus route, a 45-minute ride which leaves from the main (1 May) square off Yingze Lu (a couple of blocks before the Yingze hotel, if you're coming down from the station). Getting there (and getting back – amid the crowds of Chinese tourists) should take up most of your time in Taiyuan. **Other possible diversions**, however, if you're waiting trains, might include the **Provincial Museum** and the **Zhongshan Monastery**.

The **Shanxi Provincial Museum** is in fact two separate exhibition halls, a fair way apart from each other. **No.2**, in the **Chunyanggong** palace (centre of town – off the 1 May square), is the more impressive. Housed in a huge Taoist temple, it takes in excellent collections of ceramics, bronzes and stone sculpture, including a fine statue of Lao Tse. **No.1** museum is the **Daibedian**, a classic example of early Ming temple architecture – a fair walk from the centre in the south-east corner of the old inner town. With its upper roof supported by external pillars, it is a graceful and imposing building. The exhibits, however, are essentially specialist – a large collection of Buddhist Sutras.

Zhongshan Si – or at least what remains of it – stands over the road from the Daibedian. Damaged and substantially destroyed by fire in 1864, this was once an important and apparently enormous Song dynasty monastery. There are still hints of grandeur in the twin 50m pagodas, the town's emblem, built in very skilfully crafted brickwork, and within, in the main hall, are three fine golden Buddhas. You can climb one of the pagodas, which has been restored, for a sweeping view of the industrial scenes around.

Jinci Temple

Set at the foot of Xuanweng Shan, the **JINCI TEMPLE** is distinguished by some of the finest surviving Song architecture in the country. And with its canal, its bridges and pavilions, it is a pleasantly cool and aesthetic spot for a sultry Shanxi summer afternoon.

You enter the complex at the so-called **New Gate**, passing in to the **Water Mirror Terrace**, first of the temple's various Ming additions, used originally as an open-air theatre. Beyond, crossing the bridge over the canal, is the 11C Song **Iron Man Terrace**, complete with its four warrior statues – one of which, cast in iron, has needed no restoration. If you continue along the same axis from here, you reach another Song structure – the white marble Flying Bridge, impressive and quite different from any other you'll see in China.

Behind this bridge is the most important of the Song buildings, the **Yi Jiang Temple**, its double roof supported by beautiful bas relief dragon pillars. Inside is a statue of the Mother Goddess – Yi Jiang – surrounded by an exquisite, informal group of secular terracotta figures. Dating from the 12C, the statues depict ladies-in-waiting, elderly matrons, elegant young women, servant-girls and a cook; their attitudes, talking and daydreaming, and their costume revealing much of the period. Such naturalistic portraiture and realism was characteristic of the refined art of the urban-dwelling Song.

Off to the south-west is the main Ming temple, the **Shuimu Miao** – Water Mother, built in 1545. The goddess has a statue and shrine on the temple's upper storey. It is the shrine on the lower floor, however, that attracts most attention – and offerings. This houses a bronze statue of a peasant girl called Liu, who, so the legend goes, was forced by her mother-in-law to spend her life drawing water from a well. Her release, in time-honoured fashion, came about through an act of kindness to an unknown traveller, a tired old man to whose horse she gave water. Possessed of no mean magic power, he caused a spring to flow, releasing her from drudgery. The same spring – of course – you can see today, in the octagonal pavilion before the shrine. It is said that it flows at exactly the same volume and temperature in summer and winter, flood and drought.

SHANDONG

It is in **Shandong** that the Yellow River – the **Huang He** – forges its way to the sea. 'China's Sorrow', the Huang He, has changed course frequently over the centuries – at times finding release to the south in the Yellow Sea, at others twisting hundreds of kilometres north to the Gulf of Bohai.

These sporadic shifts – and the way that the river elevates the land rather than carving out a depression – have always meant disaster, flooding the towns and rich agricultural plains at the heart of the province. On the last occasion (the eleventh recorded), in 1899, the flooding fomented the Boxer uprising, the ruined population striking out against foreign influence and eventually laying siege to Beijing.

Control of the Huang He in this, China's third most populous province, has been a major priority since Liberation. Around **Jinan**, the industrialised provincial capital, massive flood-control dykes have been constructed, and there is constant monitoring of the river's movements. Even so, it is far from certain that the river has finally been tamed; central administrations have taken similarly ambitious measures in the past.

Historically, Shandong's fame centres on **Confucius**, who was born here at the small town of Qufu in 551BC. Rehabilitated by Deng's administration (with massive celebrations on the sage's 2,535th birthday), the Confucian temples at **Qufu** are today a major touristic focus, as is **Tai Shan** – perhaps the holiest of China's five sacred Taoist mountains. Both reward visits. So too do the province's main coastal towns, and seaside resorts, **Qingdao** and **Yantai**, each redolent of fin-de-siècle European colonisation.

Yantai, if you are making for the north-east, has a useful **ferry link to Dalian** – an easy 8hr ride which allows you to avoid doubling back through Beijing.

JINAN, TAI'AN AND TAI SHAN

Heading west by rail from Beijing, you will pass through **JINAN**. Passing through, though, is about all you should do. A busy industrial city, with 2m inhabitants, it is touted in the official guides for its many springs. But most of these have run dry and there is little else you can conjure up into a sight. If for some reason you have **to stay** (Jinan, like Qingdao, is open without permit), the *Jinan Hotel* on Jingsu Lu is accessible from the station on the no.5 bus; prices are high (¥30 for a double). Better, however, to limit your exploring to the bizarre city **railway station**, raised in hearty Bavarian style in 1904 as part of the German concession in Shandong. The Germans were responsible for Jinan's original industrialisation, linking the town by rail with their port at Qingdao. This line still operates – which may well be why you find yourself here; connections, fortunately, are good, both north to Beijing and south-west to Nanjing and Shanghai.

Continuing on the main line south, towards Jiangsu and Anhui, **TAI'AN** is just 2hrs on from Jinan. A bustling market town, this has for hundreds of years been the base for pilgrims visiting Tai Shan. It still is. Arriving, you'll be quickly made aware of just how popular the pilgrimage is with the Chinese. On certain holy days as many as 10,000 might be making their way to the peak – and year round there must be well over half a million visitors.

Arriving – Tai'an station is another German curiosity – you'll be met by a large and eager group of **rickshaw** drivers, all offering the 2–3km ride to one of the town's two foreign guests' hotels (there are also guesthouses on Tai Shan – see below). The rickshaws are motorised and decrepit, and the drivers overcharge (¥3 for two people), but if you have the money you may as well submit. Otherwise it's a no.3 bus ride. The *Taishan Binguan*, better of the two **hotels** (with a CITS office and restaurant, and ¥10 dorm beds), is just past the Dai Zongfan – the first archway on the route to Tai Shan; the *Taishan Fandian* (¥12) is about 700m before the arch. There is a good **restaurant**, with fried *baozi* the speciality, next door to the Binguan.

Tai'an itself is not remarkable, though it has a pleasant small town atmosphere, typified by the **market streets** just south of the Dai Zongfang. You'll find medicinal herbs gathered on Tai Shan sold here – along with sinister fungi, vegetables the like of which are not seen anywhere else in

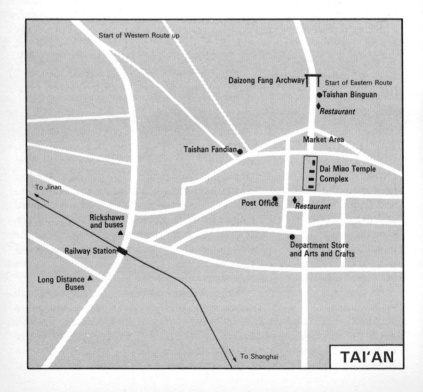

China, and bonsai trees, potted plants and intricate little tray gardens.

The main sight, however, is the **Daimiao**, the traditional starting point for the procession up Tai Shan. This is one of the most celebrated temples in the country and one of the largest, too: the main building of the complex, the *Tiankuangdian*, is matched only at the Forbidden City and at Qufu. Its origins are Han, around 2,000 years old, though construction and renovation has been almost constant since, particularly during the Song and Tang dynasties. In 1956 the whole building was restored and today it is in an excellent state of preservation. Inside is a statue of the God of Tai Shan, enthroned in a niche and dressed in flowing robes, and holding the oblong tablet which is the insignia of his authority; he looks like an emperor. The five sacrificial vessels laid before him bear the symbols of the five peaks. A huge Song dynasty mural on the three walls of the temple depicts an Emperor's pilgrimage to Taishan, with a cast of thousands portrayed in some detail.

The courtyards and temple gardens justify a full morning's visit. For calligraphy enthusiasts there is a **forest of steles**, including the oldest example of stone-carved calligraphy in China, an edict of the second Qin Emperor, carved in 209 BC. And somewhere, it is said, is the stone monolith erected by Chin Shi Huang Ti when he finally unified the Empire – this stone however bears no inscription, for it was he who burned the books. There is a little *museum* with a collection of very early sacrificial vessels and some exquisite Tang pottery; a *tea-house* and *noodle-shop*; a host of gnarled cypresses, one of which is said to be 2,100 years old, and unique and delightful, a Ming dynasty bronze pavilion.

Taishan

TAISHAN is not merely the home of the Gods, like Olympus or Sinai; it is a deity itself, and has been worshipped by the Chinese longer than recorded history. It is the eastern-most and perhaps the holiest of the five holy mountains of China – Huashan, the two Hengshans, Zhong Gao and Taishan. For over two millennia a succession of emperors worshipped at Taishan, surveying their empire from the summit, or making sacrifices, sometimes with retinues that stretched from the top to the bottom of the mountain – some six miles of pomp and ostentatious wealth. Requisitioning everything in their path to feed this gilded train, they must have been like a plague of locusts to the long-suffering local people.

To follow in their path, make your way through the **Daizongfang** arch – only the Emperor was permitted to use the middle gate – and buy a stick, a cup of tea and a mooncake to fortify you for the climb. Directly ahead are the 5,500 steps that will take you – and the crowds of Chinese pilgrims and tourists – over 1500m up the mountain. Night or day, from March through to October, you will never be alone, for this is one of the most popular of all excursions in the north. Many of the Chinese are here simply for this – the pleasure of mass tourism – but it is notable how many are genuine pilgrims. Taoism, after a long period of Communist proscription, is again alive and flourishing, attracting new adherents as well as the old women, their feet sometimes bound, you see struggling to the top of the holy mount.

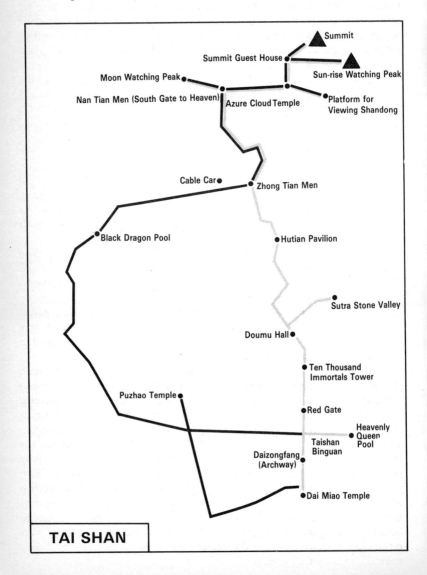

TAI SHAN

Stopping to visit all the temples on the way up, and taking the occasional cup of tea (there are refreshments every few metres), you should reach the summit in around **4–5hrs**; if you are reasonably fit, it could be done without stopping in 2hrs. An alternative – though not one I'd recommend – is to take a **bus** from the town (by the station or hotels) to the *Zhongtianmen*, the Middle Gate, well over half way up the mountain; from here the truely sedentary could rise to the summit by cablecar. If you want, it is possible to **stay at the summit**, leaving your baggage down below (the Taishan Binguan will look after it for you) or lugging it up, with the aid of one of the six hundred porters who maintain a constant ferrying service from the Zhongtianmen.

Scattered about **the foot of Taishan** steps are a number of small Taoist temples. The **Laojuntang**, off amid the trees to the right of the path, is dedicated to **Lao Zi** (for information on whom, see p. 567). Nearby, set amongst waterfalls and pools is the **Wangmuchi** (Heavenly Queen Pool), a tiny and beautiful Ming/Qing nunnery.

On **the path proper**, the first of the temples – on your left – is the **Guandi**, dedicated to Guan, god of war. Here you buy your 5mao ticket for the ascent, which begins officially at the simple stone arch of **Yitianmen** – the First Gate of Heaven. This is followed by a Ming arch, said to mark the spot where Confucius began his climb (though how he reached this point is unexplained), and by the 17C **Red Gate Palace**, built in honour of the legendary Princess of the Coloured Clouds.

Moving higher, the next group of buildings belong to the former **Dou Mu** convent. There is a tea-house here, as well as both Buddhist and Taoist temples. These, like all the buildings that line the pilgrimage way, are pleasingly simple – conceived on a far more human scale than the Daimiao in the town below. They are characterised by large flat areas of stone, painted with a blood-red wash and interfaced with small grey bricks; their beams and rafters are colour decorated, though somewhat less garishly and exuberantly than usual.

The **Zhongtianmen** – the Middle Gate of Heaven – is set on a small, flat, isolated peak. With its road access (and discreet cable car station – for a quick ascent to the summit), it is a major tourist post, equipped with a **hotel** (unexciting) and a reasonable restaurant. The sight which stands out, however, is the stream of **porters**, balancing weights of up to 125 jin (roughly 63kg) on their shoulder poles, moving swiftly up the mountain and then almost galloping down for a fresh load. A young porter told me that he made three such trips a day, six days a week. With a regulated charge of ¥2 per 100 jin, this makes around ¥45 a week – an astronomical wage for China, and, on reflection, probably more than Deng Xiaoping earns (not including perks and allowances). It ought to be said, though, that the Chinese would consider that the porter deserves more than the politician, for the porter's work output in terms of matter moved, is very much greater.

The route to the summit from the Zhongtianmen winds first downhill, along the road, then across **Yun Bu** – Cloud Stepping – bridge and up to the **Shengxianfeng**, the Archway to Immortality. From here on, the climb is considerably more strenuous, with fewer temples and pavilions in which to idle as you cover the **Eighteen Bends** – each steeply carved with 200 steps – and finally achieve the **Nantianmen**, the South Gate of Heaven.

Around the summit there is a small **village**, its buildings – guesthouses, restaurants and noodle-shops – mostly devoted to the pilgrim trade. Following the main street, to the east, you soon leave it behind and come to the **Bixia**, the Temple of the Azure Clouds. Built by the Song, the simplicity and architectural harmony of the temple make this one of the most exquisite buildings in northern China. It comprises a central pavilion with a double roof of bronze tiles surmounted by mythical figures. Within, in case you've been puzzling since beginning the ascent, is a statue of the Princess of the Coloured Clouds herself.

The **Summit Guesthouse**, to which all foreigners are likely to be directed by any of the village hotels, lies just to the north, above the Bixia. It costs ¥12 a night, which includes the hire of a heavy quilted coat – an evening essential even in midsummer. Meals in the restaurant run to ¥7 – cheaper in the village.

From the summit there are numerous **trails** to fancifully named beauty spots – Fairy Bridge, Celestial Candle Peak, etc. – and to a few further temples. It is a grand area for aimless wanderings too, with potentially magnificent views over Shandong and along the course of the Huang He: the great thing is said to be seeing the dawn rise from **Dawn Watching Peak**. In practice, however, prepare yourself for more modest pleasures. The weather up here is highly unpredictable and there are often enveloping cloud and high winds – even when it's a fine day in the plain below.

Climbing down Tai Shan, there is an alternative **western route**, slightly more circuitous and without flanking temples, but uncrowded and impressively scenic. The route veers off from the main path at the Zhongtianmen, looping round to rejoin it a little beyond the Guandi temple. Midway, just past the Bridge of Longevity, is the **Black Dragon Pool**, a dark pond, steeped in mythology and fed by a waterfall.

QUFU

There is a CITS bus **between TAI'AN and QUFU**. But it is pricey. You can as easily make your own way: by regular train to **YANZHOU** (1½hr) then a connecting bus (5 mao; leaves from outside the station; last at 5pm) for the remaining 14km to **QUFU**. The bus ride – 45 minutes – takes you across flat, fertile countryside, mostly large communes with excellent farming; beans, aubergines and potatoes are the staples, lotus fill in the wet patches; on the horizon curious blue mountains squat like toads; it is a good introduction to rural, southern Shandong.

QUFU itself is all you could ever hope for in a Chinese country town. For once no industry has intruded – save the increasingly important tourism – and rambling out from the town gates you find yourself amid fields, cut by dusty, tree-shaded lanes. Apart from which, of course, there is the **Confucian connection.** The sage, whose Chinese name is *Kong Fu* was born here (around 551BC), taught here – largely unappreciated – for much of his life, and was buried just outside the town, in what quickly became a sacred burial ground for his clan – the **Kong.** All around the town, despite a flurry of destructive zeal during the Cultural Revolution, is evidence of the stead in which he was held by successive Imperial dynasties and most monumentally by the Ming, who were responsible for the two highly dominant sights: the Confucius (or Kong) Mansion and the Confucius Temple. They, and the easygoing nature of Qufu, are worth at least a couple of days. For a run-down on Confucianism, and its place in modern China, see p. 566.

One of the most tangible pleasures of Qufu's Confucian history is the town's **guesthouse** – which occupies, with an unusually well organised and helpful **CITS**, part of the **Confucius Mansions**, or the *Kong Fu* as it is in Chinese. In a town the size of Qufu (another novelty), the mansion is hard to miss: a straight walk into town from the Drum Tower, where all the buses stop. Double rooms run for ¥18 and the luxury of their design (tea, shower, reading lamp, room key, plumbing . . .) does a neat impersonation of China travellers' fantasy. The mansions house an excellent **restaurant,** too, and have sales of both Kodak film and Scotch whisky. Another pleasantly run restaurant – earthy and tiny – is just to the east of the south gate.

Having established yourself, the **Kong Fu** mansion is an obvious first exploration. Home to the Kong clan until 1948*, it is undoubtedly the finest surviving example of a feudal aristocratic mansion anywhere in China. Like the rest of the town's aspects of clan grandeur, Confucius himself would actually have known nothing of this, but almost from his death, his successors lorded it in Qufu, retaining their wealth and influence right through from the Han to the Qing dynasties.

The mansion is essentially Ming, built in the early 16C and restored at intervals since. It is an impressive structure, with a grand triple portal like something out of a 1950s Hollywood movie, and it is currently well

---

*The last direct Confucian heir went into exile in Taiwan after the revolution. But half of Qufu, and Shandong, claims Confucian descent: the Kongs are so numerous that there's a local telephone directory dedicated to K alone! At the major Confucian celebrations in 1978, the clan was represented by direct descendants of the 77th and 78th generations – the latter a worker for a publishing firm in Beijing.

endowed. A **tour** through the halls (arranged at the hotel reception) gives a startling insight into the life of an important Mandarin family; the collections – furniture, pottery, books, musical instruments, robes – spanning a thousand years of power.

The **Kong Miao** – the principal **Temple of Confucius** – stands just to the south-west of the Kong mansion amid some 50 acres of parkland. It is approached through the *Lingxingmen* (South Gate), across a stretch of parkland with ancient cypresses and steles (and a rash of tea and trinket

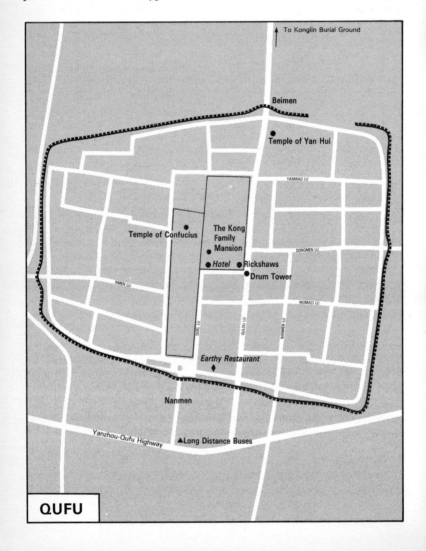

stalls), and finally a moat, spanned by three classical marble bridges. The ensemble in all ways dominates the town, and its size, and collections, demand a lengthy visit. They were damaged only to a small degree by the visit of Red Guards during the Cultural Revolution. The curators, much as they had done 2,000 years before when Qin Shi Huang Ti burned the Confucian books, managed to secrete away the more precious documents and relics.

The first exhibition rooms comprise the three *gate pavilions*, just across the moat. These house collections of pottery, sculpture and steles – some dating from the Eastern Han, around 100–200AD. Beyond them is the *Guiwenge* – the Great Pavilion of the Constellation of Scholars – which until modern decades housed the Confucian library. The oldest building in the temple complex, simple and dignified with its three roofs of glazed tiles and wooden gallery, it dates from the Jin, about 1190.

Next, past an interior gate – the *Dachengmen* – you enter the *Great Courtyard*, to your right a Kuai tree legendarily planted by the master, at the centre the distinctive *Xingtan pavilion* – built reputedly on the site of an apricot tree under which Confucius gave his lectures. Of these tree tales, the latter is the more realistic (apricot trees being in key with the style – near poverty – of Confucius's life); the former, the real life tree, has been unromantically dated as 18C, though the local authorities hopefully hold out that it took root from a genuine original.

On two sides of the Great Courtyard run long galleries, perfectly ordered with unornamented red stone columns. The third side, partially obscured by the Xingtan, is taken up by the *Dachengdian* – the principal temple hall of the sanctuary. Nearly 30m tall, this is one of the largest wooden buildings in existence. It was constructed under the Qing dynasty, in 1724, and it represents the zenith of their architecture. The focus within is a sequence of twelve vast wooden columns, each a complete tree trunk, soaring away into darkness. On the outside there is astounding stone carving on the eave supports – protected with wire netting from both birds and pilgrims (who, over the generations, have worn much of it away in their enthusiasm to touch and feel). The hall's function was in part for sacrifice – in Qing times it is said that the temple owned 8,000 acres of land solely for raising animals for the ritual.

A much smaller replica of the Kong Miao – dedicated to the master's favoured disciple, the most virtuous and wise Yan Hui, stands to the north of Qufu, just inside the Beimen (north gate). Known as the **Yan Miao**, or Fusheng Miao, this is a quieter, more relaxed spot to visit, beautifully set amid a garden with pools.

From here you could walk out of town a couple of kilometres to the **Kong Lin** – the Kong family graveyard, a vast man-made forest, where Confucius and several thousand of his clan lie buried. (Or you could, very pleasantly, take a rickshaw tour: ¥5 for half a day's pedalling, easiest arranged around the Drum Tower.) The Kong Lin is approached along a much revered Spirit Way, lined with ancient cypresses and carved stone *pailou* arches. Wandering along the numerous paths through the forest, you come across small pavilions and arches, stone lions, horses and rams, and stele-bearing tortoises. (The tortoise is an Imperial symbol of longevity; despite this, the Chinese disapprove of the unfortunate tortoise which are all believed to be male and consequently not above reproach in their sexual habits.) The **Tomb of Confucius** is itself an unpretentious affair, consisting of a mound surrounded by a low brick wall, before which are two simply inscribed steles. Nearby is an unpleasing 'hut', like a brick potting shed, in which the disciple Zi Gong mourned his master's death for six years.

On from Qufu

To reach anywhere other than Tai'an, it is best to go **via Jinan** (4hrs by direct bus – daily at 6am and 1pm. This avoids the problem of connecting with trains at Yanzhou, which will almost certainly arrive full.

The **Qufu bus station** (for Jinan departures) is a short way out of town beyond the Nanmen (south gate). Leaving the gate behind you, continue south for 500m to a T-junction: turn left and the station is on your left.

QINGDAO

QINGDAO makes a remarkable first impression. The seafront and inner town buildings are almost all Germanic and above them rear the twin red-roofed towers of a cathedral. They are the legacy of Kaiser Wilhelm's industrious attempts to extend a **German imperial** 'sphere of influence' in the east at the turn of the last century. The Kaiser's annexation of Qingdao – along with the surrounding Jiazhou peninsula – was justified in terms typical of the European actions of the time. It was prompted by concern for 'safety', following the murder of two German missionaries by the Boxer movement. The Kaiser simply raised the incident to inter-national crisis, making a near hysterical speech (which coined the phrase 'Yellow Peril') that demanded agreement from the enfeebled Manchu government. He got his concession, shortly extended to include Jinan, and set about constructing the two towns. Qingdao had previously been an insignificant Chinese fishing village – but the German choice was carefully calculated, the ubiquitous Baron von Richtofen having carried out a survey and found it ideal for a deep-water naval base. It was to remain German until the First World War, when its defences were overrun by the Japanese – who in turn annexed the port, returning it to the Chinese only in 1922.

Modern Qingdao is still a very important port (China's fourth largest) and behind the old town has skylined a considerable city and industrial base. But this doesn't dilute the charm and a string of six superb sandy **beaches** make it one of the country's most popular tourist resorts. If you don't plan passing through Beidaihe, to the north-east of Beijing, then it is certainly worth travelling this way to experience a Chinese seaside resort. Further diversions, from the German era, include a grand scattering of villas and main street shops (the German town was kept strictly segregated from the Chinese) and perhaps most importantly the old German brewery, still brewing the famous Tsingtao beer.

The Qingdao **train station** is right at the heart of the old German town – and close by the seafront. Most of the **hotels** open to foreigners are spread along the seafront too; they are better quality than usual but also – be warned – well above normal odds. If you can afford it, the *Zhanqiao* (31 Taiping Lu: opposite the pier) is the one to go for: a really majestic pile, reputedly the old German consulate, it has doubles for ¥40 at the back, ¥60 with a verandah looking out to sea. You could try bargaining.

Friendship Hotel

Seamen's Club

Boat Station

Ferry Pier

Post Office

Zhongshan Park

PSB

Railway Station

Huanghai Hotel

Zhanqiao Hotel

Huiquan Hotel

Badaguan Hotel

No. 1 Beach

No.2 Beach

QINGDAO

Alternatively take bus no.6 (from the station) further round the coast towards the No.1 Beach and you'll pass the modern *Huiquan* and *Huanghai* – no character but slightly cheaper at around ¥38–42. Further round still, by No.2 Beach, is the *Badaguan Guesthouse*: very appealing, with a series of stone villas set amidst trees, though definitely on the expensive side (doubles from ¥50). If you can't – or won't – afford any of these, then you're down to trailing one of the Chinese guesthouses – an unpredictable operation. The *Heping* and *Friendship* hotels, up to the north of town by the Friendship Store, are possibilities, though not necessarily any more than that – don't count on a cheap bed if you come to Qingdao. If you're really stuck as to what to do, **CITS** (in the Huiquan hotel) may be able to offer further suggestions.

Accommodation aside, Qingdao is a pretty easy place to manage. The old **German concession** is inevitably the most interesting quarter to explore, but the whole seafront and port area is rewarding and there are of course the **beaches** – imaginatively designated nos 1 to 6. **No.1 Beach**, flanked by the Luxun park (with sea museum and aquarium with seals), is the nicest of them. It is always crowded, but this should be exactly what you're after. The whole beach/park area swarms with holidaymakers and ice cream vendors, trinket stalls and a good rash of kitsch photographers' stalls. There are, too, a lot of Chinese youths ready to talk to foreigners in order to practise their English.

The **Qingdao Brewery**, which the Chinese took over when the Germans moved out, can be visited on arrangement with CITS at the Huiquan hotel. It's on the 25 bus route – and easy enough to spot – though CITS may insist that you take a guide and taxi from their office.

Other sights are probably discoverable if you hire a **bike** – usually available from the hotels listed above – or by **boat trip**. For the latter (including the rides to Laoshan, below) make your way to the local ferry wharf, at the bottom of a narrow sidestreet off Laiyang Lu – close by the north end of the main drag, Zhongshan Lu.

As far as **nightlife** goes, the liveliest part of town is up to the north around the harbour and **Friendship Store** – easiest covered by the no.6 bus from the station. You'll find a good restaurant immediately above the Friendship Store and a **Seamen's Club** (open till 10.30pm) on the floor above. In the southern part of town, back from the beaches, the best **food** comes at the Huiquan Hotel. For snacks, try the cafés around No.1 beach and along Zhongshan Lu.

Laoshan

LAOSHAN MOUNTAIN can be reached by boat ride from Qingdao or – preferable – by bus from the railway station (1½hr; departures daily at 7am ¥4.50 return). This road route, on a clear day, is spectacular. It runs almost all the way along the coast, somewhat precariously at times, until arriving at a small village at the foot of the mountain. From the village, a pathway of stone steps – constructed a century ago by the enterprising German Laoshan Company to cater for their compatriots' weakness for Alpine clambering – runs all the way to the summit and then back down a different route on the other side.

The path, constructed with Teutonic cunning, is a delight, climbing through gulleys and woods, streams and pools. Midway, you reach a temple, where you can fortify yourself with fruit and tea for the final haul to the top. At the **summit** – about 2hrs if you're reasonably fit – there's another temple, sacked gratuitously during the Cultural Revolution and now housing in part a meteorological station. There are springs, too, crystal clear and the source of the widely distributed Laoshan Mineral Water. And, last, there are the views – the real Germanic object, no doubt carefully documented by countless travellers. They are suitably impressive, sweeping even further round the coast as you descend by the alternative route.

Walking without masochism, you should be able to do the circuit with time for a swim down below and lunch of steamed buns and beer from one of the small **restaurants** before the **bus** returns at 2pm.

Ferries from Qingdao

There are **ferries from Qingdao** to DALIAN (for the north-east, see p. 128) and to SHANGHAI. Each runs every four days and saves considerably on the comparative train journeys in both cost (there's no foreigners' mark up) and comfort; journey times are roughly the same as for the train (26hrs to Dalian; 27hrs to Shanghai).

Tickets can be bought in advance from the Qingdao boat departure terminal – close by the Friendship Store. There are five classes (Special, 1st, 2nd, 3rd and 4th), with severe gradations in prices as you move down the scale, rather less difference in what you get for your money; 3rd is probably the best overall bet unless you're either loaded or down and out.

YANTAI

Many Chinese talk wistfully of **YANTAI** as a watering place the rival of Qingdao. It isn't – quite – due to a somewhat over-burgeoning revival of its industry and port, but the comparisons are obvious enough. Like Qingdao, Yantai's past – it was called Chefoo prior to Liberation – is closely bound up with European adventurism. First in, in 1862, were the British, who made Chefoo a Treaty Port as a result of their successes in the Opium War. They were followed here thirty years later by the Germans, not content with Qingdao around the peninsula. Later, after the First World War, came the Americans, who used the port as a summer station for their entire Asian fleet.

All of which has left an odd and highly distinctive feel – a battered **Anglo-Chinese** seaside town not altogether subdued by the proliferation of post-1950s revolutionary and functional architecture. Nor – yet – by the insurge of investment following Yantai's designation (in the 1970s) as a Special Economic Zone.

Yantai is on the **ferry routes** from Tianjin (intermittently) and also Dalian (see the section following). By **train** you can approach direct from Qingdao (by steam if you get the no.506 – leaving Qingdao at 8.50am) or from Jinan (12hrs). The Jinan journey is an enjoyable approach through the peninsula: a green landscape, weeping willows by muddy village ponds, thick with ducks and geese, then gradually the smoky industrial areas west of Yantai.

Arriving, as at Qingdao, there is a **hotel problem**. Just 200m from the **train station** you'll find the *Seamen's Mission* – the cheap option (¥5–15), though sometimes needing a lot of persistence to win a place. Alternatives are few, since Yantai is surprisingly popular with Chinese tourists – who fill most of the hotels. The most promising is perhaps the *Yantai Shan Binguan* (¥40 doubles; *possible* dorms at ¥8) though here too you need to be wily – try sneaking past the gatehouse to reach reception and base one. If you don't get in then you'll probably have little option than the *Zhifu Hotel* – 45 mins walk east of town, a ¥12 taxi or just 4 buses daily from the Station. Rewards aren't great when you reach the Zhifu either – cheapest rooms at ¥40 – although there is a kind of beach nearby for brown seaweed swimming and the hotel does have a good restaurant. CITS, if you were hoping for other advice, are themselves at the Zhifu.

Around the town, it's the **fishing industry** that's most in evidence. A large, modern fleet goes out from Yantai to fish the Bohai Gulf and Yellow Sea, whilst on a smaller scale the seafront is always lined with optimistic anglers. (Seaweed again for them.) Crabbers, however, seem more successful and a tiny **restaurant**, midway along the promenade – *Pangcui Fandian* – serves up excellent crabs and local fish. If you're committed to such sea pursuits, don't miss out either on the *Fengwei Canguan*, a more salubrious restaurant on the main street – not cheap but highly recommended. You might be tempted, whilst there, to wash your fish down with another of the town's specialities – **Yantai wine** and **brandy**. This, however, is perhaps best resisted; the wine grapes are all skin and pip with a hint of elderberry, and the wines are . . . well, reasonably priced. Stick to beer and tea.

More ostensibly tourist 'sights' are rather thin on the ground. Yantai means 'smoke platform' – from the **Beacon Hill** on the promontory, where signal fires were once lit. But the hill today, despite tempting appearance on the CITS maps, is a sorry little park – currently awaiting the development of a high-rise hotel, bowling alley and funfair.

One single exception – which really is worth anyone's time – is the **Yantai Museum,** housed in the largest and most beautiful of the city's old guildhalls, set up for the use of merchants and shipowners. The entrance hall alone is startling – decorated with an ensemble of over a hundred stone and wood carvings. The beams are in the form of a woman lying on her side nursing a baby; beneath the eaves are Arab figures playing musical instruments, possibly reflecting the fact that Quanzhou in Fujian, where the temple was constructed, has a history of trade with the Arabian peninsula in the 19C. Other panels to the north show scenes from the Romance of the Three Kingdoms, the Eight Immortals who Crossed the Sea; and one of the finest, the story of the 2C General Su

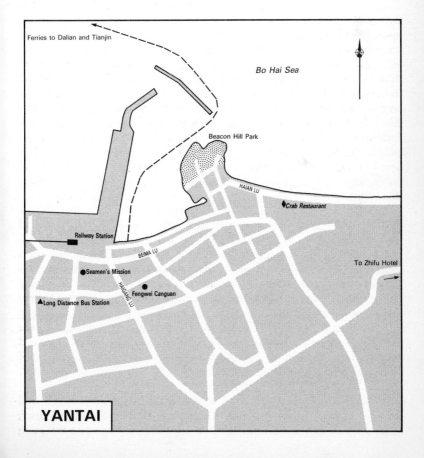

Wu, condemned to look after sheep for nineteen years for his refusal to go over to the Huns.

The main building is the temple to the Goddess of the sea. This Goddess started life as a real person, the sister of four brothers who were fishermen. It is said that she fell into a deep trance while her brothers were away on a long fishing-trip. Her parents, fearing that she was dead, woke her, whereupon she told them that she had dreamed of her brothers caught in a violent storm; later the youngest brother returned, reporting that the others had been drowned; he had been saved, by a woman who had appeared in the sky and towed his boat to safety. Generations of sailors in trouble at sea reported being guided to safety by the vision of a woman. Under the Ming and Qing she became an official deity, and temples in her honour proliferated around the coast.

The temple itself is in the style of imperial buildings of the Song dynasty. It was brought from Fujian by ship in 1864 – a unique and beautiful example of southern style in northern China, with its double roof, sweeping horns to the eaves, fancifully ornamented with mythical figures in wood, stone and glazed ceramics. Below are stone columns, their deep relief dragon motif carvings among the finest to be seen in China. The whole temple complex is set in a little garden with pools and a stage – the Goddess is said to have been fond of plays. The museum in the side-galleries houses a number of stone-age cooking-pots, axes and arrow-heads, believed to be 6,000 years old, and some fine 17C and 18C porcelain.

Out from town – Yantai county

Though you are supposed to stay only in the town, you are allowed to visit the whole of Yantai county, right out to the eastern tip of Shandong.

A rewarding day's excursion is to **PENGLAI**, two hours west on a bus that leaves the central bus-station at 7am – buy your ticket the day before – from the station or CITS. You drive for two hours past fields of maize, cotton, vineyards and estuaries – not the most beautiful countryside. Arriving at the town of Penglai, stay on the bus until it stops at the **Pavilion**, 3km outside the town. Perched on a cliff, overlooking a restored 16C fortified harbour, is a most unusual Taoist temple complex. There are six main buildings, dating from 1056, with extensive restoration and additions. The temple contains a fine gilt Sea Goddess, behind whose dais is a spectacular mural of Sea- and Cloud-dragons disporting themselves in their customary disagreeable fashion. The group of buildings, set in a garden on the slope of the cliff, is crowned by a lighthouse-like tower. You can swim or catch crabs in the sea, which is a little clearer here, while you wait for the return bus. People talk excitedly about the 'Penglai Mirage', a rare occurrence about which accounts vary wildly, from a wispy, low-level sea-mist, to islands in the sky with trees and people.

One thing is clear; if it happens not to be manifesting itself when you arrive, you may have to wait twenty years to see it – the return bus leaves at 2 pm.

Yantai ferries
From Yantai there are **boats** to a number of destinations: Dalian, Tianjin, Shanghai; tickets can be bought any time from the harbour ticket-office, or the hotel will arrange them for you.

The journey to DALIAN, directly across the Bohai Gulf, takes 8 hours; boats leave at 8pm. There are three classes: 1st – ¥29, 2nd – ¥17, and 3rd – ¥10. Third is adequate, but noisy and crowded; second is very comfortable, in a four-berth cabin. This trip has been made by tens of millions of Shandong peasants, travelling deck-class as they headed north for the seasonal harvest work in Manchuria, or emigrating permanently, as many millions did in the earlier part of this century.

TRAVEL DETAILS

FROM BEIJING
Trains
Tianjin (6 daily, 2½hrs), Shijiazhuang (4, 5hrs), Chengde (4, 4hrs), Beidaihe (4, 6hrs), Datong (4, 7hrs), Taiyuan (4, 8hrs), Jinan/Tai'an/Qufu (4, 7½hrs/ 9½hrs/11hrs), Qingdao (1, 20hrs), Yantai (1, 19hrs).
Beyond: Changsha (1 daily, 23hrs), Guangzhou/Canton (2, 33hrs), Harbin (3, 16hrs), Nanjing (4, 15hrs), Shanghai (4, 19hrs), Wuhan (4, 12hrs), Xi'an (5, 19hrs), Zhengzhou (4, 12hrs).
Trans-Siberian: Every Wednesday at 7.40am.

Flights
Services to all major cities, including Chengdu (daily, 2½hrs), Guangzhou/ Canton (6 daily, 3–4hrs), Shanghai (7 daily, 1½hrs), Urumqi (5 weekly, 4hrs) and Xi'an (4 daily, 2¼hrs).

AROUND BEIJING
Trains
From Shijiazhuang: Beidaihe (2 daily, 4hrs), Beiging (6, 2½hrs).
From Chengde: Beijing (4, 4hrs), Shen-yang (4, 8hrs).
From Beidaihe: Beijing (4, 6hrs), Tianjin (2, 4hrs).

From Datong: Taiyuan (2, 8hrs), Beijing (4, 7hrs).
From Taiyuan: Datong (2, 7hrs), Beijing (4, 8hrs).
From Jinan: Yantai (2, 12hrs), Qingdao (2, 13hrs), Tai'an (4, 2hrs), Beijing (4, 7½hrs)
From Tai'an: Jinan (4, 2hrs), Qufu (4, 1½hrs), Beijing (4, 9½ hrs).
From Qufu: Tai'an (4, 1½hrs), Jinan (4, 3½hrs), Beijing (4, 11hrs)
From Yantai: Jinan (2, 12hrs), Beijing (1, 19hrs).
From Qingdao: Jinan (2, 13hrs), Beijing (1, 20hrs).

Ferries
From Tianjin: Datian (2 a week, 20hrs), Yantai (3 a week, 24hrs)
From Qingdao: Datian (2 a week, 26hrs), Yantai (2 a week, 20hrs), Tianjin (2 a week, 40hrs).
From Yantai: Datian (Daily, 8hrs), Tianjin (3 a week, 24hrs), Qingdao (2 a week, 20hrs).

Flights
Airports at Tianjin, Yantai, Qinhuangdao (for Beidaihe); Qingdao, Jinan, Shijiazhuang and Taiyuan.

BEIDAIHE	北戴河	QUFU	曲阜
BEIJING	北京	SHANHAIGUAN	山海关
CHENGDE	承德	SHIJIAZHUANG	石家庄
DATONG	大同	TAI'AN	泰安
JINAN	济南	TAIYUAN	太原
LAOSHAN	崂山	TIANJIN	天津
PENGLAI	蓬莱	YANTAI	烟台
QINGDAO	青岛	YUNGANG	云岗

Chapter two

DONGBEI: THE NORTH-EAST

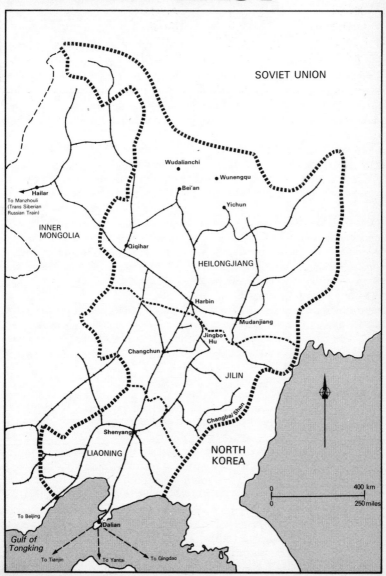

SOVIET UNION

Wudalianchi

Wunengqu

Bei'an

Yichun

Hailar
To Manzhouli
(Trans Siberian
Russian Train)

INNER
MONGOLIA

Qiqihar

HEILONGJIANG

Harbin

Mudanjiang

Jingbo
Hu

Changchun

JILIN

Changbai Shan

Shenyang

NORTH
KOREA

LIAONING

400 km

0

0

250 miles

To Beijing

To Tianjin

Dalian

Gulf of
Tongking

To Yantai

To Qingdao

LIAONING – JILIN – HEILONGJIANG

Dongbei (or, more evocatively, **Manchuria**) is a region that few tourists reach – and with good reason. There's little here that's of real appeal, distances are long and arduous, and the climate, out of the spring and summer months, is inhospitable to say the least. A huge area of some 970,000 square kilometres (roughly the size of Germany and France), most of it brimming with mineral wealth, virgin forest and as yet unexploited natural resources, travel here can be tough, and notwithstanding an excellent network of train-links (avoid buses – roads are rarely better than dirt) will only reward the really determined – and then only marginally.

Manchuria's history is, however, more interesting than the place itself. The region was for a long time a thorn in Beijing's side, its 17C rulers grabbing power from the capital to establish their own dynasty, the Qing. Later, at the turn of the 19C, the region's boundaries were contested by China, Russia and Japan – disputes that only resolved themselves with liberation in 1949. Now Manchuria is China's industrial heartland, boasting some of the country's largest steelplants, oilfields and the like, alongside a land and countryside which remains, even for most Chinese, something of an unknown quantity – and even in its most attractive reaches, in no way picturesque. Of the region's cities, the old capital **Shenyang** is easiest to reach from Beijing or Shandong, though as a goal for tourism or pleasure it's hardly enticing. **Harbin**, much further north on the main rail line, is interesting as a curiosity, although again it's a long way to go. **Changchun** and **Mudanjiang** frankly have nothing to recommend them at all.

Some history

The **history** of Manchuria proper begins with Nurhachi, a strong and warlike leader who in the 16C united the warring tribes of the northeast against the corrupt central rule of Ming dynasty Liaoning. He introduced an alphabet based on the Mongol script, administered Manchu law and, by 1625, had created a firm and relatively autonomous government that was in constant confrontation with the Chinese. His successor, Dorgun, the Regent of his grandson, Shunchih, went a stage further and with the help of the defeated Ming general, Wu Sankuei, marched on Beijing and in 1644 proclaimed the Qing dynasty – and the beginning of what was to be a long line of Manchu emperors.

The first of these – Shunchih, Kang Xi and Qian Long – were keen to establish the Qing over the whole of China, and did their best to assimilate

Chinese customs and ideas. They were, however, even more determined to protect their homeland, and so the whole of the north-east was closed to the rest of China: this way they could protect their monopoly on the valuable ginseng trade, and keep the Chinese from ploughing up their land and desecrating the graves of their ancestors. It was a policy that couldn't last forever though: the 18C saw increasing immigration into Manchuria and by 1878 the laws had been rescinded and the Chinese were moving into Manchuria by the million, escaping the flood-ravaged plains of the south for the fertile lands of the north-east.

All this time Manchuria was being coveted by its neighbours. The Sino-Japanese war of 1894 left the Japanese occupying the Liaotung peninsula and the only way the Chinese could regain it was by turning to Russia, who was also hungry for influence in the area. The deal was that the Russians be allowed to build a railway that linked Vladivostok to the main body of Russia – an arrangement which in fact led to a gradual and, eventually, complete occupation of Manchuria by the imperial Russian armies. This was by and large a bloody affair, marked by atrocities and brutal reprisals, and in 1904 the Japanese decided – by declaring war – to adopt the Russians' privileges in Manchuria for themselves.

Japan's designs on Manchuria didn't end there: their population had almost doubled over just 60 years, and this, coupled with a disastrous economic situation at home and an extreme militaristic regime, led to their invasion of the region in 1932, establishing the puppet-state of Manchukuo. The aims of this were ostensibly peaceful, but in spite of that Japan was unceremoniously booted out of the League of Nations and the state never really took legitimate root. Also, it was characterised by some examples of horrific and violent oppression – not least in a secret Japanese germ warfare research centre in Pingfang where the experiments conducted on people during the last war were on a par with anything that happened at Auschwitz.

There were bitterly disputed cases both for and against the Japanese occupation of Manchukuo – sovereignty over the area had always been contentious, though there is certainly no case for its ever being Japanese. The Japanese undoubtedly brought a degree of prosperity and organisation, even a certain stability, but, as before, the indigenous peoples and peasants who had flocked to Manchuria from all over China suffered degradation, oppression and brutality. The only reason the Japanese regime lasted so long was because the Chinese were occupied elsewhere with Mao's Red Armies, and it was only with the establishment of a united front between the Communists and the Kuomintang that Manchuria was finally – in 1945 – rid of the Japanese forever. Of course, the region's problems didn't stop there, and it was some time (and in spite of a vicious campaign against the Reds backed by both Russia and the USA) before Mao and the Communists fully took control of the region.

DALIAN (LUDA)

Nowhere in the north-east has changed hands as often as **DALIAN**. When the Japanese held sway here the city was their challenge to Hong Kong, a thriving port with the only deepwater icefree harbour in the region, ideally placed to handle the produce of the rich lands of Dongbei. Later, in 1898, the Russians saw Dalian as an alternative to the icebound port of Vladivostok, and would have constructed quite a city had not the Japanese wrested Dalian back from them a few years later. The Japanese were responsible for many of the port facilities that still stand, and it wasn't until after the last war that the Russians returned, occupying the city until the mid-1950s.

Today Dalian is busier than ever: it's still the north-east's only real port and remains the funnel of Dongbei's enormous natural and industrial wealth, a Special Economic Zone that looks set for a major expansion. Even now, by Chinese standards it's a cosmopolitan place: the shops are stocked with a wider variety of goods than most of the rest of the country, the city is clean and surprisingly uncrowded, and everywhere people seem just that little bit better heeled than their counterparts in the rest of China.

There is, however, little enough to do, and beyond strolling the lively shopping streets of the town centre and stopping off at one of Dalian's justly acclaimed seafood restaurants (the town's speciality), you'll find

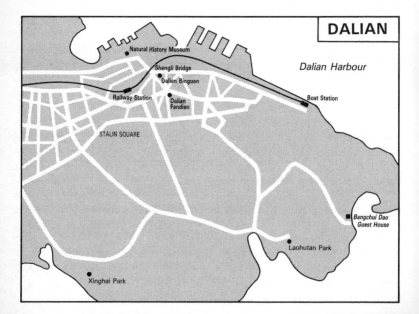

there's scant point in staying long. The **Natural History Museum**, on the north side of the railway across the curious Shengli Bridge, may be worthwhile if your connecting train is delayed, if only for the chance to have your photograph taken atop a (stuffed) Manchurian tiger. Or, for a rest from Dalian's bustle, take a no.12 bus to the **Bangcui Dao Hotel** – an exclusive concoction of villas for western VIPs and high-ranking party cadres where, if you can afford ¥30 a night for a double room, the beaches are the best in the area and the sea is clean and not plagued by sharks. If your budget won't run to the Bangcui Dao, don't despair: a 102 busride from the city centre leaves you at **Fujiazhuang Beach**, which is sandy and also offers excellent – and safe – swimming.

If through some disaster you find yourself having to stay in Dalian, bear in mind that **hotels** are few and don't come cheap. The most down-beat option is the *Friendship Hotel* above the Friendship Store at the eastern end of Sidalin (Stalin) Lu; or theres the *Seamen's Mission* just opposite. Otherwise be prepared to splash out, most luxuriously on the *Dalian Binguan* on Zhongshan Square, whose tattered Russian elegance – and good English breakfast – you may decide is worth ¥50 a night. Or, a little cheaper, the *Dalian Fandian* a few blocks away has rooms for ¥40 a night. **A word on leaving**: direct and regular trains run from Dalian to Shenyang, Beijing and Harbin, and there are daily ferries to Yantai and Shanghai, less frequent ones to Tianjin and Qingdao.

SHENYANG

Capital of Liaoning province, **SHENYANG** is the major industrial city of the north-east: a centre for trade, a major rail junction (all the major train lines of the north-east meet here), and home to any number of factories that have been laid open to the public as examples of Chinese endeavour. As such its appeal is, perhaps, limited, but there's no denying the city's historical significance which, if you're prepared to look beyond the city's drab grey 20C surface, still manifests itself in a number of visitable sights. Plus its early role as trading centre for nomads and the different peoples of northern China has left it with a rich ethnic mix. If you're heading here specifically it's about a 12-hour train journey from Beijing (an hour and half by plane); better, though, to visit en route (or to use it as a base) for places further north rather than give it a special trip. Remember, too, that Shenyang can get bitterly cold in winter – down as low as −30C – so bring your warmest woollies or come during spring or summer.

Though well known in China as an important power base for the more radical – and since discredited – factions in Chinese politics (Mao's nephew, Yuanxin, was deputy party secretary here until thrown into jail in 1976) Shenyang's real heyday was in the early 17C, when it was capital of the expanding Manchu empire. Later, the Manchus turned their sights on Beijing and Shenyang was forgotten, only becoming important again when it was centre of the railway-building activities of the Russians in the late 19C. Under them, the city became a key rail and trade centre; years after, the puppets of the Japanese state set up shop here, exploiting the resources of the surrounding region and building an industrial infrastructure that sent all the profits back home.

There's no getting over it though – most of Shenyang is grimy and despite the city's latterday prosperity bleakly poor, its architecture for the most part the last word in post-war socialist overstatement. It's also

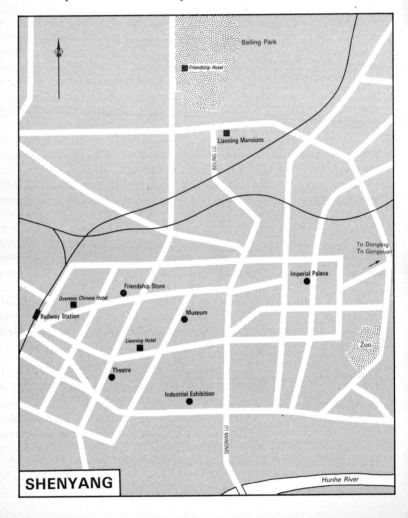

rather spread out, and to see most of the city's few attractions you'll need to use buses or hire a bike. First and most impressive of these is the **Imperial Palace** (a no.13 trolley bus ride from the railway station), built in the early 17C in homage to the incipient Manchurian dynasty. This is like the palace in Beijing on which it was modelled, but much smaller. It divides into three parts: the first, the *Cong Zheng Dian*, a low wooden-fronted hall where the emperor first proclaimed the Qing dynasty and which was used by ministers to discuss state affairs. Beyond here, in the second courtyard, stand the *Phoenix Tower*, most formal of the ceremonial halls, and the *Qing Ning Lo* – which served as bedrooms for the emperor and his concubines. Passing through to the eastern section of the complex is the *Da Zheng Dian*, a squat octagonal wooden structure in vivid red and lacquered gold, with two pillars cut with writhing golden dragons in high relief. Here the emperor Shun Chih was crowned before seizing power – and the empire – in Beijing in 1644. Just in front stand ten square pavilions, the **Shi Wang**, once used as offices by the chieftains of the eight Banners of the Empire (Banners were the districts over which they ruled), and now housing a collection of weaponry well worth a quick peek.

The palace isn't all that's left of the Manchu dynasty. Either side of town – to the north and east of Shenyang respectively and some distance apart – are the **tombs of Tai Zong and Nurhachi**, set in the Beiling and Dongling parks. Tai Zong's tomb, reachable by a no.6 or no.20 bus from the city centre and at the far end of a long drive lined with animal sculptures, is probably the most impressive of the two, well preserved and complete with altar for sacrificial offerings in the Long en Dian, and the burial mound of the emperor and empress at the rear. The park invites a closer look too: in the easternmost of the pavilions flanking the entrance subsequent emperors would wash and brush up before paying their respects at the altar: in the other, pigs and sheep were slaughtered by way of sacrifice. The tomb of Nurhachi in Dongling park is similar, perched on a hill overlooking the river and linked by bus no.18: it is, however, less monumental in layout so if you've only time, or inclination, for one, I'd go for Tai Zong's.

Practical details
Pricewise at least, there's little to choose between Shenyang's **hotels**, all of which offer rooms at broadly affordable rates. The Liaoning Hotel gives the most central location, close to the railway station and Friendship Store and within walking distance of the Imperial Palace, but on balance you may prefer to be a little further out of Shenyang's none-too-appealing centre – in which case try the *Liaoning Mansions* (huge and airy, with a CITS office next door) or the *Friendship Hotel*, both beside Beiling Park. All three hotels have **restaurants**, but service is slow and food poor so

you'd do better to sample some of the restaurants in town. Of these, the *Lumingchun*, on Nanshichang, is best, and lists 'Swimming Dragon Playing with Phoenix' among its specialities. Alternatives are the *Yingpin*, on Nanwu Lu; *Yuanlu* on Taiyuan; and *Jubinlou* in the North Market, which, like the Lumingchun, specialises in Shandong and Beijing cuisine.

HARBIN

An important junction on the Russian Manchurian railway, and even now loaded with remnants of the Russians' stay, **HARBIN** is, architecturally at least, one of the most individual towns in China. Until the late 1890s it was little more than a small and isolated fishing village on the banks of the Sungari river, but with the railway it became populated by Russian engineers and merchants. Also, huge numbers of Chinese were encouraged to move up here to look for work, and by 1917, compounded by an influx of White Russians who had fled here to escape the revolution, the town boasted a population of some 200,000.

The Russians were brutally treated by the Japanese when they took back the city in the early part of this century. But in spite of that it's their influence which is most pervasive – manifest in their large mansions and wide avenues (built by those homesick for St Petersburg), a collection of varied restaurants serving a notably un-Chinese array of different foods, and some of the country's greenest and best-kept parks and gardens. There's little tangible to see other than the peeling façades of the buildings themselves and an Orthodox cathedral which has been long closed; and in the winter months at least, the climate can be appalling, cold enough to make travel here miserable. But during the summer it's well worth the journey up to Harbin to take in a town which looks like the last threadbare outpost of Imperial Russia.

Out of the railway station you're on the city's central square, from where you can either take tram no.1 or no.3 to the *International Hotel* (good cheap restaurant, a CITS office and rooms at around ¥60 – though they assuredly do have cheaper accommodation), or slum it at the *Huaqiao* one block down the hill, where they have doubles for ¥18. **Restaurants** are easy to find, best those on and just off the main shopping street, Dazhi Jie, or towards the Songhua River along Zhongyang Dajie, one of which serves excellent steaming pots of goulash.

This, if only for its atmosphere and a handful of Russian and European style buildings, is the most appealing part of town. And though there's nothing whatever to see, you'll find it's more interesting strolling this quarter than checking out Harbin's more mainstream attractions. These include a **zoo** holding examples of Manchuria's rich fauna in some dismally cramped cages, an above-average though largely closed off **Natural History Museum**, and a set of gardens called the **Children's Park** where children aren't actually allowed to play. Rather more interesting is the **Flood Control Monument,** on the south bank of the Songhua river. This commemorates the many thousands who over the years have lost their lives in the Songhua floods, most recently in the 1930s and the 1950s, and if nothing else is a notable piece of revolutionary realism, in granite tinged with submarine green and standing on one of the miles of

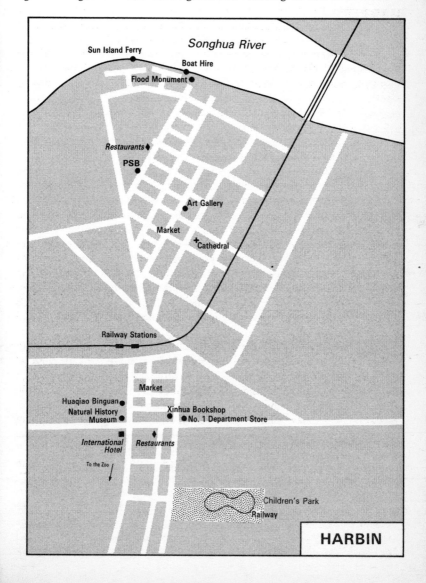

dykes built since liberation to protect the land from this notoriously unpredictable stretch of river. Along the dyke runs **Stalin Park**, a statue-crammed playground for the denizens of Harbin – the place where they come to meet, walk, wash, swim or just sit and gaze at the river. You can hire rowing boats from the steps – though with the powerful currents you'll need all your strength just to remain in one place – or in winter skate or ice-yacht your way across with the Chinese. The river freezes solid every winter and before the railway was the main means of transportation, since during the summer rains the roads up here were often completely impassable. Just west of the monument is the ferry terminal for **Sun Island**, a newly built holiday area put together as part of Harbin's burgeoning tourist infrastructure. There are beaches, boating lakes, restaurants, shops and sports facilities, all popular and all more crowded every year, but the best thing about going to Sun Island is the view you get over Harbin's industrial skyline from the river.

Harbin's most notorious – and most macabre – attraction is outside the city proper, about 30 km away in the tiny village of **PINGFANG**. This was the home of a secret Japanese research establishment during the last war and should by now have been opened to the public as a museum. Here human beings, usually prisoners of war, were injected with deadly viruses, dissected alive or frozen slowly so they could observe the prolonged effects of frostbite. Ironically enough, when the Americans got here they guaranteed the liberty of those involved in return for all the data that had been collected – something which many experts believe to have made a significant contribution to medical research in the west. To find out if it's open, and which bus to take, enquire at CITS. If you happen to be in Harbin just after Chinese New Year, it's worth hanging on for the **Ice Lantern Show** – an impressive display of ice sculpture held in Zhaolun Park. Otherwise there's nothing to stop you heading back to Beijing (18 hours by train) or Dalian (15 hours). Buying a ticket at the railway station can be difficult, even for the Chinese; the foreigners' window is no.15, but really you'd be better off getting a ticket in advance from CITS.

QIQIHAR – AND THE ZHALONG NATURE RESERVE

About six hours west of Harbin, **QIQIHAR** is Heilongjiang province's second city – one of the oldest cities of the north-east and a thriving industrial centre of well over a million people. Actually though, apart from lively shopping and some good and varied eating, there's little reason for making the trip, and the only reason most people visit Qiqihar is to visit the **ZHALONG NATURE RESERVE** 30km outside town. This, a marshy plain, flat to the horizon and abounding in shallow reedy lakes, serves as the summer breeding ground of thousands of species of birds . . .

Splendid though the birds are (at the reserve you can see white storks, whooper swans, spoonbills, white ibis and number of different kinds of crane), it can be difficult to fill in the time you're obliged to spend in Qiqihar by the bus timetable. If you're in a hurry you may be lucky enough to coincide with one of the flat-bottomed **boat tours** that take you around for ¥40 (details from CITS); otherwise the first bus of the day (from the bus station 1 km down the road from the station, on the left) leaves Qiqihar at 6.30am, arriving at Zhalong at 7.45, and the first connection goes back at noon. If you want to bypass the constrictions of the buses, try hitching: there's little enough traffic but if someone does come along they're bound to stop. Walking around the reserve, while not forbidden, is not encouraged by either the keepers or the murderous swarms of mosquitoes, so if you want to see the place in any detail best take a tour. It's a good idea to take binoculars too, since although many of the cranes are up to 1.5m tall, the reeds they hide behind are even higher.

As regards **somewhere to stay**, there's a *hotel* at the reserve that does rooms for ¥10 a night. In Qiqihar there are two opulent hotels for foreigners, the *Beifang* and the *Hubin*, which have dormitory beds for ¥10 and double rooms ¥18.

THE FAR NORTH: WUDALIANCHI, YICHUN AND WUNENGQU

Seven hours north of Harbin the train reaches **BEI'AN** – not open to foreigners but no one seems to mind you **stopping over** if you say you're on the way to Wudalianchi. You can stay at the spartan *Chinese Hotel* for just ¥1.50, and the next day take one of two buses on to Wudalianchi: at 6.20am if you're an early riser, or at midday.

Two and a half hours' bumpy journey away, along poplar-lined roads and across an undulating plain patched with vast communal farms, are the volcanoes of **WUDALIANCHI**. The name refers to the 'five great linking pools', which curl around the foot of the biggest volcano, **Laohei-shan** or *Old Black Hill*. Wudalianchi is best known, though, for its mineral waters (a bit like drinking soda water from a rusty bucket but, despite that, not unpleasant) and several springs around the village feed a bathing pool and a number of individual outdoor baths. A clinic and several sanatoria service a flow of people in search of relief from skin disorders, blood problems, baldness and other ailments.

Rooms can be had at the tatty *Wudalianchi Hotel* for ¥5–15, where there's a good **restaurant** serving locally-caught fish and from where you can hire a jeep to take you to the volcano. Laoheishan last erupted in

1719, making it the youngest 'fire mountain' in China, and around its lower slopes spreads a plain of fantastically contorted lava and pumice stone. It's only 300m high and the climb takes only 20 minutes, emerging above the tree-line to give daunting views of the lava plain, dotted with lesser sleeping volcanoes and fields of wheat and barley stretching down to the Wu da lian chi set with brand new pavilions just below. It *is* a long way to go, true, but as the official guidebook is at pains to point out, there are few better or more remote spots in which to recuperate, whether you're here for a cure or not.

East of here the train crosses the Songhua River and continues across the seemingly endless Manchurian plain. You won't want to get out here, but gazing across the fertile fields of wheat, maize and cotton, stretching forth as far as you can see, gives some idea of why this part of China was so bitterly contested in the last century. Several hours on and you're approaching the foothills of the **Xiao Xingan**: low misty mounds cut by swift clear rivers and fringed by forests of birch and pine. It's a bleak, unwelcoming environment, with winters that are long and hard: by early September it is cold and wet and the streets of the villages are little more than black mud bogs, impassable by all but the most determined of inhabitants and lined with shabby *pingfangs*, half buried beneath heaps of firewood.

YICHUN lies 10 hours on from Harbin, an unattractive town that scratches a living from logging and the trickle of tourists (mainly Japanese) who venture up here to ski or take pot-shots at the game in the surrounding forests. But Yichun's principal claim to fame is as springboard for nearby **WUNENGQU**: a small village that boasts a natural history museum set in a natural forest of 200-year-old Korean pines. The flora and fauna is unique to the area and of considerable interest to botanists.

To **get to Wunengqu** you need to hire a jeep and driver, which'll set you back ¥50 for the day and is only really worthwhile if you're an enthusiast. The distance is only about 70km, but the condition of the roads (rough) means the journey can take anything up to 2 hours – in winter even longer. Neither is it that impressive a trip, through some dismal new Dongbei settlements to a two-storey blockhouse that holds the shabby **Museum of Natural History** containing the much-heralded flora and (stuffed) fauna. More interesting is the forest around, where you might even encounter some of this animal life alive, but honestly the appeal of the place is out of all proportion to the determination you need to get here . . .

If that hasn't put you off, and you want to make Yichun a **base for some hiking**, the town's main **hotel** is the *Songxue Binguan*, five minutes bus-ride from the station, which offers beds for as low as ¥6 a night if you haggle – plus its **restaurant** charges just ¥2 for an eight-course meal. Other hotels include the *Yichun Lushi* and *Gonglu Ke* – both in Zhongshan Lu and both accepting foreigners for around ¥3 a night. Bear in mind, though, that although way up here you're far from harassment by the PSB, you're also a long long way from China proper.

TRAVEL DETAILS

Trains

From Dalian: Shenyang (4 daily, 10hrs), Harbin (2, 15hrs), Beijing (2, 20hrs).
From Shenyang: Dailian (4, 10hrs), Harbin (4, 13hrs), Beijing (2, 20hrs).
From Harbin: Yichun (4, 13hrs), Hailar (2, 17hrs), Manzhouli (2, 20 hrs), Beijing (4, 21hrs).

Ferries

From Dalian: Yantai (daily, 8hrs), Tianjin (3 a week, 20hrs).

Flights

Airports at Hailar, Harbin, Shenyang, Dalian, Changchun and Jiamusi.

BEI'AN	北安
DALIAN	大连
HARBIN	哈尔滨
PINGFANG	萍坊
QIQIHAR	齐齐哈尔
SHENYANG	沈阳
WUDALIANCHI	五大连池
WUNENQU	武嫩渠
YINCHUN	阴春
ZHALONG	扎龙

Chapter three
SHAANXI AND HENAN

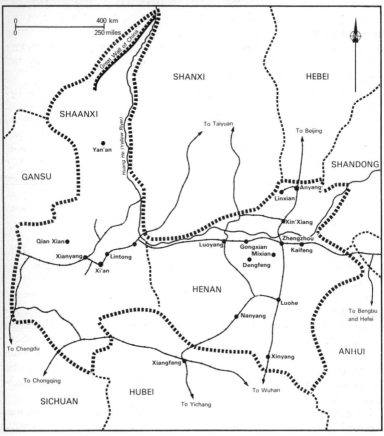

Shaanxi and Henan are provinces remarkable for the depth and breadth of their history. The *Huang He* – **Yellow River** – flows through both provinces and here, in the fertile soil of its basin, Chinese civilisation first took root more than 7,000 years ago. The river, whose shifting course and frequent floods make it a dangerous ally, creates the character of the region, a character seen above all in the pale greyish yellow-brown of the great loess plains. In its twisted course from the mountains bordering Tibet the river carries vast quantities of silt – 37kg of it in every cubic metre of water – whose choking nature has clogged and confused its course throughout history. Sometimes it has flowed into the sea near Beijing, at others into the lower Yangzi valley. In winter strong winds – the climate is one of extremes – bring yellow dust storms, depositing yet more fine silt on the plateau (where the loess lies in places 150 metres deep) and on the surface of the river: it is from this dust that it takes its name. Summer is hot, officially the rainy season, though the rains are capricious. One year torrential downpour's may burst the river's banks where the sediment it carries has raised its bed high above the surrounding plain and then vast areas are drowned; another year the rain may fail completely and there is famine.

It seems a dusty, harsh and unwelcoming region, but the river silt is fertile, and easily cultivated with the most primitive of tools. Sites of neolithic habitation are thick along the river – the homes of farmers, fishermen, excellent potters – the earliest known at **Banpo**. 3000 years later, the Yellow River was dominated by a much more advanced people under the Shang dynasty, the first of which there is a written record. They had an early capital near Zhengzhou, 480km downriver from Banpo, later moving north to **Anyang**.

For the next 3000 years, this small strip of the Yellow River basin saw the development of the Chinese state and Chinese civilisation – a development constantly threatened by tribes from the north and by the perils of the river itself, but steady nonetheless. The Zhou dynasty, masters of North China from about 1000BC, established a capital near **Xi'an**, moving on to Luoyang after this had been sacked. After them came the great emperor *Qin Shihuang*, who by 221BC had established a domination which stretched from the Great Wall in the north to regions far south of the Yellow River. It is his tomb near Xi'an which now provides the region's most remarkable attraction, the **terracotta warriors** set around as guards. They stand as an army – life-size – not far from the mound which still covers the mausoleum itself; archers, charioteers, horses, swordsmen, pikemen and officers arranged in a square with scouts in the van, sentries at the rear.

The next dynasty, the Han, also had their capital near Xi'an. This was a period in which the establishment of the **Silk Road** through Central Asia to Syria, and the rich trade with the west which followed, greatly strengthened the influence of the Yellow River area. Other influences came down the road too – most importantly **Buddhism**. The area is crowded with temples and other relics which reflect the development of Chinese buddhism from its earliest days – some of the earliest are at **Luoyang** where the Han made their capital when they too were forced to retreat eastward. The cave sculptures at **Longmen**, near here, are among, the most impressive works of art in China. By the end of the Tang dynasty there were over 100 temples in Xi'an alone, and five of the ten main schools of Buddhism in China originated here.

Under the Tang (AD618–907) the cities of the Yellow River basin appeared to reach the zenith of their prosperity and power, but with hindsight it is clear that the economic balance had long been shifting to the south. After the Han crumbled in AD220, the north was devastated by centuries of war and invasion while the Yangzi Valley flourished. When in 608 the Sui completed the **Grand Canal** to link the Yangzi and the Yellow River, its purpose was to carry grain to the north: in practice it confirmed the Yangzi valley's role as China's food bowl and the main source of the empire's finances. **Kaifeng,** which became the Song capital in 960, was the last on the Yellow River: in 1127 a further wave of invasions forced the imperial court to retreat to the south. Kaifeng had already proved its vulnerability to **flood,** and the problem became increasingly serious after the cutting of the Grand Canal disturbed the drainage of the lower reaches. From 1194–1887 there were fifty major Yellow River floods, with 300,000 people killed in 1642 alone and another major catastrophe in 1933. Soon after, in 1937, Chiang Kaishek used the river as a weapon against the invading Japanese, breaching the dikes to cut the railway line. A delay of a few weeks was gained at the cost of hundreds of thousands of Chinese lives.

Since liberation the communist regime has worked hard to try to solve the problems of the Yellow River. They are using afforestation to consolidate the light, rapidly eroded soil and since the early 1950s a whole staircase of dams has been built above Zhengzhou to control the erratic flow. But irrigation and flooding remain crucial issues.

The river valley, and the rail lines which trace it, remain the focus for visitors. A string of ancient capitals is open here, from Xi'an to Kaifeng. **Xi'an** has a great deal to show for its former glory – in particular the renowned Terracotta Army and the other **Imperial Tombs – Kaifeng,** repeatedly destroyed by floods, has very little. Over the last 50 years most of these cities have enjoyed a new lease of life as industrial centres. **Zhengzhou,** provincial capital of Henan, is one of the most important railway centres in China. **Anyang,** by contrast, has virtually no modern importance at all (and nor does it retain much trace of one of the earliest capitals) – but it is fascinating as an example of an old Chinese town, virtually untouched by the twentieth century. Outside the cities and the great archaeological sites, the plain is largely a drab, dusty and not particularly welcoming place: the lush greenery of the mountains at **Huashan** or **Songshan** makes a more than welcome contrast. In the far north of Shaanxi, as a complete change, you could also visit **Yan'an,** the isolated base high in the loess plateau to which the Long March led Mao in 1937. Or, for an impressive achievement of the 1960s, try the **Red Flag Canal** at Linxian in northern Henan.

SHAANXI

The **Yellow River** flows due south, dividing Shaanxi from neighbouring Shanxi, until at the border of Henan it turns sharply east. Here – at the Tongguan Pass – the **Wei** flows into the main stream. Shaanxi, which literally means West of the Pass, takes its name from this crucially strategic junction. The towns open to foreigners are chiefly **Xi'an** and places east along the railway and Wei valley; **Yan'an** in the north, headquarters of the Communist Army from 1937 to 1947, may also be visited but is difficult to get to from the main tourist routes.

XI'AN

Modern **XI'AN** is a manufacturing town of 2½ million people and the capital of Shaanxi province, holding a key position on the south bank of the Wei in the fertile plain between the high loess plateau of the north and the Qinling Mountains to the south. It is also a primer in Chinese history. For more than half of the period from 1000BC to AD1000 it served as the imperial capital for eleven dynasties. So you'll find a wealth of important sites and relics hereabouts: Neolithic **Banpo**, the **Terracotta Army** of the *Qin* Emperor, the *Han* and *Tang* **imperial tombs**; and in the city itself the **Wild Goose pagodas** of the *Tang*, the **Bell** and **Drum Towers** and the **city walls** of the *Ming*, and the **Provincial Museum** which has grown around the **Forest of Steles** – more than 1000 inscribed stones, the earliest 2000 years old.

The city's history begins about 3000 years ago in the Bronze Age when the **Western Zhou dynasty**, skilled and artistic bronzesmiths, built their capital at *Fenghao*, a few miles west. Nearby one of their chariot burials has been excavated. When Fenghao was sacked by north-western tribes they moved downriver to Luoyang and as their empire continued to disintegrate into warring chiefdoms the **Qin** kingdom expanded. In 221 BC King Qin Shihuang made himself the first – and only – Qin emperor of a much larger and unified China, with its capital at *Xianyang* near Xi'an.

His successors, the **Han**, ruled from 206 BC to AD 220. Near contemporaries of Imperial Rome, they ruled an empire of comparable size and power. Here in Xi'an was the start of the Silk Road along which, among many other things, Chinese silk was carried to dress Roman senators and their wives at the court of Augustus. There was also a brisk trade with south and west Asia; Han China was an outward-looking empire. The emperors built themselves a new, splendid and cosmopolitan capital a few miles northwest of Xi'an which they named *Chang'an* – Eternal Peace. Its size reflected the power of their empire; records say that its walls were 17km round with twelve great gates, and the city wall can still just be made out. But later they were forced to leave for a safer base and when their dynasty fell *Chang'an* was destroyed. Their tombs remain, though, including the Emperor *Wu Di*'s mound at Mao Ling.

It was not until 589 that the **Sui** dynasty re-united the warring kingdoms into an empire, but their rule lasted hardly longer than the time to build a new capital near Xi'an and name it *Da Xingcheng* – Great Prosperity. The **Tang**, who replaced them in 618, took over their capital: now overlaid by later buildings, this Tang city was in its day the capital of a great empire and one of the biggest conurbations in the world, with more than a million people. In the north was the Palace, in the south the Imperial City; houses, shops and markets lay to the east, west and further south. The *Da Ming Gong* palace was built in 634 and a few ruins can be seen north-east of the railway station. The *Xingqing* palace in the east, now a park, was where the Emperor Xuan Gong held court.

The Tang period was a golden age for the **arts**: ceramics, calligraphy, painting and poetry all reached new heights. You can get some idea of the quality from the Tang horses in the museum, the *Classics of Filial Piety* in the Forest of Steles and the wall paintings in the Tang tombs. At the same time **trade** flourished, with goods passing readily along the Silk Road to and from the west; in the museum you can find many foreign coins unearthed here. And the open society was reflected too in its **religious tolerance** – not only was this the great period for Buddhism but the **Great Mosque** dates from the Tang, one of the steles in Xi'an bears witness to the founding of a chapel by Nestorian Christians and home-grown Daoism also prospered.

After the fall of the Tang Xi'an went into a long decline. It was never again the imperial capital, though the **Ming** Emperor *Hong Wu* rebuilt the city as a gift for his son; the great walls and gates date from this time. Occasionally, though, the city did still provide a footnote to history. When the Empress Dowager had to flee from Beijing after the Boxer Rising and the siege of the legations she set up her court here for two years. In 1911 during the uprising against the Manchu Qing dynasty, the Manchu Quarter in Xi'an was destroyed and the Manchus massacred. And in 1936 *Chiang Kaishek* was arrested at Hua Qing Hot Springs nearby in what became known as the **Xi'an Incident**.

The railway arrived in 1934. In modern times industry, the mining of coal, iron, copper and manganese, and the presence of the university and other colleges have made Xi'an an up-to-date and important city. In addition its history, and above all the 'chocolate soldiers' (as the Terracotta Army are sometimes known) have ensured it a high place in the tourist league – seeded no.3 after Beijing and Shanghai.

Arrival – finding somewhere to stay

You'll probably arrive at the **railway station** in the north-east of the city, and since the layout is still essentially that of the Ming city – rather like a Roman legionary camp – you'll find it simple to get your **bearings**. The four walls and gates, with the main north–south and east–west streets crossing at the conspicuous Bell Tower, and the grid pattern of streets between them, make this an easy place to explore on foot. But **distances** are deceptive; modern Xi'an, of course, stretches far outside the walls but even within them this is a big city, and a stroll from the Bell Tower to the West Gate, for example, can take the best part of an hour. The four streets from the Bell Tower are *Bei, Nan, Dong* and *Xi Da Jie* – North, South, East and West Main Street – and along them, especially near their intersection, you'll find most of what you want to see, as well as shops, theatres, cinemas and places to eat. Another important street, useful for shopping and eating, is *Jiefang Lu*, which runs north from Dong Da Jie to the railway station.

Hotels are quite conveniently placed. At the north end of Jiefang Lu opposite the station is *Jiefang Fandian* – Liberation Hotel; large and run-down dorms cost ¥10 in the old wing facing the noisy square. Staff here have been known to help with buying tickets and making arrangements; they've also sometimes been surly to early morning arrivals who wash up on their shores from the night train. Midway between the station and the Bell Tower, with its entrance set back from Xixin Jie, is *Renmin Dasha* – People's Hotel, an imposing 1950s pile with surly management and dorms in the old wing for ¥14: from the front gate to your bed is a long haul with a heavy case. Its western restaurant is known for its apple pie and ice cream. **CITS** is on the premises which is useful. On the Bell Tower roundabout, the best position in the heart of the town, is *Zhonglou Fandian* – Bell Tower Hotel – with 3–4 bedded rooms from ¥14; they mix the sexes in the dorms quite arbitrarily. Out **beyond the South Gate** is *Xiao Yanta* – Small Wild Goose Hotel – a modern 12-storey building with 500 beds, rooftop bar, view and all mod cons – all reflected in the price. You could also try the colleges or the Foreign Language Dept for cheap rooms, or one of the scruffy hotels in the southern suburbs.

The city within the walls – towers and gates

Xi'an's Bell Tower, Drum Tower, walls and gates are some of the best **military architecture** of the Ming dynasty surviving anywhere. Bell and Drum Towers were common features of Chinese cities, the bell being rung in the morning and the drum beaten at night. The Xi'an **Bell Tower** was built in 1384, moved to its present site in 1582 and restored in 1739: In the 1940s it held a Kuomintang garrison. An impressive building 36 metres high, it's built of brick and wood held together without nails or mortar. Rising from a square foundation, it has two storeys with a ribbed

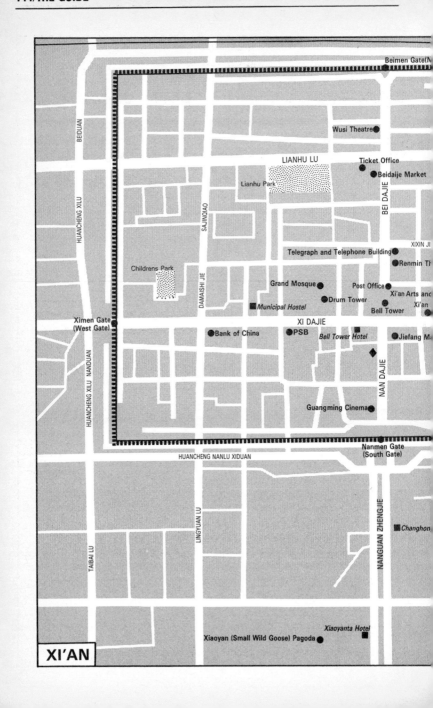

XI'AN

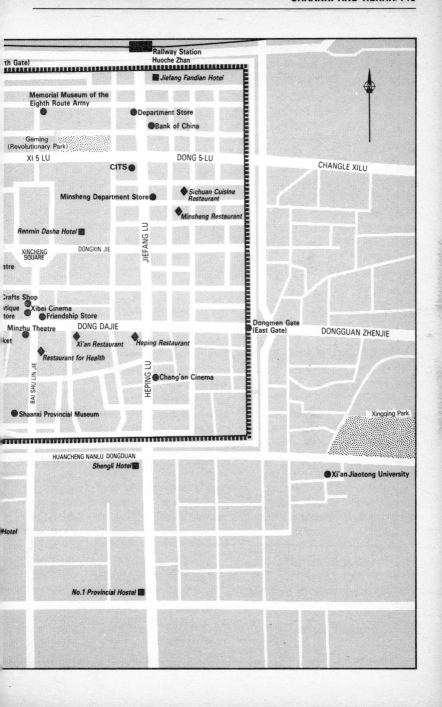

Railway Station
Huoche Zhan

th Gate)

Jiefang Fandian Hotel

Memorial Museum of the
Eighth Route Army

Department Store

Bank of China

Geming
(Revolutionary Park)

XI 5 LU

DONG 5-LU

CHANGLE XILU

CITS

Minsheng Department Store

Sichuan Cuisine
Restaurant

Minsheng Restaurant

Renmin Dasha Hotel

JIEFANG LU

XINCHENG
SQUARE

DONGXIN JIE

eatre

Crafts Shop

ntique
tore

Xibei Cinema

Friendship Store

Minzhu Theatre

DONG DAJIE

Dongmen Gate
(East Gate)

DONGGUAN ZHENJIE

ket

Xi'an Restaurant

Heping Restaurant

Restaurant for Health

BAI SHU LIN JIE

HEPING LU

Chang'an Cinema

Shaanxi Provincial Museum

Xingqing Park

HUANCHENG NANLU DONGDUAN

Shengli Hotel

Xi'an Jiaotong University

Hotel

No.1 Provincial Hostel

roof, three sets of terraced eaves supported by brackets and an original 15C bell. On the first floor there's a tourist shop and from the second floor you get good view of the city and its gates. The **Drum Tower** just to the west has the same view but its drum is gone, replaced by a large lamp.

The best place to see the **City Wall** is in the west, out along *Xi Da Jie* from the Bell Tower. Built between 1374 and 1378 it was originally a tremendous structure, 15 km round, 12 metres high and over 12 metres wide at the top, with a gate in each wall and a tower at each corner. You can see major building work going on to repair the length of the wall and dig out the moat. This will take some years but eventually there should be a walk along the top of the wall, green open spaces around, and rowing boats on the moat. Like the West Wall the **West Gate** is the best preserved, more like a fortress than a gate, with a pavilion towering at each end and an enormous courtyard. Forget the broad modern roads and imagine people 600 years ago streaming through the narrow arch into the courtyard to be checked before entering the city.

The Great Mosque and around
The **Great Mosque** is in Huajue Xiang Jie, very close to the Drum Tower at the heart of the district inhabited by the Muslim *Hui* minority, who are said to be descended from 8C Arab soldiers. It was founded in 742, about 100 years after Islam reached China, though the present buildings date at the earliest from the Ming and are probably much later. They are currently being restored. To get there from the Drum Tower take the first narrow alley on the left, bear right and follow the signs – the buildings are open to all, though you may have to wait if prayers are going on, which happens five times a day.

You enter by a pavilion with Ming and Qing steles – the grounds and the four flower-filled courtyards beyond are refreshingly peaceful – except when packed solid with tour groups – with a Chinese-style minaret and a further pavilion in the main court. Past these lies the great bulk of the **Great Hall of Prayer** (take your shoes off) with its library annexe and map with directions to Mecca. You can just make out the decorative patterns at the far end; in the centre of each is written the word 'Pray' in Arabic.

All around the mosque are the narrow streets and alleys of the **Hui district** – fascinating to explore. Xiyangshi Jie, for example, is a smoky market street, full of Muslim chefs making dumplings and stalls offering birds in cages, fruit and vegetables.

Shaanxi Provincial Museum
The **Museum** with the Forest of Steles is tucked away close to the South Gate, in a former Confucian temple off Baishulin Jie. It makes a very

useful introduction to the historic sites around the city. In the first court-yard on the left a section on the province's history covers the years 1000 BC to AD 1000, displaying a great many objects from that period. Highlights to look for include a stone drum of 800 BC with early writing, Han bronzes, a 6C map of the Sui city, Persian, Arab and Byzantine coins found in the marketplace, and Tang statuettes of polo players. A second hall contains life-size stone sculptures of horses, lions, tigers and whales from the Han period: make sure you also see the famous **chargers** from the bas relief in the Tang emperor's tomb at Zhaoling. The third section is the **Forest of Steles** itself – 1000 engraved stones dating from the Han to the 19C. The *Twelve Classics of Filial Piety* were engraved on 114 stones in 852 AD. Another stone records the arrival of a Nestorian Christian priest in 781, centuries before the Jesuits.

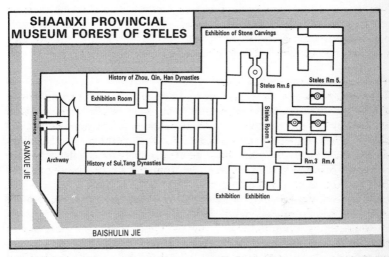

There's an awful lot of the museum, and often very little in the way of explanation, so it helps if you can tag on to a tour group with an interpreter. If time is short you should concentrate on the stone sculptures, take a quick look at the Forest of Steles and then move on to the new acquisitions. These, which include a splendid bronze tripod and bronze horse, are housed in a special section of the museum for which you pay extra.

Street walking

If you simply want to stroll around Xi'an, there's most of interest in the main east–west street. The western half, **Xi Da Jie**, runs for nearly 2 km from the Bell Tower to the West Gate and along here there really is the feel of an old city – half-timbered brown painted houses with verandahs, lopsided plastic sheets replacing the paper in their windows, old-fashioned barbers, small workshops, ancient locals with scales to weigh you in the street, and shops selling everything from medicines and mops to theatrical masks and brilliant costumes. It's interesting too to dive off into the maze of alleys on either side. **Dong Da Jie**, east from the Bell Tower, is the cosmopolitan end, with the post office, indoor market, restaurants, stores, bookshops and several cinemas.

Going north from the Bell Tower up **Bei Da Jie** there are wooden-fronted houses and the **People's Theatre**, a great ivy-covered building. South from the Bell Tower you can go through the **Jiefang covered market**, cheap, cheerful and full of everything you might need. The other important street is **Jiefang Lu** going north to the station; where it crosses Xi Wu Lu there's a clutch of restaurants and department stores. Further up on the left is the **Revolutionary Park**, with a little group of freak shows and circus acts, and beyond it in Beixin Jie the **8th Route Army Office Museum** commemorating the events of 1937.

The practicalities

Buses for moving around in the city centre are straightforward. No.3 from the station goes down Jiefang Lu, turns right for the Renmin Dasha Hotel, left into Bei Da Jie and straight on past the Bell Tower to the South Gate and beyond. No.5 from the station goes absolutely straight down Jiefang Lu. No.1 trolley bus from the station goes down Jiefang Lu to Dong Da Jie where it turns right and past the Bell Tower to the West Gate. **Taxis** can be found at all the major hotels and the railway station.

CITS is in the *Renmin Dasha* Hotel: it closes for a long lunch hour. The **PSB** is in Xi Da Jie west of the Bell Tower and the main **Post Office** in Dong Da Jie opposite the Bell Tower.

Xi'an's **restaurants** are on the whole disappointing and not cheap – mostly large mass-production diners in the main streets. In Dong Da Jie the *Xi'an* is a soulless place with seats for 1800; better nearby are the *Dong Ya Fandian* on Luoma Shi, the *Wuyi* and the *Heping Canting*. Near the Bell Tower is the *Baiyunzhang Jiaozi Gunan*, a dumpling restaurant which is good for breakfast. In Duanliumen off Dong Da Jie the *Restaurant for Health* is a small café-style place where the chef might let you into the kitchen to choose what you want. In Jiefang Lu halfway to the railway station you'll find the *Minsheng* and a little further on a Sichuan-style place. Another Sichuanese restaurant, fairly cheap, is in Xi Da Jie on the way to the West Gate. If you want a **tea-house** there's an attractive one in Dong Da Jie near the Xibei cinema – a narrow little room with low bamboo chairs and chaises longues and nice brown pots. Another is in Jiefang Lu near the station, good if you find yourself waiting about.

Shopping is best in the main streets: Jiefang Lu from the station down to Dong Da Jie and the four streets radiating from the Bell Tower. Dong Da Jie has the **Xinhua bookshop**, the Wai Wen **Foreign Language Bookshop**, the **Indoor Market**, the **Friendship Store** and **Antique Store**. In **Jiefang Market** opposite the Bell Tower, which sells a bit of everything, there's also the *Jiefang* **Theatre**. The *Renmin* theatre and the *Wusi* theatre are in Bei Da Jie and so is the *Heping* **cinema**. The *Xibei* cinema is in Dong Da Jie, the *Guang Ming* in *Nan Da Jie* and the *Qunzhong* in *Xi Da Jie*.

The city outside the walls
Beyond the South Gate of the Ming city but within the confines of the modern urban sprawl and well inside the original Tang area are a number of important temples. From the station a no.5 bus takes you nearly 4km beyond the wall to the **Great Wild Goose Pagoda**, then turns right towards **Da Xingshan Temple**; no.3 goes to the **Small Wild Goose Pagoda**.

Da Yan Ta – the Great Wild Goose Pagoda and the Temple of Grace
The **Temple of Grace**, in whose grounds the Great Wild Goose Pagoda stands, is right on the southern edge of Xi'an – the ochre-coloured pagoda rising directly from the ochre-coloured fields. As you get off the bus the temple is ahead of you, its entrance at the far end. Founded in 648 by Emperor *Gao Zong* when he was crown prince, the temple originally had as many as 3,000 monks, housed in 1,897 rooms spread about 13 courtyards: later it fell into ruin and was rebuilt much smaller in 1580. What you see now has been much restored. The Bell and Drum Towers in the courtyard are fairly dull but in the Hall are some good painted backdrops and three fine statues of Sakyamuni and attendants; there are two rows of arhats (disciples) grimacing wonderfully – look for the one with bits of twig poking out of his ears.

The **pagoda** itself, a wood and brick tower over 60 metres high, was built in 652 as a fireproof repository for the sutras brought here by the monk *Xuan Zang*. He went off to India in 629, returning 15 years later with 657 volumes which he translated into 1,335 volumes of Chinese: his achievement is recorded in two tablets by the south door, where there is also an amusing engraving of him on trek with an enormous backpack of books. The pagoda was originally called *Jing Ta* – Pagoda of the Classics. No one seems to know where the name 'Wild Goose' comes from – perhaps from the tale in which *Xuan Zang* and *Monkey*, heroes of the popular classic *Xi Yu Ji* (Journey to the West), are saved by a goose when they get lost in the desert. Over the door is an engraved tablet of Buddha preaching, which shows you something of the wooden architecture of the period.

If you climb the pagoda you'll have a good view of town and country – it's hard to believe that when built the temple was at least 3km inside the Tang city, a great beauty spot dotted with pavilions and praised by poets. High on the tourist itinerary, the grounds are likely to be very crowded: there's a tea-house where you can drink plum juice, and a hut where you can put on Tang costume to have your photograph taken!

Da Xingshan Temple
This temple, which stands in a small park, was supposedly founded in the 3C BC but has been rebuilt so often that there can be very little of the original left. Much, indeed, was put up little more than thirty years ago. It is now being restored again so you can only peer through locked doors at the fine lacquer gilt Buddha in the front hall.

Xiao Yan Ta – the Small Wild Goose Pagoda
The **Small Wild Goose Pagoda** (currently being renovated) has a remarkably similar history to its Big namesake: a temple was founded here in 684 by the empress *Wu Zetian* and in 705 the monk Yi Jung, back from his own sutra hunt in India, settled in it to translate his scriptures. The pagoda, a close-eaved structure of brick about 42 metres high, was built shortly after to house them. It lost its two top storeys in the Great Earthquake of 1555 but even so manages to look better proportioned than the Great Wild Goose. There are Buddhist figures on the west and south doors and a pleasant garden roundabout, which is where the temple used to stand.

AROUND XI'AN

You could spend days on excursions round Xi'an. Most people will at the very least want to see Banpo, the Imperial Tombs and the Terracotta Army. Much of this can be done under your own steam by public bus, which leaves you free to decide how long you want to spend looking at things and helps avoid the worst of the crowds, but such journeys are slow. A **tour bus** from Xi'an will enable you to fit very much more into a day. You can get further details, and book, at CITS or the *Bell Tower Hotel* – the trips are particularly good for the west, where there are a number of scattered sites of interest which would be impossible to combine by public transport.

East of Xi'an – Banpo
BANPO is about 8km out; no.5 trolley bus from the railway station or no.11 from the Bell Tower take under an hour. This 7000-year old village of the Neolithic *Yangshao* culture, discovered in 1952, is the biggest and best-preserved so far found and the earliest known site in the Xi'an

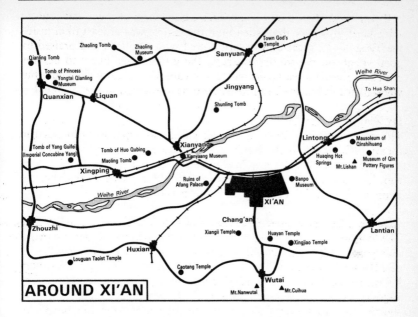

AROUND XI'AN

area. Indeed it is probably the oldest example of settled habitation and agriculture yet discovered in China: well situated near water and occupied by what was probably a matrilineal clan: a belief based partly on the much richer contents of the women's graves and partly on the theory that women invented agriculture.

Excavations have uncovered a central area protected from wild beasts by a ditch 6 metres wide and 6 metres deep – here were 45 dwellings and over 200 storage pits, foundations and post-holes. Adjacent is one of the oldest pottery-making sites in China, with 6 kilns, and a cemetery which holds more than 200 adult burials and some 50 urns containing the remains of children. One little girl was buried with 79 funerary objects.

Under a dome with raised walkways part of the **dwelling area** is displayed, with numbered sections explained in English and brought successfully to life on notice boards. The earliest houses were pit dwellings, later ones wooden: some were round, some square, but all face south and have central hearths. A reconstruction of one looks remarkably like the mud houses you still see in the country round Banpo.

The two **museum** wings have a good display of some of the 10,000 finds – stone tools, spindles, bone needles, a pot containing millet. Notice the barbed fish-hooks with weights – you can still see the local river fishermen using a similar method of flinging out a weighted net and line and dragging it through the shallows. There are ornaments of bone and mother-of-pearl, and an impressive quantity of red pottery with animal designs evolving into abstracts – some of it carefully repaired by its users. Everything is explained in detail (though the English sometimes has a quaint flavour) and illustrated with Sunday-school type paintings. I found Banpo fascinating – but very dusty. If you come independently you'll have the place to yourself during lunchtime.

Further east – the Terracotta Army

The Terracotta Army and the tomb it guards are about 28km east of Xi'an, just beyond Lintong and the Hot Springs. The tomb, now little more than a mound 40 metres high covered with pomegranates, is set into the slope of Mount Lishan. **Qin Shi Huang**, who is buried here, became king of the northern state of Qin in 246 BC as a boy of 13. Within 25 years he had annexed six other states, founded an empire with its capital near Xi'an, unified China's government, written language, laws and currency, and begun to build an enormous palace, the *A Fang Gong*. Within 40 years, following his death in 210 BC, his capital had been destroyed, his palace burnt (its ruined walls are still visible in Xi'an's western suburbs) and his **tomb** ransacked. According to the 1C BC historian, *Si Maqian* it had taken 36 years and 700,000 men to build: the records describe an 'Imperial City' below the mound, with throne room, treasure house, 'a ceiling of the heavens, a river of mercury operated by cunning device and eunuchs and officials of all ranks'. It was guarded by boobytraps which included mechanical crossbows, and secrecy was maintained by killing many of the workmen. It has been suggested in the past that all these precautions did not save the tomb from being plundered when the dynasty was overthrown and for this reason, added to fear of damaging any contents by accidentally triggering the built-in defences, work has proceeded very slowly. But excavations are now taking place, and it has recently been reported that the inner and outer walls of the underground palace have been found, with passages leading inside, ten gates and four watch towers. They've also found marked traces of mercury which at least confirms some of the description.

No record existed of the **Terracotta Army** which was set to guard the tomb; it was discovered by peasants sinking a well in 1974. Three vaults were found – rectangular, built of earth with brick floors and timber supports. Vault I is thought to hold some 6000 figures in battle order – a vanguard of 3 rows of 70 men, the main body of 38 rows, a flanking column and a rearguard. Vault 2 has about 1000 soldiers, separate units of cavalry, chariots, archers and foot. Vault 3 has 69 soldiers and a wooden chariot; some archaeologists have suggested that this represents the emperor's command headquarters.

Part of **Vault 1** has been covered by a hangar and you look down from a walkway on 400–500 figures wearing helmets and armour; they carried real bows, swords, spears and crossbows, over 10,000 of which have been found. The figures average 6 feet (1.80m) in height and are hollow from the thighs up; head and hands were modelled separately. Each figure has different features and expression and wears marks of rank: some say that each is a portrait of a real member of the ancient Imperial Guard, and certainly it is hard not to believe so. Traces of pigment show that their dress was once bright yellow, purple and green, though grey and dusty now. The horses wore harness with brass and ornaments and have been identified as a breed from Gansu and Xinjiang. The chariots were wooden; traces survive to show that they were drawn by four horses and had a driver and two soldiers, all armed.

Digging is still going on and there are plans to open **Vaults 2 and 3**. Meanwhile, in the side wings are displays of maps, photographs, the bones of workmen buried here and pieces of terracotta.

To the right of the entrance another wing contains one of the two half-size **bronze chariots**, eash with four horses and a driver, which were found in 1982 in a pit only a few yards from the emperor's mound. It is decorated with dragon, phoenix and cloud designs and has a curved canopy and gold and silver harness; behind the driver is a large compartment with a silver door latch and windows to open and shut. It's thought to be a model of an imperial chariot. You'll notice the realism of the figures; the driver's knuckles, nails and fingerprints are all shown. If you can't prove you're a student this section will cost you ¥5.

The Terracotta Army is certainly not to be missed: but be prepared to find that your view in the hangar doesn't match up to some of the photographs you've seen. I found it impressive but dusty and rather confused. Photography is forbidden and the slides and booklets on sale are disappointing; the crowded stalls at the entrance sell better-value reproductions of the figures than the shops inside. The quietest time to come is at lunchtime which means doing it independently. There are hourly **buses** from the South Gate or near the railway station which take 1¼ hours to LINTONG. Or you could stay in Lintong at a hotel near the bus station.

Hua Qing

If you take one of the day trips to the east, most of which leave the *Bell Tower Hotel* or Renmin Dasha at about 7.30am, returning by 5.30pm, you'll have about an hour at the Terracotta Army; the tour then goes on to **HUA QING** where you dawdle for 2–3 hours over lunch before continuing to Banpo. This gives you a chance to look at – and bathe in – the **Hot Springs**.

Here mineral-rich water, emerging at a constant and agreeable 43°C, is piped into a series of public bathhouses. As much as 2,500 years ago there was a Zhou palace here, and *Qin Shihuang* had a hot spring bath constructed for the Imperial family, but the resort's peak was reached in AD747 when the Tang emperor *Xuan Zong* built the pool and palace for his favourite concubine. Nothing actually survives of that original palace, but there is the **Favourite Concubine's Pool**, in which visitors are still allowed to bathe (though it was drained when I was there). Generally the place is very crowded – especially at lunchtimes – but the gushing hot water and tiled baths are certainly soothing if you've been climbing around; get your ticket near the entrance. Recent renovations have added a new block to the old bath halls, enabling the place to take as many as 400 people at once.

Round about the springs there's an artificial lake and a number of pavilions tucked into the slopes of Lishan, but the resort's real claim to modern fame lies in the **Xi'an Incident**. Here in 1936 Chiang Kaishek was arrested by his own troops and forced to sign an alliance with the Communists. The story is a little more complicated than this: as Japanese troops continued to advance into China, Chiang insisted on pursuing his policy of national unification before all else – or in other words destroying the Communists before turning on the Japanese. In December 1936 he flew to Xi'an to supervise yet another extermination campaign. Meanwhile, however, this area had fallen under the control of Marshal *Zhang Xueliang* and his Manchurian army. Although KMT supporters they, like many others, had grown weary of Chiang's policies; a disillusionment fuelled by the failure to make any real impression on the Red Army and by the fact that their Manchurian homeland was now occupied by Japanese troops. In secret meetings with Communist leaders, Zhang had been convinced of their genuine anti-Japanese sentiments. And so in the early morning of 12 December Nationalist troops stormed Chiang's headquarters at the foot of Lishan, capturing most of the headquarters staff – the great leader himself was eventually caught halfway up the slope, still in his pyjamas and without his false teeth, having bolted from his bed at the first sound of gunfire. Across the Flying Bridge a neo-Grecian pavilion marks the spot. Chiang was forced to pay a heavy ransom but was otherwise unharmed – his captors allowing him to remain in control of China provided that he allied with the Communists against the Japanese.

You could continue up to the peak of **Lishan** (Black Horse Mountain) where Zhou emperors installed beacons to warn of attack. But it is quite a haul to the top – 1200 metres above sea level – and the climb is dull, with no special views. Hua Qing as a whole, in fact, is overcrowded and considerably less romantic than it sounds.

West and north-west – Imperial Tombs
The only satisfactory way to fit in all the sites to the north and north-west is to take the day trip in an airconditioned coach; this covers the

three important tombs open to visitors, **Maoling** of the Han, where you get 50 minutes, and **Zhaoling** and **Qianling** of the Tang, also passing **Xianyang** and the museum, with its display of terracotta figures. There's 1½ hours at Zhaoling for lunch; you can eat just outside to the right of the entrance or inside, posher and more expensive. It all adds up to a 9½ hour day starting at 7.30am with the sights rather thinly spread in a lot of travelling. But the museums are stimulating and it's good to get the feel of the tombs from which so many museum treasures have come, even though most are little more than great earth mounds. The trip costs ¥10: book, as for the other trips, from CITS or the *Bell Tower Hotel*.

MAOLING is the largest of more than 20 **Han tombs** 48km west of Xi'an. The resting place of the 5th Han emperor *Wu Di* (140–85 BC), it's a great green mound against the hills, so far not excavated: records say it was over 50 years building and contains a jade burial suit and a treasure of gold and jewels. A dozen small tombs nearby belong to the emperor's court – they include those of his favourite concubine and his generals, especially the brilliant strategist *Huo Qubing* who fought several campaigns against the Xiong Nu northern tribes (the Huns) and was killed at the age of 24. A small museum displays some impressive finds from the lesser tombs. Look for the carved stone horses, frogs and a cow which stood outside the tombs, and a fine carving of a horse trampling a barbarian warrior.

A few miles further on is the tomb of *Yang Guifei* – Treasured Concubine of Tang emperor *Xuan Zong* for whom the Hua Qing palace was built. When he was fleeing from the enemy his soldiers mutinied and forced him to have her strangled. The tomb is being restored and there is nothing much to see.

At **ZHAOLING** are 19 **Tang tombs** including that of the emperor *Tai Zong*; begun in AD636 this took 13 years to complete. Tai Zong introduced the practice of building the tomb into the hillside instead of as a tumulus in an open plain. From the main tomb, built into the slope of Jiuzou, a great **cemetery** fans out south-east and south-west. The largest in China, 60km round, this includes 167 lesser tombs of the Imperial family, generals and officials: a small museum displays stone carvings, murals and pottery figures from the smaller tombs. In the museum in Xi'an you'll find four of the famous bas reliefs of the emperor's six horses which come from the sacrificial altar here.

QIANLING is 80km north-west of Xi'an, another hill tomb about 900m above sea level on the slopes of Liangshan. Here are buried Emperor *Gao Zong* and his empress **Wu Zetian**. Wu's rise to power – in a society which generally regarded women as little better than slaves, to be killed at birth or sold into slavery if they were born into a poor family – is extraordinary. Originally the concubine of Gao Zong's father, she emerged from her mourning to win the affections of the son, bear him sons in turn, and eventually marry him. As her husband ailed, her power over the administration grew until she was strong enough, at his death in 683, to usurp the throne. Seven years later she was declared empress in her own right. She finally died in AD705, when the tomb was opened at vast expense to receive her. In later years her reign became notorious for intrigue and bloodshed, but that may be in part the result of historical bias: a woman in the position of supreme power (her title was emperor, there being no female equivalent for so exalted a position) offended every rule of China's increasingly ossified society. The criticism ranged from the historian who describes her as a whore because she took male lovers (while any emperor would be expected to count his concubines in their hundreds) to the decapitation of the stone mourners along the Imperial way, the political vandalism of unknown later generations.

The **Imperial Way** leads to the tomb, lined with carved stone figures of men and flying horses, and by two groups of these now headless mourners – guest princes and envoys from tribute states, some with their names on their backs still. The tall stele on the left praises Gao Zong; opposite is the uninscribed Wordless Stele, erected by the empress to mark the supreme power which no words could express.

In the **south-east section** are 17 lesser tombs; the 5 excavated since 1960 include the tomb of Prince *Zhang Huai*. You walk down into a vault frescoed with army and processional scenes, a lovely permanent-waved tiger in the dip on either side. One fresco shows the court's welcome to visiting foreigners; you'll find a very hooknosed westerner. There are also vivid frescoes of polo playing and, in the museum, some Tang pottery horses. Another tomb belongs to Princess **Yong Tai**, the Emperor's granddaughter, who died at 17. Niches in the wall hold funeral offerings and the vaulted roof still has traces of painted patterns. The passage walls leading down are covered with murals of animals and guards of honour; the court ladies are still clear, elegant and charming after 1300 years, displaying Tang hairstyles and dresses. At the bottom is the great tomb in black stone lightly carved with human and animal shapes. Some 1300 gold, silver and pottery objects were found here and are now in the museum. At the mouth of the tomb is the traditional stone tablet into which the life story of the princess is carved – according to this she died in childbirth, but some records claim that she was murdered by her grandmother, the evil empress Wu. The **Shun mausoleum** of Wu Zetian's own mother is small, but it's worth a look for the two unusually splendid granite figures which guard it; a lion 3 metres high and an even bigger unicorn.

Southward – temples
In the wooded hilly country south of Xi'an are a number of important temples. **Xingjiao Si**, burial place of the monk *Xuan Zang* of the Great

Wild Goose pagoda, or **Xiangji Si,** which has a 10-storey pagoda covering the grave of *Shandao,* founder of the Jingtu Sect, would both make excellent focal points for a day's excursion in the countryside by anyone with time to spare. Both can be reached by country bus from the South Gate bus station.

HUA SHAN

HUA SHAN – Flowery Mountain – is about 120km east of Xi'an in Huayin County. Its five peaks are supposed to look like a five-petalled flower, hence the name: originally it was known as *Xiyue* – Western Mountain – because it is the westernmost of the Five Mountains which have been sacred to Daoism for over 2000 years. It has always been a great place for pilgrimage – and still is – though you'll see on the mountain that some of the pilgrims are rather different from what they used to be; it's an increasingly popular jaunt for Chinese from Xi'an and further afield.

Since Hua Shan is a station on the railway to Luoyang you can either take in the mountain on the way to or from Luoyang or do an excursion from Xi'an. A stopping train leaves at 8.30am, taking 3½ hours (the last train back leaves at 5.30pm) or a bus from *Jiefangnan* bus station leaves at 6am, taking 3 hours. The journey's not always as simple as it sounds – when I did it the bus from Xi'an left before its advertised time, and the train on the way back had all the carriage doors locked so that we had to climb in through the windows. From **Hua Shan station** you walk down a cinder track to the main road and either catch a passing bus or walk eastward parallel to the railway for 15 minutes. Then turn up a road lined with tea and noodle stalls to the entrance. Here foreigners wanting to spend the night on the mountain must show a **climbing pass** (the **PSB** may or may not give you one – an accident in 1983 made them nervous) but even without a pass you can wander round the temple grounds and lower slopes, and climb as high as you can without missing the last train back. The climb begins from **Yuquan** – Jade Fountain temple – dedicated to the 10C scholar *Xi Yi* who lived here as a recluse. .

There's a Chinese saying 'There is one path and one only to the summit of Hua Shan.' This **path** begins by passing under the railway, then crisscrosses a river flowing down a rocky gully; every few hundred yards a little wayside refreshment place offers stone seats, a burner, tea, soft drinks, maps and souvenirs, with the owners' makeshift tent behind. You'll be swept along in a constant stream of Chinese – some very old, some tiny children, but most in their teens and early twenties. The young rush up at a tremendous pace, stopping every five minutes to puff and wipe away the sweat; most wear totally unsuitable clothes, heavy long johns in the heat and high-heeled shoes. Crossing the river on stepping stones they all wash their feet, socks and shirts in the icy water, and drink quantities.

The deceptively easy climb up the gullies – **the Eighteen Bends** – in fact winds for about 2 hours before reaching the flight of narrow stone steps which ascend to the first summit, **North Peak**. The mountain was formerly dotted with **temples** and there are still half a dozen where you can sleep and get up very early in the hope of seeing the sun rise over the *Sea of Clouds*. Many people go on to **Middle Peak** for this, a walk that takes the best part of a day. Really energetic climbers can carry on to the east, west and south peaks.

Though the heights are not in fact great the gaunt rocky peaks, twisted pines and rugged slopes certainly look like genuine mountain scenes as they swim in and out of the mist trails. The going is rough in places too, especially for anyone with no great head for heights. Though work has recently been done to widen the path and make it safer there are still places where you negotiate very narrow ridges or walk across steep rock faces with only linked chains for support. These passages have wonderfully evocative names – Thousand Feet Precipice, Green Dragon Ridge, Ear-Touching Cliff – but as you cross them, and think of the miscellaneous crowd dashing up from the bottom, it is not difficult to see how accidents can happen.

In summer the climb can be pretty hot work; many people prefer to arrive by an early evening train and then go up the mountain by moonlight.

YAN'AN

YAN'AN is the inaccessible mountain base in which the Chinese Communists took refuge from 1937 to 1945. Here the **Long March** had brought them, an astonishing – and now semi-mythical – journey in which 86,000 men, women and children of the Red Army fled their mountain bases in Jiangxi province to escape encirclement and annihilation at the hands of the Nationalists and in a year marched 6,000 miles across some of the world's most inhospitable terrain. It was a circuitous route, taking in a vast loop to the west through Yunnan and Sichuan, and along the way the army waxed and waned, its personnel changing constantly: tens of thousands died in battle, or from exposure, hunger and exhaustion; thousands more left to spread the political message or to organise local soviets and guerrilla bases to hamper the pursuit; but at the same time thousands more were joining.

When Mao finally arrived in Yan'an there were only about 5,000 with him, but here they met up with northern Communists who had already established a soviet and gradually stragglers, and those who had been sent on missions to other parts, arrived to swell their numbers. The

Yan'an soviet soon came to control a vast tract of the surrounding country, with its own economy and bank notes to back the new political system. The people of Yan'an lived in caves cut into the loess, a scheme adopted by the Red Army: here they were safe from the sporadic Nationalist bombing raids and other attempts at harassment.

The **revolutionary sites** remain the main attraction. You can see three of the caves in which Mao lived (he moved often); a reconstruction of the building in which the 7th Party Congress was held in 1945 (a tourist site about which it is not easy to be enthusiastic); and the Revolutionary Museum – packed with interesting mementoes, photographs, weapons, documents and even Mao's stuffed horse but subject to frequent 'Historical readjustment'. They can all be covered easily enough in a day.

Few westerners make the pilgrimage up here these days, which is a pity – it is a beautiful ride up through the typical dramatic loess lands of northern China. A bus leaves the South Gate bus station in Xi'an daily at 6am, arriving some eight hours later: halfway you can stop over at HUANGLING, site of the mythical Yellow Emperor *Huang Di.* Beneath a hilltop mound are said to lie the remains of this legendary founder and first sovereign of the Han race. His reign – around 3,000 BC – was a golden age in which he united the Chinese people and invented such essentials of civilisation as the wheel, pottery, metalwork and writing. Arriving in Yan'an, you face a 20-minute walk to the *Yan'an Binguan* – cheap and comfortable, with good food. Or there is a plane from Xi'an.

HENAN

Most of Henan lies south of the Yellow River where it emerges into a vast alluvial plain. The struggle to tame and use the river has always dominated life in the province, just as the plain's fertility and strategic position once dominated China: whoever controls Luoyang controls Henan, ran the saying, and whoever controls Henan controls China.

The chief places open to foreigners are **Luoyang** and the other ancient capitals – **Zhengzhou, Kaifeng** and **Anyang** – eastward along the railway. Zhengzhou lies on the modern junction with the main line south from Beijing. Also possible to visit are the **Songshan** mountains in the south – where you'll find the **Shaolin Monastery**, famous as the birthplace of *Kung Fu* – and the **Red Flag Canal** in the north, one of the more spectacular achievements of the Communist regime.

LUOYANG

LUOYANG, in the middle reaches of the Yellow River Valley, is in effect two separate cities. There is industrial Luoyang – begun in the 1950s, drab and of little interest except in April when visitors throng to see the peony blossom – and there is the ancient 'City of Nine Capitals', occupied from Neolithic times through to AD937 and now relegated to the status of a few sites on the fringe of the modern city. Though ancient Luoyang holds an important place in Chinese history, with many finds in the museum to prove it, there is little to be seen on the ground of the once-glorious palaces and temples. Beyond the city limits, though, you can still see the **Longmen Caves** – whose Buddhist carvings provide one of the most important artistic sites in China – and the venerable **White Horse** and **Guan Lin** temples.

Much of **Luoyang's history** was revealed only by the rebuilding of the city in the 1950s and the terracing and irrigation work in the surrounding countryside, which brought to light some 60 sites and 1000 tombs. Already by 5000BC this area was quite heavily populated – the Neolithic site discovered to the west of Luoyang in 1921, which gave its name to the *Yangshao* culture, proved to be just one of a whole series of sites along the Yellow River and in the North China Plain. The city site is a fine strategic one, guarded on three sides by hills and cut across by four rivers. The Bronze Age **Shang dynasty** have left finds here for the museum, but the first real development seems to have been a walled city built by the **Zhou** around 1000BC. When their rulers were forced to retreat from Xi'an in 771BC this became their capital: tradition claims that *Confucius* studied here and that *Lao Zi* was keeper of the archives. Under the **Qin** emperor and his early Han successors Xi'an regained its title, but later **Han** emperors (from AD25–220) were once again obliged to withdraw to Luoyang, building their city east of the White Horse Temple. Luoyang's trade and communications with the west along the Silk Road grew rapidly: Buddhism was introduced here in AD68; the Imperial College was founded with 30,000 students and a great library; *Cai Lun* invented paper; and *Zhang Hen* the imperial astronomer invented the armillary sphere, demonstrating that the Chinese knew the movement of the heavens long before the west.

For a time, in the turbulent years after the fall of the Han, Luoyang remained the capital of a series of dynasties and the centre of Chinese culture. Here the poet *Zuo Si* wrote a series of poems, *The Three Capitals*, which were so popular that people copying them caused a paper famine. The *Seven Sages of the Bamboo Grove* also flourished; according to legend one of them, *Liu Ling*, drank so much of the local *Du Kang* wine (which had then already been made here for several hundred years and is still a famous local product) that he sank into a stupor which lasted three years. Finally, soon after AD300, the city was destroyed.

When the northern **Toba Wei** invaders decided to move their capital from Datong into the Chinese heartland, Luoyang was the site they chose, probably because it was believed to be the centre of the world (a belief based on the shadow cast by the sun at summer solstice at nearby Yangcheng observatory). In 493, at the command of emperor *Xiao Wendi*, they moved almost overnight to Luoyang and constructed a new capital. In 30 years it had grown to a city of half a million people, with markets selling goods from all over Asia and more than 1400 Buddhist temples. The great carvings at Longmen were begun in this period. In 534, at the command of another Wei emperor and even more suddenly than it had been taken up, Luoyang was again abandoned and its people, including the residents of all the temples, forced to move to Yeh. An account written 13 years later described the city walls collapsed and overgrown with artemisia, the streets full of thorn trees, and millet planted between the ceremonial towers of the ruined palace.

Luoyang lay in ruins once more for 70 years until under the **Sui dynasty** it was rebuilt west of the Wei ruins on a grid pattern spreading across both banks of the Luo river. Two million men were conscripted for the work and the new city rapidly became the most important market centre in China, a magnet for foreign traders, with a population of a million, three separate major markets within the walls, over 3000 shops and stalls and around 400 inns for merchants. To feed the crowds grain was brought up the Grand Canal from the Yangzi basin and stored in enormous barns: the **Hanjia granary**, discovered in 1971 west of the old city, held 250,000 metric tons and was proof against damp, mildew, rats and insects. The emperor *Yang Di* also brought 3000 musicians to live at his court and surrounded himself with scholars, scientists and engineers.

Under the **Tang** Luoyang was only the secondary capital. It's said that in AD800 the empress *Wu Zetian*, enraged that the peonies, alone among flowers, disobeyed her command to bloom in the snow, banished them from her capital at Chang'an. Many were transplanted to Luoyang where they flourished, and have since become one of the city's most celebrated attractions, the subject of countless poems and cultivation notes. Several times drought forced the court to follow the peonies to Luoyang, where the express commissioned some of the most important carvings at Longmen.

With the decline of the Tang Luoyang finally lost its importance for good; the capital moved to Kaifeng and gradually the whole balance of the nation shifted south. Although Beijing became capital under the Mongols, Luoyang never recovered: by 1920 there was a run-down settlement of some 20,000 people here. The first Five-Year Plan earmarked the city for industrial development, and its new incarnation has not looked back since. Growth has been rapid ever since the early 1950s, helped by a position astride the east-west railway and the southern spur to Yichang. Once again there's a population of around 1 million, if in rather less attractive and more polluted surroundings than of old.

Inside Luoyang

The **railway station** is in the north of the city – take care not to get off at the East Station by mistake – directly opposite the long-distance **bus station**. The bulk of the city lies between the rail line and the Luo river: the Chan river and two smaller streams flow through. Jin He Yuan Lu runs south from the station, lined with 1950s buildings, to meet Yanan Lu and Zhongzhou Lu in a T-junction at the main square: here are government buildings, office blocks and big department stores. The old quarter is in the east; over in the west are the dreary residential blocks of the industrial city.

A no.2 bus from the station will take you along Yanan Lu, past the park and across the Chan river to the main **hotel**, the *Youyi Binguan*, before turning right into Jing Hua Lu. Large and old fashioned, the hotel has a range of rooms, dorms from ¥5, a popular, varied and cheap dining room and all the usual services including **CITS**, a Post Office and a number of little shops. Alternatively you could try the *Luoyang Binguan* in the old quarter near the East Station – no.5 bus from the main station. If you want to reach the old town direct from the *Youyi Binguan* take a no.9. **Taxis** can be found at the hotels or railway station; **PSB** is in Kaixuan Lu in the centre, and there's another **Post Office** by the round-about on Zhongzhou Lu.

Looking for **something to eat** you'll do best to explore the old town – Zhongzhou Donglu, Dong Dajie and Xi Dajie are all rich in possibilities. In the same area you'll find small shops and **markets** – there's also a huge **department store** in Zhongzhou Lu opposite the Post Office and a **Friendship Store** out on Yanan Lu beyond the park. There are plenty of **theatres** and **cinemas** too: among the larger ones are *Gongren Wenhua Gong* in Hunan Lu close to the hotel, *Shanghai Juwan* in the town centre on Zhongzhou Lu, and *Renmin Yingyuan* in the heart of the old city.

The Old Town itself is fascinating in places – lovely streets with whitewashed and half-timbered houses above which poke the roofs of old temples, and narrow alleys crossed by wires on which climbing plants are trained. The best streets to wander are Nan, Xi and Dong Dajie. Near their intersection is a wonderful shop selling musical instruments, lion masks and theatrical properties. Nearby, leading up to Zhongzhou Donglu, is a country vegetable market – cabbages, cucumbers, chillies, ginger and peanuts. The next street – full of life and colour – specialises in pot plants, especially roses and cacti, and in goldfish and caged birds.

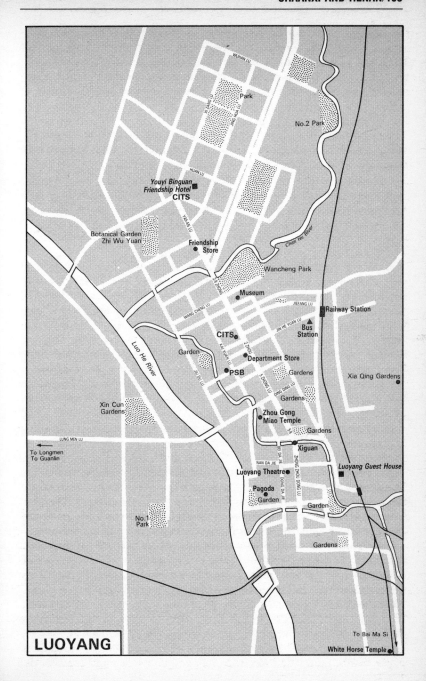

WUHAN LU

XI ZHANG LU

JING HUA LU

Park

No.2 Park

HUAN LU

Youyi Binguan
Friendship Hotel
CITS

YA AN LU

Botanical Garden
Zhi Wu Yuan

Friendship
Store

Chan He River

JI ANG

Wancheng Park

Museum

JIEFANG LU

Railway Station

JIN HE YUAN LU

WANG CHENG LU

CITS

ZHOU

Bus
Station

KAI XUAN LU

Department Store

JI DU LU

Garden

LUO He River

PSB

J ZHONG LU

Gardens

DING DING LU

Xia Qing Gardens

Xin Cun
Gardens

Gardens

LUNG MEN LU

Zhou Gong
Miao Temple

Gardens

To Longmen
To Guanlin

BEI DA JIE

Xiguan

Luoyang Guest House

NAN DA JIE

DONG DA JIE

Luoyang Theatre

ZHONG ZHOU DONG LU

Pagoda
Garden

Garden

No.1
Park

Gardens

To Bai Ma Si

LUOYANG

White Horse Temple

Back towards the hotel, the no.9 bus passes **Wangcheng Park** – the centre of Luoyang's **peonies** in the first half of April. They have been collected and cultivated until there are many thousands, of over 150 varieties, to be seen; not only in Wangcheng but also in the newer park **Zhi Wu Yuan** and indeed on every available patch or strip of ground in Luoyang – an extraordinary and splendid sight. The peony motif is also everywhere in the city, from trellis to rubbish bin. Even out of season Wangcheng is an attractive park, sloping down to a bridge across the river, and considerably less crowded. Unusually for a Chinese park it has been left quite wild in places, awaiting excavation. In the more formal areas there is loud music and a motley and depressing display of animals – snakes, tortoises and two unhappy owls on a string. These mini zoos are often eccentrically run by families who sleep on the premises – sometimes in the empty cages!

Excavations already undertaken in the park have uncovered much of the **Zhou capital** of 771BC – wall, palaces, temples and marketplace – but these are recognisable only by experts. Some fine bronzes found here are now in the museum. Across the suspension bridge there are also two **Han Tombs**, one with some good early murals. Otherwise almost all that is left of the ancient cities has been gathered into the **museum**, very near the park. A modern building, but attractively traditional in style, it is well worth at least wandering through. There are five halls arranged chronologically: look in Hall 2 for the Shang bronzes and an endearing jade tiger from the Zhou; Hall 4 has some Wei statuary which looks heavily influenced by India, as well as a model farm from a Han tomb with a sow and her row of piglets; in Hall 5 you'll find some comical Tang polychrome figures, including camels and a travelling merchant keeling over under the weight of his pack.

Outside the city

Longmen caves, Guan Lin and Bai Ma Si can all be visited in a single day's excursion from Luoyang, or each can easily be reached individually in a short trip out from the centre. If you've limited time the Buddhist carvings at Longmen are the place to head first: however little you know about Buddhism or about sculpture you cannot help but be impressed by the scale and complexity of the work and by the extraordinary contrast between the power of giant figures and the intricate delicacy of the miniatures. The only problem here is with the crowds – the caves are often quite overrun. If possible go early in the morning, late or at lunchtime. **Guan Lin** – a Taoist temple – is less striking, but beautiful nonetheless and refreshingly tranquil. **Bai Ma Si**, or White Horse Temple, is similar in atmosphere – it has a convincing claim to be the first Buddhist temple founded in China.

Longmen Caves

A no.10 bus from the *Youyi Binguan* or a no.3 from *Xi Guan* near the old town will run you out from the centre of town to the caves in a little over half an hour. They run infrequently, so check times in advance. A student card should get you into the site at local rates.

The **caves** (or grottoes or niches) are shallow recesses in the cliffs 16km south of Luoyang where the Yi river cuts through the Dragon Gate. In legend this cleft was formed when the Great *Yu*, Tamer of Floods, split the mountain to release an imprisoned dragon which was causing havoc Man has since added his bit to the tune of 1,350 caves, 750 niches and 40 pagodas containing 97,306 statues carved out of the sheer limestone cliffs bordering the river. From a distance the multi-veined cliffs, decked with green cypresses, look like a vast slab of gorgonzola cheese, and close up the different rocks provide some spectacular effects. Most of the carvings, which stretch over some 800 metres, are on the west bank.

The **Toba Wei** began the work in AD495 when they moved their capital to Luoyang from Datong, where the Yungang grottoes had just been completed. At Longmen they carried their art still further. Three caves, Guyang, Bingyang and Lianhua, date from this early period. Work continued for 500 years and reached a second peak under the **Tang**, particularly under the empress *Wu Zetian*, a devoted adherent of Buddhism. The carvings were commissioned by emperors, the imperial family, wealthy families wanting to buy good fortune, generals hoping for victory and religious groups: you can see a clear progression from the early style brought from Datong – with austere, formally modelled holy figures – to the complex and elaborate Tang carvings, including women and court characters. You can also see traces of vandalism and looting, beginning with the anti-Buddhist movement in the 9C, continuing through souvenir hunting westerners in the 19C and 20C and finally some (surprisingly muted) attacks by Red Guards during the Cultural Revolution.

Starting from the entrance of the **west bank**, the following are the most important carvings. The three **Bingyang** caves are early: the central one, commissioned by Emperor *Xuan Wu* to honour his parents, has an inscription recording that 802,366 men worked from AD500–523 to complete it. The eleven statues of Buddha show northern characteristics – long features, thin faces, splayed fishtail robes – and traces of Greek influence. The side caves, completed under the Tang, are more natural and voluptuous, carved in high relief. **Wanfuo Si** – Cave of 10,000 Buddhas – was built in 680 by Gao Zong and his empress Wu Zetian; it actually has 15,000 Buddhas carved in tiny niches, each one different and the smallest less than an inch high. **Lianhua** – Lotus Flower Cave – is another early one, dating from 527, and named after the beautifully

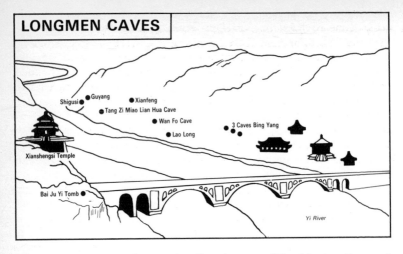

LONGMEN CAVES

Shigusi • Guyang • Xianfeng
• Tang Zi Miao Lian Hua Cave
• Wan Fo Cave
• Lao Long
3 Caves Bing Yang

Xianshengsi Temple

Bai Ju Yi Tomb •

Yi River

carved lotus in its roof. **Fengxian Si** – Ancestor Worshipping Cave – is the largest and most splendid of all. Made in 672 for Empress Wu Zetian, it has an overwhelming seated figure of Vairocana Buddha: 17 metres high with ears 2 metres long. On his left a boddhisattva wears crown and pearls and a divine general grinds a malevolent spirit under foot. This is the highest development of Tang carving and worth looking at carefully. **Medical Prescription Cave**, built in 575, details several hundred cures for everything from madness to the common cold. **Guiyang** is the earliest of all, begun in 495. Here you can still see traces of the vivid paintwork which originally gave life to these carvings: there is a central Buddha and 19 of the 'Twenty Pieces' which are important examples of ancient calligraphy.

From the end of the west bank you must at present walk back to cross to the **east bank**, but a bridge is being built at the far end to make a circuit. It's worth crossing, both to get a general view of the west bank and also to see the Tang period east bank carvings, comparatively few but of great delicacy. Here, up on the hill, is also the **Tomb of Bai Juyi**, the famous Tang poet who spent his last years in Luoyang as the Retired Scholar of the Fragrant Hill.

Guan Lin

A no.3 or no.10 bus on from Longmen or a no.16 direct from Luoyang town centre will take you to **Guan Lin**. This temple is dedicated to *Guan Yu*, a hero of the Three Kingdoms period and loyal general of *Liu Bei*, King of Shu. He was defeated and executed by the King of Wu who sent his head to *Cao Cao*, King of Wei, hoping in this way to divert on to

Wei any revenge that might be coming. Cao Cao neatly sidestepped this grisly game of Pass the Parcel by burying the head with honour in Luoyang, in a tomb behind the temple.

The buildings are Ming, highly carved and richly decorated. Through the great gate set in the outer wall is a rectangular courtyard, bounded by long low buildings with gates and Bell and Drum Towers, with the Main Hall in the middle. This, and also the second and third halls beyond, are newly painted, with remarkable action scenes, and everywhere are ancient twisted cypresses, one enormous specimen said to date from the Ming. Look at the carved stone lionesses lining the path to the main Hall – each has a different expression and a different cub, some riding boldly on mother's back, others hiding coyly behind her paws.

It's a quiet place, well restored and brilliantly coloured against the grey and green background of stone and cypresses.

Bai Ma Si – White Horse Temple

Bai Ma Si lies about 9km east of Luoyang and like Guan Lin it's a green, placid place – sometimes claimed to be the very first Buddhist temple found in China. Legend says that the Emperor *Yong Ping* dreamed of a golden figure with the sun and moon behind its head. Two monks sent to search for the origin of the dream reached India and returned riding white horses and bearing the sutras, which they then translated. The Emperor built this temple for them.

Its layout fits neatly into the legend; there are two stone horses, one on either side of the entrance, and the tombs of the two monks in the first courtyard. Ahead is the Hall of Celestial Guardians and beyond is the main Hall, where Sakyamuni is flanked by Manjusri and Samanta-bhadra. Near the Great Altar is an ancient bell weighing over a ton: in the days when there were 10,000 Tang monks here it was struck in time with the chanting. The inscription reads 'The sound of the Bell resounds in Buddha's temple causing the ghosts in Hell to tremble with fear.' Behind the main Hall is the Hall of 18 Arhats (Yuan period) and through the Jieyin Dian up the steps is the Cool Terrace where, it is said, the sutras were translated.

South-west of the temple is the **Ciyou Ta** – Cloud Reaching Pagoda – built in the 10C and restored several times since. The 13-storey brick tower with its projecting roofs is more graceful than many pagodas. You can get a bus to Bai Ma Si from Guan Lin, or take a no.6 direct from Xi Guan in the city centre.

ZHENGZHOU

Close to the south bank of the Yellow River, **ZHENGZHOU** lies almost midway between Luoyang in the west and Kaifeng to the east. 3,500 years ago there was a walled town here which was probably an early capital of the Shang dynasty and nowadays the city is capital of Henan province, though this owes nothing to its past and everything to a position astride the meeting of the main north-south and east-west railway lines. As probably the most important railway junction in China, it has a population of over 1 million and the industry to match.

It is also the post-Liberation boom town *par excellence*, making up in vitality what it lacks in beauty or antiquity. Zhengzhou is in any case virtually impossible to avoid if you are travelling in central China, so you might as well accept that it has this good point at least: there are no historic sites or beauty spots worth speaking of. From here Kaifeng and Luoyang are easily accessible, and you can take bus trips to Songshan, Gongxian and Mixian.

The modern city

Badly damaged during the war against Japan and in the subsequent struggle for supremacy up to 1949, Zhengzhou was rebuilt rapidly afterwards. Today it is an almost entirely modern city, very proud of its trees but surviving on textiles and heavy industry. Endless tracts of industrial building and workers' housing stretch out along the railway lines, but visitors will be concerned only with the central area, immediately east and north-east of the **railway station**. The main road, Zhengxing Jie, runs clear under the enormous station complex and there is a long underpass to reach the platforms: allow yourself plenty of time to catch your train.

Zhengzhou has been a railway town since it found itself at the centre of the network when the lines were completed in 1910. It was a focal point of the 1923 Communist-led strike of Beijing-Hankou railwaymen, put down with great savagery by the Warlord *Wu Pei Fu*; those who died are commemorated by the **February Seventh Monument**. A no.2 bus north-east along Zhengxing Jie from the station will take you to the roundabout where this stands – a two-towered pagoda containing a display of the events of the strike. Further north, along Erqi Lu, the **People's Park** spreads over both banks of the Jinshui river, a typical 1950s park with a period zoo, a rather seedy rockery and a grubby little canal where you can go boating.

Back towards the station the vast boulevards and characterless building blocks give way to a few less stark structures, more interesting streets. Datong Lu has low houses and shops, humming with activity, and there are busy shoping areas, too, along Shengli Lu and Dehua Lu, south from the monument. The most enjoyable of all to wander, though, is a little alley between Jiefang Lu and Erqi Lu – a lovely place crowded with food stalls where Chinese Muslims in white caps constantly turn out dumplings and golden roasted chickens.

Zhengzhou's principal **museum** lies on the no.2 bus route, an imposing building with a colossal statue of Mao outside. As the provincial museum of one of the most historically important of China's provinces, it obviously has a substantial collection – but the display is poor. There are a number of neolithic finds, especially from **Dahecun,*** and there are Bronze Age artefacts from Anyang and elsehwere in the province. The Shang capital, whose earth rampart can still just about be traced outside Zhengzhou, is also well represented. It has provided some rare and splendid bronze vessels.

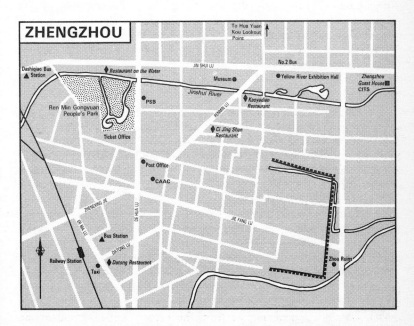

Near the museum, the **Yellow River Exhibition Hall** is also worth a visit, showing clearly what a decisive part the river's erratic behaviour has played in the life of the whole region. Although the Hall sets out to cater for groups, you can visit independently: I had the place to myself. There is a film and a presentation by a girl with a rather ferocious approach – it shows you the route of the river from its source in the mountains bordering Tibet; its deviations over the centuries, and the

---

*The site itself, a few kilometres north, can be visited by no.5 bus from the Dashiqiao suburban bus station. There are 5–6,000 year old house foundations, tombs and kilns.

floods, droughts and catastrophes it has wrought. The various methods used to control the river are also explained with grainy photographs. There are some good demonstrations with enormous cabinets and models with real water gushing through on to rusty river beds, and dams with flashing lights.

Afterwards, by taking a no.9 bus to the terminus and a no.10 on to **Hua Yuan Kou**, you can climb the lookout point and see the real McCoy. On normal form it will be a shallow trickle through the dust: it is hard to imagine that in 1937, when Chiang Kaishek breached the dikes 8km from the city to prevent the Japanese capturing the railway, the Yellow River flooded this great plain, leaving over a million dead and countless more homeless.

Practicalities

The usual **hotel** for foreigners, *Zhengzhou Binguan*, is an inconvenient 7km from the station – 40 minutes on a no.2 bus. A large, modern, soulless multi-storey block, it has **CITS**, a **Post Office** and **Bank**, but is expensive at ¥20 per head. As alternatives – no guarantee of success – you might try *Henan Binguan* or *Youyi Binguan* in Jinshui Lu near the People's Park, or *Zhengzhou Fandian* near the railway station.

Eating is no problem – the city is full of places which cater to the crowds passing through. *Shui Shan Canting* and *Guangzhou Jiu Ja*, both near the People's Park, *Datong Fanshe* in Datong Lu near the station or *Cijingshan Fandian* in Renmin Lu should all feed you reasonably well. Or try *Kaoya Dian* in Renmin Lu for duck. The Hui moslem alleys near the pagoda roundabout also offer a wealth of interesting little food stalls.

The **PSB** is in Erqi Lu virtually opposite the park entrance, and there's a main **Post Office** in the same street north of the pagoda roundabout. For your **shopping** needs there's a huge department store on the museum roundabout and small and varied shops in Dayong Lu and Dehua Lu. As for **cinemas** or **theatres**, try the *Henan* in Jinshui Lu opposite the museum, the *Dehua* in Dehua Lu near the roundabout, or the *Renmin Ju Wan* in Erqi Lu near the south end of the park.

Leaving, you'll find a **railway ticket office** in Erqi Lu as well as on the station forecourt. The **long-distance bus station** is opposite the railway station, with other ticket offices on the Renmin Lu/Jinshui Lu roundabout and at **Dashiqiao suburban bus station**, reached by no.4 bus from the main station. The **CAAC** booking office is at Erqi Lu Nantou 38.

Around Zhengzhou

GONG XIAN, on the railway east of Zhengzhou and also accessible by bus, boasts eight imperial tombs of the Song dynasty which have recently been refurbished. Though their layout is the same as that of the Tang tombs, the funeral practices of the Song emperors were very different from those of their predecessors. In particular, each emperor's tomb was built for him by his successor and had to be completed within 7 months of the death. Not surprisingly the results are considerably less grandiloquent than the tombs which earlier emperors had spent their own lifetimes preparing. **MIXIAN**, also easily reached by bus, is south of Zhengzhou and has a Han tomb.

The undoubted highlight of the area around Zhengzhou, however, is Songshan.

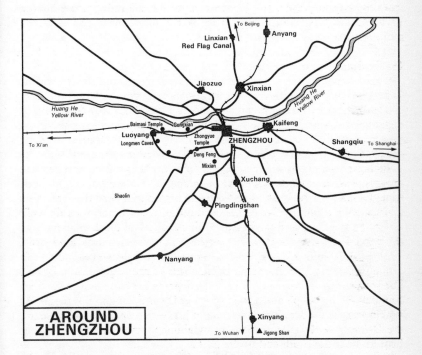

SONGSHAN – ZHONG YUE AND SHAOLIN

The seventy peaks of the **Songshan** range stretch over 64km of Dengfeng County, midway between Zhengzhou and Luoyang to the south. When the Zhou ruler Ping moved his capital to Luoyang in 771BC, it was known as *Zhong Yue* – Central Peak – being at the axis of the five sacred mountains, with Huashan to the west, Taishan to the east, Hengshan to the south and another Hengshan to the north. The mountains, thickly clad with trees, rise from narrow, steep-sided rocky valleys and appear impressively precipitous, though with the highest peak, **Junji**, at just

1500m they're not actually very lofty. With the summits emerging from a swirling sea of cloud, though, and the slopes in their brilliant autumn colours, they can certainly look the part.

Of the many sites here the two best known are Zhong Yue, a Taoist monastery 4km east of Dengfeng town, and Shaolin, 13km north-west of Dengfeng. **Shaolin** is a Buddhist monastery of considerable repute, but its fame, in China as in the west, rests far more on the fact that here **Shaolin Boxing**, better known as *Kung Fu*, is supposed to have been developed and perfected. There are **tour bus trips** to both places from Luoyang or from Zhengzhou, leaving early in the morning and returning late afternoon, for which it is advisable to book (certainly at weekends or in High Season). Alternatively there are **public buses** from Zhengzhou to **DENGFENG** several times a day. If you can get a permit to stay here or (less likely) in the hostel at Shaolin you could visit the sites at a more relaxed pace and also have time for some hiking around the less visited parts. Around the lower slopes there are numerous paths which meander along the valleys, passing temples, pagodas and guard towers – higher, there's fine scenery and some wonderful views. Setting out from Dengfeng you'd find plenty to occupy two or three days' walking. **Songyang Academy**, for example, was founded in AD484 and was one of the great centres of learning under the Song: in the courtyard are two enormous trees said to be as much as 2000 years old. The path beyond climbs to **Junji Peak** or branches off to the **Song Yue Temple Pagoda**, 5km north of Dengfeng. Built at the beginning of the 6C by the northern Wei, this 45-metre structure is the oldest in China, and also a rare example of a 12-sided pagoda. South-east of Dengfeng you could visit the **Observatory**, built in 1279 and designed by *Guo Shou Jing* to calculate the solstices.

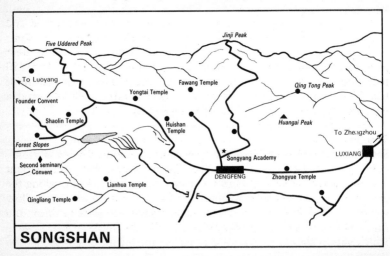

SONGSHAN

Zhong Yue

From Zhengzhou, Zhong Yue is about a 2-hour bus ride. Beyond the brick fringe of the city is a flat, dry landscape – dusty red buildings, dusty green trees, dusty brown dust – where after the city's market gardens you pass wheat fields banked up by mud or brick walls to one and a half metres above road level. Every last corner of ground is used – tiny strips of wheat grow at the bottom of deep gullies and where there is no cultivation there are brickfields, quarries, sandpits. Everywhere, too, are the caves in which locals used to live; few are inhabited now which in some ways seems strange – they are perfect for the prevailing conditions, cool in summer, warm in winter and with a handy vegetable patch on the roof.

Reaching Zhong Yue you see Huanggai Hill, with its little summit temple, in the background – independent visitors could climb this but on the tour bus you won't have time since it only stays about 1½ hours. **ZHONG YUE** itself was founded as long ago as 220BC, and subsequently rebuilt and considerably extended in 110BC by the Han emperor Wu Di. Nowadays you'll find coaches, buses and food stalls jammed together at the entrance, with locals making a killing selling everything from post-cards to plastic pagoda thermometers. Sunday is worst, but even midweek you'll probably find yourself in the middle of a constant, shuffling throng as you try to see the temple buildings – going round in reverse order may help.

Despite the crowds it's a picturesque place – its broad open spaces and brilliantly coloured buildings (some still being restored) standing out against the grey and green of the mountain. A series of gateways, court-yards and pavilions, now mainly of Qing date, lead to the Main Hall where the emperor would sacrifice to the Sacred Mountain: the **Junji Gate** has two great sentries, nearly 4 metres high, brightly painted and flourishing their weapons; in the courts are gnarled old cypresses, some of them approaching the age of the temple itself, and there are four great iron statues dating from the Song (at which time the temple had 850 halls and pavilions spread over a far larger area). The **Main Hall** itself has 45 separate compartments with red walls and orange tiles, and a well-preserved relief carving on the terrace steps.

Shaolin

SHAOLIN MONASTERY, at the foot of Shaoshi mountain, is if anything even more crowded than Zhong Yue. The pleasant country roundabout is marred by the food stalls and souvenir shops which spill out along the entrance road; there are binoculars – a few fen a go – set up to allow visitors to enjoy the views without actually having to walk to them, and inside the gate there's a hodgepodge of buildings and much new work which makes it hard to get any real feel of the layout or atmosphere of the place. The general turmoil of radios, picnics, shouting, spitting and jostling doesn't help either, and in recent years the popularity of martial arts films made here has added to the crush. Coming on the tour it takes about half an hour from Zhong Yue – make a note of your coach number or you'll never find it again in the enormous parking lot.

Shaolin was built in AD495. Shortly after, according to tradition, **Boddhidarma** came to live here. He was the Indian monk who introduced Zen Buddhism to China, visited the emperor in Nanjing, and then crossed the Yangzi on a reed to settle at Shaolin, where he sat motionless for 9 years facing a wall in a state of Illumination, which is the mystic knowledge of the Nothingness of Everything. A tablet in the temple shows his crossing of the Yangzi.

For modern visitors, though, the chief attraction of Shaolin is its role in developing *Shaolin Quan*, the specialised form of shadow boxing known as **Kung Fu**. Quite why so violent a form of exercise should have developed in the meditative atmosphere of the monastery is unclear: records suggest that monks engaged in meditation would rise and stretch to relax after long periods of immobility, and that this evolved into a set of exercises which were later adapted for self-defence. Certainly the monastery has had a turbulent history which includes being burnt down several times, though whether this caused the need for defence or was the result of the monks' power is anyone's guess. From the early 7C, when Shaolin supported the claim of the first Tang emperor, this was a rich and influential place. The damage from the last fire, in 1928, is still being repaired.

Behind the main entrance and Great Hall are a number of buildings, some crammed with unbelievably tiny cells. The wonderful murals in the furthest two are enough to justify a visit in themselves. Those in the **White Robe Hall** are a Qing vintage manual of the Shaolin method: *The Rescue of Emperor Tai Zong by Thirteen Monks* depicts a particularly heroic adventure. In the **Thousand Buddha Hall** is a famous Ming dynasty mural of 500 arhats paying homage. This is the same hall in which Boddhidarma passed his 9-year vigil and in which nowadays you can see dents in the brick floor (roped off) made by generations of monks practising Kung Fu movements.

As for modern life in the monastery, it is hard to know whether the new generation of monks (sponsored by the government) learn the secrets of the ancient art. All you see is a monk in the temple reading sutras and taking money for incense. But certainly the younger visitors believe they do: they have seen the films made here; they may be able to hum the theme from the TV series; and some can be spotted practising a few surreptitious moves in the hope that the magic of the place might wear off on them.

A few minutes' walk to the west you'll find the **Forest of Stupas**, hundreds of stone memorials erected between the 9C and the 19C, each one commemorating a monk and inscribed with the names of his disciples. An impressive layout of golden stone against the purple mountain, it would be even better without the picnickers and the litter. Another short walk beyond leads to the **Chu Zuan** Founder's Hall where the main temple, of Song date, is the oldest wooden temple in Henan. Look especially for the Four Heavenly Kings, or Guardians, unusual here in that they are carved on to pillars rather than free-standing.

KAIFENG

Just south of the Yellow River in the eastern Henan plain, **KAIFENG** is an ancient capital with a recorded history of over 3000 years. But its situation – repeatedly exposed to northern invaders and to Yellow River floods – has left few relics to conjure any past glory. Nor has it grown much this century; the role of provincial capital fell to Zhengzhou and though the town's publicity speaks of it as a rising industrial city, its unpaved streets, decrepit buildings and air of seedy poverty give more the impression of an industrial wasteland.

There are certain advantages to this – the centre is simply laid out and shops, restaurants and cinemas are concentrated in an area which is markedly unspoilt by the usual Soviet-style development. The city is small and sees few visitors: a day trip from Zhengzhou would leave plenty of time to see all the main sites and wander the streets. Recently there have been signs that the monuments are being spruced up ready for more tourists, but for the time being Kaifeng remains a provincial backwater where everything seems to close early.

The city's heyday came under the northern Song dynasty from AD960–1127. First heard of as a Shang town around 1000BC, it served as the capital of several early kingdoms and minor dynasties, but under the Song the city became the political, economic and cultural centre of the empire. A famous horizontal scroll by *Zhang Zheduan*, 'Riverside Scene at the Qingming Festival', unrolls to show views of the city of this time: teeming with life and crammed to bursting point with people, boats, carts and animals. It was a great age for painting, calligraphy, philosophy and poetry and Kaifeng became famous for the quality of its textiles and embroidery and for its range of ceramics and printed books. This Golden Age ended suddenly in 1127 when Jurchen invaders overran the city, looting palaces and temples and putting everything else to the torch. The emperor and his court were led away as prisoners. Just one royal prince escaped to the south, to set up a new capital out of harm's reach at Hangzhou beyond the Yangzi, but Kaifeng itself never recovered. Nor did much survive: what did has been damaged or destroyed by repeated floods since – between 1194 and 1887 there were over 50 severe incidents including one fearful occasion in 1624 when the dikes were breached during a siege and at least 300,000 are said to have died.

Practical details

The **railway station** and the **long-distance bus station** are at the southern end of the city. From here everything is quite walkable but if you are in a hurry there's also a cheap and convenient bus network: two of the most useful are the no.1, north from the station along Zongshan Lu and

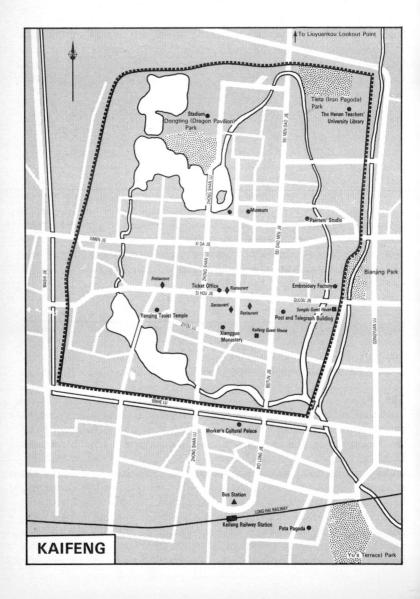

To Liuyuankou Lookout Point

Tieta (Iron Pagoda) Park

The Henan Teachers' University Library

Stadium
Dongting (Dragon Pavilion) Park

ZHONG SHAN LU

BEI MEN DAO JIE

Museum

Painters' Studio

XIMEN JIE

XI DA JIE

BEI DAO MEN JIE

Bianjing Park

MASHI JIE

Restaurant

ZHONG SHAN LU

Ticket Office

Restaurant

SI HOU JIE

Embroidery Factory

GULOU JIE

Restaurant

Restaurant

Sungdu Guest House

Post and Telegraph Building

Yanqing Taoist Temple

ZIYOU LU

Xiangguo Monastery

Kaifeng Guest House

GONGYUAN LU

BEITUN JIE

BINHE LU

Worker's Cultural Palace

ZHONG SHAN LU

MO LONG JIE

Bus Station

LONG HAI RAILWAY

Kaifeng Railway Station

Pota Pagoda

(Yu's Terrace) Park

KAIFENG

the Causeway past Longting to the Iron Pagoda, and no.10, a circular route running east from the station close to Yuwangtai, north up Gongyuan Jie, west along the central thoroughfare past the Yanqing Temple, and back south to the station. If you arrive too late for these (i.e. after 8.30pm) there are also pedicabs for hire at the station. There's a general **ticket office** in Sihou Jie near Zhongshan Lu.

The main **hotel,** very central, is the *Kaifeng Binguan* in Ziyou Lu. Sprawling over a large compound, it has an old wing with shared rooms at ¥10–15: a dining room in the pricier modern wing serves western breakfasts. Most services, including shops and **CITS**, are available inside the compound. A possible alternative is the *Songdu Binguan*, a guesthouse near Bianjing Park.

There are plenty of **places to eat** in the main thoroughfares; try the *Diyilou Baozi Guan*, a dumpling café in Sihou Jie, or *Youyi Xinfandian* in Gulou Jie. For snacks Madao Jie, with its bright blue and yellow shopfronts, is best – overflowing with milling crowds, everyone sampling the market stalls, the department stores and the **Friendship Store**. There's good window-shopping, in fact, in all the streets bounded by Ziyou Lu, Zhongshan Lu and Sihou Jie: the **Post Office** is in Ziyou Lu, the **bookshop** in Shudian Jie. Everywhere you'll see piles of green vegetables, mounds of tomatoes and melons (everywhere except in the dismal hotel restaurant, that is). **Cinemas** are also easy to find in these main streets – *Dazong Dianying* in Gelou Jie, *Jiefang Dianying* in Dong Da Jie or *Gonren Dianying* in Zhongshan Lu – but like everything else in Kaifeng they close early.

Also near the centre, Beitun Jie used to be the heart of Kaifeng's substantial **Jewish Community**. No one seems to know quite how or when Jews came to be living in this part of China, but their presence from around the 14C onwards is well documented. Nowadays, though there are a few locals who claim to be descended from these people, Judaism as a religion has entirely died out.

The city
Turn right out of the hotel on to Ziyou Lu and walk a couple of hundred yards down: the entrance to **Xiangguo Si** lies on the same side of the street. Originally built in AD555, this was one of China's foremost Buddhist temples until it was sacked in 1127. A later building put up under the Ming was destroyed by the Great Flood of 1642 and the present structure dates from 1766. The simple layout of the three remaining buildings, with green open spaces between them and plain low structures to either side, is rather pleasing – unfortunately the side wings seem nowadays to house the sad debris of an amusement park, a dusty hall of mirrors on one said and a wilting display of coral plants, like aquatic bonsai, on the other. The place has also been used as the set for a locally

produced Shaolin film. Nevertheless there are a couple of things worth seeing: the **Daxiong Baodian** – Great Treasure House – has a stunning bronze Buddha (early Song), and in the unusual and exquisite octagonal hall called **Bajiao Liulu Dian** you'll see a magnificent four-sided Guanyin carved in gingko wood and known as the *Buddha of a Thousand Arms and Eyes*.

Yanqing Taoist Temple is straight down the main road from Xiangguo Si, to the right of a major junction. All that remains of a temple built at the end of the 13C and dedicated to the Jade Emperor is a small pavilion of sea-green tiles where the Taoist master *Quanzhou* once preached. You can glimpse it from the street corner, but to get close to I had to walk through a room where a woman was cooking a meal, beyond which was a yard full of rubble with the tiny dolls' house of a pagoda tucked away in one corner.

Up Zhongshan Lu before reaching the causeway you'll find a detour to the right which leads to the **museum**. It must have been quite a substantial mansion once and is near another solid old building which still houses the library, but the major part of this one has been converted into flats. I was directed into a courtyard full of debris, tiles, workmen, packing cases, old cabinets, dusty statues, lumps of stone and rusty metal figures where the foreman said – and meant – No Photographs. The museum, apparently, is in the process of being moved, but to where, and when, remains a mystery.

Further on from the museum, past the scummy lake, is the site of the Song Imperial Palace destroyed by the Jurchen in 1127. Early writers described its imposing layout: an Imperial Way 300 metres wide lined with covered arcades; two canals covered with lotus and bordered by peach, plum and pear trees; and the concentric circles of the inner and outer cities themselves. There is little sign of that now – the causeway runs between expanses of water used both for fishing and the weekly wash to the 18C **Dragon Pagoda** (Longting), reached by a broad stairway up a series of massive terraces. Its two sagging pavilions barely mask the industrial wasteland beyond. There is a large and daunting tiled hall which used to be the site of the Civil Service Examinations; the large, square block of stone in the centre, carved with dragons and clouds, may have been the pedestal of the Imperial Throne. You can climb a stairway on either side of a carved dragon panel over which only the emperor could be carried – with a cool breeze stirring your hair and birds swooping noisily overhead there's a great view of industrial Kaifeng, smokestacks dominating, but not obliterating, the Iron Pagoda.

Actually to reach the Iron Pagoda – or **Tie Ta** – you can take off to the right on unpaved roads through dreary industrial blight or take a no.1 or 3 bus. A long avenue slices through a stripe of green park, passes a cheerful garden closed to the public and leads up to the 13-storey,

60-m tall pagoda. It is actually a perfectly normal octagonal brick construction, but entirely covered in decorative glazed tiles to make it look like iron. Get as close as you can to appreciate the detail and variety of the carving, damaged in places by weathering and Japanese bombs.

At the opposite end of town, **Yuwangtai** (terrace of Yu the Great) is beyond the railway lines not far from the station. A no.18 bus will take you close, otherwise you face a long and dusty walk through the most run-down part of town. Beyond a level crossing you'll find the entrance to a drab park – a mound topped with nondescript pavilions and encircled by a stagnant moat and an encroaching fringe of ramshackle housing. It is hard to believe now that this was originally a Music Terrace where the 8C BC musician Shi Kuang is said to have played, and later a haunt of Tang poets. Under the Ming a pavilion was built in honour of Yu the Tamer of Floods, giving the place its present name. Nearby is the **Pota Pagoda**, a dumpy brick structure originally built in 977 but now missing its topmost storeys. Close up, it has some finely detailed tiles.

Finally, if you have time to spare and haven't already seen the **Yellow River**, it's worth taking a no.6 bus from the station to **Liuyuankou Ferry** in the northern suburbs. There's a tourist area and lookout point here: you'll rarely see a wider, dustier or flatter plain.

ANYANG

Heading north by train **ANYANG** is the final stop in Henan province which is open to visitors. Since it is a place of no importance in modern times, and little of its past is visible to the untrained eye, the city hardly justifies a special trop, but it could easily be fitted into a day's visit en route to or from Beijing. Its great days, as a capital city and the source of China's earliest written records, were over 3000 years ago. Since then it has dozed in gentle obscurity and seems to have been largely undisturbed by the turmoils of the past hundred years, so that the centre has retained the character of a small, dusty, self-contained town in the old style. Anyang has escaped the flood of stark 1930s and 1950s development which has engulfed so many other towns.

When you arrive, you'll find the **railway and bus stations** together on the west side of town. The main road, Jiefang Lu, leads directly to the chief **hotel** for foreigners, the *Anyang Binguan* (wbout 15mins walk). A typical huddle of low buildings in a compound, this offers basic double rooms or dorm beds from around ¥10 upwards. **CITS** has an office in the compound and the reception will tell you about **PSB** arrangements. For other facilities – **shops, restaurants** and **cinemas** – try along Jiefang Lu and inside the **Old Town** in Zhongshan Lu, Dayuan Lu and Xi Da Jie.

The Yinxu ruins are all that is left of **ancient Anyang** – a city which vanished into the dusty fields so long ago that its very existence had been forgotten. The historian *Si Maqian*, writing in the 1C BC, mentioned the ruins of an early city on the banks of the Huan river, but this and its ruling houses were thought to be mere legend until in 1899 quantities of *oracle bones* were found. Later, in the 1920s and 1930s, excavations proved beyond doubt that this had been the capital of an historical dynasty, the **Shang**, which flourished from 1711 to 1066BC.

To visit **the ruins**, take a no.1 bus to the junction of Anyang and Yinxu Lu, cross the railway line and follow the track round to the river bend. This is an interesting walk for getting a feel of what is permanent about China: dusty yellow-walled compounds and farm buildings rise from the flat wheatfields, looking as ageless and unchanged as though they had been there since before the Shang dynasty. There are no ruined palaces, or even walls, to be seen – just a rough and tumbled site in the midst of a level, windblown and often flooded country. Fifty years ago excavations here uncovered the city of **Yin**, with royal tombs containing horses, chariots and sacrificial victims; houses and workshops with tools; splendid bronze vessels, one inscribed with the name of the royal consort *Fu Hao* and still bearing soot marks from the fire; jade and pottery of fine design; and – most important of all – tens of thousands of inscribed

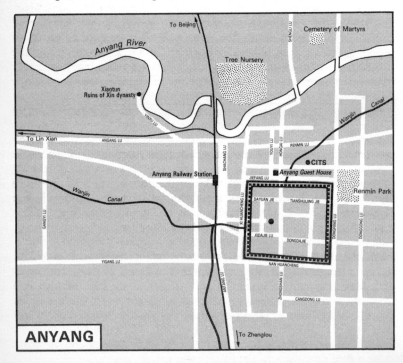

ANYANG

oracle bones. Some of these, when occasionally dug out of the ground, had been ground up and used as medicine – **dragon bones** they were called. But eventually the markings on them were identified as an early script.

The bones were used in divination – the priest or shaman applied heated sticks to them and interpreted the cracks which appeared – and they provide all sorts of useful information about hunting, war, the harvest and sacrifices because this was scratched on to the bone afterwards. The bones were also used for keeping records and reveal a great deal about the complicated organisation of the Shang city, the names of its rulers, the titles and functions of its officials and the collection and spending of tribute money. The characters used are recognisably the ancestors of the Chinese characters in use today.

Also on the site is a gaunt building which houses a **study collection**. It is not open to the general public, but if you can talk your way in as a student, you will find a fascinating collection of inscribed bones, pottery (including some from the Neolithic farmers who preceded the Shang), bronzes, animal skeletons and a number of yellowing photographs of the site and excavations.

Back in the centre of Anyang, it is well worth exploring the **Old Town** – a neat rectangle behind its moat and line of whitewashed wall. It looks much as you would expect a traditional town to look, with dusty unpaved streets and alleyways mostly too narrow for cars or lorries but full of people and carts, with bicycles swooping round every corner. From the streets you see only the long low walls of the compounds with their tiled roofs curling down towards you. But at regular intervals steps and a long dim narrow passageway lead in. Up these you can glimpse bright sunny courtyards with plants in pots and shrubs in flower, surrounded by grey tiled buildings; often there are paintings on the wall facing the entrance – mountains, birds, lakes or the characters for wealth, prosperity and long life. Traditionally this wall was there to deflect evil spirits or influences. In the alleys you may come across a rag and bone man going round shouting for any rubbish, or a night soil collector: because of the single entrance and the high walls, all peddlers, merchants or hawkers traditionally had distinctive chants and cries to attract the attention and custom of those inside. Anyang retains something of this atmosphere.

From the maze of streets the top of the **Wei Feng Pagoda** is visible, with the large bells on its eaves tinkling in the breeze. Built in AD925 it has a lotus-shaped base, five octagonal storeys with bells at each corner and, unusually, a top storey larger than its base. The entrance is a doorway to the left of a large school off Xi Da Jie and if you bang loud enough the keeper will let you in to look at the outside, which has a very fine Buddhist relief carving. To climb up you need permission from the Cultural Department – try asking at the hotel too – it would be worth it for a bird's eye view of the Old Town.

LINXIAN AND THE RED FLAG CANAL

For anyone who has had more than enough pagodas to be going on with, the side trip from Anyang to the **Red Flag Canal** makes a fascinating contrast. The mountain scenery is rugged and impressive, the canal itself a great sight, and the whole project is typical of the extraordinary feats achieved with little equipment but enormous masses of workers; in its own way a microcosm of the history and politics of the 1960s.

You can get to **LINXIAN**, which is the jumping off point for the canal, by slow train on a branch line from Anyang. The station is a crowded 40 minute bus journey from the town; get off in the main street and turn right for the *Linxian Fandian*, which charges around ¥15 all-in for **bed** and meals. Alternatively you can go by bus from Anyang, leaving about a 10 minute walk to the hotel. **PSB** is across the road.

The **RED FLAG CANAL** – *Hong Qi Qu* – is in the Taihang mountains in the far north-west of Henan. While most of the province has lived under the threat of devastating floods, this area's problem has been severe drought: the acute water shortage allied to stony, infertile hills held the peasants down to an inescapable grindstone as they attempted to scrape a living from the mountain dust. After 1949 there were numerous small-scale water conservancy and irrigation projects. By far the most ambitious was the plan to dig a tunnel through the high Taihang mountain ridge, which separates north-west Henan from Shanxi province. Water could then be channelled from the Zhanghe river in Shanxi, dammed for reservoirs and hydroelectric power and divided, channelled and diverted over a vast area for irrigation. The project took nearly two decades to complete, the work done almost entirely by human hand – hundreds of men with picks and panniers standing in for JCBs; the Chinese pamphlet for visitors speaks of the 1000 and more miles of channel dug, the 1250 hills blasted or cut into, the 143 tunnels excavated and 150 aqueducts built in this fashion.

At one time a visit to the Canal was almost obligatory for young cadres and students; key political figures and VIPs from other countries were brought up here in vast limousines to scramble up the hillside, admire the work and have their picture taken alongside local dignitaries. The flood of visitors has now dwindled to a mere trickle and you might have the place to yourself. This loss of publicity value has left the local officials a bit deflated, and they will tell you rather sadly of the great names who have come here in the past. By the same token they are very keen to impress anyone who happens along. In the hotel conference room you might find yourself treated to a solitary lecture on the history, layout and construction of the canal, using a wired-up wall map with displays of coloured lights to show you the water course, the electricity and the green irrigated areas.

They will also arrange a jeep with a driver and guide from ¥30 to 50 for a half or whole day trip, usually beginning at the **Youth Tunnel** where the water arrives in the valley through the ridge of mountain. You then climb up to follow the course of the canal clinging to the hillside high above the valley where you can see it winding endlessly across the spurs running down from the mountain ridges. It's an extraordinary and unforgettable sight. Look down into the valley at what are now fertile fields before driving on to take in a dam and perhaps the diversion lock or one of the main aqueducts – all with names entirely redolent of the 1960s like *Hero Branch Canal* and *Seizing Bumper Harvest Aqueduct*. I was given a vintage leaflet with wonderful highly coloured photographs of rosy cheeked girls with pigtails standing in ripening corn up to their shoulders and venerable elders showing the youngsters what to do; but I noticed that they were careful to remove the blurb which was less than complimentary to Liu Shaoshi who believed that the project was a waste of manpower and that the same effect could have been achieved by laying a single irrigation pipe.

If you do this trip pray for fine weather; when I came no one would have believed there was ever a drought problem – the whole mountain was knee deep in rain, water and mud, and the driver was reduced to hiring umbrellas from a local shop to keep us dry. On the way back from Anyang, at least by bus, you will be able to appreciate the end result of all the work as you pass through flourishing villages, each with its small reservoir where they swim and wash clothes and with gullies channelling the water to all the fields. It is also possible to head directly to *Zhengzhou* by bus; but this would make for a long and uncomfortable journey.

SOUTHWARD FROM THE YELLOW RIVER

As the railway line runs south from Zhengzhou to WUHAN in Hubei province it passes XUCHANG, a tobacco growing centre with an old and famous bridge. Nearby is BAISHA ZHEN whose **Song Tomb** frescoes are in the Zhengzhou provincial museum. Further south, near the border with Hubei, **XINYANG** was the furthest limit to which carriages could travel in the past before coming up against the Tongbai mountain barrier, which separates the two provinces. The **Zhou tomb** nearby, excavated in 1956, produced a huge and splendid collection of bronzes, bells and lacquerware – and even a wooden bed: the pieces are scattered among museums in Beijing and the provincial collections. A few miles south is JIGONGSHAN, a mountain zone whose hotels and bungalows survive from its former days as a refuge from the summer heat. Another spur of the railway links Luoyang with YICHANG on the Yangzi river, passing industrial NANYANG and XIANGFAN (which also connects with WUHAN).

TRAVEL DETAILS

Trains

From Xi'an: Huashan (2 daily, 2hrs), Luoyang (10, 8hrs), Zhengzhou (10, 10hrs), Bao Ji (12, 16hrs), Chengdu (8, 19hrs)

From Huashan: Xi'an (2, 2hrs)

From Luoyang: Xi'an (10, 8hrs), Zhengzhou (10, 2hrs)

From Zhengzhou: Anyang (15, 3hrs), Shijiazhuang (15, 6hrs), Beijing (15, 10hrs), Taiyuan (4, 8hrs), Wuhan (10, 9hrs), Kaifeng (7, 1hr), Xuzhou (7, 6hrs), Luoyang (10, 2hrs), Xi'an (19, 10hrs)

From Kaifeng: Zhengzhou (7, 1hr), Xuzhou (7, 5hrs)

From Anyang: Shijiazhuang (15, 3hrs), Beijing (15, 8hrs), Zhengzhou (15, 3hrs), Linxian (3, 2hrs)

Buses

From Xi'an: Huashan (3, 3hrs)

From Luoyang: Dengfeng (Shaolin) (6, 3hrs)

From Zhengzhou: Dengfeng (8, 3hrs)

From Linxian: Anyang (3, 2hrs)

Flights

Airports at Xi'an, Zhengzhou and Yanan

ANYANG	安阳	**LUOYANG**	洛阳
BAO JI	宝鸡	**NANYANG**	南阳
DENGFENG	登封	**SHAOLIN**	少林
GONG XIAN	巩县	**XI'AN**	西安
HUA SHAN	华山	**XIANYANG**	咸阳
KAIFENG	开封	**XINYANG**	信阳
LINTONG	临潼	**YAN'AN**	延安
LINXIAN	林县	**ZHENGZHOU**	郑州

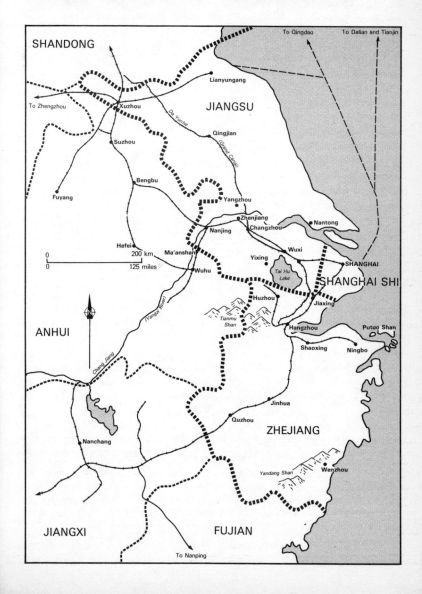

SHANGHAI SHI – JIANGSU – ZHEJIANG

Shanghai, for years Asia's leading city, still dominates China's eastern seaboard in every way. The infamy of its role as the first base of empire in mainland China, as a place of the most extreme wealth and the direst poverty, and as the most decadent city in the world was largely wiped out by liberation in 1949, but Shanghai remains a city apart. The Shanghainese have kept their reputation for style and sophistication and the city today produces one sixth of the nation's exports with the best-paid, highest-skilled labour force in the country. Even the most culture-shocked western eyes cannot fail to notice the difference.

In historical terms, though, Shanghai barely features – a fishing port propelled to prominence little over a century ago by the Opium Wars and the subsequent explosion of foreign interests in China. **Jiangsu** and **Zhejiang** by contrast, the provinces which flank the metropolitan area, have a combined history as rich as any in China. Coastal provinces both, they are linked by the Grand Canal, which flows down from the north to end at Hangzhou, and they also share the rich benefits of the Yangzi Basin. The greenery here, and the hefty crops of rice and vegetables, are instant evidence of the river's irrigational benefits, and this wealth combined with superb communications meant that the major towns developed early into important trading centres. By the 6C BC the area was part of the state of Wu, and it had already developed its own distinctive culture by the time it was annexed to the Qin empire in 223BC. After the Han empire broke up and northern tribes moved into China several southern regimes had their capitals in local cities, but the real push came when the Sui reunited China and built the *Grand Canal* to link the Yangzi with the Yellow River and ultimately to allow trade to flow freely between here and Beijing. One of three key trade routes in China, the Canal is some 1000km long.

The more important of the canal cities, **Hangzhou** and **Nanjing** above all, have always acted as a counterweight to the centralising tendencies of Beijing. Both have been capitals of China at various times – Nanjing on several occasions. Other cities – **Wuxi, Suzhou, Yangzhou, Ningbo** – have developed into significant manufacturing centres and are once again enjoying a boom which has put Jiangsu and Zhejiang back among the most prosperous provinces in China. As well as history, you'll find water wherever you go – the rivers, canals, waterways and lakes which web the plain give it much of its character. Warm, wet and fertile, bounded on the east by the sea and to north, west and south by hills, this region is intensively drained, canalised, irrigated and farmed: a country of rice, fish, fruit and silk, with tea on the slopes and wealth in the towns.

SHANGHAI

> If it was rich beyond a man's wildest dreams, the wealthy who went shopping had to pick their way carefully between corpses in the streets; it had the tallest skyscrapers in Asia – their plate glass windows overlooking the most scrofulous slums; it had the grandest boulevards, laid out with care and pride – and jutting off them narrow alleys with only open drains to carry away human excrement. It had Chinese courtesans who were maintained in the style of princesses, and penniless prostitutes at every corner. Even the climate was extreme . . . the rich cocooned themselves in furs, in a city where sables were cheap enough to be used as car rugs, while the poor, huddled in unheated tenements, died in their thousands.

When the Communists marched into Shanghai in May 1949 they were entering the most important business and trading centre in Asia, an international port where vast fortunes were made while millions lived in absolute poverty. Whichever side you were on, life in Shanghai – as described by *Noel Barber* above – was rarely one of moderation. China's most prosperous city, in large part European and American financed, it introduced Asia to electric light, boasted more cars than the rest of the country put together, and created for its rich a world of European-style mansions, tree-lined boulevards, chic café society, horse racing and exclusive gentlemen's clubs. Alongside, and equally part of the legend, lay the city famed for adventure, decadence and prostitution, of bloated bodies floating in on the tides, of beggars, starving children and coolies, of five and a half million shanty dwellers in thrall to their daily bowl of rice.

Inevitably since liberation the bright lights have dimmed – modern Shanghai is neither modern nor, except by Chinese standards, cosmopolitan. Yet despite a 35-year policy of deliberate exclusion of western influences, the city remains very distinct. Walk the streets and you'll feel it, in the people, the buildings, the air. Unlike Beijing, or almost any other Chinese city, Shanghai has never been rebuilt; it is virtually impossible to move about the centre, where the tiny streets, hung with washing, are permanently jammed. Only along the waterfront, amid the solid grandeur of 1930s architecture, is there a sense of space – and here you feel the past more strongly than ever, its outward forms, shabby and battered, still very much a working part of the city. The Shanghainese themselves are different too. They speak a dialect which is incomprehensible even to other Chinese and they have a reputation for style and for business sense. During the Cultural Revolution western excesses like curled hair and holding hands in public survived in Shanghai, and nowadays you'll find locals more eager to approach foreigners than perhaps anywhere else in the country.

Before the **Opium Wars**, Shanghai was little more than a small fishing town. Afterwards, the British moved in (under the Treaty of Nanking

(1842) to be rapidly followed by the French in 1847, the Americans (1863) and the Japanese (1895). Traders were allowed to live under their own laws in a series of privileged zones, leasing the land on an indefinite time scale. By 1900 the city's favourable position, close to the coast and to the Yangzi river, main trade route to the major silk and tea-producing regions, had allowed it to develop into a sizeable port and manufacturing centre with a cheap workforce swollen by the numbers who, during the Taiping rebellion, took shelter in the foreign settlements from the slaughter outside. Once established, peasants were attracted in their thousands to the apparent prosperity of the city, and to jobs in the factories.

Here China's first urban proletariat grew up, and the squalid living conditions, mass unemployment and glaring abuses by the foreign investors growing rich on Chinese labour made Shanghai a natural forcing ground for **revolutionary politics**. The Chinese Communist Party was founded in the city in 1921, its growth accelerated by the notoriously brutal suppression of a series of strikes in 1927. Since the Revolution, too, it has remained a centre of radical ideas – unable to get any action from the Beijing bureaucracy, Mao launched the Cultural Revolution here in 1966, and it was here that the Red Guards were most active; later, following Mao's death, Shanghai was the powerbase of the Gang of Four in the struggle for the succession.

Although some old colonials might look at the city and regret the passing of the 'good old days', Shanghai in fact remains the nation's premier industrial base, and is still something of a showplace. Following **Liberation,** the Communists set out consciously to eradicate the excesses of the foreign-dominated past and create a truly Chinese City of the People. The worst slums were knocked down to be replaced by apartments, and since 1949 the housing stock has doubled. Even now, though nothing like on the scale of the pre-War days, the variety and quality of goods in the shops attracts people from all over China: to shop on the Nanjing Road is truly to have made it.

Some problems remain. Above all Shanghai continues to suffer acute **overcrowding** – even official statistics give the average inhabitant living space little larger than a double bed and in practice this often means three generations of a family sleeping in one room. The air, too, is badly **polluted**. As a centre of huge oil refineries, chemical and metallurgical plants, Shanghai is the home of the *Yellow Dragons* – sulphurous clouds pouring from the factory chimneys. About four million tons of untreated industrial and domestic waste flow daily into the Huangpu River, the city's main source of drinking water. And finally the 10 per cent **unemployment** rate is noticeably higher than that of other major cities. It's euphemistically termed 'waiting for a job', but young people may have to wait up to a year before they get work.

Underlying all of these is a problem which applies not only to Shanghai, though its consequences are more obvious here: **overpopulation**. Ironi-cally enough it's a problem which only really arose with the improved conditions following Liberation: after years of civil war, disease and starvation were drastically reduced, slashing death rates, and at the same time the official policy was to encourage large families. Mao himself believed that more people would mean more productive labour, proclaiming that 'every stomach comes with two hands attached'. Between 1950 and 1958 the city grew by almost half, adding 2.4 million. And over a million more flocked in in search of work. Today, though closed to internal migration for over 25 years, Shanghai continues to grow, to the point where a population of over 12 million makes it one of the largest (and most congested) cities in the world.

ORIENTATION
Getting your bearings

Though the layout of Shanghai is less obviously geometrical than that of Beijing, it's quite easy to find your way around once you're familiar with the landmarks. Architecturally this is the most westernised of Chinese cities, with the former foreign concessions lending a distinctly western flavour which even the odd Soviet-inspired government building can't remove.

First get hold of a large-scale **map**. English versions are widely available in the large hotels or from the *Friendship Store* near the Bund, but the best in this case is not the cartographic production but a glossy, square-shaped one produced by the *China Travel and Tourism Press*. It has an unmistakeable Remy Martin cover and there's always a large supply in **CITS** at the *Peace Hotel*. It gives clear information on streets and sights, but not on the buses for which you'll need another, Chinese only, map. One warning: most maps imply that Shanghai is compact, with only small distances between central locations. This is not the case – even the shortest journey usually demands a two- or three-stop bus ride.

It helps to think of Shanghai (the name means 'above the sea') as built around the intersection of two waterways: the **Huangpu River** which flows from the north-east and forms a natural eastern boundary; and the **Suzhou Creek** which runs from west to east across the centre of the city and delineates the northern edge of the most interesting part of the city. Beyond it to the north lies a large industrial and council housing conurbation which, apart from Hongkou Park and a few Lu Xun monu-ments, contains little of real interest.

The best place to get your bearings is from the junction of the Huangpu and Suzhou, just opposite **Huangpu Park**. Across the Suzhou Creek to the north stands the towering red-brick fortress of the *Shanghai*

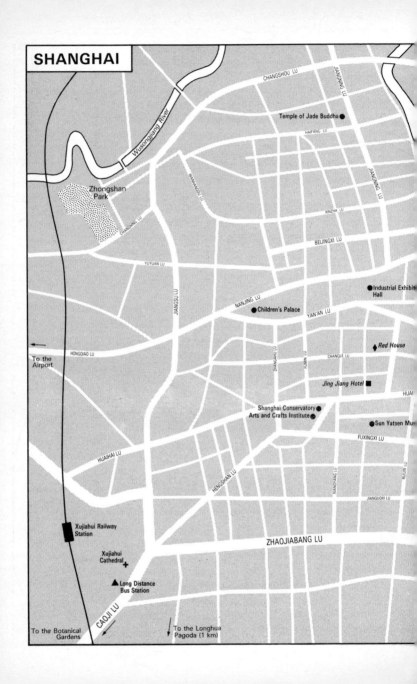

SHANGHAI

Wusongjiang River

CHANGSHOU LU

JIANGNING LU

Temple of Jade Buddha ●

HAIFANG LU

WANHANGDU LU

JIANGNING LU

Zhongshan Park

XINZHA LU

CHANGNING LU

BEIJINGXI LU

YUYUAN LU

JIANGSU LU

● Industrial Exhibit
Hall

NANJING LU

● Children's Palace

YAN'AN LU

ZHANGSHU LU

FUMIN LU

♦ Red House

CHANGLE LU

To the
Airport

HONGQIAO LU

Jing Jiang Hotel ■

HUAI

Shanghai Conservatory ●
Arts and Crafts Institute ●

● Sun Yatsen Mus

FUXINGXI LU

HUAIHAI LU

HENGSHAN LU

XIANGYANG LU

RUJIN LU

JIANGUOXI LU

Xujiahui Railway
Station

ZHAOJIABANG LU

Xujiahui
Cathedral ✚

▲ Long Distance
Bus Station

To the Botanical
Gardens

CAOJI LU

To the Longhua
Pagoda (1 km)

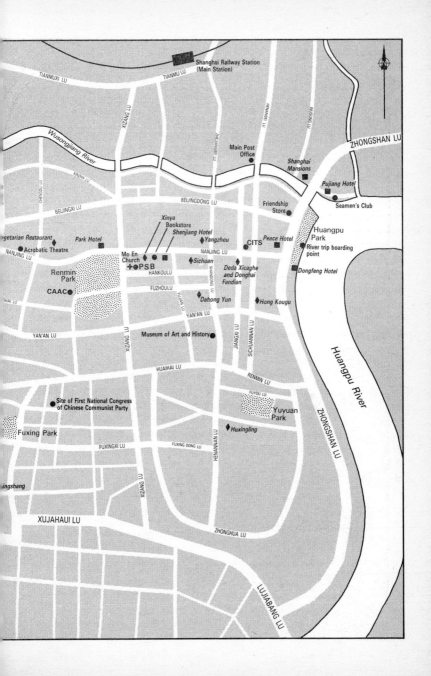

Mansions, not the most exciting of the city's relics but now a hotel whose 13th-floor roof garden offers tremendous views over most of the city. South from here, along the western bank of the Huangpu, runs **the Bund** – officially Zhongshan Lu – centrepiece of the old financial quarter. Almost immediately on the right is the former British Consulate, until recently the **Friendship Store**, first of a whole series of impressive capitalist façades which now for the most part house Chinese government agencies. On the river side, just below Huangpu Park, is the embarkation point for the **Huangpu river trip**.

A couple of hundred yards down, the Bund meets the eastern end of **Nanjing Lu**, Shanghai's principal east–west artery and reputedly the busiest street in China. Like all east–west routes it takes its name from that of a city: north–south roads are named after provinces. Heading along Nanjing Lu past the *Peace Hotel* (on both sides – **CITS** is on the right) you enter a vast commercial thoroughfare lined with restaurants, coffee houses, department stores and specialist shops. After a mile or so, the **People's Park** marks the very centre of the city. Continuing west, past the giant *Park Hotel* (on the right) and the television tower (a useful landmark, on the left) Nanjing Lu leads eventually to **Shanghai Zoo**, and to **Hongqiao Airport**, 15km away.

Xizang Lu, which crosses Nanjing immediately before the People's Park, forms the main north–south axis. Northwards it leads across Suzhou Creek towards the **railway station**, and beyond on to Baoshan Lu and the route to **Hangkou Park**, greenest spot in Shanghai and site of the Lu Xun tomb and museum. The rest of this northern area, once famous for grotesque slums, is nowadays covered in anonymous housing blocks, though in the **Fangualong district** a few hovels have been carefully preserved as a reminder. To the south the first major intersection on Xizang is with Huaihai Lu, heading westwards into the heart of the old **French Concession**. Much of the building here is distinctly French colonial, providing a marked contrast with the ghastly Russian-built **Main Exhibition Hall** on nearby Yan'an Lu. Along Huaihai you'll pass close to the *Jing Jiang Hotel*, just to the north on Maoming Lu, and to **Fuxing Park**, south, where the first national congress of the Chinese Communist Party is reputed to have met at the site of the former residence of Dr Sun Yatsen. Eventually Huaihai joins Hengshan Lu, running south-west past the **bus terminus** to **Longhua Park and Pagoda** at the city's southernmost point.

The circular boundaries of the **old Chinese city**, the longest continuously inhabited part of Shanghai, lie just to the east off Xizang Lu. It's a fascinating quarter of narrow streets, alleyways and marketplaces, and a great place to spend some time. Right at the heart lies the **Yu Garden**, a fully restored classical Chinese garden which is the haunt of every tour group in China: nearby is the **tea-house** whose zig-zag wooden bridge is the city's most famous landmark.

Planes, trains, buses and boats

Arriving in Shanghai is a revelation, particularly after the dourness of Beijing. You're immediately struck by the liveliness, the pace and the chaotic congestion of the place. What to do on arrival depends largely on your arrangements for accommodation, but if you've no fixed plans head for **CITS** and a map. The office is open from 8.30–11.30 and 1.30–5.30 and though they're reluctant to book a room for you, you'll at least get the lie of the land.

BY AIR you'll arrive at Hongqiao Airport, 15km west of the city. There's a **CAAC bus** (cost 80fen) from the airport to their office at 789 Yan'an Lu, just south of the People's Park. From here take a no.48 bus six stops east to Huangpu Park, and walk back to CITS. **Outward tickets** can be bought from CAAC (open 8.30–12 and 1–5) but early booking is essential.

TRAINS mostly come into the dilapidated old railway station just north of the city centre, across the Suzhou Creek. It's an undersized tribute to Chinese people's recently acquired travel bug, and night and day is a seething mass of people. Getting into the centre can be a gruelling process, not least the 15 minutes or so it takes just to get out of the station. Now is the time to take a **taxi**. There are buses into town, but the bus stops are all a long way from the station, and the queues around here are enormous. You'll get few of the normal good-humoured smiles as you fill up enough standing room for seven squashed bodies with your bag. The taxi rank is just on your right as you come out of the station, and though it's always busy, everyone accepts that foreigners get the first cab, and you'll be offending them if you refuse. It costs about ¥5 to CITS and up to ¥15 if you want to tour around the hotels. Or if you are really committed to **buses,** try a no.18 trolley or a 66 bus from Henan Lu, just south-east of the station. For CITS change one stop later to an eastbound 37 or 20 and, again, get off one stop later.

Rail tickets from Shanghai are sold at CITS, and if you don't mind paying the full fare plus a couple of yuan mark-up this is the place to buy them. One disadvantage is that the office only seems to have a small allocation, particularly of hard sleepers, and often they'll claim to have no tickets left at all. If you don't decide fast enough where and when you want to go, you'll have to follow the route to Chinese-rate tickets which begins at Shanghai's **principal booking office** at 230 Beijing Lu. Hundreds of foreigners trying the same thing before have made the authorities aware of what's happening, so unless you engage the services of an obliging local you may have problems. As an alternative you can always buy a ticket to an intermediary station and try again there. For **journeys within 24 hours** all tickets are sold at the station.

BUSES too run regularly between Shanghai and Hangzhou and Suzhou, though they tend to be slower than the train. The long-distance **bus**

station is in the south-west of the city: for CITS take a no.42 bus eastwards to the end of its route.

If it's in any way possible, however, *the* way to arrive in Shanghai is by – **BOAT**, either from Hong Kong or from towns along the coast or inland up the Yangzi. All of them dock close to the Bund, within walking distance of CITS: south from Gongping Lu and the **International Passenger Quay** if you've come from Hong Kong or the northern coastal towns; north from **Shilipu Wharf** for arrivals from Yangzi or coastal towns to the south.

Leaving by boat is spectacular too, and with tickets cheaper and travelling conditions better than on the train, it deserves serious consideration. Tickets for the Yangzi boats are sold at the **internal shipping office** at 222 Renmin Lu: there are four classes, and 2nd will still leave you change from the equivalent hard sleeper fare on the train. This office also handles **coastal** reservations to destinations such as Qingdao, Fuzhou, Ningbo Xiamen and Guangzhou – new routes are opening all the time, so if you want to go anywhere which looks passable by river or sea it's worth checking at one of the ticket offices (CITS are usually the last to know about any new services).

Finally the **cruises to Hong Kong**, from the International Passenger Quay, are known as one of the great journeys of Asia – though you may find them rather less exciting. Three ships, the *SS Shanghai*, *SS Jingjiang* and *SS Hanxi*, make the journey every five days – each equipped with swimming pools, restaurants, discos and clean, comfortable berths. Tickets for the 60-hour trip are available from CITS (with mark-up), the *China Ocean Shipping Agency* at 255 Jiangxi Lu or from the Beijing CITS office.

Getting about – local transport

Local **buses** are a perfectly efficient way of getting around Shanghai, though they are extremely crowded – local tradition has it that that at least three people fight over every available space. Outside rush hours – which are much as you'd expect, with long queues early morning and late evening – it's generally not too bad, and buses run from 4am through to 10.30pm. **Bus maps** mark all stops clearly with a small dot: trolley buses are marked in green and ordinary ones red. **Fares** vary between 3 and 20 fen, but a trip across town usually works out at 7 or 8 fen.

The following are the most useful **routes**:

North–south

41   From Longhua Park to the railway station via the Jing Jiang Hotel and TV tower.

46   From the People's Park to the railway station via the Park Hotel.

19	(trolley) From the Jade Buddha temple to Gongping Lu wharf via Beijing Lu.
18	(trolley) From Hongkou Park to Longhua Lu via Xizang Lu.
66	From Zhabei Park to Longhua Lu via Shanghai Museum and the old city.

East–west

| 37 | From Pingliang Lu to Jingan Park via the Bund and Nanjing Lu. |
| 12 | (trolley) From Shilipu Wharf to Longhua Lu via Renmin Lu, Huaihai Lu and Fuxing Park. |

The availability of **taxis** also tends to vary with the time of day – but most of the time they're easy enough to get hold of, either at the hotels or by telephone: 564444 for the *Shanghai Municipal Taxi Co.*; 536363 for the *Friendship Taxi Service*. Beware that the supply has a nasty habit of drying up whenever you need to be somewhere urgently. The one place they are constantly available is at the Jing Jiang Hotel. As usual fares vary according to the quality of the car but, if you can choose, some of the old Shanghai saloons are fun – well worth a ride in themselves. What you really need to explore the city is a **bike** but sadly there's nowhere yet which hires them out – perhaps in recognition of the obvious danger involved in negotiating rush-hour Nanjing Lu.

If you ever do **get lost** you'll find no shortage of locals speaking excellent English who are almost desperate to help. Shanghai has always been the major linguistic centre in China but it's only recently that foreigners have been allowed in in any numbers. I have found people taking me miles out of their way in order to be helpful, and many will try to arrange a meeting at a quieter time just to try out their English.

Finding a place to stay

Many of Shanghai's **hotels** are stunning visual legacies of the city's decadent past. If you can't afford to stay in upmarket residences like the *Peace* and the *Park* hotels you must at least take a look; especially at their dining rooms, which without exception boast some of the finest art-deco design in the world. They've been left exactly as they were, a useful contingency for the authorities in the quest for tourist income but also, one suspects, as a warning to the locals of the dire consequences of capitalist self-indulgence. Ironically enough, the *Jing Jiang*, the *Peace*, the *Park* and the *Shanghai Mansions* are all under greater threat today than at any time since 1949, not from the Chinese but from the hordes of American and Japanese tourists and businessmen who value modern comforts more than history, and plastic more than wood. Already large-scale modernisation has begun to overtake the Jing Jiang and Shanghai Mansions – it surely can't be long before the builders move in elsewhere.

The **Jing Jiang Hotel** (tel.534242) at 57 Maoming Lu in the heart of the French Concessionary District, consists of three massive blocks arranged north to south between Nanjing Lu and Huaihai Lu. In the absence of an alternative it has become the temporary base for foreign dignitaries who visit the city – the most famous being Nixon in 1972, and Reagan 12 years later. The north block is definitely the place to head for, with its charming ground-floor bars and lounges and the massive 8th-floor restaurant which serves a delicious western breakfast. The centre and south blocks have recently been extensively revamped and provide a comparatively comfortable refuge from the bustle of the city, though much of the work is superficial and the hotel's famous cockroach community remains largely intact. You can get doubles for under ¥50, and they usually have room, since they're not allowed to book up in advance on the tour groups in case important personages come to town. Opposite the main entrance is a new row of shops – the most exclusive in China – including a supermarket which sells such rare treats as chocolate and biscuits.

The **Shanghai Mansions** (tel.246260) across the bridge from the junction of Huangpu and Suzhou is a massive 22-storey skyscraper with over 250 rooms. It's the most expensive of the smart hotels (doubles from ¥150 if you don't have a specific commercial invitation from the government) and it's also the one to have suffered most from years of neglect. During the Sino-Japanese war it was occupied by the Japanese, who had little respect for its condition, and since then the most illustrious resident has been *Jiang Qing*, who issued a decree during the Cultural Revolution banning barges and sampans from travelling up the Huangpu or Suzhou while she was asleep. Today the place is worth seeing for its façade, its creepy atmospheric corridors, and for a 13th-storey roof garden with the best views in Shanghai.

The finest of the pre-Liberation hotels are the **Park** (tel.225224) and the **Peace** (tel.211244) both on Nanjing Lu and described in the text on pages 201 and 199. There are a few relatively cheap rooms in each, but they're hard to come by: the Park has doubles starting at ¥60 and triples from ¥70, usually all full; the Peace has some doubles for ¥80, most on semi-permanent loan to western businessmen. In practice you might well have to pay over ¥100.

Cheaper rooms do exist, but finding one can involve a time-consuming and frustrating journey around the city. CITS won't help out, so it's really a question of either telephoning, or if no one speaks English making a personal tour, to as many places as possible. In any event don't believe the standard CITS response that there's nothing to be had and you'll have to stay miles out, but do check out cleanliness and reports of strange wildlife inhabiting some of the dorms. Other travellers are probably the most reliable source of information on the current state of affairs. A couple of usually available standbys are the *Jing Jiang*, which has a dorm section in the wing on Maoming Lu, though the management is inexplicably capricious when it comes to allocating beds; or the *Pujiang Hotel* (tel.246388), next door to the Shanghai Mansions, whose dorms at ¥6 are comfortable enough if not the cleanest. **Students** might have more luck – some have been known to find beds in excellent student accommodation at the Shanghai Conservatory and elsewhere. In general, though, dirt and vermin afflict all cheap accommodation in Shanghai – reflecting the city's dismal standards of sanitation – and this is one place where it's probably worth splashing out a little.

If you can't afford, or can't get into, the big old places, there are several **mid-priced options**. Try, for example, the *Hotel Shenjiang* (tel.225115) at 740 Hankou Lu, off Xizang Lu. Traditionally Chinese only, it has recently started taking foreigners – excellent rooms from ¥40 double, ¥25 single. Similar prices apply at the *Rui Jin Guest House* (118 Rui Jin 2 Lu; 372653) an elegant old villa once owned by a brother-in-law of Chiang Kai-shek, complete with panelled dining room and antique furniture. Slightly further out, the *Jingan Guest House* at 370 Huashan Lu (tel.563050) has a few rooms for under ¥30 a night. It's on the no.15 trolley bus route from the railway station, set in spacious grounds; far enough away, though, to make phoning first essential.

With accommodation being at such a premium in Shanghai, you will find things very much easier if you can **arrange rooms in advance**, at least for the first couple of nights. In practice what this means is persuading a friendly hotel keeper or CITS official in some other town to ring up and do it for you. It is well worth spending over your budget to do this if necessary. Similarly, if you have nothing arranged, take the first place you are offered and think about changing later.

THE CITY
The Bund – Wall Street of the east

The most impressive street in Shanghai has always been **the Bund**, nowadays known, officially at least, as Zhongshan Lu. During Shanghai's riotous heyday it was the most famous street in the east: the city's financial centre but also a hectic working harbour where anything from tiny sailing junks to ocean-going freighters unloaded under the guns of British – and later American and Japanese – warships. Everything – from silk and tea to heavy industrial machinery – and everyone arrived here: wealthy foreigners disembarking to pick their way to one of the grand hotels through crowds of beggars, hawkers, black marketeers, shoeshine boys and overladen coolies. Named after an old Anglo-Indian term, *bunding* (the embanking of a muddy foreshore), the Bund was in every sense old Shanghai's commercial heart; the river on one side, the offices of the leading banks and trading houses on the other.

It begins at the confluence of the Huangpu and the Suzhou Creek, by **Waibaidu Bridge**, and runs south for about a mile to Jinling Donglu, formerly *Rue du Consulat*. At the outbreak of the Sino-Japanese War in 1937 the bridge formed a no-man's land between the Japanese occupied areas north of Suzhou Creek and the International Settlement – it was guarded at each end by Japanese and British sentries. Today, though most shipping docks further downstream, the waterways are still well-used thoroughfares, and the Bund itself is a popular place to stroll after dinner or to exercise in the early morning. Get here before 7am and you'll find hundreds of people taking their daily workout, while tiny Huangpu Park, at the northern end, is packed with Chinese practising Tai Chi. As an introduction to the Bund – and if you haven't already done so – try crossing the bridge and heading up to the *Shanghai Mansions'* roof garden.

On the other side of the bridge stands one of the cornerstones of British interests in old Shanghai, the former **British Consulate**.* Still set in immaculate gardens with velvet lawns, behind high walls once guarded by Sikh soldiers, its main building, nearest the gates, housed until recently the **Friendship Store**, now in an adjacent new building. Opposite is **Huangpu Park** (open 5–9), formerly the British public gardens. Here too there were Sikh troops, ready to enforce the rules which forbade dogs or Chinese from entering (unless they were servants accompanying their employer). After protests the regulations were relaxed to admit 'well-dressed' Chinese, who had to apply for a special entry permit.

Walking on down the Bund you'll pass a succession of grandiose neo-classical edifices – built to house the great foreign enterprises. **Jardine Matheson**, still flourishing in Hong Kong (though now planning to move to Bermuda), was perhaps the daddy of them all. It was William Jardine, known to the Chinese as the 'Iron-headed old rat', who did more than any other individual to precipitate the Opium Wars, and open Shanghai up to foreign trade. Initially Canton was the only port open to foreign ships, and the opium which constituted the majority of China's imports was officially illegal. Jardine succeeded in persuading the British government that in the interests of Free Trade they should use force to open China up: Canton was blockaded in June 1840, Shanghai invaded two years later, and by the eventual Treaty of Nanking Shanghai was one of five Chinese ports in which foreigners were allowed to trade and to live under their own laws in the foreign concessions. Jardines were the first

*The British have a Consul-General again, the first in 25 years, in an attempt to drum up business on the back of goodwill created by the Hong Kong agreement. His efforts to boost British tradition include driving a specially imported royal blue London taxi and going about in a cape and deer-stalker hat.

foreign concern to buy land in Shanghai and their base, midway between the Friendship Store and the Peace Hotel, is now occupied by the **China Textiles Export Corporation**. Jardines themselves maintain only a small office in the Shanghai Mansions.

The **Peace Hotel** straddles the corner with Nanjing Lu: you'll find yourself visiting at least once, if only to do battle with **CITS** which occupies a counter in the main building on the north side of Nanjing Lu (open 8.30–11.30 and 1.30–5.30). This wing of the hotel is a relic of another of the great trading houses, **Sassoon**'s and was originally known as Sassoon House. Like Jardines, the Sassoon business empire was built on opium trading, but by the early years of this century the family fortune had mostly been sunk into Shanghai real estate. Ellice Sassoon, builder of Sassoon House, was a legendary high-lifer in a city where excess was the norm, keeping a string of racehorses and proclaiming 'there's only one race greater than the Jews, and that's the Derby'. Part of his office building was occupied by the *Cathay Hotel* (you may still find its china in use in the Peace Hotel today), which was *the* place to be seen in pre-War Shanghai: it offered its guests a private plumbing system fed by a spring on the outskirts of town, marble baths with silver taps and vitreous china lavatories imported from Britain. Noel Coward is supposed to have been staying here when he completed *Private Lives*. Sassoon lived long enough to see his hotel virtually destroyed by the Japanese, but also long enough to get most of his money away to the Bahamas. The Peace Hotel today caters mainly for business people, but it's well worth a visit for the **bar**, with its now legendary jazz band, and to walk around the upper floors and take in the faded art deco elegance. The smaller wing on the south side of Nanjing Lu was originally the *Palace Hotel*, built around 1906.

Carrying on down the Bund, the **Customs House** is one of the few buildings to have retained its original function, though its distinctive clock tower has been adapted to chime *The East is Red* at 6 every morning and evening. Right next to this, and also with an easily recognisable domed roofline, the former headquarters of the **Hong Kong and Shanghai Bank** (built in 1921) is one of the most imposing of all the Bund façades; as it's the local party HQ and offices of the city government, however, there's little chance of seeing inside.

Finally you'll come to the **Dongfeng Hotel**, which until Liberation was the men-only *Shanghai Club*, a little piece of Mayfair transported east. For years now the *Dongfeng* has been a Chinese-only hotel, but like the Peace much of the interior remains intact and there's still a strong feel here of the Shanghai of the 1920s and 1930s. The lobby in particular, with its cream pillars, black and white tiled floor, sweeping staircase and panelled lift, can have changed little. The club's showpiece, the 100 foot mahogany Long Bar, where the wealthiest of the city's merchants and their European guests propped themselves at cocktail hour, has been partitioned into three. There's a restaurant which is open to foreigners (see Food section), a room used mainly by wedding parties, and, in the former smoking room, a Chinese-only dormitory.

The Huangpu river

As an alternative or in addition to the walk, a good view of the Bund can be had from the Huangpu. The **river trips**, about 3½ hours in all, leave from the waterfront by the park – you can book tickets (at a small kiosk) for the following day's journeys, though it's rarely essential. There are trips at 8.30am and at 1.30pm, but since there are often several boats leaving at each of these times you should check your booking carefully. There are three classes: in third you'll be among Chinese, on a hard seat and amid a great deal of noise – the views are perfectly good but tickets are rarely sold to foreigners; second – excellent value at ¥8 – entitles you to a plastic table outside with endless tea, sweets and orange; first has four-person cabins furnished with great overstuffed armchairs and white anti-macassars, its Chinese passengers mostly stay inside watching videos. On the way back, should you get bored with the views, there's usually a Chinese juggling act on the lower deck.

The Huangpu is still a vital resource for Shanghai, and the trip down to its confluence with the Yangzi will give some idea of the vast amount of shipping which still uses the port: one third of all China's trade passes through here. It has to be said, though, that the thick brownish waters are not exactly inviting. Almost four million tons of untreated waste are discharged into the river daily – including sewage and high levels of mercury and phenol. The Huangpu is also Shanghai's chief source of drinking water! At least it no longer serves as the burial ground remembered by J. G. Ballard:

The light advanced across the river, picking out the paper flowers that covered its surface like garlands discarded by the admirers of sailors. Every night in Shanghai those Chinese too poor to pay for the burial of their relatives would launch the bodies from the funeral piers at Nantao, decking the coffins with paper flowers. Carried away on one tide, they came back with the next, returning to the waterfront of Shanghai with all the other debris abandoned by the city. Meadows of paper flowers drifted on the running tide, and clumped in miniature floating gardens around the old men and women, the young mothers and small children, whose swollen bodies seemed to have been fed during the night by the patient Yangtse.

Nanjing Lu

From dawn to dusk, Nanking Road was one huge traffic jam. From dusk to dawn, when the neon lights were winking, it was Shanghai's most patronised promenade, filled with impassive waif-like (but tough) Chinese or sad eyed White Russians waiting for foreign "escorts" or dancing at Roxy's, which had a sign, 'This nightclub will close at 6am unless requested to remain open longer by our patrons'.

Noel Barber. The Fall of Shanghai.

Nanjing Lu stretches for six miles and intersects 26 streets. In Imperial days it was described as a cross between Broadway and Oxford Street, and it must still rate as one of the busiest shopping streets in the world – only the disappearance of many foreign and luxury goods marks the changes it has seen. There are four huge **department stores** which make fascinating visiting if you want to see what the Chinese themselves buy: take a look in particular at No.10 Store, formerly the Japanese *Wing On* department store (no.635), and the grandest of them all, No.1 store, at no.830 just before the People's Park. This is the largest store in the country, supposedly stocking every item which is available to Chinese workers. There are specialist shops for **luxury goods** too: silk from a shop at 257 Nanjing Donglu; jewellery at no.428; *Xinhua Bookstore* at no.345, pottery and porcelain at no.550 and 1698 Nanjing Xilu. You can also buy scrolls and wallhangings at the *Shanghai Arts and Crafts Store* at no.190. Bear in mind, though, if the crush gets too much, that the Friendship Store also stocks almost anything you can find here.

If you do weather the crush among the shoppers, there are a couple of treats in store. First is the **Xin Xin Barber's shop** at no.546. This, the most famous hairdresser in Shanghai, employs around 80 cutters, all of them permanently occupied. Should you fancy a trim, the ground floor is for men, the first for women and the second a beauty salon, but the true speciality of the house is traditional massage: just lie back in a special vibrating barber's chair and a wonderfully adept masseur will clear your tensions away for just ¥5. Also great for a spot of relaxation is the old **Park Hotel**, 170 Nanjing Xilu. At 24 storeys it's the tallest and for my money the most stylish hotel in Shanghai. It once had a reputation for superb food and for its dances, when the roof would be rolled back to allow guests to dance under the stars. The art deco restaurants are still in use, and the one which serves western and Chinese food is particularly good – with views right across the city. Rather cheaper, sit back in the ground-floor lounge with a coffee and brandy, and reflect on the place's past. Mao, for one, always stayed here when he was in Shanghai.

Under the windows lie **Renmin (People's) Park** and **Renmin Square**. This originally was the site of the racecourse, later converted into a sports ground by Chiang Kai-shek who decided it was unwise to pander to the Chinese passion for gambling. During the war the stadium served as a holding camp for prisoners and as a temporary mortuary. Afterwards most of it was levelled, part paved to form the dusty concrete expanse of People's Square; the rest landscaped with grass and trees to become the park. The former grandstand is now a library.

Nanjing Xilu (Nanjing Road West) was known to Shanghailanders – the Europeans who made their homes here – as Bubbling Well Road, after a spring which used to gush at the far end. In those days it was one of the smartest addresses in town, leading off into the tree-lined streets where westerners' mock-tudor mansions and immaculate lawns sheltered behind high walls. For the Chinese this was traditionally Jing'an Lu, named for the Jing'an shrine (shrine of tranquillity) which now houses a plastics factory.

If by the People's Park you turn left instead, onto **Xizang Lu**, you'll find the **Mo-En Church** a couple of blocks down on the left (no.316). Visiting a church in Shanghai is an extraordinary experience, and Mo-En is the handiest for the centre of town. The fervour of the crowd has to be seen to be believed, and though the service is in Chinese only, visitors are more than welcome – you'll be given a seat in the balcony overlooking the packed congregation; nothing like you've ever seen in a church before. There are services on Tuesday and Friday evenings as well as various times on Sunday. While you're here it's worth wandering around the cramped little downtown streets behind you: nothing in particular to see but an interesting place simply to walk about, and not far from the oldest parts of Shanghai.

The Chinese city

The old **walled city**, site of the original township of Shanghai which is said to date back to 1010, covers an area of about 2½ square miles, an oval zone delineated by Renmin Lu in the north and Zhonghua Lu in the south. The easiest approach is to walk down from Nanjing Lu along Henan Lu or Sichuan Lu. Despite the fact that the walls and moats were replaced by tree-lined ring roads in 1912, and that improved sanitation and slum clearance have played their part, the old city retains a separate, distinctive character. The tangle of narrow streets are still something of a haven of free enterprise, with people setting up shop everywhere to create makeshift markets full of cheap trinkets, clothing, and tasty delicacies like prawn crackers and steamed meatballs. In short, this is probably the part of the city to have changed least over the last 40 years, a part where *Noel Barber*'s description is still largely accurate:

Though much of it had been rebuilt over the centuries it retained a sense of intense national pride, so that the white man, if not excluded, was hardly noticed in the labyrinth of narrow, uneven potholed streets flanked by ancient houses. Here, and here alone in Shanghai, he was a pale stranger in another world peopled by grave looking Chinese in long black silk gowns or artisans working in open shops with ivory, jade, brass or gold. . . . Every narrow street was made more garish by its public display of laundry on poles jutting out like flags from the windows of the tall, flimsy buildings. And then suddenly, turning a corner, you would stand entranced before a magnificent latticed front picked out in gold leaf.

Most of the action today is in the north-eastern corner, and especially around the **Yu Garden** (open 8–11.30 and 1–4.30 daily; numerous plans printed on CITS leaflets). This Mandarin's garden may be the prime tourist spot in all Shanghai, and permanently surrounded by tour coaches, but it's certainly not to be missed, and regardless of the crowds is still used by local people simply as a place to sit and chat. The classical Chinese garden was originally created in the C16 by a high official in the Imperial court, one *Pan Yuntuan*: its pools, walkways, bridges and rockeries all planned in honour of his father. When the family fortunes declined, it passed through a number of hands before being purchased in 1760 by a group of Shanghai merchants who restored the fabric and added the west garden. Successive wars during the nineteenth and twentieth centuries also took their toll; the final restoration, and what you see now, dates from 1956.

If you want somewhere to sit awhile after your visit don't be tempted into the foreigners' teashop by the entrance – head instead for the real thing, the **Huxingting** (Heart of Lake Pavilion) **tea-house** (open 7am–5pm) set in a small ornamental lake in the middle of the bazaar, a few minutes walk from the garden. It's a favourite haunt of elderly locals, who sit for hours over their tea. And if you're here in the early morning head for the sidestreets west of the garden to catch the local **food market**. Great trains of stalls shelter under giant glass domes, selling everything from fresh meat, fish, vegetables and eggs, to cheap souvenirs of Shanghai.

Just outside the old city to the north, at 16 Henan Nanlu, is Shanghai's **Museum of Art and History** (open 9–11.30 and 1–6.30), probably the finest museum in the country. Not only does it boast superb collections of pottery, bronzes and painting, but the exhibits are housed in a converted bank which does them more than justice. Displayed over four floors, the items are set out chronologically to demonstrate the evolution of art in China, from the Shang and Zhou periods to the present day. The beauty and the striking modernity of even the most ancient works make it a museum not to miss.

Individual items are rotated, but in general the **first floor** covers the neolithic era and contains a collection of bronzes as well as various pieces of Shang pottery. On the **second** are items from the Qin and Han periods, and a collection of Tang pottery with beautiful examples of crackle glazed ceramics, calligraphy and paintings. The **top floors** include porcelain, calligraphy and lacquerware from the Song, Yuan, Ming and Qing to the present day: modern objects are arranged by province, with jade from Shanghai and Beijing, laquerware from Fuzhou, ivory from Guangzhou and Shanghai, silver filigree from Sichuan and cloisonné from Beijing. There's also a shop on the second floor where you can buy scrolls and ceramics, and a supremely quiet, relaxing rest room.

The French concession

The old **French quarter** lay to the south and west of the International Settlement, abutting the Chinese heart of the city. Through its heart ran Avenue Joffre, now Huaihai Lu, a street littered with cafés and chic tailors and boutiques. Despite its name there weren't in fact many French residents of the area: for the most part it was a relatively low-rent district inhabited by White Russians – who, despite their almost universal claims to wealth and titles back home, were looked down on by other westerners as latecomers who were forced to take jobs which should have been left to the Chinese – and by fairly wealthy Chinese. Frenchtown also offered refuge to political activists: Mao worked in Nanchang Lu (Route Vallon) for two years from 1924; Zhou Enlai lived on Sinan Lu (Rue Massenet) in the early 1940s, and Sun Yatsen, first provisional president after the overthrow of the Manchu dynasty, lived for years in a house on Xiang-shan Lu (then 29 Rue Molière) which is still standing.

Huaihai Lu, which runs parallel to Nanjing Lu and borders the edge of the old city at Renmin Lu, is a pleasant street to walk along – far less crowded than Nanjing Lu and almost equally good for shops. The window displays are delightful, especially the **bakeries** of which there are a great number here. The one at no.919 has particularly good cakes and biscuits. At no.952 there's a corner shop selling '*Face Friend*' cosmetics – with brilliant red nail varnish and 'nourishing powder' on the counter – next to this is a store stocked with home computers, and another block up there's a whole string of clothes stores; something of a haven of decadence still. When they're not buying clothes and make-up, chances are that fashionable young Chinese are up on the first floor of the restaurant at no.849. Here they serve western-style Chinese food, which most eat with knives and forks; it's a distinctly bizarre spectacle even if the food itself is barely palatable.

Just off Huaihai Lu to the south, on Xingye Lu, in the site of the **first National Congress of the Chinese Communist Party** (open 8–11 and 1–4;

closed Monday and Tuesday). The official story is that here, on 23 July 1921, thirteen representatives of the Communist cells which had developed all over China met to discuss the formation of a national party. The meeting was discovered by a French police agent (it was illegal to hold political meetings in the French Concession) and on 30 July the delegates fled to Zhejiang province, where they resumed their talks on a boat in Nanhu Lake. After Liberation this house was restored and turned into a museum: all the historical explanations are in Chinese, so take a translator if you want the full official view of recent history. Quite how much of this version is true is unclear: it's not certain that the date nor even the site of the meeting are correct, and it seems probable that there were in fact more delegates than the record remembers – not all stayed faithful to the line.

Not far from here is **Fuxing Park**, 21 acres of greenery which seems particularly popular with elderly Chinese. Head on down Fuxing Lu, then take the first right, and you'll find the **Sun Yatsen Museum**. Here Sun Yatsen lived in western style for six years, amid lawns screened by high walls and metal gates. His widow, the Communist *Soong Qingling*, stayed in the house until 1937, part of a bizarre little coterie based around her family – her sister was married to Chiang Kai-shek and her brother, *T. V. Soong*, was an international banker and sometime finance minister to Chiang. The museum unfortunately seems not to be currently open to the public, and only travellers with special connections get in to see the lavish period furnishings.

Another mansion, which you can visit, is the former home of a French millionaire at 79 Fenyang Lu, a little further west, which was converted in 1956 into the **Shanghai Arts and Crafts Institute**. Here skilled craftsmen specialising in traditional skills like lacquerwork, jade, ivory and bamboo carving, paper cutting and embroidery create original designs which are then copied in small factories and workshops all over China. There is a shop next door where the work is displayed, but ask at reception and with luck you'll be allowed in to see the craftsmen in action. If you're planning a special trip for this, though, it would be worth checking by phone beforehand. Nearby on Fenyang Lu you may catch snatches of classical music floating out from the **Conservatory** – for which see *Night Haunts*.

Western Shanghai

Not far from the Jing Jiang on Yanan Zhonglu towers the pompous majesty of the **Shanghai Industrial Exhibition Hall**. Constructed by the Russians in 1954 (when relations between the countries were considerably better, though even then they may have had doubts about how lasting – the whole place went up inside a year) it was originally known as the

Palace of Sino-Soviet Friendship and housed a permanent exhibition of industrial produce from the Shanghai area – proof of the advances achieved since Liberation. In recent years it has been turned into a vast and rather vulgar tourist shop selling everything from exquisite lacquer furniture through jewellery and silks to trinkets and souvenirs at well above the going rate. Don't even try to look for a bargain. Occasional travelling exhibitions and the amazing Stalinist architectural lines are far more worthwhile than this so-called 'Arts and Crafts Fair'.

To the west along Yanan Lu you pass **Jingan Park** on the way to the Children's Palace. **Jingan Temple** – the Temple of Serenity – was until the Liberation one of the richest Buddhist foundations in the city, headed by abbot *Khi Vehdu*, whose lifestyle was well in tune with that of the city. Six foot four and built to match, the abbot's shaven head and magnificent robes were a familiar sight around old Shanghai, and his doings legendary. His wife would be chauffered about in a brand new Buick which, whenever she stopped, would immediately be draped in sables to protect it from the elements. She, the abbot and all seven of his concubines were also shadowed wherever they went by White Russian bodyguards, each carrying what appeared to be an ordinary leather brief-case which was in fact lined with bulletproof steel and could be used as a shield in case of attack. The temple was pretty exotic too, with forty or fifty Buddhas, most clothed in gold leaf. Sadly there's not a great deal of it left to see these days, but the park roundabout is a typically popular escape from the city streets.

The **Shanghai Municipal Children's Palace** (open Sat 3–4.30, Sun 8–11am) is one of eleven converted mansions around the city where gifted or talented children get extra teaching and the chance to join in extracurricular activities. In practice it's a training college for the elite, kids between 6 and 15 who've passed a stiff entrance exam: most of them speak pretty good English which they're only too happy to practise showing tourists around and explaining what goes on. This was the first of the Children's Palaces opened in China (the idea was imported from Russia and promoted by *Soong Qingling*, Sun Yatsen's widow) and is worth seeing in addition simply for the building, a mansion formerly known as Marble House. It's yet more proof of the high life enjoyed by the few in pre-Liberation Shanghai.

Right across the street (at 53 Yanan Zhonglu) stands the **Shanghai International Club**. Re-opened in 1977 (for summer only), it offers two tennis courts, a small swimming pool, lawns, gardens, Chinese and western food, and had a great deal more atmosphere than they've managed to recreate at the Jing Jiang – this may not have survived the recent renovations. Admission is ¥2 but opening hours can vary, so it's best to ring before setting out (Tel.538 455).

Follow Yanan Lu or Nanjing Lu on to the west and they merge into

Hongqiao Lu, which leads eventually to the airport. Along the way it passes **Shanghai Zoo** (open 6–4.30), a massive affair with over 2,000 caged animals and birds: the star attraction, inevitably, is a giant panda. Next door, at 2409 Hongqiao Lu, stands the mansion which was once the Sassoons' home. It has served since as a Japanese naval HQ, as a casino and as the private villa of the Gang of Four, but now suffers the relative ignominy of being rented out as offices to *BP*. A no.57 bus will bring you out here.

The **south-western limits** of the city also offer a few points of interest if you're heading out in this direction. First is the Xujiahui **Catholic Cathedral**, one of many places of public worship which have received a new lease of life in recent years. Built in 1906, it was closed for more than ten years during the Cultural Revolution, re-opening in 1979. The chief interest here is in seeing the remarkable size and fervour of the congregations – best appreciated during an early Sunday morning service if you can drag yourself up. Easiest approach is on a no.26 trolley bus, getting off at the last stop just a couple of hundred yards from the Cathedral.

Continuing south – this time on a no.56 bus – you'll come to **Longhua Park**, on Xongshan Nanlu, which houses **Longhua temple and pagoda**. The pagoda, the sole example in Shanghai, was built by Sun Quan during the Three Kingdoms period (220–280) – it's an octagonal structure, about 40 metres high, the seven storeys built of brick with wooden balconies and red lacquer pillars. What you see has been much restored – apart from anything else it was used by the Red Guards as a convenient structure to plaster with banners – but is still fairly impressive. The temple is slightly later (c.AD345) and has seen still more reconstruction. Nevertheless it is held to be a typical example of the southern architecture of the Song dynasty. There's also a fair **vegetarian restaurant** in the park, should you feel the need of refreshment. And finally in this direction, another three stops on the 56 bus, you reach the **Shanghai Botanical Gardens** (open daily 7.30–4). Among the more than 9,000 plants on view are two pomegranate trees said to have been planted in the Qian Long era and still bearing fruit despite their antiquity. Above all, though, you should see the orchid chamber, with more than 100 different varieties of this heady bloom.

North-western Shanghai can also boast an important religious survival, the **Temple of the Jade Buddha**. With around a dozen resident monks, this is the largest active Buddhist monastery in the country. Its main attraction, though, is two magnificent statues of Buddha, both carved from a single piece of white jade. They were brought here from Burma in 1882 by a certain monk *Huigen* who had the temple built to enshrine them: the larger of the two forms the temple's centrepiece, the smaller is housed in a first-floor room. Elsewhere the temple boasts an extensive collection of Buddhist sutras and paintings. It's open daily from 8–5 (though you must find a monk to show you round) at 170 Anyuan Lu, just by the intersection of Changzhou Lu and Jiangning Lu: a no.16 bus will get you out here from the centre of town. The temple also offers a vegetarian restaurant, but this is overpriced (minimum ¥25 a head) and usually full of tour groups.

North of the Wusong

North from the Bund, across the black iron girder bridge now known as the Waibaidu, you enter an area which before the war was the Japanese Concession, and which since Liberation has been largely taken over by nondescript housing developments. The only real interest lies in **Hangpou Park** on Baoshan Lu, and its monuments to the political novelist Lu Xun. **Lu Xun**, probably the most revered of C20 Chinese authors, spent the last ten years of his life in this part of Shanghai. He died in 1936, and in 1956 his remains were removed from the cemetery where they lay to be placed in the grandiose **Tomb of Lu Xun**, complete with statue and inscription in Mao's calligraphy. Also in the park, to the right of the main entrance, is the **Lu Xun Memorial Hall** (open 8.15–12 and 1–5 except Mondays and Wednesdays). The exhibits include original correspondence, including letters from and snaps of George Bernard Shaw. The notes are in Chinese only, which is frustrating as there's little other indication of why the Chinese Communist Party regards him so highly: translations of his work are fairly widely available should you want to discover for yourself. And you can also visit the man's former home, at 9 Xinchun Dalu.

THE FACTS
Eating and drinking

Shanghai's cosmopolitan past is reflected as much in its restaurant kitchens as anywhere else – in the huge number of restaurants, snack bars and hotel dining rooms and in the great variety of the food they serve. The places themselves may be more modest nowadays, but you can still get great food at ridiculous prices all over the city. The only problem is that since eating out is so cheap, restaurants are usually full and you must arrive early. Hotels stay open later, but in restaurants you really ought to be sitting down by 11.30 for lunch and 6 for dinner, otherwise you'll be directed to the soulless and expensive foreigners' sections upstairs. The Shanghainese are also famous for their sweet tooth and the city has over 1800 coffee and pastry shops selling more than 2000 tons of pastries and confectionery each week.

Nanjing Donglu, between the Bund and Renmin Park, is the best place to start. The *Yangzhou* at no.308 serves traditional Shanghai food, specialising in wild duck and *Tofu*: book or arrive before 5.30 to beat the crowds. The *Sichuan* at no.457 is cheaper (you buy vouchers in advance from the kiosk out front), less crowded and serves tremendous sea bass. At no.719 you'll find the city's most celebrated eatery, *Xinya*, definitely worth a visit. Here you really do need to book. It's a Cantonese restaurant with beautiful, wood-panelled dining rooms and a cast of elderly waiters who almost without exception speak fluent English, learnt from the hordes of foreign visitors pre-1949. If you can't get into the restaurant try the ground-floor cake shop to get an idea of what you're missing. There's also one of Shanghai's best **vegetarian** restaurants at 43 Huanghe Lu, just north of Nanjing Lu after the Park Hotel. It's very popular and clean and prepares a mass of dishes shaped like animals, just in case you can't bear to be without meat. A meal for two here is about ¥11. Nanjing Lu also has the top **coffee bars**; the *Deda Xicaishe*, on the corner of Sichuan Zhonglu, which is renowned for its chocolate buns, and the *Donghai Fandian*, a couple of doors down at no.143.

Here too, of course, are the Peace and Park **Hotels**, two expensive but unmissable dining possibilities. Try the *Peace* for its lunch menu, especially the noodle soups, and also in the evening (arrive very early for a window table) for magnificent views. The *Park* has a western restaurant which offers both superb steaks and fish dishes and the finest art deco architecture in Shanghai. At the *Dongfeng*, on the Bund, they serve a good set lunch for ¥6 – worth it to catch a glimpse of the Long Bar and other relics of the *Shanghai Club*. The best hotel food of all, though, is to be had in the *Shenjiang Hotel*, 740 Hankou Lu just off Xizang Lu.

Further south **around Fuxing Park** are other possibilities. For a typical local's meal try the *Dashingsang*, at 129 Shunchang Lu, on the no.17 trolley bus route. You can eat masses for ¥3 a head and they serve great eels. No one speaks English. If you need this security try instead the *Dahongyun* at 556 Fuzhou Lu, near the old city. The proprieter is reluctant to let you sit downstairs with the Chinese but if you can persuade him it's still worth paying the extra for the set dinner at ¥6.50 a head. You may find yourself caught up in one of the many wedding parties which seem to be held here.

Further west, try the *Red House* at 37 Sha'anxi Nanlu, near the *Jing Jiang* hotel. It's an intriguing anachronism in the district of the site of the Communist Party's first meeting: baked alaska and cheese soufflé continue to grace the palates of the Chinese, who struggle with knives and forks to consume them. The food isn't brilliant but the experience is.

The **Old City area** boasts authentic and far less formalised catering from a series of take-aways – stuffed dough balls, noodles and all the standards. There's also the lovely *Wuxingling* tea-house next to the Yu garden. Built over an ornamental pond, this is one of Shanghai's few remaining traditional tea-houses, with tea at 15 fen a pot, and as many hot water refills as you want. As for **late night food**, hotels apart, only the handful of Moslem restaurants seem to stay open after hours. Try the *Hong Kouqu* at 2033 Sichuan Lu, open until midnight in the summer months and 10.30 in the winter. For **drinks** only the bars of the Park and Peace hotels are safe standbys – see below.

Night haunts

Shanghai probably has more **nightlife** than any other Chinese city, but even here most locals get up at the crack of dawn and are in bed by 10pm. In practice this means that most of the city comes to a dead halt at much the same time as the smallest village. By 10.30 you'll be lucky to find anything at all.

The one major exception to this rule is the **Peace Hotel bar**. Generally foreign travellers and business people in China lead totally different lives in terms of what they eat, where they stay, where they go: the Peace Hotel bar is the one place which draws them all together. Everyone seems to (and should) roll up here at least once to listen to the marvellously out of tune swing rhythms of the ageing eight-piece dance band, still belting out the numbers which echoed from the bars and dance-halls forty and more years ago. A cover charge of a couple of yuan allows you to sip cocktails amid the original 1930s decor until the breathtaking hour of 11pm. Almost as exciting are the nightly **jazz** spots at the *Yangzi Restaurant* on the Bund: these feature the first post-Liberation jazz band to play publicly in Shanghai, complete with extraordinary female vocalist.

Other hotel **bars** – notably the *Park* and *Jing Jiang* – also stay open relatively late; so does the *Seaman's Club* (ask directions at the Peace) – if it's currently in operation. Young locals tend to spend their evenings in the dilapidated old **coffee shops**, particularly those around Nanjing Lu. They may close around 9, but they're one of the few places where foreigners can mix and talk fairly freely with the Chinese, who feel at ease here on their own ground. Most serve passable coffee, which at least isn't instant, and extremely sweet cakes and buns. But the real attraction is conversation.

Culture – drama, acrobatics, music and film

Shanghai has always had a healthy cultural scene, with over 60 cinemas and theatres featuring opera, dance, acrobatics, puppets, plays and foreign and Chinese films. To find out what's on and where ask CITS to check the listings in a local newspaper – you may have difficulty persuading them that you really do want to go to anything other than a tourist acrobatics display, but they should eventually respond. For most events it's enough simply to turn up on the night but if you want to be sure CITS will arrange bookings for a small fee, or you can go to the booking office yourself (make sure you have your requirements written out in Chinese).

Operas and plays may not be easy to understand, but many performances – particularly of **opera** – are liberally sprinkled with song, dance and dramatic action: try to pick one of these. Even without them the audience's reaction is fascinating, and stimulating, in itself. There's none of the hushed reverence which you might find at the opera or ballet in the west – the Chinese slurp lollipops, talk throughout the performance, applaud frequently and sincerely and generally make sure they enjoy themselves. The best of the opera companies are probably the *Shanghai Opera Troupe* and the *Xinyihua Shanghai Opera Troupe*. As for **drama**, the *Shanghai Art Theatre* was the first Chinese company to perform modern plays (in 1929) and from the beginning had close links with the Communist party: during the 1930s the League of Leftist Dramatists was founded in Shanghai. Ironically enough the **Shanghai Art Theatre** is now based in what used to be the Lyceum Theatre, home of that essential of colonial life the British Amateur Dramatic Society. It's just up the road from the Jing Jiang Club.

Shanghai also boasts three professional **orchestras** and a Conservatory of Music, where young talent is encouraged. The *Shanghai Symphony Orchestra* performs both western and Chinese works, the *Shanghai Philharmonic* specialises in western, while the *Shanghai National Music Orchestra* plays traditional works on traditional instruments such as the *pipa*, a four-stringed lute, the *erhu*, a two-stringed fiddle, and the Chinese harp. Perhaps the most pleasant place to hear classical music, though, is the **Shanghai Conservatory**, where there are performances every Sunday evening at 7 (book by midweek to be safe). Established in 1927 as a college for talented young musicians (at 20 Fenyang Lu in the French Concession) it continues to train many of the infant prodigies who seem to appear from China at regular intervals.

Finally **acrobatics** is used here as a general term for all sorts of variety performances, including juggling, balancing, magic and animal training. Some of these skills – sword swallowing, fire eating and the simple but amazing balance acts – were being performed much as now as early as the Han dynasty; others have taken on a more modern look with props like motorbikes and spectacular costumes. The internationally renowned *Shanghai Acrobatics Troupe* can be seen at the **Shanghai Acrobatics Dome** on Nanjing Xilu. Performances, which start around 7pm, are extremely popular, so try to book to ensure a seat. The Shanghai Magic Troupe also perform here. There's a booking office – a tiny kiosk – right outside: bought here, the tickets are really very cheap.

Listings

AIRLINES *CAAC* is at 789 Yan'an Lu (Tel.533766), *Cathay Pacific* has an office at room 123 of the Jing Jiang Hotel (Tel.534242) and *Pan Am* is in room 103 of the Jingan Guest House (Tel.563050).

AIRPORT *Hongqiao airport* is 15 kilometres south-west of the centre (Tel.537664): there is a CAAC bus between here and the CAAC office, Price 80 fen.

BANKS AND CHANGING MONEY Travellers' cheques can be exchanged at most hotels. For emergencies *Bank of China* is at 23 Zhongshan Lu (Tel.217466). There is also an office of the *Hong Kong and Shanghai Banking Corporation* at 185 Yuan Ming Yuan Lu (Tel.216030). Credit cards are much more acceptable here than other Chinese towns, though watch out for the surcharge.

BOATS Tickets to Hong Kong from the *China Ocean Shipping Company* at 255 Jiangxi Lu; For the Yangzi River and Coastal destinations from 222 Renmin Lu and for Huangpu River from the office next door to Huangpu Park. Departures to Hong Kong from the International Passenger Quay; to Yangzi river and southern coastal destinations from Shilipu Wharf; to northern coastal destinations from Gongpinglu Wharf, and for Huangpu River trip from Huangpu Park by the ticket office.

BOOKSHOPS Large selection of foreign material and English translations of Chinese classics at the *Foreign Language Bookstore* at 390 Fuzhou Lu. There's also a specialist Chinese translation selection at 201 Shandong Zhonglu and the *Xinhua Bookshop* at 390 Nanjing Donglu, or western paperbacks and periodicals can be found at the Peace, Park and Jing Jiang Hotels.

CITS is located in the northern block of the Peace Hotel (open: 8.30–11.30 & 1.30–5.30). They can provide assistance on travel and entertainment tickets, visits to factories and communes, etc. but they're inefficient and keen for their cut.

EMBASSIES AND CONSULATES British Consulate-General at 244 Yong Fulu (open weekdays 9–5; Tel.374569); Australian Consulate in Wulumuqi; US at 1469 Huaihai Lu (Tel.379880); French at 1431 Huaihai Lu (Tel.371414).

FRIENDSHIP STORE at 33 Zhongshan Lu, opposite Huangpu Park, has a good hardware and silk selection, though the food choice is limited. Also visit the small arts building adjoining which sells amazing wall hangings and calligraphy tools.

HOSPITAL Shanghai No.1 Hospital the Huangdong, at 190 Suzhou Beilu is the only one which takes foreigners. Outpatients should go to 410 North Suzhou Luo.

LIBRARY Shanghai Library is at 325 Nanjing Xilu.

MAPS are available from the hotels and CITS. The best is the English language *China Travel and Tourism Press* version. Bus maps are in Chinese only.

POST OFFICE There are three main ones: 1761 Sichuan Lu, 359 Tiantong Lu, and (for air mail enquiries) 276 Bei Suzhou Lu. Telex and telegram services are available at the Jing Jiang Hotel.

PUBLIC SECURITY at 210 Hankou Lu (Tel.211997) open 8.30–12 & 1.30–5.30. Not very helpful.

RAILWAY STATION At Tianmu Lu, very busy with a beautiful first-class waiting room, worth seeing if they'll let you in.

RAILWAY TICKETS CITS for legitimate tickets, though they sometimes sell out even when there are tickets left. Otherwise advance tickets must be booked at the office at 230 Beijing Lu.

SILK is a local speciality. Keep an eye out at all material shops for the odd foreign shipment that missed the boat. There's a good supply at the Friendship Store.

SWIMMING POOLS are little in evidence though there's a mammoth one at the Jing Jiang Club, which is relatively quiet most of the day. Entrance is ¥2 to the club plus ¥3 to the pool.

TAXIS are available in a rank at the Jing Jiang Hotel, otherwise by telephone from anywhere else. *Shanghai Municipal Taxi Company* at 66 Kanjing Donglu, Tel.564444 and the *Friendship Taxi Service* at 40 Changle Lu, Tel.536363.

TELEPHONES Local calls are free from all of the hotels. Trunk calls should be made from the telegraph office next door to the north block of the Peace Hotel. There's a special foreigners section with a large, full-time staff to deal with every request. They'll even act as translators for you on the call. International calls can also be made from here.

UNIVERSITY Foreign Languages Institute, at 119 Xiti Yuhai Lu (Tel.481240).

JIANGSU

Jiangsu is a long narrow province hugging the coast south of Shandong. Low-lying, flat and wet it's one of the most fertile and long-inhabited areas of China, and also one which offers the visitor a tremendous amount. **Nanjing** is a great modern city as well as a great Ming capital, and it has relics of 19C history and of the early Revolution too. **Suzhou** and **Yangzhou** are ancient cities famous throughout China for their gardens. **Wuxi** attracts thousands of tourists to the shores of **Lake Tai** for its scenery, fruit trees and fish, and for the caves of **Yixing** across the lake.

The traditional north–south route across Jiangsu is the **Grand Canal**, which was once navigable all the way from Hangzhou in Zhejiang province to Beijing, and is still very much alive in the sections which flow through southern Jiangsu. **Zhenjiang** and **Changzhou** are canal towns (as indeed are Suzhou, Wuxi and Yangzhou) which have interest beyond the attractions of the waterside scene and the opportunities for boat rides. And Nanjing is also linked to Shanghai by the great water highway of the **Yangzi** – as well as by rail – to ensure that ancient trade routes continue to bring wealth to the region.

The north-west has traditionally been the poor and backward relation of the province, but even here **Xuzhou** is now a major rail junction with modern coal mines to supplement the fame of its early Han origins. A rail link – the continuation of the Long-Hai line – runs from here to **Lianyungang** on the coast. Wealthy in the 1930s, when completion of the rail line brought trade to the port, Lianyungang today offers a mixture of 1930s architecture, seaport atmosphere and hill temples. The centre of the province has a coast too shallow for anchorage but ideal for salt panning, always the source of its income: flat lands inland are dotted with lakes and seamed with canals.

THE GRAND CANAL

The **Grand Canal** – *Da Yunhe* – is still the world's largest manmade waterway, an extraordinary achievement which has played a key role in the nation's trade, and in the lives of the towns along it, throughout history. The first sections were dug about 400BC, probably for military purposes, but the vast bulk of the work was done in the early 7C under the Sui Emperor *Yang Di*. Records claim that as many as 6 million men were pressed into service in its construction. Its function originally was to join the rich rice-bowl of the Yangzi with the more heavily populated, less fertile lands in the north and to alleviate the effects of regular crop failures and famine. At that time the Canal's two main arms followed the nearly level ground which had at various times been the course of the Yellow River, running from the Sui capital near Xi'an south to Hangzhou: it was later extended north as far as Beijing.

The Canal was a vital element in the expansion of **trade** under the Tang and Song, benefiting all the towns on its route. Since its completion there had been a great movement of population south – by 800 the Yangzi basin was taking over from the Yellow River as the chief source of the empire's finances. A Japanese monk, *Ennin*, who travelled in China from 836 to 847, described the traffic on the water then:

> Two water buffalo were tied to more than 40 boats, with two or three of the latter joined to form a single raft and with these connected in line by hawsers. Since it was difficult to hear from head to stern there was great shouting back and forth ... Boats of the salt bureau passed laden with salt, three or four or five boats bound side by side and in line, following one another for several tens of li. This unexpected sight is not easy to describe ...

He could find remarkably similar scenes today.

From the 12C on the provinces of Jiangsu and Zhejiang became the economic heart of China, and the **canal towns** grew in stature: the Song, forced south, established a capital at **Hangzhou** and the first Ming emperor based himself in **Nanjing**, which became a capital again under the Taiping rebels and in the early years of Sun Yatsen's Republic. Throughout all this the canal was constantly maintained and regularly extended. *Robert Morrison*, travelling with Lord Amherst's embassy in 1816, journeyed from Tianjin near Beijing all the way down to the Yangzi: he described the simple locks – 'gateways with stone abutments on each side with grooves to receive planks which being let down stop the water's egress or ingress' – and noted that in places the banks were so high and the country around so low that from the boat it was possible to look down on roofs and treetops.

Not until early in the present century did the changing course of the Yellow River, the growth of coastal shipping and the coming of the railways cause a decline of the Canal. Much, falling into disuse, was rapidly silting up. But since the 1950s its value has once more been recognised, and widespread work undertaken. Certainly the stretch **south of the Yangzi**, from Zhenjiang to Hangzhou, is navigable year round – this runs through the bulk of the more interesting canal towns, journeys which for the most part are relatively easy to undertake independently. **North of the Yangzi**, too, the canal is clear virtually to the borders of Jiangsu: major works are going on to allow bulk carriers access to Xuzhou. Here there's no tourist transport, though, and less of interest along the way. Beyond navigation depends much on the level of the waters, the time of year, and the progress of local dredging programmes, but in the north the Canal can certainly not at present be seen as a reliable means of long-distance transport.

SUZHOU

Just an hour on the train from Shanghai, **SUZHOU** is the point where the Shanghai–Nanjing railway meets the Grand Canal, to run on together north-west through Wuxi, Changzhou and Zhenjiang. Only a few miles to the west, separated from the city by a range of low hills, lies Lake Taihu. The town itself – the oldest and perhaps the most attractive in this area – is built on a network of interlocking canals whose waters feed a whole series of renowned classical gardens, Suzhou's chief claim to fame these days. Ancient and moated, crisscrossed with water and dotted with greenery, it has retained its character to a remarkable degree, though by the same token this is one of China's busiest tourist cities.

He Lu, ruler of Wu, is said to have founded Suzhou in 600BC as his capital, complete with early walls and moat. Its name – Plentiful Water – was conferred by the Sui rulers (around AD600) who engineered the Grand Canal on which the city's prosperity has ever since been based: it is still crowded with local traffic. The silk trade too was established early here – it flourished under the Tang and even more so, with the Imperial Court forced to move south, under the Song. Silk is still the leading industry, though smokestacks flourishing on the outskirts testify to the growth of new light industry.

With the capital at Hangzhou, Suzhou attracted the overspill of scholars, officials and merchants, bringing wealth and patronage with them – in the late 13C Marco Polo reported '6000 bridges, clever merchants, cunning men of all crafts, very wise men called Sages and great natural physicians'. When the first Ming emperor founded his capital at Nanjing, the city continued to enjoy a privileged position within the orbit of the court and to flourish as a centre for the production and weaving of silk. In this period the business was transformed by the gathering of the workforce into great sheds in a manner not seen in the west for at least another two centuries and the coming of the Industrial Revolution. At the same time Suzhou was developing a reputation as something of a cultural centre: *Huttner*, who accompanied Macartney's embassy to China at the end of the 18C described the city as 'the school of the greatest artists, the best actors and the most nimble acrobats; meeting place of the richest pleasure seekers'.

In every other respect Suzhou's great good fortune seems to have been to manage to stay out of the mainstream of history. It suffered a brief occupation by the Taipings in the 1860s and the Japanese took it over during the last war, but unlike so many others it was never much fought

over. Which is probably why so much of the old city has survived –
moats, gates, canals, bridges, old streets and houses – to balance the
modern developments on the fringes.

Finding your way about

The clear grid of streets and canals in the old moated city centre makes
Suzhou a relatively easy place in which to get your bearings. **Renmin Lu**,
the main street, runs straight south through the centre from the **railway
station** in the north. At the other end of this street, by **Nanmen** (the
South Gate), you'll find the long-distance **bus station** and the **passenger
dock** for canal boats to Hangzhou. Most places you might want to find
downtown are between these two points, on or near Renmin Lu: the **Post
Office**, the **CAAC**, the **PSB** (in a sidestreet near the Yi Yuan Garden) and
the town centre **ticket office** (203 Guanqian Jie). The area around this
latter, Guanqian Jie, is the real city centre – cramped, animated streets
thronged with small shops, tea-houses and restaurants.

For **hotel** space, foreigners are more or less forced to head some way
out of the centre to Youyi Lu, in the south-east. Here the *Suzhou Fandian*
and the *Nanlin Fandian* are both comfortable and typical enough, with
a full complement of shops, bars and restaurants. The Suzhou has a new
wing with standard prices and an older one with 2–10 bedded rooms
from around ¥6; at the Nanlin the cheapest bed goes for ¥10, a double
room for around ¥60. It may prove worth the extra – staff are extremely
friendly and there's a wonderfully over the top formal restaurant. There
are also plenty of places to hire bikes round about. **CITS** is in the Suzhou
compound – not particularly helpful, they will at least arrange factory
visits. A morning with a driver and car costs around ¥70 (which can be
shared between 4 or 5 people); it's surprisingly interesting, an experience
of real factories (you see 3, chosen from a wide range) which appear
most unused to visitors. A more central hotel is the *Lexian Fandian*. This
is very popular with Overseas Chinese and often reluctant to find room
for anyone else, but it does have blissfully cool dining rooms which can
be handy for lunch.

If you're arriving by rail the no.2 **bus** will take you on a circuit from
the station following the moat round to the east, down Lindun Lu, west
along Daoqian Jie, up to the old quarter at Shilou and back to the station.
This takes you close to the *Nanlin* and within easy walking distance of
the *Suzhou*. Alternatively a no.1 heads from the station straight down
Renmin Lu and on through Nanmen. The no.4 crosses Renmin Lu, runs
down Lindun Lu, and goes right past both the *Nanlin* and *Suzhou* Hotels.

Seeing Suzhou

This must be one of the most enjoyable cities in China in which simply
to wander without special purpose: wherever you go you'll come across

pagodas, temples, lively shopping districts, hectic canal traffic and street scenes which look like illustrations from some ancient book on the bizarre mysteries of the east. And of course there are the gardens in which to sit and recuperate from your efforts – but of those more later. For people in a hurry the *Taxi Business Co.* at 433 Renmin Lu hires out cabs and buses and also offers a variety of **day-trips** taking in some of the highlights. But saving time means missing a lot of the atmosphere and you might prefer to hire a bicycle from the friendly **Hire Shop** in Renmin Lu near the Yi Yuan garden (from 25 fen per hour). It's an easy place to cycle, and you'll also have the opportunity to get to sites on the outskirts, including some of the scenery to the west around Lake Tai.

In town a good place to start is the **Beisi Ta** (North Temple Pagoda) which offers an excellent view of the city: the web of waterways, the low huddles of traditional grey tiled buildings with their swooping roofs, the garden enclosures, and the industrial buildings spreading beyond. And you can pick out, too, some of the more conspicuous features – the Twin Pagodas, the Taoist Temple, and in the far south-west corner the Ruiguang Pagoda. Built in the 3C AD, the Beisi Ta retains only 9 of its original 11 storeys, but it's still the highest pagoda south of the Yangzi: you'll find it towards the northern end of Renmin Lu, on the no.1 or no.3 bus route.

From here you could do worse than head to the giant Taoist **Temple of Mystery**, the *Xuanmiao Guan*, in the very heart of the city just off Guanqian Jie. Founded originally in the 3C, this has been destroyed, rebuilt, burnt and put back together over and over again through its history. The complex consists basically of a vast entrance court with at its far end the *San Qing* – Hall of the Three Pure Ones, the Taoist deities. The Pure Ones here seem always to have been thoroughly hard-pressed by Mammon – for centuries this has been the scene of a great bazaar where travelling showmen, acrobats and actors entertained the crowds. Nowadays the real market action has spilled into the surrounding streets, but a strong commercial tradition survives in the Temple: the courtyard is lined with clothes stalls, there's a craft shop at the entrance and the main hall has a tourist shop running round three sides.

Continuing south across the city, the entrance to the *Shuang Ta* – **Twin Pagodas** – is off Fenghuang Jie on the no.2 bus route. Built during the Song Dynasty by a group of successful candidates in the imperial examinations who wanted to honour their teacher, the slender towers are certainly eye-catching. It's the patch of canalside garden behind, though, which is the real attraction here: dotted with bits of statuary like some scene from classical Greece, it features a gardeners' cottage at one end, teeming with roses in pots, and at the other a tea-house crowded with old men waving their fans about and chattering like starlings.

On south, Renmin Lu passes a **Confucian Temple** – probably still closed for repairs behind its high red walls – before leaving the ancient heart of the city by **Nanmen Gate**. Cross the bridge and turn right along the banks of the canal to reach the **Pan Men Gate**, one surviving corner of the old city walls. There is a high-arched bridge here with steps up, a great vantage point for watching the canal traffic. From the top of the wall itself you'll have a good view of the **Ruiguang Pagoda**, nearly 1000 years old and now almost a ruin. Romantic when seen from a distance, the area around the base is a muddy wasteland not worth the effort of attempting to explore.

The gardens

God almighty first planted a garden and indeed it is the purest of all human pleasures.

Gardens, above all, are what Suzhou is all about. Elsewhere you'll find grounds – as at the Imperial Gardens of Chengde or the Summer Palace outside Beijing – laid out on the grand scale. Here they're tiny in comparison, but far closer to the true essence of a Chinese garden – 'infinite riches in a little room'.

Chinese gardens do not set out to imitate or to improve upon a slice of nature; they are a serious art form where, as with painting, sculpture and poetry, the aim is to produce for our contemplation the balance, harmony, proportion and variety which the Chinese seek for in life. The garden designer works with rock, water, buildings, trees and vegetation in different combinations; with subtle effects which depend on glimpses through delicate lattices or tile patterned openings or moon gates; with reflections in water; with cunning perspectives which suggest a whole landscape or which 'borrow' outside features as part of the design in order to create an illusion of distance. Nothing could be further from its intention than to look natural, which is why many western eyes find it hard to accept, or enjoy.

Gardens have been laid out in Suzhou since the Song dynasty 1000 years ago, and in their Ming and Qing heyday it's said that there were 200 of them: some half-dozen have now been restored. They were usually built by wealthy scholars and merchants, often in small areas behind high compound walls. The designers used small pavilions and terraces to suggest a larger scale, undulating covered walkways and galleries to give a downward view, and intricate interlocking groups of rock and bamboo to hint at and half conceal what lies beyond. Formerly the whole would have been completed by animals, and there are still fish and turtle in some ponds. Differences in style arise basically from the mix and balance of the ingredients – some are threeparts water, others are mazes of contorted rock, others mainly inward-looking, featuring pavilions full of strange furniture. And remember that almost everything you see has some symbolic significance – the pine tree and the crane for long life, mandarin ducks for married bliss.

It's easy to overdo the gardens: the mannered and artificial combination of nature, art and architecture often seems merely cluttered to the western eye and – the brief flourish of spring blossom apart – they can appear colourless and muted. If at all possible choose a day with blue sky and a hint of cloud – the gardens need contrast, light and shade, clear shadow and bold reflection – and don't try to see them all. The finest include the *Canglang Ting*, oldest of all; the Master of the Nets, a miracle in a tiny, lightless backyard; the Humble Administrator's Garden, big enough to get lost in; and the *Shizi Lin* for its intricate rock shapes. However, these are also the most popular and crowded so if you want to enjoy solitude and atmosphere, try some of the others.

The **Canglang Ting**, or Dark Blue Wave Pavilion, lies off Renmin Lu a short walk from the hotels in Youyi Lu. First laid out around 1044 and covering some 2 acres, it is noteworthy for 'borrowing' the surrounding landscape to integrate it within the garden. Unlike many it does not hide behind a blank wall – the carved covered gallery on the perimeter looks out, over water, as well as in to the courtyards. Notice the central hillock designed to look like a forested hill, and the undulating walkways. There is a curious **Hall of Fame** lined with stone tablets recording the names and achievements of great statesmen, heroes and poets, and some of the most hideous and contorted furniture you are ever likely to see.

For the nearby **Wangshi Yuan** (Master of the Nets garden) walk west from the Suzhou hotel as far as the no.4 bus stop and look for the narrow alleyway on the left beyond two small shops. The smallest and most intimate garden, it was first laid out in 1140, later abandoned and finally restored to its present layout in 1770. It has an attractive central lake, tiny connecting halls and pavilions with pocket handkerchief courtyards and carved wooden doors, delicate latticework and fretted windows through which you catch a series of glimpses – a glimmer of bamboo, the contrast between the dark interiors and the pool and rocks beyond, a group of banana leaves, wintersweet in a miniature rockery framed in the three windows of a study decorated with palace lanterns and scroll paintings. It needs to be seen on a brilliant day.

The **Zhuozheng Yuan** (Humble Administrator's garden) is in the northeast corner of the city on the no.2 bus route. Built in 1513 by court examiner *Wang Xianchen*, the garden was promptly gambled away by his son and sold off in three lots. It's sometimes called the **Plain Man's Politics** garden after *Fan Yue* who said 'To cultivate one's garden to meet one's needs: that is the politics of a plain man'. Much the largest in Suzhou, the Zhuozheng Yuan is very much based on water and is laid out in three linked sections: the western part consists of a small lotus pond and pavilions; the centre is largely water, with two small islands connected by zigzag bridges; the eastern part has unusually open green spaces. Some of the buildings, especially the **Mandarin Ducks Hall** with its blue glass windows, elegant furniture and open views, are well worth the visit. Right next door to the garden is the **Suzhou Museum**, housed in a former Taiping Palace. It has the usual displays – particularly good on the development of the silk industry and the history of the Grand Canal.

Not far away either you'll find the **Shizi Lin** (Lion Grove) garden. The monk who laid this out in 1350 named it in honour of his teacher who lived on Lion Rock Mountain: the rocks of which it largely consists are supposed to resemble lions in all shapes and sizes. Once chosen, these strange water-worn rocks were submerged in Lake Tai to be further eroded. Part of the rockery takes the form of a convoluted labyrinth, from the top of which you emerge occasionally to gaze down at the water reflecting the green trees and grey stone.

Still in the centre of town there's one more garden of note, **Yi Yuan**, the Garden of Harmony. Late Qing dynasty, and hence considerably more recent than most, it is supposed to encompass the four key features of a garden: white pines; rocks from Lake Tai; animals; and stone tablets over the entrance. Unusually, it also has formal flower beds and arrangements of coloured pebbles. You'll find it just off Renmin Lu, about halfway down.

Out to the west of the city, on the no.5 bus route, are two more elegant gardens. If you're heading out to Tiger Hill or Hanshan Si temple, they make a good place to stop over on the way. The **Liu Yuan** – Garden to Linger in – was built by a retired Ming official, survived the Taiping uprising and was subsequently fully restored. Its series of courtyards of varying styles and sizes are viewed through curiously shaped openings in a covered walkway called *Huo Zhang* – Windows that Live. Among the other attractions is the largest of all the Lake Tai rocks, a single lump weighing around 5 tons and known as the *Guanyun Feng* – Cloud-capped peak. The **Xi Yuan**, more a temple than a garden, lies just a few hundred yards away: great sweeps of yellow ochred walls contrasting richly with the charcoal grey rooftiles and the red woodwork. The **Zishanglu Temple** here has a striking ceiling to its main hall, and off in a wing to one side serried ranks of impressive *arhats*, including *Fengseng* the mad monk and *Jidian*, another crazed monk clutching a broken fan. It's a pleasant spot despite the droves of tourists – look out for the giant carp and giant soft-shelled turtles in the Fangsheng life-giving pond.

Canals, streetlife and sustenance

Walking between these gardens and the other sites allows you to see a great deal of the character of Suzhou. Though the factory chimneys are growing up like beanstalks in the industrial belt, there's a lot of old China here still: canals with flat-bottomed boats squeezing under humpback bridges; broad avenues lined with plane trees; narrow streets backing on to waterways, pollarded trees forming archways in front of the carved wooden house fronts; glimpses down alleys of bridges over threads of bright water; more glimpses through red wooden gates in the high white-washed walls of old compounds.

The south-western corner of the moated city is one of the most atmospheric stretches – every few hundred yards the cobbled way is interrupted by the simplest of stone bridges, buried in weeping willow and washing. Or walk down from the hotels in Youyi Lu past the canalside houses, choosing a bright day if possible. Like the gardens the canals need sun to enhance the shadows and give an edge to the reflections. Sunshine brings out the inhabitants too. Every bit of pavement has bamboo cross poles set up to hang the washing on, and everywhere will be busy with people scrubbing mats and furniture and banging clothes as everything in the house is turned out into the street: quilts, shoes, wooden pails, noodles and coal – they all get an airing.

Zhongshan Lu and **Jingde Lu** heading west each have colourful stretches leading up to bridges from which you can watch the boatmen unloading along the wharves. **Shi Lu**, bounded by walls, canal, watergate and Yanan Lu, is another raucous stretch. There are old barber shops with latticed half doors; workshops making wooden pitchers and rolling pins; a theatrical costumier selling ceremonial swords and glorious opera rig from ¥60. I watched in awe as a street tailor, tape measure round his thin neck, cut a suit for a young man who had just handed him the material, bought in the department store behind: instant chalk lines for the pieces, darts and sewing lines, all freehand, then snip snip with huge shears and a neat pile of pieces handed over to the boy sitting at the treadle sewing machine beside him, and all with the speed and dexterity of an Olympic competitor.

Guanqian Jie, though, is the real centre of Suzhou. A narrow, tree-lined pedestrianised street, packed with everything, it's an entertainment in itself, whether you're window shopping, treating yourself to cakes and ice creams, or simply waiting for one of the men in red armbands to leap on some unsuspecting cyclist who has strayed into the pedestrianised zone by mistake. For **shopping**, this is *the* place. The *Friendship Store* is here, there's a large bookshop with a foreign section upstairs, a throng of arts and crafts stalls in the Taoist Temple, and above all there's the *Daoxiancun* cake shop. Jingde and Shi Lu, on the other side of Renmin Lu, have cheaper stores selling hardware and basic groceries.

As for **eating**, Suzhou's cooking is justly renowned, and the area around Guanqian Jie is once again the place to look. The *Songhelou Caiguan* is the most famous of all, a restaurant which claims to be old enough to have served the Emperor Qianlong: its menu is elaborate and long on fish (crab, eel and squirrel fish among them) but it's also expensive. Close to the back of this, on Qingnian Lu, are three rather cheaper possibilities: the *Laozhenxian*, with Shanghai cuisine; the *Gongdelin Caiguan*, which offers a vegetarian floor; and the *Deyuelou Caiguan*. The *Huimin Fandian* in Jingde Lu serves Muslim food. For lunch try around Shi Lu or in the Xi Yuan garden, and of course there are plenty of good noodle shops everywhere.

For cinemas, theatres and local **nightlife** – which here means strolling around after dark eating an ice cream – head for Renmin Shichang Square, near Guanqian Jie. Or for something rather more western there's always the penthouse bar in the new wing of the *Suzhou Hotel*, open till around midnight.

A few excursions

Setting out from the centre of Suzhou there are a number of places which make easy day or half-day **trips** by bike or, in some cases, local bus. To the **south** of the city a no.13 bus (from Renmin Lu) will take you out along the canals to the main section of the **Grand Canal** where it heads off towards Hangzhou. Here, you'll find the **Baodai Bridge**, a 53-arched Tang dynasty construction: it's not wildly exciting, but with traffic now rerouted over a newer crossing, it does make a tranquil spot to sit and contemplate the canal traffic and the local anglers. There's much more of interest to the **west**, towards Lake Taihu.

Huqiu Hill – Tiger Hill – is the first, easily reached by bike or on a no.5 bus. Here, according to legend, is the tomb of the Wu king *He Lu*, guarded by a mythical white tiger so effectively through the centuries that it has never been found, nor its treasures plundered. There are terraces laid out with shrubs and trees, a tea-house, and everywhere rocks and pools each with their own name and hoary legend. They include the **Thousand Men Rock**, where the men who built the tomb were supposedly executed to keep its whereabouts secret, the **Sword Testing Stone**, where *He Lu* broke his sword in legend, and the **Third Spring under Heaven**, just one of thousands of third springs dotted across China. At the summit stands Suzhou's famous **leaning tower**, the *Yunyan* or Cloud Rock Pagoda. Octagonal, with seven brick storeys, it seems to need constant attention to prevent it from toppling altogether – during one such operation in 1965 workmen found a box dated 961 containing, among other treasures, eight Buddhist sutras wrapped in silk. On the way to Tiger Hill you'll come across a good market in the nearby village and, if you cycle, can take a fascinating (albeit boneshaking) route along the cobbled towpaths lining the canals, past the former splendour of the merchants' houses with their imposing façades and watergates, and children larking about in the water on rafts and inner tubes.

Han Shan Si (Cold Mountain Temple) also lies in the suburbs, on the no.6 bus route where two canals intersect near the splendid arch of **Feng Qiao** bridge – you can also get here along the canals, on a tour boat from Pen Mei Gate. Dating from around AD502 the temple is named after the Tang monks *Han* and *Shan* whose grinning faces appear in an extraordinary painting behind the main altar as well as on postcards, fans and scrolls in the shop. It's quiet but very much a working temple; inside are a handful of simple halls likely to be full of country women, their hair braided with scarlet thread, chanting away endlessly in the traditional ceremonies. Being on a busy waterway has always brought travellers here, and the temple, and especially its bell, are celebrated by several poets. The Tang writer *Zhang Ji* wrote a famous verse which is inscribed on a stone stele in the temple:

Moonset; through the freezing air the caw of a crow;
By Fenqiao, breaking my rest, the fishing lamps glow;
To me as I lie in my boat the dark hour brings
The plangent repeated sound as the temple bell rings
At Han Shan beyond Suzhou.

Further out, Lingyun Shan and Tianping Shan lie close to each other in the low hills: together they make a good day's outing. At **Lingyun Shan** – Divine Cliff Hill – you climb stone steps past a bell tower to reach a walled enclosure with a temple hall, a seven-storey pagoda and a well. **Tianping Shan** – Sky Level Hill – 3km beyond, was already a well-known beauty spot under the Song: wooded paths meander up to the summit past pavilions and small gardens, the hillside is cut with streams and dotted with strange rock formations, and in Autumn the maples which cover the slope seem to blaze. There are also tremendous views from both these hills.

Beyond, the road continues **westwards to Lake Tai** and a scenic area liberally sprinkled with pagodas and tomb ruins, or else runs south some 35km to **Dong Shan**, where a peninsula juts out into the lake. A circuit road links everything of interest here including **Zijin** or Purple Gold Nunnery, famous for its southern Song statues of arhats. There are also ferries to nearby **Xishan Island** which boasts several more temples. All this is too much to handle in a single day under your own steam, but it would be well worth it if you had time to make a leisurely circuit of the lake. Otherwise the *Taxi Business Co.* in Renmin Lu promises tourist excursions to all these places.

WUXI

WUXI straddles the Grand Canal and the Nanjing–Shanghai railway immediately north of Taihu Lake, set in a landscape of water, flat plain and low hills known for its fertility as the 'Land of fish and rice'. One of the four largest freshwater lakes in China, Taihu is considered a great beauty spot, liberally sprinkled with islands and surrounded by wooded hills. Only around 2 metres deep on average, it is a natural reservoir of relatively unpolluted water: fish can be bred here, and lotus and water-chestnut are grown in ideal conditions on the islands. Other plant and wildlife is rich too – the shores are clad with tea plantations and orchards of loquat, pear, peach, apricot and plum.

Wuxi itself, though, wins few prizes for beauty, or for anything else. The tin mines which brought the earliest settlers were already exhausted under the Han (Wuxi means No Tin) and it was the construction of the Grand Canal which brought importance to local trade and industry, as it did for so many other canal towns. The result here is something of a hotch-potch: of the lakeside cities, Hangzhou is much more appealing, and as a canal town with traditional gardens, Wuxi cannot hope to compete with Suzhou. Moreover, new expansion of industry has brought poorly planned and confusing modern developments to the centre as well as worries about pollution. It's a sprawling city with no heart and little soul. Nevertheless Wuxi remains one of the largest resort cities in China: Overseas Chinese come here in droves to sample the scenery and mainland Chinese arrive in even larger numbers to fill the honeymoon hotels and sanatoria. If nothing else you can happily spend a day on an outing from Suzhou (around an hour by train), the fruit (though with the local canning industry it's hard to come by fresh) and the fish are great, and of course there's the lake.

Getting about

Perhaps the real trouble with Wuxi is that although the lake has some mouthwatering scenery and hotels, there are few other amenities and without the benefit of the tour-group system you can find even getting from the bus or railway station to a hotel a frustrating and time-consuming business.

The **railway station** is in the north-east of the city at the top of Tongyun Lu; a new long distance **bus station** has been built in the south-east, between Hubin Lu and Liangxi Lu near the new canal. Two main streets cross the city – Renmin Lu, west to east from Gongnong Bing Square to the Grand Canal, and Zhongshan Lu, north–south right through town. **Renmin Lu** is the main shopping drag with the giant Dongfanghong Market and other stores as well as the **Post Office**, the general **ticket office**, and a number of decent restaurants. South on **Zhongshan Lu** there's the *Xinhua Bookshop*, **PSB** just off down Chongning Lu, the **Friendship Store** and, nearby, **CITS** in Xinsheng Lu. Almost everything else of interest is on or near these, too: for **theatre** and **cinema** try the *Dazhong* in Renmin Lu, the *Wenhuagong* Cultural Palace in Jiefang Lu, just off Zhingshan in the south, or the *Gongnong Bing Theatre* in the square of the same name; **restaurants**, in addition to those on Renmin Lu, include the *Liangxi Fandian* in Zhongshan Lu and the *China Restaurant* in Tongyun Lu near the station – all have excellent fish. Perhaps the biggest downtown attractions, though, are the **canals** – interesting particularly around the busy wharves in the north, near the station.

If you're looking for a **hotel**, a no.2 bus from the railway station will take you via Gongnong Bing Square and out to the lakeside Meiyuan Garden in around 30 minutes: from the end of the line it's a further 20 minutes walk to the *Taihu Hotel*. The gardens here are a delight – especially first thing in the morning – but they can get a bit wearing as you tramp through carrying your bag, and there are the additional disadvantages of its being isolated (last bus at 7pm), expensive and often full. The lakeside alternatives – the *Hubin* and its annexe the *Shuixi* – are little better despite being on the no.1 bus route direct from Gongnong Bing Square: jerry-built motel style accommodation at ¥25 a head. The *Wuxi Hotel* in Gongnong Bing Lu would be a more central and probably cheaper option – that is if they were prepared to take you in and not already bursting at the seams with Overseas Chinese.

Lakeland walks and waterways
It is in Wuxi's **parks and gardens** – either on the lake shore or in the hills overlooking it – that you should plan to spend most of your time here, though be warned, you will not be alone. Getting on a no.2 bus will take you first past **Xihui Park**, not the most attractive perhaps, but large and central, with hills which offer a good overview of the region. The main entrance on Huihe Lu leads directly to the **Dragon Light Pagoda** (*Longguang*) on top of **Xishan Hill**. There are fine views from the topmost of its seven storeys and underneath, through the hill, a dank cave has been tunnelled as an additional tourist attraction. On the far side rises the more substantial **Huishan Hill**: the path leads down from the pagoda to a small lake between the two, surrounded by a group of tiled pavilions and paved stairways which look, as you descend, like the curving ribs of some mammoth skeleton. Here are the remains of the 1500-year-old **Huishan Temple** and the **Datong Hall** – now a small museum – then the **Second Spring Under Heaven**, and on through the Guhuashan Gate the **Jichang Yuan** (Carefree Garden), laid out in 1500. From Huishan comes the special black clay for the ugly painted figurines which are sold all over the city, and which have been made here since at least the Ming Dynasty.

At the end of the no.2 bus route, on the lake shore, **Meiyuan** (**Plum**) **Garden** is considerably more attractive, and emptier. Here 3,000 years ago was the capital of the Zhou period kingdom of Gouwu, and later under the Qing there was a small peach garden on this site. Much expanded and landscaped, the park now offers a springtime sea of blossom, best appreciated from the Pagoda at the highest point, and in autumn the heady scent of osmanthus blossom, used to flavour the local delicacy of honeyed plums. You can also get to Meiyuan by ferry from the no.1 bus terminus near the entrance to Turtle Head Isle (see below).

The **Liyuan Garden** is also on the lakeshore, on the no.1 route shortly before it crosses Baojie Bridge. Built in the 1930s, this is a water-based park: you pass through a rockery maze made of strange stones from the lake, to emerge on a long promenade overlooking the water and leading to a series of fishponds and the **Pavilion of the Four Seasons**. Tucked away at one end are several decaying courtyards marooned in water – and apparently sinking – with the ugly faces of the Hubin and Shuiziu hotels rearing up behind. Not the most exciting of parks, maybe, but worth seeing if the lake itself is swathed in mist and rain.

Yuantou Zhu – Turtle Head Isle – lies right at the end of the no.1 bus route, and can also be reached by intermittent pleasure boat from the Liyuan garden pier, or from Meiyuan. The most popular spot with Chinese visitors, the peninsula (which is supposed to look like a turtle's head) boasts a small lighthouse and a scattering of tea-houses and pavilions – formerly summerhouses of the wealthy, these are now look-out points where you can take tea and soak up the views. At the highest point stands the **Guangming Pavilion**, just below which you'll find the **Guangfu Temple**, a huddle of tiny rooms each with its own altar and crowd of worshippers blurred in the heavy coils of incense smoke. Nearby is a small restaurant where you choose from a horrid display of fake dishes in a cabinet.

From a pier inside the park a ferry shuttles regularly to and from the tiny former bandits' lair of **Sanshan** – Three Hills Island. A central knob of land is linked by causeways to minuscule outcrops on either side. Neat paths lead up to a tea-house, pavilion and pagoda. If you're lucky you will have magical views of tree-clad islands, winding inlets, fishing boats under sail and, they say, wonderful sunsets: on an averagely grey day it's all thoroughly flat and uninspiring.

Finally, if you still have the appetite for more of the lakes and canals, the obvious way of getting it is to take a longer **boat trip**. There are services across the lake to Huzhou, from where it's easy enough to continue to Hangzhou (p. 256), to Yixing or along the Grand Canal in either direction, to Changzhou or Suzhou. Check with CITS for details of what seems currently practicable. The trip **to Suzhou** is probably the one they'll try to sell you, since it's a regular tourist route, and it's also one of the most interesting and varied. There is a daily sailing at 6.30am, but you'll probably be forced on to the fancy glassed-in tourist boat which leaves around 8.30 and can cost as much as ¥40. This sets out from the Jinyuan jetty below the Taihu Hotel, huge sanatoria looming mysterious from the misty shore, to thread your way along the seams of canals which fringe and fragment the lake shore, before joining the Grand Canal proper. Early fishing boats are being launched by men and women in enormous flapping black oilskins; narrow waterways lead off towards nowhere in particular, some of them blocked by great nets which sift for small fish and are winched in and out to be emptied by a man sheltering in a thatched hut; there's a constant stream of boats – small fishing vessels poled by a husband-and-wife team, long strings of cargo barges piled with everything from green vegetables to bricks, a row of plants bright along the cabin roof, concrete hulks laden gunwhale deep under a load of lime and seaweed, a solitary figure steering under an umbrella in the stern. At every town the canal narrows, the boats crowding three or four abreast and bumping like dodgems at a fair. For two or three hours it makes a great alternative to the train.

YIXING

Yixing County lies on the western shores of Lake Taihu about 60km from Wuxi – a mild, fertile plain whose smattering of small lakes make it ideal for the cultivation of tea and bamboo. These are important local products, but it is Yixing pottery which does most to attract visitors, that and the celebrated underground caverns hollowed out of the karst hills in a skein running south-west from Yixing town. The area makes an easy excursion from Wuxi (2 or 3 hours by slow bus skirting the lake) but you'll need more than a day. Better, perhaps, stop over en route from Wuxi to Changzhou.

You'll need to visit **YIXING** itself, since this is where the only hotel for foreigners is situated – the *Yixing Binguan*, half an hour's walk from the bus station and ¥15–20 per head – but the town has little else to recommend it. Your time should be spent instead around **DINGSHAN** (as the bus timetables know it – **Dingshuzen** on the map showing buses to the caves) which is the centre of the ceramic industry and the base for the major cave groups. If you do the Cave Trail be prepared to spend a deal of time queueing for tickets and hanging around for buses: perhaps better to join a tour group, with transport and guide laid on, or to hire a bike for a more leisurely exploration of the lakeside attractions.

Primitive unglazed **pottery** from as far back as the Shang and Zhou periods – some 3,000 years old – has been discovered around Dingshan and certainly since the Han Dynasty at least, some 200 years BC, this has been a major centre for glazed wares. Its heyday came under the Ming from the 14C, but manufacturing is still going strong today. A sandy local clay is used to produce the famous **Purple Sand** pottery, a dull brown unglazed ware whose properties of retaining the colour, fragrance and flavour of the tea are said to make for the best teapots in China. All along Dingshan's main street you'll find stalls and pavement displays with these teapots and blue-ware plant pots on offer at ridiculously low prices. In the pottery **Exhibition Centre** you can see more ambitious pieces – anything from fabulously delicate Song Dynasty teapots to flamboyant and highly glazed modern lamps – as well as more down-to-earth lavatory bowls and sparkplug insulators. The enormous pots decorated with writhing dragons are extremely fine and so are the round, heavy blue-glaze tables found in so many Chinese gardens: though in general the mastery of techniques seems greatly to outstrip any use of imagination in their application. With luck (and preferably advance arrangement) it may also be possible to visit the Pottery Institute and one or two of the factories.

As for **caves**, there are three chief groups. The first, **Zhanggong**, is just ten minutes on the bus from Dingshan or a relatively easy walk when the heat is not too oppressive. There are 72 caves in all, communicating on two levels by over 1500 steps (flat shoes essential) – only the odd bare bulb breaks the pitch darkness as you creep along low tunnels, slipping and being dripped on all the while. Although the stalactites, stalagmites and other rock formations are all named for their resemblance to exotic beasts or everyday objects, you'll need a powerful imagination to work out which is which – and preferably a permanent stoop and a miner's headlamp to go with it. The only real highlight for me was the **Hall of the Sea Dragon King** where the rock soars upwards in strange contortions to open onto the green hillside far above; here there is an eerie patch of swirling mist, dripping moisture and mystery.

A further 15 minutes on the bus will take you to the most recently discovered group, **Linggu Caves**, where human remains were found along with Tang inscriptions. For the locals these are the best of them all because their rocks are even more bizarrely contorted than elsewhere.

The third group, **Shanjuan**, is 25km south-west – or an hour on the bus – from Yixing. The caves are set on three interconnecting layers, most impressive of them undoubtedly being the **Water Cave**, at the bottom, where you are poled through subterranean passages in a punt while the boatman picks out highlights with his torch. I emerged, blinking and damp, after some half-hour of this, to memories of disappointed mystery boat rides at fairgrounds as a child. You'll notice that though the caves are great crowd-pullers, even most of the Chinese in coach parties show little desire to linger below the ground – they spend far more time outside buying snacks and haggling for pottery.

Other sites in Yixing County which are expected to open soon include the Jin dynasty **Zhouwang Miao** (Temple of King Zhou); the **Yunu Tan** (Jade Maiden Pool) and **Fuwang Fu**, the Mansion of King Fu built by the Taiping rulers. All of these will no doubt obey the old rule of thumb – the more evocative the name, the less interesting the place. The countryside all round, however, is good for walking and local peasants likely to invite you in for a jam jar of tea while their neighbours gather round to take a look. Put together a picnic and set off.

CHANGZHOU

CHANGZHOU is yet another of those towns taking advantage of the dual axis of the Canal and the Shanghai–Nanjing railway – just an hour or so on the train from Wuxi or from Zhenjiang and an easy day-trip from either. Like its neighbours, it has reaped the economic benefits, but here at least new-found wealth has not meant the wholesale destruction of the ancient city centre – instead a ring of new villages and industrial estates has grown up along arterial roads in the suburbs. In the centre, riddled with small waterways running off the main canal, you'll still find an attractive quarter of narrow alleys, street markets and tiny stone bridges. So far it is not much of a tourist attraction, though the number of potential sites currently undergoing renovation or repair indicates a clear intention to make it one. Providing the canalside atmosphere is not thereby destroyed, it should prove thoroughly enjoyable.

Perhaps the greatest concentration of interest is just to the east of the centre, where the impressive **Tianning Si Temple** has already been restored. When you walk out from the centre it's easy enough to spot – you cross the canal and see, to your left, a crowd of locals selling incense and miniature Buddhas from the doorways of their houses. 1300 years old, this 'Temple of Heavenly Tranquillity' suffered under the Taiping rebels and again during the Cultural Revolution, but the simple grace of its two immense halls survived, and nowadays the gilding is bright, the lacquer fresh, and the silken hangings seem to have lost none of their sheen. In the main hall a great Buddha sits in the centre with his two attendants; behind there's a row of *arhats* and an enormous drum for beating the chants – so huge that there are steps leading up for the player to reach it from. In the rear building you'll find stone tablets set into the walls with relief engravings of arhats and monks, and two shapely tripod burners in the courtyard.

Behind the temple is **Hongmei Yuan** – Red Plum Park. Large, with several entrances, a well-maintained central area, a tea-house and a restaurant overlooking the boating lake, this is nonetheless, taken as a whole, something of a mess. There's an entire section of the park which looks as if it was once turned into allotments or communal gardens and that this policy is now being reversed in a hurry. The 14C **Hongmei Ge** (Red Plum Tower), hidden behind lowering trees and dense foliage, has a keeper who enjoys a three-hour lunch break, effectively denying most visitors access to the displays inside. And the area around **Wen Bi Ta** (Writing Brush Pagoda) is so churned up by landscaping works as to make access virtually impossible. No doubt once all the works are complete it will all be a great deal more pleasant.

If you leave by the gate near the pagoda you can cross the main Jiefang Qiao Lu to find another small park, surrounded on three sides by water, which contains the **Pavilion for Mooring Su Dongpo's Boat**. The Chinese are notorious name droppers and the hope here is clearly that some of the cachet of the great poet's name will rub off on the pavilion. Much more interesting is to climb up behind the pavilion to where you can

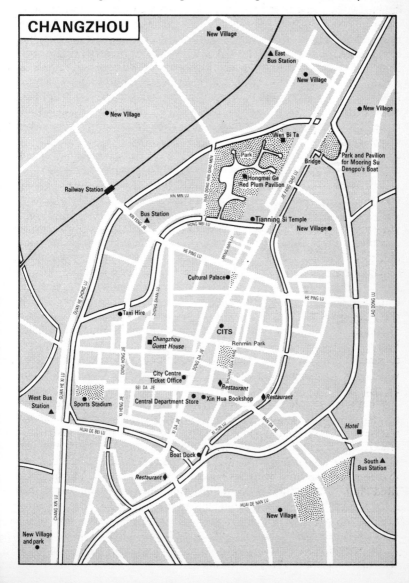

look down over the chaotic traffic on the canal and the great convoys of barges strung together.

There's a third garden in Changzhou – **Mu Yuan** off Dongheng Jie – which you'll find illustrated on postcards and brochures. It looks rather fine, especially covered in snow, but until its restoration is complete CITS seem determined to deny all knowledge of it.

Simply for **wandering**, the area in the centre of town, inside the inner-most ring of the canal network, is much the most interesting. There's a crowded market by the canal, full of wriggling eels, and were you'll find the main shopping streets, the busiest wharves, and most of the things you might need. Shops everywhere are rich in locally produced silks and fabrics at good prices, and Changzhou is also where the painted wooden combs come from – available here in every conceivable shape and size. **Dong Da Jie** is effectively Changzhou's High Street: there's a giant depart-ment store here, the *Xinhua bookstore*, an unusual antique shop selling beaten and fretted metal containers, coins and bottles, a number of **restaurants** (try the *Loyang Fandian* near CITS) theatres and cinemas – the Cultural Palace and the *Hongxin Juwan*. **Nan Da Jie**, heading off to the south, is also important; there are several more good **places to eat** here – look out for the *Courtesy Cafe*, good for coffee and cakes with the additional bonus of staying open late, a lovely rickety old tea-house perched on the canal further down, and others in nearby Fang – and the *Jiefang Dianying* cinema. Away from these, down the back alleys, you'll find more peaceful corners where whitewashed houses back on to the waterways, linen and bedding slung out to dry between them.

Practical details

You're almost certain to arrive in Changzhou by train. While it's theoret-ically possible to get a boat from Zhejiang or Wuxi, foreigners are not encouraged to do so, and in any event it's a long, slow trip. Bus is considerably slower than the train too. The **railway station** is in the north-east of town at the top of Xinfeng Jie, with the long-distance **bus station** just a short distance away down the same street. Should you be on a boat you'll arrive at the **jetty** near Huaide Lu in the west. For tickets out, head for these termini or the **general ticket** office on Dong Da Jie.

From the bus and railway stations a no.2 bus runs south and along Juqian Jie for the **Hotel Changzhou** in Changsheng Gang. This is delightful, if pricey at ¥28 for two – set in its own walled garden with ponds where the staff fish for supper, and very comfortable. Cheaper hostels and hotels for the Chinese are near the jetty, along Xiyun Lu and Huaide Lu – it might be worth trying the one on the square in Jiefang Lu if you really need to save money.

Other **bus routes** around town are somewhat baffling, since wherever possible they follow one-way routes. Broadly, though, nos **1** and **10** do a circuit from the railway station around the edge of the inner town; no.2 continues past the hotel to head south on Nan Da Jie, and no.3 crosses the city from east to west, following Xi Da Jie, Dong Da Jie and Jiefang Qiao past the park. This is also handy for the **Post Office**, on Xi Da Jie, and **CITS** on Dong Da Jie. **PSB** is just south of the centre on the canalside Qingguo Gang.

ZHENJIANG

ZHENJIANG is a canal town, too, and it lies on the Shanghai–Nanjing railway, but here the focus is very much on the great **Yangzi** river, and towards Yangzhou across on the northern bank. Protected on three sides by low hills, on the fourth by the Yangzi, Zhenjiang has offered safe harbourage and a strong defensive position for over 2000 years. During the Three Kings period one of the rulers of Wu built a walled city here as his capital: it grew rapidly, boosted over the centuries by the 'southern branch of the Grand Canal, running from here to Hangzhou, and by proximity to the Ming capital at Nanjing. After the Opium Wars the British and French were granted concessions here. Still an important Yangzi anchorage, Zhenjiang is set in the next few years for yet more expansion as a giant new harbour terminal complex nears completion.

From the start river transport has been crucial: Marco Polo remarked on the richness of the local silks and gold fabrics and these are still renowned, as, less romantically, are local vinegar and pickles. The river brought wealth, still visible in the older parts of town, and it brought outsiders – relics of early missionaries and traders survive, as do marks of the resistance put up to the British during the Opium Wars and the Japanese in 1937–8. If not the most characterful of cities, Zhenjiang does at least offer a redeeming vitality and enough to see to more than fill a day trip from Nanjing or a longer stop en route up the canal.

Arrival

This is a relatively easy place to get your bearings, though sheer size means that walking is rarely a practical way of getting around. To the north, the Yangzi stops the city spreading; in the south, the railway forms another barrier, and through the middle, running north–south across the city centre, is the Grand Canal. The **railway station** is on Laodong Lu in the south-west, the long-distance **bus station** (which is where you'll arrive if you take bus and ferry from Yangzhou) to the south along Jiefang Lu. You're less likely to be **arriving by boat**, though Yangzi cruises do stop here (at piers along Laobei Lu) and there's also a canal boat jetty very near here at the entrance to the canal.

The foreigners' **hotel** is the *Jinshan Fandian*, up in the north-west of the city near the river: a no.2 bus, which starts at the railway station and swings round through much of the city centre, will drop you at the entrance to Jinshan Park and Temple, 5 minutes from the motley collection of huts which make up its motel-style accommodation. It's expensive unless you have a very persuasive line in chat, but since the **CITS** and

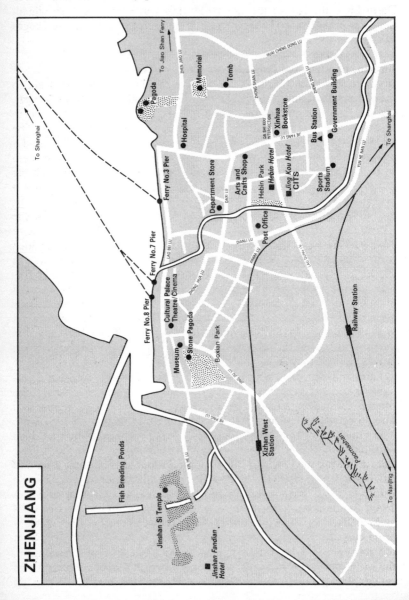

PSB are both out here, and since downtown hotels like the *Zhenjiang* (Boxian Lu) and *Luyou* (Jiefang Lu) are highly unlikely to 'have room', you have little choice. **Shops**, **restaurants** and **cinemas** are almost all concentrated on the stretch of Jiefang Lu between the bus station and Dashi Lu – the rest of the city is flat, laid out with broad, tree-lined, nondescript avenues. The points of interest all seem to lie on the fringes of town, in the low hills.

Jinshan, Jiaoshan and Beigushan

If you're staying at the Jinshan Hotel, you'll have only a short walk to the **Jinshan Park and Temple**. At one time a small island in the Yangzi, Jinshan has silted up over the years to create a lowlying peninsula, where a series of rectangular fishponds are overlooked by a small hill. The temple buildings wrap themselves dramatically around this hill behind a series of heavy yellow-ochre walls, twisting stairways leading past them to the **Cizhou Pagoda**, renovated in 1900 at great expense to celebrate the Dowager Empress Cixi's birthday. From the top of this 7-tiered octagonal tower you get a fine view down over the jumbled temple roofs, and across the ponds as they reflect every change in the sky. As for the temple itself, despite a 1500-year history and a former complement of 3000 monks, the physical remains are less impressive than the tales which it spawned. When *Li Shizhong* led the southern Song army into battle in the 12C, his wife stood here beating a drum to encourage him and strike fear into the northern invaders. And here lived *Fahai*, the monk who did all in his power to separate the young scholar from his love in the famous legend of *The White Snake*. There are several caves in the hill associated with this haunting story, but in the flesh they turn out to be dank and empty holes, while the displays devoted to the legend in several of the temple rooms are little better – cheap and tawdry.

Jiaoshan is an island which still is, some 5km downstream from Zhenjiang. It takes its name from the scholar *Jiao Guang* who was three times offered a key post at court by one of the Han dynasty emperors, and three times had the temerity to refuse, preferring to stay on his island. You can see his point – it's a wonderfully cool and refreshing spot, lush with bamboo and pine through which a path climbs up to the **Xijiang Lou**, a viewing tower which commands a florious stretch of the river and city beyond. Below are the remains of the gun batteries used against the British in 1842, the Japanese when they invaded, and *HMS Amethyst* in 1949. At the bottom, to the right of the jetty, there's a cluster of halls and pavilions among which the **Dinghui Temple** stands out for its elaborate carved and painted interiors and fine gilt Buddha. Dotted about too are several hundred stone tablets including the famous **Yihemingbei**, the memorial stone to a buried crane by one of China's most revered calligraphers. To get here take bus no.4 east (it runs from the station, up

Jiefang Lu, then out of town on Zhen Jiao Lu parallel to the river) to the end of its route, then walk through the gates to catch the small ferry, which runs from around 7.30am to 5pm. An hour or two should be enough to see everything.

On the way back, get off the bus just before it turns left away from the river. Here you'll find **Beigushan** perched on the natural fortifications of the river cliff, with the **Tieta** – a small iron pagoda from the 11C, its upper storeys destroyed by lightning but impressive nonetheless – and the **Ganlu**, or Sweet Dew Temple. 1400 years ago an enthusiastic emperor christened this area the 'Best Hill in the World above a River', which may be exaggerating a little. Nevertheless Beigushan does have a good tea-house and two **pavilions** connected with the *Romance of the Three Kingdoms* – one commemorates the marriage of *Liu Bei* of Shu to the sister of his rival *Sun Quan* of Wu, the other is dedicated to the widow, who drowned herself after *Liu Bei*'s untimely death.

Back in town one of the few points of real interest is the former British Consulate, at the corner of Boxian Park in Xiao Matou Jie (just off the no.2 bus route). This is now a local **museum** with a collection which includes the anchor from the *Amethyst* and the body of an early Chinese scholar, still clutching his Imperial examination certificate.

Further out of town, heading south into the hills, there are a few more places to visit, though until a bus service is introduced you'll have to beg or hire a bicycle to get to them. 5km or so out are the **Tomb of Mi Fei**, the great Song dynasty painter, the **Zhao Yin Temple**, and the **Tiger Running Spring**.

YANGZHOU

Straddling the Grand Canal north of the Yangzi, **YANGZHOU** is a mellow and relaxing city just a couple of hours from Nanjing. Its origins go back to around 500BC when the Wu rulers had channels dug here which were later to be incorporated into the Grand Canal. Thanks to this position at the junctions of the Yangzi, the Canal and the Huaihe river, Yangzhou rapidly developed into a prosperous and cultured city, aided by a monopoly on the lucrative salt trade. Under the Tang and later, many foreign merchants – some from Persia – lived and traded here: there's a 12C mosque and a much-quoted tale that Marco Polo governed the city for three years.

It was a city renowned too for its beauty (and the beauty of its inhabitants) and for its story-tellers, who handed their oral tradition on from one generation to the next. As such it frequently attracted the Imperial Court and its entourage, as well as artists and officials moving here in retirement – they endowed temples, created enclosed gardens and patronised local arts. In the 18C and 19C you could have found crowds scattered round the city listening to the storytellers holding forth – reciting episodes from the classic sagas and poems – from their raised platforms. It's said that you can still find them on the main roundabout near the *Shi Ta*, but even without this, and despite the industrial belt which now stretches round the south and east of the city, there's a strong sense of a cosmopolitan, cultured past here. It's evident in the famous gardens, in the layout of roads, waterways and bridges in the city centre, in the range and quality of goods in the shops, the unusual museum, the paintings, fans and materials for calligraphy sold in the backstreets. And it's clear, from the way the parks and temples are being refurbished, that the tourist machine intends to start exploiting them.

The **centre of Yangzhou** is delineated by a rectangle of narrow waterways crossed by a plethora of ornate bridges. Ganquan Lu runs across here from east to west, with Guoqing Lu coming up from the bus station to cross it at right angles: most of the big shops and restaurants are around this junction. It's an easy enough area to explore on foot, and it's only for a couple of the further-flung sites that the bus* is really necessary.

The **museum** is in the north of this central area, at the top of Guoqing Lu near the *Xiyuan Hotel*. A delightful group of assorted old pavilions, this is set among refreshingly informal, almost haphazard grounds – to Chinese eyes, no doubt, a total wilderness. The collection itself is small and arranged apparently at random, but there are enough fascinating odds and ends to justify a quick visit: a group of cast bronze bells, some of them huge, statues of horses and sheep, a Tang period wooden burial boat and several Han coffins.

In the west of the central area, the **Xianhe Si Mosque** is just off Ganquan Lu, up the last turning on the right before the junction with Yanhe Lu. Small and austere, its only real decoration is one wall covered entirely with arabic script – you may have to sign your name in the book before being admitted. The streets roundabout conceal several more buildings worth a look: the **Shi Ta**, a small stone pagoda on Yangtian Gong Lu built in 837; the **Wenchang Ge** pavilion built in 1595 at the entrance to a college established some 200 years earlier by the first Ming emperor; and the 13C **Si Wang Ting**, a three-storeyed octagonal pavilion. To the east across the canal there's more evidence of the early Muslim presence in Yangzhou – the Muslim cemetery and the **Memorial to Puhaddin**. Puhaddin was a 16th-generation descendant of Mohammed who came to China when the Mongols were in power, spent ten years in the city, and was buried here in accordance with his deathbed wish: the memorial, though, has been much closed for repairs recently.

*This is just as well since Yangzhou's one-way system and its **bus network** are a mess: prepare yourself by getting the most up-to-date map and checking the bus number and route at the bus stop before getting aboard.

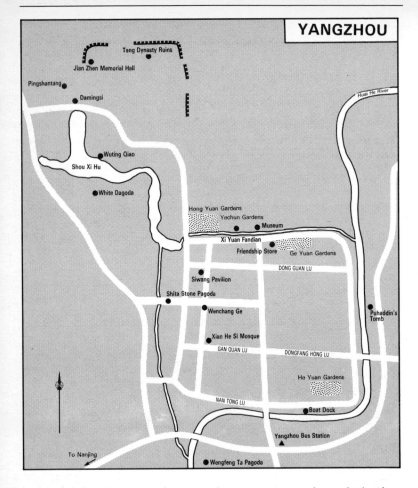

Around the city centre there are also numerous **gardens** which, if not so numerous or so famous as those in Suzhou, do offer an interesting blend of northern and southern styles and far fewer crowds. **Ye Chun** is an attractive strip running along the canal immediately to the west of the Xiyuan Hotel. Almost adjacent, **Hong Yuan** offers a veritable sea of Bonsai and an enormous collection of pot plants which make it look like nothing so much as an overcrowded nursery. **Ge Yuan**, in the other direction from the hotel across the canal past the Friendship Store, is by contrast very much a classical rock and water Chinese garden. The former home of a prosperous salt merchant, its entrance just off Dongguan Jie leads to a clutch of rather ponderously styled pavilions and to a rockery landscaped by the painter *Shi Tao* and supposed to suggest the four seasons. With a great deal of brown paint, trellis work, and contorted rocks reflected in pools, it's very much in the Chinese taste, and disappointing even if you share that, in that the stone is chipped, the walls stained and the paint peeling. Properly to work its magic, this kind of garden needs to be kept spanking clean and freshly painted. A restaurant near the entrance serves banquet-style meals: worth exploring if you're in a large group. One final spot is **He Yuan**, or Jixiao Mountain Villa, over in the south near the boat dock. Designed only in the 19C, this tiny area uses trees, shrubs and a raised walkway to give an ingenious illusion of variety and depth – the very essence of this type of gardening.

Further out, on the no.5 bus route, are two sites perhaps more worthwhile than any in the centre. The first is **Shouxi Hu** (Slender West Lake), a stream which was incorporated into the Tang city moat in the 8C and later dredged and landscaped into the narrow twisting shapes which give it its name. On a clear day it is alive with colour; grey skies and a breeze on the water lend a faintly melancholy air, with the outlines of the shabby buildings softened by the mass of weeping willow. There are some unusual structures here: an elegant white **Dagoba**, smaller copy of the one in Beijing, which could desperately use a thick coat of whitewash; the **Chui Tai** (Happiness Terrace) whose three moon gates each frame a different scene, and nearby a pavilion with an extraordinary collection of butterflies. Above all though, there's the much-photographed Five Pavilion Bridge – **Wutang Qiao** – an 18C construction with massive triple-arched and yellow tiled roofs. South of the lake the canal flows east to what used to be the landing place for the Imperial barge near the palace; now the site of the Xiyuan Hotel.

Take the no.5 to its terminus and you'll find the second site, **Daming Si Temple**, amid the ruins of the Tang city of Yangzhou. Get off the bus and you'll see stone steps leading up to a building on your right – here, in a huddle of tiny interconnecting rooms, are displayed a strange assortment of finds from the Tang ruins (the ruins themselves are of little interest unless you're an archaeologist). Follow a track from here past a row of food stalls and you'll come to the Temple of Bright Light, the Daming Si, built in the 5C and still going strong. Much of what you see is in fact a reconstruction – the Taiping rebels wrought severe destruction here – but it seems little the worse for all that. In any case the centrepiece was built only in 1973, a **Memorial Hall** to honour the monk *Jian Zhen* who is credited with having introduced *ritso* Buddhism to Japan. A profound scholar of the 8C, he was invited to teach in Japan only to find that on five successive occasions storms and misfortune drove him back to Chinese waters. Finally, on his sixth attempt at the age of 66, he made it, and sensibly decided against trying the return trip. He is still much revered in Japan – you'll see masses of photos in the hall showing Japanese monks visiting for various ceremonies. Other worthwhile structures include the *Pingshan Tang*, built in 1048 by the then prefect of Yangzhou, and the main temple hall with its fine stone Buddha. Nearby you'll find the **Pingyuan Lou**, a three-storey building offering three different views which is said to illustrate the perspective theory of the Song painter *Guo Xi*. Below are parks and gardens laid out in 1751 to incorporate the **Fifth Spring under Heaven**: you can sample its waters and the local tea from a blissfully cool tea-house overlooking the water, where plump goldfish and carp glide through murky depths.

Finally, in the far south of the city, a no.1 bus will take you to the conspicuous **Wenfeng Pagoda**, standing by a bend in the river in a small plot crammed with hollyhocks. Seven storeys high, built in 1582, it was intended to bring luck to local candidates in the Imperial examinations, though its function now is as a great vantage point over the intense activity on the water. Walk back alongside the canal and wharves for a closer view of the heavy river traffic and the small family boats, each with its swelling at one end, queueing in vast jams to be laden with anything from grain and bottled drinks to gravel and truck tyres.

Some practicalities

Since Yangzhou is not served by rail, and canal services appear reluctant to take visitors travelling independently, you're almost certain to arrive at the **bus station** on Dujiang Nan Lu in the south of the city. From here a no.1 or no.8 bus should take you as far as the Friendship Store north of the centre, from where you bear along the line of the canal until you see the entrance to the *Xiyuan Fandian*, the only **hotel** open to foreigners (at least until the adjacent skyscraper opens). This miscellaneous cluster of buildings sprawls over a vast area of walled-in park – head for the older, cheaper wing where there are rooms from around ¥10 and be prepared to stumble around in the dark hunting for the dining hall, the **CITS**, post office and shops. **CITS** have a small branch, handy for maps and info on arrival, directly opposite the exit from the bus station; **PSB** and the **main Post Office** are on central Ganquan Lu. The centre is also the **place to eat**: try the *Caigenxian Fandian* in Guoqing Lu, the *Gonghe Qunjia Miandian* in Ganquan Lu, or the *Guanglingling Jiulou* in the street of the same name.

If you want to try to get a boat out there is a **passenger jetty** to the south of the town centre where Taiping Lu meets the water. Here, though, the bus can be an experience in itself, especially if you're **heading for Nanjing**. For this is real motorway driving – a genuine dual carriageway which until recently was the only one in China – complete with road markings and multilingual international signs. Needless to say the bus does not match up to such pretensions and nor have the Chinese fully adapted yet to high-speed motoring: local peasants use the tarmac as a convenient threshing floor, spreading their grain across the road so that the heavy traffic does the hard work. Your journey will be enlivened by constant near misses as the farmers attempt to dodge the traffic and gather the fruits of their labours.

NANJING

NANJING occupies a strategic site on the south bank of the Yangzi river in a beautiful setting of lakes, river, wooded hills and mountain defences. Its situation brought importance from earliest times under many different names; it was one of China's ancient capitals, and the shift of the country's economic centre from the Yellow River to the fertile, rice-rich Yangzi valley made its position yet more crucial.

Six to seven thousand years ago there was a primitive clan society here whose stone tools and pottery are in the museum. Later, Bronze and **Iron Age** peoples found metal ores, and by 600BC there were the beginnings of a walled city. After the Han empire broke up in AD220, Nanjing was the capital of half a dozen dynasties, and when the Sui re-united China in AD589 the building of the Grand Canal increased the city's economic importance further. It became famous for its forges, foundries and weaving, especially for the veined brocade made in noble houses and monasteries. The **Sui and Tang periods** have left monuments in the Qixia octagonal pagoda and the Tang tombs. In 1368 an ex-Buddhist monk turned bandit captured Nanjing and became the first emperor of the **Ming dynasty**, with his capital here; there's much to see from this period too. Later, Nanjing was for 11 years in the mid-19C the capital of the Heavenly Kingdom of the **Taiping rebels**. After the Opium War the **Treaty of Nanking** which ceded Hong Kong to Britain was signed here: Nanjing was itself a Treaty Port and after the 1911 revolution it became the Provisional Capital of the new Chinese People's Republic, with *Sun Yatsen* as the first President. From 1945–49 it was again the nominal capital of China, as headquarters of the KMT administration.

Nowadays the city is an important railway junction – a great 1960s bridge carries the Beijing–Shanghai line over the Yangzi – a major river port for large ships, and the capital of Jiangsu Province with a population of over 4 million. It is one of the most attractive of the major Chinese cities to the visitor – the broad tree-lined boulevards and balconied houses within its Ming walls and gates give it something of the feel of a French provincial town. There are streets cramped with old houses, tiny workplaces and small shops – including plenty of pastrycooks – and there are large, airy parks. Outside the east gate are the wooded green hills of **Zijin Shan,** with the Ming tombs and other Ming sites alongside the Sun Yatsen Mausoleum.

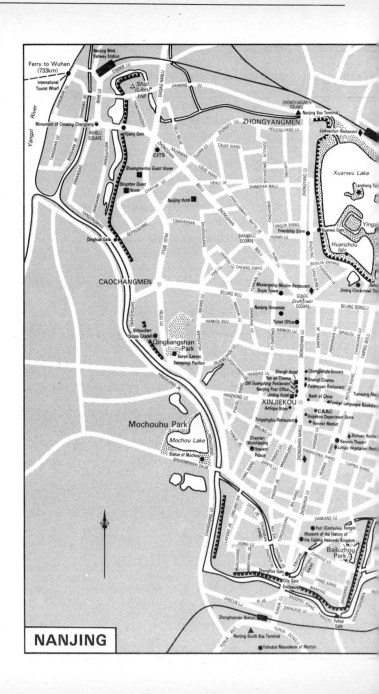

Ferry to Wuhan
(733km)

International
Tourist Wharf

Nanjing West
Railway Station

CHENGE LU

DADAO MALU

JIANNING   LU

JIANING

Shizi
(Lion)
Hill

ZHONGYANGMEN
SQUARE

Nanjing Bus Terminal

ZHONGYANGMEN

Lizhuachun Restaurant

Yangzi
River

Monument of Crossing Changjiang

REHELU
SQUARE

Yijiang Gate

CITS

Shuangmenlou Guest House

Dingshan Guest
House

Nanjing Hotel

Dinghui Gate

HELONGJIANG LU

ZHONGSHAN   BEILU

SAJIAWAN

FUJIAN   LU

CAIJIA XIANG

XINMOFAN MALU

Xuanwu Lake

Lansheng Te

Yingz

ZHONGSHAN LU

TONGJIA XIANG
Friendship Store

Xuanwu Gate

Huanzhou
Isle

Xuanwu Isle

LUDANG LU

TONGJIASHAN

SHANXILU
SQUARE

HUNAN LU

QINGSHICUN

MATAI   JIE

JIANGSU LU

BAIZI TING

BEIXIA DAFANG

TAISHAN XIE

GAOLOUMEN

JINGSU LU   DAFANG XIANG

YIHE JIE

Maxiangxing Muslim Restaurant

Drum Tower

GULOU
(Drum Tower)
SQUARE

BEIJING DONGLU

Jiming (Cockcrow) Te

Jiming (Cockcrow) Te

CAOCHANGMEN

BEIJING XILU

NINGHAI LU

Nanjing University

Ticket Office

HANKOU XILU

HANKOU LU

SIPAILOU

XIKANGQIAN JIE

CHENGXIAN   JIE

TAIPING   DONGLU

Shitouchen
(Stone Citadel)

Qingliangshan
Park

Saoye (Leaves
Sweeping) Pavilion

GUANGZHOU   LU

HUAIHAI LU

GUANGZHOU LU

HUAQIAO LU

HANZHONG LU

FENGHUANG   JIE

Shengli Hotel

Yan an Cinema

Old Guangdong Restaurant

Nanjing Post Office

Jiming Hotel

XINJIEKOU

Antique Store

Tongqinglou Restaurant

Changjianglu Grocery

Shengli Cinema

Dasanyuan Restaurant

Bank of China

Foreign Languages Bookstor

CAAC

Xinjiekou Department Store

Renmin Market

Sichuan Restu

Renmin Theatr

Lvliao Vegetarian Rest.

Mochouhu Park

Mochou Lake

Statue of Mochou

ZHONGSHAN NANLU

MOJING LU

SHUIXIMENWAI   DAJIE

JIANYE   LU

Chaotian
(Worshipping
Heaven)
Palace

ZHONGHUA LU

JIANKANG LU

JIANKANG LU

Fuzi (Confucius) Temple

Museum of the History of
the Taiping Heavenly Kingdom

Bailuzhou
Park

CHANGLE LU

DANZI XIANG

CHANGFU   JIE

CHANGLE LU

CHANGLE LU

XIAOHUANG JIE

MA   LU

Zhonghua Gate

City Gate

Enclosure

BIANYING

JHECUN LU

KI   JIE

ZHENGXUE LU

YASHU   XIANG

BAOZHOU   XIANG

Yuhua
Gate

YUHUA

YUHUA LU

Zhongzhuan Station

Nanjing South Bus Terminal

DONGLU

Yuhuatai Mausoleum of Martyrs

NANJING

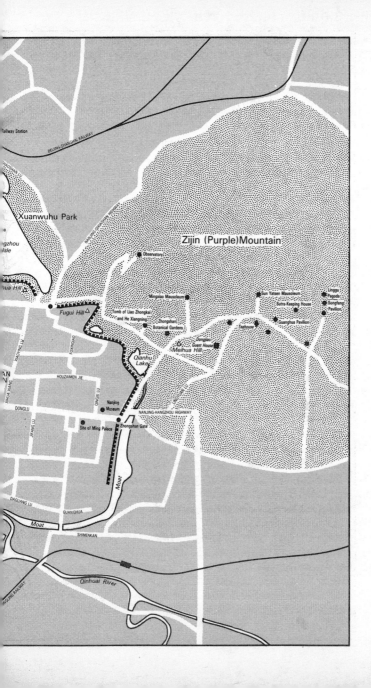

Railway Station

BEIJING-SHANGHAI RAILWAY

ZHONGSHAN LU

Xuanwuhu Park

gzhou
Isle

ua Hill

Observatory

Zijin (Purple) Mountain

NANJING-CHENGDU HIGHWAY

Mingxiao Mausoleum

Fugui Hill

Tomb of Liao Zhongkai
and He Xiangning

Zhongshan
Botanical Gardens

Sun Yatsen Mausoleum

Lingu
Pagoda

Sutra-Keeping House

Songfeng
Pavilion

Guanghua Pavilion

Teahouse

Dongliao
Guest House
Meihua Hill

Qianhu
Lake

FUXINGGANG

HOUZAIMEN JIE

QINGXI LU

XIHUA XIANG

'AN

DONGLU

JIEFANG LU

Nanjing
Museum

NANJING-HANGZHOU HIGHWAY

Site of Ming Palace

Zhongshan Gate

Moat

DAGUANG LU

GUANGHUA

Moat

SHIMENKAN

NANJING RAILWAY

Qinhuai River

Modern Nanjing – finding your way about

Within the Ming walls the layout is still very much that of the Ming city. In the north-east, just outside the city wall, is the **railway station**. From the **Zhongyang Men** roundabout nearby, the broad main street (called *Zhongyang Lu*, then *Zhongshan Lu*, then *Zhongshan Nan Lu*) runs south through the city and out at the **Zhonghua Gate**. This street is crossed from east to west, first at Drum Tower Square – **Gulou** – by *Beijing Lu* and then further south at **Xinjiekou** by *Hanzhong Lu* running west and *Zhongshan Dong Lu* running east to the **Zhongshan Gate**. Drum Tower Square and Xinjiekou are the two centres of Nanjing, the first being the administrative area and the second the 'down-town' centre, full of shops and restaurants.

A no.33 trolley bus from the railway station goes via the nearby Zhongyang Men roundabout (where you'll find the **long distance bus station**) right down Zhongyang Lu to the **south bus station**. Just north of Xinjiekou it passes the *Shengli* – **Victory Hotel** – cheap and central, with a good dining room, a western-style restaurant which is popular with the locals, especially students, and a western-style café with space invaders. The reception here is good at making arrangements. Other hotels include the giant and expensive *Nanjing Binguan* (¥60 for the cheapest double) in *Zhongshan Bei Lu*; its two wings offer all services including bicycle hire at a steep ¥2 per hour. This is on the no.16 bus route which runs from **Nanjing West Station**, near the **river-boat jetty** and ticket office in *Jiang Bian Lu*, down Zhongshan Bei Lu to Drum Tower Square and south to Zhonghua Gate. The *Jinling* on Xinjiekou roundabout has still more expensive rooms – its revolving rooftop restaurant makes it the city's pride and joy. And finally there's the *Dingshan Guest House* in *Chahaer Lu*; large, modern and charging ¥10 upwards (though just ¥4 for a dorm bed) this is closer to the river and not so convenient for the town.

Two other useful **bus** services are no.10 from the main railway station to the river-boat jetty and ticket office (Nanjing is a major port for Yangzi boats) and no.9, east from Xinjiekou along Zhongshan Dong Lu; the **CAAC** office is in this street quite near the roundabout. The town centre **ticket office** for trains, boats and long-distance buses is in Zhongshan Lu just south of Drum Tower Square. The **PSB** office is in a side street off Zhongshan Nan Lu, and **CITS** is at 313 Zhongshan Bei Lu, past the Nanjing Binguan towards the river.

Walls, gates and towers

Nanjing was walled as much as 2500 years ago but the present **city wall** is basically the work of the first Ming Emperor, who extended and strengthened the earlier walls in 1369–73. Built of brick and over 32km long, his wall followed the contours of the country, skirting the *Xuanwu lake* in the north, fringing the *Xijin Hills* in the east, and tracing to west and south the *Qin Huai* river, a tributary of the Yangzi which doubled as a moat. The wall was mainly paid for by rich families resettled here by the emperor: one third of it 'donated' by a single native of Wuxiang in Zhejiang province. Its construction employed 200,000 conscripts from the five nearby provinces. The bricks too were made in the five provinces, all to the same size and specification, each one bearing the names of the workman and overseer. They were held together – to an average height of 12 metres and a thickness of 7 – by a mixture of lime and glutinous rice paste.

The best place to see the fortifications is at **Zhonghua Men**, now isolated in the middle of a traffic island, just inside the river-moat near the southern end of the no.16 bus route. You walk through the central archway and climb up two levels, passing arched recesses on the first floor which are used for displays and selling snacks – beautifully cool in summer. Up above there's a view of the gates of the enclosure with the city spread out beyond. Zhonghua Gate is also known as *Wengcheng* – Jug Fort – because of its shape: its three gated enclosures could hold 3000 men in case of enemy attack, making it one of the biggest of its kind in China.

Another impressive bastion is the **Stone Fort** (*Shitoucheng*) in the west of the city high above the Qin Huai river. This is part of the original fortifications erected by Prince Wei of Chu around 500BC, and enlarged by Sun Quan of Wu 200 years later; his navy is said to have trained on the river below. The fort was constantly strengthened and eventually became part of the Ming defences, but the red rock of the original structure is still plainly visible.

Right in the city centre you'll find the **Drum Tower** on the west side of Drum Tower Square, a solid structure on a mound entered through a traditional style gateway. It was built in 1382 and from here the drum used to call the watch seven times a day or sound warnings at times of danger. The interior now has shows of amateur paintings. The **Great Bell Pavilion** sits just north of the Square in a well-kept garden. The enormous bell which it houses was cast in 1388 and weighs all of 23 tons: legend has it that the emperor ordered it to be cast in an alloy of iron, silver and gold which could be fused only by the blood of a virgin; the blacksmith's two daughters threw themselves into the furnace so that he could obey the emperor and escape death.

Parks and gardens

Nanjing is a pleasantly green city; as well as its tree-shaded streets it has many open spaces, ranging from the tiny **Zhanyuan Garden** and **Bailu-zhou** (Egret Isle Park) to the great water park of **Xuanwuhu** and the stretch of wooded country outside the Taiping Gate. Their freshness is very welcome in the summer heat of one of the 'three furnaces of China'.

Qinglianshan – Cool Hill

In the west of the city, just inside the wall and above the river, this was the site of the old Chu town of Jinling – Golden Hill. The Song emperors had a residence here for the torrid summer months. The **Sweep Leaf Pavilion** on a small rise was occupied in the 17C by one of the Eight Famous Painters of Nanjing, who lived here as a hermit after the Manchus conquered China: these days it's an enjoyable walk with a good view of the Stone Fort.

Mochou Lake Park

Across the river to the south lies the entrance to **Mochou**, whose far gate, round the side of the lake, leads out to open country. An open-air stage juts out into the lake, with a substantial tea-house behind, and everything is knee-deep in lotus leaves now that they've managed to halt pollution from the factories at the far end. A clutch of pavilions and walkways includes the **Square Pavilion**, with a statue of the legendary maiden Mochou, after whom the lake is named: she was called 'Sorrow free' because her sweet singing could soothe away all unhappiness. Other buildings include the **Victory in Chess Pavilion** and the **Huayan nunnery**, both part of a pleasant group hugging the shore – when I was here a regular gathering of men were playing old instruments and singing; they welcomed me eagerly as an audience. There's also a roller-skating rink and a photographic studio where you can dress up in traditional costume to have your picture taken.

Yuhuatai – Rainflower Terrace

This small hill, now a park, is not far outside the southern ramparts beyond Zhonghua Gate. In legend it was here that the sermons of a 5C Buddhist monk were so moving that flowers rained down from the sky upon him. Chinese tourists still grub around for the multi-coloured stones – *Yuhuashi* or Rain Flower Pebbles – associated with his legend and you'll find tables near the entrance piled with bowls of pebbles for sale, kept in water to brighten their colours. Hopeful treature seekers pick them over with chopsticks in search of rare specimens. Under the Ming – as well as being a renowned beauty spot dotted with temples – this was a pottery centre with 72 kilns. Most of the temples, including the

Porcelain Pagoda built by emperor Yong Le to honour his mother, were destroyed by the Taiping rebels and after 1927 the hill was an execution ground; more than 100,000 people are said to have been executed here by the Kuòmintang. It is now a **Martyrs' Memorial.** The Memorial itself is a dull statue but the park is pleasantly laid out on a slope thickly forested in pine trees among which you can witness locals giving their cagebirds an airing in the cool of the morning: the birds arrive on shoulder poles with their cages demurely curtained, to be hung up in the lower branches of the trees for a singsong while their owners gossip and play cards underneath.

Xuanwu Lake Park
Off *Zhongyang Lu* just after the Friendship Store, the **Xuanwu Lake Park** is mostly water, with hills on three sides and the city wall skirting the western shore. The lake is 5km long and nearly 3km wide and is said, not very convincingly, to have got its name (which means Black Military Lake) partly because in AD448 a black dragon appeared there – perhaps just a black alligator from the Yangzi – and partly because Song emperors reviewed their navies on the lake. Formerly a resort for the imperial family, it became a park in 1911. There are several small islands linked by causeways and bridges, with restaurants, tea houses, pavilions, rowing boats, paddle boats with awnings, places to swim, an open-air theatre and a zoo. **Liangzhou** is the busiest island, with skating rink, exhibition hall and shop. From here a bridge leads on to **Luizhou,** which is deserted – you can enjoy the grass and hear birds sing. The zoo occupies most of **Lingzhou** – it has the inevitable panda and is rather down at heel – but the best part of all is the inner lake round **Yingzhou** island, covered with lily pads and surrounded by fantastical trees with trunks shaped like corkscrews.

Walks in Nanjing

In a bus Nanjing's broad, tree-lined streets seem deceptively short, but the stretch between *Xinjiekou* and the *Zhonghua Gate*, for example, can take a full hour to walk. One way to get a feel of the city is to take a no.16 bus from the north-west, near the river. If you do this you might take the opportunity to look at the huge doubledecker bridge over the Yangzi, still a source of great pride to the Chinese because they built it under their own steam after the Russians pulled out in 1960: before the bridge was built trains took an hour and a half to ferry across the river. The no.16 will take you via Drum Tower Square and Xinjiekou down through the city to the Zhonghua bus station, where you start to walk.

Just outside the ramparts the **Qin Huai** river used to be lined with red and green-painted houses and in its Ming-Qing heyday was crowded with pleasure boats. The road across the river, between the Gate and the nearby Yuhuatai Garden, is an interesting stretch. It has 2-storey wooden-fronted houses, many with balconies above; below, open to the street, are small shops selling snacks, hardware, tools, and jasmine to pin on your shirt; also little workshops making bamboo steamers, fishing nets and spare parts for bicycles. The all-purpose trees lining the pavement provide shade as well as room to hang birdcages, pot plants and the washing. These trees are characteristic of Nanjing streets; many are French planes and it's claimed – though I found it an effort to believe – that 30 million trees have been planted in and around the city since 1949.

Going north from Zhonghua Gate the first main turning on the right, *Changle Lu*, leads to **Bailuzhou** – Egret Isle. This corner of the city remained the Chinese quarter after the Manchus took over, and the old canal and bridge, **Wuding Gate** and the city wall running behind the small park make it a rich and varied district to stroll in, full of traditional low-slung houses. Straddling the canal is the **Temple of Confucius Recreation Area** and by poking your nose down the maze of alleyways behind, all named for Confucius, you can find some of the temple buildings, including the **Examination Hall** which is now being restored. All around here is also a busy and interesting shopping area, with open and covered meat and vegetable markets.

The **Taiping Museum** is a little further north on *Zhonghua Lu*, off to the right in the former palace of Taiping's Eastern Prince. The Taiping Rising is a fascinating story – the man from Canton who failed his Civil Service examinations, then decided he was Jesus Christ's younger brother, gathered a vast army of followers, captured Nanjing from the Imperial forces and held it from 1853–64 as the capital of his Kingdom of Heavenly Peace. It was recaptured in 1864 after a 7-month siege by a Chinese army under the British general 'Chinese' Gordon, and 100,000 of the Taipings were slaughtered in the three days after it fell. It's a pity that the museum has so little English explanation – but you might be able to tack on to a tour-group and eavesdrop. The ornamental gardens here – **Zhanyuan** – were laid out by the first Ming emperor.

Continuing north, take *Jianje Lu* on the left and you come to the **Chaotiangong**. This large square, bounded by a high vermilion wall on one side and a gateway protected by tigers on the other, is the legendary site of *Ye Cheng*, 'the metal founders' settlement' which was one of the forerunners of Nanjing around the 7C. A palace was built here under the Song and extended by the Ming. It was used for audiences with the Emperor and was named *Chaotian* – Worshipping Heaven Palace. In 1865 it became a seat of learning and a temple to Confucius and nowadays its main building houses the collections of the **Municipal Museum**. The square itself is a through route for thousands of pedestrians and cyclists, emerging from the archways at either end.

Back on the main street continue north, first to the Xinjiekou round-about and then on to Drum Tower Square. **Xinjiekou** is busy, packed with shops, restaurants and commerce. The **Jinling Hotel** here – Nanjing's most expensive – is regarded by the sort of tourist who can afford to stay as the best Chinese-run hotel in China. It is also a source of immense pride locally, with a constant queue of Chinese visitors lining up to buy plastic bags saying *Jinling Hotel* – a status symbol for them and a profitable sideline for the hotel staff. Once a week locals can buy tickets to visit the rooftop bar: people staying in the hotel know when to expect the sudden rush because the staff suddenly remove all soap and towels from the loos. Shops in the hotel include a CAAC booking office and an upmarket arts and crafts store. **Drum Tower Square** is the admin-istrative centre in what used to be the heart of the city; when Nanjing became a Treaty Port in the mid-19C the foreign consulates were all based here. Round these two centres and the streets radiating from them you'll find most of what you need for living. For **shopping** there's the giant *Xinjiekou* Department Store just south of the roundabout, and the *People's Market*, a vast emporium not far away. In *Zhongshan Bei Lu*, just off Drum Tower Square, you'll find *Drum Tower Department Store*, *Shanxi Lu* Department Store and the *Gulou Grocery*. The **Friendship Store** – a good one – is further north near the entrance to Xuanwu Park.

There are many **eating places** in the same area. Between Drum Tower Square and Xinjiekou are the *Dasanyuan Jiu Jia* and *Lao Guangdong Cai Guan*, both Cantonese, *Maxiangxin* in Drum Tower Square for Muslim food. South of Xinjiekou is the *Tongqinglou* for northern and Peking food, especially dumplings, and in Taiping Lu, running parallel to the east, are the *Liuliuju Vegetarian* Restaurant (not enthusiastically recommended) and the *Sichuan* Restaurant. If you happen to be in Xuanwu Park the *Baiyuan* serves local dishes. And the whole street between Xinjiekou and Drum Tower Square is crowded with pastry shops and ice cream parlours. In the same stretch you'll find the main **Post Office** and **Bank of China**, also a choice of **cinema/theatres**: the *Shengli* Cinema and the *Yanan* in Zhongshan Lu, the *Dahua* in Zhongshan Nan Lu and the *Renmin Theatre* in Taiping Lu opposite the Sichuan Restaurant.

If you turn east at the Xinjiekou roundabout and go along Zhongshan Dong Lu you pass the **Foreign Languages Bookshop**, the **CAAC** office and then, on the left just after the Taiping Lu crossing, the **Tianwang Mansion** with its garden behind it. This was the palace of the Heavenly King of the Taiping Heavenly Kingdom but it is not normally open to visitors. Further along, just before the Zhongshan Gate in an area of office buildings in Ming style put up under the Republic, is the **Nanjing Provincial Museum**. Because this has always been an historical and important city and the centre of a wealthy province the collection is substantial and of high quality, and there are a number of important objects. They include a jade burial suit from Xuzhou – you can see another in the Xuzhou museum and lay bets as to which is the copy – and also an early figure showing acupuncture points and lines of energy.

Outside Nanjing

Not far outside the Zhongshan Gate to the east is **Zijin Shan** – Purple Gold Mountain (from the colour of its rocks), with many famous sites. Further afield are the **Tang tombs** to the south and the **Qixia temple** to the north-east.

ZIJIN SHAN is a short bus ride, either by no.9 from Xinjiekou to the Sun Yatsen Mausoleum or on a half-day bus tour from the **Tourist Bus Station** by the Drum Tower. *Zhu Geliang* of the Three Kingdoms period likened this hill to a coiled dragon and the Stone Fort to a crouching tiger – this has become a catchword for Nanjing. Traditionally the area has been regarded as a cool and shady spot to escape the furnace heat of Nanjing's summer. Here also are the most visited sites in Nanjing. Out through the gate the first port of call is the **Ming Tombs**; an agreeable evening stroll if you treat it as a separate excursion. Then comes the **Sun Yatsen Mausoleum**, the main stopping place for all buses and tours, and beyond is the group including the **Beamless Hall**, the **Songfeng Pavilion** and the **Linggu Pagoda**.

The **Sun Yatsen Mausoleum** is the most popular site with Chinese tourists and its great flight of steps is always thronged with them. An imposing structure of white granite and deep blue tiles set off by the dark green pine trees, it was built in 1929 by the architect who was responsible for the Memorial Hall in Guangzhou. From the large bronze statue at the bottom you climb 392 marble steps to the Memorial Hall, dominated by a 5 metre tall seated white marble figure of Sun Yatsen. Beyond is the burial chamber with another marble effigy lying on the stone coffin. The Three People's Principles – Nationalism, Democracy and People's Livelihood – are carved here in gold on black marble. The Mausoleum itself is impressive and the view down the steps and across to the hills is beautiful – but most people could do without its enormous marble statues of elderly civilians in marble trousers.

The **Beamless Hall** – Wuliang Temple or Hall of Eternity – was completed in 1381 and has been much restored since. Unusually large (53 metres long by 37 wide and 22 high) it is also unusual in its self-supporting brick arch construction with five columns but no central beam; the mortar used was lime mixed with glutinous rice. The Hall was used to store Buddhist sutras before the Taiping rebels made it a fortress. Behind the Hall stands the Songfeng Pavilion and behind this again is the **Linggu pagoda**, octagonal, 9 storeys and 60 metres high, built in the

1930s. Linggu temple was first built in AD513 but was moved in 1381 to make room for the Ming Emperor's tomb. Although the Mausoleum and the Linggu buildings are connected by a shuttle bus it is worth walking one way in order to take in the **Liuwei waterside pavilion**, built out on stilts over a stretch of water with a peaceful open vista of hills beyond. The road is much patronised by jogging students from the university.

The **Ming Xiao Tomb** is the burial place of *Zhu Yuan Zhang*, founder of the Ming dynasty and the only one of its 14 emperors to be buried at Nanjing. It took 2 years – from 1381 to 1383 – and 100,000 soldiers and conscripts to complete. Although originally larger than the Ming tombs near Beijing, its halls and pavilions, enclosed by a 22km long vermilion wall, were mostly destroyed by the Taipings. Nor are the 1000 deer mentioned by some writers any more to be seen, though perhaps the descendants of some of the 100,000 pine trees do survive. By the **Da Jin** (the main gate) is the **Si Fancheng** stele, the largest example of its kind from the Ming era, standing nearly 5 metres high on a *Bixi* – a mythical creature like a tortoise, said to be the ninth son of a dragon. Beyond is the **Shandao** – Sacred Way, sometimes called the Shixiang Lu or Stone Statue Road – lined with 12 pairs of great stone animals and 4 pairs of officials. Each statue is carved from a single block of stone weighing over 80 tons. This is far more pleasant, and less commercial, than the Sacred Way to the Ming Tombs near Beijing: the pairs of animals here are grouped together on a central grass verge, with the road passing either side – the officials stand among the trees further off. Through the **Lingxing Gate** at the far end across a stone bridge you can see the 56 stone column bases of the main hall, the **Xiaoling**. Beyond is the **Dulong** (Single Dragon Mound) containing the tomb of the emperor and his wife and the 50 courtiers and maids of honour who were buried alive to keep them company. The approach road ought to be straight but in fact it does a bend to avoid the tomb of *Sun Quan* of Wu.

The **Zijin Shan Observatory** was built in 1929 on one of the three peaks where the Taiping formerly had a stronghold: the third largest in China, the observatory boasts 6 observation towers and a small exhibition of early instruments. They include a gnomon column where the sun, shining through a small hole on to a gauge, allowed the observer to calculate the seasons and days of the year, and also an armillary sphere of Han date for locating the constellations. Above all, though, the peak offers coolness and a spectacular view.

The Southern Tang tombs
Dating from 937–75, the tombs of *Li Bian*, the first Southern Tang emperor, and his successor *Li Jing*, are about 20km south of Nanjing on **Niu Shou Shan** – Bull's Head Hill. All that remains is an underground

chamber with wall paintings and bas reliefs; the moveable finds from here are in the Provincial Museum in Nanjing.

Qixia

If you have time and would like a day in fresher air than Nanjing, **QIXIA** (Lingering Sunset Temple) on the Three-Peaked Qixia mountain 25km north-east of the city makes another worthwhile excursion. There is a one-day bus trip from the Tourist Bus Station in Drum Tower Square. The mountain has always been known for the medicinal herbs which grow here and about AD480 a temple was founded which became during the Tang era one of the four largest in China. The present building, though, dates only from 1908. Behind it is the **Thousand Buddha Cliff** with 515 Buddhas carved in 394 niches. The carvings were begun in AD484 and continued for at least 28 years, which ranks them among the earliest of Buddhist 'cave' sculptures. In front of the cliff is a 7-storey pagoda in stone, octagonal in shape and 18 metres high. It is thought to date from about AD601 and was built to house Buddhist relics.

NORTHERN JIANGSU

There's considerably less of interest once you get away from the historic canal towns in the south of Jiangsu province. The canal north of the Yangzi is navigable all the way to the borders of Shandong and with luck, silt from flooding allowing, on to the Yellow River. And there are ambitious plans to dredge enough to allow large vessels to get at least as far as Xuzhou and its mines. However, there's no tourist traffic along here, and frankly not a great deal to see. For the most part the country is flat and wet, ideal for salt panning but little else. **HUAIAN** is an open town, but only because it's the birthplace of *Zhou Enlai* and hence very popular with Overseas Chinese – there are a few interesting pavilions and pagodas. If you want to break your journey somewhere in this region though, Xuzhou is a better bet.

In the hilly north-west of Jiangsu where it rubs shoulders with Shandong, Henan and Anhui, **XUZHOU** lies on the old course of the Yellow River, close by a branch of the Grand Canal and is nowadays an important railway junction – meeting point of the Peking–Shanghai and Longhai lines. As such it's a transport centre for all four provinces, and has been throughout a long history. Perhaps not quite so ancient as the legends would have it (this is supposed to have been the kingdom of Peng in 2000BC), Xuzhou certainly is old: the capital of several early dynasties and birthplace of *Liu Bang*, founder of the Han dynasty. Over 3,000 terracotta figures have recently been discovered nearby in three pits, probably the most important archaeological discovery in China since the Terracotta Army was found near Xi'an. The hills all around also house a number of royal tombs and defensive positions, but nowadays they're important mainly for the coal on which Xuzhou thrives. The mines lend an industrial air to what is increasingly a large city, a dusty place with dusty trees, but which at its heart remains attractive enough – refreshed by waterways and small lakes.

The old Yellow River runs more or less diagonally through town from north-west to south-east; the Longhai railway runs past the north side of town; the Beijing–Shanghai line cutting down the east to meet it. The main **railway station** is at the eastern end of Huaihuai Lu, a major thoroughfare, while the **North Station**, on the Longhai line, is at the top of Zhongshan Lu. The core of the city lies in a rectangle bordered by these two streets along with Heping Lu and, in the east, the old river. A no.2 bus will take you on a circular route from the main station passing close to many of the places you might want to go: up Haicheng Lu to the North Station, down Zhongshan Lu through the centre and past the long distance **bus station** then along Heping Lu and up Fuxing Lu towards the station again. The *Nanjiao Binguan* lies on this route in Heping Lu, set in its own comfortable grounds complete with pavilion and rockery. Prices are average to high, food average to bad, and CITS is on the premises. Other **hotels** which you could try include the *Pencheng* and

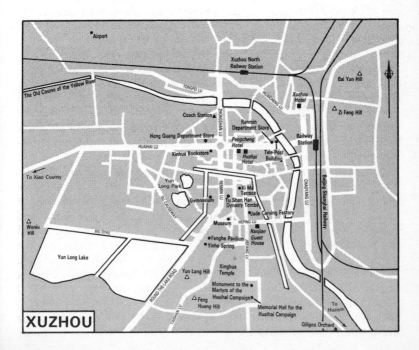

Huaihuai, close to each other in Huaihuai Lu, and the *Xuzhou* in the station square, but although all these serve reasonable food they're at best reluctant to take in stray foreigners as guests. There is a **ticket office** in Huaihuai Lu for all outgoing train, bus and air services: **PSB** is near the People's Park in the centre. Huaihuai Lu and Zhongshan Lu are where you'll find most of the **shops, cinemas** and other action – Huaihuai Lu in particular livens up as you cross the river and approach the centre, with a packed vegetable market along one side, street barbers doing a brisk trade and crowded ice cream and cold drinks parlours. If you're looking for a **restaurant** other than the big hotels, try the *Goulu Fandian* in Zhongshan Lu.

Which should leave you ready to see the city. For a general view climb up from Zhongshan Lu between the Tushan tomb and Jiefang Lu. Here a maze of tiny back alleys skirt the high walls of traditional compounds – once, as the heavy studded doors guarded by battered stone figures attest, magnificent dwellings, now packed to the rafters and surrounded by peddlers, washing and the smoke of outdoor stoves. Finally you'll emerge onto the **Xi Ma Terrace**. It takes some imagination to visualise the wealthy merchants and officials living on this hill in immaculate private enclosures with neat steps leading up on all sides to the terrace, from what is now a flattened mound of henpecked wasteland shared by a shabby pavilion and a public urinal, but you do at least get a good view of the city and the contrast between the great modern buildings along Huaihuai Lu and the small houses, shops and market stalls hugging the canal.

The nearby **Tushan tomb** looks like a giant's sandpit – a mess – but you can see a reconstruction of the inner tomb and most of the important finds at the **Museum**, not far away on the corner of Heping Lu. Small, modern and well laid out, it contains a larger than usual number of important objects for its size, including the jade burial costume sewn with silver which was found in one of the tombs (though see p. 250), an early board game complete with pieces, some beautiful jewellery and jade and some impressive stone engravings. Sidestepping the repetition and stodginess of so many provincial collections, it concentrates on illustrating the history of the area with good maps and scale models which you can enjoy even without reading the Chinese explanations. Outside, the long halls overlook a central pond and gardens where you can see the **Pavilion of the Tang Tablet**.

On the west side of Zhongshan Lu is the entrance to **Yunlong** – Dragon in the Cloud Hill – overlooking a man made lake. It looks unpromising to start with, gritty stone slopes held together by tired looking pine and cypress and scattered with lumps of rock – one of which is supposed to have been the bed of the poet *Su Dongpo*, though this really does stretch the imagination. Higher up, however, the grey stone walls of the **Xinghua**

Temple have the imposing feel of a fortress, you'll find the enormous **Sakyamuni Buddha**, hewn out of the rock in the 5C, and a delicate figure of **Guanyin** looking rather like Red Riding Hood with a baby on her knee, several tiny pairs of red slippers on the altar in front and a red shawl over her shoulders. On the lower slopes enterprising locals have set up amateurish shooting ranges, heavily patronised by Sunday crowds.

At the southern end of Jiefang Lu is another mound – **Fenghuang** (Phoenix Hill) – where you can visit the Memorial Hall and the **Monument to the Martyrs of the 1949 Huaihuai Campaign**. The Huaihuai campaign was a vital stage in the Communist victory – by winning here the PLA inflicted a fatal blow to the Kuomintang, who lost three-quarters of an army of half a million, defectors to the Red camp or prisoners. The memorial itself though is a typically dour 1960s tiled hall faced by a massive obelisk, not overly exciting.

Lianyungang

In the extreme north-eastern corner of the province, on the Yellow Sea coast at the end of the Longhai railway line, **LIANYUNGANG** is rather out on a limb from the traveller's point of view. It's a working town rather than a tourist attraction and needs to be taken as such, though the surroundings – it has a fine harbour with mountains at its back – and the 1920s and 1930s architecture do at least offer something to look at. **Yuntai Hill** in particular has a reputation as a 'scenic spot'. Mostly, though it's an atmospheric fishing town with a busy port and, on the coast to the south, a flourishing salt industry. Local cuisine is thoroughly coastal too – strong on prawns and crab.

ZHEJIANG

ZHEJIANG, one of the smallest provinces but a wealthy one, is made up of two quite different areas. The north shares climate, geography, history and the Grand Canal with Jiangsu; it is highly cultivated and netted with waterways. The south borders on, and resembles, Fujian, mountainous and sparsely populated. There's a long history in the fertile north. Recent excavations have shown that the Yangzi delta had Neolithic settlements every bit as old as those which in the Yellow River valley preceded the Imperial capitals: at **Hemudu** on the Shaoxing–Ningbo plain settled farmers were growing cultivated rice and building with stone tools 2-storey houses with precisely worked mortise and tenon joints as much as 7000 years ago, when rhinoceros and elephant still roamed here. After the Grand Canal was built, and especially under the Southern Song when the Imperial Court had to retreat to the south, northern Zhejiang enjoyed a spell of remarkable growth, ending only when the capital moved back north to Beijing.

The whole province is attractive, but most of the towns open to tourism are in the north. **Hangzhou** is the terminus of the Grand Canal; once a great capital and still a centre for silk, papermaking and printing. The West Lake here, former resort of emperors, now offers its temples and tea gardens to hordes of honeymoon couples and tourists. **Shaoxing** is a floating city threaded by canals, its beautiful surroundings best seen by boat. **Ningbo,** once a major port for coastal trade, has long been superseded by Shanghai, but remains a major fishing centre with a rich port atmosphere and some unusual temples nearby. The famous Buddhist island of **Putuoshan** offshore has recently been opened to foreigners. In the south is **Wenzhou,** a former treaty port which is still busy and noisy: it's renowned for its oranges and close to some magnificent mountain scenery.

HANGZHOU

HANGZHOU lies in the north of Zhejiang at the head of Hangzhou Bay, capital of the province and southern terminus of the Grand Canal. The canal has been the instrument of the city's wealth and fortunes, making it for over a thousand years a place of great wealth and culture. Surprisingly though – and despite the fact that *Yu the Great*, tamer of floods, is said to have moored his boats near here – it has little in the way of a legendary past or ancient history. The fact is that the present site, on the east shore of West Lake near the point where the Qiantong river flows into Hangzhou Bay, was originally under water. West Lake itself started life as a wide shallow inlet off the bay: it's said that Emperor Qin Shihuang sailed in from the sea and moored his boats on what is now the northwestern shore of the lake. Only around the 4C did river currents and tides begin to throw up a barrier of silt where this inlet opened to the estuary and the sea, a barrier which eventually closed off what is now West Lake and on which Hangzhou grew up.

As a city it rapidly made up for this slow start. The first great impetus came from the building of the **Grand Canal** at the end of the 6C. The southern terminus of the Canal, Hangzhou developed with spectacular speed as the centre for trade between north and south. Under the Tang dynasty it was a rich and thriving city, but its situation between lake and river made it vulnerable to the fierce equinoctial tides in Hangzhou Bay. A missionary writing in the 1850s described 'the bore, a tidal wave that rushes into the river with a frightful roar and the aspect of a wall of water . . . in October when it rises highest the magistrates meet it with prostrations and burning incense, believing it to herald the approach of a sea god.' A thousand years earlier, when Tang dynasty governors were building locks and dykes to control the waters round Hangzhou, the technique was different. A contemporary writer, describing the beginning of a sea wall in 910 says that 'archers were stationed on the shore to shoot down the waves while a poem was recited to propitiate the King of Dragons and Government of the Waters; the waves immediately left the wall and broke on the opposite bank so the work could go on.'

It was during the **Song dynasty** that Hangzhou received its second great impetus when the encroachment of the Tartars in the north destroyed Kaifeng, sent the imperial family into captivity beyond the Wall, and drove one prince to take refuge in the south. From 1138–1279 Hangzhou became the Imperial Capital, with all that implied for wealth, luxury and learning. Many rich families moved to the city and the population grew rapidly. A writer of the 12C describes the city as 'a rectangle 4 miles by 1 mile with high ramparts, five gateways for canals and thirteen monumental gates for great thoroughfares'. Onto its sandbank Hangzhou crammed a population as large as that of Chang'an under the Tang, but in a quarter of the space; tall wooden buildings up to 5 storeys high were crowded into narrow streets. There was a constant risk of **fire**. One writer describes how in 1132 13,000 houses were destroyed and he and his family had to take refuge in the lake. In 1137 another 10,000 were burned and in 1208 a fire which lasted for four days destroyed 57,000 houses. The risk was so regular that the merchants built special warehouses surrounded by water.

This was a great city of the silk and brocade industry, and indeed of all the trades that waited upon the court and the wealthy. When Marco Polo wrote of Hangzhou towards the end of the 13C he spoke of 'the City of Heaven, the most beautiful and magnificent in the world. It has ten principal market places, always with an abundance of victuals, roebuck, stags, harts, hares, partridge, pheasants, quails, hens, ducks, geese . . . all sorts of vegetables and fruits . . . huge pears weighing ten pounds apiece. Each day a vast quantity of fish is brought from the ocean. There is also an abundance of lake fish.' Of this last he adds (perhaps it sounded more attractive to the 13C than it does to us) 'Thanks to the refuse from the city these fish are plump and tasty.'

After the Southern Song dynasty was finally overthrown by the Mongols in 1279 Hangzhou ceased to be a capital city. But it remained an important centre of commerce and a place of luxury, with markets selling flowers, pearls, precious stones, books; with big taverns and fashionable tea-houses; with parks and gardens outside the ramparts and with hundreds of boats on the lake. Later the Ming rulers repaired the walls and deepened and restored the Grand Canal so that large ships could go all the way from Hangzhou to Beijing. Under them and after-

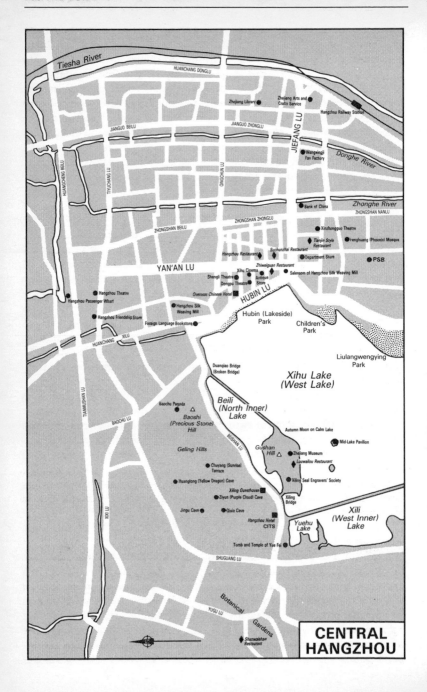

Tiesha River

HUANCHANG DONGLU

Zhejiang Library

Zhejiang Arts and
Crafts Service

Hangzhou Railway Station

JIANGUO BEILU

JIANGUO ZHONGLU

JIEFANG LU

Wangxingji
Fan Factory

Donghe River

TITUCHANG LU

QINGCHUN LU

HUANGCHENG BEILU

Bank of China

Zhonghe River

ZHONGSHAN NANLU

ZHONGSHAN ZHONGLU

Xinzhongguo Theatre

ZHONGSHAN BEILU

Tianjin Style
Restaurant

Fenghuang (Phoenix) Mosque

Suchunzhai Restaurant

Hangzhou Restaurant

Zhiweiguan Restaurant

YAN'AN LU

Xihu Cinema

Department Store

●PSB

Shengli Theatre

Antique
Store

Saleroom of Hangzhou Silk Weaving Mill

Dongpo Theatre

HUBIN LU

Hangzhou Theatre

Overseas Chinese Hotel

Hangzhou Passenger Wharf

Hangzhou Silk
Weaving Mill

Hangzhou Friendship Store

Foreign Language Bookstore

Hubin (Lakeside)
Park

Children's
Park

HUANCHANG

XILU

Liulangwengying
Park

TIANMUSHAN LU

Duanqiao Bridge
(Broken Bridge)

Xihu Lake
(West Lake)

Baochu Pagoda

△

Beili
(North Inner)
Lake

BAOCHU LU

Baoshi
(Precious Stone)
Hill

Autumn Moon on Calm Lake

BEISHAN LU

Gushan
Hill △

Mid-Lake Pavilion

Geling Hills

Zhejiang Museum

Chuyang (Sunrise)
Terrace

Louwailou Restaurant

Huanglong (Yellow Dragon) Cave

Xiling Guesthouse

Xiling Seal Engravers' Society

XIXI LU

Ziyun (Purple Cloud) Cave

Xiling
Bridge

Jingu Cave

Qixia Cave

Xili
(West Inner)
Lake

Hangzhou Hotel
CITS

Yuehu
Lake

Tomb and Temple of Yue Fei

SHUGUANG LU

Botanical
Gardens

YUGU LU

Shanwaishan
Restaurant

CENTRAL
HANGZHOU

wards the Qing, Hangzhou became one of China's most famous resorts and beauty spots. Two great Qing emperors, *Kangxi* and *Qian Long*, frequented the city and built villas, temples and gardens by the lake. But all this, and the city itself, was largely destroyed when the Taiping rebels besieged and captured Hangzhou in 1861 and even more when the imperial forces recaptured it in 1863. It's said that three-quarters of the buildings were destroyed and that 90 per cent of the population died or fled. Hangzhou recovered surprisingly quickly, though, and the foreign concessions which were established towards the end of the century, followed by the building of the railway line first to Shanghai and then to Ningbo, stimulated the growth of new industries alongside the traditional silk and brocade manufactories.

Modern Hangzhou

Since Liberation the city has grown to attain a population of around 1 million, much the same as under the Song. There are a few traditional streets of whitewashed, wooden-fronted houses and the shopping streets are lively enough, but frankly what the Taiping rebellion has left is not the most exciting of cities, especially as with the crowds of tourists it can be thoroughly crowded and noisy.

It's the **West Lake** that matters, though, and despite the destruction of many of its temples and pagodas, the natural beauty of lake and hills, which have given Hangzhou its name as a beauty spot down the centuries, was not so easily destroyed. Today it's one of China's most popular destinations for honeymoon couples, and one of her busiest resorts. This has advantages: there's no shortage of things to do, a wealth of reasonable restaurants and several good hotels. And much of the Taiping destruction on the lakeside has been repaired – the temples rebuilt, the gardens replanted. Most of the places to visit are on the lake or immediately around its shores, but there are a few more distant attractions: Lingyin temple is in the western hills in the midst of attractive walking country; further afield you can take day tours to Moganshan and to the Yaolin stalactite caves.

Arrival and orientation

Since the canal has been so important for Hangzhou, it would seem appropriate to arrive here by boat. Unfortunately the trip **from Suzhou** is a lot less attractive than it might be as you're not allowed to buy tickets for the day boat, being forced instead to travel by night, boarding about 5pm in Suzhou and disembarking at Hangzhou at 7am. Don't visualise a romantic night under the stars either – I managed to get a berth, but berth or seat you are herded into the bowels of the boat, a narrow passage with small slatted cubicles on either side. There are 4 wooden slatted bunks in each with rush mats, rush pillows and just enough room to stand between the bunks. From the top bunks you can peer through the slats at the Canal outside. There's plenty of action on the water – a constant stream of traffic and young boys taking their lives in their hands as they jump in among the hurrying boats to cool off. I watched a fine sunset and saw, 7km from Suzhou, the elegant 53-arched **Baodai Qiao** – Precious Girdle Bridge – with the new bridge behind. Peering out is tiring, though, and you can't expect much sleep when you finally lie down – the intense heat and the mosquitoes will see to that. If you can't face this, the alternative is a straight forward 3–4 hour train journey from Shanghai.

Hangzhou and its lake are sheltered from the north, west and south by hills. The city is further restricted by West Lake on one side and on the other by the railway and the Teisha river, a tributary of the Qiantong. The Grand Canal cuts across the north of the city to meet the Teisha: the **passenger wharf** is in the north-west of the city on Huancheng Bei Lu. For the rest, it's very much a grid pattern – the Central Canal and the Eastern Canal flow from north to south, paralleled by the main roads **Zhongshan Lu** and **Yanan Lu**, and with two major east–west roads, **Qingchun Lu** and **Jiefang Lu**, cutting across them. From the city a road also runs right round the lake shore. The heart of Hangzhou lies on the lakeside, in and around a small area bounded by Hubin Lu along the lake, Qingchun Lu, Zhongshan Lu and Jiefang Lu. The **railway station** is in the east on Jiancheng Lu, with a booking office there and a down-town **ticket office** in Yuan Sha Lu, while the long-distance **bus station** is in the north-west, not far from the canal jetty.

Hotels are mostly round the lake. The *Hangzhou Fandian*, on Beishan Lu around the north shore, is the most convenient for visiting the lakeside sites and is easily reached from the railway station by bus. Enormous and old-fashioned, it is nowadays jointly run with a Swiss hotel company: a lobby coffee bar serves coffee and cakes; the second floor restaurant serves a mammoth breakfast buffet, and the ground floor restaurant, open only in the evenings, has a live band playing old time dance music. It is, however, expensive – prices ranging up to ¥150 for a suite with a lake view. *Hua Qiao Fandian* is the cheap alternative if the Hangzhou is full – a rather shabby building, nearer town on Hubin Lu in the north-eastern corner of the lake. More pricey: the *Huagang Hotel* in Xishan Lu, a 4-storey building in traditional style, some way off in the south-western corner of the lake overlooking Huagang Park; or the *Xiling Binguan* not far from the Hangzhou. A no.7 trolley bus from the station heads along Jiefang Lu then round the north shore serving the *Hua Qiao*, the *Xiling* and the *Hangzhou*. For the *Huagang* take a no.4 bus from Yanan Lu around the south of the lake. From the canal wharf of bus station a no.51 trolley will take you down Yanan Lu and Jiefang Lu to the station, crossing both these other routes.

Finding somewhere to eat is no problem at all in a resort of this size, with a choice of good **restaurants** on and all around Yanan Lu. Among those to look out for are the *Hangzhou* in Yanan Lu, one of the city's largest, and the *Kuiyuanguan* in Jiefang Lu, over a hundred years old and specialising in noodles cooked in dozens of different ways. Out around the lake, *Louwailou* on the Gushan peninsula occupies a prime site overlooking the Hangzhou Hotel and is famous for West Lake Sweet and Sour Fish and other local specialities: the **vegetarian restaurant** at the Lingyin Temple is handy for lunch. The **nightlife** is hardly going to rival Broadway, but this is a resort so Hangzhou at least has its own acrobatic troupe and song and dance group as well as numerous theatre/cinemas. There are regular shows at the Hangzhou Hotel and at *Xin Zhongguo* in Qingnian Lu, *Shengli* in Yanan Lu, *Hangzhou Theatre* in Tiyuchang Lu and the *Railway Workers' Cultural Palace* in Chengzhan Lu. One thing to look out for is Shaoxing Opera, established here for some 80 years. The performers are all women, and it has its origins in an era when men and women were not allowed to touch on stage: the single-sex cast got round the problem.

Shops are mostly in the centre where you'd expect to find them, though there's a large Friendship Store near the bus station in the north-west. Another big department store is at 739 Jiefang Lu: **specialist shops** include the *Dragon Well Tea Shop* on Yanan Lu and outlets for silks and other materials in Youdian Lu and Hubin Lu. You might well find more choice, though, by simply wandering around the smaller shops in the centre, where there are also a number of antique and craft shops.

CITS is on the ground floor of the Hangzhou Hotel – more efficient than most, it will arrange onward tickets (for example by air-conditioned bus to Huangshan for ¥18) while you relax and can also set up visits to silk factories. The **PSB** is rather tucked away on the corner of Ding An Lu and Hui Min Lu; they say they're open any time but you have to ring the bell.

Seeing West Lake

The **West Lake** forms a series of landscape designs in water, rock, trees, grass, buildings and their reflections – all backed by luxuriant wooded hills. On a sunny day the colours are brilliant, but even with grey skies and choppy waters the famous lake views are delicate, soothing and tranquil. For the Chinese they are also laden with literary associations, few of which you are likely to come to terms with. Only the crowds are liable to detract from your enjoyment of the peace – the sightseeing is far from strenuous, but there still seem to be queues for every park bench.

Enjoy it while you can though, for crowds will no doubt get far worse when Japanese plans for an amusement park beside the lake become reality.

The lake is shallow, as you would expect given the manner of its formation, and not very large – just over 3km from north to south, just under 3km from east to west. As well as for its beauty, it has always been important to Hangzhou as a source of relatively unpolluted water. Sometime in the 13C there's a record of a Censor at the court lodging an accusation against two officials who had built houses on piles over the lake and were washing their hair and doing their laundry there. That anyone should dream of complaining about such a universal Chinese practice shows the great importance attached to the lake.

Already under the Tang dynasty they were working to control the waters with dikes and locks and the two causeways which now enclose sections of the lake – Bai Di in the north and Su Di in the west – originated in those embankments.

Bai Di and Gushan

Bai Di causeway is a short one; it starts off near the *Hangzhou Hotel*, along the outer edge of Gushan (sometimes called Solitary Island, though it's really a peninsula) and runs back to the north shore, enclosing the small strip of North Inner Lake. Bai Di has two bridges, one of which, **Duan Qiao** – Broken Bridge – gets its name because the snow melt early on the hump of the bridge and there seems to be a gap. In the famous legend this is where *White Snake* in the form of a beautiful girl met the young scholar *Xuxian*. The walk along this causeway on a fine day is sparkling blue with fine vistas on every side.

There's a great view from the top of **Gushan** too. This tiny promontory crammed with pavilions, pagodas and other buildings was originally landscaped under the Tang, but the present style dates from China's last dynasty, the Qing, when the Emperor Qian Long built himself a palace here. Part of his building is now the **Zhejiang Provincial Museum** – strong on history, closed on Mondays. The **Xiling Seal Engravers Society**, founded in 1904, occupies the western side of the hill. Its tiny park encloses a pavilion with a pleasant blend of steps, carved stone tablets, and nearby a small early Buddhist stupa of 16 facets, with carvings of *lohans*, or disciples. Seal engraving has a long history; in earliest times bronze was used but from the 14C stone seal engraving developed – a name or saying cut in stone and impressed in vermilion on a painting or piece of calligraphy. On the northern side of Gushan is **Fanghe pavilion**, where a Song poet lived in retirement, tending a pair of cranes. At the eastern end of the hill by the water is another of Qian Long's buildings, the **Autumn Moon on a Calm Lake Pavilion** which was and is the perfect place to watch the full moon. It's a tea-house now, very popular after sunset and full of honeymooners. The *Louwailou* **restaurant** is very good too.

On Gushan you can hire little paddle boats which are fun in the cool of the evening. At the other end of the day, if you are prepared to get up early – about 4.30 am – you can walk out to the end of Gushan to watch the sunrise, and see the blob of the sun heave itself with a jerk above the line of willows for an audience of early-rising Chinese, young and old, jogging, doing Tai Chi, racing skiffs on the lake, or simply lying on their backs on the park benches.

Su Di Causeway

The longer causeway, **Su Di**, named after the Song dynasty poet-official *Su Dong Po* who was governor of Hangzhou, starts near the Huagang Park in the south-west and runs the full length of the lake on the west side to the **Feng Yu Di** (Wind and Rain Pavilion) in the north. The causeway consists of six stone-arched bridges linked by an embankment planted with banana trees, weeping willows and plum trees. The stretch of water it encloses – **West Inner Lake** – includes **Huagang Park**, where under the Song a stretch of water was sealed off and a pavilion built from which to watch the unusual fish in it. Today there's a pond full of enormous fish in a garden which connects with the causeway. There are also wonderful stretches of grass, exotic trees and a strong flavour of Kew Gardens.

On the water

A voyage on this lake offers more refreshment and pleasure than any other experience on earth. On one side it skirts the city so that your barge commands a distant view of all its grandeur and loveliness, its temples, palaces, monasteries and gardens with towering trees running down to the water's edge. On the lake itself is an endless procession of barges thronged with pleasure seekers.

Marco Polo's description may be marginally over the top, but it's still broadly accurate today, and a trip on the lake is certainly a pleasant way to fill in a few hours. At the **Jetty on Gushan** you can pick up one of a constant stream of small, battery-powered, canopied boats which glide across to the many small islands on the lake, dropping and picking up passengers at each one. You can explore as many as you have time for.

Further out in the lake, you can also embark for **Three Pools Reflecting the Moon**. This is a roughly circular embankment thrown up in 1607: bridges link across from north to south and east to west so that the whole thing seems like a wheel with four spokes and a central hub just large enough for a pavilion/shop/restaurant. The four stretches of water thus enclosed are like small lakes within the lake – they are covered with lotus and the whole effect is quite charming. At the southern edge are three stone pagodas in the water, said to control the evil spirits lurking in the deepest spots of the lake: each has five openings in which lights are placed, and these join with the moon to make sixteen reflections in the water. It is from the pagodas that the place takes its name.

There are three jetties on the embankment, serving Huagang Park and Hubin Lu back in town as well as Gushan. Along **Hubin Lu** the waterfront is perhaps Hangzhou's one really attractive feature, albeit an extraordinary one of pistachio green colonnaded department stores and Brighton-style hotels. From here you can also set out on an **evening trip** round the lake – the boat sets out around 7pm, its searchlight picking out clouds of midges along with stretches of shore and bits of bridges as the guide recites in Chinese the legendary, literary and historical import of everything you see. It might be more revealing if they did it in daylight.

Around the Lake

Most of Hangzhou's other sights are on or near the lake shores, but while many are attractive spots or good viewpoints, few deserve a major excursion on their own. One good way to see a number of them is by **bike**: there's a **Hire Shop** near the Bai Di causeway where it meets the square. It opens at 7am – leave a ¥10 deposit with some identification and pay 25fen per hour, or keep it overnight for ¥3.50. If you set out clockwise round the lake from Hubin Lu you'll first pass *Liu Lang Weng*, **Listening to the Orioles among the Willows Park**. As so often, the name is its best feature. The park was converted from wasteland after the Liberation and is well kept but dull.

Wushan Hill lies at the southern end of the city, the site of the Town God's temple when Hangzhou was Imperial capital. It gives a good view of the lake, of the city proper, of what is left of the canal network, and of Zhongshan Lu, the main road which roughly follows the Imperial Way. This originally led to the Song Palace on **Fenghuang** (Phoenix Hill) just south of Wushan.

On your right a little further on is **Xizhao** – Sunset Hill – with the ruins of the **Leifeng Pagoda**. According to legend, it was beneath here that the abbot of Jinshan imprisoned *White Snake* until she was rescued by her faithful maid. Built in the 10C, the pagoda was burned down in the 16C by Japanese pirates to stop it sending warnings of their raids. The remains finally collapsed in 1924 after locals had been 'borrowing' bricks from its base for years. Some of the inner bricks contained Buddhist scrolls, now in the museum.

Nanping Hill is immediately on your left after Xizhao. The monastery here – *Jiang Si* or the **Monastery of Pure Compassion** – was founded in 954 and in its heyday was one of the two largest in Hangzhou. That day has long passed, and for years the monastery was left to decay behind two dreary apartment blocks and a baseball pitch. It never quite died, though, and is now in the early stages of a major restoration programme. When I was there workmen were boring test holes in the wooden pillars and building brick supports so that the rotten wood could be removed and replaced. It's interesting to see the structure uncluttered by statuary and decorations. While the temple is out of action you can walk up the slope to a temporary altar with all the paraphernalia in miniature – small white statue, tiny drum and bell, bowls of fruit and flowers. I saw hot food placed in front of the statue so the temple is certainly functioning.

Just past Nanping turn left down Hupao Lu away from the lake and the **Zoo** is on your right. It is better laid out than most, set among lush wooded slopes has the usual two pandas, as well as tigers, leopards, bears, and an interesting collection of water birds. From the opposite side of Hupao Lu a path leads up to **Yuhuang hill**, between the southern end of the lake and the Qiantang river. Here is the old **Fuxing Taoist temple**, a few caves with Yuan rock sculptures and, below, a view of the **Eight Trigrams** surrounding a mound which was once the Altar of Heaven. Here the Song emperors used to come for the ritual of the spring ploughing and sowing.

Beyond the zoo you can walk up on the right to a hill covered with dense trees, bamboo, springs and pools. A shady path climbs beside an ice-cold stream, where all the Chinese paddle to cool their feet and drench towels to mop their faces. It's likely to be crowded, and can seem quite a climb in hot weather. Higher up beyond a miscellaneous clutch of buildings the **Tiger Running Spring** – *Hupao Quan* – emerges from gloomy, sweating rock beside a hideous plaster tiger, popular with the Chinese as a background for photographs. For centuries connoisseurs have rated this the Third Best Spring in China for tea-making, and a fine match for **Dragon Well tea**, grown not far away. Masses of tea-houses dotted about the hillside invite you to sample both. The water is full of minerals and has a high surface tension – the game is to see how many coins you can add to a brimming cup before it overflows. The spring's name is said to have been given by a monk who prayed for water so that he could found a temple here; he dreamt he saw two tigers clawing the ground at a certain spot and there he found his spring.

Continuing down Hupao Lu and bearing right near the estuary, you'll come to the **Six Harmonies Pagoda** overlooking the river from **Yue Hua** hill. Built in AD970 to ward off the spirit responsible for the regular tidal bores up the estuary which caused so much flooding, it's now the most popular advantage point for the crowds who flock here to watch the great bore at the autumn equinox. A notice warns the over-enthusiastic among them not to perch on the upturned ears of the eaves, which are hung with bells. A solid wood and brick construction, 60 metres high, octagonal in shape and supported on 24 pillars, the pagoda has seen use as a lighthouse in one of its many rebuildings. The Six Harmonies of the name are the six codes of Buddhist practice – harmony of body, thought and speech, abstention from temptation, the accumulation of wealth and the expression of opinions. Its the harmony of the view which strikes most, though: dark, lush mountains behind, the muddy estuary and its bridge in the foreground, Hangzhou emerging from the silted-up river bend in the middle distance.

Upriver from the pagoda a road known as **Nine Creeks and Eighteen Gullies** runs off at right angles to the river and up through Dragon Well. It's a delightful narrow lane for a bike ride or a half-day stroll, meandering through paddy and tea terraces with the hills rising in swelling ranks on either side and not a soul about except the occasional teapicker with her basket, who tries to sell you her tea. Halfway along the road the **Xizhongsi restaurant** straddles the water where it widens into a serene lagoon. It's an exquisite spot with a tiny pavilion nestling into the woody slope above, and it serves excellent tea and food. Leaving the restaurant to your right, you continue up a bumpy rock and cobble track, constantly crisscrossed by streams where you have to get off your bicycle and wheel it through the water alongside the neat stepping stones.

At **Dragon Well village** the tea terraces rise on all sides behind the houses and everyone is busy cutting and sorting tea tips. You can see old men picking through the dried tea, and you may be offered the chance to sample some in someone's house. The local shop is full of jars of pickle. Dragon Well itself is at the end of the village, a group of buildings around an unimpressive spring, all got up in a rather touristy fashion. The no.27 bus terminates here, and all the locals wait to pester passengers to buy their tea.

From Dragon Well there is a road which forks right and leads back to Hupao Lu, passing a number of caves, a tea factory and a weaving factory, and so back to the lake. This will probably be enough for a day's bicycle ride. If you don't want to try a bicycle a no.4 **bus** will take you to the zoo, the Six Harmonies Pagoda and the turn-off for the Nine Creeks, while the no.27 goes along Beishan Lu to Dragon Well. There are also tourist shuttle buses between the zoo and Dragon Well. And there are other sites which can be visited by bus or on foot.

The tomb of Yue Fei

The **Tomb and Temple of Yue Fei** is near the north end of the Su Di causeway, not far from the Hangzhou Hotel. Yue Fei, a Song general who helped to keep the Jin invaders at bay after the fall of the northern capital at Kaifeng in 1126, fell foul of the Prime Minister who along with his wife and two accomplices laid false charges against him. Found guilty, Yue Fei was executed at the age of 39. Twenty years later, however, the next emperor annulled all charges against him and had him reburied with full honours in the capital – there is now a large memorial with a statue. The four characters above read 'Protect the Country with Great Integrity' and were said to have been tattooed on his back by his mother. There's an appealing tomb with everything in miniature – a tiny bridge over water, a small double row of men and animals in stone, steles, a small mound with old pine trees – and four cast iron statues of the villains of the piece, kneeling with their hands behind their backs looking shamefaced.

The Botanical Gardens and the Jade Spring
A no.7 bus will take you from here to the entrance of the **Botanical Gardens**, some 200 acres at the north of the lake where they managed to grow *Metasequoia*, hitherto thought to be extinct in China, as well as some 200 varieties of bamboo. There is also a small 'Garden of a Hundred Herbs' where aromatic and medicinal herbs are grown in a rock garden. It's more peaceful here than in most places in Hangzhou, a good place to sit and write your postcards. **Yu Quan** – Jade Spring – is a natural spring which flows out behind the Gardens near the site of Qinglian, or Monastery of Clear Apples.

Lingyin Temple
The no.7 goes on to Lingyin. Get off at the terminus, walk back on your tracks and turn up the side entrance to the **cable car to the top of Beishan**. On a fine day there's a stunning view of the lake cradled in trees and the temple buildings below. Keep to the right going down and you come to the **Daoguang** – Restful Temple – with its hollowed-out rock altar and the spring below, where the locals fill their plastic water carriers.

A path edged with swathes of grey-green bamboo continues to the temple proper, **Lingyin** or Spirits' Retreat. Founded in AD326 by an Indian monk, Biu Li, who is buried nearby, it was the largest and most important monastery in Hangzhou and once had 3000 monks, 9 towers, 18 pavilions and 75 halls and rooms. It has been restored at least 16 times and was so badly riddled with woodworm in the 1940s that the main crossbeams collapsed on to the statues. In 1956 the government provided the money for restoration and the Zhejiang Academy of Fine Arts produced a replica of the Tang statue of Sakyamuni, 18 metres high and carved from 24 pieces of camphorwood. It's said that Zhou Enlai himself intervened to save the temple from the Cultural Revolution, and it remains an active temple with daily (early evening) services.

Here the old brushes against the new all the time. The **Hall of the Heavenly King** contains four large and highly painted Guardians of the Four Directions made in the 1930s, while the *Wei Tuo* Guardian of Buddhist Law and Order who shields the Matreya was carved from a single piece of wood 800 years ago. The two stone pillars with Buddhist inscriptions at the entrance to the hall date from 1969. The main hall was built under the Qing and is single-storey with multiple eaves and two early stone pagodas in front.

On the other side of the water, facing the temple, is **Feilaifeng** – the peak which flew here – so called because it is of limestone rather than the usual sandstone and is small and separate from the surrounding hills. The founder of the temple is said to have believed the hill had come from India; he swore a white monkey would be found in one of its caves – and so it was. It's worth wandering up the hill which is liberally pitted with caves in which hide more than 300 Buddhist carvings dating from 900–1400. There are usually enormous crowds here but the area is big enough to absorb them.

Other hills
Behind the tomb of Yue Fei is **Qixia Shan** – Mountain where Clouds Linger. There are a number of interesting caves and a fine walk along the ridge north of the lake, to **Gelingshan** and **Chuyang** (Sunrise Terrace) which is traditionally the spot for watching the spring sun rise over the lake. Behind is **Huang Long**, Yellow Dragon Cave. On nearby **Baochu** – Precious Stone Hill – is the pagoda built to pray for the safe return of a king of Wu Yue who was summoned to Kaifeng in 968 and did not return for many years. The present needle-like pagoda was built in 1933.

SHAOXING

SHAOXING, a smaller and more intimate version of Suzhou, is, I am almost sure, my favourite Chinese city. South of Hangzhou Bay in the midst of a flat plain crisscrossed by waterways and surrounded by low hills, it is one of the oldest cities in Zhejiang. During the Warring States period, from the 5C to the 3C BC, this was the capital of Yue – *Gou Jian* rallied his forces here after a series of defeats to finally overcome Wu. His watchtower stood in the west of the city on Wo Long hill, where the Viewing Sea Pavilion now stands. Much later, under the Song dynasty, Shaoxing flourished along with its neighbours, especially when the court moved to Hangzhou; there are southern Song tombs nearby. At the same time the lack of direct access to the sea kept it out of the front line of history, and it remains very much a provincial centre, one which has retained much of its character. At the end of the 18C *Grosier* described it 'in the middle of a wide fertile plain, the water all around making it resemble Venice, with its shores banked with white and pavements of the same stone on either hand'. And a century later the missionary *Martin* wrote: 'As in Venice the streets are canals and boats the common vehicles.'

It remains very like this – a town which is attractive in itself rather than for any particular sights. Though in the centre there are some modern roads, elsewhere it is a city of running streams, black-tiled white-washed houses, narrow lanes divided by water and alleys paved with stone slabs. From here have come some of the more colourful characters of Chinese legend and history – *Yu the Great*, Tamer of Floods, the Song poet *Lu You*, wife-murdering Ming painter *Xin Wei*, *Qiu Jin*, an early woman revolutionary, and the great writer of the revolutionary period, *Lu Xun*. Shaoxing is famous too for its yellow rice wine, tea, lace, opera and the foot-propelled boats on its canals. Although often recommended as a day trip from Hangzhou, a single day is not enough to do justice to the town itself, which demands to be wandered around at leisure, or to the buildings associated with Lu Xun, the Yu temple and tomb, or to the many places of interest in the beautiful countryside roundabout. And so far all of these are mercifully free of tourists.

Around the town
The **railway station** – virtually deserted when I arrived – is in the north. The line, a spur from Hangzhou to Ningbo, swings across this side of the city, keeping clear of the circuit of canals which encloses the city centre. Jiefang Lu, one of the few main streets, heads south from here, past the long-distance **bus station** and the **boat jetty** at Cheng Bei Bridge, and then crossing the east–west thoroughfare, Renmin Lu, before heading off out of the south gate. **Buses** 1 and 2 connect all three arrival points, no.1 turning east along Renmin Lu, no.2 continuing all the way to the south gate before turning off along the canal. A no.3 from Jiefang Lu will take you to the foreigners' **hotel** – *Shaoxing Fandian* – in the west of the city below Fu Shan hill, on Huai Shan Lu. It has one modern block, but the rest of the buildings, which used to be part of a temple, are grouped in charming old courtyard style. Prices start from around ¥5, the food is excellent and reasonably priced and the staff are friendly.

Fushan Park close to the hotel – also known as *Wo Long Shan* – is as good a place as any to start seeing the town. There's a large temple near the entrance (which closes at 4.30), a number of small pavilions as you climb the hill and, from the top, a bird's-eye view of the city, its canals and bridges. These **bridges** – almost all of them elegant, many of them ancient – are a pleasure wherever you come across them: 13C *Baziqiao*, on the east side near the Wuyun bus station, is particularly worth seeking out.

Shaoxing's principal 'sight', though, is the **Lu Xun Museum**. *Lu Xun* (1881–1936) was a revolutionary philosopher as well as being officially regarded as the greatest of modern Chinese writers. His childhood and early youth were spent in Shaoxing, and local characters populate his books – since the city has been relatively sheltered from violent change, much can still be recognised today. The buildings associated with him are in the town centre, close together in Lu Xun Lu, which runs east from Jiefang Lu. His birthplace has been turned into a museum – you can wander through the rooms with their 'original' furnishings, stroll in the garden, and have tea in a small hall hung with yellowing photographs. Having seen the high, secretive outer walls of so many compounds, it makes a change to get a look at the spacious interior and numerous rooms of a traditional house; probably scores would live in a place like

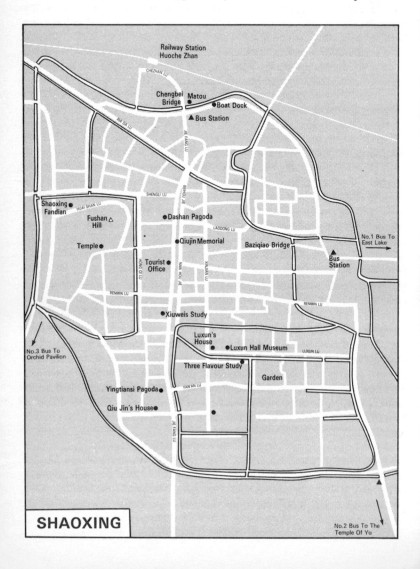

SHAOXING

this now. Next door is the **Memorial Hall**, crammed with personal odds and ends – manuscripts, cuttings from newspapers, photographs ancient and modern. And across the road is the **Three Flavour Study** where he was taught as a young boy.

Ten minutes walk south on Jiefang Lu, the **Yingtiangsi Pagoda** stands on low Tu Shan Hill. Part of a temple founded by the Song, restored by the Ming and Qing, burnt down by the Taiping rebels and rebuilt, this has recently been encased in bamboo scaffolding as it undergoes yet another restoration. Close by is the house once occupied by **Qiu Jin**, born here in 1875. After studying in Japan, *Qiu Jin* returned to China to work as a teacher, joining Sun Yatsen's *Tong Men Hui* for which she edited several revolutionary papers in Shanghai. After taking part in a series of abortive coups, she was captured and shot in Hangzhou in 1907. The house is full of background material to all this, and though there's no explanation in English the photographs and paintings manage to convey sharply the atmosphere of the time.

Back in the centre, turn left up Hou Guan Hang then left again to find the delightful studio of Ming painter **Xiu Wei** tucked away in a courtyard. Though its a simple place – bare rooms enlivened only by the odd piece of calligraphy – there's a very real feeling of the man who lived here. Or at least of someone who lived here. You can't help feeling that *Xiu Wei* himself, a leading artist of his age, ghost writer for criminals and a man who ended up in jail for murdering his wife, would have lived somewhere rather more exotic. Continue north on Jiefang Lu and you'll see another Song dynasty pagoda, **Da Shan Si**, though to get anywhere near it you'll have to struggle through factory yards on the left hand side of the road. It's hexagonal, 7 storeys and 45m high, and was built in 1004 and restored in 1228.

By now you'll have seen a good deal of *Jiefang Lu*. One side of the street is set-back low housing in traditional style – the other is modern with large shops, department stores and cinemas. Not far from Lu Xun Lu you'll find the Xinhua **bookstore** and the Antique Shop, while a little further up, near the junction with Renmin Lu, there's the **Tourist Office**. The north of the street is the noisier end, with small shops and street hawkers; in the south where it's quieter are a number of tea-houses. **Restaurants** are mainly to be found in the central stretch between Lu Xun Lu and Shengli Lu: freshwater fish is a great speciality in Shaoxing, as is the **yellow rice wine** which they claim to have been making round here for over 2,000 years. It's made from locally grown glutinous rice and – most important – water from Jianhu Lake, a 80km stretch of water to the south-west. The city is supposed to have had 3 wineshops to every 10 houses in its day, and there are still a good number of them around.

East Lake and the Temple of Yu

East Lake – **Dong Hu** – is half an hour out of town on the no.1 bus, wandering along rivers and through villages with tiny ponds, always with a line of blue hills bulging steadily over the horizon. In the 7C the Sui rulers quarried the hard green rock east of Shaoxing for building: later the hill streams were dammed, and the quarry became a lake, to which the Qing added a causeway. Not very large, the lake is nonetheless striking – with the massive cliff edge of the quarry leaning over its whole length, the colours and contortions of the rock face reflected in the water. A flight of steps leads up to a path running along this ridge.

Rather than return on the bus, **hire a boat** to take you to the Temple of Yu, threading through the network of waterways. These long, slim, flat-bottomed boats have a curved awning of matting amidships where you sit in the shade with a wonderful view through the circular opening up front. In the stern the boatman steers with a paddle and propels the boat with his bare feet on the loom of the long oar. You glide past the paddy fields, the peace broken only by the occasional rudely awoken goose or duck, while the blue mountains swing back and forth as the channel twists. It's a wonderful way of seeing some lush and watery scenery, and just about the best value for ¥3 to be had in China.

After about an hour you nudge round a bend and see the **Temple of Yu** tucked into the hillside – rather shabby 18C buildings in a beautiful setting. Legendary founder of the legendary Xia dynasty, around 2000BC, Yu earned his title of 'Tamer of the Floods' by roaming China tossing great rocks around and dealing with the underwater dragons who caused so many disasters. It took him eight years to control a great flood in the Lower Yangzi, after which he settled, and died, here. The first temple was probably built around the 6C AD, and the nearby **Tomb of Yu**, which survives, must have been closely contemporary. The temple contains a large painted figure of Yu and scores of inscribed tablets; the tall red-lettered tombstone is sheltered by an elegant open pavilion. Frankly, though, it's the boat journey which makes it all worthwhile. You can get back to town by infrequent no.2 bus or on a boat along a different route.

A final excursion is to **Lanting** or Orchid Pavilion, where the 4C poet and calligrapher *Wang Xi Shi* wrote his preface to the *Orchid Pavilion Anthology*. It's another pleasing combination of mountains, gardens and water, reached by no.3 bus from Shengli Lu Kou.

NINGBO

The rail spur from Hangzhou through Shaoxing ends at **NINGBO** – Calm Waves – an important coastal and ocean-going port in the north-east corner of the province. The city is actually set some 20km inland, at the point where the rivers Yuyao and Yong Jiang meet to flow down to the ocean together. All around is flat watery plain and paddy fields, with a line of low hills behind and along the coast, heavily indented and sprinkled with small islands, the signs of local salt-panning and fishing industries. Though there were settlements to the south some 2500 years ago, Ningbo itself has no very long history. Under the T'ang a complicated system of locks and canals was begun to make the shallow tidal river to the sea properly navigable: at the end of the 12C a breakwater was built to protect the port and from that time on trade, particularly with Japan, began to develop in earnest. As well as sending their gold in exchange for Chinese silk, the Japanese sent their pirates – on a small hill at the end of the estuary is a fort constructed by *Qi Jiguang*, who freed these waters for a while in the 16C.

There was early European influence too: already in the 16C the Portuguese were using the harbour, building a warehouse downstream and helping to fight the pirates. In the 18C the *East India Company* set up shop and in 1843, after the Opium War, Ningbo became a treaty port with a British consulate. The town was swept briefly into the Taiping rebellion in 1861, and thereafter lost ground to Shanghai very rapidly. Since 1949 it has begun to expand once more – the river has been dredged, passenger terminals built, one new bridge over the Yuyao completed and another planned, two cargo docks built at the mouth of the estuary, and port facilities generally expanded to handle the output of the local food processing and canning industries. Despite all this Ningbo still wears a rather dilapidated, provincial air – it's the sight and smells of the fishing port and the relics of the Treaty Port, including a prominent church, which you'll notice above all.

Ningbo is small enough to explore on foot, and the best place to start soaking up some of its atmosphere is around **Xin Jiang Bridge**, where the two rivers join. Like any busy harbour, it can hardly fail to be interesting: on the estuary side are moored the boats of the fishing fleet; groups of sailors crowd the pavements, their shouts competing with the cries of wheeling gulls; there's a strong smell of fish, laid out to dry on the corrugated roofs of houses all around, and there's a scent of adventure too – the salt smell of foreign parts and the high seas. The elaborate porticoes and verandahs of the old Treaty Port help, blistered and crumbling but still very exotic in this setting, with the distant church spire rising above them (the church, incidentally, still functions as a place of worship). And in front of them along the waterside, stalls are set up to sell fish, fresh and dried, great quantities of matting, and produce from the local countryside.

Zhongshan Lu cuts west from here straight through the heart of the inner city. The first part is a broad avenue lined with modern buildings where you'll find Ningbo's big department stores – beyond the Drum Tower the street gets narrower and older. For more atmosphere, though, turn left down **Kaiming Jie**, crowded with little shops and stalls, and with some of the better places to eat local seafood. At the bottom, near the junction with Jiefang Lu, you'll find the **Tianfeng Pagoda**, a 14C octagonal brick building, 30m high with a wooden staircase to the top. Or in the other direction pass under the arch of the **Drum Tower** into Cong Yuan Lu, a street in the old style, full of half-timbered houses and arched trees. If you walk here in the late afternoon you'll see all the families outside, eating supper, reading the paper, doing the washing, lounging around in their underwear. At the end is **Zhongshan Park**, a small and rather scruffy open space which teems with martial arts enthusiasts in baggy trousers doing sword practice; outside are more market stalls.

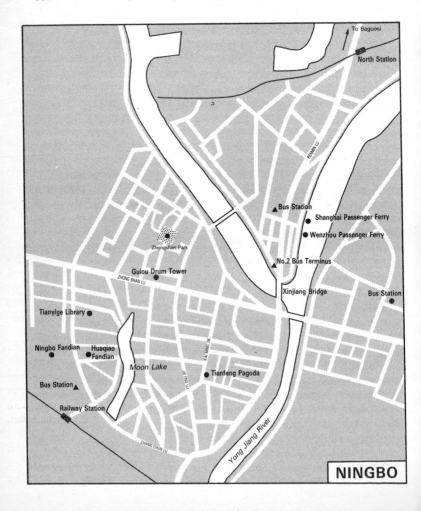

In the south-west of the centre, near the hotels, is **Moon Lake**. Little more than a large version of the usual village pond, it has an enclosed area for swimming and the usual crowd of people doing their washing on the stone steps. From the walkway along the western shore, though, you can search through the maze of narrow alleys to find **Tianyige Library**. Built in 1516 and said to be the oldest surviving library building in China, it was founded by Ming Official *Fan Qin*, whose collection went back to the 11C and included woodblock and handwritten copies of the Confucian classics, rare local histories and lists of the candidates successful in Imperial examinations. Nowadays there are around 300,000 volumes, the most valuable being 270 local chronicles of the Ming dynasty. There are small displays of old books and stone tablets too, and a tiny shop where you can buy materials for calligraphy cheaply. It's also a lovely place: the buildings, their bamboo groves, pool and rockery are austere and withdrawn, preserving an atmosphere of seclusion, contemplation and study.

Practicalities

The Yuyao river flows into Ningbo from the north-west and the Yongjiang from the south-west – the city centre crowds into the crook thus formed, to the west of the confluence. The **railway station** and the **south bus station**, for services to Wenzhou, are close to each other in the south-west of the city; the **north bus station**, for Shaoxing, is just across Xin Jiang bridge, and the **east bus station**, for suburban services to temples and pagodas in the environs, is in Ningbo Lu to the east of the rivers. The **ferry piers** are all slightly downstream from the confluence, near the north bus station.

There's a ring road which runs around the central city area. A no.1 **bus** will take you from the railway station, round the south and east sides of this ring, over Xin Jiang bridge and out on Renmin Lu, passing close by the north bus station and the jetties (or vice versa). No.10 runs right around the inner ring, past the station and hotel; no.2 shuttles back and forth along Zhongshan Lu; no.8 runs from the north bus station, over Xin Jiang bridge, and across to the east bus station.

If your bags are light you can walk from the railway station to the **Huqiao Hotel**, otherwise take a no.10. The place is damp, unfriendly, caters mainly for Chinese businessmen and has rotten food, but it seems to be the only place you can stay. The *Ningbo Fandian* across the water is the exclusive preserve of the Chinese. Rooms go for ¥18, though with a student card you might just manage to halve that. **CITS** is in the hotel, **PSB** in Zhongshan Lu near the Drum Tower.

As for keeping yourself amused, the best selection of **restaurants** is along Kaiming Jie: **theatre/cinemas** include *Ningbo Ju Wan* in Jiefang Nan Lu, *Gong Ren Wen Hua Gong* in Yao Xing Jie and *Renmin Ying Wan* in Jiangfu Jie.

Temples outside Ningbo

There are numerous temples and pagodas to be visited in the country around Ningbo. Perhaps the most interesting is **Baoguo Si**, some 15km west on *Biaoqishan* hill. A no.11 bus – every half hour or so – runs from the northern bus station out into a landscape of endless green paddy fields broken only occasionally by a village with its obligatory duckpond. After about 40 minutes you reach the temple, nestling into a hill which rises from emerald green at its base to a deep green, darkly forested summit. With luck you may have the place entirely to yourself as you climb up flights of steps past a waterfall to the **Dragon's Head** waterspout which feeds it. It's a modern concrete dragon now, but the temple itself is one of the oldest wooden buildings in China – fast approaching its millennium. The first hall has an exhibition on the history of the place, including a great many early photographs. The main hall, built in 1013 and restored under the Qing, has been left bare so that its structure can be clearly seen. The wood is unpainted and there's no statuary or decoration to get in the way: workmanship is superb, the structure relying purely on mortise and tenon joints with its roof, supported by the *Duosong* dovetailed bracketing system, held up by just sixteen columns. The ceiling consists of three pieces of hollowed-out *ciasson* (a hard mature wood). A third hall acts as a small museum. Beyond, continue up the steps to a pavilion – the temple is half-concealed by trees from here but there's a fine vista of the flat lands beyond the ridge, with ribbons of water threading through the paddies into the distance.

South-east of the city are three more sites which can easily be combined into a single excursion, setting out from the east bus station. **A Yu Wang Si**, the temple of King A Wu, is about an hour out on the slopes of *Tai*

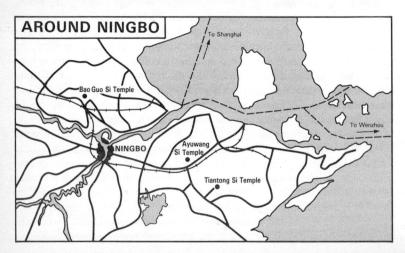

AROUND NINGBO

To Shanghai

Bao Guo Si Temple

To Wenzhou

NINGBO

Ayuwang Si Temple

Tiantong Si Temple

Ba Shan. Built in the 5C, it is famous for its miniature *stupa* which contains a bone of *Sakyamuni*, founder of Buddhism, and is one of only 18 of its type left in the world and of only two in China. The architecture is rightly renowned too – a spectacular blend of orange tiles and dark red wood against the green of the hill, with cool grey steps and platform and a refreshingly shadowy interior. **Wu Fo Ta** – Five Buddha Pagoda – is in the same hills. Small and with little specific to see, it is again beautifully set: ochre buildings below a white pagoda on a hillside platform where blue hills rise in the distance over thickly wooded slopes.

The Children of Heaven Temple – **Tiantong Si** – is an hour's journey further on, a splendid collection of buildings in the forest. Founded in the 3C AD this is one of the largest monasteries in China, with 963 halls and many famous Buddhist works of art. At the centre of it all there's a very large, very fat Buddha with an enormous smile. You may also see a crowd of Japanese visitors – the Japanese monk *Dogen* came here to study in 1223 and on his return home founded the *Sotoshi* sect which now has some 8 million adherents in Japan.

THE SACRED ISLAND OF PUTUOSHAN

Not far off the coast from Ningbo, **PUTUOSHAN** is divided by a narrow channel from the much larger Zhoushan Island. Recently opened to foreigners, it is reached by a ferry ride of about 5 hours from Ningbo. Just 12 square km in area, the isle rises at one end to a peak of some 300m – it has been attracting Buddhist pilgrims from all over north-east Asia since at least the 10C.

For this the **cult of Guanyin**, Goddess of Mercy is responsible. There are many legends to account for the island's status as its centre: according to one the goddess attained enlightenment here; another tells how a Japanese monk travelling home with an image of the goddess took shelter from a storm here and was so enchanted by the island's beauty that he stayed, building a shrine on the spot. More colourfully *Guanyin* is said to have arrived here on a ship floating on waves of fire, always burning yet never consumed – a tale some put down to the phosphorescent waves which, breaking on the shores in the evening, look like great billows of flame. In any event it became one of the leading Buddhist sanctuaries, where over the years more than a hundred monasteries and shrines were built, with magnificent halls and gardens to match. At one time there were as many as 4000 monks squeezed on to the island, and even as late as 1915 the Buddhist community numbered around 1000.

Although there was a great deal of destruction on Putuoshan during the Cultural Revolution, many treasures survived – some are now in the Zhejiang Provincial Musuem, others remain in situ. And under the present regime the great places of Buddhism are being preserved and restored:

from only 29 monks in the late 1960s there are now over 100, paid ¥25–50 per month by the State, plus grain. The government also undertakes the upkeep of the buildings, and the Abbot is a member of the province's Political Consultative Conference. Three principal monasteries survive – *Puji* the oldest, *Fayu* on the southern slopes, and *Huiji* at the summit – and there are too fantastical **rocks**, often carved into images and inscriptions, with the usual wonderful names. My own favourite here is the '*Two Tortoises Listening to the Bodhisattva*' rock.

This is a very scenic island too, considered one of the great beauty spots of South China, which is probably what attracted many Europeans in the last century. Certainly they had little time for Buddhism. The Rev. W. Medhurst wrote in 1835 that 'the whole island with its beautiful scenery, its 100 temples, its thousands of priests, exhibited to the mind nothing but useless waste of property, gross misemployment of time and a pernicious fostering of error.' And the missionary *Martin*, some 40 years later, had little more sympathy. Despite noting that 'the island is exclusively the abode of monks, no women being allowed to stay on any pretext',* he and his party insisted on being accompanied by their womenfolk: moreover, when they found themselves sleeping in a room with an image of the goddess, they insisted that a priest cover it with a sheet. The rest of their time was spent climbing and 'surfbathing' – Martin describes one place they discovered as 'an abrupt precipice overhanging a curious cavity. As the waves rush in and out with an awful roar it is believed to utter in praise of Buddha a syllable of the language of Magadha. So sacred has the place been rendered by this fiction that it has become a favourite place for religious maniacs to commit suicide.'

At the great archway 2½km from the wharf, all visitors to Putuoshan were required to descend from sedan chair or horse and walk. Beyond it is the **Duobao Pagoda** built in 1334, 5 storeys tall with Buddhist inscriptions on all four sides. Further up is **Xianren** – Cave of Immortals – where the Immortals once distilled the Elixir of Life. Today clear water still drips steadily from the cave roof into a pool where visitors drink, and which never runs dry.

1014 steps climb steeply to **Huiji Monastery**. Here you can see pilgrims, many of them elderly women from the fishing villages, struggling up, sometimes on their knees. At the top the Ming buildings stand in a flattened area between hoary trees and bamboo groves – in sunshine their tiles gleam magnificently, enamelled in greens, reds, blues and gold. **Puji** is the largest and the oldest of the monasteries, built in 1080 and enlarged by successive dynasties. It stands among camphor trees with a stone bridge and an elegantly tall pagoda: there's an enormous iron bell weighing 3500kg and a great three-legged bronze censer.

*This is no longer the case – indeed there are now nuns on the island, no doubt a no discrimination policy courtesy of the PRC.

Fayu is built on several levels along the southern slope of the hill. Its **Daxiong Hall** has just been brilliantly restored, and the **Dayuan Hall** has a unique beamless arched roof and a dome, round the inside of which squirm nine dragons of sculptured wood. This hall is said to have stood originally in Nanjing, and to have been moved here by the Emperor Kangxi in 1689. Its great statue of *Guanyin*, flanked by monks and nuns, is the focal point of the goddess's birthday celebrations on **3 April**. That day sees as many as 8000 people, pilgrims and sightseers, crowding on to the island for chanting and ceremonies which last from 7pm until midnight.

TRAVEL DETAILS

Trains
From Shanghai: Suzhou (4 daily, 1hr), Wuxi (4, 2hrs), Changzhou (4, 3hrs), Zhenjiang (5, 4hrs), Nanjing (5, 5hrs), Xuzhou (5, 9hrs), Beijing (5, 20hrs), Hangzhou (10, 3hrs), Shaoxing (4, 4hrs), Ningbo (6, 7hrs), Nanchang (3, 16hrs), Changsha (3, 25hrs), Guangzhou (3, 33hrs)
From Suzhou: Shanghai (14, 1hr), Wuxi (11, 1hr), Changzhou (11, 2hrs), Zhenjiang (5, 4hrs), Hangzhou (5, 4hrs)
From Wuxi: Shanghai (6, 2hrs), Zhenjiang (6, 2hrs), Nanjing (8, 3hrs).
From Zhenjiang: Wuxi (3, 2hrs), Suzhou (3, 3hrs), Shanghai (5, 4hrs), Nanjing (4, 1hr).
From Nanjing: Zhenjiang (4, 1hr), Wuxi (5, 3hrs), Suzhou (5, 4hrs), Shanghai (5, 5hrs), Wuhu (4, 3½hrs), Hangzhou (2, 7hrs).
From Xuzhou: Qufu (7, 5hrs), Jinan (7, 7hrs), Kaifeng (7, 5hrs), Zhengzhou (7, 6hrs), Nanjing (15, 5hrs)
From Hangzhou: Shanghai (6, 3hrs), Shaoxing (5, 1½hrs), Ningbo (7, 4hrs), Nanchang (2, 13hrs)
From Shaoxing: Hangzhou (5, 1½hrs), Ningbo (6, 3hrs), Shanghai (5, 4hrs)
From Ningbo: Shaoxing (6, 3hrs)

Buses
From Shanghai: Hangzhou (3, 3hrs), Suzhou (2, 2hrs)
From Wuxi: Yixing (10, 3hrs)

From Zhenjiang: Yangzhou (10, 1½hrs), Yixing (several, 4hrs)
From Yangzhou: Nanjing (10, 2½hrs), Zhenjiang (10, 1½hrs)
From Nanjing: Yangzhou (10, 2½hrs), Huangshan (daily service)
From Hangzhou: Huangshan (daily service)

Ferries
From Shanghai: Hong Kong (every 5 days, 60hrs); Tianjin, Qingdao, Lianyungang, Ningbo, Wenzhou, Fuzhou up to 5 boats a week. Yangzi river boat (daily): Nanjing (14hrs), Wuhu (18hrs), Jiujiang (36hrs), Wuhan (50hrs).
From Suzhou: Wuxi (daily, 6hrs), Hangzhou (overnight and daytime, 14hrs)
From Nanjing: Wuhan (daily, 2 days), Chongqing (6 days), Shanghai (daily, 10hrs)
From Hangzhou: Suzhou (overnight or daytime, 14hrs)
From Shaoxing: Putuoshan (daily, 5hrs), Shanghai (daily, 9hrs)

Flights
Airports at Shanghai, Nanjing, Hangzhou, Changzhou and Lianyungang.

CHANGZHOU	常州	SHAOXING	绍兴
HANGZHOU	杭州	SUZHOU	苏州
LAKE TAI	太湖	WENZHOU	温州
LIANYUNGANG	连云港	WUXI	无锡
NANJING	南京	XUZHOU	徐州
NINGBO	宁波	YANGZHOU	扬州
PUTUO SHAN	普陀山	YIXING	宜兴
SHANGHAI	上海	ZHENJIANG	镇江

Chapter five
THE YANGZI BASIN

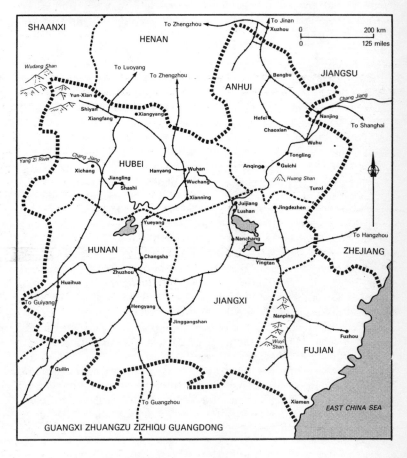

ANHUI – HUBEI – HUNAN – JIANGXI

The great artery of the **Yangzi** beats through all four of the central provinces covered in this chapter – **Anhui, Hubei, Hunan** and **Jiangxi** – and dominates their lives. As one of the key routes for trade and transport throughout Chinese history, it has been a centre of development and habitation since the earliest days. It is still a vital resource: the present government has plans to dredge the entire course, and many tributaries, to form a 14,400km navigable waterway, and to establish hydro-electric power stations in the gorges.

Not surprisingly, most of the places open to visitors are on or close to the river banks. In an ideal world you would travel on the river in your own boat, stopping off to suit your tastes. In practice the express cruise boats visit only the larger ports – reaching the lesser sites often involves tiresome fiddling about on buses and trains. But at least this gives you a chance to see something of the countryside.

Despite the long history, there's not a great deal to see here in the way of relics – this was a working area, the source of the empire's food and income rather than the site of their palaces. Only the Warring States period has really left any mark, on the middle reaches of the river. Nevertheless most of the ports can offer at least one ancient building of interest, and in the Han tombs of Mawangdui, near **Changsha** in Hunan province, there's an archaeological site of real importance. The river towns are, in any case, of interest in themselves, as working ports and vital centres of modern China. **Wuhu**, in the relatively poor province of Anhui, is typical – a historical centre of commerce which continues to fulfil its role in the distribution of locally produced rice, bamboo and grain as well as a more recent trade in manufactured produce. **Jiujiang**, similarly, still sees ships being loaded up with the famous porcelain made at nearby **Jingdezhen**, and it benefits too from a position on the shores of Poyang Hu, the country's largest lake. These days the most important of the ports is **Wuhan**, the great triple city with its vital railway links and bridge across the Yangzi which seems almost impossible for travellers in China to avoid. **Yueyang** is another lakeside port with a history, this time on Dongting Hu. And on the fringes of Sichuan, **Yichang** is an industrial city, now famous for the Gezhouba Dam, where most of the travellers who have followed the river down through its gorges disembark.

Before the construction of the railway and modern roads, areas away from the river, especially in the mountain regions, were isolated and often poor. They became a focus for rebellion and, in their more remote reaches, a base from which to resist central authority. There is much 20C history here: Wuhan was a centre of Sun Yatsen's 1911 uprising; Mao was born in **Shaoshan** and educated in **Changsha**; **Nanchang** saw the birth of the PLA; and there were revolutionary bases in the mountains at **Wudang** and **Jinggang**. The mountains also have their beauty spots and resorts, which through history have provided a welcome respite from the low-lying basin – swelteringly hot and steamy in summer. **Lushan**, in Jiangxi, and **Hengshan**, in Hunan, are traditional hill stations; **Huangshan** and **Jiuhuashan** in Anhui are sacred mountain areas, sprinkled with temples, which still make enormously popular climbing country.

ANHUI AND HUBEI

Traditionally one of the poorest provinces in the east – and a region regularly hit by flood and famine to boot – **Anhui** is divided by the broad lower reaches of the Yangzi. Divided is the right word, for there are no bridges in the whole breadth of the province and the two banks are very different. The northern half forms part of the north China plain, arid, eroded, poor and backward. South, the country is warmer and wetter with fertile wooded hills running up into rugged mountain terrain. Here tea and tobacco can be grown, but not much in the way of food. Nor are communications very good. The Yangzi may be a great river highway, and **Wuhu** an important port, but internal transport is sparse – part cause and part consequence of the poverty. There are just a couple of rail lines: one follows the river from Nanjing up to Wuhu, with a spur continuing west to Tongling; the other heads off from the north bank opposite Wuhu and passes through **Hefei**, connecting with northward lines to Beijing.

There are few places open to visitors, and neither Wuhu nor Hefei really justify special trips, though Wuhu is of course a stop for the Yangzi cruisers and you may find yourself passing through on the tortuous route to the southern mountains. These can be spectacular – **Huangshan**, with its celebrated beauty, attracts hordes of Chinese throughout the year; **Jiuhuashan**, one of the four Buddhist sacred mountains, is easier to get to and less overrun. The long slow journeys you must endure to get to them do at least offer a fascinating look at a peasant way of life which can have changed little for generations.

Hubei province also has two very different characters, although in this case it is not the river which divides them – the great bulk of Hubei lies north of the Yangzi. In the east of the province the low-lying Jianghan plain is drained by the Yangzi and Hanshui rivers, a region so spliced by waterways and dotted with lakes that it is known as the 'province of a hundred lakes'; intensely cultivated, the plain is one of China's major rice suppliers. In the west a harsh and threatening highland region borders Sichuan – it is in these remote fastnesses that China's Yeti-like wild man is said to live.

Skirted by mountains and midway between Shanghai and Chongqing on the arterial route of the Yangzi, Hubei has always been of great importance both as a strategic and a transport centre. The central area around Wuhan, and the Yangzi ports upriver, feature prominently in the classic *Romance of the Three Kingdoms* – the story of the struggle for supremacy between the states of Wu, Shu and Wei after the break-up of the Han Empire in the 3C. The ports – **Yichang, Shashi, Jiangling** and **Chibi** – all have sites and temples from this period: and not much else. More recently Hubei became the first area in the interior to feel the effects of industrialisation, with great iron and steel plants – hence industrial **Wuhan** with its Treaty Port legacy. The development of the railways further boosted Wuhan's position at the 'Gateway of Nine Provinces' – it played a key role in China's early revolutions. In the west, remote and difficult of access as they are, the **Wudang Mountains** make a worthwhile excursion from Xiangfan – if you can get permission.

HEFEI

North of the Yangzi in the very heart of the province, **HEFEI** is Anhui's capital. Until 1949 this was a place of little significance and a population of some 50,000; since, it has become a major industrial centre with a population approaching 1 million. Railway links with the north and the establishment of a number of important schools and colleges have been the major driving forces; neither has done much to make the place attractive to chance tourists. Despite associations with the Three Kingdoms period – the battlefield of Xiao Yao Jin is here, as is the site where Cao Cao, ruler of Wei, trained his army – there is little to see. Only the **Provincial Museum**, which boasts a magnificent jade burial suit, is really worth going out of your way for – though if you have time to kill Mingjiao Temple and Chao Hu lake, are both attractive spots.

The **railway station** and long-distance **bus terminal** are close to each other in the east of the city. For these the most convenient **hotel** is the *Jianghuai* in Changjiang Lu – more central is the *Daoxianglou* at the junction of Dazhai Lu and Yanan Lu. **CITS** and **CAAC** are not far from each other, or from the hotel, in Changjiang Lu.

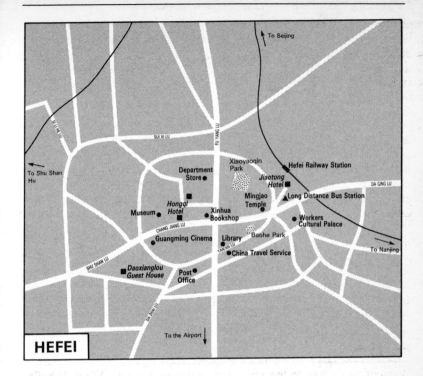

To Beijing

SUI XI LU

FU YANG LU

SHI HE LU

To Shu Shan Hu

DA QING LU

Xiaoyaoqin Park

Hefei Railway Station

Department Store

Jiaotong Hotel

Mingjao Temple

Long Distance Bus Station

Hongqi Hotel

Museum

Xinhua Bookshop

Workers Cultural Palace

CHANG JIANG LU

Guangming Cinema

Library

Baohe Park

YAN AN LU

To Nanjing

SHU SHAN LU

China Travel Service

Daoxianglou Guest House

Post Office

DA SHAN LU

To the Airport

HEFEI

WUHU

In the east of Anhui the Qingyi river flows into the Yangzi: here, at the confluence, stands the busy port of **WUHU**. The river junction supported a town as early as the Warring States period (400–500BC) and since at least the Ming Wuhu has been a brisk market and trading crossroads. It is still a crowded stretch of water, and the harbour continues to handle substantial cargo traffic as well as being a regular stop for Yangzi passenger services, but the scale of activity must have slumped considerably since the days, 100 years ago and more, when this was a Treaty Port. Then, Wuhu was as far as steamers could go. They would unload here for their cargoes to be carried on in smaller vessels and here load up again with goods coming downstream for Shanghai or the oceans beyond. There was other traffic, too, as described in Carl Crow's 1933 *Handbook for China*: 'here the great Yangtsze timber rafts are broken up and smaller ones formed to be sent into creeks and estuaries. The foreshore of the city is lined with wood and timber rafts.' Today you can still see boats piled high with bamboo bound for Nanjing or Shanghai and there is plenty of fish – mandarin and shad – but much of the modern traffic is carried by the railway and the focus of Wuhu itself is increasingly towards new light industries. At least tradition is not entirely forgotten: always fairly independent, the city was one of the first to experiment with private markets and it continues to be a leading light in China's new capitalism.

There is not a great deal for the visitor to see, but if you are waiting for bus or train connections, a waterfront walk makes an obvious way of passing the time. Where the rivers meet you can admire the **Mid-River Pagoda** – seen at its best in the evening light against the background of ships and the broad sweep of the Yangzi. Not far from here towards the centre of town is **Mirror Lake** – little more than an overgrown pond overlooked by a small pavilion – and beyond that you can walk into **Zeshan Park** where the hills come right into the city. Clamber up a steep slope here and you'll find a semi-ruinous little 3-storey pagoda which has great views over the town including, on the other side of the hill, a thousand-year-old pagoda – very whiskery looking with bushes and young trees sprouting from its broken bricks.

Wuhu's **railway station** is on the edge of town furthest from the river; the long-distance **bus station** is a little nearer in. Of the **hotels**, the *Tieshan* is attractively sited near the park, the *Wuhu* and *Jiujiang Fandian* are more central. There are two local handicrafts – on display in all the hotels and public buildings – which must come close to being the nation's least attractive: pictures made of wrought iron or of feathers.

HUANGSHAN – YELLOW MOUNTAIN

Once you have climbed **Huangshan** you will never want to climb any other mountain – so at least goes the old saying, and certainly the peaks are quite staggeringly scenic. The mountain range is regarded as sacred in China – it's an ancient pilgrimage route which has been trodden by emperors and Communist leaders alike – and it is the ambition of every Chinese to climb it at least once in their lifetime. Consequently there are droves of visitors, and mountain paths which used to require serious climbing have been tidied up and provided with concrete walkways, stairs and railings. When the new road and cable-car are completed the crowds will no doubt be still thicker. At times it feels less like a mountain than an amusement park littered with food stalls and rest stops. But then you'll turn a corner and nature will reassert itself – precipitous rock faces and wild spiralling peaks, often half hidden in swirling mists, thick bamboo forests and contorted ancient pine trees, wracked by lightning and leaning at improbable angles from narrow rock crevices. Sometimes you will see one of these views and it will seem instantly familiar: probably it is, for these hills have had a powerful influence on Chinese art. Painters still come in their hundreds (and nowadays photographers too) and as you climb the paths you'll see them at every bend, huddled into padded jackets and sheltering their art beneath umbrellas from the frequent drizzle – the most serious of them may spend months here.

Wherever you come from – and Huangshan has regular **bus connections** with Hangzhou, Nanjing and Shanghai as well as with Wuhu and other more local centres – you're in for a long journey. Wuhu is about 6 hours away by bus, which means spending a minimum of two nights here (buy a ticket out as soon as you arrive or it may be more). As long as you accept that there are going to be crowds and don't expect too much of the weather (rain clouds and ragged mists are an essential part of the views) it will be well worth it. At the foot of the range, where the bus drops you, is the *CITS Hotel*, and not far away across the small stream the *Huangshan Hot Springs Hotel* – a **bed** in a triple room at the CITS goes for around ¥8, a double room in the barracks at the side for ¥18 and there's a fair **restaurant** out the back. A shop near the hotel sells maps of the mountains and walking sticks – both of which are useful – and will even hire you a guide or a porter, or for that matter someone to carry you up the mountain in a sedan-chair type contraption. These are extravagances – the path is sometimes hard work but it's easy enough to follow and excess baggage can be stored at the CITS Hotel for a small fee. The only special equipment you need are strong shoes and something warm to wear at the top.

The highest of Huangshan's peaks is in fact less than 2000m but as you **climb** it begins to feel very high indeed. Following the main track from the hotel a rough flight of some 2500 steps leads up, past a series of honeymoon huts, to the terrace of the **Halfway House Temple**. This is where things really start to get interesting as you continue up an increasingly steep and narrow gorge, its sides overgrown with witch hazel, azalea and wild plum. The rocks here are huge, their weirdly contorted forms giving some sort of credence to the usual gamut of bizarre names, and the broken mountainside is riddled with caves. In one – the **House of Clouds** – you can scramble up a flight of ragged steps and clamber over an enormous boulder to emerge, squeezing out of a fissure, 30 metres higher up the path. Eventually the forest is left behind, exchanged for a scene of bare rocks with only the occasional solitary tree, where a new broad vista opens up at every turn. After one final narrow defile you reach the **Welcoming Pine**, immortalised in countless pictures and instantly familiar from the wrought iron ones for sale in the shop below.

Very near here is the *Yupinglou* – a **mountain hut** which looks more like some great barracks. It's damp, there's no water for most of the day, and a double goes for ¥24. By now you've been climbing for around 3 hours and have reached 1680m: if you decide to stay there are plenty of side paths which you can spend the afternoon exploring. Try the steps cut into the sheer rock face leading to the **Peak of the Heavenly City**. This climb, not for those nervous of heights, takes about an hour – from the peak there are usually superb views looking down over a sea of cloud.

The main path leads on towards the **Bei Hai Hotel**, up among the topmost peaks. It winds from the Yupinglou up to a pass between the

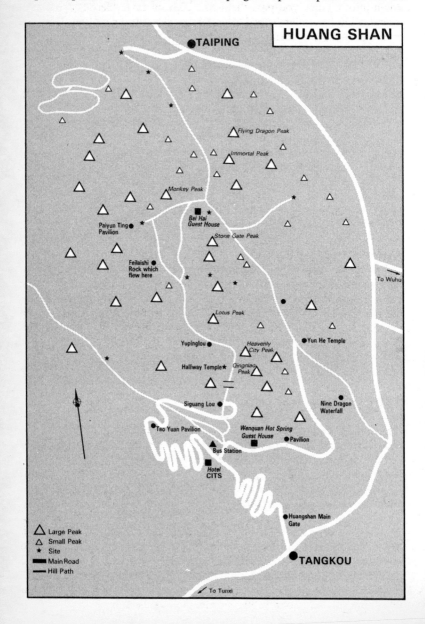

Peacock and Lotus summits where more strange rocks jut out of the mist – among them the Tortoise, the Snake and the Fantabulous Fish, climbing towards the mountain top where it will turn into a dragon. Dropping down into a valley you pass through a narrow cave. Here according to legend a kindly spider helped *Zhu Yuanzhang*, the first Ming emperor, to escape from his enemies by spinning a web over the cave entrance after he had passed. At the *Bei Hai* double rooms go for ¥24, although some foreigners have managed to find them for as little as ¥14. Each room has a pair of heavy jackets which you can wear when you get up to watch the **sunrise** – everybody is up at this hour and you'll need the jacket (unless, of course, you find pouring rain as I did).

Continuing, you could head north to meet up with the road which skirts the mountain, but the normal route doubles back to base along a more easterly path. In **Cloud Valley**, where excellent tea is said to grow, there are caves once inhabited by hermits. At least one man supposedly still lives here, surviving on leaves and roots except when, twice every lunar month, another holy man brings him rice with which to make his offerings and afterwards eat. Down at **Yuhe Si** there is a guesthouse in front of the temple where you can eat and pick up transport back to the hotel. The Hot Springs bathhouse, when you finally make it back, makes a great way of soothing some of the stiffness out of your bones.

All this is really too much to cover in a **single day**, though with determination it is possible. If you don't want to spend a night on the mountain, though, try following the route in reverse – by bus (from near the Hot Springs Guesthouse) to Yuhe Si, up to Bei Hai and then down the long way from there. This may be cheating, but it will still take a full day and leave you gasping for breath at the end. The other advantage is that you get to enjoy the spectacular scenery of the west side as you relax on the way down.

JIUHUASHAN AND ON DOWN THE YANGZI

If you want an alternative to Huangshan, **Jiuhua Shan** is both closer to the river and easier to get to. It has other advantages too: not so high – at little over 1300m – the walking is considerably easier, the landscape less austere and there is interest in more than just the scenery. For this is one of the four sacred Buddhist mountains (the others are Emei, Wutai and Putuo) and has been a place of pilgrimage since before the Tang. There are at least 60 temples, many of which date back as far as the 7C and 8C – some of the more important are being or have been refurbished. Within are an extraordinary number of sculptures – some 6,000 all told – as well as ancient scriptures and examples of early calligraphy. Among the highlights are **Roushen Hall**, perhaps the most famous of the buildings; **Baisui Temple** with its gold-plated mummy of the monk *Wu Xia* which dates from about 1600; and the **Qiyuan Temple**.

There's a daily bus from Huangshan to Jiuhuashan and you can also get here direct from Wuhu or from GUICHI which is the next major stop up the Yangzi. Guichi, though, is otherwise a closed town. If you're following the Yangzi up here Jiuhuashan is plain to see off to the south. The next place you might want to break a river journey for any amount of time is in Jiujiang on the edge of the vast Poyang Lake, both of which are in Jiangxi province (see p. 311): after this the river turns north into Hubei province, and Wuhan.

WUHAN

WUHAN is the modern portmanteau name for the three cities of **Hankou**, **Hanyang** and **Wuchang**, straddling the waters where the Hanshui River flows into the Yangzi and linked by two great bridges – one of which is the twin of the famous bridge in Nanjing. Ideally placed for water traffic linking Sichuan and the eastern seaboard, this triple city is one of the biggest inland ports in China and also occupies a central position on the main north–south railway. Thanks to these transport links you are likely to find yourself at the very least passing through Wuhan. Its strategic position, set on flat land protected by a curve of hills to the south, has long made the place an administrative centre, and it remains the capital of Hubei province.

This history, and Hankou's role as a foreign concession, have produced an extraordinary mix of architectural styles ranging from 19C classical to stolid 1950s, with a large helping of industrial art deco in between. The docks and riverside promenades give the place in addition the stimulating character of any waterside city: not strong perhaps on historic sites Wuhan nevertheless has a couple, including the Guiyan Temple, which are well worth seeing, as well as a handful of buildings linked with the revolution. It's a busy shopping centre, too, with many stores opening late to meet the demand. On the minus side Wuhan has a well-earned claim to fame as one of the 'Four Ovens of China' – so don't be surprised in summer to find the streets melting and the population apparently kept alive by a constant diet of ice lollies.

Hankou

Wedged between the Hanshui and Yangzi rivers, **HANKOU** was no more than a minor river port and fishing harbour until the 19C when it was opened up as a Treaty Port where foreign merchants could live and trade. From 1861 Britain, France, Japan and Russia set up concessions which occupied a thick slice of ground between the river and where the railway now runs. They and their buildings, from the grandiose **Custom House** down, imparted a distinctive flavour to the city centre – and still do;

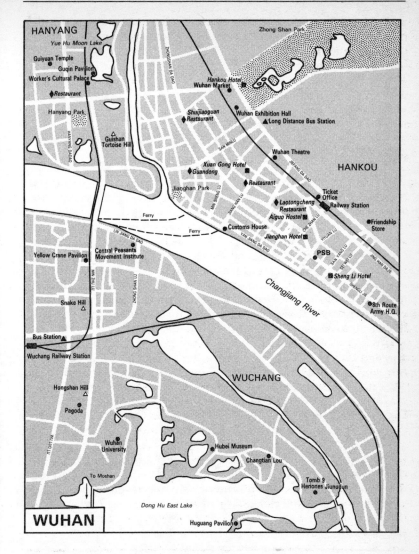

HANYANG

Yue Hu Moon Lake

Guiyuan Temple
Guqin Pavilion
Worker's Cultural Palace

◆Restaurant

Hanyang Park

ZHONGSHAN DA DAO

Zhong Shan Park

Hankou Hotel
Wuhan Market

Shuijiaoguan
◆Restaurant

Wuhan Exhibition Hall
▲Long Distance Bus Station

SAN MINLU

△Guishan
Tortoise Hill

HANYANG DADAO

Wuhan Theatre

JIEFANG DA DAO

HANKOU

Xuan Gong Hotel
◆Guandong

Jianghan Park

Ferry

MIN SHENG LU

JIANGHAN LU

◆Restaurant

◆Laotongcheng
Restaurant
Aiguo Hostel ■

Ticket
Office
■Railway Station

CHE ZHAN LU

SAN YANG LU

YIYUAN LU

JING HAN DA JIE

■Friendship
Store

Ferry

LIU JIANG DA DAO

●Customs House

YAN JIANG DA DAO

Jianghan Hotel ■

PSB

SAN WEI LU

Yellow Crane Pavilion

Central Peasants
Movement Institute

MIN ZHU LU

ZHONG SHAN LU

Changjiang River

SHENGLI JIE

■ Sheng Li Hotel

△
Snake Hill

●8th Route
Army H.Q.

Bus Station▲
━Wuchang Railway Station

WUCHANG

Hongshan Hill
△

XIONG CHU DA DAO

●Pagoda

Wuhan●
University

●Hubei Museum

Changtian Lou

To Moshan

Tomb 9
Heriones Jiunudun

Dong Hu East Lake

WUHAN

Huguang Pavilion●

though much of the old town was destroyed in the 1911 rising, the solid
1920s and 1930s buildings which served European trade still remain.

Essentially, though, Hankou is a 20C city, and it has a 20C history to
match. In 1906 the Beijing–Hankou section of the north–south rail link
was completed, opening the way for rapid industrial expansion. But the
foreign influence which this brought, exacerbated by the proposed
Hankou to Chongqing extension, helped to spark off the 1911 rising

against the Qing – a rising which had its headquarters across the river in Wuchang. Later, in the great strikes of 1923, the railway workers were once again leading forces in riots which were bloodily suppressed. In 1937 the Kuomintang briefly established a national government here as they fled westward. And as late as 1967 Wuhan saw fighting again when it became the base for a movement opposed to the Cultural Revolution and its Red Guard leaders; the rebels controlled much of the city before being put down, at considerable cost, by the PLA.

As it's the largest of the three cities, you are likely to find yourself **arriving** in Hankou, whether by boat or train (though most trains also stop at Wuchang), and you'll probably want to stay here too. The **railway station** is conveniently central in Chezhan Lu, a mostly pedestrian street which is gloriously and garishly lit up at night, transforming itself into a boisterous film set of crowded shops and restaurants with the station illuminated like some Gothic castle in the background. The main street, **Zhongshan Dadao**, runs nearby, heading south-west, parallel to the river, right through the heart of the city. CITS is here and PSB is close at hand in Yiyuan Lu: for the **ticket office** turn right out of the station along Jinghan Dajie. The **river boat jetty** is just below the **Customs House** in Yanjiang Dadao – you can also buy tickets here and squeeze aboard one of the **ferries** which shuttle across the Yangzi to Wuchang. The **long-distance bus station** is in Jiefang Dadao near the park; buses run from here to a number of small tourist towns in the area, including Huangpi, Echeng (Western Hill), Dongpo, Chibi and Xianning. If you want to fly out, the **CAAC** office is in Liji Bei Lu. Distances, even within Hankou, are considerable – useful **local buses** include the no.2 trolley, which ranges the length of Zhongshan Dadao, and the nos 24, 42 and 45 buses which run through the concession area.

Hankou's **hotels** are all pretty central: the *Jianghan Fandian* in Shengli Jie, walking distance from the station, has the most character, all the usual services and a wonderful café with a live band which kept the staff and me as the solitary punter well entertained. It fills up in spirts with tour groups off the river cruise and is reluctant to offer shared rooms, so you might have to shell out ¥40. The *Xuangong Fandian* in Jianghan Si Lu is a great barracks of a place right at the heart of things; walk or take a no.7 bus from the station. This also fills up with tour groups, so you may have to try your luck at the *Aiguo* only 5 minutes from the station in the main street. A small and shabby hostel offering 2-20 bedded rooms from ¥5, with no food or services, it is spartan and extremely grubby: fortunately the staff make up for these deficiencies by being very friendly. Finally, in Siwei Lu you'll find the *Shengli Fandian*, a standard 5-storey building further from the mainstream and hence less likely to be crowded. For **something to eat** the best place to start looking is around Zhongshan Dadao between Sanmin Lu and Chezhan Lu. The steamed dumplings are good at the *Dehua*; you can sample a host of mutton dishes at the *Donglaishun*, a Muslim restaurant in the main street; or pick one of the three floors at the *Laotongcheng* in Dazhi Lu which has unusual fish dishes. One morning for breakfast, with a long bus journey ahead of me, I tucked into a huge and delicious bowl of slippery steamed *jiaozi* at the *Shuijiao Guan* near Liqiao Lu.

There are practically no specifically tourist sites in Hankou. **The Monument to the Martyrs of the February 7th Strike** comes closest, a tall white cenotaph in the far north of the city which commemorates the railway workers who were victims of the 1923 strike. In that year of depression, the young Communist Party had masterminded a series of strikes including one of Rickshaw Pullers and one of the Unified Railway Workers. The latter were massacred at their headquarters in Jianghan Station near here by the soldiers of the warlord *Wu Peifu*. **Zhongshan Park** is one other place you might consider visiting – a thick wedge of ground running north from Jiefang Dadao, once a private garden and racecourse, now housing a zoo and a collection of rare trees.

The apparent lack of excitement matters little – for Hankou is above all a place to walk, eat, window shop, spend money; and watch others doing the same. You sense that plenty of people have cash and that the shops are well equipped to take it off them – piled high with TV sets and ghetto blasters (mostly imported) and a booming trade in electronic gadgetry for DIY enthusiasts. There is a sense – rather appropriate in the old concession area – of almost mid-Victorian affluence: you may be looking out for something small enough to take home, but the Chinese next to you is more likely preparing to splash out on a Japanese-made photocopier for the family business. Flowers in heavy pots line the pavements and litter bins shaped like pandas and pagodas liven up the central streets; those running off towards the river have ice cream booths and weighing machines on street corners, clothes markets and busy hairdressers before you reach the dusty wharves. There is an enormous range of **stores**. The *Arts and Crafts* at the corner of Zhongshan Dadao and Minsheng Lu has hideous green frog-shaped watering cans and vulgar gilded table lamps selling alongside delicate silk flowers. The *Friendship Store*, north of the station at the corner of Sanyang Lu and Jiefang Dadao, is packed with local goodies. Two other giant emporia worth a visit are the *Wuhan General Market*, opposite Zhongshan Park, and the *Wuhan Central Department Store* in Jianghan Lu near the Xuangong Hotel. **Jianghan Lu**, which was the main street of the old concession, also has a wealth of deco architecture, masses of sweet shops and a deliciously cool ice cream parlour. There are a host of **cinemas** and **theatres** in these same shopping streets – you may also have the chance to see the **acrobats** doing their stuff in the *Wuhan Juyuan*.

Hanyang

From Hankou a no.24 bus along Zhongshan Dadao, a no.42 from the park or a no.1 trolley from Sanmin Lu will take you across the Hanshui to **HANYANG**. The smallest of the three cities, Hanyang is known to have been settled as far back as AD600, but it remained quite insignificant until the late 19C, when it benefited from the growth of Hankou. Then the Viceroy *Zhang Zhidong* built China's first large scale iron and steel foundry here as part of the 'Self Strengthening Movement' – a last-ditch attempt to drag China into the industrial era and reduce foreign influence during the twilight years of the Qing dynasty. Hanyang is still the principal manufacturing sector of Wuhan: tourist facilities are thin on the ground.

There are, however, a few places worth a visit. **Guishan** (Tortoise Hill) is on the left of the road approaching the Yangzi bridge – it faces Snake Hill across the water. From here *Yu*, Tamer of the Floods, is said to have subdued the Great Flood 4000 years ago: there's still a great view from the top of the hill and you can also see the 14C Qingchuan Pavilion. **Guqin** – Ancient Lute Pavilion – is closer to the Han river bridge; off to the right overlooking **Yue Hu** (Moon Lake). The pavilion is named for *Yu Boya*, a great lute player who in legend played here for the last time at the grave of a friend and then smashed his instrument because the one man who truly appreciated his music was dead. The story is more interesting than the pavilion – which has been rebuilt many times – but at the adjacent **Workers' Cultural Palace** they have regular musical gatherings which are a real treat. Packed tight on a verandah, there's a band which plays traditional music on traditional instruments and take it in turns to sing. Most of the audience are retired and pass the day ensconced in sagging rattan chairs, drinking tea or dozing.

Guiyuan, the Temple of Original Tranquillity, is off Hanyang Dadao on the no.42 bus route. Still a busy functioning Buddhist Temple, with a shop and a vegetarian restaurant, it boasts a collection of ancient relics and scriptures in a series of unremarkable buildings. The *Longcang Scripture* housed here is one of the few complete Buddhist canons – some 54,000 volumes. Many of the interiors, with their red pillars and dark beams, feel almost like the cavernous hollow of some great ship's hold: in the Arhat Hall – where several hundred saints sit on high plinths, each with a different gesture and expression – there is a fine darkwood Buddha, and in the Main Hall a giant gilded version. Everywhere, with the statues dustily shrouded in glass cases and the temple paraphernalia bundled up and tied with red cotton, there is a fusty, stuffy feel. Perhaps this is because the real activity of the temple goes on behind the scenes in the Meditation Chamber: in the public parts Original Tranquillity is hardly the keynote, as people wander about lighting cigarettes from incense burners, having their pictures taken and munching their way noisily through substantial picnics. In one courtyard stands a bronze incense burner which is permanently ringed with visitors – they're trying to make coins stick to the (partially magnetised) surface. Success brings great good fortune.

As well as the vegetarian restaurant in the temple, Hanyang has a famous **game restaurant**: the *Ye Wei Xiang* in Yingwu Dadao. There's also a **railway station**, not far from the Guqin Pavilion, and a **bus station** behind the Guiyuan Temple. To Wuchang you can continue on a no.1 trolley, crossing the spectacular two-tier bridge over the Yangzi. Only completed in 1957, the bridge saves hours on the north–south railway journey, for which goods and passengers had formerly to be ferried across.

Wuchang

WUCHANG, on the right bank of the Yangzi, is historically the most important of the three cities. It was the walled capital of Wu during the Three Kingdoms period and later the Tang rulers made the city a major centre for trade and shipping, a role it maintained under the Mongols as the administrative centre of a vast region which included present-day Hunan, Hubei, Guangdong and Guangxi provinces. Well into the 19C Wuchang remained dominant – in 1894 Morrison wrote 'it is here that Viceroy Zhang Zhidong resides in his official yamen and dispenses injustice from a building almost as handsome as the American Mission house which overlooks it. He has erected a giant cotton mill with 35,000 spindles covering acres and lit by electric light and has also built a large mint.' Even today, the provincial administrative offices are all concentrated on this side of the river.

Until 1911 Wuchang had been some way from the centre of Chinese events but on 10 October of that year a bomb exploded prematurely at the headquarters of a local revolutionary group. The police moved in, a pitched battle ensued, and a chain of events was started which brought forward the planned date of Sun Yatsen's uprising and led directly to the downfall of the Qing dynasty and the establishment of the provisional republican government in Nanjing in 1912.

More a residential area than Hankou, Wuchang has fewer shops and none of the solid European buildings; along the river is a poorer workers' district. A large part of its outskirts are taken up by **Dong Hu** (East Lake), a natural expanse of water surrounded by a park laid out in 1949. This park occupies some 35 square miles around the winding lakeshore – by day the green open spaces make an outdoor living space where whole families eat, play and doze in the shade while the young wander around looking dégagé in tracksuits and dark glasses. On summer evenings it becomes a lovers' trysting place – the authorities try to turn everyone out but many hide in the trees and spend the night here. As for sights, they're mainly concentrated near the entrance or are miles away on the far side at Moshan: you can hire boats or take a 'taxi' across the lake. There are several places for swimming, too, though I was told that in mid-May it is still too cold.

Probably the best way to see the lake is to take the no.1 trolley to the Wuchang side of the Yangzi bridge and from there pick up a no.14 bus to the park's main entrance. Walking along the shore from here with the water on your right you pass a series of pavilions and gardens. They have evocative names – the Billow Listening House or the Strolling and Reciting Pavilion – but they tend to be scruffy modern buildings with stairways covered in peanut shells and spit, since most Chinese have no concept of Keeping China Tidy. You can get a good view of the area from **Changtian Tower** and carry on to the **Jiunudun Memorial**, the Tomb of the Nine Heroines, where nine women who fought in the Taiping Army during the great rebellion of 1851–64 are buried. From here a causeway crosses to **Huagang Pavilion** in the middle of the lake (where you can have lunch) and on to the Botanical Gardens.

Alternatively you can get a boat across to **Moshan**, where there's another restaurant before you reach the **Botanical Gardens**. These are a not particularly attractive attempt to recreate a traditional garden, over-elaborate and addicted to pot plants – in rows, on stands, in piles and even in kitsch arrangements against highly painted landscape backdrops. To the south of the lake are various hills dotted with institutes and colleges. **Wuhan University** has an intriguing looking campus on Luofia Hill. Founded in 1913 in a traditional pagoda style, it's worth a visit.

Back near the main entrance is the **Hubei Provincial Museum**, an important collection with a section devoted to general and folk history up to the Opium War on the upper floors and plenty which can be looked at and easily understood like old banknotes and photographs: the modern section is strong on revolutionary history but closely written panels in Chinese are not a great help to the casual visitor. The 7000 items unearthed in 1978 from the 2400-year-old tomb of the Marquis of Zeng are particularly impressive: the famous set of bronze chime bells – the earliest fixed-tone 12-scale instrument discovered – are alone worth going to see. There are also 120 other musical instruments – stone chimes, drums, bamboo flutes and zithers. You could potter about for a day here or fit it into a morning, and from Moshan, if you have had enough by then, you can get a no.36 bus back to the terminus and hop on a **ferry** across to the Custom House in Hankou. The water looks murky and unappetising, but there are good views of the trains pounding along the upper tier of the bridge and the steamers churning upriver to Chongqing.

With more time, Wuchang still has a couple of places to see. **Snake**

Hill, near the bridge, is the site of the **Yellow Crane Pavilion,** built in the 3C and seemingly featured in half the poems written since. The story goes that an Immortal paid his shot at the inn by drawing a crane on the wall – the bird would fly down at intervals to entertain the guests. A few years later the Immortal returned and flew away on his creation: the landlord, who no doubt could afford it by then, built the pavilion in his memory. It was burnt down in 1884 and is being rebuilt from scratch to provide a convenient tourist site for the high-rise hotel going up nearby.

Just south of Snake Hill is the **Hong Ge** (Red Building) which was the headquarters of the 1911 uprising. There is a bronze statue of Sun Yatsen out front, though at the time he was abroad raising funds. More recent history is represented by the **Central Peasant Movement Institute** at 13 Hongxian Lu near the river. Mao was director of this institute from 1926–7 and is supposed to have trained some 800 peasants here; nearby is the house in which he lived. The Institute has an entrance lavishly furnished with flowers and plants – it looks good on postcards – four long compounds and, in the centre of a grassy area, the platform from which Mao and others gave their speeches. There is the canteen with wooden tables and benches where he is said to have eaten with the trainees; the dormitory with its dusty mildewed bunks, a wide-brimmed hat hanging on each and a rack of guns; the room where the leaders discussed strategy, with a dusty desk bearing Mao's name and a huge 4-character slogan poster behind. It's all pretty gloomy, only really worth a visit if you are eager to retrace some revolutionary footsteps. Perhaps the dust is symbolic – on my visit I was the only one there and they had to open up specially for me.

Further from the river, **Hongshan Hill** and its pagoda lie to the left off Wuluo Lu. The park is very scruffy and backs on to a dismal housing estate but you can climb above this to the pagoda which has some interesting external decoration showing amongst the weeds. Seven octagonal storeys – with windows and double eaves – rise to 40m, originally they formed part of the temple complex of the long vanished 14C Baoyu Si. Wuchang's long-distance **bus station** is not far from here at the junction of Wuluo Lu and Zhongshan Lu; the **railway station** is a short walk on down Zhongshan Lu. There is a **theatre,** the *Hubei Juchang,* in the central square and a good **fish restaurant** (as an alternative to the places round the lake) at the corner of Pengliulang Lu and Jiefang Lu.

ON UP THE YANGZI

Wuhan is not only the gateway to several other central provinces but also at the heart of the river-rail-road network within Hubei itself. The towns on the river route between Wuhan and Yichang can be seen at a distance from the deck of the cruise boats: actually to reach them you'll probably have to go by bus.

Chibi and Xianning

From the boat you can hardly fail to notice the red cliffs for which **CHIBI** is named, but the town itself is not a regular stop for the river cruises. To get here you have to take a local bus from PUQI, a stop on the north-south rail route about two-thirds of the way from Wuhan to Yueyang. On the ground Chibi seems little more than a large village – low dark houses with the pig and the family stove out in the front under a porch. But it has an interesting history: a morning's walk from the bus stop in the high street will take you to a series of fascinating little sites. These may not really justify a visit, but if you want to get off the beaten track, and are not put off by the avid curiosity of the locals, the place has a lot to offer.

Into the rock face of the southern bank of the Yangzi just outside town are carved the two characters meaning *Chibi* – **Red Cliffs**. They refer to an episode recorded in the 'Romance of the Three Kingdoms': *Zhu Geliang*, the famous strategist and adviser to the ruler of Shu 'borrowed the east wind' in order to set fire to the fleet sent against his forces by *Cao Cao* of Wei. The fiercely burning ships reflected redly against the cliffs – hence the name.

Turn right up a flight of steps near the bus stop and you will come to **Feng Chu Temple** on Jingluan Hill. Here *Pan Tong* studied military strategy and so helped to conceive the plan which defeated Cao Cao. It is a simple whitewashed building containing several statues. The path leads on and up to a stele and the small **Yijiang pavilion** – a former guard post which still commands a glorious view of the terracing and paddy fields below. Continue along the High Street, bearing left where it peters out, and you'll come to Nanping Hill where you can climb past two stone lions to the **Wuhou Palace** and **Baifeng Terrace**. Inside the palace are statues of the 'four musketeers' of the Three Kingdoms wars, Zhu Geliang, Liu Bei, Guan Yu and Zhang Fei: across the courtyard a rather gloomy building offers proof that the legends have historical basis – a vast number of spears, lances, arrow heads and pottery sherds from the period, all dug up nearby.

The only **hotels** are in **PUQI**, an unremarkable market town, neither very poor nor very rich, with unpaved muddy streets, lots of stalls and street cafés and nothing in particular to see. There is a fleabitten hostel opposite the railway station where you can occupy a lumpy mattress for ¥5: there are enamel washbowls in the rooms which overlook a courtyard where locals throw their dirty water; the kitchen feed you through a tiny hatch, throwing your choice of prepared food into an enormous wok, or you can try your luck at a food stall in the railway square, where all the action is. Whether you love or hate this depends very much on your attitude to travel – it's certainly interesting. The other hotel, rather more respectable and also the place to go for local public security clearance, is a half-hour walk through the town (turn left out of the station). Basic accommodation here costs around ¥10. Nearby is the bus station from where the bus – all its windows smashed and the rest apparently held together only by a copious layer of mud – lurches off several times a day on its 1½hr journey to Chibi.

Before it reaches Puqi the train stops at **XIANNING**, about 100km from Wuhan. This is a tourist region famed for its cassia blossom, bamboo and tea through which runs the Ganshui, a tributary of the Yangzi. There are three towns in the area: XIANNING, GAN SHUI, named after the river, and the county seat of WENQUAN which is renowned for its hot springs. Near this last the *Quanshan Binguan* – more of a sanatorium than a hotel – is hidden among the trees on Qian Hill above the river. Naturally hot, mineral-rich water is piped to each room here but the hotel, like the lush surrounding countryside with its tea gardens, bamboo groves and local handicrafts, is geared mainly to domestic and Overseas Chinese tourism.

Jingzhou and Shashi

So far, from Wuhan this route has been steadily south-west, and following the river on you'd enter Hunan province at Yueyang (see p. 308) before swinging back into Hunan. Here, on the north bank of the river as it approaches Yichang, neither **SHASHI** nor **JINGZHOU** are visited by express boats. Both are towns steeped in legends of the Three Kingdoms period and neither has much to show for it. If you do fetch up here – and people have been known to get off a cruise boat by mistake – Shashi can offer accommodation at the *Jiangjin Fandian* in Jianshe Lu or the *Zhanghua Fandian* in Zhongshan Lu (with a CITS branch on the premises): in Jingzhou the main hotel (again with CITS) is in Jingnan Lu.

Yichang

After it has stormed the gorges and negotiated the Gezhouba Dam, the Yangzi reaches **YICHANG**. Here the stream broadens out, to flow more sedately on to Wuhan, and here most of the people who have followed the river down in its exciting course from Sichuan disembark, leaving the river behind and boarding trains bound north for Luoyang, east via Xiangfang to Wuhan, or south into Hunan and Guanxi provinces. The downstream boat usually arrives mid-afternoon and most of its passengers climb straight aboard the no.3 bus to the railway, seeing no more of Yichang than the docks and the station waiting room.

The town really deserves more than this – a major trade centre under the Han, it has remained an important port to this day. In the 19C it became a Treaty Port, an era still reflected in the waterfront architecture, and more recently the building of the huge Gezhouba Dam has given a fillip to its development. That said, there's little specifically to see. For a **room** try the *Yiling Fandian* in Yunji Lu or the *Taohualing Fandian* in Taohualing Lu: **CITS** is in Hongxing Lu, **CAAC** in Hanyi Lu. There are regular buses to Jingzhou and Shashi.

NORTH-WESTERN HUBEI

XIANGFAN is the major city of northern Hubei, an important railway junction which lies on the line linking Yichang and the south with Luoyang in the north and on a spur from Wuhan into Sichuan. The Hanshui River runs through, too, navigable from here all the way to Wuhan where it feeds into the Yangzi. Except as a transport centre, however, Xiangfan has little to offer: if you need to stay the main hotel is the *No.1 Guesthouse* in Changzheng Lu where you'll find the CITS office; you could also try the *Xianyang Guesthouse* in Youyi Lu. Some 20km to the west lies the ancient hill resort of LONGZHONG, a peaceful mountain and water landscape with various shrines and pavilions associated with Zhu Geliang, who lived here as a recluse. The mountains further west are rather wilder: from the area of SHENGLONGJIA come a whole series of reported sightings of the Chinese apeman – a sort of local Yeti – which in this mountainous wilderness seem far from impossible. More realistic if you want to visit a mountain area is Wudang Shan.

Now that Shaolin Temple in Henan has become so popular and overcrowded, **WUDANG SHAN** could well become an alternative. Long a sacred Taoist area, it spawned Wudang Boxing in just the same way as Shaolin Boxing (or Kung Fu) was practised in Henan. Tourist literature is available in English and a road has been built from the railway station at SHIYAN to the main peak: getting permission to visit, however, can still be a problem as some officials claim it is for local and Overseas Chinese tourists only. The area certainly has all the trimmings and statistics for success: **Tianzhu**, the highest summit, tops 1600m; there are 71 other peaks; 36 cliffs; 24 ravines; 11 caves; 3 ponds; 9 springs; 10 pools; 9 wells; 10 rocks and 9 terraces – all of them suitably named. And before you have recovered from that lot, they'll hit you with the 36 convents, 8 palaces, 2 temples, 72 cliff shrines, 39 bridges and 12 pavilions and terraces which the Ming emperor *Cheng Zi* ordered to be built in 1413 (the Tang dynasty buildings having mostly been destroyed in the previous century).

Fortunately there's no compulsion to see all of these things. Among the highlights are the **Jiulendeng** (Path of 9 Turns) which climbs to the burnished copper **Golden Hall**, its roof decorated with monkeys, deer and cranes. In the cliff face below Tianzhu is **Nanyan Hall**, an extraordinary temple carved out of the living rock in the style of a wooden building. On Zhangqi peak you'll find the **Zixiao Gong** – Purple Cloud Temple – which became the headquarters of the revolutionary 3rd Red Army in 1931 after their march from Hong Hu lake in southern Hubei. These mountains, indeed, have a long history as a hideout of bandits and revolutionaries. Here the peasant leader *Li Zicheng* massed his army when he rose in rebellion at the end of the Ming dynasty and near the temple a stone tablet records the suppression of the rebel Red Turbans by Qing forces in 1856. More peacefully, the Wudang mountains are also noted for the abundance of **medicinal plants** which they support: the 16C pharmacologist *Li Shizhen* included 400 local plants among the 1800 listed in his *Materia Medica*, including the magical mandrake root.

If you can't get permission to stay at the mountain, the nearest alternative seems to be the **Guesthouse** of the Danjiang Water Conservancy Project. This is at no.3 Huanxing Lu in JUNXIAN – where there's also a branch of CITS.

HUNAN

If you're spending any amount of time in China you'll almost inevitably pass through **Hunan**, a province which is crossed by all the major rail lines linking Beijing and Shanghai with Guangzhou and the south-west. Until 1976 it was anticipated that, as the birthplace of Mao Zedong, the province would become a major tourist attraction. It is littered with museums and monuments devoted to Mao: great modern hotels and vast railway station concourses were built in expectation of the thousands of pilgrims who would want to pass this way. But it never happened. Everything here seems to operate at well below capacity and if there is one place in China where you should have no problem finding a bed for the night it is in Hunan.

For most travellers the experience of Hunan amounts to no more than the view out of the train window – for the most part endless tracts or intensely farmed paddy fields. The fertile red earth here results in crops which provide some 15 percent of China's total rice production. In spring it rains almost continually. The rest of the year is fairly wet too, though mild always and hot in the summer.

If you are looking for somewhere to break a one- or two-day train journey, **Changsha**, the provincial capital slap in the heart of Hunan, is a convenient base from which to explore the scenes of Mao's early life. In the north, **Yueyang** sits where the Yangzi flows into Lake Dongting, the second largest lake in China. Both Hunan (literally south of the lake) and Hubei (north of the lake) take their names from this vast expanse of water. Yueyang itself, a major Yangzi port, is also an attractive city in its own right.

CHANGSHA

CHANGSHA is still proud of its links with Mao. He arrived here in 1912 from his home in Shaoshan, 90km to the south-west, and stayed 6 years – from the ages of 18 to 24. It was a period spent attending Hunan Normal School where Mao is said to have developed from a particularly naive peasant youth into a questioning student, teacher and political activist. Three years later, having moved to Beijing, he was to become a founder member of the Chinese Communist Party.

Mao's stay came at a time of considerable tension. In 1904 a treaty had been signed which allowed foreign traders access to the whole of Hunan: they had swiftly taken advantage, with an oil company establishing offices in Changsha, other businessmen flooding in and European and American missionaries opening schools throughout the province. There were anti-foreign riots in 1910, during which much of the foreign-owned property was attacked and destroyed. Partly as a defence, the western enclave moved to Orange Island in the middle of the Xiang Jiang where it flows through the city (where many of their former homes are still standing). In many ways these disturbances were simply a continuation of the peasant uprisings which had shaken the area in the 19C. Despite the abundant fertility of the fields, Hunanese peasants, deprived of land rights, starved in their thousands. The province – which saw a succession of peasant rebellions – became a breeding ground for secret political societies and for reformists and intellectuals who established educational institutions and magazines here. By 1920 there was a real movement for Hunan to become a self-governing independent state, a movement supported for a time even by the local warlord *Zhao Hendi*. Eventually however, Zhao turned on the students and workers who formed his main support in a violent campaign of repression.

In this atmosphere Mao came to study in Changsha, and he was not the only young local on whom it had a profound effect. A remarkable number of leading communist cadres were influenced by events in Hunan. They include *Liu Shaochi* – Mao's powerful deputy until he became a victim of the Cultural Revolution – *Hu Yuobang*, current head of the CCP and three other members of the current politburo. In addition *Hua Guofeng*, Mao's shortlived successor, established his power base as a party boss in Hunan. Mao himself always claimed it was the fiery local food which made the people so red.

Today Mao's presence dominates the city's formal attractions even

though most of the sites associated with his stay are reconstructions –
most of the old city was destroyed during the war against Japan when
the KMT set fire to the buildings in an attempt to flush out the Japanese
troops. There's only one small section of the old Chinese area surviving,
in the cramped streets leading off Daqing Lu. The modern parts, in the
main, are drab and grey.

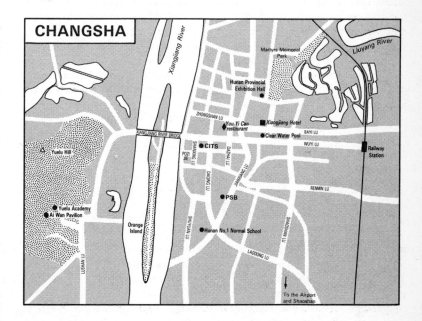

Practicalities

Probably the easiest practical task you will ever undertake in China is
finding a bed in Changsha. There's now only one **hotel** open to foreigners,
the *Xiang Jiang* on Zhongshan Lu, and it has never been known to be
full. A bed in a three-bedded room goes for ¥13, a double room for
¥34; there are no dorms. The rooms are clean and the staff helpful, if
uncomprehending: in the same building there is a small **Post Office, bank**
(open 7.30–9.30 and 5.30–7.30) and **Friendship Store**. The last is not
very well stocked, but it does have a good stock of second hand English
paperbacks – you may need them.

The choice of **restaurants** is also limited. The hotel food is no great
shakes, but at least they seem to ignore the government ruling to tone
down Hunan's traditionally hot food for foreign friends. It's also open
late, till 11pm, which is a rare luxury indeed. The *You Yi Can*, on the
first floor of 116 Zhongshan Lu, is often recommended as one of the

better alternatives but its food seems neither very fresh nor very good value. You'd be better off experimenting with some of the smaller restaurants around town – the *Huoqongdian* at 14 Pozi Lu makes a good start.

Changsha's **CITS** office is notoriously hard to find: turn right out of the hotel along Zhongshan Lu, turn left on to Dazhai Lu and keep going until you hit Wuyi Lu, the main drag – right here and left after about 200 metres you'll find the office in a large yard on the left. This is 130 Shanxing Lu, and if you get there you'll find the staff more helpful than most – probably because few people ever discover them. There are French and English speakers available and hours are from 7.30–11.30 and 2.30–6 (Tel. 22250). They will provide you with a small English **map** to find your way back: Chinese maps, which mark bus routes, are on sale in the hotel. The **bus** system here is far less crowded than in other major cities – though distances between stops are huge. **PSB** is on Huanxing Lu (left from the hotel, no.2 bus for two stops) for all standard visas: watch out for them closing early, often at 4.30. The **CAAC** office (Tel. 23820) is on Wuyi Donglu.

Arriving by air you can take a free CAAC bus to their office, from where a no.1 bus will take you to the hotel in three stops. From the nearby **railway station** you can again take the no.1, this time four stops, or get a taxi for around ¥4.

Eastern Changsha

Clearwater Pool, Mao's former home in Changsha and the site of the first local Communist Party offices, is not far from the hotel, one stop east on the no.1 bus. It's open from 7.30–11.30 and 2–6: walk through the gates and you'll see a huge white marble statue of Mao and then, as you approach, there's a small cabbage patch beside the lake. The building at the back here contains the (reconstructed) room in which Mao and his first wife lived and worked. Further on is a scaled-down copy of the Soviet-inspired buildings in Beijing's Tian'anmen Square which house Mao's mausoleum. Here they're occupied by photographic records and a commentary – in Chinese – on Mao's life and achievements; in a side room are similar photo-historical displays on Zhou Enlai, Liu Shaoqi and Zhu De. The images are all very idealised and unless you're with an interpreter the explanations can be frustrating. The three red flags are those of the Party, the PLA and the nation.

Also in the north-east of the city are a couple of sites not directly associated with Mao. Most important of them is the **Hunan Provincial Museum**, which you can reach by taking a no.3 bus from the hotel. Here is displayed the perfectly preserved corpse of the Marquess of Dai, who died around 160BC. Her tomb was one of two from the Han dynasty discovered in 1972 during construction work at **Mawangdui**, about two miles to the east. Its clay and charcoal walls appear to have kept out damp, and the body's excellent state of preservation was additionally ensured by a triple wooden sarcophagus and wrappings of linen and silk. So well protected was it that modern pathologists were able to establish that the Marquess – who was aged about 50 – was suffering from ailments which included worms, TB and a slipped disc, and that she had been eating melon shortly before she died (the pips were found in her stomach). Nowadays the mummy is displayed in the museum basement, surrounded by specimen jars which contain her pickled internal organs and by some of the funerary offerings found with her – clothing, jars of food, clay money and artworks.

As you leave the museum, retrace your steps south along the main road and after about ten minutes you'll reach an entrance to the **Martyrs' Memorial Park**. Approached from this direction (there are several other entrances) you climb a bank of steep steps to be confronted with a magnificent view of the huge lake with its ornamental bridges and pagodas. There is a coniferous wood in the park and the well-watered greenery is beautiful – though ideally avoid Sunday crowds.

The **commercial centre** of Changsha is around Wuyi Lu as it approaches the bridge. It's not particularly attractive – except for the old sections to the south behind the CITS and PSB offices – but it is an interesting example of contemporary Chinese life, and there are some great little shops around. One of the best is a small **poster house** on Wuyi Xilu. Here you'll find an impressive collection of modern Chinese posters – mostly idealised social-realist images – which make an excellent alternative to traditional prints for only around 30fen each. Even if you don't want to buy it is worth a visit to see what the Chinese are hanging on their walls. Some way south of here (again on the no.1 bus route) is the **Hunan Normal School** where Mao studied and later taught. There's not a great deal to see.

Orange Island and the west bank

Chang Sha – literally 'long sandbank' – takes its name from the spit in the middle of the Xiang Jiang which is now better known as **Orange Island**. Here the foreigners built their homes and consulates in the early years of this century, protected by the river from the threat of rioting mobs (the bridge was completed only in 1972). It is still one of the most attractive parts of the city, with the mansions partitioned now into one or two-roomed apartments for local families. Every inch is under cultivation and you can still see the famous mandarin oranges growing all over the place. From the southern tip Mao supposedly used to swim regularly across to the shore, a feat he repeated on his 65th birthday as one of his famous Yangzi swims and which nowadays is re-enacted annually by thousands of swimmers on 24 June. A no.16 bus will take you from Wuyi Lu across the bridge and down to the southern end of the isle; it runs only every 45 minutes, so check times.

On the far side of the river, **Yuelu Hill** is a famous beauty spot. Take a no. 3, 9 or 12 bus over the Xiang Jiang bridge and change to a no.5 at the bus station. Get off this where you see the huge statue of Mao in the university complex and, armed with some cakes or fruit from the local hawkers, you can start the 40-minute ascent to Wangxiang Pavilion at the summit. There are views back across Orange Island and the city. On the way up you pass a couple of other noteworthy monuments. About two-thirds of the way a path leads off to the right for the **Aiwan Pavilion**. Rebuilt in its present form in 1952, this was one of Mao's haunts as a young man; there is a tablet bearing his calligraphy. The place's name – it means 'loving dusk' – is taken from a verse by the Tang poet *Du Fu*:

> A stony path winds far up cool hills
> Toward cottages hidden deep among white clouds
> Loving the maple trees at dusk I stop my cart
> To sit and watch the frosted leaves redder than February flowers.

Not far away are the Lushun Temple, its garden overflowing with bonsai, and the Yuelu Palace and Tomb.

SHAOSHAN

Mao's birthplace lies some 90km to the south-west of Changsha, once a pilgrimage for tens of thousands of visitors, now seen by at most a few hundred curious souls daily. Its decline demonstrates dramatically the battering which the ex-leader's reputation has suffered over the last few years. From Changsha there are two direct trains daily, at 7.30am and 4.30pm; the three-hour journey costs ¥5 each way for a hard seat. There's also a direct bus, which leaves Changsha at 7am (¥2.10) or a more frequent but much more complicated bus route, via XIANGTAN where you change buses. Not officially open, Xiangtan nevertheless seems to be an easy enough place to wander around, a sizeable river port with important textile and engineering industries.

SHAOSHAN itself is noticeably wealthier than the surrounding villages, though whether this is due to favoured treatment over the years or simply to the tourist revenue is impossible to say. At any event Mao dominates the place. There's a small white village school (where he was educated), a village pond (in which he swam) and the typical mudbrick farmhouse in which he was born. This momentous event took place on 26 December 1893 (like all great leaders Mao has an actual and an official birthday) and Mao proceeded to have a thoroughly uneventful upbringing as one of four children of an affluent peasant family. It was not until he completed his teacher training in Changsha, at the age of

24, that Mao first left his native province. The Mao family name is still a common one in Shaoshan, and another of the buildings you can visit is the former ancestral temple, now a memorial to the leader's early work with the peasants here. Not far from the Mao farmhouse is the centrepiece of Shaoshan, the **Mao Zedong Exhibition Hall**. Opened in 1967 at the height of the Cultural Revolution, this museum originally had two sections, each with identical displays, to cope with the crowds of idol-atrous Red Guards: no more. Nowadays a single showing of the photos and knick-knacks tracing Mao's career is more than enough – the final room has been closed for several years as Party historians decide how the story should end. No doubt it strongly featured Hua Guofeng, who as Hunan Party boss must have played a part in developing Shaoshan as a showplace.

All this can be done easily enough as a day-trip, but should you decide to stay there's a small guesthouse, where a bed in a three-bed room costs ¥10. This also serves excellent food at very reasonable prices. Once you've finished with the village itself there's some beautiful country roundabout, with quiet villages dotted among miles of peaceful rice paddies. Up on the hillside, too, there's a reservoir in which you can swim.

SOUTHERN HUNAN

Heading south from Changsha travel is basically a question of where the railway stops, for this is essentially country you'll traverse rapidly on the lines to Canton, Guilin or Kunming. If you can get the visa, however, there's at least one place worth visiting for its own sake – **HENGSHAN**. From the railway station here (2 trains a day from Changsha, ¥6 and almost 3 hours travel) a bus runs to the southern end of the Heng Shan mountain, also known as Nan Yue, which is one of the five sacred Chinese mountains. In all there are 72 peaks strung out for over 80km, but in the south are concentrated most of the temples, Buddhist and Taoist, which have accumulated in the holy place over the centuries and around here too are numerous modern villas and guesthouses which cater for the thousands who pour in at times of pilgrimage and for the more modest numbers who arrive throughout the summer to take advantage of the mild climate. There's a small guesthouse, the *Nanyo Hotel*, in Hengshan town.

On the way from Changsha you'll have passed through **ZHUZHOU**, a dull, modern manufacturing town which is also a major rail junction at the crossing of the Shanghai–Kunming and Beijing–Guangzhou lines. Should you need to stay there's a hotel not far from the station (right out of the entrance and right again across the tracks) but little else to detain you.

HENGYANG, forty minutes beyond Hangshan, is little more enticing. Hunan's second largest industrial city, it lies at the point where the lines to Guangzhou and Guilin part company: travelling south you may well have to change here and if you're following the circuitous path between Canton and Guilin by train you will certainly have to stop for a while. The only thing this has to recommend it is that it is easy: there's a good restaurant right across from the station – look for the sign on the first floor which says *Jiang Fandian* – and a small hotel about ten minutes' walk along the road opposite the station.

YUEYANG

YUEYANG, a major river port as well as a stop on the Beijing–Guangzhou railway, lies in north-eastern Hunan along the shore of Dongting Hu – the Long Lake through which flows the Yangzi. Always an important trading centre, Yueyang was opened to foreigners as a Treaty Port in 1898 but it never figured large in China's history. If you catch it now you'll find it still retains, unspoilt by too many visitors, the atmosphere and disinterested hospitality of a small town. Once the authorities decide it has been tidied up enough it will almost certainly be fully opened to foreigners – there are certainly enough attractions. The lake itself, second largest in the land and extolled by poets up to and including Mao Zedong, is the obvious lure: there's also Yueyang Tower, architecturally unusual and recently restored; Junshan Island, famous for its tea, tortoises and bamboo; and a small surviving old quarter. For the moment all of these can quite easily be seen in a day. If you're here in the evening, bear in mind that Yueyang is also famous for its opera – less formal and rigid than the Beijing version – and that there are performances most nights. These can be spectacular.

The city's name, taken from its position to the south of Mt Tianyue, means 'sunlit side', but it has to be admitted that the modern parts – still in the throes of major rebuilding – are grubby and unappealing. You should confine your activities as far as possible to the old sector – crowded round the lake in the north-west corner of town. Practical pursuits are relatively straightforward: the **railway station**, **shops** and **restaurants** are all close together in Jianshi Lu. From here a no.4 bus will take you to the main **hotel**, the distinctive concrete *Yunmeng Fandian* in Chengdong Lu (around ¥15 a room; CITS and Security at reception). The **bus station**, both for long-distance and city buses, is in Yuedong Lu near the railway bridge; a particularly unattractive part of town which compensates by having good fish restaurants. **Yangzi ferries** dock at the pier in the north-east of town – a 40 minute bus ride in. An upstream ferry departs daily at around 8pm for the 4-day journey to Chongqing.

The **Yueyang Tower**, rising from walled ramparts overlooking the lake

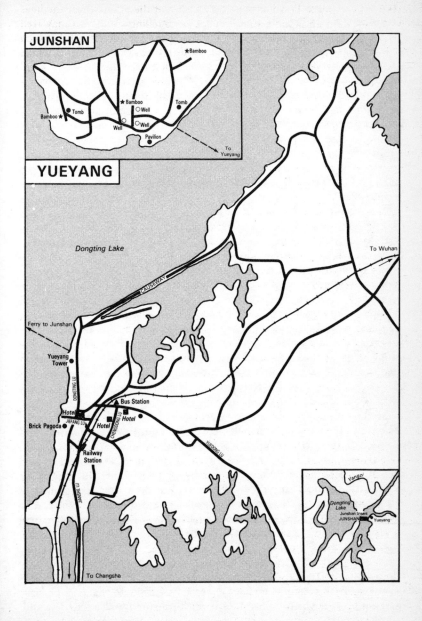

JUNSHAN

★ Bamboo

★ Bamboo
○ Well
● Tomb

Bamboo ★ ● Tomb
○ Well
○ Well

● Pavilion

To Yueyang

YUEYANG

Dongting Lake

To Wuhan

CAUSEWAY

Ferry to Junshan

Yueyang Tower

● Bus Station

Hotel ▲
Brick Pagoda ● Hotel ■ Hotel ●

JIEFANG LU

Railway Station

DONGTING LU

CHENGDONG LU

YUDONG LU

JIANSHE LU

To Changsha

Yangzi

Dongting Lake

Junshan Inset
JUNSHAN ■ Yueyang

in a small park the north-west, is the obvious place to start any city tour. On Sundays it's packed with Chinese tourists from Changsha and Wuhan. The tower itself was built in AD716 but its green site has a long history: over 2000 years ago the state of Ba made a grave mound here for its soldiers. 65 feet high, built of wood held together without benefit of a single nail, the tower has been many times destroyed and rebuilt – most recently a major restoration in 1983. There are three upward curving yellow-glazed roofs, all supported centrally by four huge red pillars of nanmu wood; 24 more columns support the ground-floor eaves, and another 12 the second storey. Even were it not architecturally important it would make a striking and brilliant spectacle – from the top you get a great view out over the lake, which looks like a stormy sea-scene the minute the wind gets up, and down over the yellow tiles to the gateway and ramparts beyond. Inside there are dusty displays of bits of wood removed during the restoration and tablets engraved with verses of praise from famous poets. Outside there are two lesser **pavilions**, *Xianwei Ting* (Fairy Plum) and *Sancui Ting* (Drunk Three Times): the latter takes its name from *Lu Dongbin* who failed his Civil Service exams and went on to become a Taoist priest and one of the Eight Immortals. Among his supernatural works was to populate the lake with its teeming silvery fish by tossing woodshavings into the water – rather less godlike, he used to come to this pavilion to get drunk.

Running down to the lakeside all around here are lively narrow streets crammed with food and clothes stalls, while between the tower and the jetty for boats to Junshan are a maze of alleys which make for a fascinating stroll. Actually to reach **the jetty** most efficiently, walk down the road, leaving the tower on your left and turn down the first alley after the walled enclosure. Boats run from 7am approximately every hour (with a break for lunch) and the trip out to the island takes about 30 minutes. Unless it is raining heavily you should buy a ticket for the upper deck – but if the weather is bad the trip is probably not worthwhile at all, for you need clear skies to appreciate the lake views and the island itself is somewhere to be wandered around at leisure. The lake is in any case at its best in the summer, when the water is higher. In the past it would drain almost entirely every winter, leaving a vast area of boggy marshes and mudflats traversed by steams, and in the summer there was serious danger of flooding: modern engineering works have done much to control the level and reduce the flood problem, but it remains noticeably lower during the winter months.

Junshan itself is for the meantime quiet and unspoilt – the sort of place where you are liable to find yourself invited into a local home. But there's a new concrete pier in the making, easier to negotiate than the present mud causeway, which will no doubt encourage more visitors. It would take little to swamp the island, which covers an area barely more than half a square mile. This land consists of what according to the Chinese are 72 hills – all of them densely cultivated with the famous Silver Needle Tea. The spring-picked tips of this look like gold sprouts – pour boiling water on and you'll see them rise to the surface, sink, rise and sink again: the highly valued brew used to be paid in tribute to the emperor and it remains the chief livelihood of the 200 or so people who live out here. Pear, plum and peach trees also blossom and you may recognise the rare Luyehong tree (or you may not until you know that its leaves are green on one side and red the other) and the speckled bamboo. The last, according to legend, was stained by the tears of the two widows of the Emperor Shun, who died in 2500BC: having speckled the bamboo they died of grief and are buried here beneath a suspiciously modern-looking tomb and stone tablet. The bamboo looks most attractive growing in clumps, but you'll see more of it which has been turned into horrendously elaborate furniture. There are long-lived Golden Tortoises on the island too – the tea-house keeps a few scruffy specimens to prove it – and a vast number of birds: swans, white egrets and tiny finches. And there are great quantities of legends – some as carefully made for visitors as the Dragon Path which skirts the shore, taking most of them in. The Bell Which Flew Here is always a favourite: a large bell which looks distinctly foolish wedged halfway up a tree – the 12C rebel *Yang Yao* is supposed to have used it to summon meetings in his cave.

JIANGXI

Long and thin, Jiangxi stretches far to the south from the Yangzi which forms its northern border. The northern half is the part longest settled and most intensively developed, especially the great plain around China's largest lake, **Poyang Hu**, with its network of rivers and waterways. An easily navigable river, the Gan Jiang, runs into the lake from the south and when, early in the 7C, the construction of the Grand Canal system opened up the route through Yangzhou and the lower Yangzi, **Nanchang** became a key point on the great north–south link of inland waterways. Coastal shipping and the opening of the Treaty Ports from the mid-19C took away much of this trade, but Nanchang remains the provincial capital. In the early years of this century Jiangxi became a battleground for warlords and later, in the struggle between Communists and National-ists in the 1920s and 1930s, its mountains were a Communist stronghold. There are legacies of this period in Nanchang and in the **Jinggangshan** mountains in the south.

The resurgence of industry came with the railway to the coast in 1936; coal mining, steel and machine tool industries have all flourished. More traditionally, the waterborne links provided by Poyang Hu and the Yangzi tributaries benefit the hilly area to the east – here, **Jingdezhen** retains its title as China's porcelain capital. North of the lake, **Jiujiang** is a key Yangzi port on the doorsteps of Anhui and Hubei, though its 19C prosperity as a Treaty Port and the province's main trade outlet did not survive the coming of the railway from Shanghai. But the nearby mountain area of **Lushan**, once a hill station with bungalows for missionaries and merchants and before that a famed retreat for poets and authors, survives as a pleasant reminder of better days.

NANCHANG

NANCHANG – Southern Prosperity – lies in the flat plain south of Lake Poyang, so shut in by mountains that it seems hot as a blast furnace in summer. Dirty, noisy and crowded, it is nothing of a tourist attraction, but thanks to its transport links you may well fetch up here en route to somewhere else. Provincial capital and trading centre or no, it saw little of history until this century, when the conflict between Communists and Nationalists thrust the city into centre stage. When Chiang Kai-shek broke the marriage of convenience between the KMT and the Communists by ordering the massacre of his former allies, Zhou Enlai and Zhu De found themselves isolated in Jiangxi with a sizeable army under their command. On 1 August 1927 they stormed Nanchang with some 30,000 men and took control of the city. It was a shortlived victory, and within a few days they were forced to retreat, but the day is still celebrated as the foundation of the People's Liberation Army: the PLA red flag bears the Chinese characters for 1 and 8, the day and month.

In recent years the rail link to Changsha in the west and Hangzhou and Shanghai to the east has encouraged Nanchang's re-emergence as a centre of iron and steel, machinery and chemical industries. Sprawling as it is, however, you'll find that most of what you'll need lies fairly close to the People's Square or along the main street, **Ba Yi Dadao**, which runs from the roundabout by the station north through the heart of the city and then turns east to approach the great bridge over the Gan Jiang. The **railway station** is in the south-east of the city and the **CAAC** office is in the station approach. From here you can take a no.2 bus for a circular tour of the city – it covers the following route in either direction. Leaving the station, it turns right up Ba Yi Dadao, passing the **long-distance bus station** and the People's Square, both on the right. Some way further, on the left, is the city's main **hotel**, the *Jiangxi Binguan*, a large and – at ¥40 – expensive place with a **CITS** office in the compound. Another hotel, the *Jiangxi Fandian*, is virtually next door; you might get in by pleading poverty. Or try *Nanchang Fandian* near the station. Soon both Ba Yi Dadao and the bus turn left, passing **PSB** on the right, to the roundabout by the bridge. Here the bus turns left again down Shengli Lu, a lively street for walking, its northern end crammed with small shops and family workshops, the southern stretch more upmarket, with department stores: this is the place for **shopping** and also for **eating**. There are cake shops to try and a couple of good restaurants – *Dong Fang Hong Can Ting* and *Bei Wei She Can Lou*. In Duan Jin Beilu,

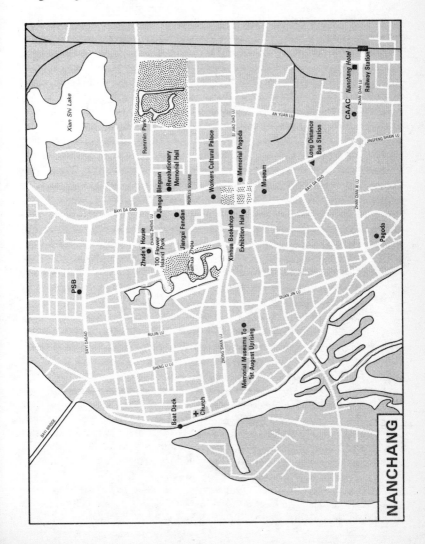

parallel to Shengli Lu, you could also try the *Qin Zhen Fang Hua Lou*; this is a quieter street with a number of **cinemas**. Finally the bus turns left into Zhongshan Lu, past solid 1930s frontages, and so back to the station.

Everywhere you go you'll find that its modern history has made Nanchang something of a period piece – the architecture, especially in the centre, reflects both the Civil War years and the later Soviet-inspired industrialisation of the 1950s. The monumental buildings are concentrated above all on Ba Yi Dadao, and in particular around the typical triumphal layout of **People's Square** – an enormous open space, bare, hot, impressive only for its size. At one end stands the tall, white **1 August Memorial**, surrounded by clumsy buildings. Here too is the **Provincial Museum**, with a large collection of ceramics from Jingdezhen. There are too a host of other buildings associated with the 1927 uprising, notably the **Memorial Hall**. Formerly a hotel, this was occupied by the Communists as their General Headquarters for as long as they held the city. Gloomy nowadays, its three floors are stuffed with mildewed furniture labelled in Chinese. Not far from here **Ba Yi Park** occupies a large slice of the city centre: there is a bridge across a little lake to Bai Hua Zhou – Island of a Hundred Flowers. Not ravishingly attractive, it does at least make for some green peace after the dust and din of the city streets.

If you want to escape the noise and crowds more effectively, take a no.1 bus to Bayiqiao and then a suburban bus to **Qing Yun Pu**. Here is the studio of the early Qing painter **Zhu Da**, known as *Ba Da Shan Ren*, who came in 1661 to live in the former Mei Xian temple. A descendant of the Ming imperial house, Zhu Da became a wandering Buddhist monk: he is said to have painted in a frenzy, often while drunk. As you will see, his works certainly show great spontaneity. From the main road you turn right over the railway line; a 15-minute walk brings you to what is now a small museum surrounded by water, with the artist's tomb outside. There are a number of originals displayed inside, and good reproductions are on sale.

JINGGANGSHAN

When Zhou Enlai and Zhu De were driven out of Nanchang after their uprising had been crushed, it was to **JINGGANGSHAN**, 300km southwest in the mountains along the Hunan border, that they fled. Here they met up with Mao, whose peasant revolt in Hunan had also been defeated, and the remnants of the two armies joined to form the first real PLA and to organise for a series of guerrilla attacks on the KMT forces with some success. This first revolutionary base was near the county town of CIPING, and here the Communists stayed – with Mao steadily consolidating his leadership – until 1935 when the Nationalists were finally stung into a major campaign against them. Withdrawing, the Red Army embarked on its Long March north.

Inevitably the base was isolated and hard to approach, and despite a programme of road building it remains difficult to get to. The mountain area – now a protected zone – is one of great beauty; the town of Ciping less so. Completely flattened in the fighting at the time, it was rebuilt in the 1950s as one enormous revolutionary relic – the more recent attempt in 1979 to transform the place into a 'Garden Town' was clearly an uphill struggle.

JIUJIANG AND LUSHAN

When **Jiujiang** was a prosperous Treaty Port with a large foreign population, **Lushan** was the hill resort in which its wealthier inhabitants would escape the torrid summer of the Poyang plain. Jiujiang has declined considerably since then, but Lushan is still a busy resort, albeit with rather different customers now.

Jiujiang

The name means Nine Rivers; here on the south bank of the Yangzi and immediately north of Poyang Hu is a region where many tributary streams feed into river and lake. With river connections to Wuhan upstream and Nanjing down, **JIUJIANG** makes a convenient jumping off point not just for Lushan and other sites nearby but also for places further afield such as Huangshan and Jiuhuashan in Anhui province. Largely destroyed during the Taiping rebellion, the city was rebuilt as a Treaty Port from 1862, but for at least 2000 years before that it had been a major river port trading in tea and Jingdezhen porcelain. The docks are still busy. If you have time to spare, the most rewarding part of the city to explore lies between the river docks and the Yanshui Pavilion on the lake. The Tang poet-official *Li Bai* was responsible for the causeway here and the much-restored moon-shaped sluice gate.

Jiujiang is a regular port of call for the Yangzi cruisers – the **passenger docks** are in Bing Jiang Lu. The **railway station** is in the west of town across the Long Kai river: the **long-distance bus station** – with services to Nanchang, Jingdezhen, Jiuhuashan and Huangshan as well as Lushan – in Chao Yang Donglu. The main **hotel**, the *Nan Hu Binguan*, is well out of the centre near the lake – it has an annexe close to the Yanshui pavilion. Alternatively the *Jiujiang Fandian* near the docks or *Dong Yang Fandian* in Chao Yang Lu may also take in foreigners. If you are unable to get to Jingdezhen to go **shopping** there are a number of shops in the centre – notably the two Friendship Stores – which are well stocked with porcelain and other local crafts. The **Cultural Palace** and a cinema/theatre are both near the Yangshui Pavilion.

Lushan

This cluster of wooded hills overlooking Poyang Lake is about 30km from Jiujiang. The hills rise to about 1700m and a public bus from the city does the sharp and twisting climb to **GULING** in 2 hours, giving you a sparkling view, widening as you get higher, of the great lake and its junction with the Yangzi. Guling itself is an old hill station set among fir-covered slopes: there's something very European about the shape and set of its stone-built villas and bungalows – indeed the place hardly seems Chinese, except in its shabbiness.

Rambling rather than climbing country, the hills have been praised since ancient times by poets and travellers for their beauty and freshness, and the area has long been a retreat from the sultry Yangzi valley. A few of the temples which in those days were said to crowd the slopes survive. In its present form, though, the resort was built for wealthy Chinese and for European missionaries, businessmen and diplomats, who would be carried up in sedan chairs. In the 1930s Chiang Kaishek had a summer residence here and there was a training school for high KMT officials. These have been preserved, as have the sites of several meetings of the communist Central Committee in more recent years. Nowadays the town is taken over by groups of teenagers, portly retired cadres with their wives and busloads of Overseas Chinese. They pack out the restaurants and troop up the paths to enjoy the views and the clean air: for their benefit the villas have been converted into hotels, sanatoria and army rest homes and one former church has become a cinema. If you wished, you could spend several days here with ease, but one full day's walking is enough to give you a good sample of the waterfalls, temples and mountain scenery.

Within easy walk of the centre of Guling, the **Floral Path** starts at the far end of Rujin Lake near the Dragon Head Cliff, with an impressive view of the Jinxui Valley below, and then runs past a cave – *Xian Ren Dong* – said to have been inhabited by a Taoist monk. Or follow He Xi Lu parallel to the small river – pass the museum and the **People's Theatre** and bear left to **Lulin Lake**. Here the road runs east to the **Botanical Garden** – the only sub-alpine garden in China – and then to **Hanpokou**, the best place for watching the sunrise. We missed the sunrise but climbed the path to the **Three Waterfalls** – quite hard work – and then took a roundabout way back via **Five Immortals Peak**. Unfortunately the Immortals must have descended to blank out the view for us – it really demands a clear blue sky. This is a rare commodity on Lushan whose peaks are often shrouded in mist – the local tea is suitably called Cloud Fog tea, but tastes much nicer than it sounds. This makes a fair day's excursion.

On **arrival** the bus – 2 hours up from Jiujiang, 3–4 from Nanchang – will set you down in **Shan Bei Gong Lu** near the central garden. The **ticket office** is here; be prepared to get up early to buy any return tickets.

Buses leave from a compound through a tunnel off the main street. The most convenient **hotel** is *Lushan Bingguan* in **He Xi Lu** about 10 minutes walk from the centre, with 2–5 bedded rooms from ¥10. Otherwise try *Lulin Fandian* near the Lake. The **CITS** is set back off He Xi Lu before the hotel and the **PSB** is not far from the bus station through the tunnel. For **eating** turn right out of the hotel, walk 5 minutes and cross a small

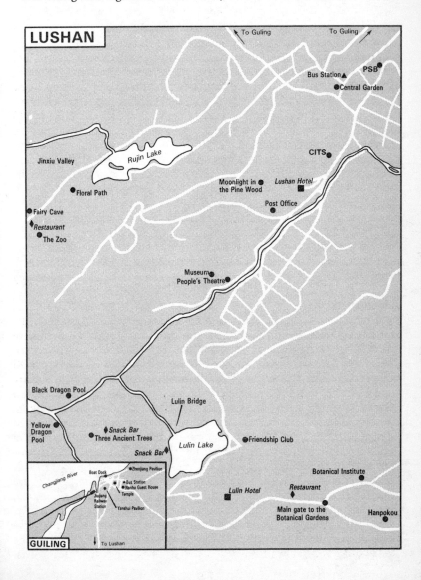

LUSHAN

To Guling   To Guling

PSB
Bus Station▲
●Central Garden

CITS●

Jinxiu Valley   Rujin Lake

Moonlight in   Lushan Hotel
the Pine Wood
●Floral Path   Post Office

●Fairy Cave
◆Restaurant
● The Zoo

Museum●
People's Theatre●

Black Dragon Pool

Lulin Bridge

Yellow   ◆Snack Bar
Dragon   ●Three Ancient Trees
Pool   Lulin Lake   ●Friendship Club
Snack Bar◆

Botanical Institute
●
Changjiang River   Boat Dock
●Zhenjiang Pavilion
● Bus Station
●Nanhu Guest House   Lulin Hotel■   Restaurant
Temple   ◆
Jiujiang
Railway   Yanshui Pavilion
Station   Main gate to the   Hanpokou
Botanical Gardens

GUILING   ↓ To Lushan

bridge to find a cheerful canteen, such good value that the food runs out by 6.30. There are masses of food stalls dotted along the hill paths. In the evenings it is pleasant to mill about with everyone else in the one main street till the shops shut, amble about the small park eating whipped ice cream and stuff yourself with the tiny fish from the rivers.

At the southern foot of Lushan is **XINGZI COUNTY**, right on the edge of Lake Poyang and home of many rare birds. From here a road leads to Guanyin Bridge, 25m long and 900 years old.

JINGDEZHEN

Pottery was being made in **JINGDEZHEN** at least 2000 years ago and – despite the efforts of the authorities to build up new industries – pottery is still its main source of income. This is the sole reason why the city comes high on most tourist itineraries. As early as the 4C ceramic ware from Jingdezhen was being used in building the palace at Nanjing; during the Tang dynasty the demand for local wares increased dramatically, partly because tea drinking was becoming more popular, partly because the use of copper for anything but coins was forbidden. During the *Jing De* period of the northern Song dynasty – about AD1000 – porcelain was made here under the control of court officials and marked with the emperor's name (in honour of which the city was renamed), and from the 14C Jingdezhen came to dominate China's porcelain production. China clay takes its name – kaolin – from the major source at GAOLING just 40km to the south.

From this period **Jingdezhen porcelain** was recognised to be the finest in the world – 'as white as jade, as thin as paper, as bright as a mirror, as tuneful as a bell'. There was a wide range of the highest quality: *Qinghua*, blue and white; *Jihong*, rainbow; *Doucai*, blue and white overglazed; *Fencai*, famille rose. The Qing dynasty established Imperial workshops and foreign demand grew so great that special Export Ware was made, much of it to special order with European patterns or coats-of-arms. The famous **Nanking Cargo**, salvaged from a wrecked cargo ship and auctioned in 1986, was manufactured here. By the 18C there were more than 500 kilns here – travellers reported that seen at night the city appeared to be on fire. After a decline earlier this century the industry is once again in a period of growth: 14 state-owned kilns and scores of smaller ones employ some 50,000 people.

As a city it is thoroughly scruffy, marred at present by extensive engineering works which will bring a new railway station, flyover and ring roads, it is also visibly suffering from severe pollution. There are no sights other than the pottery – but this alone makes the trip worthwhile. Start in the **Pottery Exhibition Hall** – to the left out of the hotel – where you can see some magnificent early works. By comparison the modern stuff pales. For all its undeniably accomplished technique, allied to swirling designs and accentuated shapes, the delicate simplicity of the old days has been lost. In the streets tableware, plant pots and all manner of gaudy decorative objects are piled for sale, and in the department and tourist stores along Zhuishan Lu you'll find extraordinary displays, with bowls and mugs stacked from floor to ceiling in the weirdest shapes. It's an incredible sight – as are the Chinese visitors who buy by the cartload.

The new **railway station** is in Tongzhan Lu: from here a no.1 bus runs through the town centre, back along the river, and over the bridge to the **bus station**. There's a **ticket office** in Nan Men Tou, at the top of the main street near the river. Looking for **somewhere to stay** you have a choice between the expensive and secluded *Guest House* in the north or the *Jingdezhen Fandian* in the main street up from the square – ¥12 for

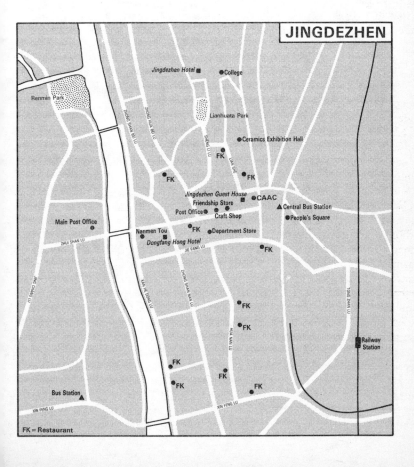

JINGDEZHEN

Jingdezhen Hotel ■   ● College

Renmin Park

Lianhuata Park

ZHONG SHAN BEI LU
ZHONG HUA BEI LU

SHENG LU

● Ceramics Exhibition Hall

● FK
LIAN SHE

● FK

● FK

Jingdezhen Guest House ■   ● CAAC
Friendship Store
Post Office ●   ● Craft Shop   ▲ Central Bus Station
Main Post Office   Nanmen Tou ●   ● FK   ● People's Square
●   ● FK   ● Department Store
ZHUI SHAN LU   Dongfang Hong Hotel
JIE FANG LU   ● FK

JING CHANG LU

KAN HE DONG LU

ZHONG SHAN NAN LU

HUA NAN LU

● FK

● FK

TONG ZHAN LU

■ Railway
Station

● FK

● FK

Bus Station ▲   ● FK   ● FK

XIN FENG LU   XIN FENG LU

FK = Restaurant

very basic accommodation. **CITS** is in the Guest House, **PSB** close by and **CAAC** in the main square near the hotel.

To explore a little of the **city** itself, try the area running down from the square and small park to the river. Here are cinemas and eating places, and in July or August you'll find the town knee deep in melons to supplement the otherwise rather basic fare. The **river**, a tributary of the Yangzi, used to handle all the pottery shipments until the coming of the railway. Even now, if you climb onto one of the bridges, you can see a good deal of activity as junks load up with local cargoes.

TRAVEL DETAILS

Trains
From Hefei: Bengbu (5, 4hrs), Xuzhou (5, 8hrs), Nanjing (5, 6hrs), Wuhu North (4, 4hrs)
From Wuhu: Nanjing (5, 3½hrs), Tongling (5, 3hrs)
From Wuhan: Xinyang (10, 4hrs), Zhengzhou (10, 9hrs), Xiangfan (6, 9hrs), Yueyang (8, 3hrs), Changsha (10, 5hrs), Guangzhou (10, 17hrs)
From Xianning: Yueyang (3, 2hrs), Wuhan (3, 1½hrs)
From Yueyang: Wuhan (8, 3hrs), Changsha (8, 2½hrs), Guangzhou (8, 14hrs)
From Yichang: Xiangfan (5, 4hrs), Wuhan (5, 9hrs)
From Changsha: Yueyang (8, 2hrs), Wuhan (10, 5hrs), Nanchang (5, 9hrs), Guangzhou (5, 15hrs), Guilin (5, 8hrs)
From Nanchang: Changsha (5, 9hrs), Guangzhou (5, 22hrs), Jiujiang (6, 3hrs), Yingtan (6, 3hrs), Jingdezhen (3, 7hrs), Hangzhou (2, 13hrs)
From Jiujiang: Nanchang (6, 3hrs)
From Jingdezhen: Guixi (3, 4½hrs), Nanchang (3, 7hrs), Hangzhou (3, 11hrs)

Buses
From Wuhu: Huangshan, Jiuhuashan and Huzhou (daily)
From Huangshan: Wuhu, Tunxi, Tonglin, Jingdezhen and Hangzhou (daily)
From Jiuhuashan: Huangshan, Guichi and Tongling (daily)
From Nanchang: Lushan (4, 4hrs), Jingdezhen (daily, 5hrs)
From Jiujiang: Jingdezhen (2, 4hrs), Lushan/Guling (6, 2hrs)
From Lushan/Guling: Jiujiang (6, 2hrs), Nanchang (daily, 4hrs)
From Jingdezhen: Jiujiang (2, 4hrs), Nanchang (3, 7hrs)

Ferries
From Wuhan: Chongqing (daily, 5days), Wuhu (daily, 30hrs), Nanjing (daily, 36hrs), Shanghai (daily, 48hrs)
From Yichang: Chongqing (daily, 2½days), Wuhan (daily, 1day)

Flights
Airports at Nanchang, Kingdezhen, Chansha, Wuhan, Hefei, Tunxi and Yichang

ANQING	安庆	JIUHUASHAN	九华山
BENGBU	蚌埠	JIUJIANG	九江
CHANGSHA	长沙	LUSHAN	庐山
CHIBI	赤壁	NANCHANG	南昌
DONGTING LAKE	洞庭湖	POYANG LAKE	鄱阳湖
ECHENG	鄂城	PUQI	浦圻
GUI XI	贵溪	SHASHI	沙市
HEFEI	合肥	TONGLING	铜陵
HENGYANG	衡阳	WUDANGSHAN	武当山
HENGSHAN	衡山	WUHAN	武汉
HUANGSHAN	黄山	WUHU	芜湖
HUANGSHI	黄石	XIANG FAN	襄樊
JIANGLING	江陵	XIANNING	咸宁
JINGDEZHEN	景德镇	YICHANG	宜昌
JINGGANGSHAN	井冈山	YUEYANG	岳阳

Chapter six
THE SOUTH: GUANGDONG AND FUJIAN

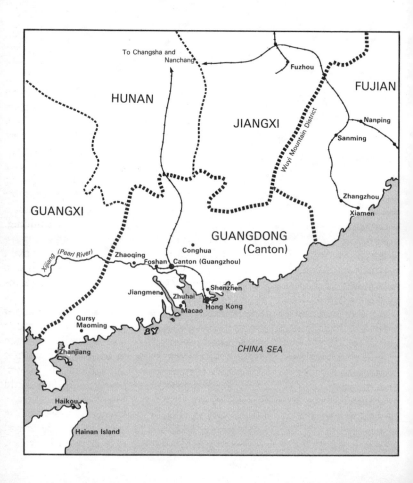

GUANGDONG – FUJIAN

Guangdong province – Canton – is both culturally and economically unique in mainland China. For years the site of strong attempts by western traders, particularly those from Hong Kong, to find new markets and sources of cheap imports, it has a quite distinct atmosphere, reinforced by its differing dialects, its customs and eating habits. Certainly the province's close ties with Hong Kong, South-East Asia and the West, and the consequent exchange of goods and ideas, has led to large parts of Guangdong seeming more like western 'Chinatowns' than the People's Republic. That said, it's Guangdong's diversity which is probably most striking, ranging from the affluence and cosmopolitanism of downtown Canton to the poverty and economic backwardness of parts of Hainan Island.

Guangzhou (**Canton City**), so often the visitor's first glimpse of China, can be misleading. Coming from Hong Kong, it seems a poor imitation of a thriving free market economy, while compared to much of the rest of China it's streets ahead economically – and most of the time seems a far less artificial product of political absolutes than some of the drab and soulless districts of, say, Beijing. Still closer to the west in feel is **Shenzhen** to the south, which acts as a taster of China for day-trippers from Hong Kong and is being developed accordingly, both as a tourist and a business destination. **Foshan** and **Zhaoqing**, both only a day's jaunt from Guangzhou, are interesting too, the former a large and bustling provincial city currently being hyped for tourists by the authorities, and the latter not especially attractive in itself but a useful base for the stunning **Seven Star Crags**, a dramatic limestone formation a few kilometres outside. Half a day's journey west of Guangzhou is the old French town of **Zhanjiang**, these days primarily a Chinese naval base and oil town but with a more ancient half spattered with colonial architecture – plus it's the point from which to make the bus and ferry journey to **Hainan Island**. This, a tropical island as yet largely untouched by modern life, sometimes seems like something out of the pages of a Graham Greene novel. However, its isolation is under threat from the country's industrial drive forward so if I were you I'd get there before it's too late. Remember, though, to check with CITS as to whether the island is actually open: due to its delicate military significance they tend to close it fairly frequently and without warning. At time of writing, only Hainan's capital, **Haikou**, and a town in the south, **Sanya**, were on-limits to individual travellers, but this could well have changed by the time you arrive.

Immediately east of Guangdong, **Fujian province** is worth idling through on the way up to Shanghai. Other than the **Wuyi Mountain Nature Reserve** in the north, much of the interior of the province remains firmly closed to foreign visitors, but the coast, notwithstanding some fast-moving development, is open and for the most part unspoilt – and home to some of China's most devastating natural scenery. **Xiamen**, the first city you'll reach if you're coming from Guangdong, is the urban highspot, smaller and prettier than the province's capital, **Fuzhou**, which despite its long history has little to tempt you beyond its convenience as an overnight stop.

As far as **climate** goes, both Guangdong and Fujian are sub-tropical: in winter the temperature hovers around the 14°C mark; summer is hot, sticky and unsettled, with heavy rainstorms and a humidity which can be overpowering. Watch out, too, for the typhoon season which lasts from July to September – the strong winds have been known to play havoc with local shipping and even upset Ghangzhou's boat and hyrdofoil connections with Hong Kong. If you have any choice in the matter, the best tim's to visit are early spring and late autumn.

GUANGZHOU AND AROUND – AND EAST TO SHANTOU

GUANGZHOU (CANTON CITY)

'I came in through Canton, but got out of there as fast as I could' is an often-heard statement. Understandably, because of its traditionally close ties with the capitalist west, a relative accessibility to tourists, its Imperialist past and present-day importance as an international trading centre, many visitors regard **GUANGZHOU** as no more than a business city – and as such worth little more than a passing glimpse on the way in or out of China. They're wrong. Though a great many of Guangzhou's visitors are indeed businesspeople, many others are Overseas Chinese seeing relatives, and it's they, rather than any kind of direct contact with the west, who have contributed to the city's cosmopolitan air: more Chinese have left Guangdong province to make a living abroad than any other part of China. Guangzhou is different, that much is true, but of China's three large cities it's the most immediately likeable – and, in its own unique way, no less Chinese than anywhere else.

Which said, I'd leave Guangzhou until the end of your trip. If you go there before seeing something else of the country you're more likely to be disappointed and view it merely as a paler, less striking version of Hong Kong. Unless you've been surrounded by a sea of people and a million bikes you'll fail to be impressed by the sheer amount of traffic on the roads; the Japanese-style taxi-cabs which cruise the city in search of business; the Pointer Sisters and Joe Jackson blaring out of car radios; the latest Hong Kong street fashions; the way couples hold hands openly in the street; the garrulous, approachable nature of the people; and the cleanliness of the city, especially when compared with Beijing and Shanghai.

There's little enough left of Canton's rebellious and eventful **history**, which dates back around 2800 years. In the 9C BC it was known as Chuting and received its present Chinese name only 600 years later. It has been called Canton by foreigners since the last century, when British traders used the city as a base from which to export silk and tea (fuelling the newly acquired British habit of tea drinking) and then to import opium into China, illegally, as a means of improving their trading balance. Opium had been used in China for some time, first as a medicine, then, from the 17C onwards, as a drug. In the early years of the 18C opium imports soared (as did levels of addiction), making huge profits for the British and their Chinese distributors but putting enormous strains on the economy – no taxes were being paid and trade was dangerously diminishing Chinese stocks of silver. When in 1839 the Qing government attempted to suppress the trade and confiscate all the opium, Britain declared war on China, attacking Canton and forcing the Chinese, under the first Unequal Treaty, to cede five ports (Hong Kong, Canton and Shanghai among them) to British control. This ended Canton's opium monopoly and the prosperity that went with it – something which, in an area already suffering from lack of land and a growing population – and with a strong tradition of independence and revolutionary activity – could only mean unrest. It was here that Hong Xiuquan, a mad religious fanatic who saw himself as the younger brother of Jesus, mobilised anti-Manchu elements to instigate the Taiping Rebellion; later Sun Yatsen made Canton the base for much of his underground activity – and for a 1911 uprising which helped finally topple the Manchu dynasty the following year. By the 1920s the Communists had established a foothold in the city, helping to organise a General Strike of dockers and seamen that lasted 16 months and founding the Peasant Movement Training Institute to mobilise support for the Party in the countryside. 1927 saw an abortive attempt to put down the Nationalists in which thousands lost their lives, but it wasn't until 1949 that the Communists were able to wrest control of the city from its then Japanese occupiers.

Arriving – and getting your bearings

Baiyun, Guangzhou's main international **airport**, is four miles north of the city centre, a 15-minute drive from all the principal hotels. There's no CAAC bus service, and local buses are erratic so its usually a better idea to splash out on a taxi into town; cost will be about ¥10. Guangzhou **railway station**, at the northernmost end of Jiefang Road, is a massive 4-storey building perpetually crowded with travellers. The hawkers and fruit-sellers who crowd outside can be useful for picking up a cheap bus map of the city or for some assistance in buying tickets for onward rail travel, something becoming increasingly difficult in Guangzhou owing to police crackdowns on the practice. The **CITS office**, on your left as you come out of the station (daily 8–11.30 & 2.30–5.30), seems a large and efficient outfit but in fact caters almost exclusively for tour groups, and even the most courteous request for information is usually met with a surly sigh and what is obviously no more than a guess at the answer. Best bypass them altogether and jump on a bus into the centre – a no.31 will take you direct to Shamian, and a no.5 to Yide Road.

The **long-distance bus station**, point of arrival from Zhanjiang, Haikou, Guilin, Shantou, Jiangmen and Fujian, is five minutes' walk west of the train station and is connected with Yide and – almost – with Shamian by a no.5 or no.15 bus.

Boats and hovercraft services from Macao and Hong Kong, and ferries from Haikou, put in at the **Zhoutouzui Wharf**, on the south bank of the Pearl River in the Honan district of town, from where you can take a taxi or a no. 9, 10 or 31 bus from Gongye Road across the river. If you're coming from Shanghai, Wuzhou or Xiamen you'll arrive at **Dashatou** in the south-eastern corner of Guangzhou, from where you can pick up a no.7 bus to the Liuhua Hotel in the northern part of the city, or bus no.12 to Xicun in the north-west.

Unlike Beijing or Shanghai, Guangzhou, for a city of its size, is surprisingly compact, and a difficult place in which to get lost. It was originally divided into three distinct parts: an inner city, closed within city walls and split into old and new quarters, and a surrounding district outside. The walls were demolished in the 1920s but it's this area, bounded south by the Pearl River and to the north by Huanshi Lu, and cut by the main arterial roads of **Jiefang** and **Zhongshan**, that makes up central Guangzhou today. Heading north from their junction, Jiefang takes you past the Luirong Temple and, on the right, the Memorial to Dr Sun Yatsen, to the imposing white façade of the Dongfang Hotel and, beyond, Huanshi – the main northern ringroad. The way north leads out to the airport and the distant White Mountains; turning left takes in, successively, CAAC, CITS, the railway station, the telegraph office and the Liuhua Hotel (see below). East of here the ringroad runs into the sprawling district of **Xiao Bei**, residential enclave of the city's thousands of civil servants, past the huge Friendship Store, and meets Xian Lie Lu. Take this and you'll come to Guangzhou Zoo and the city's deserted Botanical Gardens.

Guangzhou's **southern half** is more rundown – **Binjiang Lu** for example, which used to be the city's notorious red-light district where opium dens, brothels and gambling houses thrived before 1949. Today this is a predominantly industrial quarter of faceless warehouses and, further south, equally faceless housing estates. Past the Cultural Park is Guangzhou's busiest commercial site, a net of tiny streets spread between Xiali Lu and the riverbank route of Liuersan Lu, most of which make up the crowded and compulsive **Qingping street market**. Across the water **Shamian Island** is the former foreigners' quarter, noticeably quieter than the rest of the city, where western merchants plying the opium trade were forced to establish their base in the 19C.

These, then, are the city's major parts. **Getting around**, by way of **bus and trolley bus services**, is easier and a lot less congested than most other Chinese cities, but the huge lumbering buses are painfully slow: it takes almost half an hour to go from Haizhu Square to the railway station, a 10-minute ride by car. But if time is no problem it can be a fascinating way of viewing local life, and very cheap with tickets averaging 10fen. Trolley buses, which run on four north–south/east–west routes make the buses look fast and are extremely uncomfortable – though, apart from the useful no.4 line from Dashatou to the western end of Zhingshan Road, you shouldn't need to use them as each route is covered by a bus. **Taxis** are plentiful though impossible to book, and in season you could well have a long wait for one: as always in china they're hailable in the street if they're empty, but otherwise the best place to stand is outside a hotel; the average fare works out about ¥2 for the first kilometre and 80fen for each one after that. **Minibuses** are another option, a new development from Hong Kong with routes so complicated that often the Chinese themselves don't know where they're going. Still, if you wave a map at the driver there's a good chance he'll let you know the route he's taking, and the fixed fare of ¥1.5 makes this one of the best ways to get around if you're going any distance.

Somewhere to stay

As Guangzhou's business traffic increases, so inevitably do its **hotels**, which isn't all to the city's good for here more than anywhere else in China room prices reflect the belief that all businessmen are rich and can therefore afford the equivalent of the going rate in their own country. Plus, the growing number of tour groups has tended to shift resources towards the short stay/high pay end of the market, with the result that although dormitories and cheap rooms are available you either have to fight for a bed or accept dismal levels of sanitation. Where you look will depend largely on where you choose to stay, but if you're in town for more than a day or two the Pearl River-Shamian Island area is much the

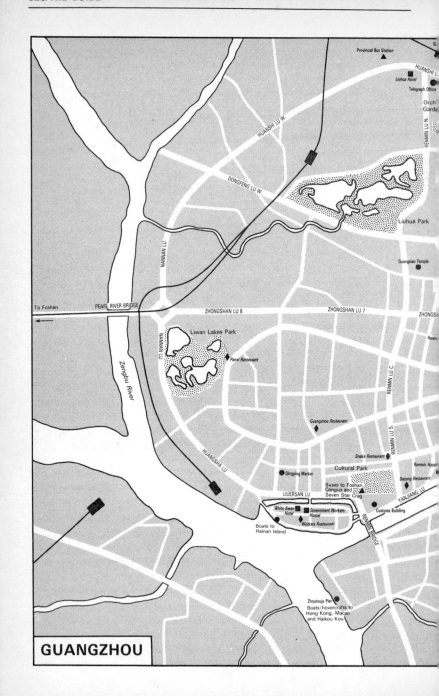

GUANGZHOU

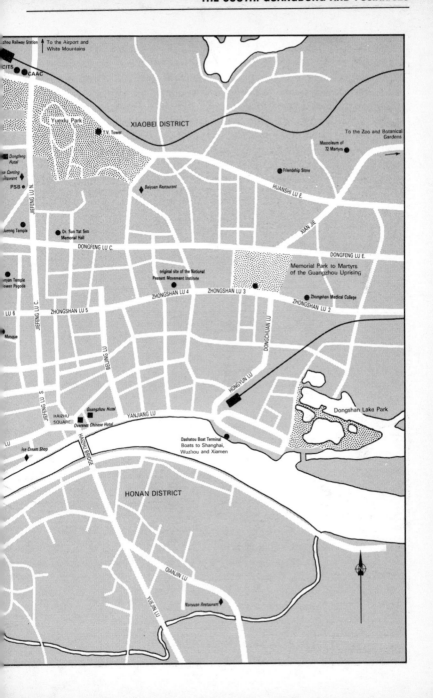

zhou Railway Station

To the Airport and
White Mountains

CITS

CAAC

Yuexlu Park

XIAOBEI DISTRICT

T.V. Tower

To the Zoo and Botanical
Gardens

Mausoleum of
72 Martyrs

Dongfeng
Hotel

a Canting
estaurant

Friendship Store

PSB

HUANSHI LU E.

JIEFENG LU N.

Beiyuan Restaurant

XIAN JIE

Jurong Temple

Dr. Sun Yat Sen
Memorial Hall

DONGFENG LU C.

DONGFENG LU E.

nyun Temple
lower Pagoda

original site of the National
Peasant Movement Institute

Memorial Park to Martyrs
of the Guangzhou Uprising

JIEFENG LU C.

ZHONGSHAN LU 4

ZHONGSHAN LU 3

Zhongshan Medical College

LU 6

ZHONGSHAN LU 5

ZHONGSHAN LU 2

Mosque

BEIJING LU

DONGCHUAN LU

JIEFENG LU S.

HONGYUN LU

Dongshan Lake Park

HAIZHU
SQUARE

Guangzhou Hotel

YANJIANG LU

Overseas Chinese Hotel

LU

HAIZHU BRIDGE

Ice Cream Shop

Dashatou Boat Terminal
Boats to Shanghai,
Wuzhou and Xiamen

HONAN DISTRICT

QIANJIN LU

YUEIN LU

Nanyuan Restaurant

N

best place to head for. Cheapest, though by no means the most comfortable option – there's no hot water and the washing facilities are somewhat primitive – is the *Government Workers Hotel* in the centre of Shamian, reachable on a no.31 bus from the train station (get off before it crosses the river and walk across the footbridge). This charges just ¥4 for a dorm bed; a three-bedded room is ¥6 and a double ¥15. If you can't get in here there are a number of other hostels in the same street, all of which will admit foreigners. Further upmarket, the *Shamian Island Hotel* is opposite the ritzy *White Swan* on the south-eastern shore of the island and has doubles at ¥25.

If you've got the readies, though, it's well worth shelling out a bit extra for some comfort – especially if you're planning on spending some time in Guangzhou. The *Renmin Daxia* (People's Hotel) is worth trying, both for its situation overlooking the river, and for its general atmosphere, preserved through years of a Chinese-only admittance policy. Doubles vary between ¥33 and ¥43, and there's a great inexpensive restaurant upstairs where locals come for a night out and frequent wedding receptions: around the beginning of the Chinese year (according to custom this is a good time to wed) there are at least half a dozen thunderous firecrackers every night. The hotel is on the no.5 bus route ... get off the stop before Haizhu Square. Further east, actually on Haizhu Sq, the *Guangzhou* and *Overseas Chinese* hotels are convenient if rather dull, with beds at ¥12.50 in three-bedded rooms. And whatever the person on the desk might say, the Guangzhou *does* have dormitories, so stand your ground and argue if you have to – it could mean the difference between ¥5 and ¥15.

Those only in Guangzhou for a couple of nights will probably find it makes more sense to hole up in the northern end of town, near the railway station. The *Liuhua*, on Huanshi Road, has long been the traditional base of independent travellers, both for its location and size, but unfortunately the constant stream of penny-pinching tourists has encouraged the staff to become indolent and aggressive. Prices, too, seem to be rising monthly, but at the last count it was ¥10 for a dorm bed, ¥35 for a double and ¥13 for a place in a three-bed room. The Liuhua's main advantage is that it's a good meeting place for travellers on their way in and out of China, and since the policy on what's closed and what's open tends to vary so much it's useful to get the latest word. The hotel also has a couple of large notice-boards on which it's possible to pin messages for a few days, or even advertise for a travelling companion. A little way along Huanshi Road, the *CAAC building* also has a couple of dorms in which it lets foreigners stay, if you can persuade them you're 'between flights'; or there's the *Dongfang*, opposite the Trade Fair Centre on Xicun Lu, once Guangzhou's most exclusive hotel though now considered old fashioned and downmarket, with doubles at around ¥30.

Food and drink

According to tradition, a Chinese should be born in Suzhou, live in Hangzhou and die in Liuzhou. He/she should, however, eat in Guangzhou, and judging by the sheer quantity and quality of the food the average Cantonese consumes each day things haven't changed. Disabuse yourself first of one notion: what we in the west call **Cantonese food** would, with one or two exceptions, be utterly unrecognisable to a Canton resident. And while much of the food in China can be poor quality, with the worst cuts of meat and the stringiest vegetables, Cantonese food has the taste, variety, texture and colour to make eating the best part of your stay here, whether you're spending a lot or just a little. It's said that the Cantonese will eat anything with legs except a table, and anything with wings except an aeroplane, and this, too, is borne out by menus on which snake, monkey, pigeon and dog are all regular features. But what matters above all else is the freshness of the food: most meat and fish is sold alive and, usually, kicking – in the case of fish often with organs still attached and lustily pumping blood. It's said that if a fish is more than two hours old it's not fresh anymore. Local cuisine seals flavour into the food by cooking it very quickly in a wok and at very high temperature. Ordering, being served and consuming your food is as much an aesthetic experience as a physical one: presentation, particularly, is a highly regarded art form and many restaurants have small intricately designed ornamental gardens, both in and outside the dining rooms, to enhance the atmosphere. A word of warning, however: even though vegetables are often of higher quality in Guangdong than the rest of China, Guangdong remains in every sense a meat eater's paradise. Vegetarian restaurants are almost non-existent, and waiters gaze in amazement if you ask for only vegetable dishes when you could order meat ones.

Breakfast, served between 5 and 9, is the best Cantonese meal of the day, when people eat *Dim Sum*, very small, fried, steamed or baked buns and rolls filled with various combinations of pork, chicken and prawns and washed down with gallons of Chinese tea. In all hotels and restaurants this is standard breakfast fare, but if you want to eat *Dim Sum* with the Chinese the best place is the *Workers Restaurant*, diagonally opposite the White Swan Hotel on Shamian Island, a vast and convivial eating palace in which dishes are pushed around on massive trolleys and, as always with *Dim Sum*, you pay according to the number of empty containers on your table at the end. You can drink as much tea as you like, and the total cost for three dishes and tea is ¥1.80. You'll feel more inspired still if you pop into the White Swan afterwards and see what people are paying for a western-style breakfast. At the other end of the market to the Workers Restaurant, the **Dong Feng Hotel** is another good place to eat *Dim Sum*, and though it'll work out around ¥5 a head the food is top quality and the decor fascinating. Otherwise *Dim Sum* are everywhere, and good wherever you go, even off a street stall.

Lunch, served between 10 and 1.30, is often a large meal for the Chinese, but if you want to stay fit for sightseeing I'd recommend you try something in the street, or go to one of hundreds of *noodle houses* such as the one at 79 Xiajiang Road, off Renmin Lu. The *food stalls* in the south-western quarter of the city, between Xialu Lu and Liuersan Lu, are excellent and cheap, with a choice of dishes varying daily from meat and chicken dumplings, prawn balls, egg and rice snacks and battered checken legs. There are also a number of small stalls and noodle houses south of the Liuhua Hotel off Huanshi Lu, and left and right off the eastern half of Zhongshan Lu. Those suffering from culture shock can try the *fast food kiosk* inside the station, which isn't as good as the one in Beijing but still leaves MacDonalds standing.

Dinner, between 5 and 8, is highlight of the day – well worth putting a few extra yuan by to enjoy in style. Providing you don't go overboard, and steer clear of the banquets and western restaurants in hotels, you can eat in the best places in town for under ¥25 for two. Many restaurants have small partitioned rooms if you want to go in a group, but it's far better to sit with the Chinese, as not only can it work out cheaper but Cantonese of all classes eat out and it's much more enjoyable to get involved. Try and give hotels a miss too, even Chinese ones, as the food they serve tends to be much less tasty than the straight restaurants.

The best restaurant in Guangzhou has to be the *Nan Yuan*, at 120 Qianjin Lu in the Honan district of the city, a no.14 or 25 busride from north of the Pearl River. Try the mushroom, fish and pork dishes, the Maotai chicken which is a speciality, and the Pomfret fish with pine nuts. Better still walk around until you spy something you like. Most other restaurants are in the south-western part of the city near Shamian. The *Datong*, 63 Yangjiang Lu, is a huge 8-storey building near the Customs House which specialises in roast suckling pig, and has a cheaper 6th floor restaurant; west off Renmin Lu, at 43 Jianglan Lu, is the amazing *Shecanguan* or snake restaurant, which serves a range of dishes from different parts of the snake: it's a good idea to come here in a group so you can try one of everything (the liver is delicious, honestly!) though if I were you I'd avoid the tourist highlight of the meal which is having the snake skinned alive at your table. Nearby, at 2 Wencheng Lu, is the *Guangzhou*, the city's oldest restaurant and still its largest, with over 10,000 diners a day passing through in high season. Prices vary according to where you sit; the ground floor seems cheapest. The *Panxi* is also good, overlooking Liwan Park in the west of the city (try the scallop soup here); the *Beiyuan*, opposite Yuexiu Park at 318 Dongfang Lu, prides itself on its shredded chicken and shark's fin dishes. There's also the very trendy and crowded *Diaxa Canting eating house*, underground on Jiefang Road, near the Dongfang Hotel. This, very popular with the local youth, is, if nothing else, a good chance to see the latest Guangzhou street fashions.

If you feel like eating on your feet, **night time street food** is available in profusion off the southern end of Renmin Lu, behind the Liuhua Hotel. Small *one man cafés* serve basic meat and vegetable dishes for around ¥1.50 each, and though the quality doesn't compare with the larger restaurants the food's fine. Delicious, too, are the fresh lychees sold in spring from a handful of *stalls* on Yangjiang Lu: in the past the Guangdong lychee crop was so succulent that the Emperor used to send for them in Beijing; today they are still like no other lychees you'll ever have tasted. Close by on Shishanang Lu is an *evening market* which deals in delicacies like frogs, snails and turtles tossed alive into massive woks and cooked on the spot. Guangzhou is also known for its ice cream, and one of the many *sweet parlours* where you can glimpse the newly liberated young Chinese holding hands and eating their ice creams is at 123 Shangjui Lu, near the Haizhu Bridge. **Drinkwise**, Guangzhou beer is palatable enough, though you'll have to drink a fair bit of it to get even slightly drunk. Various lethal rice liqueurs and wines are offered in restaurants, but check with someone who knows something about them before over-indulging.

The waterfront and Shamian Island

Guangzhou's most vigorous quarter, and easily the most interesting for idle strolls, abuts the **northern bank of the Pearl River**. This, together with Shamian Island across the water, the former foreign enclave, forms the oldest and most congested part of the city, where the buildings cluster closer together and life is more abundant, teeming, than in Guangzhou's newer areas, most of which were built during the 1920s as part of an ambitious slum clearance scheme. To get down here take bus no.5 from the long-distance bus station, railway station or the centre of town to **Yanjiang Lu**, the waterfront's main boulevard. As in Shanghai, this is a favourite spot with older residents, particularly early morning when they come down here to practise Tai Chi; in the evenings it's taken over by younger Chinese, who walk along hand in hand, arm in arm, even indulging in the western habit of kissing in public. Walk west from here, towards Shamian Island, past the old **Customs House** and a tight grouping of colonial buildings, and turn right onto Liuersan Lu. This takes its name from the Cantonese for 6 2 3, referring to 23 June 1925 when British and French troops fired on Chinese workers during the Hong Kong-Canton strike of that year. Much beyond, opposite the first bridge to Shamian Island, and you're in **Qingping market**, which extends from Liuersan Lu along Qingping Lu to Heping Lu, each intersecting east–west road forming a natural dividing line for the sale of different goods. This is by far China's most exciting market, and, if you're at all squeamish, a slightly taxing one too, where fish are de-scaled while alive, and chickens – not to mention turtles, owls, cats, monkeys, dogs and tortoises – slaughtered on the spot. The first section, nearest Liuersan Lu, sells medicines and herbs, the next fresh vegetables, and the third part is given over to the live animal, bird and fish stalls. Further up are plants, pottery and bonsai trees. East from here, behind the Renmin Hotel on Changdi Lu, there's a **smaller market**, by night a lively area of busy restaurants, bars and open-air stalls selling freshly cooked snails and fruit. Most of the shops open late too, many flogging good cheap pottery and bonsai trees.

Back on Liuersan, it's a short walk across the bridge to **Shamian Island**, a tear-shaped sandbank (that's what 'shamian' means) about half a mile long and just 400 yards wide which was held on lease by the British and French as part of their booty from the Opium Wars: the French were granted 44 acres and the British took the rest. Then, however, the island was around half its present size; the Europeans reclaimed the rest from the river as part of a concerted attempt to recreate their own backyard, throwing up French and Victorian-style buildings which housed all the trappings of life at home, many of which still stand. The **French Consulate** on the island's eastern tip, and the **British Consulate** on the main street, are both originals, and grand colonial villas line the water's edge along with churches, tennis courts, a football pitch and yacht club. All of these once excluded the Chinese completely, apart from those needed in service, shutting them out by means of huge iron gates on the bridges which were bolted regularly every night at 10. Thus the Europeans could get on with their own lives in peace, undisturbed by the bustle of Canton across the water . . .

And Shamian Island still retains something of that atmosphere today. By 1911 there were 300 people living here from Europe, America and Japan; today the villas are multi-occupied by Chinese families or businesses, but the wide streets, absence of traffic – so different from the rest of the city – and the few remaining dilapidated buildings give a poignant feel of melancholy only broken by the tall white landmark at the southern tip, the 35-storey **White Swan Hotel**. This is Canton's showpiece, an expensive, internationalist place, spanking new and with a swimming pool, western designer boutiques and authentic – as opposed to Chinese – foreign food among its many amenities. There's a good view of the Pearl River from the ground-floor café, and you can pick up some cheap prints amongst all the pricey antiques and souvenirs, but those apart, it's frankly best avoided.

After your walk, take a **boat trip** on the Pearl River, which will take you as far west as the Guangzhou Shipyards and as far east as the Physical

Culture Institute on Ershatou Island. Boats leave at 8.30, 3.30 and 7.30, and tickets for the 90 minute round trop cost ¥10 (¥8 to Overseas Chinese), available from the office opposite the Customs Building, from where the boats leave too. The **Pearl River** is today one of China's busiest waterways, second only to the Yangzi in importance as an industrial channel. Its name, oddly romantic for such a businesslike stretch of water, is the result of ancient legend, which tells how a monk, Jiahu, lost a pearl in the river, and though it was seen shining on the riverbed night after night, no one was ever able to find it.

Though you may not find the pearl, these trips give fine views of Shamian Island and Guangzhou's busy waterfront, the bridges, Haizhou Square and the new homes of the city's former boat dwellers on **Ershatou Island**. Before liberation, when Ershatou was still a German concession, an estimated 68,000 people lived on the Pearl River, working as fishermen, boatmen or ferrymen, and all used their boats as homes. For centuries these people were treated as outcasts, as indeed they were, and they shared little in the everyday life of the rest of Canton: during the Ming Dynasty they were forbidden from marrying anyone who lived on land and were not allowed to set up homes or own property ashore; later, in the Qing Dynasty, they were excluded by law from taking Imperial exams. After the revolution, however, they were moved to dry land and resettled into a purpose-built estate of apartment blocks along the south bank of the river – actually on Erstatou Island – which now goes under the name of the New Riverside Village.

Other sights

Revolutionary monuments
The Sun Yatsen Memorial Hall Dongfeng Lu, south of Yuexiu Park. Though none of the revolutionary monuments are exceptional, this is at least the most eye-catching – a massive 5000-seat theatre roofed with deep blue ceramic tiles and sitting in a broad expanse of almost unnaturally green lawns, where you can watch clouds of dragonflies circling in the heat-haze. Built in 1931 on the spot where Sun Yatsen took the presidential oath, there's nothing much to see inside, and on the whole it remains closed except for conferences and displays.
The Memorial Gardens to the Martyrs of the 1927 Guangzhou Uprising Zhongshan 3 Lu Laid out in 1957 on the spot where thousands were slaughtered by nationalist troops during the unsuccessful 1927 insurrection, the interest of this is, frankly, fairly limited.
The Mausoleum of the 72 Martyrs Xianlie Lu. This commemorates the earlier but equally brutally supressed uprising of 1911 under Sun Yatsen. Funded by contributions from Overseas Chinese, it's a slightly odd

agglommeration of architectural styles, with an Egyptian obelisk, a miniature imitation of the Trianon at Versailles capped by a stone pyramid,
and, on top, a bronze replica of the Statue of Liberty. The symbolism is
obvious, but like so many of these monuments leaves you cold.

The Peasant Movement Training Institute 42 Zhongshan 4 Lu. Once a
Confucian temple, then a school for training young Party members (Mao
was director here in 1926), this has been turned over to a museum of
mildewed revolutionary memorabilia, straw hats, sandals, rifles and
fading photographs. Worth a brief look but no more.

Temples and mosques

Huai Shang Mosque Guangta Lu. Said to be the oldest mosque in China,
and probably dating from the 7C when the city had a sizeable community
of Persian and Arab traders. Its minaret, actually inside the mosque, well
deserves the name Guangta – bare pagoda.

Temple of the Six Banyan Trees Liurong Si Lu. An 11C visitor, the
scholar-poet Su Dongpo, was so charmed by the banyan trees in the
courtyard here that he rechristened the temple with an example of his
calligraphy – Six Banyans. Things have changed quite a lot since then:
the trees have gone, and a reception hall for foreigners absorbs seemingly
endless contents of tour buses, all eager to see one of the few truly old
buildings in Guangzhou. Once you've glimpsed the temple, clamber up
the Hua Ta or Flowery Pagoda, a 6C 9-storey octagonal structure where
Boddhiddharma, the Indian monk who traditionally founded Zen
Buddhism, is supposed to have stayed and rid the place of mosquitoes.
The inner walls are covered in footprints – a few, somehow, on the ceiling
– and though the inside niches are empty, the view from the top is
spectacular enough to warrant the climb.

Guangxiao Si A short walk from the Six Banyan Trees and much less
frequented – probably because, until recently, it was officially closed to
individuals – this is Guangzhou's oldest Buddhist temple, its main hall
dating from the 4C and today backing on to a fascinating huddle of
alleyways and workshops. The Indian monk Dharmayas preached here
in the 4C, and hair shaved from the head of the monk Hui Neng (founder
of the Southern School of Chinese Buddhism) is buried beneath one of
the small Buddha-encrusted pagodas in the courtyard, both of which date
from AD960. When I ambled through, the locals were using these as a
quiet place for a smoke, for their evening meal or a game of hide and
seek. If you can, take a look in the Hall of the Sleeping Buddha whose
statue, women believed, could induce fertility through contact with their
bedsheets.

Parks and gardens

Yuexiu Park Jiefang Bei Lu. The biggest park in the city, which seems to have effortlessly swallowed up a huge sports stadium, an olympic-size swimming pool, two lakes and a clutch of tea-houses, restaurants and pavilions. You can do virtually anything here: rent a rowboat for a few mao, roller skate to a deafening symphony, swim in the 1930s style pool or just join one of the long queues for ice cream. And if you were wondering why a grotesque sculpture of five rams should figure on so many Guangzhou postcards, this is the place to find out. For here, on a small mound and surrounded by Chinese posing for photographs, is the sculpture itself, a reference to the mythical founding of the city when five sages rode in on five rams each carrying a stalk of rice. The park rises in its centre to a hall, topped with a 19C tower known as Zhen Hai Lou (Tower which commands the Seas), the only survivor from the original city wall, which has been, variously, a palace for high-ranking officials, a nationalist hospital, and, currently, a museum of local history. Of the five floors of exhibits, the ceramics are interesting and the maritime history section particularly strong. Your ticket will also buy you tea on the top-floor verandah, from which you can look down on sunhatted children astride the cannon in the courtyard below and the hazy sprawl of the city beyond.

Orchid Gardens Jiefang Bei Lu. An oasis of calm after a hot dusty walk or the battle for train tickets. Stone-flagged paths weave past great hangar-like greenhouses brimming with hundreds of varieties of orchid – all for an entrance fee of just ¥1, which also entitles you to unlimited tea and hot flannels in one of the elegant pavilions.

Liuhua Park Renmin Lu. Not far from the Dongfang Hotel, this is an enormous manmade lake dug in 1958 as part of Chairman Mao's Great Leap Forward. It's somewhat less inviting now, stagnant for the most part and skirted by mud paths pitted by the heat, but outside weekends – when, incidentally, you should avoid it like the plague – it has the gentle feel of an out-of-season resort.

The Cultural Park Liuersan Lu. Great for an early evening stroll, when you'll find gangs of children queueing under the eagle eye of their custodian for space invaders machines and the park's fairground amusements, as well as exhibitions, an aquarium and open-air cinema and opera house.

Listings

Airlines *CAAC* are at 181 Huanshi Road, two doors east of the railway station. Open evenings only, 6–10pm.

Antiques Mainly reproduction these days, but try *Kuantung Antique Store* in Hungshu Road N, which sells jade, porcelain, pottery and ivory. The *shop* at 146 Wende Road, off Zhongshan Road, also has scattered bargains.

Banks The *Bank of China* is at 137 Changti Road; most larger hotels will change travellers cheques and foreign notes. The black market operates outside the Liuhua and Overseas Chinese hotels, but take care.

Boats and hovercrafts From Zhoutouzui Wharf to Hong Kong, Macao and Haikou (Hainan Island); tickets from the ticket office there, from a small office opposite the Customs Building on Yanjiang Lu, or from large hotels or CITS. These last will probably charge you a ¥2 mark-up, but it's worth paying for the convenience. **From Dashatou**, in SE Guangzhou, for all other services. Tickets only from the office opposite the Customs Building.

Books The *Foreign Language Bookstore*, 326 Beijing Lu, specialises in English translations of Chinese classics and American magazines. Good selection, too, at Xinhua Bookstore, 336 Beijing Lu.

Buses For services to Foshan, Zhanjiang, Haikou, Beihai, Guilin, Jiangmen and Zhaoqing, use the long-distance bus station on Huanshi Lu, west of the railway station. Buses to Foshan, Congua and the Seven Star Crag leave from opposite the Cultural Park. (If you're going to Foshan, the bus station on Da Xinhu also offers a service.) Tickets for all destinations from the bus station office (730-930) or the Overseas Chinese Hotel on Haizu Square (830-1130/230-530)

Canton Fair Twice yearly between 15 April and 15 May, and 15 October and 15 November, at the Fair Building on Xicun Lu, opposite the Dongfang Hotel. Be warned that rooms are much scarcer during these times.

Cinemas and theatres The large cinemas on Beijing Lu, like the Xinwen and Yinghung, show a number of Chinese and Western films each week. Opera and acrobatic shows perform all over town: try the *Youyi Theatre*, near Linhua Bridge, and the handful on Dongfang Lu. Check with CITS for details of what's on.

CITS Two offices, one at 179 Huanshi Lu, nextdoor to the station (8-1130/230-5), which is unhelpful and apathetic, and another in room 2366 of the Dongfang Hotel (8-8) which is even worse. Both are only really interested in western hard currency, so if you want some information be prepared to persevere.

Consulates *American* on the 11th floor of the Dongfang Hotel (1100), *Japanese* on the 7th floor (69900 ex 2785).

Department store Guangzhou's finest is the *Nang Fang* on Liuersan Lu, opposite the Cultural Park. Good stock of Chinese products.

Friendship Store Next door to the Baiyun Hotel on Huanshi Lu, on the no.30 bus route. Large food market on the ground floor, first floor leather and arts and crafts. Open 8.30–9.

Hospital The Zhongshan Medical College, near the Memorial Garden to the Martyrs on Zhongshan Lu; 1 or 2 bus.

Interpreters Can be hired from *Guangzhou Friendship Labour Service*, room 2207, Dongfang Hotel. ¥4 an hour.

Jogging and Tai Chi Both endemic among the Cantonese. Go to the Cultural Park before 6.30 and see for yourself.

Maps Good English city and bus maps are available from hawkers at the station, or from CITS or hotels.

Poste restante Guangzhou has the most efficient service in China: at the two main post offices on Huanshi Lu, next to the train station, and at Changdi Damalu, just off Renmin Lu. Stemps and telegram facilities are available at hotels.

Public security At the foreign affairs section, 863 Jiefang Beilu, 15 minutes' walk from the Dongfang Hotel: all standard visas, except for Behai, which you can only get in Nanning. Open 8.30–11.30/2.30–5.30.

Railway station Huanshi Lu, in the north of the city. Advance ticket office open evenings 5–11.30, but you can get same-day tickets 24 hours a day. Tickets also available from CITS.

Silk Good supplies at the Friendship Store and at the Trade Fair Exhibition Hall, which doubles up as a shop when the fair isn't on. Handmade silk padded jackets can be ordered at 8 Xiajui Lu, off Renmin Lu.

Telephones Local calls are generally free at hotels. International and long-distance calls are best made from the Telegraph Office next door to the Liuhua Hotel; hotels work out considerably more expensive.

AROUND GUANGZHOU – AND EAST TO SHANTOU

BAIYUN SHAN or the White Cloud Mountain, 14km north of Guangzhou, is reachable by quarter-hourly bus from Guangwei Road – a 25 minute journey which leaves you a good 3 hours' climb from the summit. This, called Moxing Ling (Star Touching Peak), is at 382m the highest point in an otherwise flat region, providing fine sunset views over the whole of Canton and the Pearl River delta. Make a point of climbing up to the **Cheng precipice**, a ledge which gained its name when a Qin dynasty emperor sent his minister, Cheng Kee, here to find a herb which would bestow immortality on whoever ate it. Cheng duly found the herb but on eating it found to his dismay that the rest of it had disappeared. Sure of his fate if he dared to go back with this story, he flung himself off the mountain – only to be rescued by a stork (he was, after all, by now immortal) and taken to heaven.

If this story seems slightly dubious, the views from the precipice are most definitely not, said by the Cantonese to be one of the eight great sights of Guangdong. These hills, once covered with numerous monasteries and hermitages, have been heavily reforested and unfold in a lush panorama of green, dotted with tiny tea-houses and pavilions. Two luxury hotels, reputed to be China's finest, hide away up here too, and though they are largely kept for distinguished Party members and visiting foreign dignitaries you can bask away for hours in the marbled splendour of their sunken baths.

More scenic beauty, and a popular watering hole of Guangzhou residents, can be found about 60 kilometres south-west of the city in the **XIQIAO HILLS**. These number around 70 peaks, and, pitted with caves and crags and carved with waterfalls, rise to something like 400m at their highest point, exuding a quiet, calm kind of beauty which makes them a good place to unwind after the tensions of Guangzhou; it comes as no surprise to learn of their popularity with local artists. The foothill village of **GUANSHAN** makes the best place to head for: to get there take a bus from the small bus station on Daxin Road, just off at Jiefang Road, at 7 in the morning.

About the same distance north of the city, **CONGHUA** is an equally good bet for a couple of days hiking through the Qingyuan mountains – though the town is most famous for its Hot Springs. These lie around 15 kilometres outside Conghua, surrounded by luxuriant vegetation – plum, cassia and lychee orchards – and with hotels in which you can take the waters. These are clear and odourless, ranging in temperature from 35°C to 70°C, and are said to cure illnesses like neuralgia, high blood pressure, rheumatism and various skin diseases. Local buses leave Guangzhou from opposite the Cultural Park's front entrance at 6.40 am, Saturdays and Sundays only; or CITS run a daily tourist bus, but you had best check with them for details.

If you've got time on your hands, it could, too, be worth a trip down to the Pearl River delta, much of which is taken up by ZHONGSHAN COUNTY. ZHONGSHAN the town is of little interest, but **JIANGMEN**, a few kilometres west, sports an array of cobbled streets, unusual in China, and rows of European-style 19C mansions – the homes of Pearl River traders during the opium wars – that would repay a quite considerable trek. This region is perhaps best known for being the birthplace of Dr Sun Yatsen, who was born in the nearby village of **CUIHENG** and whose former home still stands and is open to the public for small fee. Four buses daily make the 2½ hour journey from Guangzhou to Jiangmen, and, if you want to stay, there are basic but inexpensive rooms on offer at the Jiangmen Mansions Hotel, next door to the bus station.

The other side of the delta, the south China border town of **SHENZHEN** is very much the pride of the region, at least in economic terms. For over the last five years, spurred by its status as a special economic zone and benefiting greatly from its proximity to Hong Kong, it has made a major transformation, from sleepy, rather nondescript frontier crossing – for many people, their first taste of China – to a thriving manufacturing and tourist centre.

This development has come, inevitably, at a price, since the Chinese, with their usual sharp eye for a money-spinner, have gutsily promoted above all else Shenzhen's ideal position for Hong Kong's day-trip trade, and for much of the year the town is now flocked with tours just here for a very brief glimpse of life under Communism – something you don't even need a passport for if you're staying in Hong Kong. Dull monuments have been smartened up, and an ersatz handicraft industry created from nothing, together with countless business ventures in the outlying province which rely on Hong Kong money and expertise.

All of which, while the benefits to China and its people can't be denied, makes Shenzhen sound awful, which is unfair because the town does have its moments, and especially if you've come in on the blundering old Kowloon train from Hong Kong, is well worth a quick browse around. Certainly it does have a quite potent atmosphere all of its own, notwithstanding the glaringly obvious tourist-trap restaurants, newly built on a shoestring and hung with English signs. However, you no longer have to take the slow train, for since 1978 there's been a direct express to Guangzhou, so basically I'd recommend you only stop if you've got bags of time or are particularly interested in examples of Chinese enterprise . . . For those who do decide to break their journey, there's a **CITS office** inside the train station and a small **hotel**, the *Overseas Chinese*, on the far side of the railway line, reachable via the station underpass. This, at ¥45 for a double, is predictably expensive and has no dormitories, so unless you have a specific reason to linger in Shenzhen I wouldn't bother to spend the night. There are five trains a day to Guangzhou, but a word of warning: the last one leaves at 4.30 pm so don't leave it too late.

SHANTOU

Further east along the coast and chief port of eastern Guangdong, **SHANTOU** makes an ideal stopover on the long and arduous journey between Guangzhou and Xiamen. And, like most ports, it's an interesting place to wander around, though you should be able to see everything inside a day. Shantou first opened its doors to foreigners in 1858 as a result of the Treaty of Tianjin, which brought to an end one in the long series of opium war battles and established the British here as the main entrepreneurs. Under their initiative, Shantou became a major trading post – which, to this day, it remains.

Coming out of the long-distance bus station, the first thing to do is equip yourself with a map, which you can do at the small kiosk outside. After that, jump on a no.3 bus to either the *Overseas Chinese Hotel* on Shanzhang Lu (doubles for ¥14, triples for ¥18), or, 10 minutes' walk further on at the Shanzhang/Jinsha junction, another, cheaper hotel.

The town's most interesting reaches lie south of here, on a swollen thumb of land that juts west into the sea. This is Shantou's **harbour quarter**, an exhilarating if squalid blend of tumbledown buildings, crumbling mud shacks, narrow, filthy streets and new but already aged concrete apartment blocks – in short, a typical portside slum. There's nothing here to see specifically, but there's a fine and vital atmosphere to the place that's well worth soaking up: Shantou is a nice place just to walk around, even if you wouldn't want to live there. Apart from anything, there are some great **restaurants** around, not least two at the top end of Zhongshan Lu and an excellent one on the corner of Yongyi Lu and Yuejin Lu. And once you've walked, seen and eaten, you'll be more than ready to move on.

SOUTH-WEST TO HAINAN ISLAND

FOSHAN

Though only 25 kilometres south-west of Guangzhou, **FOSHAN** is very much a town in its own right, with a recorded history of some 1300 years as one of the four ancient centres of old China. Originally called Jihua, it was renamed Foshan or 'Hill of the Buddhas' in AD628 after the excavation of three Buddhist statues which, according to legend, had been enshrined by a wandering Buddhist monk. Its proximity to Guangzhou, and a prime situation at the tip of the Pearl River delta, made it an important trading centre, and even today its clean streets and white-fronted buildings give it an unmistakeably affluent air – in all a pleasant contrast from the cramped streets of Canton.

This prosperity is nowadays the result more of the town's burgeoning tourist trade than anything else, which rests largely on Foshan's reputation as a handicraft centre. Certainly it has an impressive array of crafts, centred both in Foshan itself and the district of Shiwan, a few kilometres to the south-west. However, although the town's fabled silk-weaving and ceramics industries continue to thrive, aside from some acceptable staple ware they don't produce much apart from industrial bricks and tiles and some faintly tackly ornamental pieces for tourists.

Instead of wasting time on Foshan's souvenirs, take a look at some of the town's historic sites, foremost of which is the **Ancestral Temple** (Daily 8.30–4.30) at the southern end of Zumiao Lu. This, a massive late 11C structure from the Song Dynasty ingeniously constructed entirely out of wooden mortice and tenon joints, is probably best known for its elaborately decorated ceiling, lined with Shiwan tiles. Though severely damaged by fire in a Ming dynasty peasants' revolt, it was extensively rebuilt in

1372 with funds raised by public subscription. The building, now a museum, divides into five parts – the *front* and *main halls*, the *Tower of Rejoicing in Immortality*, the *Stage of Myriad Blessings*, and the marvellously named *Pong of Splendid Fragrance*. In the main hall stands an enormous 6000 pound bronze statue of the so-called *North God*, from the Song Dynasty. According to local tradition this figure, Beidi – or sometimes Heidi – ruled the waters of Guangdong, which made him an especially venerated god in an area prone to violent flooding: people would try to please him with numerous temples and shrines carved with turtles and sea-creatures (witness not only this statue but also the carved serpent and turtle in the courtyard). Before you leave, spare five minutes for the **Foshan Museum** in the temple grounds, and, if you've got some surplus cash, pop your head round the door of the *Antique and Crafts Stores*, also in the grounds.

A short step north-east from here, the **Linhua Market** is also worth a look, if only to confirm that the Qingping market in Guangzhou isn't

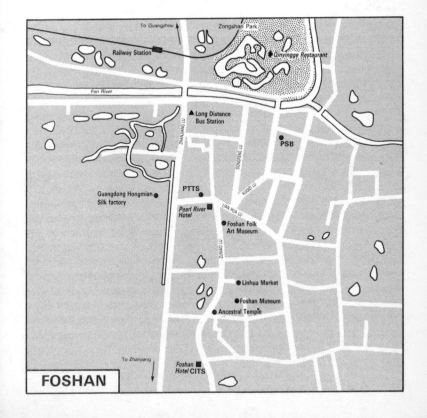

FOSHAN

quite as *outré* as it seems – at least by Cantonese standards. Again, most of the livestock is very much alive, and once more consists mainly of dogs, snakes, turtles and the like. Strangely enough, pets get a look in too, making a comeback after being declared ideologically unsound during the Cultural Revolution.

Some practical details
The **long-distance bus station**, where you'll arrive if you're coming from Canton, is on the northern side of town on the south bank of the Fen river – the **railway station** is on the far bank – and from here there's a range of local bus and taxi services into the town centre. Maps you can pick up from **CITS**, inside the *Foshan Hotel* at 64 Zumiao Lu. The *Foshan* also makes for a good place **to stay** (its doubles cost ¥28), or there's the *Pearl River Hotel*, at the top end of Zumiao Lu, which has dorms as well. **Foodwise**, it's best to eat from the *takeaway stands* near the bus station; or, if you've more money to spend, try the excellent *Qinyingge Restaurant* in Zhongshan Park (¥12 a head).

ZHAOQING AND THE SEVEN STAR CRAGS

Sixty-four miles west of Guangzhou, on the north bank of the West River, **ZHAOQING** is in itself a fairly dull town with some rather drab monuments, but it makes by far the best base for seeing Guangdong's most celebrated scenic resort – the **Seven Star Crags**. These, if you've already seen the limestone peaks of Guilin, seem rather muted by comparison; on the other hand if you haven't, they're a rewarding trip, and, swathed in mist and cut by lakes, they make a spectacular landscape in which to spend a few days.

You can get to the Crags without seeing the centre of Zhaoqing at all: just turn left outside the long-distance bus station and they're a 5 minute walk. The Crags, of which there are – obviously – seven in all, loom lugubriously before you, wierd limestone pinnacles arranged in the shape of a big dipper. Legend has them as seven stars which fell from the sky, since when they've been given tags supposed roughly to describe what they're thought to resemble – names like *Shizhang* (stone hand), *Tianzhu* (pillar to the sky) and *Chanchu* (toad). Arranged around is a series of five artificial lakes, together with an interlocking network of arched bridges, pathways, caves and underground rivers, fringed by willow trees, which you can tour either on foot, or, more efficiently, by boats which are available for hire. The park also boasts many traditional pavilions, built when the area was redeveloped in the mid-1950s, partly to encourage tourism, and partly to expand the main lake to provide irrigation and fish-rearing facilities, of which the **Five Dragons Pavilion** is most notable – a memorial to five brothers who in 2 BC were celebrated local scholars.

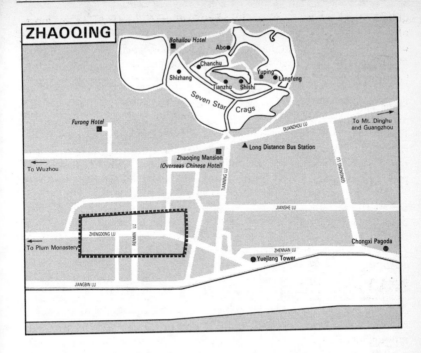

Have a look, too, inside some of the caves, embellished by ornate graffiti left over the years in tribute to the beauty of the landscape.

Back in town there's a long-established ivory-carving industry and a handful of neglected monuments, remnants from Zhaoqing's thousand-year history. None of these are especially exciting, and all are positioned, irritatingly, far enough apart as to make them only worth the bother if you're stuck here and have nothing better to do. Roughly in order of enticement there's the **Plum Monastery**, which you'll have to climb into if you want to see, the recently restored **Yuejiang Tower**, on the bank of the West River, and, a little way east, the **Chongxi Pagoda** – a rundown and very firmly closed reminder of China's imperial past. Further out there's **Mount Dinghu**, ancient tourist hangout and low-key version of the Seven Star Crags, notable for its secluded beauty and Ming Dynasty temple. You can take a local bus there, but again, it's only really worthwhile if you're hanging around between connections . . .

Assuming this does happen – say, for example, you decide to travel to Quzhou by boat and break your journey at Zhaoqing – you may well need a room. Best place is the *Overseas Chinese Hotel*, south of the entrance to the Seven Star Park on Tianming Lu, which has doubles at ¥20–28 and dormitories for ¥8; or there's the dull but reliable *Bohailour*

Hotel inside the park itself. For **food**, use the *street cafés* grouped around the Overseas Chinese Hotel.

ZHANJIANG

There's really only one reason for coming to **ZHANJIANG**, and that's to pick up the frequent bus and ferry service to Haikou on Hainan Island. Otherwise the town, with a population of 310,000 south-west China's largest port, is almost entirely without interest. It was leased to the French in 1898, and they remained here for around 50 years, leaving behind a few tatty reminders of their stay. Today, along with the British and Americans, they're back again – for what has contributed more than anything to Zhangjiang's rather dreary prosperity is offshore oil, plenty of it, which has attracted a glut of western cash and labour in the hope of rich pickings in the South China Sea. Drilling began in 1975, overseen by the newly created Nanhua West Oil Corporation, and since then the town's facilities have expanded to accommodate large tankers and a heliport to ferry workers and supplies to the outlying rigs. Signs of western money are everywhere, not least the large and luxurious Hai Bin hotel complex just outside town, where businesspeople languish beside pools and pay anything up to ¥4 for a drink. But in spite of this, Zhanjiang remains a grey, bleak place – a boom town very much in its infancy ...

The town splits evenly into two parts, oddly divided by a stretch of open countryside. The old city, **Tsu Kan**, where the long-distance buses pull in from Guangzhou, is of most interest, its streets winding narrowly over the town's low hill. If you're staying overnight and want to keep close to the bus station, there's a small **hotel** on Chuang Shan Lu (turn right out of the station) which has dorms at ¥4 and doubles for ¥18, though the facilities, those that there are, can be a little austere. Otherwise most hotels are in the new part of town. A few doors away the **Public Security Office** (7.30–11.30 & 3–6) is the place to get a permit to visit the **islands** off Zhenjiang. These, though closed when I was last in town, could well be easier to visit now, and offer some of the finest swimming in the whole of southern China. Back towards the bus station are the **Post Office** and **No.1 Department Store**, and a small market which harbours a number of **cafés** for lunchtime **eating** – that's if you can stand the sight of the local speciality: whole dogs skinned and barbecued, complete with tail. Instead try the locally caught seafood, cheap and tasty.

You can get to New Zhenjiang, or **Xia Sang**, by taking a no.1 or no.2 bus from the long-distance bus station – a trip that can take anything from 20 to 40 minutes depending on which route you take. Once in Xia Sang, the first thing that strikes you is the contrast, its wide tree-lined boulevards and large modern apartment blocks quite at odds with the

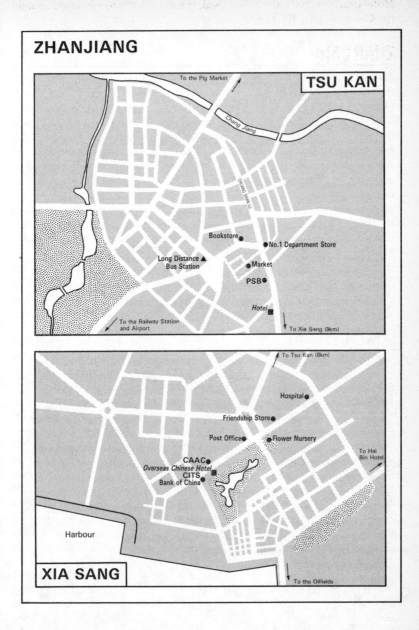

ZHANJIANG

TSU KAN

To the Pig Market

Chang Jiang

CHUNG SHAN LU

Bookstore

No.1 Department Store

Long Distance
Bus Station

Market

PSB

Hotel

To the Railway Station
and Airport

To Xia Sang (8km)

To Tsu Kan (8km)

Hospital

Friendship Store

Post Office

Flower Nursery

To Hai
Bin Hotel

CAAC
Overseas Chinese Hotel
CITS
Bank of China

Harbour

XIA SANG

To the Oilfields

dilapidated houses and tortuous alleys of Tsu Kan. Many of the buildings here were put up by the French during their occupation, but though more imposing, nowhere are they particularly attractive. Cheapest of the **hotels** is the *Overseas Chinese* on Renmin Lu, which has dorms at ¥4 and doubles for ¥18, buckets rather than taps of hot water, and a **CITS office** which hands out city and bus maps. **Food** is good here too, and at ¥5 a head for a filling meal is popular with locals as well as tourists. However, other than a lush **Park and Flower Nursery** off Renmin Lu, there's little more to see here than in Tsu Kan, and for anything of even remote interest you have to head outside the town itself. About 10km south west, a no.3 and then a no.6 bus ride, the **Last Crag Lake** and **Sub Tropical Garden** are popular local landmarks, their volcanic formation typical of the coastal region and making for a refreshing breather from the greyness of the city. **New Zhon Island** is, assuming you can procure a visa, another rewarding short trek, principally for its wonderful beaches, crystal clean water and fresh-caught lobster, on sale in all the restaurants. To get there, take bus no.5 to the tip of Tonghai Island and then pick up a ferry.

HAINAN ISLAND

If you're not flying direct, you can reach **HAINAN ISLAND** by regular ferry from **HAI-AN**, not a typing error but a mainland village on the southern tip of the Guangdong peninsula. Arriving here, you have to check into a small office to the left of the administrative building and exchange your ticket for a voucher for the boat. Each seat is numbered and the crossing, though only 1¾ hours, can often be rough so however long you have to wait on the sometimes tediously slow embarkation you'd be well advised not to gorge yourself before leaving. If – and only if – you should miss the boat, there's a small hotel in Hai-an which will put you up for just ¥1.50 a night.

Hainan is the closest thing in China to a tropical island, an intriguing mix of windswept, coconut palmed beaches, stunning mountain scenery, different ethnic groups and, because of its proximity to Vietnam, China's closest and most bitter enemy, battle-primed military installations. It has, however, one major drawback at least for the visitor, in that only its capital Haikou and Sanya in the south are for the moment open to the individual traveller. It is possible to visit selected areas of the rest of the island – principally Jiaji, Tongzha and a couple of sites around Haikou – but only on organised tours (CITS have details).

Quite why this is no one seems to know for sure. Until 1982 a visa for Haikou allowed travel all over the island but since then, for some reason, the rules have been considerably tightened. This could be a case of the Chinese trying to make as much money from the island as possible, but it's more likely that it's down to Hainan's substantial and ultra-sensitive military significance as the last frontier before Vietnam. The hostilities between the two countries date back to 1978, when the Vietnamese expelled around a quarter of a million Chinese from their country and China retaliated by invading its northern borders. They soon pulled back, but not before some heavy losses had been inflicted by the Vietnamese, and ever since China has been determinedly wary of Vietnam, not least because of that country's long-standing alliance with their other mortal enemy, the Soviet Union. So it goes, and bearing in mind this recent history, Hainan's minority peoples and the presence on the island and in Zhenjiang of 300,000 Chinese naval troops, it's perhaps surprising you can come here at all.

In a sense, Hainan has always been something of a trouble-spot for the Chinese. Its indigenous inhabitants, the *Li* and *Miao* tribes, who live

HAINAN ISLAND

in the central and densely forested mountain areas of the island, rebelled against the domination of Imperial China more than once, but each time they were soon – and cruelly – put down. The Li, who make up around 750,000 of Hainan's 5½ million population, are known best for their language (quite unlike Chinese and dividing into different dialects) and their often exaggerated sexual morality, which at one time led them to tattoo their daughters' faces to prevent the Chinese from stealing them. The Maio, with a population of only 100,000, are a traditionally nomadic people, hunters constantly in search of new sources of food, originally confined solely to the mountains but now moving down to the foothills and the village of MIAO'AN. The Japanese arrived in the 1930s, and systematically murdered half the islanders, most of whom they believed to be Communist sympathisers – as, in many ways, they were. After the defeat of the Kuomintang, mainland Communist forces took refuge here under the protection of the local Li and Miao people. Almost in return, after Liberation part of the island's central portion was granted semi-autonomous status. This, however, was short-lived, and the invasion of Lin Biao in 1950, and, more recently, heavy influxes of Han and Overseas Chinese during the 1960s and 1970s, as well as large numbers of Vietnamese refugees, has left the Li and Miao by far the minority.

In spite of its popularity with outside immigrants, and notwithstanding as yet unexploited valuable mineral resources, Hainan remains possibly China's poorest region, with a *per capita* income averaging just ¥150 a year. This could change however: the island has been declared a Special Economic Zone, hydro-electric, mining and oil projects are already under way, and there are plans in hand, despite the current no-entry policy, to develop Hainan's considerable tourist attractions. How things will go it's impossible to say, but you should expect some big changes here in the future. Large numbers of tourists and a massive military presence may make uneasy bedfellows, but Hainan could be on the brink of a huge breakthrough in popularity. In anticipation of the island's eventual opening-up, we've included details on individual travel to selected points on the rest of Hainan.

Haikou and around

HAIKOU, the island's cultural and commercial capital, is a vibrant and exciting town, much freer than most in China for private enterprise, its streets congested with traders and hawkers selling all manner of different goods, unrestrained by the surprisingly low-profile authorities. It's also extremely rundown, to a quite alarming degree when you delve deeper, and some areas of the town betray a poverty worse than anything you'll have seen before in China.

Arriving by ferry, pick up a (Chinese-only) *bus and city plan* inside the terminal concourse and take a no.2 bus or pedicab to the *Overseas Chinese Hotel* on Daitong Lu – much the cheapest and most convenient **place to stay**. This is far from luxurious – hot water is still only available by the bucket – but rooms here range from ¥18 to ¥45, ¥6 is you settle for a dorm bed, and there's reasonable restaurant on the second floor. Other facilities include a **CITS office** (7.30–11.30 & 2.30–5.30), a *CAAC* rep on call the same times as CITS, and a **coffee bar** which acts as hangout of local Haikou hipsters. They don't change money, however, so use the *Bank of China* across the road – that's assuming you can't strike a deal with one of the black-market dealers hanging about outside the hotel door. Finally, if you don't want to stay at the Overseas Chinese, the *Hainan the First*, on Hai Fu Lu, a no.1 bus ride, offers rooms at similar prices and an authentic siting in the local CP Headquarters. No one would pretend there's actually much to see in Haikou, but the vigorous nature of its street-life, and its bustling 'South-East Asian' atmosphere, make it well worth exploring. Best place to start is Jaifong Lu, whose western end – small businesses and import and export dealers for the most part – becomes, past the main Post Office, Haikou's liveliest

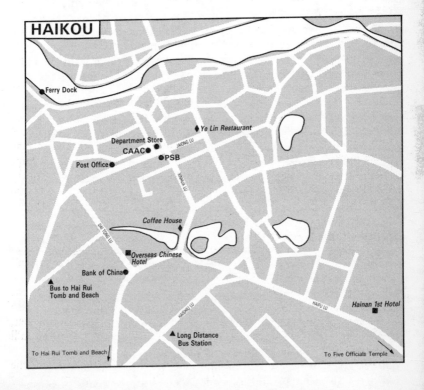

district, where tiny streets and alleys hide away unusual small shops selling leather goods and locally-crafted basketware. At the far end of Jaifong, on the left, the Ye Lin restaurant serves Haikou culinary specialities (try the chicken in coconut sauce), and countless tea-houses cluster nearby, popular places crammed with young people in the evenings. South of this part of town Haikou also brags some fine parks, cut with shimmering lakes and because of the humid climate (it tends to rain at least once each day) a lot greener than most other Chinese cities.

As for **getting out of Haikou**, two local buses, nos 1 and 2, ply the routes south-east and south-west of the town respectively. It's worth a ride on bus no.2, which you can pick up outside the Overseas Chinese Hotel, to see the **Tomb of Hai Rui**, built in memory of a Qing dynasty administrative official. Hai Rui is something of a local hero, since while here he campaigned vigorously for the local people, determinedly putting their arguments to the Emperor in Beijing. During the Cultural Revolution he was no more popular with the authorities and his tomb was desecrated – principally because of one Wu Han's opera, 'Hai Rui removed from office', which was uncovered as a thinly veiled attack on Mao. Bus no.2 also takes you on to about the best place for a swim within reach of Haikou, **Shui Ying Beach**, a 20-minute ride out of town. Get off where the bus makes a sharp left turn, walk back to the crossroads, do a left, turn first right, continue down for 400m and take the left-hand fork; the beach is about 25 minutes further on. The beach is quite secluded and has a small café but generally, you'll find Hainan's best beaches on the southern side of the island.

Bus no.1 takes you to the **Five Officials Memorial Temple**, 15 minutes out of town and built to commemorate five exiled rulers who lived during the Tang and Song dynasties. They were installed on Hainan, like all officials of the Imperial era, to persecute the local people; like Hai Rui, however, they refused, instead working full out for the welfare of the island as a whole. Their temple is a fitting memory, decorated with paintings, porcelain and calligraphy.

South to Sanya

Hainan has two main road networks: a coastal road around the whole island, and a mountain road over the Limu Ling range. An efficient bus system connects the major towns, and all of the cheap hotels generally take foreigners. On the east coast, **XINCUN** and **XINLUNG** are the largest centres, Xincun the centre of Hainan's cultured pearl industry, run by members of the tiny Danjia minority, and Xinlung famous for its hot springs and tropical fruit. But it's **SANYA**, a large naval base on the southern coast, which should occupy most of your time, not only for itself but also as jumping-off point for the rest of the southern coastal strip. Sanya has a long and venerable history, dating back 1500 years to its establishment as the port of Yazhou. AD748 saw the monk Jianzhen forced to land here by a typhoon on his fifth unsuccessful attempt to cross by sea to Japan. During his stay he oversaw construction of the Dayun Monastery, which still stands, and scattered the town with Buddhist inscriptions. It's the modern era, though, which marks Sanya out: its wide bay plays a crucial role in southern Chinese trade, shipping salt, rubber, lumber and tea to domestic and international markets, and 10 million yuan have been invested in what is hoped will be a major tourist resort within 3 years, built partly with Hong Kong money and expertise. Air passenger services are planned not just to Guangzhou and Zhenjiang but to Tokyo and Hong Kong as well – harbingers of a time when Hainan as a whole will be a stop on the international tourist circuit.

Heading west, around a spacious bay, **TIANYA HAIJIAO**, known locally as 'the end of the sky and corner of the sea', is a large group of grotesquely shaped rocks facing out to sea. Take a closer look and you can see inscribed on two of the rocks the four Chinese characters of Tianya and Haijiao. If you had gone east out of Sanya you'd have reached the legendary scenic resort of **LUHUITOU** or 'the deer turns its head' (the name actually refers to the mountain just behind), well-equipped with a number of **villas and bungalows for rent**. Villa no.1 is reserved for Party officials, who travel down here in the winter months, but it's possible for ordinary beings to stay in the other villas for rates that begin at ¥10. The name Luhuitou is, like so many Chinese place-names, the result of ancient, in this case Li, legend. Apparently, a young hunter, Ah Tun, once chased a deer down here from the centre of the island, crossing 99 rivers and climbing 99 mountains in the process. When he saw the only way forward was into the water he took aim with his bow, and just as he was about to fire the deer turned its head and changed into a mountain – the same mountain you see now. Out of this mountain walked a young and beautiful girl, a fairy, and the two went off together and lived happily ever after, their offspring, the legend goes, the original Li people. Along the bay from Luhuitou is **Dadonghai Beach**, a crescent-shaped beach between two mountain peaks whose waters, warm, clear and wonderfully welcoming, are ideal for winter swimming.

Pushing on back to Haikou by way of the mountain road, it's worth a brief stop at **BAOTING**, capital of the Li and Miao autonomous region. There's not much to keep you in the town itself, only a small hotel, but a walk up into the mountains that surround takes you into the heart of the minorities' area. Don't be afraid to do this: the Li and the Miao people, though perhaps a bit surprised to see you, will make you incredibly welcome, probably inviting you in for a cup of Chinese tea. Further towards Haikou is **QIONGZHONG**, centre of the minority crafts industry where you may pick up a bargain but don't count on it – most of the stuff I saw was cheap and nasty.

FUJIAN

Fujian province splits neatly into distinct halves – one made up of the large towns that line its beautiful coastal stretch, 19C trading ports for opium and other products of western merchants, and the other a rugged, mountainous and largely inaccessible interior, home to around 140 different local dialects and with a history of poverty and backwardness. The contrast could not be greater: while inner Fujian stayed remote – indeed so remote that it's claimed that when the Red Army got there in the 1960s they were asked who the Emperor was – contacts between the coast and the west grew and grew, and large parts of Singapore, Malaysia, the Philippines and Taiwan were colonised by Fujianese. Nowadays things haven't changed much. It's the coast that's open to foreign visitors while the interior remains firmly shut, and it's the coast that's become a prime site for government development, generous injections of cash helping to encourage the area's attractiveness as a tourist spot and, Beijing hopes, persuade the thousands of overseas Fujianese to come back and invest in their home country.

XIAMEN (AMOY)

XIAMEN, better known to locals and on Chinese menus in the west as **AMOY**, is one of the country's most likeable cities, smaller and prettier than Fujian's capital of Fuzhou, and with a lot more to see. Until the mid 1950s it was on an island, but since then it's been connected to the mainland by a 5 kilometre-long causeway. This hasn't ruined the atmosphere, however, and the town's European-style buildings, built during its 19C heyday, the ancient streets with their bustling shops and stalls, and the white sandy beaches that enclose the town, all combine to lend a somewhat Mediterranean feel. Compounding this impression, is the tiny island of Gulangyu, a 10-minute ferry ride to the south-west, old colonial home of the Europeans and Japanese and with their huge decaying mansions still lining the island's traffic-free streets.

Xiamen was founded in the mid 14C and grew in stature under the Ming dynasty, becoming by the 17C, under a steady and rather secretive succession of Portuguese, Spanish and Dutch fortune-hunters, a thriving port that acted as centre of revolt against the invading Manchu armies. The pirate Koxinga led the hostilities but was eventually defeated, setting up base in offshore Taiwan until he finally died and that too was colonised by the Manchus. A couple of hundred years later the British arrived, increasing trade and establishing their nerve centre – Shamian style – on the nearby island of Gulangyu and formalising the manoeuvre with the

Treaty of Nanjing in 1842. By the turn of the century Xiamen was a relatively prosperous community, supported partly by a steady turnover in trade and by the trickle of wealth back from the city's emigrants, who over the centuries had continued to swell in numbers. The 1950s, though, saw decline, when Chinese troops exchanged fire with the nationalist armies that still occupied Taiwan and the smaller islands of Quemoy and Matsu. And the entire area became the scene of continual skirmishes that nearly plunged China into what could have been a vicious and bloody confrontation.

That was 30 odd years ago, and though the offshore islands are still occupied by Kuomintang sympathisers, things have quietened down quite a lot since then. Five years ago Xiamen was declared a Special Economic Zone – and given the attendant privileges – and recently the town's fortunes have picked up substantially: like Guangzhou in the main benefiting from Hong Kong and western cash. As if in anticipation of a massive trade and tourist boom, the harbour has been enlarged and the airport, built only in 1983, is being extended to cater for jumbo jets from places like Bangkok and Hawaii.

Though there's no livelier place in the whole of China, especially at night, apart from a couple of markets selling Hong Kong fashions, you won't find anything tangible to detain you in Xiamen's city centre. Better instead to make the short no.2 bus journey three miles east of the city to see the **Nanputuo Temple**, built over a thousand years ago on the slopes of Wulao mountain. This is one of China's most impressive Buddhist temples, its roofs a gaudy jumble of flying dragons, human figures and multi-coloured flowers and with among its collection of treasures a set of carved tablets dating from the Qing dynasty and recording Manchu atrocities. Inside the main hall, behind the Maitreya or Fat Buddha, is a statue of Wei Tuo, the deity responsible for Buddhist doctrine, who holds a stick pointing to the ground – a sign which by tradition means the monastery is a rich one and can provide board and lodging for itinerants. If he had been balancing the stick straight he would have been saying that the temple was poor and you had better go elsewhere. The temple is still used today and boasts a vegetarian restaurant but is at its busiest on 13 October, birthday of Avalokitesvara, when crowds gather annually to pray for luck and happiness.

Nearby Nanputuo, on Daxue Lu, stands **Xiamen University**, and you can cut through here, to get to the **beaches** – really, one of the principal reasons anyone comes to Xiamen. These are fine, but don't swim out too far as there's a notoriously strong tide.

Walking west along the beach road takes you down to **Huli Mountain Cannon**, a 19C hunk of German heavy artillery which had a range of 10,000 metres and was used during the Qing dynasty to fend off foreign imperialists. You can hire binoculars to look across the East Sea to the tiny, islets, and to the larger Taiwanese island of JINMEN, which faces the mainland opposite Xiamen. Until 1984, because of the close proximity of Taiwan, this whole area was out of bounds, and the beach under a dusk-till-dawn curfew.

Still in the east of Xiamen, a no.1 bus links the temple with the **Wanshi Botanical Gardens**, where a stock of 4000 varieties of plant life includes a Redwood tree brought here by Nixon on his last official visit to China. Part of Xiamen's attempt to improve its tourist infrastructure, you soon won't have to take the bus to get to the gardens as they're currently constructing an underground walkway. The no.1 bus will also take you to the **Overseas Chinese Museum**, which has a wide collection of pottery and bronzes going back as far as the 14C, and a display of photographs depicting the life of Chinese people abroad – though there are perhaps more evocative signs of overseas influences here in the amusement arcade down the road, which has a skating rink, space invaders machines and a western-style disco . . .

Living – a few points

Staying over in Xiamen presents no problems at all, since there are plenty of hotels, many of them thrown up recently as part of Xiamen's tourist drive. Cheapest for foreigners is the *Overseas Chinese*, ten minutes walk from the junction of Zhongshan and Siming Lu, in the direction of the railway station; or you can catch a no.1 or no.3 bus, direction 'Huaqiao Dasha'. Here, though conditions are a little on the primitive side, you can find a bed in the hotel's old wing for around ¥7–27 if you want a double – or in the much plusher new building for ¥36; plus it's also the home of **CITS**. If, however, you find the Overseas Chinese full, try the *Xiamen Guesthouse* or *Tiger Garden Hotel*, both nearby and on the no.1 and 3 bus routes, where rooms start at about ¥36. A rather more peaceful alternative is the wonderfully secluded *Gulangyu Guesthouse* on the island of the same name, or, also on the island, a small *private hotel* which you can reach if you turn right rather than left where the boat lands. Beds here go for as little as ¥2.50 a night, but you may find they only accept foreigners in close season. For a taster of Xiamen's future as an upmarket western resort, look in at the Liyang and Guanhai Hotels in the town centre, just opened and expensive, with facilities like sports centres, discos and, believe it or not, an imported coffee shop. The local **food** is one of Xiamen's main assets, with plenty of fresh fish and seafood, particularly oysters, crabs and prawns, and, uniquely, liberal use of peanuts (the Shaohamian noodles in hot peanut soup is outstanding). A good **restaurant** to try is the *Xinnan xuan Juiuia* on Siming Lu, 50 metres from the Zhongshan–Siming junction. Here you can get snacks downstairs and a range of peanut and seafood specialities on the upper floor. Close by are two small **coffee shops,** one with Chinese coffee at just 2 mao a cup, and another, up a small alley on the right, where the owner is so proud to have western customers you'll be asked to sign a visitors' book. Two further restaurants, popular with the locals, are the *Seafood Restaurant,* opposite the Overseas Chinese Museum, and the *Nanputuo Temple* vegetarian restaurant. Eating on your feet is best done from the food stalls around the station and ferry areas, where you can pick up some marvellous fishy delicacies, not least a wonderful oyster omelette.

The best way to **get around locally** is, as usual, by bus. Four services connect the major points of importance, a no.1 travelling between the university and railway station, another (no.2) going from the ferry port to the university, and a third, no.3, connecting the railway station with the ferry. A fourth, un-numbered service runs out to the Huli special economic zone. Minibuses, a new idea from Guangzhou, have also been introduced of late, but though frequent and reliable, operate a fare system which is three times the price of the buses; taxis are available from city hotels but come even pricier ... The **Gulangyu ferry** runs every 10 minutes from 5 o'clock till midnight, and will also, at different times, take you on trips around the small offshore islands. Between Xiamen and Gulangyu is a retired Danish cruiseship which now serves as a hotel (beds for ¥7), restaurant and disco, open from 2pm, admission ¥3.

Gulangyu Island

GULANGYU, or the 'Garden of the Sea' is the highlight of any visit to Xiamen – a small, hilly floral island where it's said the inhabitants are lovers of music, and since the ending of the crackdown on 'decadent' western composers you can hear the practice and playing of Beethoven and Mozart emanating from the windows of its main street. It's here, at the end of Longtou Lu, that the ferry deposits you, from where it's a minute walk and 10 minute climb to the island's highest point, **Sunlight Rock,** which gives panoramic views of the rest of the island, Xiamen and the surrounding islets. Also up here, or at least in the same park, is the **Koxinga Memorial Hall,** a colonial-style building which remembers the pirate hero's efforts to slay the Dutch, Manchus and just about anyone else who got in his way – though there is sadly little captioning in English. Coming back down the northern slope of Sunlight Rock brings you to the **Wanzai Pavilion,** where carved into the rock in Chinese characters is an inscription saying 'When the strength of your feet is exhausted, the hill looks more beautiful.' Whether it does or not is for you to judge ...

Walking back towards the ferry you'll see a sign for **Shuzhuang Garden,** full of small pavilions and with a walkway leading to Gulangyu's largest beach, the *Guangzi Hou Bathing Beach.* The original owner of the garden was an Overseas Chinese who came from Danshui in Taiwan. After the

Qing lost the Sino–Japanese war of 1894–95 Taiwan was ceded to Japan and Shuzhuang – for that was his name – moved here, building the garden facing east so he could sit and contemplate his lost home. The garden is lovely but the beach tends to get over-crowded. Those apart that's about it as far as Gulangyu's attractions go, but that doesn't mean you should hotfoot it back to Xiamen. Gulangyu's principal pull is that it's a nice place just to idle, wandering around its streets, alleyways and parks (all of them banned to motor traffic) until the sun sets and it's time for dinner, which you can get at any number of places on the main street, afterwards catching the night ferry back to Xiamen.

WUYI MOUNTAIN DISTRICT

Though closed to foreigners until recently, the **WUYI MOUNTAIN NATURAL RESERVE**, running along the southern side of Fujian–Jiangxi border, offers some of the most unspoilt and picturesque scenery in southern China. It's the only inland part of Fujian you can visit and consists of two parts, known, in rough translation, as *Three Three* and *Six Six*, a strange timetable way of referring to the Nine Crook Stream (the former) which meanders at the feet of the mountains, and the Thirty Six Peaks that rise up from the river. The reserve makes for a tremendous place to relax for a few days, its clear fresh mountain air and brisk though not over-demanding walks as yet untainted by any kind of commercialism. Having said that, though, it's as well to point out that this could all change, since the Fujian government have big plans for Wuyi, and they've made no secret of their intention to pack the park's 60 square km area with around 2000 hotel beds by 1990, at a cost of a cool 10 million yuan. Get here quick then, for the people are starting to increase already, and enjoy the lush green vegetation, deep red sandstone mountains and some unique rockpools, waterfalls and caves. Even now Wuyi gets crowded in summer, and it's unbearably hot, so I'd advise a winter visit if you can make it then, when the mountains are cloaked with snow.

To get to Wuyi you can either catch a bus from Nanping, 4 hours to the south-east, or from Shaowu, 5 hours south-west. The Nanping bus, which leaves at 6am each morning, drops you at WUYIGONG, the nearest town, and the Shaowu bus, which departs at 1am and travels through the night, takes you straight to the Jiuqu Guesthouse, both journeys costing around ¥7. If you happen to be at a stop on the main Shanghai–Beijing train line, the best way of getting to Wuyi is to go to SHANGRAO in Jiangxi province and take a bus from there. A word of warning on leaving: the bus from Wuyi to Shaowu is timed to arrive at exactly the same time as the Xiamen train, so unless you make sure you buy your onward ticket on the train and make a dash for it when you

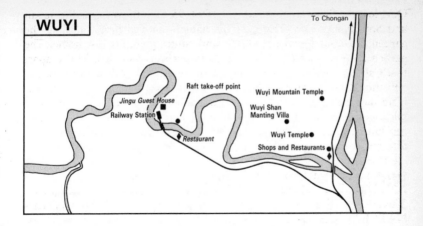

get there you'll have to stay overnight in SHAOWU – not a pleasant prospect and only compensated by the possibility of tasting the local wild gooseberries which look and taste like Kiwi fruit. Another way of getting to and from Wuyi is by special tourist bus which, though reliable, will set you back twice the price of regular public transport: details, if you're interested, from CITS. There is also an airport now, at nearby CHISHI, which has made travel to Wuyi a lot easier; if you can afford it, flights are from Xiamen, Fuzhou and Hong Kong.

The best way to appreciate Wuyi is to take a bamboo raft trip along its main artery, the Jiugo River, which runs a crooked course for 5 miles between XINGCUN village and Wuyi Temple. The rafts leave daily between 7.30am and 2pm all year round, and though you can pick one up from more or less anywhere on the river, much the best place is about halfway along, between the fifth crook in the river (more of stream really) and the Juiqu Guesthouse. For around ¥6.50, the raft will take you from the first crook in the meandering river right up to the ninth, and though there's little enough to see beyond the scenery – and some odd boat-shaped coffins in caves above the fourth crook, said to be 4000 years old – the journey gives a useful initial orientation of the reserve as a whole.

The **mountains** look quite large and imposing but in fact are relatively easy to climb. One of the ones you'll have seen from the raft, and the nearest one to the Juiqu Guesthouse where you may be staying (see below), is the *Heavenly Tour Peak*, whose summit is no more than a half-hour clamber away. Best time to get up here is early morning, when you can if you're lucky catch the sunrise and the early morning mists start to clear to reveal a good view of the nine crooks in the Jiugo River and the sweeping countryside beyond. You can, too, get a good breakfast at the small temple on the summit, and there are a number of tiny pavilions and tea gardens on the lower slopes should you need sustenance on the way up. Another peak well worth the ascent is the *Dawang Fengon King of Peaks* at the easternmost end of the river, more of a gentle walk than a climb and taking about two hours from its foot to the summit. Also, if you have time, take a three-wheeled motor taxi, cost around ¥4 (the buses are infrequent) to the **Shuilian Cave**, which features a large waterfall if you're here out of the summer months; if you're not it will probably have dried up. Actually, it's not a real cave but a hill with a tea-house set into the cliffside and, alongside, a crumbling hut made of the same red sandstone as the mountain. You can sit in the tea-house and sip your tea (the local Wuyi or Oolong variety, expensive but apparently one of the best in China) while the waterfall literally cascades over your head. Nearby, a short walk through the tea bushes and over a small stone bridge, is **Eagle Beak Hill**, whose main attraction is the remains of the railings and walkways leading into a set of caves where, during the Taiping Revolution, local bigwigs fled to escape persecution.

As far as a **room** goes, the *Jiuqu* is the cheapest and most convenient hotel, with double rooms at ¥8 and ¥6 for a single bed in a triple. The showers have cold water only but there's a small restaurant where you can eat for a pittance. Or you can stay in **WUYIGONG** itself, principal settlement for the area, where the *Wuyi Shan Manting Mountain Villa*, just north of the town, has a branch of **CITS**, prices between ¥11 and 30 and a western-style nightclub complex with bar, dancehall and plush restaurant. However, the Wuyi Mountain Villa nearby is much preferable, with colour TV in each room, 24-hour hot water and, if you're lucky, rates from about ¥15 a night. The location, too, is marvellous, resting hard under the King of Peaks and with a skilfully designed Suzhou style ornamental garden. Plus there's a restaurant which will serve you an excellent lunch or dinner for about ¥4 apiece.

Foodwise, it's the local Shilin frogs which make Wuyi cuisine special, for along with other popular dishes like bamboo shoots and fungus they're served almost everywhere and taste fine. If you want to get out of the hotel restaurants and eat with the locals, try the small restaurant 5 minutes' walk from the Juiqu Guesthouse, across the bridge, which sells most dishes for around ¥2 and has a small takeaway stall that serves delicious steamed buns and bread. Shops, however, there are not, and you'll have to be content with fruit stalls. A couple of useful places in Wuyigong itself are the large Travel Centre, where you can hire taxis and buy bus tickets to Shaowu or Nanping, and the nearby bus stop for the irregular local service to the Juiqu Guesthouse.

QUANZHOU

'I tell you that for one shipload of pepper which may go to Alexandria or to other places to be carried into Christian lands there come more than a hundred of them to this port', wrote Marco Polo when he visited **QUANZHOU**, then called Zayton, in the late 13C. Then, 700 years ago, Quanzhou was a great port, one of the two largest in the world, exploiting its deep natural harbour and position on the important Perfume Sea Route. Now there's little doubt that those days are long gone. The harbour silted up centuries ago, and what trade there is now carries on in piecemeal form.

Quanzhou is, however, a lively and stimulating city, and though a pale reflection of its glorious past, easily worth an overnight visit. Of the remnants of that past, best is the **Kai Yuan Temple**, built originally in 686, supplemented in the 13C with two 5-storey stone pagodas and rebuilt under the Ming dynasty after it had been destroyed by fire. Formerly known as the Lotus Flower Temple and home to around 1000 monks, the Kai Yuan was built, legend has it, after the owner of a small mulberry grove on this site was visited in a dream by a Buddhist monk who asked him to erect a place of worship on his land. 'Only if my mulberry trees bear lotus flowers' replied the cunning owner, whereupon the flowers duly appeared and he had no option. In memory of this, an ancient mulberry in the temple courtyard bears the sign 'Mulberry Lotus Tree'. As regards architecture, the temple is widely regarded as a peculiarly fine example, not least in its details which include a hundred stone columns supporting the roof of the main hall, most of which are carved with delicate musicians holding instruments or sacrificial objects. Look at the pagodas too: carved on each of the 8 sides are two images of the Buddha, and inside, one of them has 40 ancient Buddhist stories inscribed on its walls. The temple grounds hold a special exhibition hall, whose exhibits number among them a 200 ton wooden sailing vessel said to be from the 12C or 13C – Quanzhou's one and only reminder of its magnificent trading past and, in its design, a fine example of just how far advanced Chinese shipbuilders were compared to their counterparts in Europe. The vessel was found in 1974 (a series of photos detail the stages of the excavation), still with the herbs and spices it had been carrying preserved in its hold. Also in the museum are a number of Arab tombstones, those of merchants who traded here during Quanzhou's golden years, most of whom were from the Middle East – as were many of the sailors who manned the ships. Further evidence of their presence is the **Qingzhen Mosque**, back in town behind the Kai Yuan Temple, which with an age of getting on for 1000 years ranks as one of the three oldest mosques in China. Renovated in 1313 and now, if only because of its uniqueness in a country not exactly overrun with Muslim architecture, a nationally protected monument, it sports a gate tower said to be an exact copy of a Damascus original.

Once you've seen all this – which, frankly, shouldn't take you long – take a walk (or a 30 minute tri-shaw ride) up Zhongshan Beilu to where, 3km outside the city, lies **Mount Qing Yuan**, which gives good views over Quanzhou. Most people come out here not for the views, however, but for the huge stone **statue of Lao Zi**, a Song dynasty sculpture which is said to aid longevity if you climb on to his back and rub noses. The effectiveness of this has yet to be proven, but loads of people try it nonetheless, much to the dismay of the authorities who not surprisingly are more concerned with the life-span of the statue. Incidentally, to get to Qing Yuan I wouldn't bother waiting for a local bus – for some reason there aren't any.

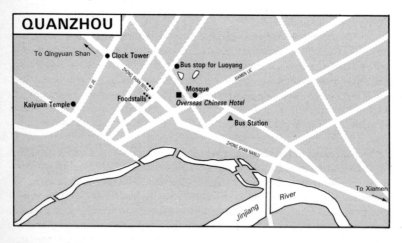

Some practicalities

There are no choices to be made on **where to stay**: you have to use the *Overseas Chinese*, just a short walk from the bus station in the centre of town (see map). You can, however, choose between the old and new section, bed prices for which are ¥4 and ¥13 respectively. As far as **eating** goes, you can either use the *hotel*, or, more cheaply, the *street stalls* which line Zhongshan Lu late at night, and cluster around the market by day. Here a filling bowl of rice noodle soup, crammed with seafood, will cost you just a few fen. Failing that, there are a couple of *seafood restaurants* on the same street as the Overseas Chinese Hotel and around the corner near the mosque, where you can get good shellfish or sample the local speciality – frogs. If you're into doing a bit of consuming, perhaps picking up a few souvenirs, try the streets and alleys of Quanzhou's old quarter, along and around Zhongshan Lu and the market, where you'll find a better than average selection of handicrafts – pottery, cane-ware, tea pots, dishes and the like.

FUZHOU

Though capital of Fujian province, and a venerable city with a good 1000 years of history behind it, **FUZHOU** is something of a letdown after Quanzhou and Xiamen: less colourful, with few historical relics and none of the flavour of the other coastal towns. It is, however, neatly placed between Guangzhou and Shanghai, so if you're travelling between the two, you could do worse than use Fuzhou as a stopover.

Like Quanzhou, Fuzhou was in its day an important trading centre, again visited by Marco Polo, but, again, only officially opened up to foreign merchants by the treaty of Nanjing which ended the second Opium War. One thing Polo noted when he was here was the high-profile presence of Mongol armies here to suppress any potential uprisings, and though for rather different reasons, the city is no less well defended today, since it forms the heart of Fujian's military opposition to Taiwan. Attempts to liberate the island are rather more low-key these days, but still its sensitive positioning gives Fuzhou something of a frontline feel. And it's worth noting that, much like Xiamen, it was the post-war bickering between the Nationalists and Red Army that led, in part, to Fuzhou's decline.

What is there to see then? Frankly, not a great deal: the city walls have long since been razed and the broad boulevards of the refurbished town centre harbour little beyond a couple of crumbling pagodas in terms of historical interest. Of these, much the best is the **White Pagoda**, which stands at the foot of the Yu Mountain (Yu Shan) and gives, if you mount the rickety wooden staircase inside, far-reaching views of the city and the surrounding offshore islands. Just east of here, overlooking the vast expanse of Wuyi Square, stands a gargantuan statue of Mao Zedong, erected here to commemorate the Ninth Congress of the Chinese Communist Party in 1969, which was significant in that it ratified Maoism as 'state religion' of China, and named the late Defence Minister, Lin Piao, as official heir to Mao's throne.

Beyond those, however, Fuzhou's attractions are pretty thin. There's the **zoo**, of course, which a couple of renowned performing pandas (bus no.1 if you're a zoo fan), or, next door, **West Lake Park**, which is pleasant enough and houses the **Fuzhou Provincial Museum**. Or you could catch a bus to Drum Hill, around 11 km east of the city centre, where stands a rather depleted 10C temple, the **Yongquan**, and a couple of early Song dynasty pagodas. Best, though, to kill time between connections just wandering around the old waterfront area, which has a vaguely picturesque dilapidation, or to walk across to the old foreign merchants'

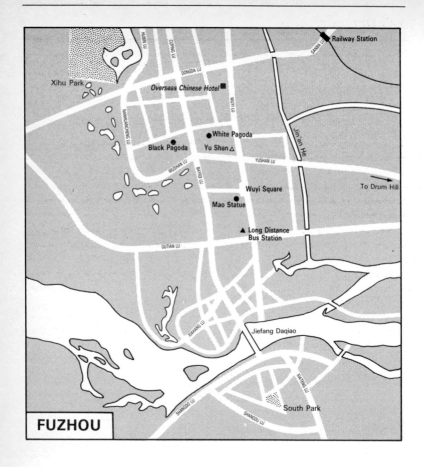

FUZHOU

Railway Station
Xihu Park
Overseas Chinese Hotel
HUBIN LU
CUPING LU
DONGDA LU
WUYI LU
SANBA LU
Jin'an He
White Pagoda
Black Pagoda
Yu Shan △
NANJUNCHENG LU
WUSHAN LU
BAND LU
YUSHAN LU
To Drum Hill
Wuyi Square
Mao Statue
▲ Long Distance
Bus Station
GUTIAN LU
XIAHANG LU
Jiefang Daqiao
XIATING LU
SHANGOU LU
SHANGOU LU
South Park

Nantau Island, where a handful of the former European buildings still stand. If, however, you've seen Shamian Island in Guangzhou, or Xiamen's Gulangyu Island, even this will be a disappointment.

More importantly, you're going to need **somewhere to stay**, and, once again, the *Overseas Chinese Hotel* should be first choice – on Wuyi Lu, a short no.2 bus ride from the railway station – where you can get a bed for around ¥15. Slightly cheaper, though not nearly as comfortable, is the *Qiaolian Hotel* a little further along Wuyi Lu, which offers beds for ¥12. Fuzhou's **restaurants** specialise in Yuwuan fishballs and Bai guo, a pasta made from glutinous rice, baked in cakes, and of them, I'd recommend the *Weizhing Wei* and, for seafood, the *Haiweiguan*, both of which can be found near the Dongie Koa. And don't forget to try *Laojin*, the strong and tasty local liqueur.

TRAVEL DETAILS

FROM GUANGZHOU (CANTON CITY)

Trains
In this chapter: Shenzhen (5 daily, 2hrs).
Beyond: Hong Kong (2 express trains daily, 2hrs; 5 via Shenzhen, 3hrs), Changsha (2, 14hrs), Shanghai (1, 33hrs), Beijing (1, 33hrs).

Buses
In this chapter: Shantou (2, 15hrs), Zhaoqing (6, 3hrs), Zhanjiang (1, 13hrs), Fuzhou (11, 6hrs), Xiamen (every other day, 24hrs).
Beyond: Wuzhou (Daily, 12hrs), Macao (3 daily, 4hrs), Haikou (1, 20hrs).

Ferries
To Hong Kong (daily, 8hrs) or Hovercraft (3 daily, 8hrs; departures from the Whampoa port). Also to Macao (1 daily, 20hrs), Wuzhou (1 daily, 18hrs), Haikou (1 daily, 26hrs) and Shanghai (1 a week, 5 days).

Flights
Services to most major cities, including Beijing (8 daily, 3hrs), Chengdu (5 a week, 2hrs), Fuzhou (4 a week, 1¼hrs), Shanghai (2 daily, 2¼hrs), Hong Kong (5 daily, ¾hr), Bangkok (2 a week, 2hrs), Manila (2 a week, 2hrs).

GUANGDONG/FUJIAN

Trains
From Zhanjiang: Nanning (1 daily, 9hrs), Guilin (1, 13hrs).
From Fuzhou: Yingtan (1, 15hrs), Xiamen (1, 10hrs), Shanghai (1, 21hrs).

Buses
From Zhanjiang: Guangzhou (Local service 2 daily, 12hrs; CITS bus daily, 10hrs), Haikou (2, 7hrs), Beihai (2, 5hrs).
From Haikou: Guangzhou (express service daily, 18hrs; local bus daily, 24hrs), Sanya (1, 10hrs), Baoting (2, 4hrs), Zhenjiang (2, 7hrs).
From Shantou: Guangzhou (2, 15hrs), Shenzhen (1, 11hrs), Xiamen (3, 9hrs), Zhangzhou (6, 4hrs).
From Fuzhou: Xiamen (3, 9hrs), Hong Kong (Express service 2 or 3 times a week), Shenzhen (daily CITS bus).

Ferries
From Xiamen: Once weekly to Shanghai (Monday at 11am) and Shanghai (Sunday afternoon). Twice weekly (Tuesday and Friday) to Hong Kong (20hrs).
From Fuzhou: Irregular boats from Fuzhou's port of Mawei to Shanghai (Usually 2 a week).
From Shantou: Irregular ferry services to Hong Kong and Guangzhou.
From Zhenjiang: Twice daily to Haikou (5hrs), every 2 weeks to Hong Kong (Leaves on the 10th and 22nd of each month, 17hrs).
From Haikou: Twice daily to Zhenjiang (5hrs), daily to Guangzhou (27hrs), sporadically to Singapore (check the Overseas Chinese Hotel for details).

Flights
Airports at Shantou, Zhenjiang, Haikou, Xiamen and Fuzhou.

BAOTING	保定	QUANZHOU	泉州
CONGHUA	从化	SANYA	三亚
FOSHAN	佛山	SHANTOU	汕头
FUZHOU	福州	SHENZHEN	深圳
GUANGZHOU (CANTON)	广州	WUYI	武夷
GULANGYU ISLAND	鼓浪屿	XIAMEN (AMOY)	厦门
HAI'AN	海安	XINCUN	辛村
HAIKOU	海口	XINLUNG	兴隆
HAINAN ISLAND	海南岛	ZHANJIANG	湛江
JIANGMEN	江门	ZHAOQING	肇庆

Chapter seven
THE SOUTH-WEST

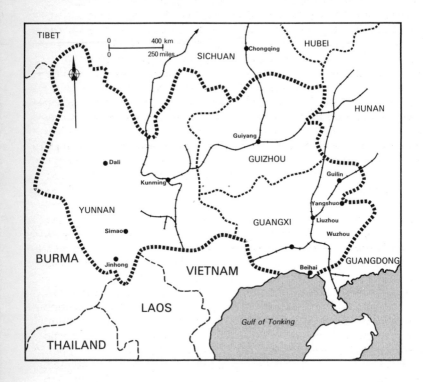

GUANGXI – YUNNAN – GUIZHOU

The three provinces of south-western China, **Guangxi**, **Yunnan** and
Guizhou, share a geographical and historical isolation from the rest of
the country which for many travellers makes their chief attraction. The
semi-tropical climate, the lush greenery and the relaxed pace of life all
make for a very real change from the tensions and frustrations of Beijing,
Guangzhou or Shanghai. In the most remote and recently opened parts
of Yunnan – accessible only by day-long bus journeys through the mountains – the traveller can still feel like a privileged pioneer, seeing parts of
the world which for decades have been totally out of bounds.

But there is another side to this coin: the mountains make for poor communications, and if you do decide to explore the south-west you'll need to set aside a least a week for travel alone. Most journeys between the major towns require at least one full day. What's worse, most routes are also horribly crowded: on the trains, especially, passengers are often hanging out of the windows. You're well advised to travel a class better than usual (if you can get the tickets) or at the least to carry with you plenty of food and other distractions to help pass the time away.

In all three provinces there are large numbers of '**minority peoples**', and historically much of this area was self-governing until relatively late. Even after the whole region had officially been included in the Chinese Empire in the 13C, it continued in practice to pay no more than lip service to unity for much of the next six centuries – there were frequent rebellions and little chance of effectively suppressing them: the rebels could simply hide in the mountains. Today, though, there's surprisingly little to show for this long-held autonomy beyond the dress and facial features of some of the people. The surviving minorities have either thoroughly adapted to Chinese ways or they continue to dwell in remote mountain and border areas, off limits to travellers. What you do see of 'quaint' customs comes largely in the form of tourist entertainments or carefully cleaned-up villages. Nevertheless you may see something of the genuine modern life of some of these peoples if you travel to the remoter regions of Yunnan or simply in hanging around any large town on market day.

For centuries China's rulers regarded the south and the tribes who inhabited it as culturally barren and as late as the Cultural Revolution many high officials, students and intellectuals were banished to the south-west. In **Kunming**, the capital of **Yunnan**, you can still meet people who will openly tell you that though they have since been given the opportunity to return home – to Beijing or wherever – they have refused, preferring the easygoing lifestyle and the year-round availability of fresh food. Maybe officialdom has woken up now to the area's charms: **Dali**, a delightfully unspoilt rural town couched in Yunnan's western mountains has recently been opened, and **Xishuang Banna**, an area in the south of Yunan bordering on Burma, Laos and Vietnam is now receiving a steady stream of visitors.

Guizhou, though its capital of Guiyang is a major rail junction, remains little visited and hard to get to or through except on the main rail lines. Here the prospect of exile might still be worrying – the only attractions are natural ones, including China's highest waterfall and a whole series of lesser falls, underground rivers and caverns. Natural phenomena are high on the agenda in **Guangxi** too, where **Guilin** has been a tourist attraction for centuries. Easily accessible from Hong Kong or Guangzhou this is on every tour group's schedule but it remains worth it for all that

– some of the most extraordinary natural rock formations anywhere and the perfect postcard image of China. From here you can take a spectacular trip down the Li River to **Yangshuo** or head south, to the tropical capital of **Nanning** and on to the coast. To the far south-west of the province, however, you cannot venture, for this is the Vietnamese border where sporadic fighting has been going on since 1969.

GUANGXI

Sub-tropical, lush and green the year round, GUANGXI boasts some of the most spectacular scenery in China. Its extensive tracts of Karst hills – dramatically shaped needles of grey rock – have been a source of inspiration to Chinese artists for centuries: it's this sort of bizarre landscape you think of when asked to produce an image of China.

The geological process which created Guangxi's weird scenes began some 325 million years ago when the entire area lay covered by the ocean. Movement of the earth's crust over subsequent millennia saw it emerge above the waves and sink again, to be finally thrust above sea level some 200 million years BC. The limestone then began gradually to be eroded into its present state – a forest of individual peaks poking out from the plain.

The finest examples are to be found around **Guilin** in the north-east. This is one of the biggest tourist draws in China but, commercialised as it is, the scenery is worth it. And as compensation there's the sublime ride down the Li River to **Yangshuo**. In the south of the province **Nanning**, the capital, and **Beihai**, on the coast, offer rather different attractions: Nanning as a tropical city with a powerful feeling of the south, and of a colonial past; Beihai as a remarkably unspoilt fishing port with some fine beaches.

Guangxi's full title should properly be the **Guangxi Zhuang Autonomous Region**. Set up in 1958, the autonomous region is named for the **Zhuang** people, 90 per cent of whose 13 million number live in the province. Though they make up only about 30 percent of the population here – other minority peoples include the *Yao*, the *Jing*, the *Hui* and the *Shin* – they occupy around two-thirds of the province. In practice you'll notice little difference: though the Zhuang were originally independent, and their language is closely linked to Thai, they have thoroughly assimilated Chinese culture. The other minorities, mostly hill peoples, are for the most part off any routes you'll be allowed to tread – regular restrictions are further complicated here by the proximity of the hostilities along the Vietnamese border.

GUILIN

GUILIN, renowned for its unique natural oddities for centuries, is perhaps China's worst tourist trap. On the itinerary of many package tours, it depends on visitors for the bulk of its income and has a well-established – and expensive – service industry. Locals are far more

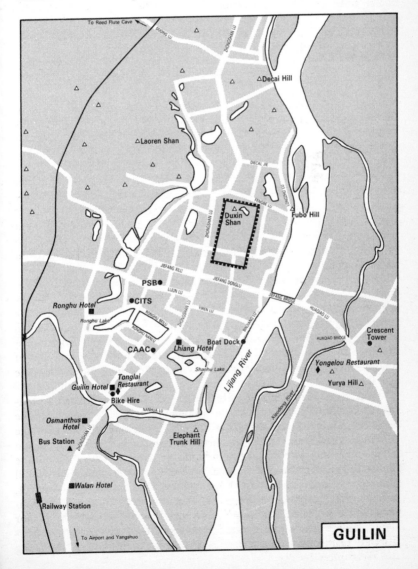

To Reed Flute Cave

DOONG LU

ZHONGSHAN LU

△Decai Hill

△Laoren Shan

DECAI JIE

FENGBE LU

DECAI LU

△
Duxin
Shan

Fubo Hill

ZHONGSHAN LU

JIEFANG XILU

JIEFANG DONGLU

JIEFANG BRIDGE

PSB●

LIJUN LU

HUAQIAO LU

Ronghu Hotel

●CITS

VIREN LU

Ronghu Lake

RONGHU BEILU

ZHONGSHAN LU

BINJIANG LU

RONGHU NAN LU

Crescent
Tower

Boat Dock●

HUAQIAO BRIDGE

CAAC●

Lhiang Hotel

Lijiang River

Yongelou Restaurant

Shanhu Lake

△

Tonglai
Restaurant

Yurya Hill△

Guilin Hotel ■●

Bike Hire

Xiandong River

NANHUA LU

Osmanthus ■
Hotel

ZHONGSHAN LU

Bus Station
▲

Elephant
Trunk Hill

■Walan Hotel

■Railway Station

To Airport and Yangshuo

GUILIN

worldly than almost anywhere else in China, and out to milk you for all you are worth: you can't walk down a street without being approached to change money or to buy something. Accommodation, too, is costly and poor. None of which in the end should deter you – Guilin's landscape is as impressively beautiful as it has always been.

Founded in the 3C, Guilin was the capital of Guanxi from the Ming dynasty until 1914, though strangely it only started to play any significant role in history after losing that rank to Nanning. Sun Yatsen launched his northern expedition from here in 1926 and during the war with Japan the city was a Chinese stronghold and a place of refuge for upwards of 1 million people (from a pre-war population of some 100,000). The Japanese bombing during this era explains the grey drabness of the city centre, most of it built since Liberation.

If you can, you should visit Guilin in early summer or autumn, which is when the **Cassia trees** from which the city takes its name (Guilin means Forest of Cassia) are in full bloom. 900,000 new trees have recently been planted, and in season they pervade the whole town with a marvellous jasmine-like odour. As far as **weather** goes, though, any time will do – winters are mild, summers hot (28°C average in July) and humid. Hustlers aside, Guilin is also thoroughly relaxing: small enough in the centre to be got around on foot, its roads refreshingly clear of traffic. Hire a **bike** and you can really take advantage of the place and its surrounds.

Whatever else you do, though, the highlight of your stay can hardly fail to be the 6-hour boat trip **down the Li River** to Yangshuo. This is where the most spectacular country lies, and Yangshuo itself also has much to offer, even if most visitors do get straight on to a bus back to Guilin.

Practicalities

If you're arriving by air, Guilin's **airport** is 14km south of the city, a 25-minute bus ride courtesy of *CAAC* to their office at 144 Zhongshan Rd, right in the centre. Arriving by **bus** or **train**, a no.1 or 2 bus will take you into the centre, or you can get a taxi just in front of the station for ¥5. Alternatively it's only a 10–15 minute walk to the main hotels (turn left and keep going), which is just as well since most east–west trains, **to and from Kunming**, seem timed to arrive in the middle of the night and buses and taxis both stop running at midnight.

Hotels are not Guilin's strong suit. At the cheaper end of the range you've a choice of three, all a couple of bus stops north from the station along Zhongshan Lu, the city's main drag. First there's the *Walan*, a modern place where a shared room with three beds costs ¥6 each; on the left, is the *Osmanthus*, with dorm beds at ¥10; then comes the *Guilin*, with dorms at the same price, singles for ¥7 and doubles at ¥16. The *Guilin*, with cold water only and wall-to-wall filth, is the worst by some way, but it's also likely to be the only one with a bed for you. More upmarket, the *Ronghu Hotel* is comfortable but overpriced, with identical doubles ranging from ¥25 to ¥70 depending on what they think they can get from you. You'll find it by continuing up Zhongshan and then turning left on Ronghu Beilu: it has a reasonable restaurant. Marginally cheaper, and much better if you can get in, is the *Lijiang Hotel* (turn right opposite Ronghu Beilu) where doubles go for ¥38, singles for around half that. The Lijiang, though, is often fully booked by tour groups.

All these hotels sell useful English **maps**, though you may want to get a bus map (Chinese only; from bookshops or the hawkers by the station) to supplement it. **CITS** (open daily 7.30–11.30 and 2.30–5.30) have a plush office at 14 Ronghu Beilu – most of their information, though, is misleading or inaccurate. **PSB** (same hours; more helpful) are at the corner of Zhongshan Lu and Sanduo Lu; **CAAC** (daily 8–5) are at 144 Zhongshan Lu. **Bikes** can be hired from the *Lijiang* or *Ronghu* hotels at ¥1 per hour or ¥6 for a day, but there's a much cheaper dealer who operates from the corner of Zhongshan Lu and Nanhuan Lu by the *Guilin Hotel*. Look for his handpainted cardboard sign, and prices about half of those quoted above (you'll need ¥100 or your passport as a deposit).

In general it's hard to know what to advise about other **hustlers**, and especially the **money-changers** who will hassle you all over town. In theory the consequences could be pretty severe: Chinese can be shot if found guilty of corruption and it's not entirely clear what happens to foreigners. On the other hand, it all seems so established here that it's hard to believe the authorities aren't consciously turning a blind eye. You should, however, consider what you're going to be able to do with your Renminbi: the going rate seems to be around ¥130 for every ¥100 FEC, but in Guilin even local shops are likely to insist on Foreign Exchange Certificates. Throughout the south, in fact, you'll have difficulty spending Renminbi so it's only if you're heading north for a while that it would be worth attempting any major dealings. One good wheeze is to buy all your **train tickets** in Guilin – there are always locals outside the railway station who will offer to buy tickets for you at the Chinese rate in exchange for payment in FEC.

Food in Guilin is renowned for being exotic, and it certainly is varied. Wild game is a speciality which you'll find in particular at the *Yongelou Restaurant* in Seven Stars Park and at the *Tonglai* just north of the Guilin hotel. The Tonglai even has a series of cages outside in which are masked civets, bamboo rat, pangolin, snakes, turtles and other live animals – all of which are to be found on the menu (there has been official criticism of Guilin restaurants in the past for serving up endangered species). Perhaps more enticingly, hot chilli sauces and fermented bean curd are also popular, along with fresh fish from the Lijiang. For less ambitious food the *Lijiang Hotel* restaurant isn't bad, with a decend breakfast for under ¥3, or there's a pleasant café open for lunch beside the entrance to the Reed Flute Cave. Down by the railway station, too, you'll find stalls set up to serve reasonable, cheap food.

As for **shops**, Zhongshan Road seems to be lined from top to bottom with uninspiring tourist junk souvenirs. You might find a few fair examples of local jade and bamboo work at the **Arts and Crafts Store** opposite CAAC, and there's a reasonable department store at 115 Zhongshan Lu, but the **Friendship Store** at 119 isn't worth visiting. More worthwile than any of them is the interesting little **market** on Xicheng Lu just north of the Guilin Hotel – it has a substantial section devoted to fruit and vegetables. One stall I saw here had three dead rats laid out for inspection: their exact purpose was unclear, but the authorities have recently been trying to persuade people to eat rats as part of an anti-vermin campaign – even issuing recommended recipes. One of these, which involves steaming the animals, marinating them in ginger and pepper, pressing them into a steak and cooking with rice and sesame oil, is supposedly a traditional Guangxi dish.

The town and its hills
As a town, Guilin has virtually nothing in the way of sights to offer – even right in the centre it is natural beauties which draw the attention. Zhongshan Lu forms the barrier between two **lakes** – *Ronghu* (Banyan) and *Shanhu* (Fir) – in the very heart of the city. Taking their names from the ancient trees which once stood here, they were originally part of a moat which surrounded the city walls during the T'ang dynasty. In the Song era they were divided in two by the construction of the Green Belt Bridge, and since Liberation, with the walls long since crumbled away, the area around them has been relandscaped to form a small park. With its bamboos, willow, peach and kumquat trees, it makes a pleasant escape from the city streets, though unfortunately not always from the money-changers who like to conduct business here.

Elsewhere the famous **hills** remain the focus of interest. Some are well within the city limits, though since none are very tall they're not exactly major landmarks from ground level – climb to the roof of the *Lijiang Hotel* for the best **views**. **Fubo Hill** is the closest to here, a pleasant walk along the river path which runs parallel to Binjang Lu. As ever, the hill is surrounded by a whole series of legends: here the giant *Jie Die* appeared in response to the apparition of a giant demon over Chuanshan Hill in the south. With his bow and bright sword Jie Die slew the demon and the snakes and fierce animals which accompanied him – from that day on evil spirits and wild animals have left Guilin in peace. At the foot of the hill is the **Returned Pearl Cave** (*Huanzhu Dong*) where a dragon lived in a pool playing with a brilliantly shining pearl. One day an old boatman, attracted by the light, stole the pearl while the dragon slept, but later, stricken by conscience, brought it back (hence Returned Pearl) – both dragon and boatman, we assume, lived happily ever after. The cave entrance faces south across the river, and in the morning is spectacularly illuminated by the early sun; inside is the *Shijian* rock, a 3m stalactite on which the Han general Fubo is said to have tested his sword. Nearby is the **Thousand Buddhas Cliff**, with over 300 carved figures dating from the Song and Tang dynasties. For the summit there's a flight of stone steps which lead to the River Kui pavilion, halfway up, and then on to the top: on the eastern face a winding corridor zigzags above the river and there's another pavilion, the *Tingtao*, and a tea-house in which to recover from the steep ascent.

Carrying on up the riverbank, *Decai* or **Folded Brocades Hill** is a further 10 minutes' walk. The variegated erosion of its limestone seams have given it a whole series of small peaks – Siwan, Yuyue, Heavenly Crane Peak and Bright Moon Peak – and an appearance which is supposed to resemble a pile of interlaced brocades. There are dozens of caves, too, many with Tang and Song Buddhist statues, some of which were defaced during the Cultural Revolution. At the peak, *Nayunting* or **Grasping Gloud Pavilion** offers spectacular views of the surrounding area – the stools and stone benches here are a favourite haunt of old men who come to sit and contemplate. On your way up, the stone pathway passes through an arch, to the left of which is the **Yan Zhi Hall**, a memorial to the late Ming national heroes *Qu Shisi* and *Zhong Tongchang*.

Duxiu Feng stands just to the west of Fubo Hill, not far off Zhongshan Lu – it's also known as the Pillar under the Southern Sky or **Solitary Beauty Peak**. This latter comes from the poet *Yan Yanzhi* who wrote:

Nothing is more beautiful than the peak of Solitary Beauty
Rising straight from the level ground in the midst of the city.

The hill now stands within the grounds of the mansion of *Zhu Shouqian*, a grandson of the Ming emperor Hongwu who was made King of this area in 1369. There's little of the original left beyond a gate, and the present building, which had been used as an office by Sun Yatsen and as a venue for provincial exams, is now the home of Guanxi Teachers' College, 306 steps lead to the top, and, tough going as it is, the view once again makes it all worthwhile.

West of the city

Heading west on Lijun Road, you reach **Yinshan**, Hidden or Secluded Hill, shortly after crossing the railway line. This peak was once totally surrounded by water – the bulk of it long since drained away – and was used as a retreat by the Tang poet *Li Bo* who built a pavilion and planted trees and flowers. It's especially beautiful in midsummer, when the many small lakes and ponds which survive are covered in flowers. **Xishan** – the Western Hills – are further out along this road, some 3km from the town centre. The peaks here include Avolakitesvara's Peak, Stone Fish Peak, Dragon Head Peak and Qianshan. The whole area has long Buddhist connections: hundreds of Buddhas were carved into the high rocks, most of them now destroyed, and the impressive **Xiqinglin Temple** survives as one of the five important Buddhist centres in South China. Here you can see hundreds of exquisitely carved Buddhist statues, ranging from miniatures of 10cm to oversized figures more than 2m tall.

A no.3 bus (starting from the railway station) will take you past both these hills before curving round to the north for **Reed Flute Cave** – you can follow this route by bike. Situated in the south side of Guangming Hill, on the west bank of Peach Blossom River, this cave is one of the most extraordinary examples of limestone erosion in all south China; if you had time to see only one of Guilin's caves, this should be it. You have to go round in a guided tour (at 20-minute intervals from 8.30–11 and 12.30–3.30) so try tagging along with a tour group if the official Chinese version doesn't appeal. Basically, though, the natural formations are impressive enough even if you don't know that what you're seeing is supposed to resemble 'Rosy Dawn in a Lion Forest' or a 'Waterfall Splashing Down from a High Valley', and the awestruck reactions of the Chinese visitors are enjoyable in themselves. Throughout, and despite some rather crude coloured lighting which sometimes makes the place look like Indiana Jones' Temple of Doom, the size, colour and variety of the rock formations are genuinely spectacular, reaching their peak in the huge **Crystal Palace Grotto**, which can house a thousand people with ease.

Reed Flute Cave, which gets its name from the reeds growing immediately outside the main entrance, was only developed as a tourist site in the late 1950s. For years before that the local population had kept its existence a secret, relying on this and the tortuous paths inside to provide a safe refuge in case of attack or banditry. Nowadays the place has been landscaped, there's a reasonable restaurant (open 8am–2pm) just to the right of the entrance and a large bike park.

Continuing, you could ride out to the west for several kilometres through settlements rarely visited by westerners before eventually being turned back at the city limits. Alternatively **Laoren Shan**, Old Man Hill, is also to be found in the north-west of the city, on the way back towards the centre. Here according to legend lived a group of celestial monkeys, living off what they could steal from the fields and homes roundabout. An old man who came to Guilin settled on the mountain and declared war on the monkeys who, thinking that the mountain was the old man, fled.

East of the Li River
The scenic highlight of Guilin lies on the other side of the Lijiang – the dramatic area known as **Seven Star Park**. Here seven great peaks are laid out in the shape of the Great Bear constellation (the star of the title) and there are six major caves: the whole can easily fill a day's wandering. Cross the Lijiang by the Jiefang or **Liberation Bridge** and continue across the narrow stream of the Xiaodong via **Huaqiao Bridge** to reach the main entrance. The second of these bridges is worthy of a little attention in itself – built in the Song Dynasty and recently reconstructed, it features a tiled roof overhead with palisades and arches below to control the flow of the river.

To your left as you enter the park is the huge expanse of **Patuo**, named after one of the four Buddhist sacred mountains. On this hill are the four northern peaks of the star, *Tianshi, Tianxuan, Tianji* and *Tianquan*. Patuo Gate leads to a stone stairway which heads up the hill's western slope: just inside the gate is **Yuan Feng** (Deep and Windy Cave), famous for its cooling breeze all year round, and, to the right, the **Pavilion of Stone Tablets** with a plaque on which the three characters *Xiao Yao Lou* (Carefree Tower) were handwritten by the Tang calligrapher *Yan Zhenqing*. As you climb Patuo you have a choice of routes. The left-hand path leads down through an area known as 'Pure Land Transcending the Mortal World' to the Yonglui Pavilion and the Xiaopenglai Corridor before emerging in the Patuo Stone Forest. Close by here is the **Patuo Temple**, 22 storeys high with views back over the city, and behind it is **Guanyin Cave** where Bodhisattva, 28th teacher of Suddhana Kumara, reputedly preached to his pupil. To the right of the temple is Yonguan or Clear Water Spring and below this the small Patuo Cave.

To the right, you reach **Xuanwu Pavilion** (God of the Northern Sky) through the windows of which is framed the great Ming cliff sculpture 'Turtle-Snake Union'. Close at hand is White Crane Cave, named after two stalactites said to resemble the legs of the bird. Pass between them and you emerge in *Sixian* or Four Immortals' Cave which leads in turn into the **Seven Star Cave**, most spectacular of all. This huge cavern – over 1km in length, 27m at its highest point and over 40m at its broadest – was originally a subterranean river channel, and indeed in the lowest level the river is still flowing. This, though, you don't see, and nor do you get to visit the upper reaches of the cave, but the central section is quite impressive enough. It is like some vast geomorphic art gallery (with a constant temperature, year round, of about 20°C) in which, as always, every last rock has been given its own exotic title. The cave itself is variously known as the 'Verdant Void' or 'Lingering Sunset Glow', but my own favourite is the rock formation known as 'Magpies spreading their wings to form a bridge across the Milky Way'.

In the south of the park, **Yueya Shan** (Crescent Moon Hill) sports the three remaining crags of the seven stars – *Yuleng, Kaiyang* and *Yaoguang*.

At the foot of the hill is **Crescent Moon Pavilion** – a handy spot to rest up where you can buy drinks – and on the way up you pass Banqu (Moon's Companion Pavilion), Xiao Guanghan (Lesser Moon Tower), Crescent Cave and the Jinjiang Pavilion, with more good views. Descending on the south side, past Dangui or Red Osmanthus Cave, you reach the celebrated **Dragon Refuge Cave** where centuries of erosion by trickling water has left the rock face looking as if covered in Dragon-size scales. There's a constant ray of light which shines through a crack in the ceiling to illuminate thousands of poems inscribed on the walls by visitors. In the **Guilin Stele Forest** a little further on (and supposedly the former home of a ferocious dragon) you can see over 2,000 inscriptions on stone, their subjects ranging from Marxist economics to history and literature.

Lutuo Shan (Camel Hill, for obvious reasons) rises to the east of Yueya Shan near the zoo. Here are many peach, osmanthus, and cassia trees and even a Japanese gingko, planted by a delegation from Kumanto in Japan when Guilin and Kumanto became Friendship Cities. From Lutuo there's a fine view south to **Chuan Shan** – the Hill with a Hole Through It. To its right is **Tashan** – Pagoda Hill – which takes its name from a hexagonal brick pagoda built during the Ming dynasty. This has a legendary foundation: on Chuan Shan lived a cock whose daily crowing would inspire the people of Guilin to rise early for work. Then a demon, in the shape of a giant centipede, settled on Tashan and began to harass the locals and rob them while they slept. One misty day the cock chased and attacked the centipede, wounding it – the demon retreated into a cave on Tashan over the entrance to which the people of Guilin promptly erected the pagoda, sealing the centipede in to this day.

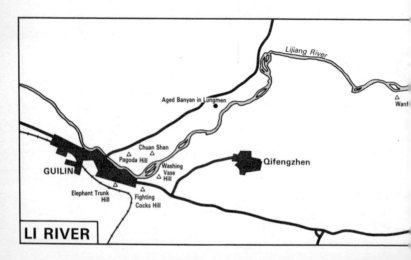

THE LIJIANG AND YANGSHUO

Expensive as it is, the **Li River trip** is worth every penny. Every morning around 8am some sixty boats leave Guilin for the 85-kilometre, 6-hour trip south to Yangshuo. It's a spectacular ride, through some of the finest scenery that even this part of China can provide. At the same time the boat itself is comfortingly tranquil: although they say that every sailor ever drowned in the Lijiang has been transformed into a demon who rocks the boats as they navigate the rapids, the skill of the boatman is such that the passage almost always feels totally calm. Along the way you'll pass fishermen on their bamboo rafts, selling freshly caught fish to the boat crew as they pass, and water buffalo wallowing in the shallows – you'll also be fed a tasty lunch by your boatman's family, who usually live on board.

You can **book** the trip through CITS for ¥40 or through any of the ticketsellers on the main streets of Guilin for about ¥33 – don't think you're paying for any extras with CITS, you're not, it's exactly the same trip. If you can't run even to ¥33 there are still two alternatives, starting **from Yangshuo**. One is to take a short trip downstream – around ¥5 for a couple of hours – run by a local commune: you'll find a man offering this ride outside the main hotel (he also speaks good English and is a very helpful source of information on the area). Alternatively you can negotiate a price for a return trip with one of the crew from the Guilin boats. Because they're navigating upriver, against the stream, this journey takes about 4 hours longer, even with an empty boat. If you set off at 1pm you won't arrive back in Guilin until 11pm, with the last few hours of the journey in darkness. But this doesn't matter too much since

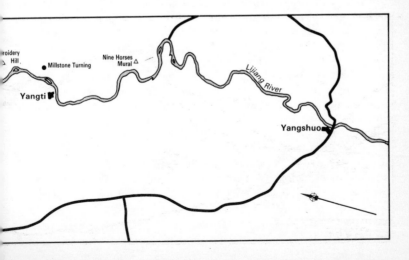

the most beautiful part of the journey comes between Yangshuo and Yangti, about halfway. Indeed **in winter** the river is frequently too low for navigation in Guilin, and river trip passengers are taken by bus to Yangti, to sail from there to Yangshuo.

There's very little specific to say about the ride – it's simply a marvellously restful journey through gorgeous scenery. Inevitably, though, almost all the peaks along the way have obscure or exotic names, and most have an associated legend to explain their bizarre appearance. First of these is **Elephant Trunk Hill** just a few hundred yards from the departure point, which is supposed to resemble an elephant drinking from the river (and, for once, just about does). This elephant was originally brought to the south by a celestial emperor touring the south; it fell ill and was abandoned near Guilin where some locals found the beast and nursed it back to health. Recovered, the elephant showed its gratitude by working for its human helpers, but the emperor was so outraged by this display or man's hubris that he sent his soldiers to kill the beast – they trapped it unawares as it drank, and promptly turned it to stone.

A little further down on the opposite bank is **Chuan Shan** – Pierced Hill or the Hill with a Hole Through It – and nearby Tashan (p. 376). The hole in Chuan Shan is, according to the Chinese, in the shape of the full moon – which means it is round. It was formed when *Jie Die* (see p. 372) loosed off an arrow at the demon here – one shot was enough to pierce demon and hill. Near here too are **Washing Vase Hill** – supposed to resemble a water jug being washed by the river, the hill and its reflection making up a whole vase – and, best seen by looking back as you pass this, **Fighting Cocks Hill**, with two peaks about to leap on each other. This area just south of Guilin also has many maple trees – particularly striking in the autumn as their leaves turn to flame.

As you continue downstream you'll have many more scenes pointed out. At **Oxen Gorge** the rocks which line the ravine edges are supposed to represent a herd of oxen looking down over the river. **Wanfu** (Yearning for Husband Hill) takes its name from two stone figures in the shape of a man and a woman holding a baby: the story goes that as the family sailed down the river they discovered they had only one bag of rice left. Mooring on the little island in the stream, the husband climbed the hill looking for another boat which might help – when he failed to return the wife followed, carrying the child, but found only a stone statue. She stood mourning in front of it for so long that she too turned to stone. The brightly coloured rocks on **Embroidery Hill** are said to resemble a giant piece of embroidery. **Millstone Turning Hill** looks like an old man industriously grinding his corn. Further along, **Nine Horses Mural Hill** has nine steep peaks, each supposed to be the outline of a horse. After a while you can start to invent your own.

Yangshuo

YANGSHUO (Bright Moon) plays host to thousands of trippers who descend on the place by boat, stay an hour or so, then climb into their coaches and head back to Guilin. The face that Yangshuo turns to these visitors is undoubtedly its worst: a main street crowded with shops selling overpriced souvenirs and refusing point blank to accept local currency. Stay overnight, however – as more and more independent travellers seeking to escape Guilin's crowds are doing – and you'll get a very different impression. Outside its rush hours this is a wonderfully restful place, easygoing, laid-back and surrounded by beautiful countryside which is easily explored by bike. The *Yangshuo Hotel* is on Feng Binguan (right off the main street under the archway), charges ¥38 for a double room and apart from a lack of hot water is thoroughly pleasant. The *Xi Lang Hill Hotel* is rather cheaper at ¥14 for a double.

Bikes can be hired from a place under the archway for ¥2 a day: get out among the villages and you'll find lush green fields sprinkled with cypress and poplar and dotted with fantastically shaped hills. Highest of these peaks is **Green Lotus**, by the river, which is worth climbing for the views. Alternative vistas can be had from **Yangshuo People's Park**, a group of hills right in the village best appreciated from the *Pavilion Nestling in the Clouds* on its south side, and from **Moon Hill** in the neighbouring village of Li.

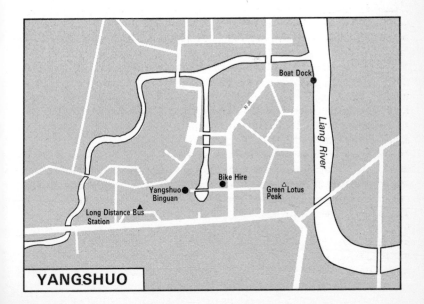

YANGSHUO

ON FROM GUILIN – THE ROUTE TO GUANGZHOU

Getting from Guilin to Guangzhou, or vice versa, is no easy matter. You can fly, of course, but it's expensive: overland is slow, but as long as time is not a prime concern it can make a fascinating journey. By train, with no direct line, you're looking at a two-day journey; far more interesting is the more direct (though even slower) **bus and boat trip** which takes you through remote villages to WUZHOU and then on down the Xi Jiang to Guangzhou in local passenger boats.

The bus from Guilin to Wuzhou leaves from near the Lijiang Hotel at 7am; you can buy tickets (for the entire journey) the day before at the small green kiosk opposite the hotel entrance. It's a reasonably comfortable ride – albeit packed for the full ten hours – and there are rarely any other foreigners along. For a good while after setting out the scenery is quite breathtaking, and even after the limestone peaks disappear the landscape opens out to broad, lush agricultural valleys. This is a side of China you'll see only rarely – rural villages and market towns through which the bus crawls, stopping frequently for drinks and snacks.

Arriving at **WUZHOU** in the early evening, the bus stops at a large hotel on the far side of the river. For the ferry terminals you must cross back to the main part of town – ask at the hotel for exact directions. Wuzhou was closed, except for transit, until 1985, but if you're expecting a backwater you'll be surprised: perched high on the river banks, it's a lively, crowded place, prosperous looking and full of energy. In the 19C this was an important trading centre where wealthy Cantonese merchants settled and in 1897 the port was opened up to foreign traders – principally British – whose steamers ran regularly between here and Hong Kong. Despite a certain shabbiness, Wuzhou retains an air of thriving activity; the street leading down to the ferries is full of shopping complexes and cinemas, and the shops sell a surprisingly wide and upmarket range of consumer goods. Along the road behind the wharves, above the river, plenty of stalls give you the chance to enjoy fresh fish and seafood. There is a ferry depot where you can leave your luggage while you explore, or if the ferry is delayed.

The **ferry** is supposed to leave Wuzhou at 9pm, but it rarely does. Once you board you'll find conditions very basic: there's only one class and on any other boat it would be about 5th. You lie on rows and rows of foam mattresses, separated only by narrow wooden battens. If you're over 5'6", forget sitting up. Food is brought round periodically (not bad food either) and there is a narrow platform outside where you can escape for a breath of fresh air. The whole thing is a definite experience – scheduled to take 12 hours, the boats drop anchor at the slightest hint of fog on the water and almost always take much longer, so take plenty of things to keep you amused. After a bad trip Guangzhou can seem like paradise, but strenuous as it is this trip is well worth it.

Travelling in the other direction you may find easier ways of getting from **Guangzhou to Wuzhou**. There are some larger ferries, or with luck you might even get aboard a hovercraft which would drop you there.

Liuzhou

Heading south from Guilin by train, whether to Guangzhou or Nanning, you'll probably have to change at **LIUZHOU**. For most Chinese this is a city with unfortunate connotations, where by tradition you come to die: the local cedar wood is of exceptional quality and much prized for coffins. In the Tang dynasty, when this was still regarded as the barbarous south, Liuzhou was a regular posting for disgraced officials. One such was *Liu Zongyuan*, transferred here as governor in 815. The poetry which his tribulations inspired has recently become popular again, as expressing the arduous life facing the common people. Liuzhou's main sight today is a temple built in his honour after he had successfully driven off a band of marauding bandits. Otherwise modern Liuzhou is a standard small market town, gradually developing into a manufacturing centre: two hotels are available to independent travellers, the *Liuzhou* on Wenge Lu and the *Liujiang* on Gongyan, each a short pedicab ride from the station.

NANNING

Fly into **NANNING**, China's southernmost city, and you're immediately struck by its tropical atmosphere. The humidity, the palm-lined streets, the steady whirring of the three-pronged ceiling fans and the dilapidated cane furniture all conspire to make this seem the setting for some Graham Greene novella. And it is a very attractive place, certainly by Chinese standards: there are fewer concrete blocks here than in other centres and a marked absence of the normally ubiquitous blue or green Mao-suits – most locals adopt more traditional forms of Chinese clothing. You'll also find very few other travellers, but in spite of a reputation for being rather dull, Nanning is ideal if you're happy to spend a couple of days simply wandering round and absorbing a southern city rather than seeing specific 'sights'.

The modern capital of Guanxi province, Nanning was founded during the Yuan dynasty and remained a medium sized market town right through to the end of the 19C. Then European traders opened a navigation route from the mouth of the Xijiang and Nanning moved into a period of spectacular growth. Made capital in 1914, it grew first through being a relatively safe haven from the fighting of the first half of the century, lost its status to Guilin from 1936–49, then regained it and saw a real boom with the building of the **railways**. The line to the Vietnamese border at Pingxiang was completed in 1952, and not long after was extended to Hanoi: Nanning was a vital supply centre throughout the Vietnam War and to some extent it still is – feeding the troops engaged in continuing border hostilities little over 160km away. Fighting allegedly reached Nanning itself during the Cultural Revolution: such stories are always and inevitably vague, and you hear tales of pitched battles between rival factions throughout the province, but in Nanning the street fighting is supposed to have been particularly vicious, fuelled by arms looted from trains bound for Vietnam.

None of this – apart from a certain boom-town atmosphere and occasional signs of hasty construction – is particularly evident on the streets. It's simply a bustling southern city. To get a feel of it, try wandering around some of the lanes at the river end of **Xinling Lu**, north of the *Yongjiang Hotel*. Crowded shopping streets, these sell nothing particularly out of the ordinary, but they're enjoyable simply to wander around, checking out what's on offer and, in season, drooling over some delicious tropical fruit. Xinling Lu itself also offers some of the finest **cake shops** in China (better even than Shanghai's) and the Foreign Language

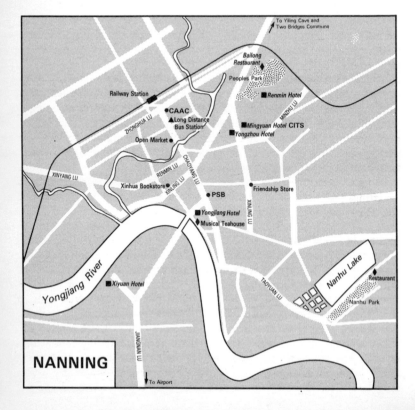

Bookstore, which seems to stock nothing more exciting than English–Chinese grammar primers. Just off Chaoyang Lu, the town's main street which runs from the railway station to the centre, there's also one of the largest and most varied **open air markets** in the province – get there on a no.5 bus. There are hundreds of stalls selling live snakes, chickens, ducks, turtles and frogs; others with great heaps of fruit and vegetables. You can find Chinese pharmacists specialising in such exotica as rhino horn aphrodisiacs and when I was there one stall in the clothes section sold terrific fluorescent plastic sandals: locals are very friendly and only too eager to get into photographs.

For a bit of escape, head for the south of the city and **Nanhu lake** and park. There's a sizeable expanse of water here and interesting, peaceful gardens, but it's most famous as the location of the annual **Dragon Boat Races**, held on the fifth day of the fifth lunar month (usually early June). Dating back some 2,000 years to the Han dynasty, the races have only recently been reinstated after falling out of favour during the Cultural Revolution. Nowadays a thoroughly colourful, joyous occasion, they attract over a quarter of a million people annually, with prizes being awarded for the best designed and fastest boats. You can get to Nanhu Park on a no.2 bus from Xinling Lu, or by no.3 which runs from the railway station, down Chaoyang Lu, and winds up by the northern side of the lake.

One final thing to do in Nanning – and this is definitely not be be missed – is to visit the appropriately named **Musical Tea-house** by the river, opposite the Yongjiang Hotel. Open every evening (¥1 including tea and biscuits) this is one of the few places in provincial China where you'll find people going out at night solely to enjoy themselves: set up and run by young people for young people, its open air setting attracts hundreds of them and is a popular dating place. Live music is very much Irish jig Chinese style with various soloists backed by an eight-piece band of strings and percussion, nattily fitted out in collarless suits, shirt and tie. They look eerily like the early Beatles.

Practicalities

Air travellers can take the CAAC bus from the airport into town – it goes to the **CAAC office** (64 Chaoyang Lu) but will also drop you at the main hotels. The journey takes around 45 minutes and costs 20fen. If you arrive by either **bus** or **train**, a no.5 bus will drop you outside the *Yongjiang Hotel* or take a no.5 followed by a no.1 for the others. Alternatively you can hire a pedicab, which shouldn't cost more than ¥2.

Looking for a **hotel** in Nanning, it's worth remembering that you're now far enough south for some of the less pleasant aspects of tropical life to make themselves felt – rock hard beds are surrounded by musty mosquito nets. The only dorms in town are at the *Yongjiang Hotel* for

¥6 a night; they also have beds in three-bedded rooms for ¥10 and double rooms with baths for ¥32. It is in Linjiang Lu on the north bank of the river. Two other places might have rooms, though the Yongjiang seems to be the mainstay for independent travellers. The *Minyiang Guest-house* is a lovely old building in spacious grounds but is expensive – usually upwards of ¥50 though doubles are theoretically available for ¥28. The *Yongzhou Hotel*, directly across Xinmin Lu from here, is a rather ugly tower block with double rooms for ¥35. On the south side of the river (no.1 or 5 bus) there's also a smart new hotel, the *Xiyuan*; rooms are expensive (¥60 up) but the **restaurant** has a nationwide reputation.

Other **food** in Nanning is along Guangxi lines, but with a little Cantonese influence creeping in. There's a good fish restaurant beside Nanhu Lake (open 8–4, try to establish a price before you order) and the *Bailong* in Renmin Park is also worth a try. Otherwise the hotels are adequate, there are food stalls in the market and numerous reasonable street cafés – remember too the cake shops on Xingling Lu.

You'll find the **CITS** office by the back entrance to the Minyiang Guesthouse. They have **maps** (as do the hotels) and are helpful enough, but have little experience of independent travellers – they may try to dissuade you from travelling on local buses, for example, and it takes considerable perseverance to persuade them to provide tickets, even at a ¥2 mark-up. The **Friendship Store** is south of here at the bottom of Xinmin Lu – it stocks mainly western drink and cigarettes. **Public Security** is on the large roundabout at the southern end of Chaoyang Lu; this is the place to get your **visa for Beihai**, unobtainable anywhere else.

Out from Nanning

Setting off from the city, there are a number of trips which can easily be done in a day. **Yiling Cave**, about 25km north-west of Nanning near the village of YILING, is closest at hand. If you're keen on caves this is well worth seeing – more spectacular than many of the caves in Guilin and every bit as garishly lit: if you're not, it's just another cave. CITS organise occasional trips, or you can catch the local bus which runs twice daily (7.30am and 1pm; ¥1.30) from the long-distance bus station. The **Two Bridges Commune**, strictly a CITS trip, is further out, some 45km away near the town of WUMING. It's a chance to see the Zhuang people on their home ground and is also handily close to swimming spots at **Lingshui Springs**. On a rather different tack, **BINYANG**, a town famous for its pottery, lies a little over 90km to the north-east. You'll need a travel permit to get there but otherwise it's easy enough – around two hours on very regular buses.

BEIHAI

The only way in or out of **BEIHAI** overland is by bus, and wherever you're coming from that's a long, hard haul. Which is the main reason why very few foreigners ever seem to get here and a good justification for making the effort yourself. It's a pleasant little town, sleepily subtropical, with a superb beach and, quite unexpectedly, one of the largest fishing fleets in China. One of a number of potential resorts earmarked for development as China opens up to the outside world, Beihai is worth seeing now, before the bulldozers move in.

Historically, Beihai is part of Guangdong province – it became part of Guangxi only in 1954 when the government decreed that without a major port of its own Guangxi could not meet its economic development targets. Its people still speak Cantonese and culturally remain closer to their traditional than their adopted province. The port first began to develop when the British signed the Yangtai Trading Agreement with the Qing rulers in 1876; in 1885 a further agreement with the French consolidated its position as a bridgehead for foreign traders. It grew rapidly as outsiders set up schools, churches, offices and banks – you can still see the former French Consulate and a British hospital. Nowadays the town is entering a new phase of expansion. When the railway link from Nanning to Fangcheng (on the coast nearby) is complete, Beihai's importance as a trading centre for the inland regions of Sichuan, Yunnan, Guizhou and

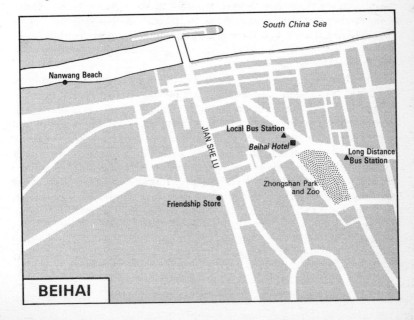

Guangxi should grow. And in recent years there has been a major influx of Vietnamese refugees, absorbed remarkably successfully into the expanding fishing industry.

The **sea front** is the most interesting, and the most ancient, part of town. At the northern end there's a small island which you can walk across to on a narrow bridge. And the harbour itself is fascinating – many of the fishing boats are traditional Chinese-rig sailing junks, aboard which entire families make their home, sailing out every evening and returning at dawn laden with the night's catch.

Not far from here, along the northern shore of the peninsula, lies the **town beach**. Here are held the races of the annual Dragon Boat Festival, a spectacle closely akin to that of Nanning, and here too the locals go to swim in relatively clean water – though be prepared for a crowd of onlookers should you decide to join them. **Nan Wang beach** is a considerably more enticing option, unspoilt, beautiful and virtually deserted (apart from a couple of rusting hulks which are being dismantled for scrap). The only problem is getting there, which involves a short hike. Take a no.2 bus past the fishing harbour and on for a little under 1km, to where a brown mud track leads off from the road – follow this for about an hour (on foot) and you'll sight the beach at the tip of the peninsula. On a clear day you may also see **Weizhou Island** offshore – a naval base said to have some 13,000 inhabitants.

In addition to the no.2 (for the port and towards Nan Wang) Beihai has three more **local bus services**, all starting from the local bus station. Nos 1 and 4 both run around town; no.3 heads out to the **refugee camp** which houses some 13,000 Vietnamese 'boat people'. Built by the Chinese government and the UN High Commissioner for refugees, the camp is something of a model – it has its own port and upwards of 700 fishing boats which since 1983 have produced enough fish to make the place self-sufficient. Most of the residents arrived in the late 1970s when some quarter of a million refugees, mostly ethnic Chinese, fled Vietnam – victims of an apparently premeditated attempt by the Vietnamese authorities to remove the Chinese minority, and with them Chinese influence. This was one of the major causes of the 1979 outbreak of hostilities between China and Vietnam and the sporadic fighting which continues along the border. Refugees continue to be a headache for the government in Guangxi and Yunnan provinces, with few yet absorbed as successfully as here.

Staying in Beihai

Arriving in Beihai you'll be dropped at the **long-distance bus station**, just to the east of the only **hotel** in town, the *Beihai Hotel*. It's an easy walk, turning left out of the terminus and on for about 200 metres to a fork in the road where the hotel lies on the right. Dorm beds go for ¥4, double rooms for ¥14 and it's a clean enough place, if a little musty. The only real problems are the lack of running hot water (though you can ask for buckets to be brought to your room) and the fact that none of the staff speak English – practise your mime. The hotel is the centre of most other activities: you can **change money** here (though foreigners are so rare that even the hotel staff have little experience of Foreign Exchange Certificates and most local shops will insist on Renminbi); there are **bikes** for hire (most of the time); and the best **food** is served on the premises. There are three restaurants within the hotel – downstairs you can either queue for a self service set meal or pay slightly more for waiter service. Either of these costs around ¥2 a head (serve yourself slightly cheaper) for a limited choice from a fixed menu. Upstairs, for about ¥3–5 each, you can order from a wide range of local seafood dishes, perhaps the best in the province. Here you must order in the morning (for lunch or dinner) so that your food can be brought in fresh: specialities of the local fishing industry include red snapper, cuttle fish, squid and four varieties of prawn. Apart from this there are few restaurants of any note, though there are several small **ice-cream parlours** which serve very welcome ice cold beer. Try the one opposite the Department Store.

To fill any more spare time in Beihai you could try **Zongxian Park**, right across the road from the hotel. It's a pleasant hangout in the early morning, to exercise or simply to sit and watch the locals taking theirs, but you should avoid the zoo: a cramped and depressing gathering of mournful, ragged beasts. There are also some interesting **shops**, especially along Zuhai Lu. This is a good place to buy **bamboo** wares – it's a local speciality and there are plenty of sturdy, well made pieces around, none of them intended for the tourist market.

Four buses a day **leave** Beihai, and any of them will theoretically pick you up from the hotel (though the bus station still seems much safer). Two go to Zhangjiang (6.30 and 11.45am; ¥5.35; 5 hour journey), one to Nanning (7.05; ¥6.65; 7hrs) and one to Haikou (5.40am; ¥10.55; 10hrs). And remember that even to get here in the first place you need a **travel visa**, available only from the PSB in Nanning.

WEST TO KUNMING – GUIZHOU AND YUNNAN

Heading west from Guangxi you're travelling still further into isolation. Mountainous, difficult terrain and hostile inhabitants have always made the provinces of Guizhou and Yunnan something apart from China and even today they are poor and scantly populated. It is only recently that outside tourists have been permitted to travel here at all, and even now only to very restricted areas. But the effort is worth making – Yunnan in particular is spectacularly scenic and in its western fringes, towards Burma, are some of the most relaxed and tropical rural parts of the country.

Like Guangxi, both provinces are the home of substantial numbers of China's **minority peoples** – there are as many as 22 distinct ethnic group-ings in Yunnan – though here no one group is in the majority. And while the area has in theory been under central Chinese rule since at least the 13C, it remained in practice the domain of local rulers who at best paid token obeisance to the national government, until well into the 19C. Today, though, the rebel spirit seems finally to have been crushed and the minorities marginalised – in Guizhou they occupy the southern and eastern mountain regions, leaving the lowlands and fertile valleys to the Chinese; in Yunnan they tend to be found in the closed border regions. You'll see little evidence of the region's diversity on the roads you're allowed to follow.

For the traveller **Yunnan** is the more rewarding region. **Kunming**, at the heart of its central plateau, is a thoroughly pleasant capital – an excellent base from which to explore the beautiful country roundabout. Here above all you'll find the **Stone Forest** around Lunan, a smaller but if anything even more spectacular outcrop of the bizarre karst mountain scenery found around Guilin. Then there are **lakes** – Dianchi near Kunming and Erhai outside Dali – and a climate which guarantees warmth year round. In the far west **Dali**, the former capital of the *Bai* people, is perhaps the least spoilt, most relaxing country town you'll be allowed to visit anywhere in China.

Guizhou, still thoroughly backward despite considerable industrial-isation in recent years, is less attractive, but if you're moving on from Guangxi by train you're almost bound to have to make a connection in its capital, **Guiyang**. The average altitude of the entire province is 1100m and Guiyang itself is over 1000m above sea level: communications are notoriously difficult and the rain is legendary (according to the proverb Guizhou has 'no three feet of flat earth, nor three days of sun') but there are at least some spectacular views, and the limestone mountains are riddled with underground rivers and lakes. Nowadays too this is an important mining region, with resources of silver, copper and coal, and the lowlands are increasingly exploited for agriculture – one area where the warm temperatures and heavy rains are an unalloyed boon. As far as stopping here for long is concerned, though, there's just one undeniable attraction, **Hangguosho Falls**, the largest waterfall in China.

GUIYANG AND ONWARDS

GUIYANG's population is exploding towards the million mark (from 50,000 in 1900) but it remains a thoroughly backward place, and makes for rather grim visiting. Still, it's a lot more interesting than the station so if you're stranded between trains or plan to visit the Falls from this direction, you might as well catch a bus into town (assuming you have a Guiyang permit: no.1 is best, circling around town and past the hotels before returning to the station; no.2 follows much the same route in the opposite direction). If you need **somewhere to stay** try the *Yun Yen* or the *Zhao Yan*, both on Beijing Lu, or the *Jinqiao Fandian* at Daximen, all of them on the no.1 bus route – should you encounter problems getting a room **CITS** (further round the same route or tel.25121) are remarkably enthusiastic and helpful. A very long way out to the south of the city, en route to the airport, there's also the official tourist hotel, the *Huaxi Binguan*: highly impractical for transport.

Looking around town you'll find a few interesting shops and backstreet markets, but the streets which house them are crowded, dirty and unattractive: more enticing perhaps are the **parks**, which feature local cave and lake scenery. There are two large ones on the fringes of town – the Daxia Gongyuan boasts a waterfall and one of the more impressive caves, the mythical home of the Monkey King.

The only reason you might actually choose to stay in Guiyang, however, is to visit the **Hangguosho Falls**, some 150km west. China's biggest, the falls – pictured on the 10fen FEC – certainly are spectacular, plunging well over 70m into the Rhinoceros Pool and sending up a great cloud of misty spume which drifts, sometimes for miles, over the forest roundabout. And in the area all around are many other waterfalls, caves and subterranean rivers, some easily visited, others involving serious hiking expeditions. At the main falls you can follow a series of slippery stepping stones across the pool to stand in the small Water Curtain Cave right behind the plunging water.

The problem with visiting the fall is one of logistics and expense – there's a good chance of having to spend two nights at least in this area. Most straightforwardly, you can take an early morning **bus from Guiyang** (leaves the bus depot around 7am) direct to the falls (arriving towards noon) and catch the same bus back in the afternoon. This, though, will give you only around 4 hours at the falls – not enough to explore anything beyond the main cataract – and will probably still mean spending two nights in Guiyang. You could also do a **CITS trip** from Guiyang, but these are very pricey and only run once a week at best. The alternative is either to stay at the falls, where the foreigners only **hotel** is comfortable but expensive, or to go in one direction via **Anshun**, on the Guiyang–Kunming railway. Anshun is only 1½ hours from Hangguoshu and has several buses every day which should connect with onward trains. There's a hotel here too if you get stranded, but otherwise the town is closed.

KUNMING

KUNMING, literally translated, means 'Brilliance for Generations' but it's always described in English as the city of eternal spring – a claim which for once is not entirely without basis. 2150m above sea level in the heart of the fertile Yunnan plateau, it enjoys warmly temperate conditions throughout the year. Wander about and you'll sense a distinct atmosphere of well-being; the quality of life here is noticeably better than in most Chinese cities.

Ironically enough Kunming has always been regarded as something of a backwater and a place of exile for dissidents. The authorities took rather longer to wake up to its newfound attractions than did their opponents – many of the people banished from Beijing or Shanghai during the Cultural Revolution or other upheavals have since refused the offer of a return to the north. People in Kunming will tell you how much more relaxed life is here, how much better the climate and friendly the inhabitants. And there are tangible advantages too, in such obvious areas as the abundance of fresh fruit and vegetables throughout the year. It also makes a good base for travellers: there are plenty of attractions in the countryside roundabout and so far little overt commercialism – the free-spending guided tours have yet to penetrate this far in any numbers.

The two most significant factors in changing Kunming from a barbaric place of exile into a prosperous modern city were the rail link to Haiphong and the 1937–45 war against the Japanese. The railway, completed in 1911, opened a significant trade route, above all allowing the French to exploit Yunnan's considerable mineral resources for the benefit of their colonies in Indo-China. During the war against Japan Kunming was a place of haven for east-coast Chinese fleeing the hostilities – their wealth helped the city to grow, as did its vital position as a supply centre. This was the end of the infamous Burma Road and, when that was cut, the centre of a major air supply operation. Factories were also developed to help supply the Chinese war effort. It is a process which has continued steadily since (and Kunming has again played an important role in war supplies during the Vietnam war and the subsequent border fighting) leaving modern Kunming with a substantial industrial base, with broad new boulevards and solid workers' tenements.

Not packed with historical monuments, Kunming nevertheless has very real pleasures. As a city you notice above all that it is a place in which you can get real enjoyment simply walking the streets, something which certainly could not be said of most northern cities. And when you tire there are scores of traditional tea and coffee shops, surviving here – a rarity indeed – in much their original state. Outside the city you'll find Buddhist temples scattered across the land, but it is the landscape itself which stands out – especially the vast extent of Lake Dianchi and the spectacular stone forest at Lunan.

Practicalities

Kunming **airport** lies to the east of town – a 10 minute ride on the CAAC bus will take you to the airline's downtown office on Dongfeng Donglu, right next to the Kunming Hotel. The **railway station** is 2km to the south of the centre, a straightforward ride in on the no.23 bus up Beijing Lu. **Buses** are rather more complicated, but the main terminus (from which

buses leave for Dali) is in the west of the city at the end of the no.1, 2 and 5 local bus routes. On the subject of local buses, watch out for pickpockets, who have gained some notoriety here in recent years.

Looking for a **room**, you'll find the cheapest beds in the *Kunhu Hotel*, though it has little else to recommend it. Dorm beds go for ¥5 and hot showers are available in the afternoon: it's about a 10 minute walk (or short bus hop) from the railway station up Beijing Lu. Reception here is a good place to buy rail tickets out of Kunming. The *Yunnan Hotel* on Dongfeng Xilu is only marginally more expensive and only marginally better. If you can afford it, the *Kunming Hotel* is in an altogether different class, clean, comfortable, friendly and helpful. There are dorms here (¥8) in the older section at the front, but foreigners rarely seem able to get one; the luxurious new building costs ¥16 for a bed in a three-bed room or ¥50 for a double room. The hotel also runs a left luggage operation (50fen per day) which can come in useful if you're making the trip to Dali. There's one final hotel in the north of town with prices very similar to the Kunming – the *Green Lake Hotel* (*Cuihu Binguan*) opposite Green Lake Park. This is twenty minutes on the no.2 bus from the station and a good choice if it's peace and quiet you want – do check that they have rooms, though, as this is where tour groups stay when they come to Kunming (tel.22912).

The centre of **downtown Kunming** lies around the junction of Dongfeng Lu and Zhengyi Lu – in a relatively small area here you'll find the vast majority of the shops and offices you might want to visit, as well as the bulk of the more interesting places to eat. Right on the central junction is the *Kunming Department Store*, on the third floor of which houses the **Friendship Store**. Straight across the road is the **Foreign Language Bookstore**, with a good collection of Chinese classics (in translation), some fascinating Chinese cartoon books and even cassettes of local music. This is also the best place to get a map (CITS issue free ones but they're very poor). Just a few doors from the bookshop along Dongfeng Lu the western **chemist** has a vast array of imported drugs; if you prefer traditional Chinese therapy there's a large local pharmacy to the south at 119 Jinbie Lu and a **Chinese medicine hospital** in the backstreets behind the department store. Still on Dongfeng Lu close to the western chemist you'll find two of Kunming's three **Minority Stores** which sell traditional artefacts and clothing of the province's minority peoples. As for more practical pursuits, the woman in the **Public Security** office has a reputation among travellers throughout China for her helpfulness: if you're here at the beginning of your journey you should stock up with all the visas you'll need. The office, on Beijing Lu, is open from 8–11.30 and 2.30–6 except on Fridays when she attends political study classes. **CITS**, at the front counter of the Kunming Hotel, is also unusually cooperative. The staff speak fluent English and are perhaps the most co-operative in China – even to the extent of providing details of local trips which run in competition to their own. The **Post Office and Telecommunications** building, from where you can make long-distance phone calls, is halfway between these two at the corner of Beijing Lu and Dongfeng Donglu.

Restaurants are again concentrated in the central area – food in Kunming is surprisingly varied, and some of it is very good indeed. As ever, though, most travellers tend to stick to the hotels – the *Kunming* boasts 10 dining rooms (though only 2 ever seem to be open) including a Yunnanese restaurant which specialises in spring rolls – infinitely better than the western version – and also serves ten-course goat or deer banquets. The *Green Lake Hotel* also has a number of different places to eat and serves a good lunch for ¥10, though to this they add a 10 percent service charge, no doubt a sign of the times in China. Local specialities include chicken steamed in the pot, toasted goat's cheese (a tasty side dish) and various Muslim meat dishes, but most famous of all is **Noodles across the Bridge**. According to the story this dish was invented by accident: once upon a time there was a scholar who retreated from the world to study on an island in a lake in the south of the province. His wife had to carry his meals to him across a long wooden bridge, and by the time she arrived the food was always cold – one day, however, she left a rather fatty bird to stew for too long and was amazed to discover that the resultant soup stayed hot all the way across the bridge: a layer of grease sealing in the heat. What you get nowadays is a bowl of rather oily soup and a delicious variety of side dishes to go with it – this is served all over town but for the real thing, and plenty of atmosphere, try the *Yunnan Restaurant* on Nantong Jie just off Jinbie Lu to the west of its junction with Zhengyi Lu. For more **basic meals** there are two small places very near the Kunming Hotel which are popular with travellers and young locals alike: the *Cooking School* and the *Olympic Bar*. There is also an excellent café – again crowded with young locals – right next to the front entrance of Yunnan University on Chin Yuin Lu, on the no.2 bus route.

For snacks, breakfast or simply to sit and rest the traditional **tea-houses** and **coffee shops** take some beating. In most of China these old talking shops were closed during the Cultural Revolution, but Kunming's seem to have been far enough from central authority to have escaped more or less intact. On almost any side street you'll see groups of old men sitting, talking and sipping their tea – there's a particularly popular example in a side-street which runs between Jingxing Jie and Guanghua Jiie behind the department store; this is in the middle of a large market and is a meeting place for bird fanciers who bring their caged birds along with them and hang them from the roof to provide music. Less traditional spots sometimes have more tempting goodies – best of all is the *Vietna-*

mese Coffee House on the north side of Jinbie Lu which specialises in ice cream sodas as well as serving excellent coffee. There's a less crowded coffee shop, along with numerous other noodle stalls and food retail stores, on Baoshan Jie, a small street which runs off Zhengyi Lu immediately behind the Foreign Language bookstore, and there are larger bakery/ice cream shops on the main roads around the centre.

In the evenings there's a tea-house right opposite the Kunhu Hotel which has musical performances and many of the other tea-houses have late night storytelling performances – as enjoyable as they are meaningless to an outsider. Other **nightlife** is distinctly limited: there are cinemas, occasional regional dance or drama performances if you're lucky, and the hotel bars (open till midnight in the *Kunming*!). One more interesting possibility is to catch some local **opera**: walk north along the east side of the canal, past the riverside café, until the land opens out into allotments – amongst these there's an old temple/barn in which for 20fen (including tea) you can enjoy local performers (around 8pm). During the day look out too for the **storytellers** who shelter under huge black umbrellas on the bridge by the canal.

The city

Despite the modern aspect of many of its main streets, much of central Kumming can in fact have changed little since before Liberation: a maze of narrow lanes crowded with market stalls, shops and tea-houses. **Green Lake Park**, a no.2 bus ride from Dongfeng Lu, makes a good place from which to start exploring – if you rise early you'll catch thousands of locals here, practising their Tai Chi. Reclaimed from marshland towards the end of the Yuan dynasty, the park's chief attraction, not unexpectedly, is its lake. At the right time of year you'll find the water carpeted in lotus and other water plants but it's a pleasant place to wander at any time, with a maze of bridges and walkways heading out to the mid-lake pavilion – its arched roof resplendent in glittering, yellow glazed tiles. Around the park you'll also discover a separate boating lake and a small children's playground.

Out of the eastern gate, Cuihu Nanlu leads onto Yuantong Jie. Take the first right, a small side street, and you emerge into a colourful little **market**, its stalls laden with fresh vegetables, herbs, spices, meat and massive slabs of bean curd – another local speciality. Yuantong Jie itself leads on past the small public park in which stands the **Yuantong Buddhist Temple** (open 7.30–7). There are fine gardens here and the temple itself, originally Yuan dynasty (13–14C), features three large bronze Buddhas and roof support beams exquisitely carved with intricate dragon motifs. From the Hill behind the temple there are good views over Kunming and further back in this direction (though to get there you must go out and round by the roads) is the local **zoo** (open 7.30–9) a typically shabby little affair which again offers excellent views.

For a more interesting walk back to the centre, retrace your steps along Cuihu Lu past the park and turn left onto Dongfeng Xilu. Almost immediately you're in an area full of traditional houses and shopfronts: left on Wucheng Lu you'll come across particularly good examples; right on Daguan Jie are more, fronted by the stalls of a regular street **market**. From Wucheng Lu you can thread your way back downtown through more market activity – head along Wuyi Lu and then Minsheng Jie, behind the hospital, to find a particularly lively area brightened by the vociferous activity of songbird vendors and their wares. On Dongfeng Lu and Zhengyi Lu you emerge briefly again into a modern commercial centre, but with Jinbie Lu you're back in provincial China – a haven of Chinese dentists, opticians and hairdressers. Just to the south of Jinbie Lu lie two Tang dynasty **pagodas**, rebuilt after being severely damaged during a 19C rebellion of local Muslims, and now crumbling again.

Perhaps the most exciting of all Kunming's 'sights' comes last – the **Xishuangbanna people's market**. Head up Beijing Lu from its junction with Jinbie Lu and turn left a few yards after PSB. This is the site of a unique trading outlet for the tribesmen. One stall in particular has a gruesome array of human and animal skulls and bones. But keep your cameras out of the way: these are a people who believe that a photograph captures the spirit, and when my companion tried to take one a sword was pulled on him.

AROUND KUNMING – LAKE, HILLS AND FOREST OF STONE

The country around Kunming is rich in interest – above all there's the vast expanse of Lake Dianchi, whose northernmost tip is just a few kilometres south of the city; the heights of Xishan, the Western Hills, overlooking the lake; and the Stone Forest off to the east. Between them are dotted various small temples and villages of interest.

Daguan Park, at the end of the no.4 bus route, hardly qualifies as out of town, but it is from here that you can set off around the lake. The park itself (open from 5.30–9) consists of a maze of elegantly carved rainbow bridges and paths dividing landscaped gardens from small lotus-covered pools. Its centrepiece is the magnificent 3-storey **Daguan** (or Grand View Tower) in the north-west – a large whitewashed building, beautifully decorated with white stone walls, yellow glazed tiles on curved eaves and traditional blue wooden windows; on the doorpost is a famous inscription by the Qing poet *Sun Ranweng*. Nearby are a small botanical garden and a rose garden – well worth the 5fen entrance fee. For a quick trip around the nearest sections of the lake there are boats available for around 50fen per hour: this is much better value than the ¥4 tour which you may also be offered.

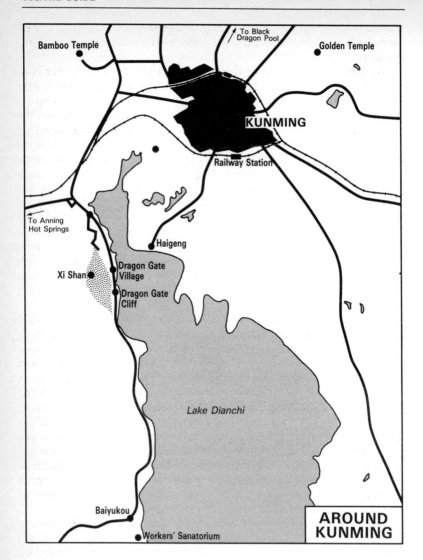

Lake Dianchi and Xishan

The sixth largest freshwater lake in China, **Dianchi** covers an area of some 270 square kilometres, filling a vast fault in Yunnan's central plateau. The quality of its fish has been renowned at least since Marco Polo passed this way in the 13C, but it is the scenic beauty which attracts more people now. The colours in particular are spectacular: the deep blue of the water fading to pale at the shores; the green and brown of the hills to the west and the low lands to the east; the white sails of the junks dotting the surface.

To appreciate the scale of this great water plain, your best bet is to head for Xishan on the local workers' **ferry**, which departs from a jetty near Daguan Park at 8am daily. Take a no.4 bus to the first stop on Daguan Jie after its junction with Huancheng Xilu, just before the terminus – continue walking west and you'll see the departure point on your left. The boat has four stops. First is an hour away at **Haigeng** on the north-eastern shore, a large beach which is a popular spot for swimming. There are facilities here including restaurants and also a fairly regular bus service for central Kunming. The ferry then crosses to the more interesting west bank where it stops at **Dragon Gate Village**, directly below Dragon Gate Cliff in the western hills. The final calls are at **Baiyukou**, a workers' sanatorium, and just beyond this at **Haikou**, a small settlement further south. The whole journey takes 3 hours and the boat leaves Haikou on its return trip at 2pm. The entire trip costs less than ¥1 each way so it's considerably cheaper than the alternative route to the hills – no.5 bus to the end of its route followed by no.6 to Gaoyao bus station.

If you want to reach the top of the hills, though, you'll probably want to take the bus one way at least. **Xizhan**'s summit is at an altitude of some 2,500m, and it is a gruelling climb of almost three hours from Gaoyao to Dragon Gate at the peak. Switchbacking directly up from Dragon Gate Village might be quicker, but this really is steep, and at times a scary ascent. Climbing from Gaoyao you come forst to the **Huatingsi** – a temple built originally as a country retreat for the rulers of the Nan Zhao kingdom, which held sway here around the 12C. It takes the form of a pavilion surrounded by gardens and a small pond, while the temple itself contains several impressive statues. There's a traditional Yunnanese restaurant in the grounds, a handy place to break your journey. Winding on through groves of ancient trees you reach **Taihua Temple**, a 14C construction famous for its 19 bronze statues of Buddha and for its picturesque botanical gardens.

The third major temple here is the Taoist **Sanqingge**, another building which started life as a royal country villa. Less than a kilometre beyond, the path runs into a narrow tunnel carved from the rock, surrounded by carvings and statues. All of these were the work of a Taoist monk, *Wu Laiqing*, and his assistants in the closing years of the 18C – look out especially for two large caves, the Ciyundong and the Yunhuadong. Finally, you reach the great Dragon Gate with its balcony leaning precariously over the wide expanse of Lake Dianchi. The view is tremendous.

There's a local **tourist bus** which makes occasional trips from Gaoyao bus station to the summit if you're feeling lazy (last down at 4pm; last from Gaoyao to Kunming at 8pm), and also various day-trip operators who cover the lake, Xishan and usually one or two other places from the Kunming hotels. Details from CITS.

North and west

There are a number of other sites, north and west of Kunming, which are covered by day-trip coaches or easily done on local transport. If time presses, however, none of these are as worthwhile as the lake and hills or the stone forest.

Anning is a small village 39km west of Kunming or about 18km west of the lake; it's possible to walk from the foothills of Xishan but, frankly, it's not worth the effort (or the 4 hours it takes). Far easier to take a no.18 bus from Kunming's Nantiqiao bus terminus (about 800m west of the Kunming Hotel) which costs 80fen and takes 70 minutes. Buses leave at 8, 11.30 and 2.30, returning at 10.30, 2.00 and 4.30 – book in advance to avoid a real possibility of standing all the way: return tickets are sold at a small shop behind Anning's hotel. The village is dull – though the hotel is very cheap and its restaurant reasonable – and known mainly for its **hot springs**, which for over 500 years have been exploited as a treatment for arthritis, high blood pressure, heart disease and other disorders. You can hire one of the hotel's bathrooms for ¥3 and spend as long as you like soaking in the soothing warm waters. Other than this the surrounding countryside is the only real attraction, criss-crossed with easily explored tracks. Half a mile away – cross the bridge and fork left up the hill – **Caoxi Temple** has a number of unusual statues. Recently restored, the temple was originally constructed by princes from the province of Dali during the T'ang period. Following the road further into the hills, past a number of health resorts for high officials, you are rewarded with increasingly good views of the Yunnan plateau.

North-west of the city, some 12km out, lies the Tang dynasty **Bamboo Temple**. The draw here is an extraordinary series of *arhats*, life-size clay figures, of Buddhas and monks in an orgy of bizarre postures and actions. They were executed by the Sichuan master *Li Guangxiu* towards the end of the last century and are well worth seeing. A no.5 bus followed by a no.7 and an uphill walk for an hour or two will get you there, but it's a lot easier to tag along with a tour for this one.

In the north are two more sites. **Black Dragon Pool** is a rather dull spring set about with gardens and pavilions. The **Golden Temple** is better, although what you see is actually only a copy of the original. Even so it's a spectacularly large and richly adorned building, roofed in copper and standing on a white marble base. Here in the 17C the Manchu rebel *Wu Sangui* set himself up as a warlord, having been sent at the head of an army to suppress one of the constant rebellions. For either of these, buses depart from the northern *Chuanxingulou* terminus (no.3 or 23 to get there): bus no.10 for the pool, no.9 for the temple.

The stone forest

A sight that attracts large numbers of visitors, both Chinese and otherwise, is **Shilin** – the **Stone Forest**. It is situated well over 100km to the east of Kunming and to do it justice you really need to stay overnight in the small resort that has been built right next to the 'forest'. A forest of limestone pinnacles, eroded and weather-split into fantasmagorical shapes, this striking landform has become the centrepiece of a quiet, but nevertheless thriving, tourist resort. There are many such stone forests in Yunan. The addition of steps, walkways and several pavilions to this particular landscape seems to represent the Chinese tourist's seal of approval. Broken bottles and copious litter quickly take the novelty out of a stroll through the pinnacles, the tallest of which are not much higher than a two-storey house. The frequency with which local tribespeople jump out from behind the different rockforms offering embroidered bags, hats and dresses for sale only adds to the sad feeling that the place has been over-commercialised already.

The Stone Forest needn't be the only reason for making your way out from Kunming. The resort's *Shilin Hotel*, with accommodation between ¥4 and ¥25 (dormitories to double rooms), puts on a first-class **dance** display every evening. Performed by Sani people from a village backing onto the Shilin resort, these dances have an authenticity and sponaneity that contrasts starkly with the tackiness that packages the Stone Forest.

If you are able to get out to Shilin on a Tuesday you'll be able to catch **market day** in the nearby town of Lunan every Wednesday. Two streets play host to large numbers of tribespeople selling their wares and sporting their colourful and proudly worn costumes. Motorbike taxis outside the main gates of the resort regularly make the 30minute run into Lunan.

The Shilin Hotel is not the only **accommodation** option at the Stone Forest. There is a hotel opposite the point at which the bus from Kunming unloads its passengers. Non-Chinese, and non-overseas Chinese, have stayed there for less than ¥4 per night.

To get to the forest you have two basic alternatives. There's a **tourist minibus** which leaves from the *Kunming Hotel* at 7.30am daily. Return tickets cost ¥12 and should be bought at least one day in advance: the bus is cramped, but gets there at least an hour quicker than the local bus, in around 3 hours and your ticket will be valid next day if you stay. The **local bus** costs ¥4 and leaves from the Xishan terminus in the north-west of Kunming. Take a no.2 there followed by a no.17 to Shilin. Again, buy your ticket in advance unless you want to risk standing much of the way.

ONWARD TO DALI

The bus journey to Dali takes 11 hours – a nightmare passage over twisting mountain roads with a maniac at the wheel: the drivers' habit of coasting down every hill is particularly alarming. When you arrive, however, you'll tell yourself it was all worthwhile, for **DALI**, open only since February 1984, is a place where few modern travellers have ever been: a rural town, 2000 metres up, bordered on one side by snowcapped mountains, on the other by a lake 25 miles long and 2 miles wide. The one hotel offers only the most basic accommodation, its outside toilet serves as the local public convenience, you wash in the local bathhouse and you eat in the converted living rooms of a couple of enterprising local families who ask you to sign their visitors' books as you enter. Already there's a new 'luxury' hotel under construction (bathroom and toilet in every room) and locals are planning to set up bike and taxi hire businesses – so catch it before the commercial boom. The place is particularly exciting during the annual Spring Fair – 15–22 April – when there are horse races, dancing and a week-long market.

The daily **bus** leaves Kunming at 7am from the long-distance bus station in the west of the city (at the end of the no.1, 2 or 5 routes) or less reliably from the back of the Kunhu Hotel. Seats are allocated on a first-come-first-served basis starting from the front of the bus, so get yours early – the nearer the back, the more you'll be flung around by the bumps en route. Demand for tickets is considerable. You should go to the west bus station 48 hours before your intended departure time. There are two very brief (20 minute) stops along the way, plus a half hour for lunch at a transport canteen – food can be excellent, or it can be inedible. Half an hour before Dali the bus passes through XIAGYUAN, a larger and more industrialised town. Here there's a **hotel** – the *Erhai Number One Hotel* – which offers considerably more luxury than the one in Dali (and is also much more expensive at around ¥15 for a bed). It's at 140 Renmin Lu, left out of the bus station, right at the crossroads and straight on for half a mile. Buses run fairly frequently between Xiagyuan and Dali, but to no apparent timetable: they only leave when the bus is full.

On arriving in Dali the bus will probably drop you off inside the town gates in which case you'll be only two minutes from the *Dali Number Two Hotel* (No.1 is in Xiagyuan). You might be off-loaded at the terminus outside the town gates in which case you'll have a 15-minute walk on your hands to get to the Number Two Hotel (the only one at which foreigners can stay in Dali). Turn left out of the terminus and walk through the South Gate. Once in the old town you should keep an eye out for a sign, on a wall to your left, that gives clear directions in English to the hotel. A **bed** in a 4- or 5-bedded room here costs ¥1.60; in a 3-bed room they're ¥4 each and for a double room (this is one of the few Chinese hotels with real double beds) you pay ¥14. All prices are 25 percent cheaper for students studying in China, but you'll need valid identification. None of the hotel staff speaks English but a teacher from one of the local middle schools calls round each evening to help translate.

Look for him around 7pm when the bus arrives – he speaks excellent English and is a useful source of information for anything you might want to know about the area. To get to the hotel washroom walk through a small temple area to the left of the hotel: toilet facilities are revolting. There's a public **bathhouse** just 200 yards away where you can get a bath for 60fen – turn left out of the hotel, left and left again (open 8–12 and 2–6).

As for **food**, you're best off buying breakfast from one of the small cake shops along the main street, just down the road from the hotel. For lunch and dinner there's a choice of the *Happy Restaurant* or the *Garden Restaurant*. These are almost next door to each other on the road leading down to the lake: both family-run affairs set up to cater for travellers after Dali was opened up. The *Happy* has better atmosphere, but the food is slightly better at the *Garden* – both serve beautifully fresh fish from the lake and a variety of vegetable dishes. Despite the English names and menus, food and prices remain genuine; gorge yourself for ¥4. If you want to get some of your own food there's a weekly **market** in Dali too. This is held on different days in each month, so check locally. Better still is the Monday market at SHAPIM, an event worth going out of your way for. You can take a bus from Dali or hitch a ride on one of the hundreds of tractors and carts headed that way: be prepared to bargain for embroidered wares brought along by the Bai people, or to catch the odd piglet which breaks loose through the crowds.

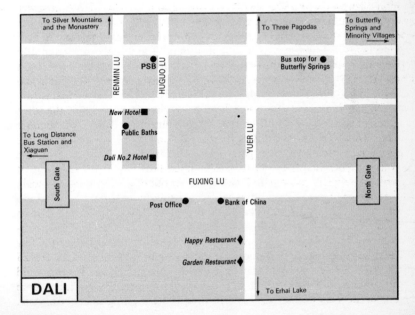

Other facilities are thin on the ground. There's no CITS at present and although there is a **Public Security** office (up the street from the hotel) they can only issue permits in exceptional circumstances. The **Bank of China** and the **Post Office** are both on Fuxing Lu, the main street – they open from 9–12 and 2–6. So far there's nowhere to hire a bike. For a **taxi** you have to telephone to Xiagyuan, easiest done through the interpreter.

Seeing Dali

Dali has a long history: as much as 2000 years ago it was a stop on early trade routes from China into Burma and India, and from around the 9C to the 13C it was the capital of a kingdom known as Nan Zhao County and later as the Kingdom of Dali. The influence of local *Bai* rulers spread well into modern Thailand, Vietnam and Burma. In 1253 the state of Dali became part of the Yuan Chinese Empire and so the area has remained – in name at least – ever since. Today the **Bai people** still make up 80 percent of Dali's 400,000 population, the rest being mostly Han Chinese or Muslim.

The city also has long been renowned as a beauty spot and four aspects of its beauty in particular are singled out by local mythology: the Shanguan flower which grows in the hills, said to rival even the loveliness of Bai women; the snow on Cang Shan; the moon on the lake; and the Xiagyuan wind. These can still be experienced, though the Shanguan flower will require some luck.

Cang Shan, Silver Mountain, has 19 peaks which remain snowcapped as late as the beginning of June – it can be reached by an occasional bus which runs along the high mountainside road above the village. There are several Buddhist monasteries here – lowest in Zhong He on the tenth peak, known as middle peak, a climb of two hours or so. You are advised by locals against climbing any higher than Zhong He towards the 4000m summit: weather conditions can change with alarming rapidity. While I was in Dali a party of eight Chinese botanists had to be rescued by a local search party. Even in town the weather can change very fast: warm sun giving way to thunderstorms and back to sun as clouds build up in the mountains, sweep down and are rapidly dispersed by the Xianguan wind. At any time, be prepared for rain.

Erhai Lake lies in the other direction, about an hour's walk across the fields. It's a beautiful setting and a boat trip here is a tempting prospect. Once again locals will try to warn you off because of the dangers – in this case the Xiagyuan wind, which gusts down from a gap in the mountains towards Xiagyuan and is subject to capricious shifts – but this seems to be taking caution too far; there are plenty of fishermen about who survive well enough. One of them may well be persuaded to take you out. One of the fishing methods here, which you may see, seems pretty barbaric: they use cormorants to do the work for them, tying their throats so they cannot swallow the fish.

On the west side of the lake lies Butterfly Spring, about 30 minutes by bus to the north of Dali. On the way you first pass three tall, white, **Buddhist pagodas** – the largest of them, a Tang structure dating from around AD750 almost 70 metres high. The smaller structures are a few hundred years younger – all stood close to a monastery which has since been destroyed, but there are small buildings nearby which house its historical records, and if you pass this way on a Sunday you'll find many elderly Chinese at prayer. During the April Fair, on Beggar's Day, locals visit the pagodas dressed in rags, collecting alms from passers-by. It's about half an hour's walk from here back to Dali. Further on, the bus passes through the lakeside village of **Xizhou**, with some delightful traditional buildings, and then stops at the Bai village of **Zhou Cheng**. Before Liberation the people here were skilled dyers. As a trade that has largely died out, but the survival of the craft is evident in the locally dyed materials for the villagers' bright costumes. **Butterfly Spring**, when you get there, is supposed to be the haunt of a number of beautiful rare butterflies and of a variety of unusual plants which attract them (including the Shanguan Flower). None were much in evidence on my visit. The spring itself is unremarkable – you'd probably be better off spending your time at Xizhou or Zhou Cheng. In late May/early June Dali celebrates the **Feast of Butterflies**, a round of festivities lasting about three days during which young men and women are allowed to go off into the mountains together!

On the northeastern corner of Lake Erhai lies the small fishing town of Wase. With no road link whatsoever running around the northern end of the lake, and only a rough track heading south to Xiagyuan, Wase and its neighbouring villages provide a glimpse of life untainted by any attempt to cater to western travellers. (The only place you'll be able to stay at is Wase's Public Security Office. In mid-1986 the register here had recorded less than 20 visitors.) Wase's main street, flanked by mud-brick buildings and narrow, unpaved alleyways, is endlessly photogenic. Running from a cluttered and continually used harbour front through the town's main square and eventually into rice fields beyond, this thoroughfare is lined with market stalls and shops manned by Bai people in their red and blue tribal outfits. Pigs, cows and goats forage their way up and down the street. Wase depends on its fishing as much as its rice cultivation and its small harbour is a mess of majestic, bulky square-rigged fishing boats.

All the paths from Dali lead down to the jetty from where a boat makes the crossing over to Wase. Leaving late afternoon when enough passengers have boarded, you should aim to be at the jetty around 4.30pm. You can carry bicycles across with you. The return journey is at dawn daily. A track leads east out of Wase through smaller villages and townships before it heads south behind the hills lining the lakes eastern side. From Wase back down to Xiagyuan is at least 20 miles.

An eight-hour bus journey north of Dali takes you to Lijiang. At an elevation already of close to 12,000 feet and only 130 miles (the way the crow flies) from the border with Tibet, the road north from Dali can be thought of as another of the Tibetan roads. (See below)

On first impressions, Lijiang is uninspiring. The modern town has all predictable marks of a hastily constructed functional outpost. One of the few towns where the Mao statue dominating the main boulevard wasn't torn down, Lijiang's modern streets are no different to other uniformly planned Chinese towns. Yet tucked away behind the main street is the start of Lijiang's extensive old town. Wooden buildings overlooking cobble-stoned streets lead up and over a hill to Lijiang's river. The old town's main thoroughfare divides into two here, running along both banks of the river until it joins the central market square. Here more single-storey houses built over uneven cobble-stoned streets fan off in four directions. Much of the streetscape in Lijiang's old town is more than 200 years old. Such an extensive and well-preserved remnant of China's feudal past has not survived by accident. Chou-en-Lai, it is said, managed to place a preservation order on Lijiang's old town. Consequently it escaped the ravages of the Cultural Revolution that has made such proudly kept evidence of the past a rarity in so much of China. Yet the dogmatic destruction of the Cultural Revolution certainly extended to the upper reaches of Yunnan. Buddhist temples around Lijiang bear the marks of desecration visitors to China soon come to recognise. Yet Lijiang survives. An old man sits on a humpbacked bridge in the shade of a willow tree smoking a long bamboo pipe and watching the stream pass below. An old lady, wearing the blue, black and white tunic of the indigenous Nakhi minority tribespeople, makes her way down a twisting cobblestoned street and disappears through the entrance into a small wooden dwelling whose walls slant with old age. Doors, windows and shutters remain open to the curiosity of a passer by. A cottage industry thrives: a tailor in one house, a carpenter in another, a circle of Nakhi women busily embroidering tunics in a wide courtyard. It is as if the whole village were a film set constructed to portray a sentimental scene of Chinese provincial life. Yet it is unself-consciously genuine.

While the younger generation no longer wear the traditional tunic, the older women in Lijiang's old town and in surrounding villages in this part of Yunnan hold to the tradition. The Nakhi are descendants of Tibetan nomads, who centuries ago made their homes in Lijiang. The Nakhi introduced agriculture at 12,000 feet. In summer today the roads in northern Yunnan are intermittently smothered with wheat for passing vehicles to perform threshing. The religion the Nakhi brought with them was Tibetan Lamaism. It thrived alongside Chinese Taoism and animism. The dress of the Nakhi women has survived unchanged for hundreds of years. The cape they all wear is the cosmos on their back. The upper part is a band of dark blue representing the sky; the lower half of creamy silk or sheepskin stands for the light of day. The two halves are separated by a row of discs that symbolize the stars.

In mid-1986 there was one hotel catering to foreigners. It is about five minutes from the main intersection; your bus driver from Dali will provide directions. Four-bed and three-bed dorms cost ¥6 and upwards. A few miles north of Lijiang is a herbal pharmacy run by a most welcoming gentleman by the name of Dr. Ho. Ask for Dr. Ho, The Clinic of Chinese Herbs in Beisha village at the reception of the foreigners hotel. Dr. Ho, who began studying herbs in 1950s, provides free medical service to anybody who cares to call. He places great faith in the curative powers of a kaleidoscopic stock of herbs. Since he received official sanction from the local authorities to practise medicine, he has added a modest medicine chest of modern drugs to his surgery. Whether or not you are impressed by his claims to have restored to health patients with ailments ranging from chronic bronchitis, stomach ulcers to TB and cancer, his personal account of persecution between 1949 and 1976 certainly deserves a sympathetic hearing. A few minutes cycle ride beyond Beisha village lies Yufeng Si – Jade Dragon Monastery – a beautifully preserved temple lying in the shadow of snow-capped Jade Snow Mountain. Dr. Ho will provide directions.

To leave Lijiang you do not have to double back to Kunming. A daily bus makes a ten-hour run east to a small town called Jinjiang. Jinjiang is on the Kunming to Chengdu railway line. Journey time to Chengdu is just under 15 hours, though by getting on the train midway between two major stations its not possible to buy a hard sleeper ticket unless you try to upgrade your hard seat once on board. The fact that the Lijiang bus makes an evening connection with the train makes it highly unlikely that you will be able to upgrade to hard sleeper. Hard seat tickets to Chengdu are ¥15.

The most exciting alternative after Lijiang is of course Tibet. A daily bus doubles back west for a short distance and then heads 100 miles further north to Zhongdian. Though still within the northern extremities of Yunnan Province, Zhongdian marks the beginning of the Tibetan Plateau – geographically and ethnically. The town's buildings are unmistakably Tibetan in style. A predominance of people of Tibetan origin, yak butter and *chang* mark Zhongdian as the first Tibetan town on the Tibetan road.

North of Zhongdian the going becomes less predictable. There is a real possibility of being turned back by Public Security Officials who consider the route into Tibet unsuitable for foreigners. In mid-1986 travellers heading out of Yunnan into Tibet were being turned back at Deden – the last major town before the border with Tibet. Likewise, in mid-1986, it was easy to find people in Dali or Kunming who had made it successfully from Tibet out into Yunan.

Less than 100 miles beyond Deden the road reaches Markam having followed the dramatic upper reaches of the Mekong. At Markam you are on the Chengdu to Lhasa route; a steady stream of determined travellers has to all intents and purposes rendered this road open.

XISHUANG BANNA

The area of **XISHUANG BANNA** lies in the far south of Yunnan, bordering Laos and Burma. It was deemed out of bounds while I was in Yunnan, but travellers before and since have made it there; it's reputed to be a stunning tropical region, beautiful and relaxed. Originally inhabited exclusively by the **Dai people** (who are also found across the borders) the area has to some extent been consciously resettled to affirm Chinese control. The Dai, though, remain the majority and their culture survives relatively intact: they are Buddhists and in the jungle countless temples lie in ruins – some are being reconstructed. There is no official reason why Xishuang Banna is closed at certain times; certainly tour groups and Overseas Chinese seem to have less problems than independent travellers – but persistent rumour has it that the place is used by high ranking Party officials in need of a break. If this is true, you'll have better luck with permits in summer.

To get a permit for **JINHONG**, capital of Xishuang Banna, apply to Public Security in Kunming. The journey involves flying to SIMAO, two hundred miles west of Jinhong, and embarking on a 5 hour bus journey from there. This almost inevitably means spending the night in Simao – there's a reasonable hotel on the main street which offers dorm beds for ¥4. In Jinhong you must have your permit endorsed by Public Security – they'll rarely grant you more than a 3-day stay, though on occasions this can be extended. The hotel here is said to be pretty good, and in the immediate surrounds are Dai villages which can be visited by local bus, or even on foot.

TRAVEL DETAILS

Trains
From Guilin: Liuzhou (3 daily, 3hrs), Nanning (1, 15hrs), Kunming (1, 33hrs), Zhanjiang (2, 13hrs), Guangzhou (1 – via Henyang, 24hrs).
From Liuzhou: Nanning (1, 8hrs), Guiyang (1, 21hrs), Zhanjiang (1, 12hrs).
From Nanning: Liuzhou (1, 8hrs), Zhanjiang (2, 10hrs).
From Guiyang: Liuzhou (1, 2hrs), Kunming (1, 15hrs).
From Kunming: Guiyang (1, 15hrs), Chengdu (1, 25hrs).

Buses
From Guilin: Yangshuo (10 daily, 2hrs), Wuzhou (2, 12hrs), Guangzhou (1, 36hrs – including an overnight stop in Wuzhou).
From Kunming: Dali (1, 12hrs).

From Nanning: Beihai (1, 7hrs).
From Dali: Kunming (1, 12hrs).
From Beihai: Zhanjiang (2, 5hrs), Nanning (1, 7hrs), Haikou (1, 110hrs).

Ferries
From Guilin: Three a week to Wuzhou (from the port at Pinglo).
From Nanning:PB Occasional service to Wuzhou – when the river's high enough.
From Wuzhou: Daily to Guangzhou (13hrs), occasional service to Nanning (as above).
Several other cities have sporadic river ferry connections: check CITS for details.

Flights
Airports at Guilin, Kunming, Nanning, Guiyang, Baoshan, Simao.

BEIHAI	北海	KUNMING	昆明
DALI	大理	LIUZHOU	柳州
GUILIN	桂林	NANNING	南宁
GUIYANG	贵阳	SHILIN	石林
JINHONG	景洪	YANGSHUO	阳朔

Chapter eight
SICHUAN

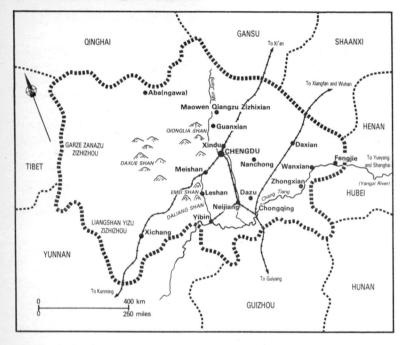

China's largest province, with a population of over 100 million and rising, **Sichuan** – literally the Four Rivers – lies in enforced isolation, the great mountain ranges of Tibet at its back and further peaks enclosing the rest of its borders. Historically, the only ways out have been either over the ancient mountain paths, crossing sheer hillsides by means of wooden galleries driven into the cliff, or by way of the Yangzi River which hurtles out through narrow gorges into central China. The 9C poet, Li Bai, wrote that the road to Sichuan was more difficult than the road to heaven, and it wasn't until 1956 that its capital Chengdu was finally connected to the rest of the country by rail. Despite this isolation, or maybe even because of it, Sichuan, once the kingdom of Shu, has for centuries been one of China's most prosperous regions – a result both of its innovative farming methods, beginning with Li Bing's great irrigation scheme of the 3C BC, and its tradition of resistance to authority, which had long made it a refuge for displaced peasants who brought with them tools and new skills. Its climate, too, meant that Sichuan could become almost self-sufficient: sheltered from the harsh north-west winds by the mountains, and with an abundant rainfall, mild temperatures and fertile soil, there's almost nothing that won't grow on its terraced hillsides and plains. Significantly, when the Japanese invaded China in 1937, it was to Sichuan that the nationalist government retreated for safety . . .

In politics, too, Sichuan has historically played the maverick, rebelling early on against the viciousness and implacability of the Cultural Revolution (which had left the province in the early 1970s poor, hungry and agriculturally devastated) and in part instigating the country's drive towards decentralisation and greater freedom of enterprise. Zhao Ziyang, current premier of China and local party leader at the time, instituted under the auspices of fellow native of Sichuan, Deng Xiaoping, flexible farming reforms and the 'responsibility system', which left peasants free to sell their own produce. As a result, Sichuan is firmly back on its feet and well on the road to becoming, once again, China's foodbowl. You'll notice also that the province's industrial face, with the resultant pollution, is daily more manifest as it competes energetically with the eastern seaboard for foreign markets.

But above all Sichuan is a province of variety, ranging from its lively and well-to-do capital, **Chengdu**, to the modern, massive and crowded industrial port of **Chongqing**, coal city and wartime capital. Outside Chengdu are a number of interesting day-trips: principally **Xindu** with its Tang dynasty monastery and remarkable 3C BC **Dujiangyan Irrigation System** – and, 3 hours south by train, **Emei Shan** mountain and some of Sichuan's most breathtaking scenery.

Everywhere you'll find the influence of **Buddhism** predominates, not least at **Leshan** where a giant Buddha, for foreigners at least one of the most grandiose and evocative symbols of China, stares stonily across the water, and further east at **Dazu**, whose isolation has left a set of stone carvings which have been marvellously preserved from destruction. **Western Sichuan** is by contrast more remote and little visited by tourists, the only foray most of them make being the 9-hour trip from Chengdu to the **Wolong Nature Reserve**, best known of the province's nature areas, where, controversially, the government is resettling indigenous Tibetans so as to give the giant pandas more room to roam. There's a marked Tibetan element here, in faces, clothes, colours and buildings – a flavour which appears in Sichuan's **food**, whose hot, spicy individuality has never been entirely smoothed away by the tide of Han cultural uniformity. Actually, minority peoples make up a large part of Sichuan's population, and three **autonomous areas** in the north, south and west occupy half the province. You may be able to visit the nature reserve at **Juizhaigou** – Nine Village Gully – in the **A'ba Tibetan Autonomous Area** in the mountains north of Chengdu; nearer is the **Maowen Qiangzu Autonomous Area** – listed as open to foreigners though few authorities seem to be aware of the fact. As regards routes: come or go to **Wolong via**

Kunming and you'll find much of the journey spectacular; so too, on the other side of the province, the **river cruise down the Yangzi** as far as Yichang.

CHENGDU

If you come into Sichuan from the north, **CHENGDU** may well be your first stop, smaller than Chongqing but nevertheless provincial capital for something like 2400 years. Bang in the middle of the Western Plain, practically the only flat stretch of the province, it's a city with two faces – broad avenues lined with trees and flowers, and small narrow streets of half-timbered houses with wooden porches crowded with pot plants in the traditional style. Once ringed by 12 miles of battlements and gates (damaged in 1949, pulled down in the 1960s), the city's remoteness meant it played little part in mainstream Chinese history, but for all that it remained a wealthy and sophisticated centre for industry, crafts and learning for more than 2000 years. As far back as the Han dynasty it earned the name of 'Brocade City': its silk, washed by local women in the Jinjiang – Brocade River – south of town, travelled westward along the caravan routes as far as imperial Rome; and records speak of the thousand and more goldsmiths, silversmiths and lacquer craftsmen working here at much the same time. Under the Tang dynasty Chengdu was much praised by poets, and the Emperor Xuan Zong chose it as his refuge from a rebellion sparked off by his infatuation with his beautiful concubine Yang Guifei. Later, under the Song, this was a great printing centre – as well as books and dictionaries, paper money was first printed here. Sacked by the invading Mongols in 1271, Chengdu recovered soon enough to astound Marco Polo, a visitor from the court of Kublai Khan, by its great host of trading boats moving up and down the river. And since then Chengdu has survived more than its fair share of punitive wars and revolution to become a major industrial centre, with a university founded in the 1920s, an important School of Chinese Medicine, and a strong cultural tradition enjoyed by a million and a half people. Very few key sites or buildings have survived this chequered history, and although you can visit the poet Du Fu's thatched cottage, and a sprinkling of temples and tombs, you may find some less interesting than the streets you walk through to reach them. Don't despair though: things to see outside the city more than compensate.

Finding your way about

Two of Chengdu's three rivers make a loop which encloses the city centre on three sides, while beyond the city the railway line describes a great curve to the north east and south. The **main railway station** – dilapidated

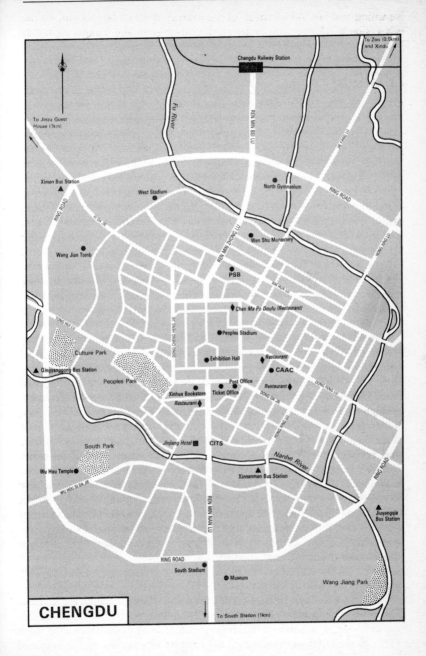

To Zoo (0.5km) and Xindu

Chengdu Railway Station

To Jinzu Guest House (1km)

Fu River

REN MIN BEI LU

JI FANG LU

RING ROAD

DONG HONG LU

Ximen Bus Station

West Stadium

North Gymnasium

RING ROAD

JI DA JIE

Wang Jian Tomb

REN MIN ZHONG LU

Wen Shu Monastery

PSB

XIN HUA LU

Chen Ma Po Doufu (Restaurant)

TONG HUI LU

DONG CHENG HENG JIE

Peoples Stadium

Culture Park

Exhibition Hall

Restaurant

Qingyanggong Bus Station

CAAC

Peoples Park

Post Office

Restaurant

DONG FENG LU

Xinhua Bookstore

Ticket Office

DONG DA JIE

SI TH LU

Restaurant

RING ROAD

South Park

Jinjiang Hotel

CITS

Nanhe River

Wu Hou Temple

WU HOU SI DA JIE

Xinnanmen Bus Station

REN MIN NAN LU

Jiuyangqia Bus Station

RING ROAD

South Stadium

Museum

Wang Jiang Park

To South Station (1km)

CHENGDU

and chaotic with repairs – is in the north at the top of Renmin Lu, a long main road which dives south, over the Fu river, through a city centre of ponderous public buildings and across the Nan river to the **south railway station**. The no.16 bus (if you can find it among the confusion of the main station's roundabout) follows this road and passes the main hotel for foreigners, the *Jinjiang Binguan*, which counts among its many facilities (**bank, post office, CITS**, etc.) several dorms for about ¥10. There are, too, masses of shops and a number of reasonably priced **restaurants**, as well as a delightful rooftop bar blessed with a cooling breeze, plenty of rattan chairs and even a billiard room. Another useful bus is the no.1 trolley, which runs from the main station through the city centre to one of the **long-distance bus stations** at Xin Nanmen (a further bus station is at Ximen – West Gate). For **tickets**, there are booking offices at all of the main stations and in the central city square at the top end of Renmin Nanlu; **CAAC** are centrally placed at 31 Beixin Jie and **Public Security** on the 16 bus route in Xinhua Donglu.

The city and its sights

First on many Chinese itineraries, **Du Fu Caotang** or the Thatched Cottage of the Tang dynasty poet Du Fu is something of a misnomer, since not only is it not remotely like a thatched cottage, but Du Fu never even lived here at all. Instead the poet, when he came to Chengdu as a minor official from the imperial court of Chang'an in 759, holed up in a grass-roofed dwelling outside the west wall – a simple place where he wrote some 200 of his 1400 surviving poems. In an age of great poets he was considered one of the greatest, his achievement his originality, writing about people as well as nature – about poverty, war and human suffering. Two centuries after his death this temple was built in his memory: rebuilt and enlarged several times, it now includes a main hall with a statue of Du Fu, a museum wing with some marvellous early woodblock and handwritten versions of his poems and an extensive garden – rather characterless unless the crab apples, azaleas and camellias are in flower to soften a crowded, dingy and formless collection of buildings. Getting to the temple is easy: a no.35 bus will take you direct from the hotel, or you can pick up a no.27 as far as the Wenhua Gongyuan Culture Park and walk for 15 minutes through the rather smelly gardens.

An erratic shuttle bus connects the temple with the much restored Tang dynasty **Wu Hou Temple** in the south of the city – also accessible by a no.27 bus or a no.1 from Renmin Lu. This is dedicated to Zhu Geliang, the famous strategist of the Three Kingdoms period (AD220–265) and prime minister of the state of Shu (of which Chengdu was capital), housing his statue, a tablet from 809 recording his achievements and the tomb of the emperor he was loyal to, Lui Bei – who lies buried here, it's said, alongside his two wives. Historical associations apart, though, there's little here of much interest, and on the whole it makes a dank and gloomy place to pass any time.

More lively, however, and also on the no.1 trolley bus route, is the **Wen Shu Monastery**, whose four halls, swathed in incense smoke, are well weathered and, unlike Wu Hou, not over embellished. The second hall is cordoned off, but you can peer in to see the floor awash with brightly coloured patchwork prayer cushions; the next contains a row of gilt *arhats* under glass – look for the one whose eyebrows droop on to his chest – while the last hall sports a wonderful painting of a creature (cat or dog?) behind a smiling Buddha. In each hall sits a monk, and the temple is full of locals posturing to Buddha and showing their children how to do it – nice for once to see the worshippers outnumbering the sightseers. Outside, the atmosphere of the monastery compound is no less busied, its centrepiece – other than a peaceful garden with water and bamboo – a noisy tea-house jam-packed with Chinese clamouring for refreshment. Clearly, Wen Shu is very much a working monastery, and worth a visit for just that reason.

The rest of Chengdu's sights are rather scattered, so while you're in the north of the city best drop in on the **Tomb of Wang Jian**, on the no.25 bus route between the main station and the Cultural Park. Wang was ruler of Shu during the Five Dynasties period (907–60) and this, though not one of Chengdu's most spectacular spots, has sculptures, engravings and imperial trinkets, that are worth the short detour if you're not pushed for time.

If you are, better head straight south of the city centre, where the **Wangjiang Lou** (Pavilion for Viewing the River) sits in a small park hugging the river bank just beyond the gates of Sichuan University – reachable by the no.27 bus. A Ming dynasty building, this is said to be the spot where the Tang poetess Xue Tao lived and used the local well water to wash and dye a special kind of red paper – her own technique and still available today. These days there are three southern-style buildings given over to displays of scrollwork and bonsai, and, outside, some muted surrounding gardens, brushed by the breeze from the river and cut with paths arched with a hundred varieties of bamboo. Still on the no.27 bus route, there's the **Provincial Museum** (closed on Mondays), quiet and airy and refreshingly free of the gloom that pervades so many of these buildings. Often overlooked by guidebooks, this displays finds from Sichuan, conveniently gathered into one place from all the corners of a province you could never hope to see in its entirety. The ground floor takes in ancient history, with an amusing figure of a Han court jester and a Qing brocade loom, as well as some fine stone rubbings and ceramics – all heavily influenced by the art of Tibet and south-west China.

Upstairs a wealth of photographs and ephemera tells of the revolutionary period and the Long March – extremely good.

Eating, shopping and culture

You'll find Chengdu a cheerful and relaxed city – relatively affluent, full of activity and a nice place just to be, with girls in colourful dresses and permed hair window-shopping arm-in-arm, streets full of flowers, especially during the spring flower festival, and market stalls heaped with oranges, plums and apricots. In fact, stalls cram most of Chengdu's narrow central streets, along with countless other small businesses: street butchers with great dollops of meat on fierce hooks, shops given over to repairs, papermaking, tin beating; elsewhere an entire street devoted to cobblers, in another a clothmarket composed of whirring arrays of sewing machines. And, of course, hordes of bicycles, some with squawking geese strung from handlebars heading for market, others hung with small children strapped tenuously to the rider's back. If you fancy joining in there's a *hire shop* left out of the hotel (open 8am–10pm) which charges just 30fen for what makes a good value and ideal way of exploring the city and nearby market towns. But take care – one of the chief local amusements seems to be standing at street corners watching cyclists and jaywalkers being fined for traffic offences.

Eating-wise, bear in mind that the lavish use of red pepper and spices in Sichuan cooking can feel like it's taking the lining off your stomach, and eat accordingly. Dish titles should be enough to remind you: choose from *Maoshi Yishangshu* (ants climbing up a tree), *Chen Mapo Doufu* (grandmother's spicy beancurd) or *Dandanmian* – carrying pole noodles – which street vendors used to sell from pots slung on a carrying pole. If you feel lazy it's possible to order speciality dishes in advance from the hotel's main *dining room*; more adventurously, try the *Chengdu Canting* in Shengli Zhonglu, the *Furong Canting* in Renmin Nanlu or the *Tianfu Jiujia* in Cidong Jie. Or, if you feel in need of a cure, try the *Tongrengtang* restaurant where you state your ailment and they serve up the dish most suitable. For **cheap snacks** let your nose do the choosing down Dongfeng Lu.

For **shopping**, the best streets are Renmin Lu for brocades, crafts and fabrics, and Chunxi Lu for large stores (not least the Friendship Store), old books and Chinese medicines (from Derentang Yaodian); for antiques there's a shop in Shangye Chang Jie. On the whole you'll find that Chengdu offers a better range of better quality goods than most Chinese provincial cities.

Chengdu's centre is similarly well loaded with **theatres and cinemas**. If you decide to go to the opera, eat first or else treat the performance as an aperitif rather than sitting out the full two hours or more, for though the costumes are beautiful the story lines can be pretty heavy going. Many of the locals prefer to spend their evenings queueing up to have a flash photo taken in front of the long row of luridly lit fountains near the Mao Statue and Exhibition Hall – a raucously successful business that must rank as one of the best examples of China's new western-style enterprise.

OUTSIDE CHENGDU

Some 18km north of Chengdu (buses half-hourly from the railway round-about bus station), a pleasant 40-minute journey through market garden and paddyfield, lies **XINDU** – a market town knee-deep in summertime in spring onions, tomatoes and green vegetables, and stalls selling a locally made and highly coloured basketware. It's pleasant enough, and well worth an indolent stroll, but what really draws people here is the **Bao-guang Si** (Monastery of Divine Light) – a large and still influential complex from the Tang dynasty, reconstructed in the 17C in an odd mix of grandeur and austerity and now comprising 5 halls around 16 courtyards. These days it's something of a tourist blackspot but worth seeing nonetheless, its treasures including a *stone tablet* from AD540 cut with the figures of 1000 Buddhas, an unusually wide range of paintings and calligraphy from the Qing and Ming dynasties and some tiny jewel-like gardens that hide away in secluded corners. Look, too, for the 13-storey leaning *stupa* and, in the Arhat Hall, a set of comical statues sculpted in 1851. These all represent Buddhist saints but for two, which depict the emperors Kangxi and Qianlong, clearly noticeable by their beards and royal boots and capes. If after all this you're hungry, there's a *vegetarian restaurant* in the monastery compound, delightfully airy, clean and cheap, and close by, **Gui Hu** (Osmanthus Lake), where if you have time you can let your meal go down and visit the **memorial hall** to the Ming scholar Yang Shengan – on an island in the centre.

Further west is **GUANXIAN**, and its principal attraction the 3C BC **Dujiangyan IRRIGATION SCHEME**, connected with Chengdu by frequent buses from the West Gate station – a 1½ hour journey through rice paddy dotted with busy peasants and languid water buffalo, cooling off in ditch water. The town itself is worth only scant attention, however, so on arriving turn left down the main street and head straight for the park which encloses the original heart of the irrigation scheme (it's been much expanded over the years) – really the only reason anyone comes to Guanxian at all. First thing you see here is the **Fulong Guan**, Subduing Dragon Taoist Temple, a faded wooden building with a rickety upper storey and magical animal carvings on the curved tile roof, erected during the Jin dynasty to commemorate the building of the dam, and with a

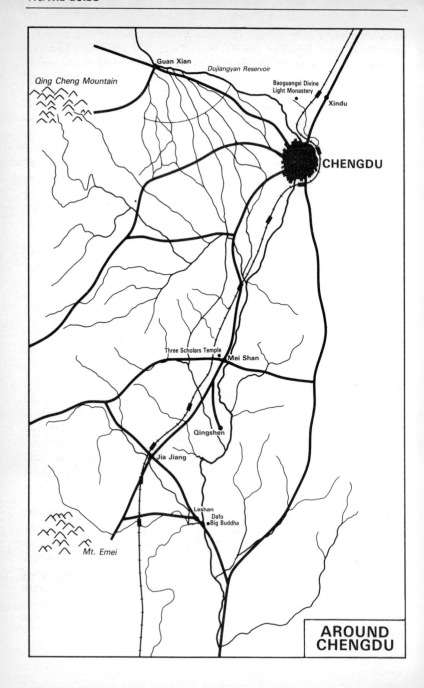

AROUND CHENGDU

rundown on its history inside. This was, in short, a remarkable achievement for its time. Begun in 256 BC by Li Bing, then governor of Shu, to control the capricious flow of the mighty Min river, it was engineered in three parts. A central dam – Fish Mouth Divide – created an inner flow for irrigation and an outer channel for flood control; the Feisha Spillway directed the flood water, regulated the outflow and allowed the silt to be dredged, while an opening carved through the hillside called the Bottleneck Sluiceway controlled the flow of oncoming water. Work was continued by Li Bing's son and the scheme has been maintained and developed ever since, so that the present system of dams, reservoirs and pumping stations irrigates some 3.2 million hectares of the Sichuan plain. There's a stone statue of the innovative Li Bing in the temple, dated AD168, and a memorial tablet preserves his immortal line, 'Dig the channel deep, keep the spillway low' – wise words indeed. Climb up to the upper floor for a breathtaking view of the river, frothing angrily past and bouncing great logs in its wake.

For the finest vista of the dam, make your way to the **Two Kings Temple**, across a gaudily coloured galleried footbridge and along a slender street banked with precariously overhanging houses. Left up a series of crumbling steps and along the river takes you to the temple, commandingly positioned in steep tiers near a hanging bridge. Posthumously dedicated to Li Bing and his son, who are remembered by statues in the two main halls, this is beautifully unspoilt and holds a wedge of tree-trunk said to be 4000 years old. Down by the gates are a number of interesting market stalls – selling remedies like bear's paw, snake and dragon bones, some of them – and further up a beaming, wizened old woman will invite you to take part in ceremonials at her hilltop altar. Nearby, the old **Billow Taming Bridge**, once a key route into Tibet, has been replaced by a modern suspension bridge but remains a perilous enough crossing, alarmingly unsteady above the rushing water and bobbing tree trunks. If you can face it, cross and walk back to Guanxian on the far side – though be warned that most of the rest of the walk is rather dull.

The third of Chengdu's surrounding places of interest, **QINGCHENG SHAN** or the Azure City Mountain, is linked with Chengdu by a daily 7.30am bus from Ximen station. This, the quietest spot under heaven they say, makes a good alternative if you haven't the time or energy for Emei Shan (see below). The summit, topped with the **Shang Qing Gong Temple**, is about a 6km climb up tree-covered slopes scattered with pavilions, bridges and temples, best of which is the Taoist Monastery of **Tianshi Dong** – Grotto of the Heavenly Teacher – which has a main hall decorated with Ming dynasty panels.

EMEI SHAN AND LESHAN

It's a good idea to organise these two places into a single trip: there is a strong Buddhist element in both, they are quite close together and there are several buses a day between them, taking just 1½ hours.

Emei Shan

A 3-hour train ride from Chengdu, on the line to Kunming in south-west Sichuan, lies the mountainous district of **EMEI SHAN**, one of China's most spectacular and untouched regions of natural beauty. The name means 'eyebrows of beauty', since the Chinese say that from a distance the two main peaks – there are three in all – look like the eyebrows of a moth(!). Though steep, hilly and rocky, this is not so much a climber's as a hiker's mountain, cloaked with dense trees and undergrowth and scored by manmade paths, sometimes rough steps or uneven paving, sometimes no more than muddy switchback tracks or ankle-twisting boulders. And it's a wonderful place to explore: the warmth, at the least on the lower slopes, the abundant rain, the fault blocks of cliffs and eroded rocks mean that Emei Shan is rich in plant and animal life. There are over 200 kinds of butterfly, along with gingko and cedar trees, azaleas, rhododendrons, tea bushes, medicinal herbs and brilliant un-nameable flowers; and amongst all this live bearded frogs, lesser pandas, silver pheasant – and, most prominently, monkeys.

Emei Shan has, too, been a place of pilgrimage since the first Taoist temples were built here more than 1800 years ago, and by the 6C it had become one of the country's four mountains sacred to Buddhism: the Boddhisatva Samantabhadra is thought to have preached here, and these hallowed slopes once held around 150 temples and monasteries. Of these, only about twenty remain (the others were destroyed by the Japanese and later by the Red Guard during the Cultural Revolution), all of which have been renovated and enjoy a religious freedom which would have been unthinkable a couple of decades ago. It's in these, dotted all over the mountainside and offering simple refuge, that you spend each night. The landscape changes markedly with the seasons: most people come in spring and summer – weather-wise much the best time, when the mountain is clothed in dense lush green and often wreathed in cloud and mist. Certainly, in summer Emei Shan provides a welcome escape from Sichuan's scathing heat. Autumn brings brilliant colours and cooler temperatures, and some Chinese climb in winter when the crowds have gone, and the light is clear and the snow lends grandeur.

On the mountain

If you're not pushed for time, you could easily enjoy three or four days walking the lower slopes, thereby giving a better chance of picking a fine day for the assault on the top and, perhaps, the highest point at the end of the ridge – **Wanfoding** or 10,000 Buddha Peak. It's only really worth climbing this high if the weather's good; if conditions look uncertain then all you'll see is a weather station, a broadcasting mast and a down-at-heel temple. On the whole, if you prefer a richer bag of views, temples, streams and vegetation, stick to the lower paths. If you're intent on reaching the summit(s), and time is short, best take the most direct route, which means taking a bus to Wannian Si and then making your way on foot via Xi Xiang Chi to Jinding – the first summit at 3075m – either coming back to Wannian Si the same way or by the longer southern route. At a pinch you can always bucket down the rough mountain roads by jeep . . . Those with bags of time should hike the 12km from Baoguo Si to Qingyin Ge and then weave their way up the mountain from there.

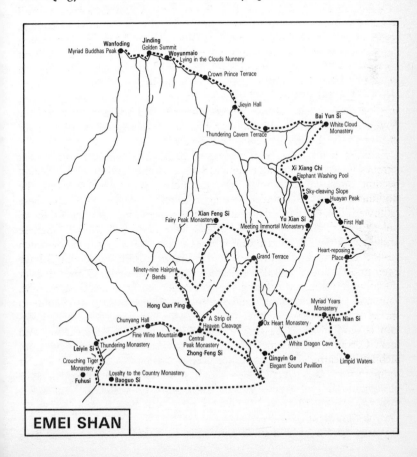

EMEI SHAN

Whatever you plan to do, and however you arrive (by bus either from Leshan or Emei town), you'll have to start your explorations at **BAOGUO SI** (Protect the country monastery), which acts as gateway to the whole area. Here, up on a slope to the left of the bus station, there's a quiet **hotel** overlooking a lake, the *Hongzhushan Binguan*, where you should be able to find a room (and good food in the restaurant opposite). In the other direction a road leads off in a riot of stalls selling food, maps, walking sticks and souvenirs, to the **temple hostel** – convenient but clamorous, with basic accommodation for ¥3 and a branch of **CITS**.

Baoguo Si is a large and busy temple built under the Song, later burnt, and rebuilt and enlarged in the 17C. Four main halls rise one behind the other up the slope, with fine garden courtyards and elaborate latticework and carved doorways. The porcelain Buddha in the **Sutra Hall** is eye-catching, with its red-lined black garments covered with tiny gilt images of Buddha, but the temple is likely to be awash with guided tours so it's well worth the short walk to the restored **Fu Hu Si** – Tiger Taming Temple – where people can also stay. About the same period as Baoguo Si, it is much more peaceful, set in thick forest beneath great nanmu trees. Here you will find the **Huayan Pagoda**, 14 storeys but only 7 metres high, cast of bronze in the 16C and engraved with 4700 images of Buddha and the full text of the Huayan Scripture.

Walking out of Baoguo Si, the path takes you past Lei Yin Si (Thundering Monastery), the Emerald Bamboo Bridge, the Jade Maiden Pool, said never to run dry, to Chunyang Hall where you can spend the night and take in some panoramic views of the summit. From here the track leads down past the enticingly named Fine Wine Fountain and through a dense copse of nanmu trees to Qingyin Ge. This is the hub of several paths: you can either join the shorter north route to the top by walking the few kilometres to Wannian Si (Myriad Years Monastery) – where, had you taken the exhilarating half-hour bus ride from Baoguo Si, you would be starting your ascent anyway – or take the southern route up to the Ox Heart Monastery. Here you can see the famous bearded frogs (at least the males have beards – females make do with stripes) – and hurry on to Hong Chun Ping, the age-old trees terrace, where if you wish you can stop the night. Climbing higher, the path takes you past Jiu Lao Dong, a large limestone cave thickly shaded with bamboo, up to Xian Feng Si (Fairy Peaks Monastery), another place to spend a night, clustered by conifer forest, and on to join the north route at Xi Xiang Chi – the Elephant Bathing Pool.

However, most people take the northern route from **Wannian Si**. High enough for good views to the south and east, this is one of the earliest surviving temples, having been first built in the 4C AD and rebuilt by Tang Emperor Xi Zong about 880. It's famous for the brick hall in front, rather square and dumpy with an arched entrance and windows in ochre and red, with blue latticework. The roof has a little stupa at each corner and another on top of the squat dome. Inside, a stunning Buddha sits on a gilt lotus on a great white elephant whose feet are planted delicately in four lotus blossoms. The huge statue was cast in bronze about 980 and brought from Chengdu in bits. You may have to persuade them to let you **spend the night** here though, since at just ¥1.30 per person it's considered too primitive for westerners. And certainly conditions are pretty frugal – hot water is provided by a coal-fired stove, you wash out in the open at a stone slab and accept your dinner from an anonymous hatch – but you should find the feel of the place more than compensates for any discomfort. This is the only temple, among those that I saw anyway, that gives the impression it is putting up visitors and pilgrims much as it has done for centuries: at dusk you listen to the chorus of frogs around the temple croaking at the tops of their voices – like guitars, say the Chinese – and later the drone of the monks' chants and the sing-song of their bells reverberates through the thin walls.

Early starts are the norm here, so aim to be on the road by 6, trekking up the steep slippery path through swirling mist and thick swathes of bamboo and pine. The traffic in spring and summer can be fairly dense and there are any number of wayside halts, some selling drinks, maps, nuts, others covered with tarpaulins and offering more substantial fare – rice and gruel, garlic soup and noodles. A steady 3 hours, past the reassuringly named Heart-resting Place and the First Hall and Huayan Peak, and you should be mounting the last steps to **Xi Xiang Chi** – the Elephant Bathing Pool.

This is where the Elephant stopped for a dip on his way up the mountain carrying Samantabhadra, and everyone now stops for a drink and a photo call. Finely set on its hilltop, it is not as imposing as Wannian Si but has a wide view, lots of little paths through ancient trees and many kinds of rhododendron. You can have a drink or snack or spend the night here before tackling the 4 hours to the top; as a meeting of the ways it's likely to be crowded, so get here early to be sure of a bed. Beyond here the path gets easier, though you may have to fight off gangs of vicious monkeys crossing the jeep track which snakes its way round from behind the mountain. There are still lots of people on this stretch of road: old women (and fat young ones!) being carried on panniers, teenagers climbing on cross-looking horses to have their photos taken in pre-war army uniform; follow them through the thick woods and before long you're at Thundering Cavern Terrace, balanced delicately between a high cliff to the right and a sheer precipice on the left.

The top, **Jinding** or Golden Summit, so called after the bronze roof of its temple which reflects the light, is a short walk from here but can be a sad disappointment, especially if the weather's murky and obscures the views. Best of these are the *Buddha's Halo* (a rainbow-like halation on the afternoon clouds), the sunrise – spectacular, they say, but I didn't catch it – and the *Sea of Clouds*. Otherwise there's just a huge broad-casting mast, a handful of dilapidated buildings and a temple on wooden legs – a ramshackle affair hooked onto the side of the mountain. Tourism, inevitably, is rife: bored teenagers shuffle through the temple hall, pay mock homage to the Buddha and giggle sheepishly, watched over by an impassive monk. You can **stay the night** at the temple (it's 15°C colder up here so they hire you a padded coat), and then pick up a jeep first thing next morning to take you down to Baoguo Si for around ¥10. This journey can be exciting, often enlivened by the driver's rundown of Emei Shan's attractions in groups of four: 'scenery, temples, animals, plants'; the four best temples 'Baoguo Si, Wannian Si, Tiger-taming and Elephant Bathing Pool'; the four summit views 'Buddha's Halo, Sunrise, the Sea of Clouds and Chengdu'. At most times of the year he might well add: 'fog, clouds, rain and gales'.

Some hints for climbers
Don't forget **warm clothing** for the top and some protection against rain – a cycle cape is just the thing. A **stick** is useful, especially for going down, which is harder work. Temple **accommodation** costs from ¥2–10 depending on the degree of comfort; try to get there early in the afternoon to be sure of a bed. **Food** is usually vegetarian, always cheap, but there's often no running water and hot water must be fetched from the kitchen. There may be no electricity so carry a torch for nocturnal visits to the loo.

Leshan

In **LESHAN**, a tiny 1300-year-old market town in southern Sichuan, the Qing, Yi, Min and Dadu rivers join in a froth of muddy dark waters, the different colours of their separate currents clearly visible. Though undergoing some reconstruction of late, it's a lively little place, a good opportunity to experience Chinese provincial life outside of the large cities, and it looks across to Lingyun and Wuyou, the twin hills for which the town is famous, and the great carved Buddha in a niche in the river cliff. It's for this that people come here, but you can quite easily combine it with a trip to Emei Shan.

The town
Leshan has no railway link, and the nearest station is Xia Jiang on the Chengdu line – though Emei is more convenient as the bus from there can have you in Leshan in 1½ hours. Failing that, if you want to give Emei a miss you can come direct from Chengdu by bus, a rather tiring 5 hour trip but passing through some agreeable countryside. The **bus**

station is in the high street, from where a special bus connects with Lingyun Hill (for the Great Buddha) and a city bus drops you back in the centre. Four stops from the station on the no.1 bus is the *Jiazhou Hotel*, where rooms for ¥18–25 in the central block or dorm beds for ¥5 in the shabby building across the street both give stunning views of Emei Shan and the huge Buddha. Last buses to here leave quite early, and the first bus in the morning doesn't leave until 6.20am which may be too late to catch your long-distance connection – something worth bearing in mind. As regards **eating**, the hotel does a set menu that isn't dagger cheap but may well include sweet and sour fish fresh out of the courtyard pool; or there's a handful of small restaurants and shops, and a further seedy *hotel*, in Leshan's cheerful main street. The Wuyou temple across the river has a restaurant and offer basic accommodation, but don't be surprised if they turn foreigners away. Finally a note on **leaving**: remember that if you want to head on to Dazu and Chongqing you're not, idiotically, allowed to take the bus on to Neijiang, the obvious connecting station, but must instead go back the way you came.

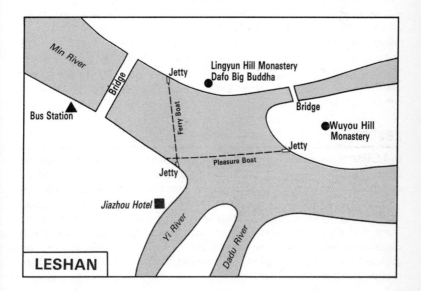

The Great Buddha and the Two Hills

Carved into the sandstone cliff of Lingyun, the **Great Buddha** (Dafu) sits stolidly staring across the water, 70 metres high and said to be the largest in the world. Size apart, the Buddha is unusual in many ways, more like a solid middle-aged politician than a religious effigy, squat and chunky with hands firmly planted on his knees, and feet mounted sure and steady by the river – an uncharacteristically worldly pose. Legend has it that the statue was begun by a monk called Haitong in 713 – a local effort that took 90 years to complete and was supposed to pacify the rough waters of the river which were destroying so many boats. The Buddha is startlingly well preserved. Haitong and his engineers devised a cunning network of drains, burrowed inside the body, to protect it from weathering. Today, the only real sign of the Buddha's age is the grey-green ferns and foliage that sprout from its every niche and cranny.

It's fun – if slightly daunting – to clamber about on the stone staircases cut into the body of the great Buddha, but you get by far the best view from the water, from one of the pleasure boats from Leshan which hover midstream while the Chinese take endless photographs of each other with the Buddha as backdrop. These boats drop you at the foot of Lingyun's twin hill, **Wuyou** or Greenest Hill, so called for the dense woods that spread dappled shade over its paths and steps. This was originally a small peninsula, but a couple of thousand years ago Li Bing, famous engineer of the Dujiangyan Irrigation Scheme (see p.415), cut a channel through the rock to divert the treacherous spring floods and so turned Wuyou into an island. Follow the steep steps from the waterside up to the warm pink-walled **monastery** which crowns the top, founded in 742 and restored last century. It's a charming group of buildings, especially the pavilion hugging the hillside like a spread fan and the lattice-windowed tea-house where you can enjoy a cool drink. The Hall of 500 Arhats is empty, but the prayer cushions in the Main Hall show the temple is still functioning, and the large wooden fish is still struck to call the monks to the refectory. For the rest, the complex's main purpose is as museum. Certainly the gilded camphorwood statues of Sakyamuni, Manjusri and Samantabhadra are worth the climb, as is the monastery's assortment of calligraphy and paintings, but really it's the fine panoramas of Leshan and beyond which draw people here.

Drop down from here to the water's edge, where a rope hanging bridge links the island with **Lingyun**. This tends to close from time to time but no matter: when I was last here everyone took off their shoes and paddled across – the waters are actually quite shallow. Once on Lingyun you can, if you've enough energy left, climb up to another group of **temples**, this time founded under the Tang dynasty, where there are wonderful vistas over the Great Buddha's head of Emei Shan, swimming in haze beyond the water. The 17C statues were placed here when the place was rebuilt and include one of the patron saint of the mountain. You can also refill on tea in a small and pleasant restaurant, and look down on the Buddha's pendulous ears, afterwards chancing the vertiginous descent down the **Staircase of the Nine Turnings** which wriggles its way down the statue's

slopes of the two main hills: Eling (Goose Neck – you'll see the goose on the map), and Pipa Shan (Loquat Hill) – seamed by narrow winding roads and steep flights of steps, and topped by two parks. Bicycles cannot cope with the hills, and the sedan chairs of old have long gone, so transport is mainly crowded buses which skirt around the edge of town on the lower slopes, something which gives Chongqing a look curiously at odds with other Chinese cities. Morrison, writing in 1890, described an enormously rich city, with unscalable walls, many temples and pagodas, spacious *yamens* and great public buildings. The source of this wealth, he perceived, was opium: there were numberless opium shops here and the drug was widely grown in Sichuan. However, while the wealth may be still here, the buildings and walls he saw were either bombed out of existence by the Japanese in the last war or sacrificed to Chongqing's rapid and merciless expansion, both in the 1930s and today. An extensive network of tunnels and air-raid shelters remains, but otherwise the city is best characterised by the relative modernity of its city centre and the ungainly sprawl of its suburbs, which spread north and south, linked by large bridges, on the farther banks of both rivers.

Chongqing's **railway station** is south-west of the centre; once off the train a funicular takes you up and deposits you on the main road. From here a no.5 bus will take you to Shangqingsi roundabout, and, 10 minutes walk away along Renmin Lu, the *Renmin Da Litang Hotel* – much the best place **to stay** in town with beds from about ¥6. This, a 1950s Ming-style palace, has a fine and friendly atmosphere and staff, and a mini Albert Hall used for concerts, but beware the prices for foreigners and non-students in the dining rooms and bar. There's also a **CITS** office, though it wins no prizes for efficiency. An alternative, and though rather a dreary pile much more in the heart of things, is the *Chongqing Binguan* in Misheng Lu, a no.5 bus ride east, with dorms from ¥6 and all the usual amenities. Or there's the *Yuzhou Guesthouse* – a large and characterless hotel in the suburbs . . .

As far as further vital addresses go, the **long-distance bus stations** are at the junction of Xinhua Lu and Zhonghua Lu, and – for routes north and to Dazu – across the Jialing River in Jianxin Bei Lu; **ticket offices** and a handful of further buses can be found in Qingnian Lu, near Jiefang Bei. **Public Security** are in Linjiang Lu and **CAAC** in Zhongshan Lu, near the Shangqingsi roundabout (see map). Apart from the no.5, **useful buses** are the no.12, which takes you along the southern fringe of the centre; the no.13, which does the same to the north; the no.1 eastward along the goose's head from Shangqingsi to Chaotianmen; the no.3 from the funicular past to Yuzhou Guesthouse and zoo; and the no.71 right across both rivers and the entire city.

The city: parks, streets, shops and food

Chongqing's sights, those that there are, centre on the city's parks. Best is the **Pipa Shan Park** on Loquat Hill, reachable on foot from the Renmin Hotel by walking south and following the yellow arrows which lead you gradually up hill by way of narrow stepped streets. Though not much to see in itself, this is the highest point in the city – over 200 metres – and offers good orientation and excellent if alarming views of Chongqing's horrific smogline, especially by night when the lights flash on. Rest up in the busy *tea-house*, full of cheerful twittering old men playing cards (bring your own mug and tealeaves) and then set off for the local **museum** (closed Mondays), which has finds from hereabouts of mild interest, a coffin that once served as a hollowed-out boat of Chongqing's original inhabitants, over 3000 years old, and an impressive display of Han bricks. Look out also for the Ming and Qing paintings – a surprisingly fine collection – though you can easily give the bronzes and ceramics a miss, two a penny in any Chinese museum. The city's other main park, the **Eling** on Goose Neck Hill, is rather scruffy and, unless you're going that way, not really worth the bother, with an ugly modern concrete pagoda whose only saving grace is a pretty collection of bonsai trees.

Parks aside, the only other specific thing to see in Chongqing is **Hongyacun** or Red Crag Village, on the north shore of the peninsula beyond Renmin da Litang hotel. This was used by officers of the Communist wing of the alliance against the Japanese during the war and has been opened up to the public with a broad-ranging display of photos and documents of the era. Zhou Enlai and other big names were here at least once during those years, and Mao himself stayed here in 1945 when involved in negotiations with Chiang Kaishek and the Kuomintang. Forgetting the history, though, there's nothing here now of paramount interest to a foreigner.

For a more stimulating time it makes more sense to head east to the city centre, where the streets grouped around the Liberation Monument, a large clock tower, make an interesting quarter to wander through – and, if you're flush, do a spot of shopping. Browsable **shops** include the *Medicine Shop* on Minzu Lu, which sells 57 varieties of royal jelly and antler horn, the *Chongqing Arts and Crafts Shop*, a rather seedy *Friendship Store* and the *Western Clothes Market* – all stationed along the same street. Just north of here, in Qiangbai Lu, a **cable car** straddles the Jialing River, giving fine views of the bankside's sprawling settlements – though I wouldn't bother if it's raining since then the contraption tends to break down. Afterwards, take a no.13 bus as far as it goes and walk down Xinhua Lu to the docks, **Chaotianmen**, where a hubbub of activity focuses on loading and unloading, street-traders trotting to fill up their panniers and a line of food and clothes stalls that stretches way back to the town centre. Walk back west from here for more busy commerce, most interestingly a jam-packed street crammed with clothes stalls selling bright nylon and pleated crimplene items, some made locally, some 'high fashion' from Shanghai, but all amazingly tacky. Look in on the *Xinshancheng Pharmacy* on Zhongshan Lu, where old-style wooden cabinets hold countless bundles of herbs and you can see the chemists making up medicines for a long and constant queue of customers.

By the time you've waded through all this you'll most likely be feeling hungry, and for that there's no problem. A cluster of **restaurants** serves the city centre: choose from the *Yizhishi* in Zourong Lu – smart with excellent steamed dumplings; the *Chongqing* in Xinhua Lu, large and black-tiled, like a gloomy bank; *Old Sichuan*, in Bayi Lu, with a roomy ground floor and a wide range of different dishes; or the *Huixianlou* in Minzu Lu which has roof terrace that's a nice escape from the dust and, next door, an ice-cream, cold drinks and cake parlour. For **cultural life**, the *Renmin Da Litang hall* is the best bet for concerts and theatre; otherwise there's the *Renmin Theatre* in Xinhua Lu and the *Heping Cinema* in Zourong Lu. And lots more.

Outside Chongqing

A possible place to visit immediately outside Chongqing is the **US-Chiang Kai-shek Criminal Acts Exhibition Hall**, at the foot of Gele mountain in the north-western suburbs of the city – a 20 minute ride on the no.17 bus. This is actually two prisons, set up by the Sino-American Cooperation Organisation (SACO) during the last war to house Communists and those found guilty of acts against the Kuomintang government. Their record is pretty dismal: hundreds of political prisoners were kept here, and of those plenty were executed or tortured. Myriad photographs and some macabre instruments of torture illustrate those years as best they can, but, all in all, if you have a day to kill between connections, there are pleasanter possibilities . . .

The **Nanshangongyaun** (South Mountain), for one, offers enjoyable hilly walks and the dark and cool Laojun Cave, one-time home of the philosopher Laotzi, and is just 20km to the south – reachable by ferry from Jiao Yang and then a short bus ride. A few kilometres further out **Nanwenquan** (Southern Hot Springs), is set idyllically among green hills, pine woods and bamboo groves and has a stalactite cave and hot spring water at 38°C for your entertainment – and rheumatism. To get here you'll need to take bus no.41 from Xinhua Lu. If you're serious about hot springs, bear in mind that the **Beiwenquan**, North Hot Springs, are better and a lot more organised, accessible in an hour on bus no.30 and then a local bus. Here you can swim in three enormous pools, filled with the warm spring water, and then take a boat along the river for lunch.

The nine peaks of **Jinyun Shan** or Red Silk Mountain are visible a few miles away. Two thousand species of sub-tropical plant grow here, as well as a famous local tea, and you can visit the mountain's 1500-year-old temple. To get there, simply stay on the no.30 bus.

DAZU

About 180 kilometres west of Chongqing lie the much-touted cliff sculptures of DAZU, amid a beautiful lush countryside of green rolling hills cut with gentle terraces. It's a 6 hour bus ride from Chongqing (or a 1-hour bus journey from nearby YOUTINGPU, on the Chengdu–Chongqing line) but well worth it, for although Dazu itself is rather a boring little place, the sculptures are, by anyone's standards, remarkable. To see everything you'll need to stay overnight, in which case the **hotel** in the town centre offers the best chance of a room for foreigners – small, fairly shabby, but with generous set meals and beds for ¥10–15.

There are about 50,000 pieces of sculpture in all, concentrated mainly at Beishan or the North Hill, and Baodingshan, Precious Summit Hill, although sporadic examples are scattered all over the outlying countryside. The work began in 892 and continued on and off for the next 400 years, taking in themes and imagery that are on the whole Buddhist but include some Confucian and Taoist elements. Indeed, sometimes the founders of all three religions appear together in the same carving. Later than the better-known Yung Gang and Longmen sculptures, it is, however, the secular themes that make them special – real people and animals figure highly, in what amount to cautionary tales on aspects of everyday life. You also see these sculptures much as they would have looked when they were finished, since an ingenious drainage system, not unlike the one at Leshan, has protected them from the ravages of weather; plus their relative isolation has made them no easy target for native vandals and foreign looters. And their scale and layout enable you to enjoy the detail close to, and the vitality of their colour, variety and frequent humour, makes them easier for a western eye to appreciate than the more impersonal work of earlier periods.

Beishan

Walk north from Dazu's main street for about a mile, up a flight of steps and along a path lined with hollyhocks and peonies, and you're at the **Beishan** group of sculptures: earlier than those at Baodingshan and consequently a lot less animated and more filled with Buddhist iconography. Ten thousand statues gather round the hill in 264 recesses, looking from a distance rather like rabbit burrows. Wei Junjing, governor of Changzhou and commanding general here at the time, started the work and is suitably remembered by one of the earliest statues, carved in his honour by a Shu general he had defeated. Other statues were paid for by donation, some military, some given by monks and nuns, many of whom have their names recorded by inscriptions or appear in the arrangements themselves. For the utterly overwhelmed, *cave 245* (they are all numbered) is considered outstanding, with over 600 figures and some nice details of contemporary Tang life – ornaments, dress, musical instruments and the like.

It's just north of here, though, in the carvings from the Song dynasty, that the detail and craftsmanship is best. *Cave 113* has an elegant Avalokitesvara Gazing at the Moon's Reflection; in *cave 125* Avalokitesvara appears again with rosary, looking more like shy debutante than a girl renouncing the world. The largest cave, *no.136*, depicts Sakyamuni, flanked by the feature-filled figures of 20 Boddhisattvas, among them Manjusri riding a blue roaring lion and Samantabhadra sitting elegantly in lotus position on a sturdy elephant.

Baodingshan

You can reach the sculptures of **Baodingshan**, 16km north-east of Dazu, by regular bus: the journey takes about half an hour and the last bus back leaves at 5pm. These sculptures are more exciting than those at Beishan: later and more realistic, even comic in places, they were funded by subscriptions collected between 1179 and 1245 by Zhao Zhifeng, a dedicated local monk. The 10,000 carvings divide into two clear groupings – those at Dafowan, and another bunch at Xiaofowan, both of which subsequently became popular places of pilgrimage. Xiaofowan was the first group carved, in grottoes built with stone walls, pillars and beams, but most people spend their time at the later and more impressive Dafowan, where the sculptures have been cleverly incorporated into the natural landscape, occupying 31 numbered niches on the inner side of a horseshoe curve of hills around a narrow valley.

Here Zhao Zhifeng aimed to depict stories from the Buddhist scriptures: because he was in charge of the project so long there isn't the repetition you find in so many other sculpture series; plus, as at Beishan, you can get close enough to enjoy some quite incredible – and illuminating – detail. The first, the *Fierce Tiger Coming Down from a Mountain*, greets you with superb elan, and leads on to another striking group, the *Six Ways of Transmigration*, in which a brightly coloured Atlas holds a great disc of six carved segments, each representing one of the courses of predestination. Further along, *niche no.5* holds a gigantic group of three saints, Vairocana, Manjusri and Samantabhadra, each 7 metres high, the last holding out a stone pagoda said to weigh half a ton. No less imposing is niche no.8, the *Dabei Pavilion*, where the figure of the Thousand-Armed Avalokitesvara is the largest ever carved in China –

and, if you're prepared to count them, actually has slightly over its designated 1000 arms, 1007 in fact. Each hand is different, fanning out in glowing blue and gold like peacock feathers. Impressive in a different way are no.11, *Reclining Buddha*, 30 metres from head to knee, and no.15, *Requital of Parents' Kindness*, which is full of vitality: below, seven Buddhas represent the stage's of man's life – praying for a son, conception, birth, feeding and washing the baby, arranging marriage, right through to old age. By way of contrast, the next but one along shows *Buddha Requiting His Parents' Kindness*, with figures recalling his goodness to his parents while on the left heretics slander him as unfilial. My personal favourite, though, was no.20, *Eighteen Layers of Hell*: a chamber of Horrors type scene interspersed with delicate and amusing comic strip cameos like the Hen Wife or Drunkard. Near the exit *no.30* continues the naturalistic theme, showing ten buffaloes with their herdsman – a symbol of meditation, but also a tranquil picture of pastoral life.

THE YANGZI RIVER GORGES

From Chongqing, many people take one of the river boats that ply the route down the **YANGZI RIVER** as far as Shanghai – a welcome respite from thrashing around on trains and buses. Most don't go all the way, but disembark at Yichang or, sometimes, Wuhan: easily the most spectacular stretch of the river, and, you'll probably find, quite enough. There are four classes on board the boats, beginning, strangely enough, with 2nd class, which gives double berths in the bows, washbasins, carpets and a

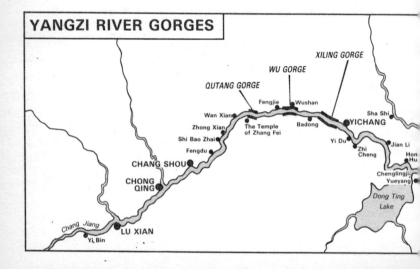

viewing lounge; 3rd class gets you a place in a 4 or 8-bed cabin, 4th in a 14–16 bed cabin, and 5th just a mat on the floor in the bilges. Not surprisingly, the difference in price between 2nd and 5th class is pretty wide . . . Showers are available to all and, though in almost constant use, come piping hot, but the food can be unspeakable. Of two canteens, the lower one has short hours, long queues and, when you can get one, abysmal meals, while the upper deck canteen is expensive and restricted to 2nd class passengers only (¥12 for breakfast and evening meal). On the whole, if you're travelling anything lower than 2nd class, best bring your own food and drink.

Boats leave Chongqing from Chaotianmen dock at 6.30–7am each morning, stopping at Wanxian the first evening, Yichang the second evening, and then heading on to Wuhan, Nanjing and Shanghai. **Tickets** are available either from the booking office at the terminal or from CITS, and you should book 2 or 3 days in advance to be sure of a place. You can make your own way down to Chaotianmen or catch a special bus from the Renmin Hotel at 6am (fare ¥1.20, bookable at reception). A rough guide to downriver fares: at the last count 3rd class to Yichang cost around ¥35; to Wuhan was about ¥50.

The Changjiang, the Chinese name for the Yangzi meaning 'Long River', is the third longest river in the world, rising north-west of Tibet, sweeping east for 6400 kilometres, receiving 700 tributaries and spilling its muddy waters into the East China Sea near Shanghai. Different stretches of the river have different names: Dajiang, which means 'Great River', is one; Jinshajiang – Golden River – is another, referring to the waters above

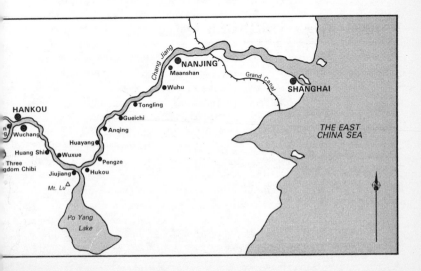

Chongqing where gold was once panned; and, of course, there's Yangzi-jiang, derived from a ford near Yangzhou and applied by foreigners to the river as a whole. Nowadays the Yangzi is navigable well beyond Chongqing, but although people have travelled up and down the river for a good 1000 years it wasn't always so easy. People braved the angry moods of the Yangzi because it was the only link between Sichuan and the rest of China, and the horror stories of early travellers – of the impossibility of moving after dark, of the reefs, icefloes in spring and torrid heat in summer – are common. And though farming and industrial communities along its banks have benefited for centuries, it was also dangerous to be too close to the unpredictable Yangzi: spring floods could raise the water level by as much as 50 metres in some places, sweeping away the makeshift shanty towns on the banks. Rivercraft also had to beware of the Yangzi currents, none too kind at the best of times but particularly hazardous when the water level sank to expose difficult reefs and shoals. Most dangerous of all were the three **Gorges**, now on the borders of Sichuan and Hubei provinces, which were formed around 70 million years ago when two mountains squeezed together and a vast inland sea draining east cut into the limestone faults in zigzags, throwing up the gorges' precipitous cliffs and sharp hairpin bends. As recently as the late 19C no-one could navigate this stretch of the river alone: steamers couldn't pass at all, and small boats were hauled through the rapids by teams of trackers in a journey which could and often did take several weeks.

Having read all this, probably the last thing you want to do is negotiate the Yangzi gorges. Suffice to say that since 1940 the rocks and reefs which created the rapids have been blasted away, and though the trip is still impressive enough, it's no longer the frightener it was. First, though, the early stages of the journey, which begin quietly and gently, with you slipping out of Chongqing at dawn, the water flat and still and the mountains uncurling far ahead. As you proceed, the shore grows more interesting: green grassy slopes, terraces and little bobble-headed trees form a pastoral backdrop for the billowing sails of sampans and junks, and everywhere you look there are pagodas and temples built to appease violent river gods, and wierd shaped cliffs named after mysterious local legends. All of this, if you understand Chinese, you can pick up from the tannoy, which keeps up a consistent commentary; if you don't, however, better to switch off completely and simply enjoy the view. Past **CHANG-SHOU**, an old town on the north bank of the river, the boat reaches **FULONG**, which sits at the mouth of the Wujiang river, ancient capital of Ba and site of its royal tombs and now a stopover for river traffic travelling between eastern Sichuan and Guizhou. A little way downstream a great rock, the **Baihe Ridge**, sits plum mid-current, bearing on its side a set of carvings centuries old that are thought to have served as water-level marks – though these days they're only visible if the waters are running particularly low. FENGDU comes next, glowered over by the mountain of Pingdu, once thought erroneously to be the hideaway of some kind of Chinese Satan, and with scores of temples and shrines built to that effect, all with names like 'Palace of the King of Hell' and 'Between the Living and the Dead' and crammed full of sculptures of demons.

Unhappily the boat doesn't stop so you can't go and see for yourself; and it's a similar story with the next town, ZHONGXIAN, which sits in a bamboo grove on the north shore, famous for its fermented bean curd and, rather more venerably, the Hall of Four Virtuous Men where the poet Bai Ju Yi is commemorated. One thing you do get a good look at though, further on, is **Shibaozhai** (Stone Treasure Stronghold), a lumbering rock buttress on the north bank. Thirty metres high, it's topped with an 18C temple, pagoda-shape, encasing a spiral staircase for reaching the temple's main sanctuary. A legend says there was once a tiny hole in the temple, through which poured enough rice to feed the monks. Greedily, they tried to enlarge it, and the frugal supply stopped forever – a Chinese version of the Western goose with golden eggs story. By late afternoon you should be docked at **WANXIAN** – an old trading city clinging precariously to the hill like a fortress; steps lead up through slits in its enormous walls. It's a relief to get off the boat, and an opportunity well worth taking advantage of: walk up to the clock tower to find a flowery park cupped in the hill, then wander down the main street when the stalls are lit and visiting Chinese are buying bamboo and rattan. Wanxian is famous for this, and you can pick up some lovely pieces – brightly coloured baskets, huge steamers, rattan tables, chairs and matting.

Once you've staggered back to the boat with your prizes, and grabbed a few hours sleep, the boat will be off, timing its journey so as to reach the gorges as daylight breaks. You pass **YUNYANG** and the Zhanwang Temple, **FENGJIE**, with its high wall and gate, and at **BAIDICHENG** the Yangzi Gorges begin – 200 kilometres of wind-driven rapids from Mount Wushan – Witches' mountain – to Nanjinyuang near **YICHANG**. Liu Bei, 3C ruler of Shu, is said to have died of despair at Baidicheng after failing to avenge the death of his sworn brother Guan Yu in the war against Wu. Both of them, and also Zhu Geliang and Zhang Fei, the remaining two of the 'four musketeers' of that war, are commemorated by statues and tablets in the Baidi Temple. It also has eight sandalwood chairs, supposedly used by the leaders of the Heavenly Kingdom during the Taiping Rebellion. Opposite, you'll see Meng Liang's Staircase, chiselled into the cliff as far as a platform around half way up, where, the story goes, the Song general Yang was killed by traitors. When his bodyguard climbed up to recover the body, he was confronted by a monk, whom he promptly up-ended and hung by his feet from the cliff face;

try, if you can, to recognise the unfortunate monk, petrified, they say, in the shape of a huge hanging rock.

The first of the gorges, **Qutang Gorge**, is 8 kilometres long, the river weaving between great limestone cliffs plunging sheer down to the water, and the banks closing gradually in to form Wui Gate where, as the poet Su Dongpo put it, the angry waters pour through the narrow channel 'like a thousand seas poured into one cup'. **Wuxia Gorge**, the next one, is much longer, snaking for 45 kilometres past fantastic peaks and valleys that are often wreathed by rain and mist. The so-called **Twelve Peaks** represent the goddess Yao Ji and her eleven sisters – come to earth to help Yu the Tamer of Floods stem a flood stirred up by twelve dragons. Yao Ji killed the dragons and the sisters were transformed into twelve mountains – more petrified rock – stationed by the river to guide ships downriver. Nearby is the **Kong Ming Tablet**, a Three Kingdoms period rock inscription that proclaims 'Wuxia has peaks rising higher and higher.' Still visible, it's said that this once so worried an enemy general that he and his army turned tail and fled. Further downstream, **ZIGUI** was the birthplace of the great poet, Qu Yuan, who drowned himself a couple of millennia ago when his country, Chu, was conquered by Qin. Every year, in his memory, the people hold dragon boat races and throw *zongzi* (rice dumplings in bamboo leaves) into the water to protect the poet from a dragon said to lurk at the bottom of the river . . .

Xiling, the longest gorge, begins at **Fragrant Stream**, where shoals of tiny fish glint like peachblossom in the crystal clear water. It was this stretch of the river that was always the most dangerous, described by Morrison in 1894 as 'a swirling torrent with a roar like thunder.' He goes on, 'barriers of rocks stretched like a weir athwart the water. Crowds of trackers squatted on the banks. A dozen men with iron-shod bamboos sheered the vessel off the rocks. Once through, stupendous walls of rock shut in the boat. We glided over the sunless waters between them . . .' The scenery hasn't changed a great deal since then, just clothed itself with a thick forest of orange trees, but the rocks, rapids and trackers are gone and the boat passes through with relative ease, sailing on to a number of smaller gorges – Sword and Book, Ox Liver, Horse Lung and Cow – until you reach Shadow Play gorge, where the shifting rocks by moonlight look like figures in a shadow play.

Finally, the river runs into the sheer cliffs and twisting currents of **Nanjin Pass**, and, after that, out on to the broad gentle plain above Yichang. Here you'll find the **Gezhouba Project**, an enormous complex of dams, power stations, locks and floodgates that, when finished, will be the largest hydro-electric power producer in China. The boat squeezes through the lock, which can take some time, to dock in **YICHANG**, of no special interest for itself but nonetheless the place where most people disembark – the scenery is much less striking further downriver. If, however, you are going on to WUHAN, you may as well stay on the boat as take a train, passing SHASHI, JIANGLING and CHIBI, described more fully in chapter 5. After Wuhan the Yangzi becomes the border of five provinces, curving its way slowly but surely past JIUJIANG, WUHU and NANJING (chapter 5) before arrival in SHANGHAI (chapter 3).

TRAVEL DETAILS

Trains
From Chengdu: Bao Ji (8 daily, 16hrs), Xi'an (8, 19hrs), Neijiang (8, 4hrs), Chongqing (4, 11hrs), Emei (4, 3hrs), Kunming (4, 25hrs)
From Emei: Chengdu (4, 3hrs), Kunming (4, 21hrs)
From Leshan: Emei (4, 1hr), Chengdu (4, 4hrs)
From Chongqing: Chengdu (4, 11hrs), Guiyang (5, 12hrs)

Buses
From Chengdu: Guanxian (8, 1½hrs),

Xindu (16, 1hr), Leshan (5, 5hrs)
From Emei: Leshan (8, 1hr)
From Leshan: Emei (8, 1hr), Chengdu (5, 5hrs)
From Chongqing: Dazu (2, 7hrs)
From Dazu: Chongqing (2, 7hrs)

Ferries
Daily to Wanxian (12hrs), Yichang (36hrs), Wuhan (3 days)

Flights
Airports at Chengdu and Chongqing

CHENGDU	成都	LESHAN	乐山
CHONGQING	重庆	NEIJIANG	內江
DAZU	大足	WANXIAN	万县
DU JIANG YAN	都江堰	XINDU	新都
EMEI SHAN	峨眉山		

Chapter nine
THE NORTH-WEST

GANSU – NINGXIA – QINGHAI – XINJIANG – INNER MONGOLIA

'China beyond the Wall', as the north-west used to be called, has an atmosphere quite different from the central, Han Chinese areas of the People's Republic. Traditionally remote and with climates as unwelcoming as any in Asia, these vast areas of steppe and grassland, desert and mountain, are the ancient homelands of the Barbarians – the Mongols, Uighurs, Kazakhs, Tufans and others – who for centuries plagued Chinese administrations. They are today officially designated **Autonomous Regions**, in deference to their 'minority peoples', though to all intents there is little actual independence. The history of dissent, and of highly sensitive border machinations with the Soviet Union, is too recent. In predominantly Muslim, Turkic-speaking Xinjiang, there was armed resistance by Uighurs opposed to Chinese rule into the 1960s. Resentments, fuelled by atrocities committed against Islamic targets during the Cultural Revolution, still erupt from time to time.

You do not have to be much more than a casual observer to notice this – nor, indeed, the reluctance of Qinghai's Tibetans, or of the Mongols, to integrate with the officially sponsored influxes of Han Chinese settlers. But whilst your sympathies are likely to take a pro-Minority turn during travels in these regions, it is important to be aware how much Beijing's own policy has shifted over the last few years – from strict 'integrational' dominance towards a degree of cultural acceptance (or at least token respect) of the minority cultures. The presence in the north-west of important natural and mineral reserves has inevitably played its part in this, and so too has the newly discovered potential of tourism. But it would be overly cynical not to give some credit for the government's attempts to institute industry and agricultural aid in what are in general the poorest fringes of the PRC.

Travel in this part of China, unless you have the money for flights and tours, is hard going. But on the positive side there are fewer restrictions – or at least they are easier to flout. An Uighur or Mongol official will often sell you a bus ticket that would worry a Han Chinese, partly through mentality, partly since you are so far from centralised control. And there is, of course, an obvious magic in the **routes** – the old Silk Road through the desert oases of Gansu and Xinjiang, the great grassland plateau of Inner Mongolia, and if you're really into roughing it the tortuous (but now thoroughly open) overland approach to Tibet, through Qinghai. Individual highlights for each of these disparate regions are detailed in their specific chapter introductions. However, you should certainly not pass through the north-west without seeing the Buddhist caves at **Mogao** (near Dunhuang) or the spectacular **Taersi Lamasery** (near Xining). If you are looking for isolation – and this is possible up here in these underpopulated wilds – there is also some tremendous **hiking** to be had in the **Tian Shan** (Mountains of Heaven), which bisect Xinjiang.

A note is necessary on **climate**. The north-west regions take in both high mountain plateau and desert basins. Xining (in Qinghai) is reckoned in summer to be China's coolest town – for what that's worth, whilst Turfan (in Xinjiang) is certainly the hottest. But throughout these regions there is extreme variation, between summer and winter temperatures. The summer is just about manageable, wherever you go, although be prepared for the dryness of southern Xinjiang and for temperatures well into high 20sC, possibly even higher. Winter is another matter altogether. By October, it is getting very cold at nights, making sleeping-bags essential on the long train journeys along with multi-layers of cold-weather gear. Later than this, through to about early March, you would have to be very determined to venture much past Xining. Xinjiang and Qinghai temperatures average out around −10°C, and often hit −15°C, in January.

The Silk Road

The pass of Karakoram, linking Xinjiang with Pakistan and points west, is once again open. But it is still very little travelled, and an extremely hard road to take. Yet a thousand years ago this was a crucial and well beaten trade route. The foundations for this, the **Silk Road** to the west which was to become one of the most important arteries of trade and culture in world history, were laid over two millennia ago. In the 2C BC little was known in China of the existence of people and lands beyond her borders, but there were constant rumours. In order to investigate these, the Imperial Court at Chang'an (Xi'an) despatched one *Zhang Qiang* to investigate the world to the west and to seek allies in the constant struggle against the Huns. Zhang set out in 139BC with a party of 100 men. Thirteen years later he returned, with only two other members of his original expedition and no alliances; but the news he brought nevertheless set Emperor Wu Ti and his court aflame. It included tales of Bactria, Sogdia, Parthia, Persia, Ferghana and its famous flying horses, and even of the Roman Empire.

Expeditions were despatched to secure some of these 'Blood-sweating, flying horses' for the Imperial cavalry – the horse played an important

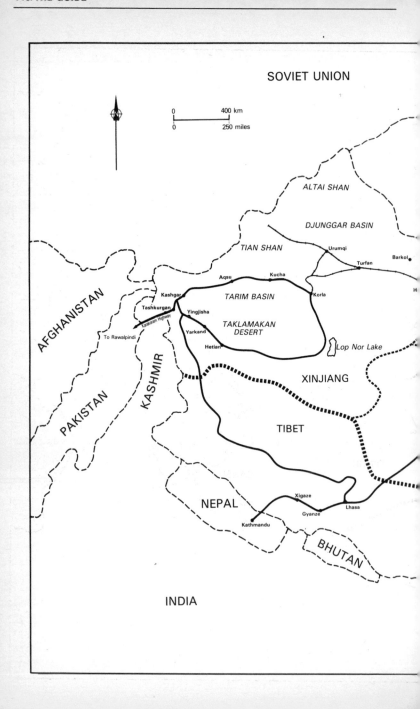

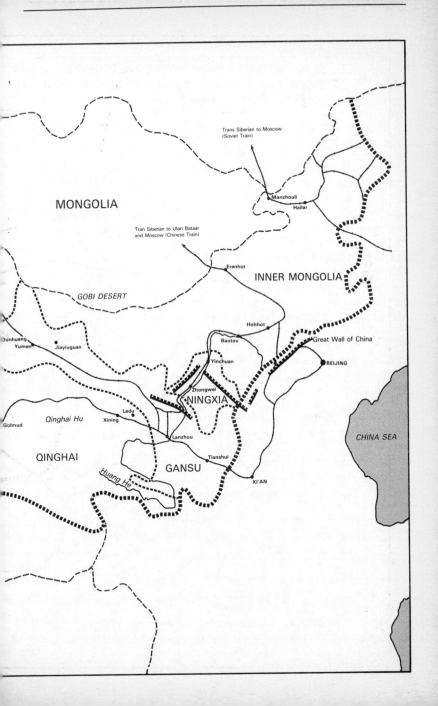

Trans Siberian to Moscow
(Soviet Train)

MONGOLIA

Manzhouli
Hailar

Tran Siberian to Ulan Bataar
and Moscow (Chinese Train)

Erenhot

INNER MONGOLIA

GOBI DESERT

Hohhot

Great Wall of China

Dunhuang
Yumen
Jiayiuguan

Baotou

Yinchuan

BEIJING

Zhongwei

NINGXIA

Ledu

Golmud

Qinghai Hu
Xining

Lanzhou

CHINA SEA

QINGHAI

Tianshui

GANSU

Huang He

XI'AN

role in the life of the Han Empire (hence the many magnificent representations in the art of the time). From these beginnings trade developed with astounding alacrity: by 100BC a dozen caravans a year were heading west into the desert from **Yumen** – Jade Gate. Each consisted of about 100 men and as many as 500 camels, each carrying 150–250kg of merchandise. West from China flowed jade, porcelain, lacquerware and, of course, **silk**.

The silkworm had already been domesticated in China for thousands of years, but in the west this exotic material, believed to be combed from the trees, was little more than a legend. The Chinese took great pains to protect their monopoly, punishing any attempt to export silkworms with death: it was centuries later that sericulture finally reached the west, silkworm larvae having been smuggled out by Nestorian monks in their hollow sticks. When the Romans first saw silk, snaking in the wind from the banners of their Parthian enemies, it filled them with terror and resulted in a humiliating rout. They determined to acquire it for themselves, but the Parthians discouraged any missions to the east, thus gaining themselves the position of middlemen in a highly profitable trade. Meanwhile Roman society became obsessed with the fabric, which around AD14 was said to change hands for its weight in gold. By 380 everyone was wearing it, 'even to the lowest', and the drain on the Roman exchequer was causing serious concern. According to one calculation, by the 4C two-thirds of the empire's stock of gold and silver had set off towards the east. But silk was not all that passed along the route: from China came oranges, peaches, rhubarb, pears, roses, azaleas, peonies, camellias, chrysanthemums, cast iron, gunpowder, the crossbow, the wheelbarrow, paper and printing; from the west came cucumber, figs, alfalfa, chives, clover, sesame, pomegranates, walnuts, grapes (and winemaking), wool, linen, ivory, jewels, rugs, asbestos cloth, fine steel and copper and potency-restoring rhinoceros horn.

Starting from Chang'an (Xi'an), the Silk Road curved north-west through Gansu to **Yumen** – where it split. Leaving the protection of the Great Wall, travellers could follow one of two routes across the terrible deserts of Lop Nor and Taklamakan, braving the attacks of the Huns, to **Kashgar**. The southern route ran through Dunhuang, Lobnor, Moron, Niya, Khotan and Yarkand; the northern branch through Hami, Turfan, Karashahr, Kucha and Aqsu. Many of these – once important cities – are now buried in the sands. High in the Pamirs beyond Kashgar, perhaps beneath the legendary stone tower of Tashkurghan, the merchants would trade their goods with the middlemen who were to carry them on the next stage, to Kashmir, Bactria, Afghanistan and India, or north to Ferghana, Tashkent and Samarkand. Laden with western gold, the Chinese merchants would turn back down the mountains for the 3000-kilometre journey home.

The **oases** which were staging posts and watering holes along the route inevitably prospered, each taking their rake-off and becoming important cities in their own right. Here were maintained garrisons to deal with the ever-present threat from Huns and Tibetans who, seeing the immense wealth lumbering to and fro at the foot of their mountains, were determined to exact their own tributes. With the decline of Chinese domination many of these cities became independent Khanates – self-sufficient feudal city-states.

As far as the Silk Road's importance in the development of China goes, the physical traffic takes second place to the cultural influences which it brought. New ideas included Nestorian Christianity and Manichaeism, but by far the most influential was **Buddhism**. The first Buddhist missionaries appeared during the 1C AD, crossing the High Pamirs from India, and their creed gained rapid acceptance among the nomads and oasis dwellers of what is now western China. It represented here the first budding of culture and art, filling a religious and spiritual vacuum. All along the road monasteries, chapels, stupas and grottoes proliferated; while, retracing the steps of the missionaries, pilgrims would travel from east to west in search of the roots of their religion. As Buddhism spread, wealthy merchants of the oases commissioned artists to build shrines and temples to ensure the safety of their caravans or to give thanks for their safe return. By the 4C Buddhism had become the official religion of much of northern China and by the eighth it was accepted throughout the Empire. Little remains today of the early flowering of Buddhist art along the road: the Muslims, for whom such figurative works were an abomination, western 'archaeologists', Red Guards, peasants and the forces of nature have all taken their toll. But some examples do survive – in particular the cave sculptures at **Mogao** (near Dunhuang) and **Bilingsi** (Lanzhou).

The Silk Road continued to flourish for centuries, reaching its zenith under the Tang (618–907) and bringing immense wealth to the Chinese nobility and merchants. But it was a slow, dangerous and expensive means of transport: predatory tribes to the north and south harried the caravans despite garrisons and military escorts; at times they took whole cities and even the entire Tarim Basin would periodically shake off the Chinese yoke and have to be 'repacified'. The route took its toll in purely physical terms too – whole caravans could be lost in the deserts and literally millions of pack animals perished in the passes of Karakoram and Pamir. Today a journey from Xi'an to Turfan by train, and thence by bus to Kashgar, takes about a week; a caravan, travelling between 18 and 25km a day, would have taken at least five months. Not surprisingly, then, the opening of sea-routes between China and the west took away most of the road's trade: the Empire's increasing isolation under the Qing completed the job.

GANSU AND NINGXIA

Gansu – the opening corridor of the Silk Road – is essentially desert. Except when the Han empire took in Xinjiang, under the Qing and Manchus, it was considered the edge of the empire, a realm of desolate landscape and barbarian peoples. Today, over half of its 19m population are Han, settled in the cities along the rail line, which in turn follows the thin belt of irrigated oasis created by the passage of the Huang He (Yellow River). But there are significant numbers of Hui, Kazakhs, Mongols and Tibetans – all, save the last, Muslim and usually actively so. For these traditional inhabitants life in Gansu is generally hard: the province includes some of the poorest parts of China, with herdsmen still eking out a semi-nomadic existence in the southern mountain foothills.

The great monumental highlight for travellers in Gansu is **Mogao** – the site of a spectacular sequence of Buddhist caves near **Dunhuang**, in the north of the province. Considered the finest surviving examples of Chinese Buddhist art, these are the most obvious legacy of the Silk Road's passage through the province. Hardly less exciting, by all accounts, are the **Maijishan Caves** near **Tianshui**, en route on the rail line from Lanzhou. (Unfortunately we have only slight information on Tianshui/Maijishan, which has only just been opened to travellers.) As counterpoint to such splendours, there is also the fortress of **Jiayuguan**, the last along the Great Wall.

Ningxia, a small autonomous Hui region, north of Gansu's capital, Lanzhou, has rather less of note. Like Gansu, it is largely desert, though increasingly reclaimed under the ambitious 'Green Wall' scheme to prevent the Gobi spreading further south. If you are travelling between the crossroads of Lanzhou and Hohhot, however, you will pass through this province. **Yinchuan**, its capital, is open for stopovers, so too is the whole county of **Zhongwei**.

LANZHOU

Few tourists are enthusiastic about **LANZHOU**. Marco Polo spent a whole year in the town without finding anything of note, and for modern-day travellers it is often the industrial pollution (amongst the worst anywhere in China) that makes the most forceful first impression. Don't, however, let this put you off. The city, long an important junction as the crossroads for routes to Lhasa, Siberia, India and Central China, has a plethora of sites to awe, delight and instruct – and an interesting mix of cultures that includes a thriving Muslim community. A two-day stopover here is time well spent.

Arriving

Coming into Lanzhou **by train** it's important to get off at the Dongzhan – the east station; Lanzhou Xizhan, the west station, lands you at the heart of the city's industrial quarter some 3–4km out from the centre.

From the Dongzhan, it's a straightforward 15 minutes walk (or no.1 bus ride) down Tianshui Lu to the main travellers' **hotel**, the *Lanzhou Fandian*. This is a reasonable place, easily spotted at the north-west corner of the roundabout; dormitory beds go for ¥5, double rooms around ¥16. But if they have space, a slightly preferable alternative is the newly opened *luxury hotel* next door – its entrance a couple of hundred yards up the same road. The hotel staff here are extremely friendly (and English speaking) and they let out double rooms in a rather less luxurious annexe for just ¥6 a head – including hot showers morning and evening. The third hotel here, the 'Sound Sleeping Guesthouse' across the road, is currently Chinese-only.

If for any reason both these hotels are full, and this is unlikely, the one other possibility is the *Friendship Hotel*, way over on the other side of the city centre by the Provincial Museum. Dormitory beds here are again ¥6. Access is simplest just by staying on the no.1 bus – about fifteen stops.

Some of Lanzhou's more interesting restaurants – and Muslim food-stalls – are detailed in the main text, below. But you'll find a couple of very reasonable places in the main hotel area. One of them is in fact the Fandian's own restaurant – moderately good food and inexpensive. The other, just outside the hotel gate, advertises itself with a picture of a glazed rat, lying on a bed of lettuce with its head on a beetroot: it's excellent, and again very cheap.

As far as other practicalities go, Lanzhou's **Public Security Bureau** (in the centre of town – see our map) deserves a mention: efficient, knowledgeable and English-speaking, they seem to know much more about the town (and possible excursions) than CITS. **CITS**, however, are co-operative enough and handily positioned on the first floor (room 201) of a building immediately behind the Fandian. Use them to buy train tickets when the railway station's foreigners' section (in a separate hall at the west end) is closed. Lanzhou's **Post Office** is reliable, if you want to pick up poste restante.

The city

Were it not for the Yellow River, roaring its way through the centre of the city, Lanzhou's pollution might well be lethal. But the river provides a kind of wind corridor, clearing at least some of the petrochemical fumes deposited by the vast Lanzhou Chemical Industry Company. In earlier days, the river here played no less crucial a role. For Lanzhou was one of the most important of the Huang He crossing points – no casual matter, as you realise just looking at the flow today. Until this century the bridge in fact comprised a series of boats, lashed together. They were superseded by an iron bridge around 1910, then in the 1960s by an ambitious four-lane highway – quite a feat of modern engineering, spanning nearly half a kilometre. Hardly less impressive is the locals' summer pastime of throwing themselves into the river, to hurtle (at an estimated 8 knots) through the city.

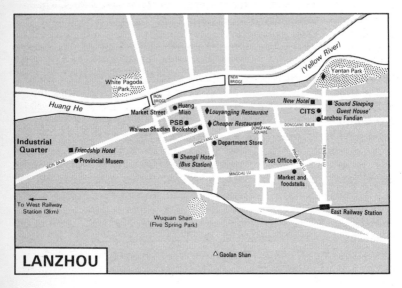

The iron bridge, just north of the city centre, is a good point to start exploring Lanzhou. Walk across and you will find yourself at the base of **Baita Shan**. Strung out along a quiet hillside park are a group of Qing dynasty pavilions – with an earlier, Yuan dynasty, White Pagoda at the summit. The pagoda is a kind of landmark to Lanzhou; the views from it are a useful orientation, spreading over the city centre and out to the bleak industrial suburbs on either side. At the foot of the hill, if you feel like whiling away an hour or two, there's a large tea-garden where local musicians play most afternoons.

Lanzhou's centre is marked by the crossroads at **Nanguan Shizi** square, flanked – distinctively – by a department store. The streets between here and the river are lively and interesting, full of little markets, noodle stalls, Huimin (literally Hui Muslim – though a word the Chinese use as a general term for Muslim) restaurants and a weird mix of shops – at which you can buy anything from a microwave to a dead rat. There is also a foreign language bookshop, the *Waiwen Shudian*, about 80 metres up from the square on the street going directly north. On the same street are two of Lanzhou's best restaurants. If you've the money, head for the *Louyangjing*, relatively expensive but with excellent food on each of the three floors. The alternative, next door but one (back towards the square) is a more modest-looking, unnamed eating house – again high quality cooking. Between the two, exotic if none too outstanding on the crafts- manship side, is a traditional music instrument shop.

Continuing along this street towards the river, and turning left at its end, you will come to the **Huang Miao**, the old town gardens. This is a marvellous, timeless place – a tea garden set amid another of Lanzhou's complexes of Qing dynasty pavilions. Sitting in the shade of mulberry trees, you can sip tea all afternoon for just 2 jiao. It is used for occasional exhibitions and concerts – probably worth catching if anything's on. Between exhibitions, unfortunately, the garden is sometimes closed.

The main city park is the **Wuquan Shan** – Five Spring Mountain – a no.8 bus ride (or a 20 minutes or so walk) from the Nanguan Shizi. Named from the tale of an ancient Chinese general who raised five springs by striking the ground, this is a typical Chinese park, gay pavilions – Qing dynasty again but pleasurably dilapidated – and convoluted flights of steps sprawling up the mountainside, interspersed with tea-houses, art exhibition halls and ponds with lily stepping-stones. There are oddities, too: a rather ramshackle circus run by a group of young people from Wuhan, and bizarre educational displays of aborted Siamese twins and hairy babies. All of which you can take or ignore at will. Much of the Wuquan's attraction is simply in wandering about, alongside the locals who converge here on summer evenings and weekends. From the top there are more sweeping views, north over the city, south across endless ranges of loess.

Further afield, getting on for 2km to the east of the Lanzhou Fandian (and the end of the no.12 bus route), is the much larger **Yantan Park**, laid out along the south bank of the Huang He. On a weekday you'll have this almost to yourself, a huge area planted with shrubs and willows by the authorities as part compensation for the vain efforts to combat the inner city's pollution. There is a public swimming pool here, and a lake with rowboats by the hour. Around the east end of the park are a number of small villages, set in irrigated farmland – a good walk if the sun's not too sweltering.

Over to the west side of town, where the industrial quarter really takes hold, there is less to entice. But the Lanzhou **Provincial Museum**, near the Friendship Hotel, is unusually good. Among a large collection of Han bronzes, their layout recently modernised, is a beautiful *Flying Horse*, a sculptural celebration of the arrival of the 'Flying Horses of Ferghana', imported by the Han to replace the traditional short-legged Chinese horse, which were to change the whole balance of power in the Ancient East.

The Binglingsi caves

The trip out from Lanzhou to the **Binglingsi caves** is one of the best excursions you can make in the north-west – enough in itself to merit a stay in the city. Not only does it give you a glimpse of the spectacular Buddhist cave, art that filtered through to this region along the Silk Road, but it is a startling introduction to the Yellow River, and its continued influence.

You can arrange the trip either through CITS (¥20–40 for the tour, depending on support) or the *Shengli Hotel* (¥36; students ¥18); either should be booked at least a day in advance. If you go for the Shengli's tour – and most travellers seem to – you'll find the hotel one stop west of Nanguan Shizi on the no.1 bus route. Their tour coach leaves daily at 6am and they'll fetch you from your hotel.

First stage of the expedition is a bruising 2 hour ride – the bus has no shock absorbers – through impressively fertile loess to the massive **Liuji-axia hydro-electric dam**. This is a spectacular sight, poised above an enormous reservoir winding some 80km along beautiful, coloured rock mountains. Foreign guests, sadly, are not invited to take too close a look at the dam itself, China's second largest. But the land and river hereabout is wonder enough. A bountiful plot, whilst the Huang He stays controlled, it is full of action: fishermen and ferryboats sailing down the river, peasants cultivating patches of wheat, sunflowers and rice on the dark, deep loess banks.

You leave the coach at the dam and transfer, for the next 3 hours, to a ferry – by this time a welcome change. The next part of the trip is an insight, following the course of the reservoir, and along one dramatic stretch entering a tall, hung **gorge**, where the current of the river really makes itself felt. Even as you pass, you'll see sections of the loess slipping away into the waters. It is said that the Huang He carries some 35 kilos of silt in every cubic metre of water – hence its constant murkiness – and, of course, the name.

The ferry finally docks just below the **Binglingsi caves**, or *Lingyansi* (Supernatural Cliff Monastery), as they're popularly known. Cut into sheer cliff, above a tributary of the Huang He there are 180 caves in all. They were amongst the earliest significant Buddhist monuments in China – first dynasty and subsequently extended by the Northern Wei, the Tang, Song and Ming. Spared through inaccessibility from the attentions of Muslims, Europeans and Red Guards, most of the cave sculpture is in good condition, and some impressive restoration work is in progress on the (predominantly Song and Ming) wall paintings. The centrepiece sculpture, approached along a dizzying network of stairs and ramps is a huge 27 metre seated Buddha – carved around AD650 under the Tang. The work at **Binglingsi** reached its artistic peak later under the Song and Ming dynasties. Though the wall-paintings of this period have been virtually washed away, there remains a considerable number of small, exquisite carvings.

Unfortunately you have just one hour to look around before the boat leaves – hopelessly inadequate but, unless you decide to go your own way and camp in the hills, the only option. As yet, and hopefully this may change, there is nowhere to stay, nor anywhere to eat either – buy your own lunch in Lanzhou the night before. Be sure, too, to take both warm clothes for the early morning bus and boat ride (it can be *very* cold!) and an umbrella or some kind of head protection for the intense sun on the ferry trip back.

Other trips around Lanzhou
At the time of research Binglingsi was the only properly open excursion from Lanzhou – but the situation has recently changed, TIANSHUI, along the rail line from Xi'an to Lanzhou, is now open, which means that you should be able to visit **MAIJISHAN**, another remote and (supposedly) magnificent centre of Buddhist art, with huge Buddhas carved out from the side of the mountain. We would welcome accounts on Maijishan for the next edition of this book.

Other possibly rewarding trips, worth at least the enquiry, are LIAN-CHENG and LABRO.

LIANCHENG was already open to Overseas Chinese when I was in Lanzhou, so if it's not open to foreigners by now it should be very soon. The attraction here is a **Ming dynasty palace**, set in an area of mountains and forests that are said to be teeming with rare flora and fauna. It is well within a day's journey of Lanzhou.

To the south-west, another likely addition is **LABRO** (or LABULENG SI). In Qing times this was the most important Lamaist monastery outside Tibet, with some 25,000 lamas under its control. It is said to be magnificent. To get there you would have to take a bus to XIAHE (again not open when I was in Lanzhou but imminent, according to the PSB).

JIAYUGUAN

One more cup of wine for our remaining happiness
There will be chilling parting dreams tonight
                              – 9C poet on a leave-taking at Jiayuguan

400km to the north of Lanzhou – and a useful break on the rail journey to Urumqi – **JIAYUGUAN** marks the traditional boundary of the Han Chinese empire. The **Great Wall** did once extend beyond here, further out along the Silk Road toward Xinjiang, but it was never effectively maintained and in 1372 the Han built here a final outpost fort. They gave it the name Jiayuguan – 'Earth's Greatest Barrier' – in quiet contempt for the territories beyond, and over the following centuries thousands of travellers passed through its gates, out of the protection of the Empire.

The modern town here has a thriving steel industry, and a sense of activity which rather belies the bleak remoteness of its past. The fort aside, it is not an interesting place. But it is open, you can stay pleasantly enough and without difficulty, and there are buses on to Dunhuang (see below). Arriving at Jiayuguan train station, you should be met by the town bus (even on the 11pm arrival from Urumqi/Turfan) which does a circuit down through the centre, passing the one foreigners' **hotel**, the *Jiayuguan Binguan*. A friendly, helpful place, the Binguan charges a standard ¥5 a night – whether in single, double or triple rooms, and you should have no problem getting a bed. There's a **bank** and **Post Office** opposite; a **PSB** and the bus station for Dunhuang just a little further down the road (ask the hotel to point you towards them). CITS have a representative (though no actual office) in the hotel.

The **Fort** is a 15 minute bus ride out of town; catch the bus from outside the hotel (4 departures daily – around 9.30, 12, 2 and 4.30). It has been substantially restored, recently and at intervals over its years of service, but its atmosphere remains very much rooted in the past. Out here, away from the modern town, the scenery is desolate beyond words, the walls, with their 20m towers, a fragile reassurance. It is not hard to imagine the despair of those for whom it must have been dark and probably permanent exile – the disgraced officials, condemned criminals and outlaws. Among the ruins and buildings, almost a secondary concern to this powerful feel, you can make out a number of pavilions, a temple and – perhaps most haunting – the foundations of an old open-air theatre.

DUNHUANG: THE MOGAO CAVES

DUNHUANG, at the borders of Chinese Turkestan, is an oasis city. To its south roll the sand dunes of the Gansu desert; west are the beginnings of the Taklamakan. It is a bleak, desolate landscape for the population, though arriving here as a traveller you will probably find it hard to resist the excitement. And arrive here you should, for, 25km outside the garrison town, stand the **Mogao caves**, the earliest (and probably the greatest) Buddhist cave temples created in China. Astonishingly well preserved in the dry desert air, they feature a brilliant sequence of murals which read like an illustrated history of Chinese painting – from Indian-influenced scenes of the 4C, through classic, elaborate Tang masterpieces, to 13C Tantric themes committed after the region's brief conquest by Tibet.

To do the caves any degree of justice – even the 40 (of a total 492) that are open – you will need a full day, or an afternoon and morning. Which means a likely two-day stay in Dunhuang. The town is nothing very much in itself – a garrison, as it has always been, approached along sticky tarmac melting in the sun. But it is very much on the travellers' circuit, and you won't exactly find yourself isolated.

Dunhuang is not on the railway, so you'll need to **approach**, by bus from one or other point along the Lanzhou–Urumqi line. The closest station is LIUYUAN (buses to Dunhuang at 7am, 1pm and 7pm), though this is a transit point you won't want to remain for long. Better perhaps to take the direct bus from JIAYUGUAN (3½hrs; at least daily departures). Moving on, you can rejoin the line by cutting across the desert to JIUQUAN (8hrs; daily at 7am), or if you have distinct masochistic tendencies, you *could* head due south over the desert and mountains to GOLMUD (8hrs; see p. 465) and on from there to Tibet.

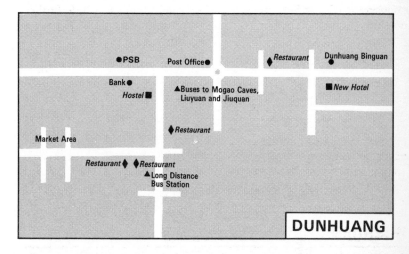

DUNHUANG

Staying in Dunhuang, there is a surprising amount (and quality) of choice. The standard foreigners' hotel is the *Dunhuang Binguan* (¥4.50 for dorms, ¥8–12 in doubles), an easygoing place with a bar and fountain – both enticing. Alternatively there's a *new tour group hotel*, directly opposite, whose friendly staff are willing to mop up extra budget tourists in very nice 3-bed rooms. Unlike their normal rooms these have no shower facilities, however nobody seems to mind if you trot over the road to the old Binguan (whose hot water is turned on from 7pm). Or, if you want to stay in more authentically north-west Chinese surroundings, there's also a wonderful little hostel run by a family near the market – very simple rooms around a courtyard (with pigs). All of these hotels are centrally positioned – see the plan – and only a few minutes walk from the high street bus terminal (where, unless you are coming from Golmud, you will arrive).

There are plenty of good **places to eat** scattered around town, many of the most interesting in the market area. Or, less exciting, you can get slightly above average fare at the Dunhuang Binguan. Lovely fresh bread is baked and sold on the corner of the market street.

There is no CITS in Dunhuang but the **PSB** – again easily found in the centre of town (opposite the **Bank of China**) is particularly helpful.

Heading to the Mogao caves, you have the choice between a bus (from the high street terminal, 7am daily, 30mins; return at 11am or 5pm) or hiring a bike or jeep from the Dunhuang Binguan. Biking allows a useful flexibility, and you can take off to see the sunset from the dunes too, but be warned that it is hot, hard going, uphill and for most of the way through straight desert. Before leaving, you may want to get your own lunch together. There is just the one restaurant at the site – and they sometimes make life hard for travellers by serving lunch only to those who book on arrival (before 9am). Lastly, if you want to get the most out of a visit to Dunhuang, you'd be well advised to buy a torch.

The Mogao caves

The Mogao caves are one of the great sites – and archaeological discovery stories – of the east. The first known Buddhist temples within the boundaries of the Chinese Empire, begun in AD366 by the monk Luo Zun, they were a crucial centre of the Silk Road's culture for over a millennium. The city of Dunhuang itself owes its origins to their creation but the most important legacy was undoubtedly a religious and artistic one. The spread of Buddhism radiated out, first across the north-west territories, later the whole Han Empire, from these wild desert cliffs, and with it, gradually adapting to a wholly Chinese style and context, came the artistic influences of India and Central Asia.

The story of Mogao's development, then subsequent abandonment and discovery, is an intriguing one. Its emergence dominated early Chinese Buddhism, as pilgrims, monks and scholars passing along the Silk Road, settled and worked here, translating (well apart from the strife of Central China) the holy texts, the Sutras. Merchants and nobles stopped too, endowing temples to ensure the success of their caravans or to benefit their souls, as they did (to a lesser or greater degree) all along the Silk Road. Under the Mongol dynasties, which really saw the establishment of Buddhism in the empire, the monastic community reached a zenith, with (under the Tang) over a thousand cave temples. Thereafter, however, as new trading links turned central China towards different directions, Mogao (and Dunhuang) became increasingly provincial, and at some point in the 14C the caves were sealed and abandoned.

Although Mogao's existence was known to Buddhist scholars, it was only in 1900 that the wandering monk, Wang Yuan Lu, fleeing from plague and famine in the central empire, stumbled upon them. He at once realised their significance, if not (in European terms) their value, and made it his life's work to restore and beautify the site, excavating caves full of sand, touching up the murals, planting trees and gardens and building a guesthouse. This work he undertook with two acolytes and financed – being himself penniless – through begging expeditions.

The reconstructions might have gone on in relative obscurity were it not for the discovery of a bricked-up hidden chamber, which Wang opened to reveal an enormous collection of manuscripts, sutras and silk and paper paintings – some a thousand years old and virtually undamaged. It was a trove that reached the ears first of the Dunhuang authorities, who, having appropriated a fair haul for themselves, suggested that the find be removed to Lanzhou, then, finding this too expensive, resealed them. So it remained for a further seven years, until the arrival of the Central Asian explorer and scholar, Aurel Stein. Stein, a Hungarian working for the British and the Indian Survey (perhaps in plainer language, an agent), had heard rumours of the caves and been offered items for sale that the Dunhuang authorities had removed. In good Howard Carter tradition, he persuaded Wang to re-open the chamber:

> The sight the small room disclosed was one to make my eyes open; heaped up in layers, but without any order, there appeared in the dim light of the priest's little lamp a solid mass of manuscript bundles rising to a height of nearly 10ft and filling, as subsequent measurement showed, close on 500 cubic feet – an unparalleled archaeological scoop.

Which was no understatement. Examining the manuscripts, Stein found original Sutras brought from India by the temples' founder, Xuan Zhang, and there were other Buddhist texts written in Sanskrit, Sogdian, Tibetan, Runic-Turkic, Chinese, Uighur – and others, unknown to the scholar. Amidst the art finds, hardly less important, were dozens of rare Tang dynasty paintings on silk and paper – badly crushed but totally undamaged by damp.

Eventually Stein, donating the princely sum of £130 to Wang's restoration fund, left Mogao with some 700 manuscripts and 500 paintings. Later in the year a Frenchman, Paul Pelliot, negotiated a similar deal, shipping 6000 manuscripts and many paintings back to Paris. And so, virtually overnight, and before the Beijing authorities could put a stop to it, the British Museum and Louvre acquired the core of their Chinese manuscript and painting collections.

All of which seems a pity, coming here after travelling through the wastes of north-west China to view the caves themselves. A museum of Tang paintings, and selected manuscripts from the find, would undoubtedly be inspiring – and the Chinese, fuelled perhaps by Greek claims on the Elgin marbles, are currently negotiating for a return. It has to be hoped that this will happen, though in fairness it was only in 1961 that the Chinese declared Mogao a National Monument. Had the trove remained, more would almost certainly have been lost. A large party of White Russians used the caves as a barracks in 1917, leaving a testimony of their disregard by scrawling their names over the frescoes. And the manuscripts might simply have met the fate of a wheelbarrow load of priceless Manichaean texts, found by a Muslim peasant at Kharakhoja and tipped into the river for fear of what the local Imam might say.

Visiting the caves

Of the original thousand or so caves, 429 survive in recognisable form. You cannot see them all. Some, by all accounts, are no longer of significant value or interest; others are, but contain Tantric murals which the Chinese reckon too sexually explicit for visitors' sight. But, so long as the guides are willing to unlock them, you should be able to look around some forty or so of the more interesting. To do this be sure to buy the **full ¥4 ticket**, which entitles you to two '**block visits**' (i.e. a morning and afternoon session); the caves close from 12–1.30 or so, so you can either turn up early and do both in one day, or take a first look in the afternoon and return the following morning to cover the rest. The **60fen ticket**, which the guides may possibly persuade you to accept, covers only the briefest of tours, highlighting half a dozen caves. And because the native Chinese visitor can be expected to take the cheaper of the two tours it is likely the guide will conduct the tour in Mandarin.

The full tours take some account of **chronology**, allowing you to get a reasonable picture of the caves' (and specifically their murals') development. The account below is structured as an additional aid.

The idea of cave temples came to China, with Buddhism, from India, where poverty, lack of building materials and the intense heat had necessitated the development of the form. The Chinese – Taoist and Confucian – tradition had been one of making temples from wood, a material well adapted to most Chinese conditions. The earliest caves here – hewn out in the 4C and 5C during the **Sixteen States** and **Northern Wei** dynasties – are relatively small in size. They centre on a sculpted figure of the Buddha, surrounded in tiers on the walls by a mass of tiny Buddhas – all brilliantly painted in blacks, whites, blues, reds and greens. The sculpture is in fact a form of terracotta: the texture of the caves (unlike that at Yungang, for example) was not suited to detailed carving, so the craftsmen would first carve a rough outline of the figure, then build it up with clay.

The style of the murals in these caves shows a great deal of foreign influence (quite obviously so, once you have seen the thoroughly Sinicised Tang paintings, later on). **Cave 101**, decorated towards the end of the 5C, provides a good example. The Buddha, enclosed by attendant Bodhisattvas, is essentially a western figure – recognisably Christ-like, in the way he appears on Greek Byzantine frescoes. Technically, however, there are distinctions: the Bodhisattvas and the stiff, strange postures are characteristically Central Asian. And there are the beginnings of Chinese influence in the wavy, flower-like angels above.

Murals like this were designed as a focus of devotional contemplation. But the arrival of a new religion also necessitated a narrative purpose, and the paintings soon move towards a wider subject matter, their story sequences arranged in long horizontal strips. **Cave 135** (early 16C) is one such. It illustrates the *jataka* story – a former life of the Buddha in which he gave his own body to feed a starving tigress, unable to succour her cubs. The narrative, read from right to left, is broken up by simple landscapes, a frequently used device.

Artistic changes – and a shift towards a resolutely Chinese style – began to appear towards the end of the Northern Wei period, around the middle of the 6C. One of the most strikingly Chinese of the Wei murals is in **Cave 120N** – with luck you will be shown this – and shows above the devotional niches a series of battle scenes. According to the art historian Laurence Soper, this 'introduces a point of view that was to remain a favourite throughout Chinese painting. [A convention] of the audience looking down onto the scene . . . onto the roof of the small buildings, but at the same time up the steps and directly at the verandah where a lady is seated. The artist felt no need for consistency . . . All the figures are drawn as though seen straight on.'

Soper adds, in comment, that these early examples of Chinese Buddhist painting were essentially provincial in character. That is to say, they absorbed influences from India and beyond, along the Silk Road, but they were well distanced from the Chinese court centres. With the founding of the **Sui dynasty** in 581 this position radically altered. The Chinese Empire had been torn apart by civil wars and there followed a boom in Buddhism – and Buddhist art. In the four decades up to the emergence of the Tang (in 618) over 70 caves were carved at Dunhuang. Structurally they dispense with the central column – a feature of the earlier grottoes. Artistically, they show the replacement of the bold, slightly crude Wei brushwork with intricate, flowing lines and an increasingly extravagant use of colour that soon included gilding and washes of silver. There is a new sense of calm, too, suggesting a rather different spiritual dimension. In **Cave 150**, for example, painted in the last year of the Sui, narrative has been dispensed with altogether in favour of a repeated theme of throned Buddhas and Bodhisattvas. In terms of sculpture, the Sui period also shows an enrichment. Interestingly, though, the figures themselves become more lifelike – the craftsmen having taken to modelling from real-life visitors and pilgrims.

The **Tang dynasty** artists, under whom (from 618–906) the caves at Dunhuang reached their zenith, drew both from past traditions and real life. Their paintings range from huge murals depicting scenes from the Sutras – now contained within one composition rather than the earlier 'cartoon strip' convention – to vivid paintings of individuals which show a startling new sense of portraiture. Line drawing was also introduced, reaching a high stage of development.

One of the most popular – and spectacular – Tang mural themes was that of the Visit of the Bodhisattva Manjusri to Vimalakirti. **Cave 1** contains perhaps the greatest expression of this story. Vimalakirti, on the left, is attended by a great host of heavenly beings, eager to hear the discourse of the ailing old king. Above him the plane is tilted to take in a seemingly limitless landscape, with the Buddha surrounded by Bodhisattvas on an island in its midst. Another version can be seen in **Cave 51E**, a mural that's also especially notable for the subtle shading of its portraiture – which includes a magnificently depicted Central Asian retinue. Other superb Tang murals include a very free, fluid landscape in **Cave 70** and, perhaps most developed of all, **Cave 139A**'s depiction of the Western Paradise of the Amitabha Buddha. This last is a supremely confident painting, working in elaborate displays of architecture and figures within a style that remains wholly contemplative and calm. The theme is the Buddha's promise of paradise: the souls or the reborn rise from lotus flowers in the foreground, with paradisal scenes enclosing the Buddha above.

The classic Tang cave has a square floor, tapering roof and a niche for worship set into the back wall. The **sculpture** includes warriors – a new theme. All are carefully detailed, the Bodhisattvas above all, with their pleats and folds clinging softly to undulating feminine figures.

Later work, executed by the **Five Dynasties**, **Song**, and **Western Xia** (906–1220), shows different period style, though little real progression from the Tang. Much, in any case, is simply restoration or repainting of existing murals. Song work is perhaps the most interesting, tending towards a heavy richness of colour, and with many of its figures displaying the features of minority races.

During the Mongol **Yuan dynasty** (1260–1368), towards the end of which period Mogao seems to have been abandoned, the standard niche in the back wall of the caves gave way to a central altar – creating fresh and uncluttered space for murals. Subject matter too signifies change. Tibetan-style Lamaist (or Tantric) figures are introduced, and occult diagrams – mandalas – become fashionable. The most interesting Yuan art is apparently in **Cave 465** – slightly set apart from the main body of grottoes. You might try asking the guides if they will open this up for view, though the odds are probably against you. In the fashion of Indian Buddhist painting, the murals include Tantric figures in the ultimate state of enlightenment – graphically represented by the state of sexual union.

Such then is the art. But a last note is perhaps due on the **artists and**

craftsmen who worked at Dunhuang. Paid a pittance – in a cave housing Buddhist scriptures, archaeologists discovered a bill of indenture signed by one sculptor for the sale of his son – they lived in tiny caves in the northern section of Mogao, furnished simply with a small brick bed. They worked, too, in very hard conditions, often lying on high scaffoldings, their light provided in the main by oil-lamps.

NINGXIA AUTONOMOUS REGION: YINCHUAN AND ZHONGWEI

Ningxia Huizhu Zizhiqu – The Autonomous Hui Region of Ningxia – shares the forbidding climate and landscape of Gansu (of which it for a time formed a part). In the north it is cut by the Huang He and encroached upon by the great wastes of the Tengger desert – part of the Gobi; in the south it is arid and mountainous. Traditionally one of the poorest and most backward reaches of the country, it is the homeland of the **Hui**, a Muslim people who now constitute around one-third of the 4m population. Historically, their most significant modern role was in the Muslim Uprisings of 1862–78, viciously put down by the Chinese in these parts with a fearful toll of lives. As elsewhere in the north-west, Han emigration has been actively promoted in the post-Liberation years.

There is no real reason for visiting the region other than travel. If you are heading from Lanzhou into Inner Mongolia (or vice versa) you will pass through the capital, YINCHUAN, and second city, ZHONGWEI, en route to BAOTOU. The **Lanzhou-Baotou rail line**, opened only in 1958, has done much to relieve isolation. It was laid, by literally thousands of labourers, over a 2 year period which involved the shifting of virtual mountains of sand and the creation of a massive chequerboard grid of straw thatch to prevent the desert reclaiming its land.

Zhongwei

A small country town, enclosed in a rich belt of irrigated fields and poplar windbreaks, **ZHONGWEI** is probably the best break of journey in Ningxia. It is a modern-looking place – though of ancient foundation. The story goes that old, walled Zhongwei had no north gate – for there was no more of China to its north.

The town has one **hotel**, open to foreigners (¥6 in a triple; ¥12 in a double). To find it, turn right on leaving the station, then right again at the Drum Tower and walk 350m up the street – the *Zhongwei Binguan* is on your right.

As far as action goes, you can hire bicycles at the hotel to explore the town and beyond, or for ¥50 you could hire a jeep and driver. The latter allows rather more scope, for there are substantial remains of the **Great**

Wall to the east and some dramatic desert routes out towards the Huang He. Slightly further afield, west of Zhongwei, SHAPOTOU has one of China's most ambitious sand-control schemes, which your jeep driver may be willing to take in.

Yinchuan

Like Zhongwei, the area around the Ningxia capital, **YINCHUAN** is well irrigated. Some of the canals, it is said, have been in more or less continuous use since the Han and Qin dynasties; so too, no doubt, have the rice fields. The city itself, however, is modern and somewhat bleak: a possible, though not a greatly recommended, stop.

If you do decide **to stay**, you'll need the no.1 bus from outside the station, which will take you, logically enough, to the *Number One Hotel*. Double rooms go for ¥15; there may also be cheaper dormitories.

Around the town, the greatest interest is in the strong Muslim flavour of the place. **Mosques** dot most quarters and there is one that looks exotically Central Asian in appearance. There are a couple of impressive Yuan dynasty brick **pagodas** too – worth the look if you decide to pause between trains, as is the **Chengtian Temple** (with its museum) in the west of the city. An additional oddity is a Roman Catholic church, legacy of turn-of-the-century Belgian missionaries.

Yinchuan lies 3hrs east on the railway from Zhongwei; (??)hrs from Baotou.

QINGHAI

Qinghai is geographically an extension of the Tibetan Plateau, an area of some 750,000 square kilometres – all of it startlingly inhospitable. In this century it has had a reputation as a kind of Chinese Siberia: apt both in terms of climate and function, for it is home to most of the PRC's labour camps and traditionally a place of exile.

Culturally and historically Qinghai's affinities are with Tibet, rather than with Han China. It became part of the Chinese Empire only in the 18C. Previously, in so much as its desolate land mass attracted attention, it was the domain of the feudal Tibetan monasteries (one of the greatest of which, Taersi, stands in fact inside the province). The population – outside of the capital and Han outpost of Xining – largely comprises Tibetans, Kazakhs, Mongols and Hui.

The province was opened late to tourism – in 1985 – but is now firmly on the travellers' circuit. This is due almost wholly to the **overland route** to Tibet, which runs through **Xining** to **Golmud** by rail, then on from there to Lhasa by bus. Returning through Qinghai there is also the option of cutting north from Golmud to Dunhuang – though this, as suggested later (p. 467), is something of an endurance test.

As far as its own intrinsic interest goes, Qinghai does not have a lot to offer beyond the perspective of a strong minority presence. This is one of the poorest parts of China – bleak, desolate and with a depressed air about it. The lamasery of **Taersi**, however, is an atmospheric and magnificent site – arguably the rival of anything in Tibet itself. And the mountains, up to 6,500m as you near Tibet, and vast expanse of **Qinghai Lake**, form a memorable backdrop to the long, hard business of travel.

XINING

4½hrs by train from Lanzhou, **XINING** is an unpromising beginning to Qinghai-Tibet, with its predominantly Han Chinese population and standard Chinese architecture. The Tibetans in this area tend to be country dwellers, shepherds and peasant farmers, and it is only really the presence of Hui mosques that creates any feel of being in such a remote, minority area. On the positive side, though, Xining does allow the opportunity of an excursion to Taersi; it is a reasonably comfortable pit-stop on the dash to Tibet; and its PSB has a reputation of being one of the most flexible in the country.

The town's foundation is ancient – perhaps as early as the 2C, during the Eastern Han dynasty. It was – and is – a strategic location, set in a fertile patch on the Huang Shui and controlling passage through the province. All around are mountains, most of them a good 5,000m above sea level. Xining itself is high, too. It is known as one of the coolest summer cities in China – and one of the most bitter in winter. If you are heading beyond (and there would be little point in coming here if you do not intend to), it is a good place to stock up on Chinese cold-weather gear.

There are two **hotels** open to foreigners. The *Renmin Binguan* is just 1km down from the station (on the left, taking the road directly opposite) and offers basic dormitory accommodation at around ¥4 a night. The *Xining Binguan* is closer to the centre of the city – buses run from the station through to 8.30pm (arrive later and it's a long walk or, if you can get one, tricycle cab) – and a little more upmarket, with ¥6 dorm accommodation, doubles or triples a few yuan extra. Both hotels have running water for a few hours a day, and both serve meals (of somewhat variable character). Other **places to eat** have to be searched out, Xining being a somewhat impoverished city. There are good noodles to be had as you turn right out of the Xining Binguan. Or you could make your way to the *Swan Restaurant*, about 10 minutes walk away, near the market area; run by a group of homesick but boisterous Shanghainese, this serves what must be the city's best food – and good value, too. A scattering of other places can also be found opposite the station, or there are stalls in the market open during the day.

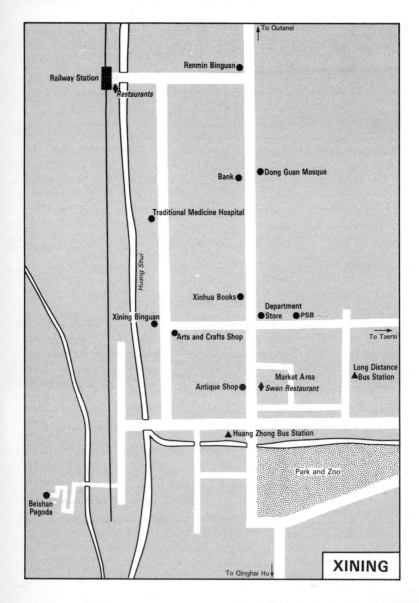

CITS have an office in the Xining Binguan, open daily and offering tours to both the Qinghai Lake and Taersi (see below). Alongside CITS there is also a **money exchange**, though this only operates for 2hrs in the morning.

Sights around the city are thin. At some point, however, make your way to the **market**, about the only place in Xining you're likely to see Qinghai Tibetans, in from the hills to sell their wares. You can also buy good Muslim bread there, or stock up on nibbles (peanuts, dates, raisins, walnuts) for long journeys ahead. The **department store**, a block down from the market, is worth a browse too; wander up to the second floor, full of Tibetan musical instruments, boots, cloth, brass and turquoise. Across the road, just north of the junction, is the **Xinhua Bookstore**, with a fair selection of titles in English.

More concretely, Xining also boasts a zoo, a medical college and two interesting religious buildings – the Dong Guan Mosque and Beishan Temple.

The **Dong Guan**, Xining's Grand Mosque, is 20 minutes or so walk north of the market. The city's most imposing and beautiful building, it was built in the 14C and remains today a thriving centre of worship and teaching. You are free to visit, so long as you're respectfully dressed (more than likely in this climate). Parallel to the Dong Guan, a few blocks to the west, you'll find the city's **Medical College** and **Hospital**. This may not be an obvious highlight but if you've a serious interest in acupuncture or Chinese traditional medicine the staff are willing to show you around. (If you want to do this, it's best to ask the hotel to phone ahead and make an appointment for you.)

The **Beishan Pagoda** stands on the mountainside at the other end of the city. From the Xining Binguan, turn right out of the hotel, right again at the roundabout, over the river and left at the T-junction by the railway and you will come upon the track which leads up the mountain. The temple is remarkable primarily for its position – perched on a cleft of the mountainside and a popular target for weekend picnickers. If you climb up to the brick pagoda at the summit, refresh yourself en route with a cup of *dragon's eye tea* – a luxury drink, tea, crystal sugar and three floating dragon's eyes (or lonchans, a kind of lychee, which should be peeled before eating!). The views at the end of the climb are generally clear and very striking. The city on one side below, on the other a landscape of utter barrenness, peppered with grey, sandy hills. At the foot of the hillside is a swift **irrigation channel**, ideal for **swimming** and popular with the Xiningese as such. As you float between banks of tall poplars, you pass through the city's village suburbs – a constantly replayed vision of mud-walled courtyards, paper windows and intensively cultivated plots of cabbages, cotton and rape. (Do not, however, get lulled into carelessness by this scenario: sluice gates lie ahead to suck you into reality; take care!)

Lastly, on the Beishan side of the city, there is **Xining Park and Zoo**; from the market it is only 10 minutes walk. This is not exactly worth travelling to Xining to see, though if you get stuck waiting for tickets you can while away a pleasant morning around here. The park flowers are wonderful – a welcome relief from all those brown, dingy buildings. And the zoo – though its conditions are sadly very confined – takes in an assortment of big cats, including various lynxes and the elusive snow leopard (found only in Qinghai and Tibet). As usual, unless you want to be treated as a zoo animal yourself, avoid going on a Sunday.

Taersi (Kumbum) Lamasery

Taersi – or Kumbum (or Gonbon) as it used to be known – is the most important Lamaist monastery outside Tibet. The current Dalai Lama came from here, and it attracts droves of pilgrims from Tibet, Qinghai and Mongolia – a startling sight, with their rugged features, huge embroidered coats, bold jewellery and open, frank manner. This alone would justify a trip out to Taersi, as would the monastery's architecture, spectacularly and defiantly un-Chinese. Added incentive, however, comes in the countryside around – mountainous, beautiful and perfect for **hiking**. The views stretch away to a panorama of Himalayan foothills, and you can ramble at will through hills of wheat, cattle or horses, and over ridges and passes strewn with wild flowers. The people you meet here are mainly Tibetan horsemen, humorous and keen to investigate you, workers in the field who will profer an ear of roasted barley by way of hospitality, or the pilgrims, prostrating their way around the monastery walls. Definitely a special place – with most to offer those who can slow down and spend a few days – and unbelievably restful after time spent travelling through the cities, stares and crowds of central China.

Taersi, as part of Huang Zhong county, can be visited without any special permit. To get out there take the LUSHAER **bus** from the Huang Zhong bus station in Xining; they run more or less every hour, the journey taking around 1½hrs. Arriving at Lushaer, walk straight uphill past the trinket stalls and rug sellers until, after about 1km, you see the row of eight stupas (or *chortens* as they're known in Tibet) at the monastery entrance. Just beyond the stupas, on the right, you'll see the *Huang-zhong County Tour Hotel*, actually a beautiful, 16C **pilgrims' hostel**, wooden and rickety, with an ancient balcony and peeling murals. With luck you will find a room here (¥7 a bed in a double) though it is becoming so popular with travellers that it is often difficult to get in. If this is so, then there's another even ricketier residence almost directly opposite. Or, as a last resort, you may have to put in a first night at the **hotel** opposite the Lushaer bus station – basic but cheap at ¥4 a bed. You can get **meals** at the pilgrims' hotel, depending on the vagaries of the cook. Or try one of the Muslim eateries on the road between the town and monastery. These are great value, providing huge warming bowls of noodles (two kinds – rice and wheat) with plenty of vegetables and, to wash it down, more dragon's eye tea. There are further eating stalls – open daytime and early evening – in the market area down the steps in front and to the left of the stupas.

The monastery dates from 1560, when building was begun in honour of Tsong Kapa, founder of the reformist Yellow Hat sect of Tibetan Buddhism (see p. 505), who was born in the Taersi estates. Legend tells how, on Tsong's birth, drops of blood fell from his umbilical cord causing a tree with a thousand leaves to spring up; on each leaf was the face of the Buddha, and in the trunk a Buddha image (now preserved in one of the stupas). History is scarcely more modest in regard to Tsong's significance; his two major disciples were to become the two living Buddhas – one the Dalai Lama, the other the Panchen (Baiqen) Lama.

Set in the cleft of a valley, the monastic complex is an imposing and wonderful sight – entirely walled, with flags blowing *Om mani padme hum* out to the wind. It is an active place of worship for about 600 monks (ranging in age from 10 to 80) as well as the constant succession of pilgrims. Visitors can see six of the monastery's temples: you buy a book of tickets (which covers them all) in the kiosk to the right of the stupas. The most beautiful is perhaps the *Dajingtang*, the Great Hall of Meditation, an enormous, very dimly lit prayer hall, colonnaded by dozens of carpeted pillars and hung with long silk tapestries (*tankas*). But it is closely rivalled by the principal temple, the *Dajinwa*, with its gilded tiles, wall paintings of scenes from the Buddha's life and brilliant silver stupa containing a statue of Tsong Kapa. And, in its own equally spectacular manner, by a long building set slightly apart on the hillside which contains yak butter sculptures – incredibly elaborate, painted tableaux, depicting Tibetan and Buddhist legends. Another of the temples is dedicated to animals.

If you are discreet, you can explore other of the monastery buildings and climb on to the slopes behind for a general perspective. You can also attend some of the religious ceremonies – though it is difficult to find out when these are taking place. Two regular chanting sessions, however, seem to be held at 5.30am and 6.30pm. Hang around and keep your eyes and ears open. There is plenty of activity, in any case, to watch. Monks in their dusty burgundy robes and huge leather boots, sitting in stately tranquillity in temple doorways, or working on their daily tasks – collecting wood, drawing water from the well, carrying food to the kitchens on a yoke. Or the young novices, fooling around on their way to sutra practice just like any other high-spirited schoolboys.

Qutan Si

If you feel inspired by Taersi, you might try to visit another Tibetan lamasery, **QUTAN SI,** off to the south of Xining. It wasn't open to foreigners when I was there (and at the time of writing I've not heard of anyone visiting). But the Xining PSB assured me it was on the cards – so ask! The monastery, built during the Ming dynasty (14C) was once among the most important Buddhist centres in China and it was maintained and added to until the 17C. According to Chinese friends, it is an extremely impressive sight.

You could get to Qutan Si by direct **bus** from the long-distance bus station in Xining, or by local train to LEDU (then bus or hitch the 17km on from there).

Qinghai Hu (Qinghai Lake)

QINGHAI HU – China's largest lake, ringed by a spectacular swathe of mountains – lies between Xining and Golmud. If you take a daytime train along this route you will get a dramatic sequence of views. Visiting the lake, however, is possible only with a CITS arranged tour. Local buses don't run anywhere very near the lake (nor anywhere very interesting), according to travellers who have tried to go it alone. And the region is said to be a sensitive one – home to some of the Qinghai labour camps and, apparently, a missile research establishment.

There are two **tours** to Qinghai Hu on offer at the Xining CITS. The short tour (¥26–32, depending on how many people join) gives just an afternoon and a night at the lake – hardly enough to see the lake. The longer, three-day version (about ¥48–55, but not always available) gives a much stronger sense of the area, taking you right round to the west end of the lake. Note, however, that CITS tour prices do not include food or accommodation, and if you join a tour made up largely by one party – say, Hong Kong Overseas Chinese – you may well find plans adapted to their whims. Also, most importantly, take a lot of warm clothes: the lake is very, very high altitude (which may cause sickness – headaches and nausea – so take things easy on arrival).

It takes about 3hrs for the tour bus to reach the eastern edge of **the lake,** a long haul which involves the crossing of a pass at 3750m. On arrival you will be taken to a village of brick barrack-like huts, where you are welcomed by CITS-approved Tibetans. After tea you are free to go for a walk or take a rough tractor ride to a pool known as the 'Garden of Eden', before a supper of excellent Qinghai Hu fish at around 6pm. And if you are on the short tour this will be about it – the bus sets off back to Xining at 8 the next morning.

The longer tour, of course, offers more chance to explore. You may even be able to get out to one of the five **islands** in the lake. One (generally closed except to ornithological experts) is a bird sanctuary, home to over a hundred different species, including the Black Necked Crane (unique to Qinghai and Tibet). Another, rather more promising, used to house a lamasery; the waters around it were considered sacred, apparently, so no boats were allowed to circulate and supplies could only be brought in when the lake froze over in winter! It is now a more conventional community, with a fishing fleet and a cannery on the southern shore. The island village is imaginatively called YUCHANG (Fish Factory). You can stay there, in tourist *yurts* just outside or in the barracks (or, if you can escape the CITS attentions, in what is said to be a good hotel in the village itself). If you are really committed to escaping from the tours, perhaps even staying on after the bus leaves, the hills are thinly populated by semi-nomadic Tibetan herders and you may be able to stay with them.

The lake is ideally visited **May–August**, when the flowers on the grassland are at their most vivid and rampant. Although the lake is totally enclosed by mountains, the landscape immediately around is lush and fertile and the plains of deep grass are full of flowers (Edelweiss roll into the distance) and wildlife – hares, lizards and fearless birds. Horses and cattle are put to graze here, whilst higher up are huge flocks of sheep.

GOLMUD – AND ON TOWARDS TIBET

GOLMUD transformed itself within a matter of months from being quite out of bounds to foreigners to a busy crossroads for travellers to and from LHASA to the south, DUNHUANG to the north, and XINING/LANZHOU to the east. The last of these links is the most (indeed the only) straightforward one. Two trains run daily between Xining and Golmud in about 10hrs, or slower but possibly more interesting, there's also a local bus. Dunhuang and Lhasa connections are detailed (in all their complexity) below.

Golmud itself is of no great interest beyond the experience of the grimness of life in this sort of area. The town's main function is as a transport link and supply base – virtually all supplies to Tibet are taken in through here – and as a military garrison (there is a large army presence).

The town is spread out, barrack-like and bleak, but it offers a reasonable **hotel** that takes foreigners, with four-bed rooms or dorms for ¥6–10; no showers, but hot water from the boiler when it's on. The hotel is located near the market, department store and hospital, in what is presumably the centre of town. If you arrive by rail you will probably be met by a bus which will take you straight there. If you arrive by bus or truck you could end up at one of several bus/truck stops in or around the town. Unless there is obvious transport to the hotel, try hailing someone in the street; many farmers will be happy to take you in their tractor-trailer for a couple of yuan a person. (Before leaving your bus/truck stop, incidentally, try to find the energy to enquire about rides to your next destination: you may be able to continue the same day, or at any rate avoid a fruitless trip to the bus stop the next day.)

Going on to Lhasa

BY BUS: If you arrive in Golmud by train from Xining, you may be met by a bus waiting to whisk you straight off to Lhasa, or by one that is leaving that afternoon and for which you can buy a **ticket** (unlike trains, there are no Chinese/foreigners distinctions on bus tickets). Otherwise there should be a chance to get a ticket at the hotel, as someone from the bus station makes a daily visit. The hotel staff, especially the manager, are happy to give information (though they are all Chinese-speaking only). Tickets can be bought at the bus station, of course, though at somewhat unpredictable times.

The **bus to Lhasa** takes about 30 driving hours, the number of stops en route (and total journey time) varying considerably from driver to driver. There will quite probably, however, be one overnight stop at a truckstop along the way. Overnight could mean from about 7pm till 5am (in which case there's time for supper), or it could be 11pm till 4am (no hope). There should though be some sort of food stops on the way, albeit brief ones – just time to order a plate of noodles and eat them, with the driver hooting to restart before you are half way through.

As luggage stays on top of the bus all the way, carry with you anything that you might need on the journey (or overnight stop – if it happens). As well as plenty to eat and drink, it is a good idea to take a sleeping bag into the bus, regardless of season. The route climbs to over 5000m and nights are *cold*.

The standard of buses varies considerably – there are a couple of new Japanese buses with reclining seats and stereo cassette players (try enquiring when these leave, if you are really worked out!) – but it is best to expect neither heating nor legroom.

BY TRUCK: Lifts can be **arranged** easily enough at Golmud's Tibet-bound truck stops and you *may* find one that turns out a more comfort-able means of travel than the bus. A ride in one of the beautiful white Toyota trucks is perhaps the ultimate in travel comfort available in the People's Republic. On the other hand, some of the trucks are very, very primitive. Pick with care.

Truck drivers tend to expect **payment** more or less equal to the bus fare. The number of stops they make is obviously variable. A possible bonus, if you find a Tibetan driver, is that they may stop off to visit family or friends en route.

Getting to Dunhuang

BY BUS: Buses between Golmud and Dunhuang run every few days depending on demand. Buying a **ticket** is no guarantee that the bus will actually leave – drivers won't set out until they've a minimum of twelve passengers. Find out from other travellers (and the hotel) what the position is and prepare yourself for frustration (there have been recent reports of fights breaking out between passengers, Chinese and foreign, and bus drivers and conductors!).

The journey takes around 8hrs, with a stop for lunch.

BY TRUCK: Arranging a truck may be straightforward – or it could mean spending four or five days getting nowhere (in which case there will be several Chinese would-be travellers in the same position).

To try it, make your way to the truck stop on the Dunhuang road. Be aware that some drivers have been fined for taking western passengers in the back of their trucks rather than in the cab – so if they appear to have space and yet won't take you, that is probably why.

BY JEEP: Hire of jeep/landcruiser/minibus (with driver)* can be arranged through the hotel in Golmud, though rates are high and fellow passengers willing to pay probably sparse. With eight people (the maximum) you would still be paying over ¥100 each.

BY CAMEL: Yes, it is possible – though the trip has probably not been done by any westerners yet. Golmud boasts a camel co-operative (round the corner from the Dunhuang-bound truck stop, where you can get directions) that sends camel trains up to Dunhuang.

The trip apparently takes three to four weeks.

XINJIANG

The Autonomous Region of Xinjiang – literally 'New Frontier' – occupies an area slightly greater than Western Europe (or Alaska, if your comparisons are Atlantic). Its population, however, is just 11m, for this is one of the least hospitable areas of China: isolated by the Tian Shan mountains and, above all, by the Taklamakan, the country's most formidable desert, which covers much of the southern part of the region.

Xinjiang's dominant culture is **Uighur**, though there are also some dozen other Central Asian minority populations. It is perhaps the 'least Chinese' of all parts of the People's Republic, and arguably also the most exciting: an extraordinary terrain, over two thousand miles from any

---

*The **minibus** may be too expensive for long trips, however it can certainly be worth hiring (if there are two or three of you) in order to get to an out-of-the-way truck stop to leave town or arrange a lift.

coast, with oasis settlements still producing the silk and cotton for which it was famed from the time of the Roman Empire. Taking the **routes through Xinjiang** – descendants of the ancient Silk Roads – is one of the real adventures of travel (in China – or anywhere) and they are opening rapidly to foreigners. If you are hardy and adventurous enough you can take the road to Kashgar in the far west – and then beyond, out of China across the 'Karakoram Highway' to Pakistan, or even across the mountains into Tibet (though this latter route remains more or less expeditionary – and officially illegal). Within Xinjiang itself, the highlights are the great oasis cities of **Turfan** and **Kashgar**, each redolent of old Turkestan, and the **Tian Shan** mountain pastures outside Urumqi, where there is the chance to hike in rare solitude and to stay with the Kazakhs in their *yurts*.

Geographically – and in its climate – Xinjiang divides into two distinct **regions**: the Djunggar Basin (to the north of the Tian Shan mountain range) and the Tarim Basin (to the south).

The **Tarim**, a great depression that covers most of the south, has at its heart the Taklamakan desert. The population (which is largely Uighur: Han settlement being mainly in Djunggaria) lives in a string of oases, mainly along the western fringes where there is irrigation from the Himalayan Pamirs. The climate here is intense – as much as 45°C in summer (in Turfan), and down to −30°C in January – and it is made harder to deal with by the dryness (and sand dust) of the summer air.

The Djunggar Basin (or Djunggaria, as it's sometimes called) is largely grassland, with large state farms in the centre, Kazakh and Mongol herdsmen (still partially nomadic) in the mountain pastures on the fringes. The climate is less extreme than that of the Tarim, only in the 20°sC in summer, though still below freezing from October through to March.

In general, it would be wise to avoid doing any travelling in Xinjiang in midsummer or midwinter.

Some history
The **Uighurs** have a long history of armed opposition to Chinese rule – a history which runs right through to the post-Liberation period when Muslim separatists attempted to halt the region's incorporation into the PRC. Even today there are outbursts of Uighur **dissent**, most recently (in 1986) in opposition to China's nuclear tests at the desert site near Lop Nor. These were the first-ever anti-nuclear protests in China, prompted by what seem to have been numerous cases of early death from cancer and a high incidence of deformity in lambs and newborn children. The import of fruit and vegetables from Xinjiang was banned for a time by Hong Kong, though following tests they have been resumed.

The region's **historical background** takes in such names as Tamburlaine, Genghis Khan, Attila the Hun, even Alexander the Great. More often, though, in counterpoint to these great movements of history, it has seen isolation and feudal warring between the rulers of its oasis kingdoms, or *khanates*.

The influence of China has been far from constant. The north-west – or eastern Turkestan as it was more commonly known pre-1949 – first passed under Han control in the 2C BC, under the Emperor Wu Ti. But it was only during the **Tang dynasty** (AD650–850) that there was anything more than a military presence. Tang period Xinjiang seems by all accounts to have been something of a golden age, with the culture, art and (Buddhist) religion of the oases reaching their zenith. The Middle Ages saw the arrival of **Islam**, which took hold throughout the region, but also of Genghis Khan and later, from the west, Tamburlaine. Both perpetrated untold slaughter. After Tamburlaine's campaigns, it is said, Kashgaria was left devastated – 'a man-made desert'.

Through this period, but particularly after the fall of the Mongols, Xinjiang began to split into the **khanates** – and to a succession of religious and factional wars. This was feudalism at perhaps its most cruel; however, it was an independence of a kind and **Qing** re-assertion of Chinese domination in the mid 18C was fiercely contested. In 1862 there was full-scale **Muslim rebellion,** led by the ruler of Kashgaria, one Yakub Beg, armed and supported by the British, seeking influence in this buffer zone between India and Russia. Ultimately the revolt failed – Beg becoming as hated a tyrant as any Chinese – and the region remained part of the empire.

At the beginning of this century, Xinjiang was still feudal, a Chinese backwater controlled by the **warlord** Yang Tsentsin and later by his successor Chin Shuren, who led his followers into civil war against the southern Muslim rival, Ma Chungying. This period was eventually brought to a close by the military intervention of Chin's commander, Sheng Shizai. Sheng was initially a reforming force, instituting religious and ethnic freedoms, and, after inviting a number of Communists to join his administration, establishing trade with the newly emergent Soviet Union. He too, however, became brutally dictatorial, slamming the door on the Soviets and on leftist influences within Xinjiang itself – where a reign of terror in 1940 resulted in the deaths of over 200,000 Communists, intellectuals, students and patriots. In 1943 Sheng's paranoia edged him into joining the Kuomintang, who promptly pushed him from control, and attempted to use Xinjiang as a base against the Red Army.

The drive towards **Liberation**, in 1949, combined numerous forces – Muslim nationalist as well as Communist. The principal Muslim Nationalist leaders, however, were mysteriously killed in a plane crash in 1949 and the impetus towards a separatist state was lost. The last Uighur guerilla leader, Osman, was executed in 1961.

In the 1950s and 1960s the Chinese government made strenuous attempts to stabilise the region and gain more control by settling Han Chinese from the east – into Urumqi and Turfan, in particular. The region, 90 percent Muslim Uighurs at Liberation, was 50 percent Han according to the census of 1982. (And this despite the minorities' exemption from the One Child policy.) The **settlement of Hans** has probably had the effect intended, watering down nationalist impulses and possibilities of action. However, it has not been without problems. Though some of the resettled Hans are happy enough with life in Xinjiang, for many others it has not lost its image of 'barbarian' country – and it certainly is bleak, dusty, furiously hot or bitterly cold, and less well provided for materially than the east. There have been reports of Han demonstrations in Xinjiang – and of Han families returning to the east and refusing to go back.

TURFAN

TURFAN (TURPAN) is an exciting beginning to Xinjiang: a distinctly Asian city, whose 180,000 population are dominated by Uighurs and Hui, and which on Sundays breaks into life with one of the largest traditional markets in the north-west (an event with which you should, if possible, plan to co-incide). It is set amid a long, fertile oasis at the edge of the Djunggar Basin, and so has the added distinction of being the lowest (500m *below* sea level) and in summer the hottest (up to 49°C) place in China.

Arriving

Turfan has a **railway station** – TURPAN ZHAN – but it is actually some 32km distant from the city, at a one-horse town called DAHEYON. Buses run fairly regularly between the two, though at somewhat peculiar intervals, so be prepared for a little industry when you step off the train. The bus station at Daheyon is obviously the first point of enquiry: it's just 450m from the station (walk uphill, turn right on the main street and it's on your left). Alternatives, if nothing seems to be stirring, are to phone the guesthouse in Turfan (who will send over a car for around ¥30, split between up to six people) or to hitch. Most of the traffic leaving Daheyon is headed for Turfan, so this shouldn't be too difficult. To get on to the road, turn left after a compound where cotton is stacked, 300m or so past the railway bridge – there is no sign. (Daheyon, incidentally, boasts no hotel, if for any unfathomable reason you were thinking of staying.)

  Once in Turfan itself, you have the choice of two – just possibly three – **hotels**, all of them centrally positioned. So long as they have room, though, the *Turfan Binguan* is the natural choice. This is a lovely old place, with running water outside in the yard and a garden of trellises festooned with grapes. Triples here run at about ¥6 a bed, doubles (in the more opulent part of the hotel) ¥30. The Binguan stays open late, runs a bar (cold beer!) and once or twice a week organises coy Uighur dancing on the patio.

The other Turfan hotel options are a flashy new *Tourgroup Hotel*, built in rather grotesque 'mosque style', 10 minutes walk up the road; doubles here (with bathroom) are around ¥40. Or, there's a chance you may be able to stay at the *Overseas Chinese Hotel*, close by the bazaar.

The Turfan Binguan has a **restaurant** where they serve cheap and eatable Chinese food. Much better, however, is the Hui restaurant around the corner (left at the roundabout, see the plan). This is a promising place to try Turfan's local wine – sweet and orange-coloured but not so bad for all that. For **snacks** there are numerous street stalls around the bazaar (see below).

The **PSB** and **CITS** offices are also in the Turfan Binguan. To get your bearings in Turfan and the immediate oasis you could do worse than to take the CITS **full-day tour** of the city and surrounding oasis – around ¥25, depending on how many of you club together for the minibus hire. You could then take in Gaochang and Bezeklik (again see below) at your own pace, either by bus, donkey cart or hired jeep.

The city and oasis

Turfan – inevitably – has evolved in close relation to its extremes of climate. Tall, densely planted poplars shade the narrow streets, and between their whitewashed trunks run swift streams of cool water, channelled from the glaciers of Tian Shan. Little bridges cross the streams to the **houses** behind, and here, on the gates and doors, there is a trace of the ornamentation and decoration so lacking throughout most of central China. The actual houses – built, like everything in this town, of beaten earth and mud-brick – are single-storeyed, their walled yards shadowed by trailing vines. In summer the locals generally sleep out in these yards to escape the still heat of the night.

This domestic architecture is very pleasing, and the streets are made lively and colourful by the people – traditionally extravagant in their tastes. On a monumental level the one really notable building is the grand mosque – the so-called **Imin Pagoda**. Twenty minutes walk from the hotel, this should definitely be a part of your ramblings. It was built in 1779 by the then feudal khan, or ruler, of the kingdom of Turfan, Suleiman Hoja, and is dedicated to his father, Amin Hoja. The mosque is unique in form – or at least its minaret (the tower from which the faithful are called to prayer) is, with its tapering shaft and dome. Its decoration, strict and austere, consists entirely of the intricate patterning of the brickwork. The mosque is today unused, but you can look inside, and climb the minaret for an overview of town and oasis, by asking

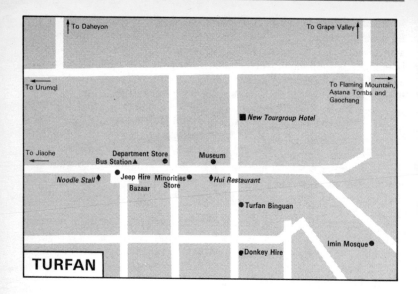

To Daheyon
To Grape Valley
To Urumqi
To Flaming Mountain, Astana Tombs and Gaochang
■ New Tourgroup Hotel
To Jiaohe
Department Store
Bus Station▲
Museum
Noodle Stall
● Jeep Hire
Bazaar
Minorities● Store
◆Hui Restaurant
● Turfan Binguan
● Donkey Hire
Imin Mosque●

TURFAN

at the caretaker's house (the whitewashed building at the side of the mosque).

Turfan's most obvious focus, however, is the **bazaar**, at the centre of town. This is open every day, though it takes on quite new dimensions on a Sunday, when the dusty roads around the city become an endless procession of peasants from the oasis, driving their flocks into the market or riding with the whole family on the donkey-powered market cart. The bazaar is pure Central Asia: a bedlam of dust and heat, packed with goats, donkeys, horses, even the odd camel. Stalls sell the region's famed grapes, melons and other fruit (alongside massed ranks of vegetables, spices, tobacco and poultry) and, still a local speciality, silks and cottons. The silks, unlike the machine-inspired patterns you normally find in China, feature earthy, folkweave patterns. And some of these, like the magnificent Uighur headwear on sale, are inspired.

Food stalls around the bazaar are equally compelling. You can buy kebabs of fat-tailed mutton, either with shashlik or nan bread, *pilaus*, a delicious meat and vegetable stew in a pastry bag, and of course the everpresent noodles. There is ice-cream, too, though somewhat lethal-looking, curdled from sheep's milk with vanilla and ice in bicycle-operated urns.

The **oasis** enclosing the city is a rich agricultural region, producing quantities of cotton, wheat and vegetables. What it is most famous for, though, are the sweet, seedless Turfan grapes. Like none other on earth, these are delicious; best of all in the main August–September season. Out in the oasis, there are vines everywhere – and the town too is full of them, for everyone seems to produce a few grapes for personal consumption and a little extra private income. The secret of the grapes is partly in the breeding, partly in the unusual system of irrigation. It doesn't rain around Turfan, so the vines never get wet. They are watered by means of **karezes**, horizontal wells which bring water dozens of kilometres from the eternal snows of Tian Shan. The karez is peculiar in China to Turfan and its neighbouring oasis, Hami. Its origin was probably Persian, The technique is to drive a well through to the non-porous strata below the base of the mountains; the snow-melt collected in this way flows underground all the way to the oasis with none of the loss through evaporation that would take place in surface canals. They were dug at some uncertain date during the Qing dynasty, by the *Chakar* (serf) labour – once a feature of all the feudal khanates of Turkestan.

Exploring the oasis close by Turfan, the CITS tour will take you out to the ruined city of Jiaohe and to the Flaming Mountain Grape Commune. You could equally well visit them using local forms of transport: either a hired jeep (from nearby the bazaar: see the plan) or a donkey cart (hired down the road from the Binguan).

Jiaohe lies an hour and a half by donkey cart (or 20 minutes by jeep) to the west of the city. Like the more substantial Gaochang (see below) this was once an active town along the Silk Road. It is an eery maze of sand-coloured hollows, almost as much natural scenery now as ruins of urban settlement. It stood at the fork of two rivers – needing no wall for its defence – but fell into decline and was abandoned after these dried up, leaving it barren and exposed. If you visit under your own steam, take plentiful water or fruit.

As antidote to such desolation, you could hope for little more wonderful than the **Flaming Mountain Grape Commune**. The commune charges a small admission fee to visitors, in return for which you are free to stroll the afternoon away, gorging yourself from the fruit of its terraces of vines, drinking crystal cool spring water (safe) and bathing in its pool. The 'Flaming Mountain' title comes from the gorge in which the commune is set: it is not actually volcanic but the bare convoluted rock of the mountain constantly changes colour, often looking like fire.

Further out: Gaochang and Bezeklik

These two excursions are some way out from Turfan: easiest of access by hired jeep (and driver) from outside the bazaar entrance. Either one should cost around ¥25 (split four or five ways) and take up the best part of half a day.

GAOCHANG (or Karakhoja, as it used to be known) is the most extensive of Xinjiang's 'lost cities', ancient Silk Road centres which were abandoned due to the shifting sands of the Talamakan. It must also have been one of the oldest; established by the western Han around 200BC as a military garrison, it later became a powerful independent khanate. The ruins, picked over by western archaeologists at the turn of the last century, yielded important finds of Manichaean documents. Today a national monument, they give a surprisingly clear impression of a traditional Chinese city. Following the walls, you can recognise the inner and outer compounds, a palace to the north, and numerous temples – Buddhist, Manichaean and Nestorian.

Just to the north of the site, at **Astana**, there is also a remarkable burial field. Several Tang dynasty tombs here have been opened up and can be looked around. One contains the bodies of an official and his wife – their hair, skin and teeth preserved virtually intact by the extreme dryness of the climate. Most of their funerary artefacts have been removed to the museum in Turfan (worth a subsequent visit if you have come out here), but there is a small and very atmospheric display here – including bowls of condiments, fruits and nuts buried to sustain the dead, as well as the more expected silks, clothes, pottery and sculpture. Most date from the Han dynasty and, again, all are astonishingly preserved.

The cave temples at **BEZEKLIK** are even more spectacular – at least in their setting, a long gorge in the Flaming Mountain to the north of Turfan. The caves themselves, 57 of them, dating from the 6C to the 13C, are sadly in very poor condition. They too were 'discovered' by western archaeologists at the end of the last century, their cultural arrogance resulting in the removal not only of artefacts but of whole walls and murals. The guide will give you the full details on this vandalism, its list of guilty names spanning most of the countries of Europe: LeCoq, Stein, Hedin, Pelliot and the rest. In the interests of accuracy it needs adding that a great part of the destruction had already been carried out by Muslims (zealously defacing the human representations) and by natural disaster – and that there was further damage from the ubiquitous Red Guards during the Cultural Revolution. What remains, however, is enough to suggest the artistic brilliance. Take a torch.

On to Urumqi

Urumqi is on the **rail line** – and you could, if you really wanted, take a bus back to Daheyon and go on from there. This is slightly less problematic than coming in from the rail line. You can buy a bus ticket a day before so as to coincide with the train's departure.

It is, however, a great deal simpler to go direct to Urumqi by **bus**. There is a daily departure for the 4 hour journey at 7.30am. Again, buy a ticket the day before (from the main bus station by the bazaar).

If you are heading **back east**, towards Lanzhou, Xi'an and Beijing, there is normally no shortage of seats available on the trains – or hard sleepers. However, this is not the case around the end of October and beginning of November when there seems to be a mass exodus of Han Chinese, presumably escaping the oncoming wintry chill. At this time of year both main express trains (the Shanghai Express and Beijing Express) leave Urumqi full beyond belief – sometimes with nowhere even to stand or put down a pack – and plane seats too are all taken up. Your best bet, if you are reading this too late to change plans, will be to go to Urumqi (whether or not you had intended to) and wait around there until you can book a sleeper.

URUMQI

URUMQI means 'Beautiful Pastures' (in Mongolian): an inappropriate name for this ugly grey city, the industrial and political capital of Xinjiang. In the early years of this century few travellers had a good word for it – 'A place of exile with a reputation of sorrow and degradation' is how Mildred Cable described it – but it has changed, if not for the picturesque, at least for the better. The opening of the rail line from Lanzhou placed Urumqi and its region firmly within the PRC's economy. And it is in this northern part of Xinjiang – the Djunggar Basin – that the province's wealth (oil, coal, gold and other mineral reserves) is concentrated.

All of which means that Urumqi, as you arrive, looks very little different from any other major city of Central China – and those 2½ days on the train from Xi'an might begin to seem on the wrong side of sanity. But architectural appearances are distracting. Most travellers reckon Urumqi one of the most interesting of all Chinese destinations. It offers the chance of a visit to Tianchi (The Lake of Heaven – see below), whilst its own city streets form a startling peoplescape – almost a directory of China's Central Asian component – with their mix of Uighur and Han, Hui, Kazakh, Kirghiz, Tadjik, Sibo and others. The Uighurs, and most of these other minorities, are Muslim and scattered about the Soviet-style blocks there are many hundreds of mosques. There are, too, specifically minority quarters – most obviously Uighur and Hui – with their own markets and restaurants. Walking about the city streets late (non-Han hours!) on a warm summer evening is bound to be enlightening.

Coming into Urumqi you may find yourself a little lost as to where (and what) is the centre of the city. As much as one exists, it is probably the area around the **Hongshan** department store and **People's Park** – a kilometre or so north-east of the **long-distance bus station**, a little further from the **railway station**. The main **hotel options** are some way out from here and best reached by regular city bus. The main travellers' place seems to be the *Kunlun* (or Ba Lou), off to the north of the city (opposite the Minorities Museum); dormitory beds at ¥6. This is on bus line no.2. Greatly preferable, however, and slightly closer to the train station, is the

Huaqiao Binguan (bus no.7, southbound) with ¥4 beds in four-person rooms, doubles for ¥24. **CITS** have an office in the Binguan and there's a reasonable restaurant as well (meals at ¥3 – payment in FECs only). A possible third alternative – cheap, clean and friendly – is a *Chinese Hotel*, three blocks north of the Huaqiao, which sometimes accepts foreigners.

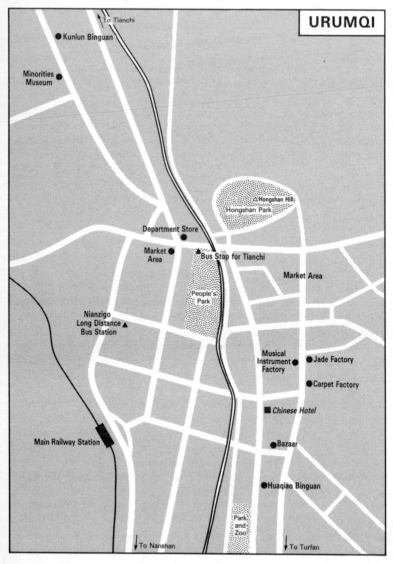

As stressed, Urumqi's major appeal lies in its population and **streetlife**. Having found yourself a room, your first move should be towards one of the Hui or Uighur areas of the city. There is an interesting quarter with a covered bazaar and numerous small Muslim restaurants 1km north-east of the Huaqiao, and another around the Hongshan department store. You will certainly do best eating in these parts of the city. The lamb kebabs here must be the lastiest in the country; the noodles too are promising.

Of the city's few (and scattered) 'monumental' sights, **Hongshan Hill** is a single obvious focus. Crowned with a 9-storey Qing pagoda, it is worth a clamber just for the views – a strange vista of industry, desert and in the far distance the high snowfields of the Bogda Feng, the Mountain of God.

After the Hongshan, you might wander southwards, down through the market towards the Huaqiao Binguan. En route there are a group of traditional handicrafts factories open to tourist visits. Facing each other – around midway between the hill and hotel – are a **Jade Factory** and **Musical Instruments Factory**: both well worth the look, unless you have been saturated with such places elsewhere. The **Carpet Factory** nearby, which sounds more exciting, is a letdown. Xinjiang used to be famous for its carpets, but those produced today bear slight resemblance to the pieces you gaze at in museums: processes have become mechanised, dyes chemical.

Just to the south of the Huaqiao Binguan, you come to a **Park and Zoo**, welcome enough on a hot afternoon (as is the People's Park, below Hongshan, currently being enthusiastically landscaped with pools and pavilions). The zoo itself, though, is like so many in China, with its impressive collection of animals kept in tiny squalid cages. In this park there once stood a magnificent palace and garden – built as solace by the exiled Lin Cixu, sent to govern Xinjiang in 1842 after burning the British opium in Canton. But someone at some time saw fit to pull it down. Today there is only a routine **Museum of the Eighth Route Army**. Not very inspired.

The city's other museum – the **Autonomous Region Minority People's Museum** – stands some way to the north, by the Kunlun Binguan. This is definitely worth your attention, its displays – clearly and imaginatively laid out – taking in exhibits, ancient and modern, from all the minority cultures of Xinjiang. There is a **shop** here too, where you can buy the region's silks, rugs and other artefacts – all much cheaper than elsewhere. There is a packing service if you want purchases reliably sent home.

Tianchi – The Pool of Heaven

For many travellers to this part of the north-west, it is **TIANCHI** – and the high mountain valleys around it – that are the real drawing point. A rarity in China, this is an area where you can wander at will and take to the hills. There are no restrictions on accommodation (you stay in *yurts*, large felt tents, with the semi-nomadic Kazakh population) and, depending on your fitness and will, there is virtually limitless hiking. The only reservation and warning is one of climate: as early as October, Tianchi may be inaccessible due to snowfalls, and it remains so through until late March or early April.

Starting point for the trip is the Hongshan **bus** stop at the top end of the People's Park, where from 8 each morning a convoy of buses (and locals – this is a popular outing) leaves for Tianchi. (There is sometimes also a bus from outside the Huaqiao at 6.50am). Tickets cost around ¥5, one way, and are best booked a day in advance. The 98km journey takes a little over 4hrs – the first two across flat desert, the last a spectacular climb through green meadows, conifer forests and along a wild mountain river – an astonishing and compact contrast.

TIANCHI, circled by steep forests and meadows, stands at some 2,400m above sea level – a 1400m rise from Urumqi. Beyond it rear the great snowfields of the Bogda Feng, awesomely high at up to almost 6100m. There is a ramshackle village beside the lake, including a **guest-house** (chalets at ¥6 a bed) and, along the far end, a gaggle of yurts (¥6 a bed). There are **ferry-boat trips**, and plenty of **places to eat** – well and cheaply in the shacks back along the road, more ambitiously at the lakeside restaurants.

But the real joy of Tianchi is in the freedom to take off and explore the remote **valleys of the Tian Shan** (the Mountains of Heaven – which bisect much of Xinjiang), a world far apart from the CITS and PSB. To reach them it is useful to have a guide (there are no maps) and there are young Kazakh boys at the lakeside who will lead you up, on horseback. Midway, there is an overnight stay at a guesthouse (¥3). Before setting out, stock up on provisions at the stalls in the coachpark – and make sure you have good supplies of biscuits for the children of your Kazakh hosts.

Once up at the snowfields, the valleys are yours. Each is dotted with Kazakh yurts, and there's nearly always one or more where you can spend the night – you'll find yourself directed as soon as you ask. The **Kazakhs**, who lead a semi-nomadic herding existence in these hills, are organised into communes, very loosely organised by the state which in theory owns both their land and animals – let on 15- or 30-year 'contracts'. Their principal livelihood is traditionally in sheep, selling lambs in spring if the winter spares them. But it is a hard, unpredictable business – the state sometimes has to bail them out if the winter is a disastrous one – and revenues come increasingly from tourism. As in Inner Mongolia, with which there are considerable cultural affinities, the Kazakhs have been roped in to perform at horse shows, mostly for tourists. Extra income from accommodation, from those prepared to move beyond the lakeside, is welcomed. There is no set official rate for board and lodging in a yurt – I paid around ¥6–7 a day, which seemed acceptable (and fair enough). If you can come in the spring – the most beautiful time – you may get to try *kumiss*, fermented mare's milk, considered a rare delicacy; the rest of the year the Kazakhs make do on a kind of tea, with an infusion of dried snow lily and sheep's milk.

Communication with the Kazakhs can be problematic – few speak Chinese and English is non-existent. If you know any Turkish you may find it functional. Otherwise you are largely dependent on whoever adopts you as a (generally Chinese-speaking) guide.

Returning from Tianchi, there is a bus back to Urumqi daily at 4pm.

Other trips from Urumqi

Another beautiful mountain area, where you can stay with local people, lies 75km south of Urumqi. This is the **NANSHAN GRASSLANDS**, wild-looking mountain fastnesses which, with the Altai mountains in north-east Xinjiang, were the breeding ground for the region's Liberation Armies in the 1940s. CITS arrange tours.

The **ALTAI MOUNTAIN VALLEYS**, further to the north, were open to Overseas Chinese but not foreigners at the time of research. They too should offer superb hiking potential.

Urumqi to Kashgar

Heading for Kashgar (or Kashi, as it's sometimes written), you have a choice between bus (detailed in the section below) or plane.

If you go for the latter, you may need to book some time in advance, since Kashgar is fast becoming one of the big Chinese travel goals. There are currently, however, daily **flights** (single fare ¥220) between the two towns. And they aren't without excitement: crossing the Tian Shan and the Taklamakan desert on board an ancient, propeller-driven machine with needs a pit-stop midway at AQSU.

By **bus** there is less competition. Tickets, at ¥40, are available from the Nianzigo bus station: reachable from the Huaqiao Binguan by taking bus no.7 (north) for two stops, then bus no.8 (west) four stops, then a ½km walk (it's on the left, see the plan). Seats are bookable a day in advance and are numbered and kept for the entire journey: if possible, try to get one in the front five seats – very much more comfortable and better for views. Luggage travels on the roof, so carry with you anything you might want, which should include a sleeping bag (October to May nights, and daytime till around 11am, are very, very cold). The buses leave, in pairs, at 9 each morning.

ON FROM URUMQI: THE KASHGAR BUS

The road to Kashgar is about as dramatic a journey as you could hope for. It cuts through the Tian Shan, and then threads its way across the dusty whirlwinds of the Tarim Basin and along the edge of the Takla-makan desert. The total distance, from Urumqi, is over 1100km – and with the rail line stopping just past Turfan at Korla, it is all done by bus. Travel time is a minimum of three days, often more like four: it is no joyride. But for the adventurous, this is one of the great Chinese trails – and one that could even be extended towards further excitements. West of Kashgar the Karakoram Highway leads into Pakistan. South, still officially closed, there is perhaps the wildest of all roads, in China or beyond, that finds its way eventually to Tibet.

Leaving Urumqi, the bus initially takes the Turfan road, running through flat, fertile countryside with the snowfields of the Bogda Feng towering away to the east.

The first stop is made at **DABANCHENG**, where streetsellers offer bowls of warm, fresh cow's milk and yoghurt – the last dairy products on the road. Beyond here you will stop for refreshments every two to three hours, though you will need a harsh constitution. Except at a couple of Han restaurants, noodles are about all that's on offer, right through to Kashgar. Tea, though, at least, is on offer everywhere – either free or for 2 or 3 fen – and there are melons on sale at most of the roadside halts.

Shortly after Dabancheng, the bus begins to climb, pushing through a dark **gorge pass in the Tian Shan** (where, among others, the forces of the Ma Chung Ying and Kuomintang were decimated) and weaving through the mountain foothills. The landscape hereabouts is frighteningly bleak and it merges eventually with the desert – the northern rim of the **Tarim Basin** – where you are likely to confront your first 'Dust Devils', whirl-winds whipped up in the still air by the intense heat, which are said to be able to lift a horse off its feet.

The road across the Tarim is good, though progress can be unpredict-able, hampered by breakdowns. Depending on how many you meet with, you will spend the night in one or other of the **oasis outposts** of TOCSUN, KORLA, KUCHA, AQSU or SANJIAKOU. **KORLA** is the end of the railway from Turfan and is not open to foreigners, except on this bus route. It apparently has an institution where 800 deaf-mutes are employed in painting landscapes; I noticed no other excitement. **AQSU**, also closed (it is said to have a Sino-American monitoring station), is more inter-esting: a large and important oasis near the foot of the Muzart Pass into the high ranges of Tian Shan. There are cave temples nearby. **KUCHA** looks as if it may be about to open to foreigners, as there is a big new hotel in the compound. You might try asking in Urumqi before setting out. If you could stay, there is the chance to see the **Kizil Caves**, supposedly among the finest Buddhist art in Xinjiang, with paintings executed in a unique Chandaran-Indian style. **SANJIAKOU**, plagued by hot dust-laden winds, is generally the last night's stop: so bleak a place now you wonder why any kind of settlement should ever have been contemplated, though it was once, before changes in the mountain glaciers, a very rich and beautiful watering-place.

In terms of the journey, the routine seems to be standard wherever you stop. The bus pulls into a compound, already mysteriously full of other buses and lorries, and everyone rushes off to join the queue to book **beds** (¥1) in the state-run compound hotel. After a night of heat and choking dryness, you're back in the bus for a 7am start.

For the **second and third days of the journey**, you will see to the south of the road the **Taklamakan desert**: its name, in Turkic, means, simply, 'Go In And You Won't Come Out'. Sodom and Gomorrah stories of lost cities abound – as do tales of piteous, crying voices luring the traveller from the path. The desert has certainly claimed countless lives, sometimes swallowing whole caravans, whilst over the last two millennia as many as 300 oasis towns have been engulfed by the sands. Their ruins, at the turn of this century, provided rich pickings for European archaeologists – who crated them up and carried them away, over the Indian border. If you are reading this well in advance, you might check out the story in Peter Hopkirk's *Foreign Devils on the Silk Road* (see p. 578), or better still take it along to read on the bus.

KASHGAR (KASHI)

KASHGAR (KASHI), astonishingly, more than lives up to the excitement of this approach. An ancient and once enormously powerful oasis city, it seems almost the essence of Chinese Turkestan: 90 percent Muslim, with its Uighur and Kazakh bazaars and teashops clustered about narrow old streets, and all set against the majestic Himalayan backdrop of the Pamirs. But for its climate – hot dust constantly blows in from the desert – it would be a really beautiful place to stay. As it is, it is certainly the most interesting city in the north-west.

The history of Kashgar is dominated by its strategic position, first as a junction of the Silk Roads, more recently as the meeting-point of three empires – Chinese, Soviet and British. Both Britain and the Soviets maintained consulates in Kashgar until 1949: the British with an eye to their interests across the frontier in India, the Soviets (so everyone assumed) with the long-term intention of absorbing Xinjiang into their Central Asian orbit. The conspiracy (and romance) of this period is brilliantly evoked in Peter Fleming's *News from Tartary* and Ella Maillart's *Forbidden Journey*. At the time of Fleming's visit, in 1935, the city was in effect run by the Soviets, who had brought their railway to within two days of Kashgar. But the war, which turned Soviet resources towards the Western European Front, brought an end to the intrigue as the Chinese, then on good terms with the Soviets, moved in to Xinjiang. Trading routes were directed back towards China and, with the break in Sino-Soviet relations, the Soviet border (and influence) firmly closed. Today, with signs of rapprochement between Deng and Gorbachev, there is talk of re-opening the border near Kashgar. Keep your ears open! For if this takes place then Kashgar will once again be one of the great travel crossroads of the world.

Arrival

There are said to be imminent plans to extend the railway from Korla to Kashgar; someone even told me there was a railway station already built at Kashgar, though if so it won't be too central – I didn't come across it. For the immediate future, therefore, you're going to be coming in on the bus. The **long-distance bus station**, for Urumqi (and, as far as I could make out, Tashkorgan – the first Chinese town on the Karakoram Highway), is on the south side of the city, about 1km from the main Id Kah mosque and square.

For a **hotel**, you are likely to be in for a long walk. At the time of writing there is just one place open to foreigners: the *Kashgar Binguan* (or 'New Hotel' as it is also, optimistically, titled). This is pretty wretched – poor reward after your half-hour trek (or 15 minutes on a donkey cart) from the bus. Beds in basic four-person dormitories go for ¥5; ¥28–56 for more luxurious doubles. Beyond telling you these prices, the hotel doesn't make much effort. It does maintain a **CITS** branch (erratic hours – but generally manned from 10–12pm), though, and there's a **shop/bar** in the garden where you can drink Xinjiang beer through to the early hours.*

Kashgar does have several other hotels and it is possible that one of these will have responded to the new burst of travel by opening its doors to foreigners. The most central is the *Renmin Binguan*, only a block away from the bus station, by the junction of Kashgar's two main streets. The others are an unnamed *Chinese-Only Hotel* up to the north of the city, near the Minorities Store, in a building said to have been the former British Consulate. And the *Lao Binguan* (Old Hotel), currently being rebuilt and presumably renamed. This should, by the time you arrive be open – in which case it will be the definite first choice.

For **eats**, the Kashgar Binguan does average Chinese meals at ¥3. More variety (and taste) is available at the city's foodstalls, around the Mao

---

*Unusually – and unofficially – Kashgar seems to keep its own time, adapted slightly to its position 4,000km from the capital to run at 1hr behind the Beijing Standard. Even so, you are still left feeling everything happens very much later in Kashgar.

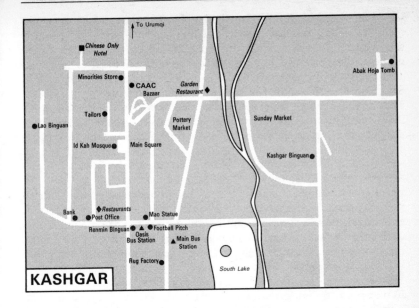

To Urumqi

Chinese Only Hotel

Minorities Store

CAAC
Bazaar

Garden Restaurant

Abak Hoja Tomb

Tailors

Lao Binguan

Pottery Market

Sunday Market

Id Kah Mosque

Main Square

Kashgar Binguan

Bank

Restaurants

Post Office

Mao Statue

Renmin Binguan

Oasis Bus Station

Football Pitch

Main Bus Station

Rug Factory

South Lake

KASHGAR

statue or up at the main Id Kah square. Kebabs are the standard here, and to follow there's a superb local speciality – bowls of chipped ice mixed with honey and yoghurt.

Getting around Kashgar – and its oasis – you are more or less dependent on walking or donkey carts (for which you need to haggle). **Bicycles** used to be hired out, though currently are not. Everyone used to cycle off to the Pamirs (only a day's ride away) and the authorities took fright. Of course, this too may well change. . . .

Around the city

There are one or two monuments of note in Kashgar but the main attractions of this city are its ordinary streets – scarcely changed over the centuries, with their markets, bazaars, street restaurants and tea-shops. The markets suffered during the Cultural Revolution – and even the tea-shops were for a while closed down – but they are now fully revived, seething with new life and apparent prosperity. If there is any chance at all that you can do so, try to be in Kashgar for the **Sunday Market** (all Xinjiang markets are held on Sundays). This is held on a large, dusty plain on the bank of the river and is really The Big Event of the region. Farmers and traders come in with their camels, horses, donkeys, sheep, goats and cattle: all timeless Central Asia.

The **bazaars** too are at their most active on Sundays, though they are open throughout the week. They are scattered amid the grid of streets just to the north of the Id Kah square. The main section is off to the right. Here you can buy rugs from Khotan, knives from Yengihissar, Astrakhan and Karakul lambskins, wolfskins, handmade leather boots and shoes, embroidered caps, sheepskin Kazakh hats, dried cormorants, toads and seahorses, bright painted cradles, brass and silver ware, jade and chalcedony from the rivers of Kashgaria . . . the variety is endless. You can also change money (preferably dollars) at *very* favourable rates. Off to the left, set slightly apart, there is a street of tailors where silks, cottons and linen are displayed in a narrow, awning-covered alley, the tailors' shops flanking the street beside it, their owners willing to run up anything you desire, to your design or theirs, very quickly.

The **Id Khan Mosque**, which as much as anything else signifies the centre of the city, dominated the main square. It was built in 1779 to imposing (though not especially interesting) effect. Roundabout, here too there are numerous market stalls, several of them selling the bizarre and fascinating Uighur musical instruments. If you've time (and energy) at hand you can watch these being made at a **handicrafts factory** a couple of blocks to the north. The instruments in the square are actually cheaper (and better made) than in the factory, since they tend to be the craftsmen's own work. At the factory (which also has an embroidery workshop) they produce less careful ware – instruments for the masses, as one explained.

The **Kashgar oasis** is up to 120km wide – very lush despite the dry dustiness of the climate, for it is well irrigated by the Pamirs. A great variety of crops are grown and the fields are often bordered with a dense growth of *Marijuana sativa*, which is used in China as a specific for stomach disorders. This is very convenient, for the standards of Kashgar hygiene tend to be low and a great many visitors do suffer such complaints.

Walking (or hopefully cycling) out to the fields, the most purposeful route would be to head north-east towards the **Abak Hoja Tomb**, around 3km from the centre. Surrounded by plane trees and still pools, this is a beautiful spot, seemingly in a world of its own. It is one of the most important Muslim monuments left in Xinjiang. Abak Hoja was a saint of great holiness – 'No such holiness had existed since the Prophet himself', runs his hagiography, 'people swooned before him, the deaf heard, the blind recovered their sight and the lame danced for joy.' His tomb was built by his daughter, Teleshat Shanimo, on her return from Beijing (where she had been sent as a consort to the Qing Emperor Kang Xi). As architecture, it is firmly Muslim and Asian in style, reminiscent of the great buildings of Khiva with its severe lines and sparse decoration. The interior is quite bare of ornament, relying simply on the strength of its proportions.

At one time the tomb was the centre of a feudal estate, owning 120,000 acres of land, a mill, numerous farms and a highschool. It houses today some 70 of the saint's descendants, among them an old woman who sells tea and bread in its shade.

Walking **further into the oasis**, amid the shade of poplars, is also recommended. You come upon old villages totally untouched by modern influence, or architecture, as you'll discover when someone invites you into their house to look around. The houses are made for the most part of rammed earth and mud-brick, perfect building material for this environment and brightened by deep, cool vine-shaded courtyards, often full of flowers.

Yingjishah

An hour and a half's bus ride south-west through the Kashgar oasis, and across a stretch of desert, will bring you to **YINGJISHAH** (or YENGI HISSAR in its Turkic form). This town is famed primarily for its knives, turned out to traditional designs in a little **handicrafts factory** to which visitors are directed. But it is also a lively example of a Tarim oasis settlement – and worth seeing as such. There is a busy market (with street entertainers) and the dusty streets, like Kashgar's are lined with irrigation ditches and poplars.

The town was once an important fort, though the walls were pulled down after Liberation, and was involved in one of the stranger, peripheral events of the Imperialist dash for Turkestan at the end of the 19C. Germany, seeing the British and Russian activities, decided to get involved and sent one Adolphus Schlagintweit to set the ball rolling. After a gruelling mountain journey he arrived at Yingjishah to find it besieged by a local Khodja (feudal lord). Presented to the Khodja, the German enquired how long the siege had been going on. 'Too long', replied the disconsolate Khodja, 'over three months.' 'Ah', said the German, 'In my country we would have had the whole thing tied up in three days.' At which point, not unreasonably the Khodja ordered him to be taken away and executed, so ending Germany's involvement in Xinjiang.

If you visit today, there is perhaps less immediate need for tact. However, bear in mind that the locals see few foreigners – you are likely to be the centre of prolonged crowd staring.

On from Kashgar

The **Kashgar–Urumqi bus** is undoubtedly worth taking once (see the account on p. 480). However, you may decide that once is enough. In which case you have the option of flying out, or trying one of the two **adventure routes** on from Kashgar – along the Karakoram Highway into Pakistan, or (officially illegal) south to Tibet.

Flights are obviously the easiest option, though at present there is just one departure a day – to Urumqi – and you may find yourself waiting several days for a seat. Best to enquire as soon as you arrive. **CITS**, in the Kashgar Binguan, will book both flights and bus tickets (which you can also buy yourself at the long-distance bus station).

The **long-distance bus station** for Urumqi, Tashkorgan and Pakistan (and a variety of other destinations in Xinjiang) is off the main east–west road running through the centre of Kashgar. The road itself is easily identifiable for its enormous statue of Mao and the fact that Kashgar's ubiquitous horse and cart traffic is prohibited along this thoroughfare. Heading east along this road the first turning on the right, once Mao is behind you, leads to the bus station. You are more likely to be coming from the other direction since the horse and cart will drop you at a junction east of the bus station. If you buy the sole city map available (pink title box and yellow built up areas) the word THE in the label for 'The Foreign Affairs office' marks the spot where the horse and cart will drop you. The road junction for the bus station lies just opposite. The Kashgar map mentioned above is grossly inaccurate and leaves the Chinese label for 'long distance bus station' untranslated. While there is a drawing of a bus it is placed in an ambiguous position. The foregoing directions to the bus station may seem laughably detailed but with only one bus per week leaving for Pakistan at present there is a frantic rush for tickets. Kashgar is a large city where you'll find it more difficult to orientate yourself than usual. There are many travellers who have spent fruitless hours trying to locate the bus station.

There are two services running along the **Sino–Pakistan Highway**. On **Wednesdays** a 'local' bus runs to Tashkorgan. This is an ineffective way of getting to Pakistan since Tashkorgan is still several hours by road to the final Chinese checkpoint out of China. If you take this bus to Tashkorgan you should be prepared to walk the final leg. On **Tuesdays** an 'international' bus runs right through to the first checkpoint on the Pakistan side – Sust. The journey is supposed to take two days though it is unlikely that anything other than a landrover could make it in such a time. Expect three uncomfortable days. **Tickets** for either the local or the international bus are sold 48 hours in advance though you could try obtaining them earlier. There is no need to panic about availability of tickets. Buses are laid on to meet demand. If you discover your ticket is marked with the figure 23 and that of a fellow traveller is marked 73, it doesn't mean you are all going to be squeezed onto the same vehicle. Those numbers refer not to seat numbers but to the sequence in which you bought your ticket. Knowing this should save you anxiety as you make the final demanding move in getting through China. Tickets cost ¥74.00.

The **journey** itself is nothing short of spectacular every inch of the way. Although the route from Kashgar to the first Pakistani checkpoint of Sust is less than 250 miles (the way the crow flies) the difficulty of the terrain and the lack of any road surface whatsoever until you get to Pakistan mean that you'll be in your bus for around 12 hours a day three days running. There are no scheduled stops and no timetables the drivers try to keep to. The first two or three hours out of Kashgar are over level ground as you leave that city's oasis landscape. Tree-lined lanes alternate with rock-strewn desert. Soon the trees and rice fields disappear as the bus begins its gradual ascent through the eastern end of the Pamir mountains. The road runs up a river valley for the remainder of the day. The landscape is arid and imposing. The mountains here are in the rain shadow of the Karakoram Range that divides China from Pakistan a little further south. By the end of the day snow-capped mountains, appearing from behind cloud or haze, become commonplace. The road itself is seldom more than a track that has been bull-dozed through an imposing glacial landscape. Continuing erosion by streams flowing across the grain of the road down the river valley often make it difficult to see exactly where the bus will go next. Frequently the surface of the road has been potholed to the extent that the entire busload of passengers has to get out and walk behind the bus as it negotiates sections of the road with its lighter load. You may occasionally have to even push. Be prepared for anything. There are few truck stops for the bus driver to choose from. Which one you actually stay at will depend on how much progress you made during the day. You should bring enough food to last you the full three days. Your truck stop may have a basic meal available but don't bank on it.

Many of the steeper inclines will have been completed on the first day. You should pass Mt. Kongur early on the second day. The road at this point is close to Tashkorgan's altitude of 12,000 feet. Between Mt. Kongur and Tashkorgan the bus passes occasional nomadic settlements.

Tashkorgan has little of interest other than the surrounding landscape. The town is nestled in a wide glacial valley. The towering mountains at its edges are snow-capped throughout the year. Tashkorgan is built around a long central thoroughfare that has a few restaurants and stores.

The climax of any journey along the Karakoram Highway is the **Khunjerab Pass**. From Tashkorgan right through the various checkpoints to Sust in Pakistan can take as long as nine hours by road. The approach to the top of the Khunjerab Pass at over 15,000 feet is slow and majestic. From Tashkorgan the road begins an almost imperceptible climb. Despite the presence of glacial rivers and streams running off every slope around, the landscape is barren and rocky for much of the way. There are no trees to punctuate the vast remote landscape, only areas of moss and grass that gather around the larger glacial streams. Two to three hours out of Tashkorgan is the customs checkpoint on the China side at Pirali. Foreigners departing China hand over their customs declaration form and can change any remaining FEC (but not Renminbi). The length of the stop at Pirali depends on the number of buses in your convoy. You are unlikely to get through in less than an hour. There is another check between Pirali and the top of the Khunjerab pass – the point that marks the Pakistan–China border. The final climb up to the two signposts that mark the border is the steepest of all. Leaving China this way really does take you over the roof of the world.

Kashgar to Tashkorgan	175 miles	one to two days
Tashkorgan to Pirali	53 miles	two to three hours
Pirali to Khunjerab	31 miles	one to two hours
Khunjerab to Sust	54 miles	two to three hours

There is the option of arranging a place on a bus rented out by Pakistani visitors. Many Pakistanis with small businesses come to China to take advantage of the relatively low cost of goods in Kashgar. In order to get their purchases back to Pakistan they group together and rent a bus from the long distance bus station to take them from Kashgar to Sust. They use exactly the same kind of bus that runs the scheduled international route on Wednesdays though they use some of the seats inside the bus to carry luggage. If you want to look into the possibility of buying a seat on such a bus you should go to the Chini Bagh hotel (to the north of the Id Kah Mosque). The majority of travellers from Pakistan can be found here. Arrangements can fall through easily as people back out of the group looking to rent a bus. You should expect to pay between 25% and 50% more than the scheduled bus from Kashgar.

And finally, the long (or, perhaps more accurately, wrong) **route to Lhasa**. This, by all accounts, has been undertaken only by a handful of travellers. It remains, at the time of writing, strictly illegal and if you are accosted by the authorities you may find yourself in for a fine . . . as well as a potential backtrack out of Tibet to return to Kashgar. But such is the stuff of adventure. The route is there, it is covered by a small flow of trucks – anything is possible. Accounts welcome for our next edition.

INNER MONGOLIA

Inner Mongolia is rather less exciting than it sounds: unless you are wily and resourceful enough to pass yourself off as a Mongol, there are very few places you will be allowed to visit. This is a border area and there is still a certain paranoia evident – until recently one of the main attractions shown to visitors in Hohhot, the capital, was the network of underground shelters equipped with hospitals and factories so that life could continue even during a Soviet attack. **Hohhot** is still open, as are **Baotou**, the main industrial centre, and **Hailar** up in the north-east. It is possible, by the time you read this, that **Bayinhot, Xilinhot** or **Erenhot** may also be open. But if you come to Inner Mongolia expecting to find something worthy of Ghengis Khan, ruthless conqueror and ruler of the largest empire the world has known, you are bound to be disappointed. The heirs of the Mongol hordes are now a mild-mannered minority, quietly going about their business of shepherding, herding horses and entertaining tourists. They are also swamped by the Chinese, who number 17 million to the Mongols' 2.

Genghis Khan (1162–1227) was born, ominously enough, with a clot of blood in his hand. Under him the Mongols erupted from their homeland to ravage the whole of Asia, butchering millions, razing cities and laying waste all the land from Beijing to Hungary, Poland and Russia. It was his proud boast that the destruction of the cities he took was so complete that he could ride across their ruins by night without the least fear of his horse stumbling.

Long before Genghis exploded on to the scene, the Mongols had been a thorn in the side of the Chinese: construction of the Great Wall, to keep them out, began almost 2,000 years before his reign. Fortunately for those beyond their plateau, the early nomadic tribes of Mongolia fought almost as much among themselves as they did against outsiders. It was Genghis Khan's achievement (or Temuchin to give him his proper name) to weld the warring nomads into a fighting force the equal of which the world has never seen. Becoming Khan of Khans in 1206, he also introduced the *Yasak*, the first code of laws the Mongols had known – few details of its Draconian tenets survive today (though it was inscribed on iron tablets at Genghis' death) but Tamberlaine, at Samarkand, and Baber the Great Mogul, in Hindustan, both used it as the basis for their authority.

The secret of Genghis Khan's success lay in skilful cavalry tactics: frequently his armies would rout forces 10 or 20 times their size. Each of his warriors would have three or four horses and nothing more. Food was taken from the surrounding country; the troops slept in the open; meat was cooked by being placed under the saddle; and when the going got really tough they would slit a vein in the horse's neck and drink the blood, still on the move. There was no supply problem, no camp followers, no excess baggage. A man's only duty was to fight:

> The greatest joy a man can know is to conquer his enemies and drive them before him, to ride their horses and take their possessions, to see the faces of those that were dear to them bedewed with tears and to clasp their wives and daughters in his arms.

Having also perfected siege techniques, at Ningxia, Genghis turned his attention on China, marching with 200,000 men into Shanxi and defeating three much larger armies to stand before the walls of Beijing.

Unsuccessful in his first attempts to take the city, he sent armies to lay waste Shandong, Shanxi and Manchuria: they smashed, burned, massacred and pillaged – sending a constant flow of caravans of loot back into Mongolia – but they also caused famine, and after that plague, which affected the invaders almost as badly as the invaded. Genghis Khan never took Beijing, but fell ill and died in Shanxi in 1227. His body was carried back to Mongolia by a funeral cortège of 10,000, who slew every man and beast within ten miles of the road so that none should report the Great Khan's death before his sons and viceroys could be gathered from the farthest corners of his dominions. He was buried beneath a tree, on a hill, in a spot he had chosen while hunting, many years before. A forest grew round the grave, whose whereabouts remain unknown to this day (though by other accounts his ashes are in the new Mongolian-style mausoleum south of Baotou).

In 1276 the Mongols finally went on to establish their **Yuan dynasty** over the whole of China, the only time the Chinese have been under foreign rule for any significant period. It is still an era about which Chinese historians can find little good to say, though the boundaries of their empire were expanded considerably, to include Yunnan and Tibet for the first time. For a sycophantic account of the magnificence of its zenith, under Kublai Khan, read Marco Polo. Finally, though, the regime's unpopularity in the countryside led to its downfall and the last Yuan emperor, *Shun Ti*, was defeated in 1368 by the 'Beggar King' *Chu Yuan-chang*, a priest-turned-bandit-turned-emperor. The Mongols returned to Mongolia and quickly reverted to their former ways, hunting, fighting amongst themselves and occasionally skirmishing with the Chinese down by the wall.

Thereafter, Mongolian history moves gradually downhill, though right through into the 18C they maintained at least nominal control over many of the lands to the south and west originally won by Genghis Khan. These included Tibet, from where Lamaist Buddhism was imported to become the dominant religion in Mongolia: the few Tibetan-style monasteries to survive the Cultural Revolution are now among the most important monuments in the country. Over the years, though, others came too – there's a sizeable Muslim minority and under the Qing many Chinese settlers moved to Inner Mongolia, escaping overpopulation and famine at home. They ploughed up the grassland with disastrous results – wind and water swept the soil away: the Mongols withdrew to the hills. Only now has a serious programme of land stabilisation – and reclamation – got underway.

Sandwiched as she was between two Imperial powers, Mongolia's independence was constantly threatened. The Russians set up a protectorate over the north, the rest came effectively under the control of China. In the 1930s Japan occupied much of eastern Inner Mongolia as part of

Manchukuo, and the Chinese reds also maintained a strong presence. In 1945 Stalin persuaded Chiang Kai-shek to recognise the independence of Outer Mongolia under Soviet protection as part of the Sino-Soviet anti-Japanese treaty, effectively sealing the fate of what is now the Mongolian People's Republic. And in 1947 Inner Mongolia was designated the first Autonomous Region of the People's Republic of China.

HOHHOT

HOHHOT (or HUHEHAOTE as it is pronounced and sometimes written, and formerly known as Suiyuan) is the capital of Inner Mongolia, set in a great plain to the south of the Da Qing Mountains. It is a pleasant city, well-planned streets lined with weeping willows, pines and well-tended flower beds; a scattering of fine modern buildings breaking up the atmospheric older quarters. The people – some half-million of them – are mainly Han Chinese, settled here to dilute the indigenous Mongol and Hui population. For most people the chief reason to visit is to head out on a tour of the Mongolian grasslands, but Hohhot itself should not be written off – wandering around the narrow streets of the old parts can be fascinating.

The temples and lamaseries of Inner Mongolia suffered a great deal of destruction in the Cultural Revolution, as everywhere, but in Hohhot enthusiastic restoration is everywhere apparent and several interesting sites survive. Heading out from the centre the first of these is the **Great Mosque**, just by the North Gate bus station. You should be able to spot the minaret. The building itself, which dates from the Qing dynasty, is a fanciful concoction of grey brick and red pillars. Since 1983 it has once again been used as a place of worship by Hohhot's sizeable Muslim community. Across the road is a rather grim Christian **Church**, incongruously set in a military barracks.

500 yards south of the Mosque, on the right, **Da Zhao Temple** lies at the centre of one of the old Mongol quarters of the city. Here traditions are actively being preserved and a great deal of restoration is going on, both on the temple itself and the area surrounding it. The shops, houses and restaurants facing the narrow cobbled streets are having their traditional wooden façades refurbished: when finished, this promises to create much the most attractive part of town. Funding for these works comes not from the city administration but from individual work units – the Mongolians are very proud of their city. As for the Da Zhao, it's a Sino-Tibetan style monastery of the Ming dynasty, its buildings centred on the massive 2-storey Hall of the Sutras, at the head of a courtyard containing bronze lions and vases. The walls of the main hall are slightly oblique, giving that impression of squat solidity typical of Tibetan buildings; they are surmounted by a Chinese double roof with horned eaves.

As a whole, it's a surprisingly harmonious bulk, though it should blend in rather better once the new paint has weathered somewhat. Across Da Nanjie is another old sector containing the **Xiao Zhao Monastery**. In a state of some dilapidation at the moment this, too, is due for restoration – again the streets around are lively and interesting.

Further south, the **Wu Ta Si** (Five Pagoda Temple) is perhaps the most worthwhile of all Hohhot's sites – a Qing dynasty structure unique in China for its Classical Indian style. A sturdy symmetrical base is surmounted by five tapering pagodas, the whole structure being ringed with narrow strips of tile to create what appear to be numerous false roofs. In the spaces between these tile roofs thousands of carved Buddhas are set into small niches, a motif continued over the entire building.

From here, a no.1 bus will take you back to the centre where the **Museum of Inner Mongolia** (1 jiao entrance; closed Mondays) has a magnificent display of palaeontological finds, including the skeleton of an immense Mammoth and of a Tyrannosaurus: there are also murals of Brontosauri, Diplodoci, Stegosauri and others disporting themselves amongst the spring flowers on the grasslands. A considerable collection of Stone and Iron Age artefacts testifies to the richness of early human civilisations, too, and past this an excellent National Minorities Exhibition leads into the Hall of Liberation. Well presented (though texts are in Chinese and Mongolian only), this has photos backed up by arms and uniforms, and some stirring revolutionary sculpture and painting: men lie magnificent and bleeding in the snow, while fine, powerful women comfort them and simultaneously hurl mighty boulders upon a craven and ill-favoured enemy! Next door to the museum is an antique shop with a splendid array of Mongolian snuff bottles, vases and pots – fascinating stuff until you see the price tags.

Survival

The *Xincheng Hotel*, centrally situated 20 minutes walk south-east of the railway station (or take a pedicab), is the best **place to stay** in Hohhot: dorm beds here start at ¥3, double rooms are ¥40, there are hot baths and showers and a reasonable restaurant. The larger rooms are really quite luxurious. Alternatives are the *Hohhot Guesthouse*, officially Chinese only, or the new and expensive *Inner Mongolia Hotel*. **Eating** outside the hotel is not particularly exciting – your best bet is the 3-storey *Qin Cheng* restaurant, opposite the People's Park, whose upper floor specialises in Mongolian food. This seems to be the only such restaurant in Mongolia, though even here local food is rarely available and you have to make do with the (very good) Chinese menu. Otherwise the **markets** scattered around town sell excellent yoghurt and other assorted goodies: there's a covered food market near the museum, a general market outside the People's Park (in the east), and another in the

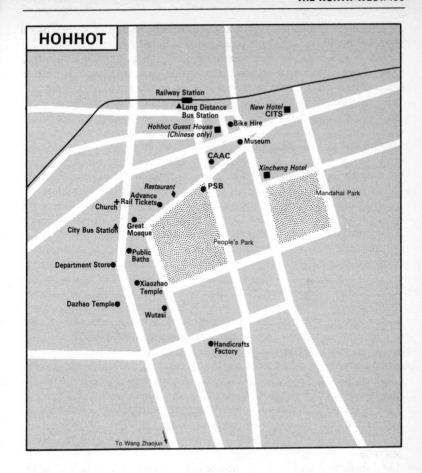

HOHHOT

Railway Station
Long Distance
Bus Station
New Hotel
CITS
Hohhot Guest House
(Chinese only)
Bike Hire
Museum
CAAC
Xincheng Hotel
Mandahai Park
Restaurant
PSB
Advance
Rail Tickets
Church
City Bus Station
Great
Mosque
People's Park
Public
Baths
Department Store
Xiaozhao
Temple
Dazhao Temple
Wutasi
Handicrafts
Factory
To Wang Zhaojun

streets north of the Da Zhao and Xiao Zhao temples. The **People's Park**, leafy and scattered with pavilions, has a boating lake and appears to be undergoing the same feverish restoration process as most of Hohhot. You can **hire bikes** at the hotel or from a place opposite the Hohhot Guest-house, and **CITS** is in the new high-rise hotel. This is where you should go to set up a visit to the Grasslands.

Around Hohhot – grassland tours

There is no chance of getting out into the famous Mongolian grasslands independently, so you may as well accept that you'll be on a CITS tour and make the most of it. This basically means getting down to some serious bargaining over price and what you are going to see: permutations are endless, depending on the type of transport, number of people, length of stay, etc. – try to include a visit to one of the factories in Hohhot in your itinerary, which is otherwise very hard to organise. There are three areas of grassland which you might be able to visit. **Wulantuge** is the closest, 90km north of Hohhot, and the most visited – outside the peak summer months it will probably be the only one open. **Baiyinhushao** is 180km from Hohhot in the same general direction – a beautiful drive up through the Daqing Mountains on to the high plateau beyond. Finally there's **Huitengxile** to which tours seem only to be run by the China Youth Travel Service – if you have student credentials you might get a cheaper and more interesting trip this way. Prices should range from around ¥40 to ¥100 depending on the number of people, the mode of transport, and the length and route of the tour.

In general, the trips all follow the same pattern. Transport, meals and accommodation in a yurt is included, as are various unconvincing 'Mongolian Entertainments' – camel and spectacular horse riding in particular – and visits to 'typical' Mongol families in traditional dress. Of these only the food is consistently good – for once the CITS leaflet is barely exaggerating in its claim that '*the Mongolian hot-pot, Finger Mutton and roast whole sheep will undoubtedly draw the mouthwater of the visitors*'. The banquet is followed by an evening of drinking, dancing and singing which normally degenerates into something quite fun. It is when you escape from the tour, however, that it can really become worthwhile; you don't have to be with the group to be invited for tea by a Mongolian family and the sheer scale of the plain, bleak as it is, is an experience. If you've been spending time among the unrelenting crowds of eastern China, it's a particularly welcome one.

For the ultimate grassland experience, though, you should try to coincide with the full moon. By day the undulating expanses of rolling prairie, deep in grass and flowers, can begin to become monotonous. The nights are something else. Stars seem brighter and bigger than anywhere else on earth and when the huge moon rises, flooding the plains with silver – you will be glad you left the other tourists in the hospitality yurt.

Other attractions which the tours could take in include **Xiang Sha Wan**, a resonant sandy gorge which, again according to CITS, is '*well known for its great mystery. It is 60m high sandy hill which resounds peculiarly when people slide downhill from it, hence the name. While digging the sand with your hands you may hear the sound like a frog-cry. For many centuries people have remained perplexed despite much thoughts about the peculiarity of the sand*'. I didn't go, so perplexed we will all have to remain.

Much closer in, just seven miles south-west of the city, is the **Tomb of Wang Zhaojun**, a Tang dynasty princess sent from Chengdu to cement Han–Mongol relations by marrying the King of Mongolia. It is fairly dull

– a huge mound raised from the plain and planted with gardens in the centre of which is a modern pavilion – but is included on the itinerary of many tours. In the rose garden, amongst pergolas festooned with gourds, is a tiny museum devoted to Zhaojun. It contains some of her clothes, including a tiny pair of shoes, jewels, books and a number of steles. To get here independently take a no.10 bus from North Gate or cycle – straight down Da Nanjie and keep going.

BAOTOU

Three hours to the west of Hohhot on the main railway line, **BAOTOU** is the largest city and the main industrial centre of Inner Mongolia. It comprises three towns: KUEN, the industrial sector whose enormous steelworks huffs out clouds of reddish-brown and white smoke; QINSHAN; and DONGHE, both residential neighbourhoods. These three, which form the corners of an equilateral triangle about six kilometres from one another, are linked by long straight avenues through a fertile area not unlike Wimbledon Common. Horses, sheep and cattle graze everywhere.

If you get off the train at **Baotou station** you will find yourself a short way south of **Kuen**: a no.1 bus will take you to the *Baotou Binguan*. This is a gargantuan hotel (dorm beds about ¥6) where tour groups are usually installed. In the westernmost building, at the end of a gloomy, unpromising corridor, you'll find **CITS** and **PSB**. At CITS – very helpful – you can arrange a tour of one of Kuen's iron works or carpet factories. **Qinshan**, reached by no.8 bus from Kuen, is a brand new residential development: there are a couple of restaurants, a park still in its infancy, and countless functional apartment blocks in red and grey brick. Young trees and flowerbeds line the streets.

The most interesting part of Baotou by some way, however, is **Donghe**, and the best plan is to head straight here on arrival, getting off the train at Donghe station. Alternatively, grab a no.10 bus from Qinshan or a no.5 from Kuen. The *Donghe Binguan* is 1km straight down from the station on the left (or you pass it on the no.5). A rotten hotel, its advantages are price (just ¥4 for a bed in a double room) and position – just south of the town's central crossroads. Here there are busy streets lined with market stalls, vegetables piled on the pavements, restaurants, shops, dust, bicycles and thousands of people. Outside the hotel is a sign which says simply '*Dining Hall*', not the greatest place to eat, but a considerable step up from the hotel restaurant – alternatively you'll find several basic Hui and Han restaurants up by the station.

Four times a day a no.18 bus leaves the station square bus terminus and heads down to the new bridge over the **Yellow River**, a 6 mile trip on dusty, bumpy roads. It's an enjoyable trip if only as an escape from the city heat and grime – the river here is nearly a mile wide, shallow and sluggish, great for swimming. On the road out you pass through acres of smoky-grey residential *pingfangs*, with sunflowers in their yards and TV aerials sprouting from their roofs. Once at the river you can stroll along the banks, stopping at some of the Mongolian villages, often very pretty places with black pigs luxuriating in black pools of mud in the streets. Near the bridge there is a large fish-farm with what is said to be an excellent restaurant.

Wudangzhao

Once you have exhausted the delights of Baotou (which won't take long) you can turn your attention to extraordinary monastery of **Wudangzhao** in the hills to the north. One of the results of the Mongol conquest of Tibet in the 13C was the spread of Tibetan Lama Buddhism to Mongolia. The road between Mongolia and Tibet was worn by the feet of countless pilgrims and wandering monks; and lama monasteries, built in a distinctly Tibetan style, proliferated throughout Mongolia. Unfortunately these monasteries, of which there were many hundreds, were decimated during the Cultural Revolution. Wudangzhao is perhaps the best example surving in Mongolia.

Set in a barren valley, sparsely planted with pines, is a group of Tibetan buildings, village houses, lamas' quarters, temples and the pilgrims' hostel. The temple complex is built up the side of a hill, giving some sense of unity to its apparent disorganisation. All the buildings are a fading white, set on plinths, with the lower storey tapering into the upper, and a flat roof. The verandahs are decorated with magnificent murals, scenes from the life of the Buddha, mandalas and interesting allegorical motifs – the purification of an elephant, changing from black to white as it ascends the path to heaven, is one such. The interiors are festooned with hanging silks, rich colour, softened by the dark, and redolent of yak-butter. There is a restaurant here, and several pilgrims' hostels, in one of which you may be able to stay for ¥1.50, depending upon the mood of the innkeeper.

CITS arrange **tours to the monastery** from the *Baoutou Binguan*, or buy a ticket the day before from the long-distance bus station, opposite the railway station – ¥1.50 and the bus leaves at 7.00am. You can also catch the no.7 bus which makes the journey twice a day. From Donghe to Wudangzhao is a 2 hour drive up a rocky riverbed, with occasional stops to cram more people into an already bursting bus. The countryside is grim: an open-cast coalmining area spreads its film of grey dust over a waste of treeless hills where the occasional mining village straggles amorphously over the river and up the slope. But Wudangzhao is worth it.

HAILAR

Hailar is in the far east of Inner Mongolia, where it curls northwards following the line of the Soviet border: take a train west from Harbin and in 18 hours you will get there. The journey is a lovely one, through curious formations of hills, mist-hung rivers and thickly wooded valleys – all quite deserted. This underpopulation is especially striking if you've been travelling in central China: the Chinese don't like the area and those who have been allocated jobs up here are often thoroughly dissatisfied with their lot; they find the country drab and the climate inhospitable. The train continues across Inner Mongolia to MANZHOULI (birthplace of the Dowager Empress) where the Chinese Eastern Railway crosses the frontier to join the Trans-Siberian Railway. This is said to be open to foreigners now, and nearby is the great lake of **Hulun Nur**, a shallow expanse of water set in marshy grazing country where flocks of swans, geese, cranes and other migratory birds spend the winter.

HAILAR itself is a small light-industrial and agricultural town on the banks of the Heilongjiang, or Amur, River. It has a small Muslim population as well as the usual Mongol/Han mix: there are a number of Huimin and Chinese restaurants, and a market which specialises in fresh river fish, edible fungi of every type, and vegetables of prodigious size and quality. Otherwise, however, there is remarkably little of interest in Hailar apart from the Minorities Shop, over the bridge on the left from the hotel. Here they sell a variety of Mongol handicrafts – saddles, rugs, pots, pipes, knives and very fine leather riding boots for a mere ¥37.

The reason for coming here is to see the North Mongolian **Hulunbuir Grasslands**, an apparently limitless rolling land of plains and low grassy mountains, traced by slow rivers which teem with fish. Hundreds of thousands of sheep, cattle and horses graze this inexhaustible pasture, spread over thousands of miles. The Han Chinese do not take to this style of life, so all their herdsmen are Mongol: they live a semi-nomadic life in villages of felt Yurts, which move with the grazing season; in summer they graze the higher pastures and in winter they come down to the lowlands, still often deep in snow, and as cold as −50°C. Transport is mostly by camel and pony.

About 20 kilometres out of Hailar is a CITS-approved village of Mongol herders; here they receive the odd tourist, mostly Japanese. The good thing about this grassland tour, as opposed to the Hohhot trips, is that you can virtually go alone. I hired a jeep from CITS at the hotel (friendly and helpful, though they speak only Chinese or Mongolian) which cost about ¥50 a day, including a driver and an 'interpreter', who was just along for the ride – he spoke nothing but Chinese. After a long drive across the grass, we arrived at the village of yurts, and were ushered inside to take milk-tea and buttered biscuits. These 'guest-yurts' are very luxurious compared to the real thing; the ordinary ones have little more than a mud floor with some rugs and a tin stove, perhaps a baby rocking in a wooden cradle, protected from the flies by a muslin bag. After the tea-feast there was time for a stroll and a jeep-ride to see some distant flocks, or you may be expected to make a fool of yourself on a camel. But the most remarkable thing is the grass itself. Thickly scattered with a variety of flowers and huge fungi you discover, as you step on to it, that it is also alive with little black toads, grasshoppers, birds and insects. It is impossible to avoid stepping on the toads: by the same token the insects find you hard to miss. Mosquito repellent would be useful.

Arriving back at the yurt, you will be expected to eat most of the sheep that has just been killed in your honour. In little more than 1½hrs the

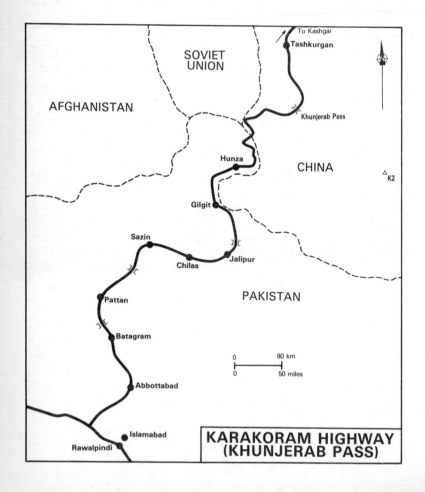

KARAKORAM HIGHWAY (KHUNJERAB PASS)

unfortunate beast has been transformed into a great number of dishes, from intestine-wrapped blood sausages to liver casserole and shredded mutton with garlic and celery. You will also be expected to drink like a horse and make a speech in whatever language you can still muster. This can be a very amusing occasion, but its darker side becomes apparent as you lurch your way back to Hailar, 1½ hours in the jeep.

TRAVEL DETAILS

Trains

From Lanzhou: Tianshui/Xi'an (4 daily, 13hrs/18hrs), Beijing (4, 34hrs), Zhongwei/Yinchuan/Baotou/Hohhot (4, 10hrs/12hrs/20hrs/23hrs), Xining (4, 5 hrs), Golmud (2, 15hrs), Jiayuguan/Liuyuan/Jiuquan/Turfan/Urumqi (4, 18hrs/26hrs/41hrs/45hrs).

From Jiayuguan: Lanzhou/Turfan (4, 13hrs/18hrs).

From Zhongwei: Yinchuan/Baotou/Hohhot (4, 2hrs/10hrs/13hrs).

From Yinchuan: Baotou/Hohhot (4, 8hrs/11hrs).

From Xining: Lanzhou (4, 5hrs), Golmud (2, 10hrs).

From Golmud: Xining/Lanzhou (2, 10hrs/15hrs).

From Turfan: Liuyuan/Jiayuguan/Lanzhou (4, 15hrs/23hrs/41hrs), Urumqi (4, 4hrs), Korla (2, 12hrs).

From Urumqi: Turfan/Lanzhou (4, 4hrs/45hrs).

From Baotou: Yinchuan/Zhongwei/Lanzhou (4, 8hrs/10hrs/20hrs), Hohhot (4, 2hrs), Erenhot (1, 20hrs), Datong (4, 8hrs), Beijing (4, 15hrs).

From Hohhot: Baotou/Yinchuan/Zhongwei/Lanzhou (4, 3hrs/11hrs/13hrs/23hrs), Datong (4, 5hrs), Beijing (4, 12hrs), Trans-Siberian Chinese train (leaves every Thursday morning at around 7.00).

From Hailar: Harbin/Beijing (2, 17hrs/38hrs).

Buses

From Dunhuang: Mogao Caves (Daily at 7am, 30mins), Liuyuan (2 daily, 3hrs), Jiayuguan (2, 8hrs), Jiuquan (2, 8hrs), Golmud (1, 8hrs).

From Xining: Taersi Lamasery (6 daily, 45mins).

From Golmud: Dunhuang (not regularly, 8hrs), Lhasa (daily, at least 30hrs).

From Turfan: Urumqi (Daily at 7.30am, 4hrs).

From Urumqi: Turfan (Daily, 4hrs), Tianchi (Daily, 4hrs).

From Kashgar: Urumqi (Daily, 3–4 days), Tashkurgan (Wednesdays).

Flights

Airports at Urumqi, Kashgar, Hetian, Kucha, Korla, Aqsu, Yining, Altay, Lanzhou, Dunhuang, Jiayuguan, Xining, Yinchuan, Baotou, Hohhot, Golmud.

BAOTOUBEZEKLIK	包头	MANZHOULI	满洲里
BINGLINGSI	壁灵寺	MOGAO	莫高
DUNHUANG	敦煌	QINGHAI HU	青海湖
GAOCHANG	高昌	QUTAN SI	曲潭寺
GOLMUD	格尔木	TAERSI	塔儿寺
HAILAR	海拉尔	TASHKORGAN	塔什干
HOHHOT	呼和浩特	TIANCHI	天池
JIAYUGUAN	嘉峪关	URUMQI	乌鲁木齐
JIUQUAN	酒泉	TURFAN	吐鲁蕃
KASHGAR	喀什	WUDANGZHAO	武唐照
LANZHOU	兰州	XINING	西宁
LABRO	拉布罗	YINCHUAN	银川
LIANCHENG	连城	YINGJISHAH	银迹山
LIUYUAN	留源	ZHONGWEI	中威
MAJISHAN	马迹山		

Chapter ten
TIBET

XIZANG

It has been a long wait, but **Tibet** (*Xizang*, in Chinese), the Roof of the World, is finally well and truly open. This isolated kingdom, ringed by the world's highest mountains, has stirred the imagination of the West since the 18C. Yet until the British invaded in 1904 only a trickle of bold eccentrics, adventurers and the odd missionary had succeeded in reaching Lhasa, and then only at serious risk to their lives, for it was firm Tibetan policy to exclude all influence from the outside world.

Inevitably this very inaccessibility only fired the imaginations of those kept out. Yet when the major breakthrough came, in the form of an invading British force of 1500 men, what they found was at first a profound disappointment. Far from the romantic Shangri-La they had anticipated, Lhasa was a city of indescribable filth and poverty, its people primitive and locked into an oppressive feudal theocracy unchanged since the Middle Ages. As one journalist wrote:

> If one approached within a league of Lhasa, saw the glittering domes of the Potala and turned back without entering the precincts one might still imagine an enchanted city. It was in fact an unsanitary slum. In the pitted streets pools of rainwater and piles of refuse were everywhere: the houses were mean and filthy, the stench pervasive. Pigs and ravens competed for nameless delicacies in open sewers.

All the traits of an archaic feudal society existed: of a population of around a million, 800,000 were serfs and a further 150,000 monks, leaving wealth and power in the hands of a tiny minority with the corrupt Lama theocracy at their head. Yet despite the squalor, no one then or later detected any strong desire for change: indeed long isolation had entrenched tradition and among many there was fierce resistance to new ideas.

Only now are these barriers breaking down, and having been breached they are being swept away fast. Ironically enough it is tourism – in search of that very dying isolation – which has become the catalyst, changing things far faster than almost four decades of military occupation could. For as the Chinese, who themselves regard Tibet as backward and barbarian, have finally woken up to the west's fascination, so have the Tibetans themselves learned to exploit it. On one level the Chinese are

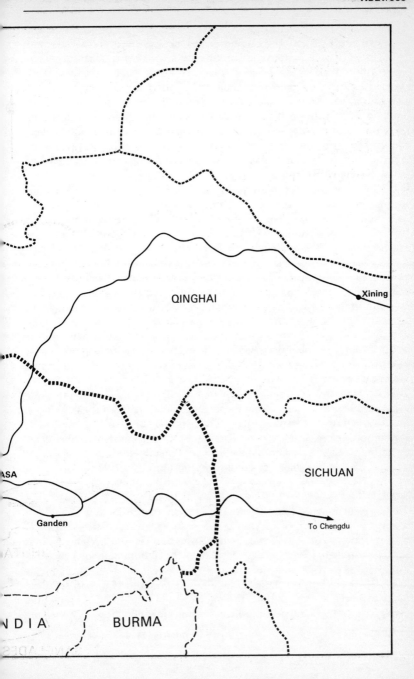

planning numerous new luxury hotels (nine in Lhasa alone), a gamepark in which wealthy visitors can hunt and new airports at Xigaze and Gyanze: on another, enterprising locals are setting up restaurants which cater brilliantly to less well-heeled travellers' needs (yakburgers have now reached Lhasa) and generally going out of their way to boost tourism along with their own incomes. To an extent, of course, these changes are undoing what you are here to see, but for the individual it means that there is a great deal more – in terms of ways to get to and around Tibet, of places to stay and of places to go. And despite a depressing lack of control on new developments, it also means a visibly raised standard of living for many Tibetans.

It has to be said that many people still find that Tibet fails to live up to their expectations: the Chinese development has to some extent been exploitative and you often get the impression that the restoration – of the Buddhist monasteries in particular – is purely for show. Certainly the real events of Tibetan religious life continue to take place in Nepal, Ladakh, or with the Dalai Lama in Dharamsala, India. But if you come without preconceptions Tibet is definitely worth it: apart from the natural splendours of the Himalayas, the people are consistently warm, with a spark of life and a willingness to make contact which sets them apart in China. Away from the main centres especially you may encounter quite extraordinary hospitality and find yourself plied with vast quantities of butter tea as your presence becomes the excuse for an impromptu party: in return recent pictures of the Dalai Lama (discreetly offered) are almost always welcome.

Most Tibetans live in the south of the country, in one of the three main towns or in villages along the trading routes between them. Villages are characterised by their high white perimeter walls, a necessary precaution against the extreme climate, and by clumps of prayer flags fluttering above them. The walls are also frequently decorated with swastikas, the Tibetan symbol of good luck and unity.

Some history

The early history of Tibet is a vague one, resting mainly on myths and legends which suggest a very ancient history indeed. Concrete evidence, however, begins only in AD625, when **Srongtsen Gampo** became the first king of a unified Tibet. In these early days the nation expanded rapidly* pushing out to control a great part of northern India and east as far as the borders of the Tang Empire: here the kingdom of Nanzhao (modern Yunnan) became for a time the subject of Tibet. At the same time Srongtsen Gampo opened the way for cultural influences by marrying

---

*From accounts by the British expedition of 1904, it appeared that their military prowess had diminished considerably over the years. One British officer wrote of the horror he felt at fighting an enemy who, put to flight, merely strolled disconsolately away.

two princesses, one Chinese (the famous Wen Cheng) the other Nepali. Tibetan nobles went to study in Chang'an (Xi'an) and brought back silk, paper and alcohol, while from India came early writing.

Most importantly, however, Srongtsen opened the way to **Buddhism**: both his brides were Buddhists and the images which they brought as dowries were ceremoniously received, the first incarnation of the Jokhang being built in Lhasa to house them. The famous Sakyamuni Buddha brought by Wen Cheng is still in place there, said to be the oldest such image in the world. Rapidly established, Buddhism gradually came to overshadow Tibet's indigenous Bon religion altogether. Some 100 years after its introduction the great Indian pandit *Padma Sambhava* was invited to Tibet by the then king, Tri Song Detsen, to take part in a formal debate against the Bon priests: after his victory Buddhism was declared the official religion of Tibet. Padma also founded the first Buddhist monastery in the country, at Samye to the south-east of Lhasa – it was built in the shape of a mandala, a cosmic diagram of the universe widely featured in Tibetan art and symbolism.

Over the next couple of centuries the country fell into chaos as strife within the royal family destroyed their authority, and organised religion, too, all but died out. In 1042, however, the Indian scholar-monk *Atisha* arrived in Tibet to revitalise the Buddhist tradition: stressing the ethical basis of the tantric practice,* he established a sect known as the *Kham-dampa*, with emphasis on enlightened compassion, and the impact of his teachings led to the foundation of two other major schools, the *Kargyud* and *Sakya* traditions. At the same time the notion of religious succession developed, a belief that all spiritual leaders, from the Dalai Lama down-wards, are reincarnations of their predecessors. These three rival traditions were the prominent schools of Tibetan Buddhism for the next 300–400 years, a period in which the religious communities began to fortify their monasteries, accumulate land and serfs, and added political control to their spiritual authority (although from 1207, when Ghengis Khan overran the country, Tibet was nominally ruled by a Mongol Viceroy). Each reigned supreme at different times: when the Sakyans held sway they forged close links with the Mongols, introducing lamaist Buddhism to Mongolia.

The first real threat to their authority came from the reforming theo-logian **Tsong Khapa** (1357–1419) who preached a stricter adherence to

---

*Tibetan Buddhism is one of the most all-pervasive forms in existence, encompassing the three systems of *Theravadin* (not harming others), *Mahayana* (helping others on the principle of compassion) and the **Tantric Tradition** (using the power of emotions to transform the energies of the mind into wisdom and enlightenment). The *Tantra*, central to Tibetan Buddhism, seeks to unify the two aspects of our being: masculine and feminine; intellectual and intuitive; active and passive. It is frequently represented in Tibetan art through the symbol of sexual union. Such erotic art, however, has been destroyed virtually throughout Tibet (though major western museums, especially the British Museum, do offer examples).

the Buddhist creed and stressed the importance of the discipline of the monastic life. Starting from the teachings of Atisha, and incorporating aspects of the other sects' practices, he established a new school of Buddhism, the *Gelupka* (Followers of the Way of Virtue), also known as 'yellow hats' (the other sects all wore red hats of different styles – yellow was chosen as a symbol of virtue). Tsong Khapa and his disciples rapidly emerged as the most powerful force in Tibet, establishing a new system of education and founding the great teaching monasteries: at Ganden in 1409, Drepung in 1416 and Sera in 1419. The fourth of the great monasteries, Tashilunpo, was established by Tsong Khapa's nephew Gendun Drub, third Grand Abbot of the Gelupka, in 1447.

Gendun Drub was also the first head of the order to be named **Dalai Lama** (Ocean of Wisdom), a title conferred on him posthumously by the Mongol prince Altan Khan. A successor of Altan Khan's later became the fourth Dalai Lama. Final supremacy over the Red Hats was achieved by the fifth Dalai Lama – the **Great Fifth** – with the support of the Mongols. He rebuilt the Potala, leaving it more or less as we see it today, travelled to Beijing to meet the Emperor on equal terms as a head of state, and was the first Dalai Lama to be regarded as a reincarnation of the Bodhisattva Avalokitesvara as well as of his predecessor. This last accounts for the powerful mix of national sentiment and religious fervour with which the Dalai Lama is still regarded. In a move calculated further to consolidate the power of the Yellow Hats and unite the country behind him, the Great Fifth also created the post of *Panchen Lama* for the abbot of the Tashilunpo monastery – Panchens are reincarnations of Amitaba, the God of Infinite Light.

The death of the fifth Dalai Lama was kept secret for thirteen years, until the completion of the Potala Palace. His successor, when eventually chosen, turned out to be something of a playboy: the Potala, which houses stupas for all the other Dalai Lamas, contains no monument to him, his only legacy to the country being a large collection of very beautiful love poems. Accounts vary as to the place and time of his death, but one way or another he was clearly bundled out of the way before he could do much damage: he was nonetheless greatly loved by his people.

It was a long time before another strong Dalai Lama emerged, a period in which Tibet drew itself in, falling further and further out of step with the world around. Its backwardness left it weak and in 1720 the **Chinese** moved in, forcing out the Mongols and leaving behind administrators known as *Ambans* and a garrison of some 1500 soldiers who were to remain for almost two centuries. Meanwhile the British, incensed by the lack of respect shown to their Imperial emissaries and wrongly suspecting Russian intrigue at Lhasa, mounted their expeditionary force in 1904. Unpopular back home, where it was seen as the violation of the right of a backward nation to live independent of worldly interference, the expedition nevertheless lasted long enough to force the thirteenth Dalai Lama to flee to Mongolia and thence to Beijing, and to allow the Chinese to tighten their grip. The Khampas, on Tibet's eastern marches, rose in revolt, but were immediately and brutally crushed by General Chao Er Feng, who established a regime notorious for its insensitivity to local sentiment – monasteries were defiled, religious relics looted and destroyed. In 1910 he took Lhasa, forcing the Dalai Lama to flee yet again, this time to the British in India.

Finally in 1911 the Manchu dynasty fell and the Dalai Lama was able to return, expel the Chinese armies, and rule in relative peace and independence until 1951. In that year the **Red Army**, reviving long-standing Chinese claims over Tibet, occupied the eastern marches again while Britain and India ignored pleas for help. The Dalai Lama sent a delegation to Beijing and reached an agreement which permitted the PLA to occupy Tibet on the understanding that they respected the religious beliefs and customs of the people. Forlorn hope! In October the PLA marched into Lhasa and set about their task of liberating the country (from whom? Pandit Nehru asked; from the shackles of feudal and religious oppression, the Chinese would no doubt have replied). Despite a cautious beginning – on both sides – serious **uprisings** broke out against the anti-religious campaigns being conducted by the Chinese. The most serious, in eastern Tibet in 1956 and Lhasa in 1959 were viciously repressed, and after the latter the current (fourteenth) Dalai Lama fled to India, where established a government-in-exile at Dharamsala in the Himalayan foothills.

The Chinese now set to earnest at their tasks of re-education and of bringing Tibet into the 20C – building roads, restructuring agriculture (often disastrously) and introducing modern medicine and hygiene. In 1960 they set up a committee to work on the administrative and political structure, and in 1965 the **Tibetan Autonomous Region** of the PRC was duly proclaimed. Religion, though, continued to be suppressed and in the Cultural Revolution these measures reached their bloody height: thousands of monasteries were destroyed and all forms of religious activity utterly forbidden.

Nowadays the situation is a good deal better. Since 1978 the Chinese have relaxed their policies, allowing greater religious and personal freedom. Monasteries are being rebuilt and monks are practising again – though where 50 years ago there were 1500 monasteries and many thousands of monks today only 10 monasteries are active with barely 1000 monks (and there are some who say that even this is cosmetic, the monasteries restored for tourism and the monks ignorant of the religion they are supposed to practise). There is a conscious policy to encourage exiles – and especially the Dalai Lama, who has begun talks with Chinese leaders – to return home. Chinese education, too, has had its effect on many of the young. Even so the undercurrent of opposition, and the memory of past abuses, continues to run strong.

Tibetan practicalities

Geographically, Tibet can be divided into four main regions: the northern plains or Chang Tang, a huge region of bare, almost uninhabited land where few crops grow because of the elevation and exposure; southern Tibet, the most fertile and densely populated region, which includes the towns of Lhasa, Xigaze and Gyanze and the three river valleys of the Upper Indus, Brahmaputra and Khaligandaki; eastern Tibet, the deeply incised mountain area between the Chang Tang and Sichuan; and the west, which is sealed off by the Kunlun mountains in the north and the Himalayas to the south. The air is thin and fresh, and the climate extreme. **Temperatures,** which can reach around 18°C in summer, plunge to −18°C in January: you're best off visiting in spring or autumn, but any time between March and November should be acceptable. You'll need warm clothing to keep off the night chill whenever you come.

The city of Lhasa is almost 4000 metres above sea level (over 12000 feet) and **altitude sickness** can be a real problem. The sudden change if you arrive by air can be a shock − overland routes allow more time to adapt, but they also go higher still (up to 5200 metres, 17000 feet), in the mountain passes. Symptoms can range from nausea and difficulty breathing to permanent, violent headaches, and insomnia is also common. The only answer is to take things easy for the first few days and to take in plenty of liquids to offset the dryness of the air. Walk slowly from the moment you arrive and avoid alcohol and cigarettes for the first day at least − it's a frustrating regime, but it works.

The staple **food** of the Tibetans is *tsampa*, which is roasted barley flour − it can be eaten as a dry powder but is often mixed to a paste with butter tea (a curious blend of tea churned together with rancid yak butter). Many Tibetans carry a small pouch of tsampa to keep them going through the day. This diet is supplemented by meat, yoghurt, eggs and root vegetables − though in the market at Lhasa a vast array of fresh vegetables, some brought in from China, can also be found. The most common drink − other than tea (*Cha Suma*, butter tea, or *Cha Namu*, sweet and milky) − is *Chang*, a milky-coloured alcoholic beverage brewed from barley.

One final warning is to photographers: you are not normally allowed to take **photographs** inside Tibet's monasteries or temples. With persist-ence − and for an exorbitant fee − it may be possible to get permission from the Chinese to do so, but even this is no guarantee that you will actually be able to take any photographs: many Tibetans object strongly and occasionally with violence.

Getting in – and out

The most common way of travelling to Tibet is still **by air** from CHENGDU. There's a daily flight which leaves at 6.55am, takes just under two hours and costs ¥424 one way. There have, in the past, been flights from Xi'an and Lanzhou, though these were discontinued early in 1986. You should check on the current situation at any CAAC office once you are in China. From 1987 there should also be an air link between Kathmandu and Lhasa, which would make visiting Tibet considerably cheaper than it has been.

Increasingly, though, independent travellers are taking the arduous but rewarding **overland routes**. Five of these are feasible: from Golmud, from Chengdu, from Kashgar, from Dali (northwest of Kunming in Yunan Province), or from Nepal along the Friendship Highway. On any of them you must be prepared for delays, for harsh conditions (cold and altitude take their toll) and poor food: take plenty to eat along with you and keep your warmest clothes easily accessible. The possibility of being turned back by Public Security Officials always exists on all routes save that between Kathmandu and Lhasa. The Chengdu route has effectively been forced open by sheer persistence of travellers and for this reason is probably a reasonable bet. Those overlanders who did run into official problems more often than not were on their way *into* Tibet. It seems that if you are making your way *out* of Tibet you are less likely to run the risk of being stopped. Shortest, and the obvious alternative to flying, is the road **from Golmud**, a rocket testing site in Qinghai province. The fact that there is a road connecting Golmud with Lhasa makes it possible to travel this route by bus or truck with comparative ease, and in the last couple of years this has become a well-established route. If you go by truck, make sure the lift goes the whole way, for more than nine-tenths of the journey runs along the Tibetan Plateau – a flat, often uninspiring landscape dotted with a handful of bleak, isolated settlements. The only town to speak of is Amdo, a haphazard cluster of wooden shacks, brick huts and rusting corrugated-iron roofs, lying to the south of the Tanggula Mountains marking the border between Tibet and Qinghai. Were you to be stranded anywhere along the route you'd have a cold, muddy landscape (even at the height of summer) and the prospect of an interminable wait to contend with – an adventure you should be able to avoid. For further details see the section on Golmud (p. 466). If the scheme for a railway from Golmud to Lhasa is ever completed, it promises to be one of the most amazing feats of railway engineering – and one of the finest journeys – in the world.

The road **from Chengdu** to Lhasa, which can take 20 days or more, is yet more spectacular – a tortuous route frequently destroyed by flood or landslide along which you may need to dig much of your way. You can get a lift with truck drivers in Chengdu or there are occasional buses: for all its difficulties, this route comes highly recommended by those with the time and stamina to endure it.

Another possibility within China is the journey **from Kashgar** to Lhasa by truck. Though this can be done it is not strictly permitted and some travellers – even several days into their journey – have found themselves turned back by officials. If you manage it, however, the trip is on a par, at least, with that from Chengdu: it can take ten days, it may need three weeks or more. Of all the overland routes, the Kashgar option is the most difficult. You should be prepared mentally, physically (and equipment-wise) to walk a substantial part of the way.

The newest option is that from Dali north through Yunnan Province to Lijiang, Zhongdian, Deden and then along the valley of the Mekong to Markam – whereupon the road heads west. Markam is the midway point on the Lhasa–Chengdu run and is the first major town on Tibet's eastern periphery. You will have no problems getting to Lijiang by bus from Dali (see the chapter on the Southwest). The remaining two hundred-odd miles north to the Chengdu–Lhasa road involve the risk of being turned back, though it's easy enough to buy a ticket in Lijiang for Zhongdian. Anyone not planning a visit to Tibet but who makes it to the northern parts of Yunnan should bear in mind that Zhongdian is, geologically and ethnically, on the Tibetan Plateau. With Tibetan-style houses, butter tea, yak butter and a good number of Tibetans, the town offers at least a glimpse of what lies beyond.

Travel **between Tibet and Nepal** is also becoming increasingly popular, though not noticeably easier. You could reach Lhasa from Kathmandu within three days, but most people take longer in order properly to enjoy the sights en route. So far this route is much more heavily travelled in the other direction, as a way out of China. You can attempt it by a combination of public bus as far as Xigaze and then lorry, but this is not always easy – trucks are few and you'll be competing with locals for any places available. The standard alternative is to **hire your own transport**. Buses – which hold up to 25 people, though 20 plus luggage is more realistic – can be hired from the coach station in Lhasa with a few days' notice; total cost about ¥2,000. You should establish that this price is for the coach (and not based on the number of passengers) as this will allow you to pick up extra travellers if you want. It is also important to have at least one Mandarin speaker along, and an itinerary in Chinese – the driver is not going to understand English. For smaller groups Land-Cruisers are a possible alternative – they take 7 but again 5 plus luggage will be considerably more comfortable. These charge around ¥300 a day for long-distance journeys, or about ¥1700 to the border: coming into Tibet, with luck, you might get a much cheaper ride with one returning empty.

In practice, you'll probably find that some enterprising soul has already organised a bus and posted a notice advertising spare seats on the hotel bulletin boards – get in touch quickly as these tend to fill fast. If you need to organise one yourself you should easily find passengers via notice-boards too. Bear in mind that you will need a **visa for Nepal** (¥30 from the Nepalese Embassy in Beijing, ¥40 at the one in Lhasa – you need photographs) and a permit from the PSB to leave China at the Nepali border; it is very useful to have the towns you plan to visit written on to your travel permit. There are, too, some additional costs to consider: overnight stops at ¥3–10 per person and food (carrying food from Lhasa, especially tins of fruit and juice, will save money and help eke out the often sparse supplies available en route). Finally, be prepared for some discomfort – the food is generally awful, accommodation primitive, and the rows between driver and passengers over when and where to stop are legendary.

Trekking in Tibet

Once you are in Tibet **trekking** is not strictly allowed, but the chances of being stopped seem very small. One obvious temptation is the hike up the Rumbuk Valley to Qomolongma – Mt Everest. If you do plan to undertake anything of this nature, however, you will have to come equipped – maps and backpacking equipment are not available in Lhasa (or, for that matter, in Beijing). At the least you will need a good sleeping bag, warm gloves, hat and socks: even thick socks seem unobtainable in China.

You also need to bring with you the right attitude. Not leaving litter and so on may seem obvious, but trekkers should also remain keenly aware of their relationship with Tibetans they might meet along the way. It is neither fair nor realistic to expect to be fed by locals – traditionally hospitable or no, their borderline existence cannot hope to support the ever-rising waves of travellers. Best to carry your own food and the means of cooking it. Firewood, too, is in short supply on the Tibetan plateau and villagers rarely have spare fuel. If they offer some you should be prepared to make a payment or practical gift in return. At the same time, while gifts of real practical value or small payments make obvious sense, there is danger in too much open-handedness; subsequent trekkers may find themselves expected to be Santa Claus too.

LHASA

LHASA is Tibet's largest town by some way and its capital in every sense. Under Chinese influence there are now two very distinct parts: the ancient Tibetan, cleared of the rabid dogs and noxious squalour but otherwise remarkably as described by early visitors, and the modern Chinese – ugly, purpose-built blocks reminiscent of every other city in China. The modern part continues to spread – and there are no less than nine luxury hotels planned for Lhasa – but at least the realisation of its tourist potential should have ensured the survival of the traditional town alongside.

The dichotomy is clear even from a distance: as you approach Lhasa the whiteness of the hilltop Potala shines out as it has always done; nowadays, though, the adjoining hill is crowned by a giant telecommunications mast. And it is reflected in smaller things too – wander round the bazaar and you'll find Chinese-made plastic shoes and leaking batteries on sale alongside the yak butter. It is tourism, however, which may do most to break down traditions which centuries of military action could not budge. Modern Lhasa is well on its way to becoming another Kathmandu as Tibetans begin to realise the potential of their visitors. For the time being, at least, this works in your favour – prices are not yet disastrous and there are more places catering for travellers every day.

Arrival

Despite the growing popularity of the overland routes, the majority of people still seem to arrive in Lhasa by air. There's a CAAC bus from the **airport,** that runs all the way to the CAAC office in Lhasa (located in the shadow of the Potala, to the east). The road to Lhasa runs due west along the valley of the Tsangpo until it joins the main Lhasa-Gyanze road. Lhasa lies to the northeast along a major tributary of the Tsangpo. The road hugs the river most of the way. Journey time is approximately 90 minutes. In spring, sections of this road can be washed away and the journey will take very much longer. En route you'll pass whitewashed villages and ruined hilltop fortresses, once regional stations of the Tibetan administration, now abandoned. Look out in particular for the rock carving of *Atisha*, the Indian scholar-monk who introduced many important aspects of Buddhism to Tibet. This is about halfway, set back from the road on the left and clearly reflected in the river running below.

Once in Lhasa, the **hotel** most travellers head for is *Snowlands*, a 2-storeyed Tibetan building in a street running off to the left in front of the Jokhang. This charges about ¥5 for a bed in a 5–10 bedded dorm, has no running water or heating and only a couple of double rooms. But it does offer a pump in the yard, a popular dining room, bike hire, and an excellent location. Similar accommodation, with more double rooms (¥10) and another good dining room, can be found at the *Banak Shol*. The *Number One Guesthouse* is also central, to the right of the Jokhang, and charges ¥5 for space in a three-bedded room: staff here can be difficult, though, despite speaking some English. The *Kirey Guesthouse*, a minute or two east of the Banak Shol, offers three- and four-bed options working out to a maximum of ¥9 per person. The Kirey's showers can be used by residents and non-residents alike. Shower tokens have to be bought from a small office on the right-hand side of the courtyard as you go in. Bicycles are available for hire though you'll have to part company with either your passport or ¥200 as a deposit.

Moving up in price, there's the *Sunlight Hotel* – ¥60 for a double room with bath and (cold) running water. Near the university, this is a long way both from where the bus drops you and from the main sites you might want to visit. More new luxury hotels are springing up all the time. Two which are definitely in operation already are the *Lhasa Hotel*, complete with marble lobby, 1100 beds, Chinese and western restaurants and oxygen supply in every room but already fraying at its plush edges, and the *Tibetan Guesthouse*, with similar facilities in a rather more attractive building. Either of these will set you back at least ¥100 per night for a double room, though the Tibetan Guesthouse is the cheaper of the two. Finally, awkwardly situated some way out in its own small park, there's the *Number Three Guesthouse*, another luxury pad with prices to match.

Seeing the city

The **Jokhang**, Tibet's most sacred temple right at the heart of the city, is the obvious place to start. Built in 642 to house the great statue of Buddha Sakyamuni brought as a dowry by the Chinese princess Wen Cheng on her marriage to King Srongtsen Gampo, it is still a magnificent building. And the statue – thought to be the oldest image of Buddha in the world – is still in place in the Great Hall.

In the courtyard in front of the temple pilgrims prostrate themselves, setting up a constant swishing as the cardboard they hold rubs along the stones, while others queue to enter. You can join this queue and, inside, make the rounds of the inner temples. Each of these, dimly lit and infused with the smell of yak butter lamps, houses a different deity. The walls are covered in carvings and paintings of scenes from Tibetan history, while on the gilded roofs, where you are also allowed to clamber, protective and sanctifying texts are inscribed. There are also spectacular views of the Potala and the mountains beyond from here. The legendary gate from the Jokhang to the underworld, though, is nowhere to be seen.

Walking around the Jokhang – or any other hall or shrine in Tibet – remember that you must always follow a clockwise direction. Circles, or mantras, are a vital piece of symbolism in Tibetan Buddhism and it is a sign of great disrespect not to follow the correct direction. Prayer wheels, too, are always spun clockwise.

Around the Jokhang, again in a circle which must be followed in a clockwise direction, runs Parkor Street with its famous **Bazaar**. This – like the Jokhang – opens at around 9am. The hour before this is one of the most interesting times to see the area – it is just light and vast crowds are making their early morning devotions around and in front of the

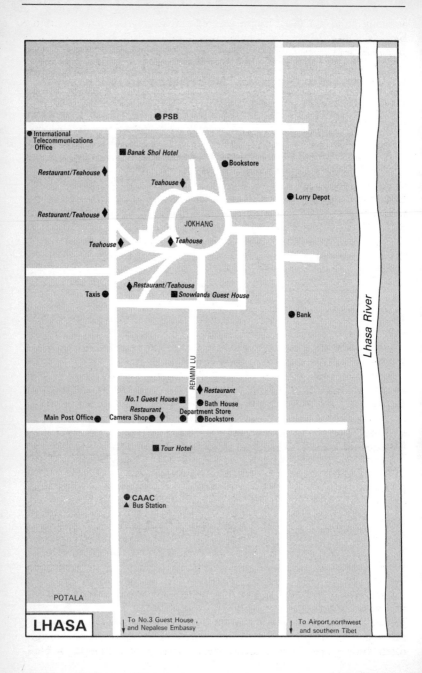

● PSB

● International
Telecommunications
Office

■ *Banak Shol Hotel*

● Bookstore

Restaurant/Teahouse ♦

Teahouse ♦

● Lorry Depot

Restaurant/Teahouse ♦

JOKHANG

Teahouse ♦   ♦ *Teahouse*

♦ *Restaurant/Teahouse*

Taxis ●   ■ *Snowlands Guest House*

● Bank

RENMIN LU

♦ *Restaurant*

No.1 Guest House ■   ● Bath House

Restaurant   Department Store
Main Post Office ●   Camera Shop ● ♦   ● ● Bookstore

■ *Tour Hotel*

● CAAC
▲ Bus Station

POTALA

Lhasa River

LHASA

To No.3 Guest House ,
↓ and Nepalese Embassy

To Airport, northwest
↓ and southern Tibet

Jokhang amid clouds of sweet scented smoke from enormous incense burners. Once the market is underway – selling everything from cheap souvenirs and knick-knacks to precious stones and old carpets – there remains a curious mix of religious devotees, tradesmen and tourists. There are few bargains to be had, if any, but the atmosphere is absorbing. Head off down the sidestreets and you'll pass haircutters and cobblers, maybe an open-air dentist plying his primitive teade, before reaching the food markets with their piles of meat, vegetables and yak butter. At night the place becomes even more animated.

The **Potala Palace**, former home of the Dalai Lamas, dominates Lhasa from its hilltop position. Originally conceived in the 7C, it was rebuilt after 1642 when the 'Great Fifth' Dalai Lama moved his seat of power from the Drepung Monastery to Lhasa as he took over control of temporal affairs. A vast and imposing edifice, it has scores of courtyards, halls and temples spread over 13 storeys. One thousand steps lead up to the great red chamber in the centre of the building: inside, you pass through countless halls, lit only by yak butter lamps, where huge stupas to former Dalai Lamas loom out of the darkness. Take a torch. There are jewel-encrusted monuments, gloomy historical and religious paintings, and nowadays too you can visit what were the private quarters of the current Dalai Lama, seeing how he lived, studied and slept. The halls of the fifth and thirteenth Dalai Lamas are the largest and richest of all, their stupas made of bronze overlaid with gold leaf and lavishly set with precious stones.

There are two ways into the Potala, the main front entrance and another at the back. The front is used by most pilgrims; tour groups use the rear entrance which can be reached by road – if you latch on to one of these you'll learn a great deal more about what you are seeing and get into parts not open to casual visitors. Opening hours are from 9–1 on Mondays, Wednesdays and Saturdays, with the last admissions at 10.30.

To the west of the city, near the new Lhasa Hotel, is the former summer residence of the Dalai Lamas, the **Norbulinka** or Jewel Park. The fourteenth Dalai Lama in particular is said to have longed for the summer months when he could escape from the prison-like Potala to enjoy the open spaces and relaxed atmosphere of his summer palace. The buildings themselves are undistinguished, but they are set in a beautiful park and you can wander at leisure through what is now an entirely deserted retreat. For ¥2 there is also a tour around the Dalai Lama's living quarters.

Elsewhere in Lhasa, if you've had enough of temples and the smell of yak butter lamps, you can visit the **Chinese hospital**, not far from the Jokhang, or the **carpet factory** on the northern rim of the city, where you can watch the dyeing and weaving processes. The factory shop, though, offers little worth buying. Lhasa also boasts a new **Exhibition Hall**, opposite the Lhasa Hotel, where there are displays of the artefacts and achievements of the Tibetan 'minority people'.

Lhasa's monasteries

Tibetan monasteries, however much they may differ in appearance, all conform to the same basic architectural pattern. At the spiritual centre is the chapel building, the main hall used for monastic gatherings and collective rituals each day: around it are colleges where the monks pass their daily lives in training, study and prayer; chapels of individual teaching establishments for less important rituals, and hotels and hospices for visiting monks. The whole gives the impression of a complete walled village. The monks themselves wear maroon robes, usually with one arm left bare, and shave their heads. Their period of study lasts from 20–25 years, though only a few go on to become 'literati' and study the enormous body of Buddhist scripture – the rest continue to work in the monastery.

One activity which you may witness if you visit is monastic **debating**. Central to Tibetan Buddhism, this takes place on certain afternoons in a designated space within the monastery – a peaceful open area, often planted with trees, guarded by a wall. Here the monks sit on the ground in groups, surrounding one of their number as he expounds on a theme drawn from Buddhist writings. He must answer any questions or challenges to his knowledge put by his colleagues and teachers and as he makes his points he slaps his hand against his wrist and shouts, the noise level increasing as the argument heats up. This duel of oratory is similar to an Indian custom known as the '*rig che*' (great test of wisdom).

There are three major monasteries which can be visited from Lhasa: two of them accessible by local buses. **Drepung** was founded in 1416 by disciples of Tsong Khapa and was the original seat of the Dalai Lamas. It is now functioning again in a small way, with a couple of hundred monks where once there were 10,000: you can visit the vast kitchens to gain some idea of its scale. Eight km west of Lhasa at the foot of the mountains, this is easily reached by bike once you have acclimatised, or it lies on the no.5 bus route. The **Sera**, founded in 1419, is just over 3 km to the north of town on the main road leading from the east gate of the Potala, reached by no.10 bus. Both Drepung and Sera are temple 'complexes' – comprising several buildings each. You should set aside a full morning or afternoon at least for a visit to either one. If you have time only to visit one of these you should choose Drepung; in much better condition than Sera anyway it occupies the centre of a relatively thriving village and offers fine views over the river valley.

Sera, however, lies close to the site of Lhasa's sky burials. If you follow the track which runs in front of the monastery wall until it disappears at the spur of a hill, and then continue along a path or groove worn in the rock by thousands of feet, you will come to the huge boulder where the ceremony takes place.

The **sky burial** is a particularly grisly ritual: when they die wealthy Tibetan Buddhists are not left to rot in the ground, but instead are ritually dismembered, their bones ground and mixed with barley flour, and the resultant mess fed to waiting vultures. The ceremony, celebrated at sunrise, occurs fairly regularly, though there is no way of predicting in advance when it will be. As numbers of visitors to Lhasa have increased in the last year or two, so have the numbers of observers at the ceremonies – sometimes rising to as many as 60 or 70 tourists. Tibetans do not appreciate even a single voyeur, and angry scenes and stone-throwing incidents have become increasingly frequent, even meriting a report in the *China Daily*. While a Chinese presence seems particularly unpopular (and photographs are out of the question) our advice must be for anyone to stay away from what should, after all, be a private occasion.

Ganden Monastery is considerably further afield, some 60km east of Lhasa or 1½ hours by road. It is possible to hitch a lift with a lorry leaving Lhasa, but you then face a very steep uphill climb of some 1000 metres – hiring a LandCruiser (around ¥50 each between four) is a considerably easier option. You may encounter some resistance from the authorities if you plan to visit, but persistence should get you there. Founded by Tsong Khapa in 1409, Ganden was one of the four most important monasteries in Tibet, its supreme abbot third in status after the Dalai and Panchen Lamas. At present there is no head Lama here but the empty thrones for him and the Dalai Lama, draped in the Yellow of the reformist Gelupka (Yellow Hat) sect, are always decked in white scarves left by pilgrims – powerful reminders of the Dalai Lama's continuing importance to his people.

Ganden occupies a stunning position, perched at some 4800 metres on a narrow col between two peaks and visible only when you are almost upon it. The road runs through a village at the foot of the mountain and begins a steep, tortuous climb: as the pass approaches a huge mountain city comes suddenly into view. On closer inspection, this is little more than a skeleton – Ganden came under particularly fierce attack during the Cultural Revolution, with widespread devastation still apparent. Restoration work has now begun in earnest, though, and a clutch of brightly painted buildings stands out in sharp contrast to the faceless ruins around them. Some 200 monks now live and work at Ganden: visitors can wander around freely and even take photographs of the deities inside, since all the images here are 1980s reproductions.

Lhasan practicalities
One of the most obvious signs of the way in which Lhasa has opened up over the last few years is the number of good travellers' **restaurants** which

can now be found. There are several where you can choose from a selection of raw ingredients – chopped vegetables and meat mainly – which are then cooked for you in a wok. The result is cheap (from ¥2.50–4), tasty and saves a great deal of wrestling with language and menus. Two particularly good examples are the *Snowlands* restaurant and the one directly opposite the *Banak Shol*. There are also several Sichuan restaurants in Lhasa, the Chinese and western hotel restaurants, and a number of traditional Tibetan places, mainly on the main road east of the Potala and side streets off it. The specialities in these include *Shapali* – flat, round, deep-fried pastries, filled with yakmeat and herbs – *Tukkpa* – noodle soup with yakmeat – and *Momo* – delicious yakmeat dumplings with spices, dipped in a hot chilli sauce.

As an alternative if you are planning to stay more than a few days you could buy a burner (¥13 in the market) and **prepare your own** meat and vegetables. A group of people clubbing together can save significantly this way, and maybe eat better too. At the market you can buy yak meat, mutton, pork and beef as well as a wide selection of vegetables, eggs, cheese and yak butter. This last is quite expensive at ¥2 per jin and it varies in flavour from quite mild to a hairy roquefort – taste before you buy. The yoghurt sold in Lhasa is ambrosial and sells out by noon – take your own container. It helps if you can become a regular shopper; prices will drop and the stallholders become considerably more helpful.

Most of the facilities you might need are reasonably central and marked on our map: only **PSB** is really any distance from the heart of things – the one you need to visit for exit visas and so on is out beyond the Potala palace. The **CAAC** office is open for requests for tickets in the afternoons only; it actually issues tickets between 9 and 12 three days prior to the flight. If you're looking to **hire a taxi** or LandCruiser the best place is near the Jokhang: take the road past the Snowlands to the end, turn right and you will see a large TAXI sign on the left. You can hire transport to Ganden from here, or to virtually anywhere else in Tibet including the Nepalese border. Most drivers are Tibetans who speak some Chinese – make sure you have a clear map on which to specify your intentions. **Bicycle hire**, for destinations closer at hand, is easy enough these days too, either from the Snowlands Hotel or one of a number of bike hire stalls which line the pavements nearby.

Finally Tibetan **nightlife**, such as it is. Every now and then there are performances of native song and dance at the Exhibition Hall – not always entirely professional, the spectacles are at least lively, colourful, folksy and quite unlike anything else you'll have seen in China. The Jokhang bazaar at night is also worth a visit. In general Tibet seems to stay open and keep going longer than most of China: by the same token, mornings start later, with nothing much open before 9am.

XIGAZE

Tibet's second city, Xigaze lies 160 kilometres south-west of Lhasa, from where it can be reached either by public bus or hired jeep. The mountainous route, passing spectacular waterfalls and plunging streams and traversing passes of up to 5200 metres amid savage scenery, can take a full day. But it is well worth it: the views are magnificent throughout.

XIGAZE itself, however, is little more than a village – bleak and very evidently poor. Only a modern Chinese quarter, with new buildings and a huge Friendship Store, hints at any affinity with Lhasa or suggests that in Tibetan terms this is an important town. The most important relic is the **Tsong Shan**, a high fortress which, although destroyed during the Cultural Revolution and now deserted, continues to dominate every view of Xigaze. This is the former residence and administrative base of the Panchen Lamas – a labyrinthine complex of religious halls, library archives and living quarters. You are free to wander around at will; on the external walls one of the more notorious Cultural Revolution slogans – *Destroy the Four Olds* – can still be deciphered.

Just outside town, within walking distance of the government guest house, is the famous – and fascinating – **Tashilunpo Monastery** (open 9.30–1, daily except Sundays). Founded in 1447 by Gendun Drub, nephew of Tsong Khapa, it was made the seat of the Panchen Lama in 1649 by the fifth Dalai Lama. The title Panchen (great scholar) and the attendant regional authority made the abbot of Tashilunpo second only to the Dalai Lama in Tibet's religious and political hierarchy. The current holder lives in Beijing where, as a senior Communist Party official, he is supposed to be deeply involved in Tibetan policy. But his role must be an ambivalent one, even if his cooperation with the Chinese does not appear to have cost him the high regard of his people.

The monastery itself huddles against the mountainside, a clustered mass of buildings similar to the Drepung at Lhasa: at its height 4,000 monks lives here. There are nothing like that now, but at least this is still a functioning place of worship, its buildings in relatively good repair and actively being restored. In the Great Hall you can see the funeral pagodas of former Panchen Lamas – the largest commemorates the fourth, a vast construction overlaid with silver leaf and crusted with jewels. The kitchens, too, are open, perhaps the most extraordinary aspect of the monastery. Once your eyes accustom themselves to the apparently perpetual gloom down here you may glimpse the monks who tend the vast cauldrons of bubbling yak butter. Nearby, the Panchen Lama's house is also open to visitors.

There are several small and rather primitive **guesthouses** in Xigaze: *Guesthouse No.1* is new, faceless, said to have a restaurant and charges ¥30 a night; *No.2* is closer to the centre, charges ¥3 for a dorm bed, and serves basic food for ¥1.50 – at 6pm you form a queue to buy your ticket from the office and hire a bowl! There is also a sizeable hotel near the department store and truck-stop accommodation on the edge of town. The town **market** has a good selection of coral and turquoise and some revolting plastic trinkets. Not far out there is also a major **Bon monastery**, one of the few survivors of Tibet's indigenous religion.

GYANZE

About 50 kilometres east of Xigaze, along a valley which in summer is lush and green, heavily cultivated with barley, lies **GYANZE**. Public buses from Xigaze take about 2 hours, so that a day-trip is theoretically feasible – but beware of erratic timetables and, in the summer, of rains which can render the road impassable. You could also get here direct from Lhasa – a rough ride of 9 hours, amply compensated by the magnificence of the scenery – or from the south, from the Nepalese border.

Gyanze itself, clustered around its citadel, is tiny. A single main road runs through and along here there is a lively market, of interest more for its atmosphere than for anything on sale. The monastery atop the hill is in poor condition and not always open to visitors – if you find the gates shut the only alternative access involves climbing the hill face.

The main attraction of Gyanze, however, is the extraordinary **Palkor Monastery**. Built in 1429, it originally contained thirteen temples, though only the main temple and the pagoda have survived intact. The architecture of the pagoda is stupendous: built on 9 storeys, its plan is that of a mandala – a circle within a square. From every side the eyes of Buddha look out, showing his concern for all mankind, and there are thirteen rings on the spire, representing the levels one must reach before attaining Buddhahood. Within there are 15C frescoes and a vast collection of images of saints and divinities (this is known as the 'Pagoda of Ten Thousand Buddhas'). Some 20 lamas still inhabit the place today.

Other Buddhist relics nearby include the **Yer Pa Hermitages**, a whole town of hermitages attached to the monastery where monks of all schools would spend some 5–7 years in total isolation. It was a hard life: once ready to enter this state, the hermit would build himself an earthen hut or find a cave, and close himself off entirely in a small space with only a latrine in the corner. No light entered the cell: there was only a small opening through which an attendant, assigned to the monk, passed food once a day, at midday. The monk was not allowed to speak or even see the attendant's hand. If no sign of life was seen over a period of three days, death or illness would be assumed and the head lama summoned.

Off the road between Gyanze and Xigaze you can also visit the **Xia Lu Monastery** above the village of XIGA. Reached by a path up a wild and wooded mountainside, this is believed to be one of the oldest monasteries in Tibet. Despite extensive damage, both Nepalese and Chinese influences can be seen in its architecture.

If you want to **stay the night** in Gyanze there are a couple of alternatives. The bus station 'hotel' is the one to avoid, uncomfortable and overpriced. Head towards town instead and you will see a large red building on the right: here, and in the place directly opposite, you can get a bed for about ¥4. There is also a good restaurant of the pick-your-own-ingredients type.

WESTWARDS

The town of Xigar is another day's journey by public transport from Xigaze, on a route which crosses three passes over 15,000 feet. Along here, 5–6 hours out of Xigaze, a road leads off to the town and ancient monastery of **SAKYA**. You could stay the night here, but an hour is enough to see what you want to see: the town is almost deserted save for the army camp, where there is a restaurant, and the monastery, which attracts truck loads of pilgrims from as far away as Gansu and Qinghai. Founded in 1073, this is one of the oldest in Tibet, and also one of the most important; it was here that the Sakya sect developed in the 13C – a powerful cult which ruled Tibet on and off for 400 years. Most of the monastery now lies in ruins but the one surviving temple is magnificent: it consists of three halls in beautiful condition and contains an extremely valuable collection of ancient sutras.

XIGAR, when you finally reach it, is the only town of any size in this remote part of western Tibet. There is a very primitive rest house here, a huge fort whose sheer walls seem to buttress the side of the mountain, and a monastery stacked up in tiers against the hillside in typically Tibetan style. A road continues west to **Mount Kailash** and **Lake Mansuvera**, and on through the Kunlun Mountains to **Xinjiang** and **Kashgar**. At Kailash you can walk around the mountain and then down to Lake Mansuvera where there is a guesthouse. Close to the mountain is the **Kingdom of Ngari**, a completely preserved ancient city with relics of weapons and armoury in the streets. Another track heads south from Xigar towards **Mount Everest**, with spectacular views of the high Himalayas: it is also possible to trek from Xigar to Everest, a round trip which will take a minimum of six days. Otherwise, there is no public transport on any routes beyond Xigar: even if you hire your own transport these are not roads to be taken lightly and are likely to prove almost as arduous as they are expensive.

SOUTH: THE ROAD TO NEPAL

The Friendship Highway runs from Lhasa to the Nepalese border by way of Gyanze, Xigaze and Sakya, in any of which you can pick up onward transport. **OLD TINGRI** is 4–5 hours beyond Sakya, a stopover point and little else. If you plan to stay the night be sure not to pass through the customs barrier, as the only hotel beyond it is an army barracks which charges anything from ¥4–20 a bed. Before the barrier you'll find a couple of clean guesthouses on the left close to the police station – even these may charge up to ¥10 per person. **NEW TINGRI**, another spectacular 4 hours switchbacking over the Himalayas, is the closest point to the Everest base camp. This stretch of road is perhaps the highest and most scenic you will yet have encountered.

Finally, another 4 hours will plunge you 2000 metres from these austere heights to the tropical forests around **KASA**. This is literally the end of the road: the monsoons, from June to September, seem to wash away the final section into Nepal as soon as it is repaired. There is a luxury hotel (where rooms are at least ¥40) and a bank on the hillside where you can change a small quantity of RMB. From here it is a matter of trekking. Nepalese porters can be hired for about Rs.100 – you will need one to guide you down the mountainside, though even carrying a 20 or 30 kilo load he is likely to leave you far behind. After about 1½ hours descent (in the other direction, a 3 hour climb) you will come to the valley which forms the border between Tibet and Nepal. This dramatic frontier is in constant use, but even so you may feel some trepidation when stepping on to the slippery wooden footbridge across the thundering weir.

Once **in Nepal** your porter will take you to the Nepalese customs. There is a guesthouse nearby or, for about 50Rs, there are trucks to the town of Bharabise. This is a lovely stopover point and has frequent coaches to Kathmandu.

NORTH – THE ROUTE TO QINGHAI

ZEDANG lies a morning's bus ride to the southeast of Lhasa. This area is the cultural centre of Tibet. Site of some of the earliest settled habitation in Tibet, the town is also surrounded by a number of ancient monasteries. Within a four-mile radius there are at least five which date from the reign of King Srongtsen Gampo: in Ze Dang itself; Nai Dong to the south; Zantong to the south-west; Yongmulakong to the south-east, and Chang Zhu to the east. The best location is Yongmulakong – an exceptionally well-preserved (though tiny) temple perching high up on a rocky crag and looking like something out of Disneyland. The climb up to the temple door from the road can take up to an hour. The effort is well worth it. Inside, the temple is in pristine condition and, on two floors, boasts unspoilt wall paintings.

The most important site culturally speaking are the Tombs of the

Tibetan Kings at Qiong Jie, some 30 miles south-east. There are eight burial mounds here, including that of Songsten Gampo and his wives. Built in three tiers, with stone steps leading to a flattened summit, the mounds rise as high as 38 feet. Getting there, on a very difficult road, can take as much as half a day. The site is primarily of academic interest; the mounds are themselves unremarkable.

A far more interesting trip from Ze Dang would be to **Samye**, around twenty miles to the west along the road back towards Lhasa. A small truck stop marks the location of a ferry that crosses the Tsangpo River. The ferry service is intermittent to say the least and once it sets out takes an hour to weave its way through the ever-shifting sandbanks to the other side. An equally intermittent truck or tractor completes the journey to Samye over rough desert ground in around forty-five minutes. This small village occupies a small oasis and is the site of Tibet's oldest monastery. Sadly, the wall paintings here have suffered from the ravages of both time and man. The damage inflicted by the latter almost certainly occurred during the Cultural Revolution. The relative remoteness of Samye gives it an air of authenticity that might not be apparent in Lhasa. A visit to Samye from Ze Dang (and back) would take up a full day. If you started out early you could hitch a lift west out of Ze Dang twenty miles to the ferry point. The bus from Lhasa to Zedang will also drop you at the ferry point (and vice-versa).

Foreigners can stay at two **hotels** in Ze Dang. Both lie to the south of the town's main intersection a few hundred meters apart. The Ze Dang Guesthouse compares favourably with the best accommodation in Lhasa and in mid-1986 was charging ¥40 for a double. The other option is an anonymous guesthouse with budget-price dormitory accommodation.

TRAVEL DETAILS

TRAVEL WITHIN TIBET

There are various **public buses**, leaving around 8am. The following information is displayed outside the ticket office in Lhasa's bus station:

Golmud	1166 km	90.00 FEC	1½ days	daily
Xigaze	355 km	35.60 FEC	1 day	daily
Ze Dang	195 km	19.60 FEC	4 hours	daily
Yadong	474 km	47.40 FEC	2 days	Friday
Bayi	406 km	40.60 FEC	1 day	daily except Wed./Fri.
Zhangmu	844 km	84.40 FEC	2½ days	Tue./Sat.
Naggu	328 km	32.80 FEC	1 day	Tue./Thur./Sat.
Chamdo	1127 km	112.80 FEC	3 days	Sat.
Chengdu	2416 km	241.60 FEC	7 days	? (sic)

No public buses go beyond Xigaze, so you need to find a truck or hire transport to go any further.

The best place in LHASA to find a **truck** is at the truck stop, either the evening before you leave or before light the next day – best to be ready by about 6am. It is possible to hail drivers on the road, of course, but competition for rides can be stiff, so get in at the start of the journey if possible.

The best truck stop for trips **west out of Lhasa** is about 10km out of town, to the west – not on the road to Drepung monastery but on the large road parallel with, and south of, it.

In XIGAZE plenty of drivers stop quite centrally, near the department store and hence hotel.

In GYANZE the truck stop is on the edge of town, though walkable in 15–20mins.

OLD TINGRI stands at a fork in the road to Kesa and Nepal – here the road branches off to Xigar (7km distant) and beyond. To travel towards Nepal the best place to get a truck is at the road barrier where all drivers have to stop anyhow – this is a good place to get a ride towards Xigaze/Lhasa, too. Unless you get an early ride originating in Old Tingri, you just have to sit it out and wait. From XIGAR to Lhasa it is probably worth walking down to the Nepal road (i.e. Old Tingri) for a ride, unless you find one at the Xigar truck stop.

TRAVEL OUT OF TIBET

Buses and trucks from Lhasa

To Chengdu: The journey is apparently possible by bus, but this may mean by a succession of local buses rather than by a long-distance one. Even though the bus information given here says 'Chengdu 7 days' you should expect the journey to take twelve days or more. By truck the journey will take as much as three weeks. Trucks are erratic and you

may have to spend some days looking for one to take you on the next step of your journey.

To Golmud: Buses leave Lhasa daily. Driving time is around 30 hours. The first day could see you spending up to sixteen hours in the bus (8am to midnight). It's unlikely you'll get more than six or seven hours sleep as the bus is scheduled to arrive in Golmud mid-afternoon (2pm/3pm). Expect the overnight accommodation to be extremely basic. Take enough food and drink to last the whole way. While there are isolated settlements on the way there are few places providing food and no guarantee that you'll stop at one anyway. Warm clothing is essential for the early hours of day two.

To Kashgar: This route isn't officially open and is covered (by truck) only sporadically. 12 to 20 days is the likely time needed. If you're feeling adventurous, it is a possibility . . .

To Kathmandu: Irregular public bus or truck to Xigaze (approx 8 hours) and then even more irregular trucks to the Tibetan border (another 2 days). Then a trek over the border and bus/truck to Kathmandu. Alternatively – see p. 510 – you can get a group of travellers together and hire your own transport, either a bus or a LandCruiser. Again, these will only be able to go as far as the border in most cases.

By air to Chengdu

CAAC flights have to be booked a few days in advance. The CAAC office is near the bus station and Potala. There are daily (morning) flights, and passengers are taken to the airport the previous evening.

GYANGZÊ	江孜	TINGRI	定日
LHASA	拉萨	XIGAZÊ	日喀则
SAKYA	萨迦	ZE DANG	泽当

Chapter eleven

OUT OF CHINA: HONG KONG AND MACAU

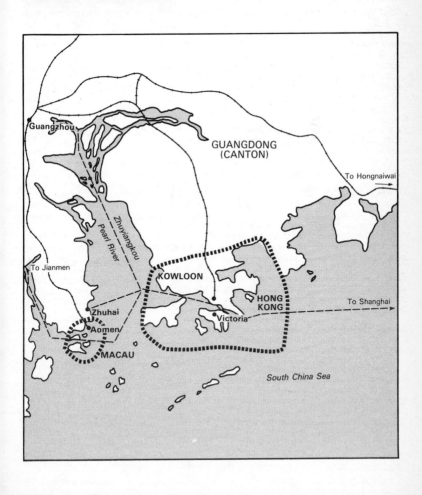

XIANGGANG (HONG KONG) – AOMEN (MACAU)

The majority of people who travel to China arrive via **Hong Kong**, or sometimes **Macau**, which is why we've included a short chapter detailing the colonies' main attractions – and their more formidable drawbacks. We should emphasise, though, that this is inevitably a fairly brief rundown, and if you're spending any time at all here it's best to get hold of a guide solely devoted to Hong Kong and Macau before you come. It's worth noting, also, that the **free information** doled out by the tourist offices is comprehensive and surprisingly useful, and as a result well worth picking up – something you don't have to go out of your way to do.

HONG KONG

There's really no more bizarre introduction to the People's Republic than **HONG KONG**: a shrine to pure unbridled capitalism whose glow can be seen many miles into China – and which, to the Chinese at least, must seem like some kind of earthly paradise, tantalisingly near after the dim-lit austerity of their own cities. Its television can be picked up all over Guangdong province and provides further material for conjecture, as do the hundreds of thousands of Hong Kong Chinese who regularly visit relatives on the mainland. All of which led, until 1980 when firm action was taken by the authorities, to a steady stream of immigrants across the Chinese border – something the Hong Kong side were acutely embarrassed about since their tiny patch of rock, paddy-field and skyscraper had already the highest population density on earth. Today well over 5 million people live in Hong Kong, on a land mass that amounts to just 370 square miles – roughly the size of the Isle of Wight – and there is little room for any more.

But what Hong Kong really means – and what the Chinese were really attracted by – is money, and lots of it. Ever since the British took the island and, later, leased its nearby peninsula and outlying islands as a spoil in the 19C Opium Wars, it's been the banking and financial centre of the Far East. And even now, though due to be returned to its rightful owner, China, at the turn of the century, Hong Kong seems unlikely to change, since it's worth so much as an earner of foreign currency. It's also, largely because of its colonial role, one of Asia's dirtiest, most crowded, most congested and visually unpleasant cities, and one where the contrasts of vast corporate wealth and bitter grinding poverty are never far apart. Even the **climate** isn't particularly pleasant: in winter temperatures stay fairly low, and summer is hot and humid, relieved only by frequent thunderstorms or, worse, typhoons which sweep in unpredictably from the offshore waters.

Why, then, should anyone want to come here? And, even stranger, why should most of those who do, come away enchanted by the place? There isn't much in terms of sights: you visit Hong Kong more for its feel, for an atmosphere which, because of its history, is unique. Beijing-based diplomats take regular all-expenses paid breaks here, to wallow in a touch of unashamed voluptuousness after the rigours of a China posting. And certainly, there aren't many cities in the world more vital than Hong Kong, and few that offer quite such a complete – and vivid – set of extremes. Twenty-four hours a day it throbs and swarms with frenzied activity, and whether you're given to gastronomy, carnality, sightseeing, shopping, swimming, fishing or sailing, or just lolling around on beaches,

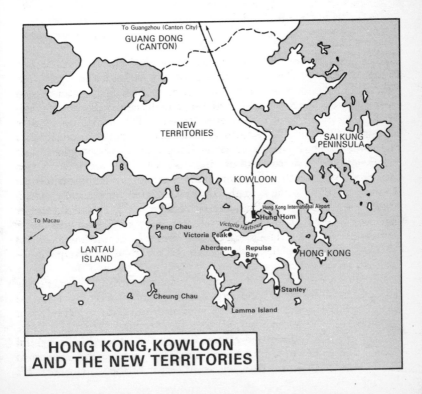

HONG KONG, KOWLOON AND THE NEW TERRITORIES

there should be something to occupy you here. As far as practicalities go, if you're a UK citizen you don't, until 1997, need a **visa** unless you intend to stay for six months or more. Nationals of Australia, the USA, Western Europe and South America can stay visa-free for a month.

Arriving

There's only one way to **arrive** in Hong Kong, and that's the one everyone tells you about: swooping into Kaitak Airport at night over the dazzling cityscape of urban Kowloon and million lights of the harbour – one of the great experiences of modern air travel and well worth securing an evening arrival flight and a window seat to enjoy. Once you've landed, the best way of **getting into the centre of town** is to take a bus, either route 201 to Tsimshatsui (for the YMCAs and cheaper hotels) or a 200 which takes you across to Hong Island proper; fares are HK$2.50 and HK$4 respectively. If, though, there are several of you, and you are heading to or near Tsimshatsui, a taxi may well work out cheaper; the HK$20 surcharge for the tunnel, however, makes taxis to Hong Kong Island prohibitively expensive.

Information – most of it comprehensive and extremely useful – isn't difficult to come by; indeed you'll be bombarded with it immediately you step inside the office of the *Hong Kong Tourist Association* at the airport (open daily 8.30–10.30). Other HKTA offices are dotted all over the city centre – principally at the Star Ferry Pier in Kowloon (Mon–Fri 8–6; weekends 8–1) and at 35/F Connaught Centre, Hong Kong (Mon–Fri 8–6; Sat 8–1). They also have a seven-day telephone enquiry service on 671111. Most **travel requirements** – accommodation, knock-down air tickets, ISIC cards, and tours, both in Hong Kong and mainland China – can be dealt with by the *Hong Kong Student Travel Bureau* (STB), who have two branches at 8/F Tai Sang Bank Building, 130–132 Des Voeux Road (414841) and Room 1020 Star House, Tsimshatsui (694847). They're also good for smoothing the way into mainland China, selling tickets, arranging visas and providing an escort for an inclusive price of about HK$300. **Tours to China** are also organised by the *China Travel Service*, 1/F China Travel Building, 77 Queens Road, Hong Kong (236055), and (other than a day-trip to Guangzhou for around HK$100) range in length from 5–14 nights, and in price from about HK$6,500 per person to well over HK$10,000.

If rates like that are beyond you, **heading on to China independently** is easy – and viable, to Guangzhou and other gateways, by train, plane, boat, hovercraft or jetfoil. For full details – and information on visas –

see p. 7. For maps, glossy leaflets, advance up-to-date info **CITS** are at 6/F, Tower II, South Sea Centre, Tsimshatsui East (7215317).

Getting around and finding somewhere to stay

Getting around

The best way of getting around Hong Kong's centre is on **foot**: there are few more compact – not to say congested – cities than Hong Kong, and few better ways of experiencing its vibrant streetlife. If you're in a hurry though, or there's a particular place you want to get to, the alternatives are numerous. Tourist bumpf always unhesitatingly recommends you hail a **taxi** – red or silver and charging around HK$5 standard fare plus 70c for every quarter kilometre – but honestly, unless it's late or there's a group of you, there are cheaper ways, and Hong Kong's perennial traffic clogs mean they're not even that fast; plus the English spoken by most drivers leaves plenty of room for error. Better, if you're heading to points outside the city, especially to certain of the beaches, to take a **bus**: double-decker affairs reminiscent of Britain, very crowded, especially during rush hours, but cheap at upwards of 80c for the shortest trip you're likely to make – pop the exact change into the box as you get on (it's a good idea always to carry a small supply). Stops are all over town (round red signs) but the main termini are near the ferry piers and at the Admiralty MTR station. If you can't find a bus, pick up a **Minibus** – confusing, with their destinations printed in Chinese characters only and with an erratic stopping policy, but just as cheap as buses; pay as you get off. Cheaper still is the **tram**, travelling one more or less straight route across the north side of the main island from Kennedy Town in the west to Shau Kei Wan in the east. This costs a flat 60c and, though slow, is probably the simplest way of getting from A to B within the city centre. *The* tram journey (funicular railway actually) is the one up to The Peak from Garden Road, just behind the Hilton Hotel – HK$4 each way, and a must for the views over Hong Kong harbour from the top (see below).

For longer distances – up to the Chinese border and around – the **MTR** (Mass Transit Railway) is a cool and spacious surprise, white tiled and completely devoid of all the garish vitality that pervades above-stairs. The fare from Central District across to Tsimshatsui on Kowloon is about HK$3.50 and is much the fastest way you could do it. Buy a ticket from the station dispensing machine, insert it into the turnstile and hang on to it – you need it to get out at the other end (*tourist tickets* are available for HK$15 from the HKTA office at the Kowloon Star Ferry terminal and inside larger MTR stations, but they don't actually save you any money). Otherwise, to cross the water utilise the best bargain in town, the **Star Ferry**: 50c for the relatively uncrowded 7-minute trip and giving spectacular vistas of the city skyline. Other **ferries** run regularly to the outlying islands, most departing from the Outlying Districts Services Pier a few hundred metres west of the Star Ferry pier in Central District. On any of these trips buy a return ticket to save time.

Somewhere to stay

There's no getting over it: finding a **room**, even a budget room, in central Hong Kong is going to be your major expense, so if you know anyone at all here, or you have a friend who knows someone, get in touch before you come out and, if you can, make use of their hospitality. If you can't do that, prepare yourself for the worst: really, the only sure way of cutting costs is to settle for dormitory-style accommodation or stay somewhere well off Hong Kong Island.

Bottom-line are **Hostels** of which there are many, official and not so official, though bear in mind that at the official ones you may have to flash a valid IYHF card to be let in. Best and most famous of the bunch is the *YMCA* near the Kowloon Star Ferry terminal on Salisbury Road (692211), co-ed despite the name and comfortable and clean with rooms at from HK$100 a night (dorm beds for considerably less) and a swimming pool and rooftop coffee shop; try also the *International House* at 23 Waterloo Road (319111). For women who want to stay somewhere away from men there's a *YWCA* north of here at (honestly) 5 Man Fuk Road (7139211). At both of these booking is essential throughout the year – direct by phone, more securely by telex, or through your home YMCA. Otherwise just walk north up Nathan Road, where there are any number of cheap dives, most popular of which is the *Chung King* at no.40 (665362-6): good for contacts with fellow travellers but, like all the places along here, none too clean or secure. **Official Youth Hostels** and **Campsites** scatter all over, most of them out in the New Territories or on Lantau Island (see the HKTA's list), but there's one in central Hong Kong at the top of Mount Davis (875715) which at the last count had dormitory beds for just HK$8 a night. Again, though, advance booking is in most instances vital.

Food, nightlife and culture

Food – the eating of it and the rituals surrounding it – is alone one of the best reasons for visiting Hong Kong. There are few places in the world where you can eat so well, and though restaurants don't always come cheap, there is an unsurpassable selection – many of which, if you know which to choose, needn't cost a bomb.

Best way to start the day is with one of the colony's – and Canton's – more renowned specialities, **Dim Sum**: literally 'your heart's delight' and in reality lots of little dishes (dumplings, checken's feet and the like) picked off a trolley and paid for when you've eaten your fill. There are any number of places serving Dim Sum in Hong Kong, but the most lavish is probably *Sun Tung Lok* in Harbour City, whose shark's fin (an aphrodisiac, they say) is the speciality of the house. **Evenings**, you can eat well enough from the *market stalls* of Poor Man's Nightclub, but if you're into something a little more luxurious, and not expensive, try the restaurants in the *Miramar Hotel*, which serve a good broad menu of Cantonese food and a range of fast foods – vegetarian, Japanese, Cantonese – in the basement. Other affordable restaurants include *Foon Luk* on Hennessy Road, *Lok Yu* on Patterson Street, and the *Green Villa* on Granville Road, which serves Sichuan food.

More upmarket, and well known outside of Hong Kong for the quality of their food, is *Fook Lam Moon* on Lockhart Road, whose seafood is wonderful and not too highly priced – as is that of the *Regent Seafood Restaurant* on Gloucester Road. If you like seafood you should also check out the tumbledown district of *Laufaushan*, situated next door to Hong Kong's most fertile oyster bed in the north-west corner of the colony (see below).

Nightlife is varied and vigorous, and, as you might expect, caters on the whole for western businessmen on freebies. There are a number of 'English-style' **pubs**, best known of which is *Ned Kelly's Last Stand* at 11a Ashley Road in Kowloon: a haunt of Aussie travellers, packed most nights and with live jazz. Others are the *Bull and Bear*, on the ground floor of Hutchinson House in Central District – Tudor decor and ex-pats drinking bitter; *The Jockey*, 1st floor, Swire House, Central – big with the after-office crowd who swarm in to monopolise the dartboard; and the *Blacksmith's Arms*, 16 Minden Avenue, Kowloon, which is small, smoky and usually extremely crowded.

Discos and nightclubs are many, but most often the choice is between swanky haunts at the top of the corporate hotels or sleazy hostess joints of the Suzie Wong variety – both best avoided unless you want to spend a fortune. Best known of the hotel discos are the *Polaris Club* on the 16th floor of the Hyatt and the *Pink Giraffe* at the top of the Sheraton, which gives fine vistas of the harbour. Rather nicer than both of these places, though, is the *1999*.

As far as **Culture** goes, until recently there wasn't any in Hong Kong, and it's only over the last 5–10 years that improvements have taken place in the arts. Time was when one museum served the entire colony; now a change of policy and more generous injections of cash have led to institutions like the **City Hall Centre**, where there's now a reference library, gallery space and museum of art with regularly changing exhibitions; the **Arts Centre** on the reclaimed Wanchai waterfront, where three auditoria host performances of theatre and dance; and Hong Kong's new annual **Arts Festival**, held early each year and lasting a month. There are, too, the more established museums, like the long-standing **Fung Ping Shan Museum** at Hong Kong University (bus 3 from Connaught Centre), which has a reasonable archaeological collection; the largely ethnographic **Museum of History**, Kowloon Park, Tsimshatsui (closed Fridays); and its satellite, the **Han Tomb**, a late Han dynasty burial chamber, five minutes from Cheung Sha Wan MTR station (closed Thursdays). More interesting perhaps is the **Flagstaff Museum** on Cotton Tree Drive, which holds a neat assortment of Chinese tea paraphernalia in what is supposed to be the oldest colonial building in Hong Kong – built in 1844 (closed Wednesdays).

Performances of **drama, opera** and **dance** have also improved drastically in recent years. Apart from those listed above, the **Cheng Yung Theatre** is worth checking out, whose posters at the Ocean Terminal detail all kinds of Chinese-type entertainments on a regular basis. Otherwise, to see what's on, pick up a copy of the monthly *City News*, free from City Hall, or the Arts Centre's monthly *newsletter*.

HONG KONG ISLAND

The urban area of Hong Kong is made up of the northern coast of **Hong Kong Island** itself (known technically as Victoria) and the southern tip of the **Kowloon** peninsula, otherwise known as **Tsimshatsui**. The rest of Kowloon, the so-called **New Territories**, and 200 or so **outlying islands** constitute the rest of the colony, in part home to Hong Kong's industry but on the whole still rural and with a pace of life far more representative of what you're likely to encounter in mainland China.

At the heart of Hong Kong Island, and bedrock of the famous thrusting skyline, is **CENTRAL DISTRICT**, hub of business and high finance and appropriately enough signalled by a statue of a bank-manager as you step off the Star ferry. Directly ahead, across from the **General Post Office**, there's another reminder of Hong Kong's real function: the vast port-holed tower of the **Connaught Building**, dubbed the 'thousand orifices' by the Cantonese and, along with the gleaming new hi-tech **Hong Kong and Shanghai Bank**, dominating the city's profile from wherever you stand. To make sense of all this, arm yourself with an information pack from the HKTA office just behind, and take in what amounts to a visual and aural feast: around the feet of the skyscrapers nestle tiny shops, stalls and street hawkers, pervaded everywhere by the smell of food and the shouts of the traders. Best way to take everything in at first is to jump on a tram – every 3 minutes along De Vouex Road, the neighbourhood's central boutique-fringed thoroughfare – and then explore the narrow side-alleys which branch off at every turn. Here hide the trappings of the oriental city, seemingly far from the opulent shrines of capitalism

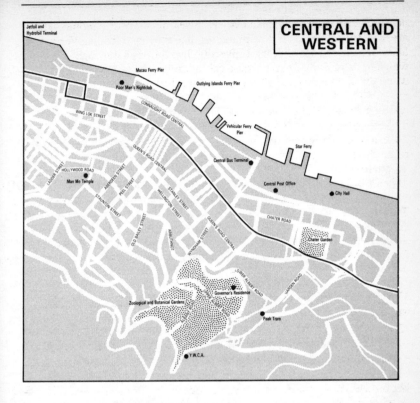

you just left: fortune tellers, herbalists, street tailors and furniture makers, vendors of weird nameless foods and swallow's nests make up a tight-knit enclave that you can delve into again and again and still feel there's more to discover. **For bargains**, Li Yuen Street (East and West) are worth nosing through; Wing On Street is best for fabric and cloth, while Wing Sing Street purveys nothing but eggs, some a century old.

Keep on the tram to **WESTERN DISTRICT** and there's more of the same: slummy lanes brimming with artisans, precipitously stepped streets (Ladder and Cat are the oldest and best) lined with rattan shops, junk and antique stores and more fortune tellers. At its centre, on the district's main street, Hollywood Road, the **Man Mo Temple** (7–5) is dedicated to the God of Civil Servants and is the oldest temple in Hong Kong. Below here, on **Hillier** and **Jarvis** Streets, shops proffer different varieties of snake alive and dead, some for eating, others for their gall bladders which are crushed into glasses of rice wine to make a well-known Chinese aphrodisiac. Back east, opposite the **Central Market** (seafood, meat, vegetables, etc.), the **Chinese Merchandise Emporium** offers goods from the mainland – vases, bowls, jade, silk, ivory and assorted *chinoiserie* – at markedly better prices than in China itself. Another market worth checking out is the nightmarket in front of the Macau hydrofoil terminal, the **Poor Man's Nightclub** – great for strolling, idling, and evening meals taken on your feet.

At the far end of Queens Road do a right by the Hilton and stroll up Garden Road to the **Peak Funicular** station, where you can take the railway up to **VICTORIA PEAK** (bus no.15 or a sharp hike up Mount Austin Road are alternatives). The funicular runs every 15 minutes during the day and the fare is HK$4 each way. The views are breathtaking, a must on a fine day – Hong Kong, Kowloon and the New Territories, sprawling tauntingly far into the distance. The inevitable tourist infra-structure – viewing tower, café and some psuedo-Chinese craft shops – adds nothing to the beauty of the place, but there's a good restaurant, with a tea garden, that's a refreshing escape from the fearful heat 1500 feet below, and any number of paths taking you down to the southern side of the island – one as far as Aberdeen on the southern shore. Another takes you to the **Zoological and Botanical Gardens**: more views, animals, plants and birds and early morning displays of Tai Chi.

Back down at sea level, **WANCHAI** is Hong Kong's ageing though still functioning Red Light District, its bars, clubs and neon being steadily encroached upon by the monied towers of Central District next door. There are a couple of interesting **temples**, the Pak Tai and Chai Kung Woot Fat, both still solidly in use despite throngs of gawkers, but other-wise little to entice you to stick around outside the evening hours. Pass on instead to **CAUSEWAY BAY** where you can spy the **Noon Day Gun** of Noel Coward's son ('Mad Dogs and Englishmen') on the waterfront – and which is still fired at noon every day – or simply drift through the herb and provisions stores of **Jardine's Bazaar** (named after Jardine, Matheson & Co) and the streets around.

The **southern side** of the island is a different world altogether: a shore of rocky coves, sandy beaches and small fishing villages, in the week slower and quieter than the mad city centre, on summer weekends awash with city-dwellers eager to escape the traumas of Hong Kong proper. Whatever else you do, make sure you visit **STANLEY** (its market sells second-hand clothes and designer seconds), but be careful to miss out **REPULSE BAY**. This has been dubbed 'Repulsive Bay' by the locals, and amid the litter, hamburgers, boogie boxes and prone sun-seekers it's not hard to see what they're getting at. Further west, **ABERDEEN**, or 'Little Hong Kong', is a suburb of around 20,000 people living on junks and sampans in a harbour sheltered naturally from typhoons. A half-hour **sampan tour** of the harbour will cost you about HK$60; beyond that there's only the 16C **Tin Hau Temple** at the top end of Aberdeen Main Road that's worth seeing, and what most people come here for is a meal on one of the famous **floating restaurants**. Buses no.7 or 70 run direct to Aberdeen roughly every 10 minutes from Hong Kong's Central Bus terminal; or you can catch a no.6 or 260 to Stanley and pick up a connection from there.

KOWLOON AND THE NEW TERRITORIES

TSIMSHATSUI, over the water at the tip of the Kowloon peninsula, is the commercial heart of Hong Kong, a vast, racey bazaar of tellies, videos, watches, cameras, hi-fi equipment and all the other electric baubles that have become so indispensable to life in the west. Really, there's no better place in the world for picking up electronic goods at cut-price rates, but remember – you can also get seriously ripped off, even in the most respectable-looking places, so be careful. Two **hotels** stand near the water-front: one, the ancient colonial style *Peninsula* whose days, it is said, are numbered, and the other, the spanking new *Regent*, whose enormous windows give awesome panoramas of Hong Kong Island opposite. The

KOWLOON: TSIMSHATSUI

★ MTR ENTRANCES

reason the building uses so much glass is simple: the hotel was built at the place a local dragon enters the harbour for his bath and the hotel didn't want to disturb him with a concrete block. In case you're wondering, the dome-shaped edifice in front of the Peninsula is the **Space Museum**, though its building is more interesting than the delights on offer inside.

The other side of Tsimshatsui Kowloon changes from tawdry shopping district to more atmospheric Chinese quarters: neighbourhoods like **YAUMATEI**, another part-floating city – and home to dozens of love-boats who ply a brisk trade in the harbour – where there's a morning **Jade market** on Kansu Street (look, don't buy) and a **nightmarket** on Temple Street. Look in, too on the **Public Square Street Temples**, the largest of which, *Tin Hau* (7.30–8.30), is dedicated to the goddess who protects those Hong Kong denizens who make their living from the sea – a sizeable few. One small point though: be warned that Yaumatei can be risky at night on your own.

North of here you start to leave the colony behind and enter a more authentically Chinese world, the glamour of Hong Kong having given way to some dismal squalour and overcrowding – and a set of streets that most visitors would be well advised to avoid. The notorious **WALLED CITY** for one, ruled by rival Triads and out of bounds even to the city police, is a no-go area for the most part, and the only place most tourists reach – admittedly in huge numbers – is the **Wong Tai Sin temple**, probably the most profitable temple in the east and one that is still used for private worship.

The temple apart, you'd be better off heading straight up to the **NEW TERRITORIES**, most of which are visitable by taking the Kowloon–Guangzhou railway. Here, despite some fast-moving industrial-isation, there are secluded coves and fine sandy beaches, rich green paddy fields spotted with water buffalo, and a smattering of forested mountain scenery, all of which you can see by getting off the train and walking, staying the night at any one of a number of campsites or youth hostels (lists from the HKTA). The walled villages of **Kat Hing Wai** and **Tsang Tai Uk** are inviting places to stop over, and, should you want to eat fish, **Laufaushan**, up in the north-west corner of Hong Kong, has a glut of fresh seafood restaurants and is linked with Hong Kong by bus no.68. Altogether a welcome and on the whole little-discovered escape from the city – further details from the HKTA.

THE OUTLYING ISLANDS

Far and away the best antidote to the speed and hassle of Hong Kong is a trip to the **OUTLYING ISLANDS** – all readily accessible from various points on Hong Kong, although you should confirm ferry times before setting out (phone 423081) – and, most importantly, have the correct change for the turnstiles; return fares range from HK$8 to HK$20. If possible avoid weekends, as they can be horribly congested, and plan your visit to coincide with one of the colourful local festivals. As always, further information from the HKTA; detailed maps, if you need them, can be bought from the Government Publications Centre in the General Post Office.

Of the colony's 250 or so islands, **LANTAU** is the largest, twice the size of Hong Kong Island but with a population of less than 40,000 (compared to Hong Kong's million). There is much here to explore, and the island's size means that although it is by far the most popular, there's no problem escaping the crowds if you're prepared to walk. The main settlement is **Tai O**, a fishing port on the south-western side; you can either take a ferry directly there or to **Silvermine Bay**, from where a 10 minute bus-ride delivers you at one of the island's best **beaches**, *Cheung Sha*. As well as beaches – and some wonderful treks across the island's hills – the island is home to a couple of interesting **monasteries**, both of which offer the chance to stay overnight to those not worried about creature comforts (bareboards are the norm for sleeping). To get to the **Trappist Monastery**, take the ferry to the tiny island of **Peng Chau** and pick up a sampan – though bear in mind that if you want to stay you have to book in advance (write to the Grand Master at PO Box 5, Peng Chau). The Buddhist **Po Lin** Monastery, high on the plateau of Ngong Ping, also does a vegetarian lunch for a nominal charge and will lay on a monk to guide you to the top of nearby **Lantau Peak** (934m) for views of what can be a memorable sunrise. Outside the monastery they're working on something that, when finished, will be the tallest **statue of the Buddha** in South-East Asia – a massive project with a forecast cost of around HK$20 million.

CHEUNG CHAU, lying just off the south-east coast of Lantau, used to be a haven for ex-pats who couldn't afford Hong Kong rents, or those who preferred a more relaxed place. But in the last two years the place has been developed out of all recognition, its tatty waterside bars demolished in favour of sterile modern apartment blocks and purpose-built resort complexes. It does, however, boast one or two reasonable **beaches** that, for the moment at least, remain relatively unspoilt – plus the fact that cars are banned, which means that the island will always seem peaceful after Hong Kong. Try and get here in May for the four-day Cheng Chau Festival, when the island takes on a carnival atmosphere with street processions, historical tableaux and effigies of Chinese gods. All should culminate in a mad scramble for consecrated buns, which are supposed to bring good luck throughout the coming year, but this has been stopped after a perilous incident several years back. To cool off, *Tung Wan* is the most easily reached beach, about 10 minutes walk from the ferry terminal, but it can get jammed, even during the week; *Nam Tam Wan*, on the southern shore, is rocky but emptier; quieter still is the sandy *Po Yu Wan*, out on the south-west peninsula.

Of Hong Kong's other small islands, **CHEK LAP KOK** can be reached by ferry from the New Territories and is good for some quiet fishing and walking; similarly **TAP MUN**, accessible by hourly ferry from the Won Shek pier on the Sai Kung peninsula. At both these islands accommodation is on hand at local guesthouses but don't expect anyone to speak English. More populated, but still relatively peaceful, is **LAMMA**, 40 minutes by ferry from Hong Kong. You can go to one of two ports (no more than villages really) **Sok Ku Wan** or, the capital, **Yung Shue Wan**, and the best way of working things is to arrive at one and leave by the other, hiking the 5 kilometres or so between the two and taking in some of the island's main attractions. These are limited but include a couple of good **beaches**, *Hung Shing Ye* and *Lo So Shing* (both with facilities), the small **Tin Hau Temple**, and some marvellous views from the summit of **Mount Stenhouse**, whose 353m take about an hour to scale from Sok Ku Wan. For **food**, the waterside restaurants of Sok Ku Wan serve some excellent seafood, and for **accommodation**, there's a guesthouse in Yung Shue Wan.

MACAU

MACAU, made up of the old peninsula city of Macau and the tiny offshore islands of Taipa and Coloane, is the oldest European settlement in the far east, founded in 1557 by the Portuguese as a trading centre for southern China, and remaining in their possession ever since – despite numerous attempts by other countries to wrest it away (notably the Dutch in the 17C). These days it's an odd sort of hybrid, dominated by the Chinese, who arrived here from Guangdong and Fujian after the last war and now make up 95 percent of the population. The Portuguese, and a small group, the Macanese, who inter-married and now speak a local patois all of their own, have little contact with the bulk of the population and an influence more or less confined to the colony's restaurants, most of which serve solidly European fare.

Details like this give Macau its charm, and as a whole the colony is altogether more friendly than Hong Kong, less caught up in the stampede for a fast buck, and, as such, more typically Chinese. It is also a good arrival or departure point for China: its plethora of backstreets and alleys, markets and squares make for some fascinating exploring, and there's a set of buildings here, in Macanese style, whose florid, almost art nouveau blend of Mediterranean and eastern influences, is unique. Also, if you're a long-term Asia traveller, Macau can offer a degree of respite from the east, at least in the chance to indulge in a different kind of cuisine. (For details on travel on to China see foot of p. 5.)

You should, however, expect some changes in Macau over the coming years. Ever since Red Guards stormed into Macau from the mainland in 1966, Portugal has been trying to hand back the colony and its half million or so inhabitants to China. Now, negotiations are underway with a view to securing a Hong-Kong-style arrangement whereby Macau is given the right to retain its capitalist system for 50 years. Frankly, though, the Portuguese government couldn't care less, and seem more concerned to get rid of Macau as soon as possible – and with as few of its inhabitants retaining Portuguese citizenship as they can manage.

THE CITY AND OFFSHORE ISLANDS

MACAU and its islands, though wonderfully peaceful after Hong Kong, are above all places for pottering rather than doing any real sightseeing. Probably the colony's most renowned attraction (it figures prominently on much of the tourist bumpf) is the Baroque façade of **St Paul's Church**, built by Japanese Jesuit priests in 1602 but destroyed by fire a couple of hundred years later. Its citadel, **Montefort**, next door, gives fine views over the rest of Macau. Back down in the city, in a park in the southern reaches of the peninsula, is the **Temple of A-Ma**, supposedly built on the spot where Macau was founded and whose deity gives the place its name, but that apart there's little that's of much interest. If money's no object drop in on a **casino** or two (for some reason Macau is the Asian gambler's Mecca) or, if it is, stroll through the peninsula's bucolic gardens and watch the locals running through their Tai Chi. Of these the **Camoes Garden and Grotto** is perhaps the best, with a museum that holds a good selection of Han, Song and Tang dynasty sculpture and portraits by emigre painters George Chinnery and George Smirnoff. Best, though, to visit one – or both (they're not hard to reach) of the colony's offshore islands . . .

These, **TAIPA** and **COLOANE**, are linked to Macau proper by bridge and causeway respectively, and are accessible by bus from outside the Hotel Lisboa. They're small islands, wooded and in the main unspoilt, but like Macau town, hold little beyond a handful of beaches and couple of minor temples. Taipa is home to **Macau University**, which has a canteen serving cheap food; Coloane is a former pirates' hangout and sports a small Catholic **chapel** whose boast is the arm of St Francis Xavier, brought here from St Paul's after the fire. Otherwise, just lounge around on the **beaches**, most appealing of which are those on Coloane's southern shore.

Getting there – and being there

There are three ways to make the 60 kilometre crossing from Hong Kong to Macau, **Jetfoil** is the quickest and most expensive at around HK$60 (HK$65 weekends) for the 55-minute trip (departures half-hourly; or there's the **hydrofoil**, which is just as frequent but takes 75 minutes and costs about HK$15 less. Cheaper still is the **ferry**, 'high-speed' (7 1½ hour trips a day and fares from HK$35) or 'regular' (from HK$18 for the 3 hour trip). It's best to book tickets in advance, especially at weekends when all these alternatives can get packed; remember, also, that there's a departure tax from Hong Kong which for those using the ferry has recently been raised to HK$15. For up-to-date information phone 457021 (ferry) or 455566 (jet/hydrofoil).

Visas can be obtained on arrival in Macau but are not necessary for nationals of Britain, Hong Kong, Portugal, Brazil, the USA, Canada or most western European countries; inoculation certificates are not needed by anyone. The currency is *Pataca*, though you can use Hong Kong dollars which are worth a wee bit more, but don't forget to exchange all your excess pataca before you leave as they're virtually worthless outside Macau. Further **information** – maps, glossy brochures, etc. – can be had from the *Macau Tourist Information Bureau* in the arrivals hall at the harbour; or, if you're coming from Hong Kong, from Room 1729, Star House, Salisbury Road, Kowloon (677747).

Macau has a good **bus service** serving the whole of the main island and there are plenty of buses and pedicabs (roughly HK$5 for the average journey or HK$20–30 for an hour's sightseeing), but much the best way of getting around is to invest in your own set of wheels – either by hiring a **bicycle** or, more expensively, a **self-drive moke**. You can hire the latter from *Macau Mokes Ltd* – in Hong Kong at 233 Hollywood Road (434190) and in Macau at Room 202 in the ferry terminal building. Rates run from HK$220 a day.

If you're not on too tight a shoestring, Macau can be an excellent place to indulge in a bit of luxury, and with this in mind many travellers choose **to stay** at the old colonial *Bela Vista Hotel* on the southern prong of the island – though a double room there will set you back around Ptc$100. If that's beyond your means there are plenty of guesthouses – *hospedaries* – (ask at the tourist bureau) and some of the bigger hotels will admit to having cheaper rooms if pushed: try the **Central** in the main street, or **Hotel Estoril** on Avenida Sidonia Pais, but beware price rises at weekends.

TRAVEL DETAILS

HONG KONG – CHINA LINKS

Trains
MTR from Kowloon's Hung Hom Station to **Shenzhen**, the Chinese border station. From Shenzhen, there are five trains daily to Guangzhou (Canton City). Also twice daily **express train** from Hung Hom direct to Guangzhou (3hrs).

Buses
Various **express services** (details and times from Hong Kong travel agents) to Guangzhou, Fuzhou and other Chinese cities.

Ferries
To Whampoa (Guangzhou's port): Daily ferry (8hrs) and 3 daily hovercraft departures (2hrs).
To Zhuhai: Daily jetfoil (1hr).
To Jiangmen: Sporadic ferry service (3hrs).

To Shanghai: Twice weekly ferry (60hrs).
To Shantou and Xiamen: Sporadic ferries.
To Wuzhou: Hovercraft every other morning from Tai Kok Tsui Wharf (11hrs).

Flights
Regular connections to Beijing, Guangzhou, Shanghai, etc.

MACAU – CHINA LINKS

Bus
Daily to Guangzhou (3–4hrs).

Ferry
Daily to Whampoa/Guangzhou (Leaves early evening; around 10hrs).

NOTE: SEE 'GETTING THERE' in the BASICS section (p. 5) for further details and addresses for all Hong Kong/Macau–China connections.

AOMEN (MACAU)	澳门	LAMMA	南丫
CHEK LAP KOK	赤腊角	LANTAU	大屿山
CHEUN G CHAU	长洲	TAIPA	氹仔
COLOANE	路环	TSIMSHATSUI	尖沙咀
KOWLOON	九龙	XIANGGANG	香港
		(HONG KONG)	

Part three
CONTEXTS

THE HISTORICAL FRAMEWORK

For centuries and centuries the history of China is the history of its dynasties, a succession of warring rulers who differed only in the degree of their autocracy. In a brief history it's easy to overlook that for 4000 years the lot of those ruled was appalling. Kept in permanent poverty by taxes to finance military ventures or extravagant courts, starvation and early death were common, and frequent famine accounted for millions among the rural population. Industrialisation didn't make things better for the worker, and as late as the 1930s children were kept at machines for twelve hours a day and women often sold as slaves or prostitutes. Whatever criticisms exist of the People's Republic, it's worth remembering that only since its birth in 1949, yesterday in historical terms, has the quality of life for the ordinary person begun to improve.

The earliest times: dragons, myths and legends

Pan Ku was born from the egg of chaos and grew to fill the space between Yin, the earth, and Yang, the heavens. For 18,000 years Pan Ku laboured, chiselling the earth to its present state with the aid of a dragon, a unicorn, a phoenix and a tortoise. When his body died his flesh became the soil of the earth and sweat from his labour the rain. The blood from his body was transformed into rivers while his eyes became the sun and moon. And while the breath of his mouth grew into wind and the sound of his voice the thunder of the skies, the tiny parasites feeding on his body transformed into human beings.

So runs the legend of creation, but little of China's earliest times is known. Traditionally a pantheon of semi-divine rulers known as **The Five Sovereigns** followed Pan Ku, each reigning for a hundred years or more and inventing fire, the calendar, agriculture, silk-breeding and marriage. Later a famous triumvirate included **Yao the Benevolent** who abdicated in favour of **Shu**; Shu toiled in the sun until his skin turned black and then abdicated in favour of **Yu the Great**, tamer of floods and builder of dikes and said to be the founder of the first dynasty, the **Xia**. Legend also says that the Xia lasted 439 years until their last degenerate and corrupt king was overthrown by the victorious founder of the Shang dynasty.

But behind all the myth and legend are some hard archeological facts. Remains of **Primitive Man**, from about 700,000BC were found in the 1960s at Lantian near Xi'an, and the later skulls of *Homo erectus* had already been discovered in caves at Zhoukoudian, not far from Peking. The earliest evidence of communities lies in the Yellow River basin, where the village of **Banpo** (4800BC) has a well-preserved dwelling area, a cemetery and kilns for pottery, and further south at **Homudu** in Zhejiang are traces of a riverside settlement of 5–3000BC.

The picture becomes clearer with the emergence of the **Shang** dynasty from myth into reality. Though Si Maqian wrote of them and the ruins of their cities near Zhengzhou and Anyang, in the earliest dynastic history compiled in 100BC, the cities had vanished so completely that they were thought legend until revealed by accidental discoveries and 20C excavations. More recent digs are pushing history further back still, since at **Erlitou** in Henan archeologists have uncovered what may be the Bronze Age capital of the Xia of legend, predecessor of the Shang.

The beginnings of Imperial China

Though the Shang occupied only a small part of modern China, they were developed into a highly organised society with a king, a class system, written records and a skilled bronze art which produced the splendid vessels found in today's museums. Between the 18C and 12C BC there were 29 Shang rulers, and excavations on the site of Yin, their capital, have found magnificent tombs stuffed with bronze weapons, jade ornaments, traces of silk, and sacrificial victims – which confirm the importance of ancestor worship. The Shang also practised '**divination by scapulimancy**' – the interpretation of fire cracks on tortoiseshell and bones – and scratched records on these bones. The enormous legacy of these **Dragon Bones** provides what are (so far) China's earliest written records, covering everything from tax records and rainfall to dreams and ancestral curses. It was at this time too that the foundations for the imperial structure were being laid: an ideographic script, the forerunner of later Chinese characters, the religion of ancestor worship, the notion of a single ruler, the growth of towns and the development of a farming economy able to support a ruling class. But around 1100BC a semi-nomadic tribe from the north, the **Zhou**, overthrew the increasingly despotic Shang. Probably as justification for their rebellion the Zhou introduced the doctrine of the **Mandate from Heaven** – a belief that heaven gives a mandate to leaders who are strong and wise and takes it from those who aren't. This concept became – and to an extent remains – an integral part of the political perspective of the Chinese. To support their mandate the Zhou stylised themselves 'Sons of Heaven', a title that stuck for the next 3000-odd years, and ruled their lands through a hierarchy of feudal vassal lords. Gradually, though, Zhou prestige declined and pressure from northern barbarians drove them to Luoyang. From here Zhou rulers exercised only a symbolic role; real power was fought over by some two hundred city states and kingdoms during the 400 years known as the **Spring and Autumn** and the **Warring States** periods. This time of violence was also a time of vitality and change, as most of the important ingredients were being stirred into the pot: the feudal system was breaking down and traditional religion giving way to new ideas based on the writings of Kong Zi or **Confucius**, and also on Taoism and Legalism (see p. 566). All the warring states were rubbing up against each other and in the process agriculture and irrigation, trade, transport and diplomacy were all galvanised; iron was used for weapons and tools and great discoveries made in medicine, astronomy and mathematics. Within 300 years war and annexation had reduced the competitors to seven states, mainly in the Yellow River basin and known as Zhong Guo or the **Central States**. The fighting only came to an end in the 3C BC with the rise of a new dynasty – the **Qin**.

The Qin Dynasty

For 500 years the Qin rulers had gradually been gobbling up their neighbours, and in 221BC First Exalted Emperor **Qin Shihuang** rose rapidly, to control a huge empire, uniting the Chinese as a single centralised state for the first time, and creating an infrastructure of roads, currency and writing that was to last generations. His rule was absolute: all literature written before his reign was destroyed to wipe out any ideas that conflicted with his own, and peasants were forced off their land into virtual slavery to work on massive defences like the Great Wall, built to protect the Empire from ever-present northern invaders. But Qin Shihuang's empire was only as strong as its leader and with his death rebels were quick to make claim to his power. By 202BC **Liu Bang** had taken Xi'an, the Qin capital, and founded a new dynasty, the **Han**. Qin Shihuang's legacies were an enduring structure of government and – one of the great sights – the giant **Terracotta Army** that guarded his tomb in Xi'an.

The Han Dynasty

Lasting some 400 years and larger at its height than its near contemporary, Imperial Rome, the **Han** was the first great dynasty, one that experienced a flowering of culture and a major impetus to push out frontiers and open them to trade, people and new ideas. Liu Bang maintained the Qin model of local government, but to prevent others from repeating his own military takeover strengthened his position by handing out large chunks of land to his relatives. This secured a period of stability, with effective taxation financing a growing civil service and the building of a huge and cosmopolitan capital called **Chang'an**, today's Xi'an. Growing revenue also refuelled the expansionist policies of **Wu Di**; from 135 to 90 BC he extended his lines of defence well into Xinjiang, opening up the Silk Road for trade in tea, spices and silk with India, west Asia and Rome. He used his sons and competent generals to beat off northern tribes, enter Korea and colonise south of the Yangzi as far as Vietnam. At home Wu Di stressed the Confucian model for his growing civil service beginning a 2000 year institution of Confucianism in government offices. But, eventually, the Empire's resources and supply lines were stretched to breaking point, while the burden of taxation led to unrest and retrenchment. Gradually the ruling house became decadent and was weakened by power struggles between rival factions of imperal consorts, eunuchs and statesmen, until **Wang Mang**, regent for a child emperor, usurped the rule to found his own brief dynasty in AD9. 15 years later the **Eastern Han** was re-established from Luoyang the new capital, where the classical tradition was re-imposed, a great academy founded and paper and the seismograph brought into use. From this high point under Emperor **Liu Xiu** and his successor, the dynasty was again undermined by factional intrigue; China's borders shrank under the encroachments of nomadic chiefdoms, and internal strife was fomented by the **Yellow Turbans**, who drew their following from Taoist cults. Local governments and land-owners began to set up as semi-independent rulers, with the country once again splitting into warring states. But by this time two major schools of philosophy and religion had emerged to survive the ensuing chaos. **Confucianism** had crystallised Imperial authority as the ideological basis for a universal order of things; **Buddhism**, introduced into the country by the Buddhist priests who accompanied Indian merchants, would enrich and transform every aspect of life and thought, especially the fine arts and literature, stimulating Taoism and Confucianism while itself being absorbed and changed.

Creative chaos and dark ages – the Three Kingdoms

Nearly four hundred years separate the collapse of the Han in about AD220 and the return of unity under the Sui in 589, and China was under a single government for only about fifty years of that time, though the idea of a unified empire was never forgotten. This was in some ways a dark age – of war, violence and genocide – but it was also a richly formative one, and when the dust had settled,

both culturally and economically a very different society had emerged. For much of this time many areas produced a food surplus which could support a rich and leisured ruling class in the cities and the countryside, as well as large armies and burgeoning Buddhist communities. So culture developed, literature flourished, calligraphy and sculpture, especially Buddhist carvings, all enriched by Indian and central Asian elements, reached unsurpassed levels. This was a rich legacy for the Sui and Tang dynasties which followed to inherit and build on.

From AD200 the three states of **Wei**, **Wu** and **Shu** held the centre of the stage in a struggle for supremacy (which was later immortalised in the saga *Romance of the Three Kingdoms*) that left China's borders unprotected. The north was invaded by the **Tobas**, who achieved unity by enforcing the adoption of Chinese manners and customs on their northern aristocracy – a pattern of assimilation that would recur with other invaders. At their first capital Datong they created a wonderful series of Buddhist carvings, but as part of their cultural absorption they were compelled to make a rapid move to a new capital at Luoyang, and within 25 years its population had swollen to half a million. But by 534 rebellion and the forced exodus of 2 million people from Luoyang to another capital at Ye signalled the end of the dynasty.

In the 5C and 6C the south saw weak and shortlived dynasties, but nevertheless there was prosperity and economic growth, with the capital Nanjing becoming a thriving trading centre. The south had a more sophisticated culture as well as a sounder economic base than the north, a polarisation which has continued to this day. But unity was eventually restored from the north, where political and military institutions made for a stronger state. One of their generals, **Yang Jian**, grabbed power in 581 from the ruler of the northern Zhou and went on to conquer the south by land and sea to found the Sui dynasty.

The Sui

The **Sui** get short shrift in historical surveys. Their brief empire was soon eclipsed by their successors, the Tang, but until the dynasty over-reached itself on the military front in Korea and burnt out like a brilliant firework, two of its three emperors could claim considerable achievements. Until his death in 604 Yang Jian himself – Emperor **Wen Di** – was an active ruler who took the best from the past and built on it; he simplified and strengthened the bureaucracy, brought in a new legal code, recentralised civil and military authority and made tax collection more efficient. Near Xi'an his architects designed a new capital, *Da Xing Cheng* – 'Great Prosperity' – with a palace city, a residential quarter of 108 walled compounds, several vast markets and an outer wall over 35km round – quite probably then the largest city in the world. After Wen Di's death **Yang Di** elbowed his elder brother out to become emperor. He improved administration, encouraged a revival of Confucian learning, and promoted a strong foreign policy. Continuing the engineering works begun by his father, Yang Di, he completed a major extension of the Great Wall and, most importantly, recognised the necessity of an efficient method of transport between the rice bowl of the southern Yangzi to his capital Xi'an, and therefore ordered the digging of the 2000km Grand Canal. Of a total work force of 5,500,000, 2,520,000 died in its construction. Eventually, harsh conscription for these and other grandiose projects along with crippling levies for his expansionist land and sea expeditions led to a revolt, and he was assassinated in 618. His successor lasted barely a year.

The Tang

The Medieval period of Chinese history is dominated by the Tang dynasty and is known as the **Golden Age**. This was a time of experimentation in literature, art, music and agriculture, an age even more cosmopolitan and sophisticated than the Han period, and one which unified seemingly incompatible elements.

The first Tang emperor, **Gao Zu**, spent a decade getting rid of all his rivals, and like his Han forerunners structured local government to prevent the rise of independent rulers like himself. Under Tang rule China expanded: the Turks were crushed, the Tibetans brought to heel, and relations established with Byzantium. China kept open house for traders and travellers of all races and creeds, who settled in the mercantile cities of

Yangzhou and Canton, bringing with them their religions, especially **Islam**, and influencing the arts, cookery, fashion and entertainment. China's goods flowed out to India, Persia, the Near East and many other countries, and her language and religion were adopted by Japan and Korea. At home **Buddhism** remained the all-pervading foreign influence, with pilgrims travelling widely in India. The best known of these, Xuan Zang, was sent by the Emperor in the early 7C and returned with a mass of Buddhist *sutras*, that added greatly to China's storehouse of knowledge.

Xi'an's population swelled to over a million and it became one of the world's great cultural centres. As heart of a highly centralised state, all power flowed from the capital and the emperor – the Son of Heaven. Under Emperor **Gao Zong**, China moved against Korea and drove a wedge far to the west before being forced on the defensive. In many ways the tide of Tang expansion had turned. The recurring concentration of land ownership and a shift of population southward for economic reasons cut the revenue needed to pay a standing army and a mushrooming civil service; Gao Zong's reign ended in crisis precipitated by natural disasters. Gao Zong's empress **Wu Chao**, once his father's concubine, then set herself up as China's only woman ruler. As a great patron of Buddhism she commissioned the famous Longmen carvings outside Luoyang, and created a civil service selected on merit rather than birth. Her successor, **Ming Huang** began well but his infatuation with the beautiful Yang Guifei led to the collapse of his rule, his flight to Sichuan, and Yang's ignominious death at the hands of his mutineering army.

During the twilight of the Tang, the reach and strength of their central authority began to fail as diverse groups built up power bases on the country's wide boundaries. In the disunity which followed from 907–960 **Five Dynasties** succeeded each other, all too shortlived to be effective, with the record for brevity going to the Han – a mere 7 years. China's northern defences were permanently weakened, while her economic dependence on the south increased and the dispersal of power brought sweeping social changes. The traditional elite whose fortunes were tied to the dynasty gave way to a military and merchant class who bought land to acquire status, plus a professional ruling class selected by examination. In the south the **Ten Kingdoms** (some existing side by side) managed to retain what was left of Tang civilisation; their greater stability and economic prosperity sustained a relatively high cultural level.

Finally in 960 a disaffected army in the north put a successful general on the throne. His new ruling house, **the Song**, made its capital at **Kaifeng** in the Yellow River basin, and well placed at the head of the Grand Canal for transport to supply its million people with grain from the south. By skilled politicking rather than military might the Song consolidated their authority over the many petty kingdoms and re-established civilian primacy. In the 12C northern invaders pushed the Song court south to Hangzhou where, guarded by the Yangzi river, culture continued to flourish. This period saw the development of gunpowder, the magnetic compass, fine porcelain and – most importantly – movable-type printing. The northern invaders occupied their lands and all remained stable until . . .

. . . The Mongol invasion

It took **Genghis Khan** just four years to capture China. Hated for their uncultured society, the Mongol tribes had united under his leadership to form an immensely powerful army, and despite Chinese resistance and dilatory Mongol infighting, sixty years after the invasion the **Yuan dynasty** was in control, with **Kublai Khan**, Genghis Khan's grandson, at the head of an Empire that stretched way beyond China's borders. From their capital at Khanbalik (modern **Beijing**) the Yuan retained control over all China only from 1278 to 1368; although they adopted some Chinese institutions and employed Chinese interpreters and officials as part of their administration, their discriminatory caste system and harsh penal code kept the Chinese well below the Mongols and their allies in the pecking order, and made alien rule deeply unpopular. Nevertheless, central control boosted the economy and helped repair the devastation of land and destruction of cities that the Mongol advance had caused.

Under the Yuan, China was wide open to western travellers, traders and missionaries: **Marco Polo** arrived in the 1270s, establishing the first direct link with Europe; Arab and Venetian traders were to be found in many Chinese ports and (believe it or not) a Russian came top of the Imperial Civil Service exam of 1341. In Beijing the **Palace of All Tranquillities** was built inside a new city wall and came to be known as the **Great Interior**, later the **Forbidden City**. Descriptions of this, along with the culture of the Yuan dynasty, were brought back to Europe by Marco Polo, who put his impressions of Yuan lifestyle and treasures on paper after living in Beijing for 17 years and serving in the government of Kublai Kahn.

It was the Mongols' inability to assimilate Chinese culture that brought about the downfall of the Yuan dynasty. Eventually famine and disastrous floods brought a series of rebellions, until in 1368 a monk-turned-bandit leader from the south, **Zhu Yuanzhang**, seized the throne from the last boy emperor of the Yuan.

The Ming dynasty

Zhu Yuanzhang took the name **Hong Wu** and proclaimed himself first Emperor of the **Ming Dynasty**, with Nanjing as his capital. Zhu influenced the development of the country in two central ways: firstly, his style of government became despotic to the point of totalitarianism – all ministries were directly responsible to him, and court protocol became so tyrannical that ministers would fear death if they were summoned. He retained a deep suspicion of the traditional scholar-official, so much so that in the late 14C he ordered two appalling purges in which thousands of officials and their families died. The Confucian notions of proper conduct, responsibility and obedience had apparently decayed into tyranny. Secondly, under Zhu's rule a tribute system was created that would in later years place China on a course of isolation from the west; culture would become inward-looking and the benefits of trade and connections with foreign powers would be lost. These two trends were to last throughout the dynasty of the Ming rulers and indeed their successors, the Qing.

But even under the terror of the despotic Ming emperors the period produced fine artistic accomplishments. The **porcelain** from the Imperial potteries of Jingdezhen is well known today and classic novels and other books survive from the period, including the *Yong Le Da Dien*, an encyclopedia compiled in 1408. Over three years 2000 scholars charted the 3000 years of Chinese history – including all known documents in full or part.

The stagnation in Chinese cultural life elsewhere was slowed only by one exception to the isolationist policy prescribed by Hong and his descendants. **Yong Le**, Zhu's 26th son, became third Ming Emperor and during his reign sent the imperial navy to the Indian Ocean and Arabian Sea for the first time, reaching as far as the east coast of Africa. But with Yong Le's death in 1424 these explorations were cancelled, since they were deemed not in accordance with the Confucian values, which denounced international trade and held a strong contempt for foreigners. Thus trading initiative passed into the hands of the Europeans, with the great period of world voyages by Columbus, Magellan and Vasco da Gama. In 1514 the Portuguese first appeared in the Canton river, and though expelled soon came back to Macau and by 1557 were permitted to plant permanent settlements there and move to Canton for the trading season; trade thus grew steadily in the 16C and 17C and contacts with the west increased. All dealings with foreigners were linked to the **Tribute System**, which reflected the imperial view of China as the largest and oldest source of civilisation condescending to permit dealings with lesser nations for the benefit of the latter – but although the court saw no advantage to China in the system for allowing foreign traders to operate, Chinese merchants and officials were eager to milk profit from it.

In later years though, as so often in Chinese history, the dynasty produced a succession of less able rulers who allowed power to slip into the hands of inner court officials; this eunuch bureaucracy grew and flourished largely unchecked, until by the last days of the Ming in the mid-17C it had mushroomed to 70,000 plus. Frontier defences had fallen into decay, the **Manchu tribes** in the north were threatening and some were already across the wall. Costly war and famine stirred up rebellion against the enfeebled dynasty, and when **Li Zicheng**, leader of a popular uprising, managed to break into the capital, the last Ming Emperor fled from his palace and hanged himself – an ignoble end to a 300-year-old dynasty.

1644 to 1911: the Qing Dynasty, war and rebellion

The Manchus weren't slow in turning internal dissention to their advantage. Sweeping down on Beijing, they threw out Li Zicheng's rebel army, claimed the capital as their own and founded the **Qing Dynasty**. It took a further twenty years for the Manchus to capture the south of the country, creating a divide which exists to this day. Once again China was under foreign rule.

Like the Mongol Yuan dynasty, the Qing initially did little to assimilate domestic culture, ruling the people as separate overlords: the Manchu language became the official language, and the Chinese were obliged to wear the Manchu pigtail. Intermarriage between a Manchu and a Chinese was strictly forbidden. Under the Qing dynasty the distant areas of Inner and Outer Mongolia, Tibet and Turkestan, once considered purely barbarian, were incorporated into the Chinese Empire, uniting the Chinese world to a greater extent than during the Tang period. Many buildings date from this period. The **White Pagoda** was a monument in honour of the first visit of a Dalai Lama to Beijing; the **Summer Palace** was also constructed at this time and various alterations were made to the **Forbidden City**. In fact, what can be seen at the Forbidden City today are reconstructions by the Qing of the Ming originals.

Though in Qing China the Manchus were firmly the ruling class, by the late 18C they had become deeply influenced by Chinese culture. For the first 140 years of the dynasty three outstanding emperors brought an infusion of new blood and vigour to government and China enjoyed a great period of peace and prosperity. **Kang Xi** (1654–1722) who became emperor at the age of 6 and reigned for 61 years was a great patron of the arts and scholarship. He assiduously cultivated his image as the 'Son of Heaven' by making royal progresses throughout the country and by his personal style of leadership. He did much to bring the south under control and by 1683 the southern **Rebellion of Three Feudatories** – military governors – had been savagely put down. His fourth son the Emperor **Yungzheng** (1678–1735) ruled over what is considered one of the most efficient and least corrupt administrations ever enjoyed by China. This was inherited by **Jian Long** (1711–99) whose reign was a golden age in which China's frontiers were widely extended and the economy stimulated by peace and prosperity. In 1750 China was perhaps at its peak; after three remarkable emperors it was one of the strongest, wealthiest and most powerful countries in the world. But in the second half of the 18C it was already coming under pressure as the emperor withdrew from active government and its expanding population pressed on its food resources. Meanwhile its closed, exclusive society came up against expanding European countries looking for trading opportunities. Though the Portuguese had been first in the field, the English had been trading regularly with Canton since about 1660 and in the 18C the **East India Company** joined in and came to monopolise the China trade from Britain. But the Qing dynasty became increasingly inward-looking and restrictive of trade, and Europeans, eager to buy tea and silk for which they paid in silver, found themselves restricted to thirteen factories on the mainland. They hoped to establish what they saw as normal diplomatic and trading relations with China but her rulers, still immensely rich and powerful and entirely convinced of their own effortless superiority, had no wish for dealings with foreigners. When **Lord Macartney** arrived in 1793 bearing the usual gifts in order to propose a treaty between George III and the Emperor, he refused to kowtow in submission and his embassy was unsuccessful; the King's 'tribute' was accepted but the Emperor totally rejected any idea of alliance with one who, according to Chinese ideas, was a subordinate in any case. Macartney was greatly impressed by the vast wealth and power of the Chinese court but later wrote perceptively that the empire was 'like an old crazy first rate man of war which its officers have contrived to keep afloat to terrify by its appearance and bulk'.

The Opium Wars and the Taiping rebellion

In fact the first leak in the ship of state had sprung twenty years earlier. A deep-seated economic crisis, caused by a rapidly-growing population and subsequent lack of land, was compounded by natural disaster and popular uprising to weaken Qing authority. At the end of the 18C the East India Company began to pay for its tea and silk with opium rather than silver: the company, along with other European powers, took advantage of the Qing crisis, realising that the domestic market for opium could easily be flooded with cheap imports from India. With a rapidly escalating number of addicts and a dwindling of the country's silver reserves, the Emperor pronounced an edict strictly forbidding the import of opium – which the addicts, traders, corrupt officials and especially the British ignored totally. Things went from bad to worse: the demand for the drug increased until the country's trade surplus became a deficit, and silver drained out of China, dislocating her monetary system and the country's finances.

An attempt by the Chinese to suspend the trade by blockading factories and confiscating and destroying over 20,000 chests of opium led to war. In 1840 a British expeditionary force sailed up the Yangzi, threatening Nanjing and forcing the Chinese to sign the **Treaty of Nanjing** in 1842. The terms – a huge indemnity, the opening up of new ports to trade, and the **cession of Hong Kong** – provided the framework for a greatly expanding trade, both by the British and others, and were the first in a long series of concessions extracted by other unequal treaties.

It was a devastating blow for the Chinese, who failed to understand the superiority which new techniques and organisation had secured the Europeans. Furthermore the country was now confronted with a major rebellion: missionaries had followed hard upon the European traders and **Hong Xiu Quan**, from a poor Hakka minority family in the south, who had failed his civil service examinations, was influenced by a

Christian tract to believe himself the second son of Jehovah and younger brother of Jesus Christ. By acting as focus both for anti-Manchu feeling and for unrest created by economic hardship, he mobilised a cross-section of society into an enormous army of over a million men and women, and known as the **Taiping**, which captured Nanjing in 1853 and occupied much of the rich Yangzi valley. From Nanjing, his 'Heavenly Capital', Hong developed a doctrine which embraced radical social reform and managed to sustain itself until 1864. A programme was put forward to prohibit drink, tobacco and opium; slavery, prostitution, arranged marriages and the practice of foot binding were to be abolished; land was to be held in common and taxation lightened. The parallels with the Communist movement of a century later are easily seen. But between the years of 1851–64 20 million people were killed as a result of the Taiping Rebellion and five provinces devastated before European powers, favouring a weak Qing government to a strong Taiping one, helped the Qing army force the Taiping back to their capital – where they were besieged, defeated and systematically slaughtered. With Hong Xiu Quan's suicide, the Taiping rebellion was at an end.

The second half of the 19C saw a series of smaller scraps as foreign powers dug in their heels for increased trade and territory. Qing government was at an all-time low, and when in 1861 the country found itself landed with a 6-year-old Emperor, the **Empress Dowager Wu Ci Xi** took over. Certain that reform or change would weaken the Qing's grasp of power, she ruled for 48 years with a deep conservatism at a time when China needed to overhaul its antiquated political structure. The result was that by the turn of the century the Qing dynasty was on its last legs and the common people impoverished.

During this period China's colonial empire was fast disintegrating. France gained control over Laos, Cambodia and Vietnam after a war in 1883–5;

Britain gained Burma; and, perhaps most importantly, in 1894 China sent 2,000 troops to support the king of **Korea** when a rebellion broke out. In reply, Japan dispatched 10,000 to keep the rebellion going, and within a few months Chinese and Korean forces were beaten. Under the treaty that followed, China was forced to cede the island of Taiwan, the Pescadores and the Liaong peninsula to Japan. This didn't go down well on the international scene. France, Germany and Russia, fearful of Japan's snowballing power, forced the country to return the Liaong Peninsula to China. By way of reward the Chinese allowed Russia to build a railway through Manchuria to their port of Lushun: with the ability to quickly move troops along this line, Russia effectively held control over Manchuria for the next 10 years. Other powers held sway over much of the country, and were only prevented from carving it up by American trade proposals.

Things weren't any better on the **home front**. Profitable mines and industries were now almost exclusively owned by foreigners, who channelled their wealth out of the country, and the increase in Christian missionary activity was undermining the traditional concepts on which Chinese society was based. In response to some of these problems, radical advisers persuaded Emperor Guangxu of 'the need for widespread reform'. **The Hundred Days Reform**, encouraged by Kang Youwei, of 1898 attempted modernisation of agriculture, industry and government institutions, but was crushed by the opposition from the Confucian establishment and in particular from the ultra-conservative Empress Dowager Ci Xi. Guangxu realised Ci Xi was a potential danger and put her under house arrest. Her power, however, proved greater than his and it was he who ended up as her prisoner. Shortly after the Emperor's confinement, she proceeded to execute the advisers of reform and repealed their measures. With this coup d'état the Empress Dowager took control once more.

The Boxer Rebellion – and the end of Imperial China

By the 1890s the country was in a poor state. The Qing rulers had done little or nothing to help the people, spent fortunes on various wars and allowed foreigners to take over domestic industry. A popular organisation was all that was needed to realise the support of the peasants and it came with the **Boxers**, as the 'Righteous and Harmonious Fists' are commonly known – a simplification of their philosophy in which callisthenics were used to prepare body and mind for battle. Their religious beliefs were a combination of magical Daoism and Buddhism, and they considered themselves so well protected by spirits as to be invulnerable to bullets in battle; and their stated aims, 'Overthrow the Qing, destroy the foreigner' were understandably close to the peasants' hearts.

After an initial defeat at the hands of her troops in 1899, Ci Xi's government revised its policy to support the Boxers as a method of ridding China of foreigners: from the winter of 1899 the Boxers systematically slaughtered missionaries, Christian converts and just about any foreigner they could lay their hands on. By the summer of 1900 the government had made a wild declaration of war on all foreign powers on its lands, and the Boxers were in the capital sieging the foreign legation compound. The German and Japanese ministers were murdered, but other foreign staff managed to hold out until an international relief force arrived on 14 August; on the 15th Ci Xi and the Emperor left the Imperial Palace disguised as peasants in a wooden cart. The Qing dynasty never really recovered.

Ci Xi fled to Xi'an, leaving her ministers to negotiate a humiliating peace. While foreign powers took great bites out of China's borders – Russia seized a large part of Manchuria – there was a growing movement to bring down the Empire from within. In 1905 in Japan **Sun Yatsen** founded the **Tong Meng Hui** with the aim of destroying the dynasty and building a new China. With the death of the Empress Dowager three years later the Empire began to crumble. Major reforms were initiated and a draft constitution published, but absolutist government is never so vulnerable as when it begins to make concessions: groups of revolutionaries proliferated and risings broke out like a rash along the eastern seaboard. In 1911 opposition to railway construction by foreigners coupled with a small rising in Wuchang triggered off a series of minor events which toppled the dynasty. In Nanjing Sun Yatsen took the lead in the provisional Republican government. When the end came it was surprisingly quiet; 2000 years of Empire vanished with hardly a struggle.

The new Republic

Almost immediately the new Republic was in trouble. It lacked any central army to reinforce its power, and in the north the former leader of the Imperial Army **Yuan Shikai** still held sway. Sun Yatsen was faced with a choice between probable civil war and relinquishing his presidency; he chose the latter, and stepped down for Yuan, who promptly dismissed the government, forced Sun to flee, and attempted to centralise power with a view to founding his own dynasty. But with his sudden death in 1916 his dynasty died with him.

China walked a precarious tightrope during the First World War. Japan had joined the Allies and claimed the German port of Quingdao and all German shipping and industry in the Shangdong Peninsula. In 1915 Japan presented China with the **Twenty-One Demands** many of which Yuan Shikai, under threat of Japanese invasion, was forced to accept. The news gave impetus to a growing unrest among intellectuals nationally, specifically in Beijing, where a group centred around **Li Dazhao**, librarian at the university, along with the young **Mao Zedong** and **Zhang Gudao**, both students. In Tianjin **Zhou Enlai** formed a Marxist study group, and those who gathered around these two centres would later become the founders of the Chinese Communist Party.

The 4 May uprising

The Chinese were optimistic that the **Treaty of Versailles** in 1919 would bring an end to Japanese aggression, as well as the unequal treaties, foreign concessions and other grievances. But their hopes were dashed when the western powers, who had already signed secret pacts with Japan, confirmed Japan's rights in China. This was the last straw. Popular feeling broke out in demonstrations and riots on 4 May in an assertion of Nationalism that had to be broken up by the police. Resistance was brief but it reflected a growing movement among the country's intellectuals of anti-foreign (especially anti-Japanese) nationalism.

A further grievance were the **warlords** in the north, whose feuding, plundering armies prevented national unification. In 1917 they had forced Sun Yatsen to retreat to Guangzhou when he attempted to form a government with the remnants of his Kuomintang party that could effectively challenge them. His defeat cost him what remained of his political clout, and almost his life. The problem of subduing the warlords remained, and would become a major difficulty for the developing Communist Party.

The rise of the Chinese Communist Party

The Chinese Communist Party (**CCP**) was formed by Li Dazhao and Chen Duxiu in Shanghai in 1921. Their party, a collection of Marxist groups, was guided by Russians who had been active in the Bolshevik revolution and who represented the Communist International (Comintern). But directives from Moscow invariably included a measure of Soviet foreign policy. When Moscow asked the CCP to join the Kuomintang (KMT) – a nationalist organisation formed after the fall of the Manchus – against the warlords, the reality was that Soviet fear of Japan attacking their eastern lands required a strong China and considered the Kuomintang the most likely party to achieve this. But the CCP thought the Kuomintang was basically unconcerned with changing the social order. Under pressure the CCP joined the Kuomintang; but they were unlikely bedfellows. When Sun Yatsen died in 1925 the differences between social reformer **Wang Jingwei** and military chief Chiang Kaishek came to a head, with Chiang Kaishek victorious. Under his leadership there was a turnaround in policy and the Kuomintang sent the National Revolutionary Army (NRA) on the **Northern Expedition** to crush the ever-troublesome warlords. As commander-in-chief, Chiang Kaishek's position was now at its strongest: after the other Kuomintang leader and Soviet advisers refused to join him in his newly captured Nanchang, and with the NRA ready to attack Shanghai, Chiang Kaishek utilised the moment to wipe out his opponents in the Kuomintang and the Communist Party.

On 21 March 1927, the NRA entered Shanghai, seized the military arsenal and armed the striking workers. Briefly they were victorious, but the industry bosses and foreign owners quickly retaliated, backing Chiang Kaishek in a duplicitous and bloody act that became infamous. Chiang was financed to disguise hundreds of thugs as members of the National Revolutionary Army, who then turned on the workers' militia and massacred 'fellow' Communists, along with anyone else Chiang had decided to eradicate. Around 5000 were murdered: Zhou Enlai escaped only by luck, and party founder Li Dazhao was executed by slow strangulation.

Two nationalist governments were now in operation: Chiang's in Nanjing and the original Kuomintang in Wuhan. With the army on his side and much of the original Communist opposition summarily executed (including Mao's second wife **Yang Kaihui**), Chiang quickly achieved supremacy and was declared head of the national government in 1928. Under Chiang the KMT was a ruthless and oppressive military dictatorship: its policies were to ignore the wretched state of the people and the increasing Japanese encroachments on China's sovereignty, and subdue all opposition to its rule by brute force. In this Chiang was aided substantially by the western powers – including the Soviet Union, who never let up on the line that the Communists should maintain their alliance with the KMT. His domestic base of power, however, was small, and despite attempts at limited social reform from within, the Party quickly came to represent the interests of a social elite. Those Communists who had escaped Chiang's increasingly rabid purges regrouped in Jiangxi province as the **Red Army**, under the leadership of **Mao Zedong**.

Mao Zedong, the peasants and the Red Army

Mao's belief was that potential social reform lay in the hands of the peasants. As a teacher at the Peasant Training Institute in Canton his belief in the peasant-workers as agents of radical change had hardened, and he appealed, unsuccessfully, for the then-Communist controlled Kuomintang to turn to the people for their power base. At this time the lot of the worker was little improved from previous centuries. Poverty and starvation were rife, caused by oppressive taxation by landlords supported by corrupt government officials, and any whiff of dissent was crushed by the landlords' private armies. The peasants had few rights and no power base within the system. Drawing from Marx's analyses, Mao recognised the parallels between 19C Europe and 20C China – and that a mass armed rising was the only way the old order could be overthrown.

In 1927 Mao organised the first peasant-worker army in Changsha in what was later to be called the **Autumn Harvest Uprising**. Dropping south into Hunan his troops moved into the Jinggang mountains where they were met by **Zhu De**, once a leader of the Kuomintang who had joined the Communists. Though the army was a rag-tag mix of peasants, miners and Kuomintang deserters it had achieved a success unexpected by the Central Committee of the Communist Party. **Li Lisan**, the leader, remained sceptical and ordered Mao's army out of its mountain base to attack the cities. After a couple of heavy defeats Mao and Zhu split from Li Lisan, refusing to carry out his orders. Their army was essentially a guerrilla one, and like most guerrilla armies best adapted to fighting in the countryside. No longer under orders from Li Lisan, Mao was able to achieve his objective – the creation of a peasant-based revolutionary movement.

Mao withdrew to the mountains he had known as a child and began recruiting the peasants to the **Red Army** (as well as being the traditional colour of revolution, to the Chinese red signifies joy).

The army was well disciplined as, dependent on peasant support for survival, it had to be. It was also didactic: the revolutionary soldier, Mao wrote, had to fight on the political front as well as the battlefield.

Mao also realised that the army's strength lay in guerrilla tactics and that in face-to-face combat with the vastly superior KMT forces it wouldn't stand a chance. The four tactics he established have become the code of every guerrilla force since.

1. When the enemy advances we retreat.
2. When he escapes we harass.
3. When he retreats we pursue.
4. When he is tired we attack.

So organised, the Red Army survived in the middle of KMT territory for five years.

In the early 1930s Chiang Kaishek's troops suffered a succession of humiliating defeats, most spectacularly when 300,000 Nationalist troops were defeated by a Red Army of no more than 30,000. And, increasingly, KMT soldiers were deserting, bringing with them much-needed weapons and munitions. Chiang's response to this was to mobilise half a million troops for an attack intended to crush the rebel forces once and for all. The KMT encircled the Red Army and its peasant supporters with a ring of concrete block-houses and barbed wire entanglements and slowly tightened it. In the process many thousands of peasants were captured, to be deported or executed. Many of those remaining inside the blockade starved to death – approximately one million of them.

Mao was facing disaster: once more he had been forced by the party leadership into fighting pitched battles with the KMT, and the Red Army had nearly halved as a consequence. The KMT's cordon drew tighter daily: the choice was between fighting it out on his own territory or cutting and running. What happened was to prove one of the most epic mass movements of modern history.

The Long March

The story of how 100,000 men, women and children broke through the KMT cordon around Jinggangshan, and marched through summer and winter across 18 mountain ranges (5 of them snow capped), 24 rivers and 12 provinces each larger than most European countries, almost defies belief. The journey of 6000 miles took a year, and only one in twenty of those who started survived; tens of thousands perished of cold, hunger, bombing and strafing by the KMT or in the innumerable battles that were fought along the way. But by the time they reached safety in Yenan in Shensi province its leaders had turned a humiliating defeat into an advance towards victory; for along the way thousands of Chinese who had never heard of Communism ('Who is the emperor now?' was a question the marchers were often asked) were made aware of their struggles and beliefs. And an army that could do this could do anything . . .

Japanese invasion and the United Front

In 1932 Japan invaded Chinese Manchuria and installed Pu Yi (last Emperor of the Qing Dynasty) as puppet leader. By 1937 they had taken Beijing, Shanghai, Canton and most of eastern China, and controlled much of the heavy industry. It seemed possible that Japan might soon be in control of the whole country, especially since they had met with little organised resistance. Chiang Kaishek wanted to rid China of the Comunists and create a common front to fight the Japanese. 'The Japanese are only a disease of the skin, he said, but the Communists are a disease of the heart.' The upshot of this policy was that the KMT waged constant battle against the Red Army while the invaders went unopposed. Mao, more realistically, wrote to Chiang (and to the warlords' bandit leaders and secret societies) advocating an end to civil war and a United Front against the Japanese. Chiang's reply was to move in his Manchurian armies down to finish off the Reds in Shaanxi. A bad move, for Zhang wanted to get at the Japanese in his homeland, and so entered into an agreement with the Communist forces. When Chiang turned up to see what was going on, he was kidnapped by his own troops and forced into signing an agreement to the United Front. Briefly, China was united – though both sides knew that the alliance would last only as long as the Japanese threat.

Full-scale war broke out in July 1937 and by 1939 the best of the KMT army had been wiped out, with the remnants retreating into the heart of Southern China to lick their wounds. The Japanese concentrated their efforts on routing the KMT, leaving a vacuum in the north that the Communists quickly filled, establishing what amounted to stable government of 100 million people across the North China Plain.

The outbreak of war in Europe in September 1939 soon had repercussions in China. Nazi Germany stopped supplying the weaponary the KMT relied on, and with the bombing of Pearl Harbor two years later all military aid from the United States to Japan ceased. As a result the United Front became dependent on the Americans and British flying in supplies over the Himalayas. But Chiang's true allegiances were never far below the surface, and he failed to distribute the arms among the Red Army, and indeed by 1941 was already ordering his troops to attack Communist forces. The United Front collapsed.

The end of the war . . . and the Kuomintang

Despite fighting with the KMT, the Communists hit the Japanese troops hard and they were already on the retreat when the two atom bombs ended the war. 1945 saw the Red Army close on a million strong, with a widespread following throughout the country; Communism in China was established. It wasn't, however, that secure: predictably, the Americans sided with Chiang Kaishek and the KMT, and so did the Soviet Union, confirming its support of Chiang with a treaty. Stalin believed that the KMT would easily destroy the CCP, and if not with ease then with the help of the Americans. In the peace negotiations between Nationalist and Communist sides, Chiang refused to admit the CCP into government, knowing that its policy had too great a popularity to be safely under his control while the Red Army still existed. It was evident to the CCP that without an army, they were nothing. The talks ended in stalemate.

Ironically, it was American military aid that decided matters in the Communists' favour. US weapons were captured en masse from KMT troops, providing the Communists with the firepower to continue and build on its victories. In 1948 the newly-named **People's Liberation Army** (PLA) began a final assault on the KMT. Massively popular and with much of the country starving as a result of Chiang's mishandling of the economy, the PLA faced little opposition after it won three great battles in the winter. Just before Shanghai fell to the Communists, Chiang Kaishek took off in a plane crammed with the country's entire gold reserves and his military henchmen bound for the island of Formosa (today's **Taiwan**) to form the **Republic of China**, where he would remain until his death in 1975, forlornly waiting to liberate mainland China with the two million troops and refugees who later joined him. By October 1949 Mao was able to proclaim the formation of the **People's Republic of China** in Beijing: the world's third largest nation and its most populous was now Communist.

The People's Republic – the Hundred Flowers and The Great Leap Forward

Massive problems faced the new Republic: the road and rail network were mostly destroyed, industrial output had slumped, much of the agricultural areas had been ravaged, and there were no gold reserves to support the country economically. But the Chinese people, still in awe of their long and hard-won victory, took to the task of repairing and revitalising the country with an energy that was obsessive. By the mid-1950s all industry had been nationalised and output was back at pre-war levels. Land was handed over to the peasants and over a million landlords were executed. Under **revolutionary education** (called 'criticism and self-criticism' by some, 'brainwashing' by others) there was enforced discussion and study of Marxist tracts in an attempt to rid the new ideology of elitism or bourgeois deviance from the revolutionary spirit. People were encouraged to criticise openly themselves, their past and those around them, for some a traumatic experience and one that broke centuries-old traditional norms.

With all the difficulties on the home front, the **Korean War** of 1950 was a distraction the government could well have done without. The US had pushed into North Korea and, despite vigorous warnings from Zhou Enlai, had continued through to Chinese territory. China's hand was forced and in June war was declared. Half a million troops steamrollered the Americans back to the 38th parallel and, after much loss of life, forced peace negotiations. As a boost for the morale of the new nation, the incident could not have been better timed.

The Hundred Flowers
In 1956 Mao decided to loosen the restrictions on public expression, in the hope that open criticism would shake up the more intractable bureaucrats and party officials. Following the slogan 'Let a hundred flowers bloom, a hundred schools of thought contend,' intellectuals were allowed to voice their thoughts and criticisms. At first there was little response, but in 1957 intellectuals began blistering attacks, not on inefficient officals as Mao had hoped but on the Communist system itself. Those who had spoken out swiftly found themselves at worst in gaol or at best undergoing a heavy bout of criticism and self-criticism. Following this, the **Hundred Flowers** episode, intellectuals as a group, and especially those who were involved in running the economy, were mistrusted and constantly scrutinised.

Agricultural revolution
Even though China had greatly boosted its agricultural and industrial outputs the Central Committee of the Communist Party decided that the revolutionary drive needed reviving. In August 1958 it announced that all land held privately by peasant farmers was to be pooled into collective farms, linked together as self-

governing **Communes**. 500 million peasants were to be spread over 24,000 communes, with the aim of turning small-scale farming units into hyper-efficient agricultural areas. Industry was to be fired into activity by the co-option of seasonally employed workers, who would construct heavy industrial plants, dig canals and drain marshes. Propaganda campaigns promised eternal well-being in return for three years of hard work and austerity. Almost from the outset the **Great Leap Forward**, as it was known, was a disaster. Having been given their land (and in many cases fought for it) the peasants now found themselves losing it once more, and eagerness to work in huge units was low. Combined with ill-trained commune management, the Great Leap Forward took China several steps back. Its aim was to match British industrial output in 10 years, and overtake American in 15 to 20: what happened was an almost immediate slump in agricultural and industrial production. Millions starved.

As if this wasn't enough, the harvests of 1959 and 1960 both failed, and in 1960 the Soviet Union stopped all aid. The commune policy was watered down and each peasant given a private house and own land. By the mid 1960s the economy was back on its feet, but the incident had damaged Mao's reputation and set members of the Communist Party Central Committee against some of his policies. Two committee members, **Liu Shaoqi** and **Deng Xiaoping** widened the gap between themselves and their supporters and Mao, believing in the necessity of creating material incentives for the peasant-workers in order to boost production and raise the standard of living. They had been responsible for the turnabout in commune policy along with creating free market and small-scale economic independence among the country's traders. Their policy spawned a large bureaucracy over which Mao held little political sway. Furthermore Liu and Deng supported the deposed Minister of Defence **Peng Dehuai** in a move to secure technological and military aid from the Soviet Union, and to free the army from non-military work – a move popular with sections of the army. Mao believed that an alliance with the Soviets was unnecessary and would end China's policy of self-reliance – and he was determined to keep control of the army.

In 1964 **Lin Biao** formed the **Socialist Education Movement**, activists whose aim was to destroy the 'spontaneous desire to become capitalists' among the peasants, as well as those in the party hierarchy who opposed Mao. Mao himself widened the SEM's aims to include the whole bureaucracy that Liu Shaoqi had founded, believing it to be revisionist, bourgeois and elitist, and a ruling caste as strong as the Confucian officials of the ancient dynasties. The military revolution had been achieved in 1949, the economic one attempted in 1958. What was needed now, Mao posited, was a third – a cultural revolution.

The Cultural Revolution

Mao had seen the successful pragmatic policies of the last few years as a dangerous tendency towards revisionism, the negation of all that he and the masses had suffered for. Feeling now that he had lost control of the Party, he sought to regain it by orchestrating the youth of China and the PLA against his moderate opponents. Initially the Great Proletarian Cultural Revolution seemed relatively harmless, a re-run of the anti-rightist campaign following the Hundred Flowers fiasco. But in 1966 a campaign following the Hundred Flowers fiasco. But in 1966 a student put up a poster at Beijing university, denouncing university administration and supporting the Revolution. Under Mao's guidance Beijing's students started to organise themselves into a political group – the **Red Guard**. Within weeks Mao had arranged their removal out of the university and on to the streets.

The enemies of the Red Guard were the **Four Olds**: old ideas, old culture, old customs and old habits. In action reminiscent of earlier xenophobia, anything redolent of capitalism, the west or the Soviet Union came under attack. Academics were humiliated and assaulted, books were burned, temples desecrated. Shops selling anything remotely western were destroyed along with the gardens of the 'decadent bourgeoisie'. Eventually, inevitably, the Party officials who had threatened Mao came under attack: half the Party's ministers were forced to resign, many paraded through the streets wearing placards carring humiliating slogans; tens of thousands of 'Rightists', 'Revisionists' and 'Capitalists' were ostracised, imprisoned or driven to suicide. The police and army were forbidden to intervene and looked on as the Red Guard beat people to death. The waste in human life and human resources was almost beyond belief.

On the 5 August 1966 Mao proclaimed that reactionaries had reached the highest levels of the CCP. Though no-one was named the targets were obvious: **Liu Shaoqi**, Chief of State of the Republic was thrown in prison and died there of ill-treatment in 1969; **Deng Xiaoping**, General Secretary of the Communist Party, was dismissed from his post and condemned to wait on tables at a Party canteen and turn a lathe at a provincial tractor plant. **Peng Dehuai** disappeared, probably to die in gaol, and many other senior officials and army officers were dismissed.

By August 1967 the violence had reached its worst and most widespread. The Red Guard's fanaticism was threatening to fragment the country and Mao intervened, instructing the Guard to surrender all weapons to the army and return to their homes. The army was allowed to use force where necessary, and the most radical Guard members were arrested. But the activities of the Red Guard were not easily stopped. Street fighting broke out in the spring of 1968 and the army responded by sending tanks into the cities. Mao was forced to desperate remedies and ordered the army into the universities to break up the Red Guard. As a result millions of the Guard were shipped from the cities and put to work on the land.

The aftermath

The damage waged on China by the Cultural Revolution was deep and wide ranging. Law and order broke down, looting and street crime increased and Chinese standing in the international community sunk to an all-time low after the Red Guard assaulted members of the British Embassy. Foreign ambassadors were called home and the country slid into isolation, backtracking on the gradual international acceptance that had brought it close to replacing Taiwan as the official representative of China at the United Nations in 1965.

The years after the Revolution also saw the rise of a **personality cult** around Mao Zedong. In a way it's not surprising that the people should consider deifying a man after the excesses committed by the ideologues of the Cultural Revolution. What is unusual is the extent of the cult and the degree to which it is denounced today. Mao's portrait had always been prominent in China's streets but it now took on a almost religious iconography as workers would bow to it and roadside shrines were built to it. In the most famous incident, a soldier spotted a school on fire: his first thought was to save the portrait of Mao in the classrooms and only then start to save those trapped inside. The media treated him as a hero irrespective (or probably because) of his priorities.

This period also saw **Lin Biao**, Defence Minister and Vice-Chairman of the Communist Party rise to prominence. Mao's closest ally during the Cultural Revolution, Lin was designated Mao's successor in 1969, but with the return to order the role of the army and its chief were less crucial Lin began to feel his power base eroded. What happened next is conjecture, as what little was written of the event was recorded by pro-Mao historians. Lin, seeing his power evaporating, may have attempted some form of coup against Mao and organised an assassination attempt. In 1972 it was announced that Lin had died the previous year when a plane carrying him and his followers had crashed en route to the Soviet Union. The story is plausible but probably fictional. Lin might well have been executed and the tale concocted to underline his treason – and to state that Mao's enemies were, of course, never liquidated. It's unlikely that the truth will ever be known.

What is certain is that with Lin's removal and the uncovering of a plot, Mao needed to broaden his base of support. This he did by rehabilitating those who had fallen from grace during the Cultural Revolution and had been reindoctrinated. Even those who, a few years earlier, would have been considered permanently ostracised were returned to differing degrees of power. With help from Zhou Enlai **Deng**

Xiaoping returned, and as Mao declined in health (he was 80 in 1973), Deng took control of the day-to-day running of the Communist Party Central Committee.

Zhou Enlai himself was still Mao's deputy but he was in his 70s; it was Deng's star that was in the ascendant.

The post-revolution years – Diplomacy, Ping-Pong and the Bamboo Curtain

America had continued to support Chiang Kaishek's Kuomintang in the post-war period for a straightforward reason. American foreign policy was determined by business and political interests that stood to gain from the collapse of Communism in mainland China, and so whatever possible was done to stir up paranoia over the possibility of a Sino-Soviet pact. In reality there was little chance of this, following the split between Kruschev and Mao in 1960, but the Cultural Revolution confirmed American fears, and a ban that had been imposed on US citizens travelling to China a few years earlier was not lifted. But, improbably, several incidents were to bring about a rapprochement with the US. In 1964 China exploded its first atomic bomb, taking it into the league of nuclear powers not automatically friendly to Washington. In 1971 the People's Republic became the official representative of the nation called China, and Chiang Kaishek's Republic was slung out. And, through the late 1960s, border skirmishes with the Soviet Union made it politic to seek friendship with America. Despite the US invasion of Cambodia in 1970, envoy Henry Kissinger opened communications between the two countries, cultural and sporting links were formed (a tactic that became known as **ping-pong diplomacy**) and by 1972 President Richard Nixon was walking on the Great Wall and holding talks with Mao, trade restrictions were lifted and China began to commerce with the west. The 'bamboo curtain' had parted, isolationism was over, and damage of the Cultural Revolution was slowly being repaired.

Right versus Left

Zhou Enlai died in 1976 and his protégé Deng Xiaoping read the eulogy at his funeral. The two had formed a political camp in latter years which saw itself as more realistic and pragmatic than Mao and his followers. With Zhou's death a split opened between the moderates and the radical mouthpiece of the increasingly absent Mao – the **Gang of Four**, a group led by Mao's 3rd wife Jiang Qing. Their first act was to cut the period of mourning for Zhou to a few days. Deng Xiaoping disappeared and the Maoist-controlled media twittered about anti-revolutionary forces at large. **Hua Guofeng** was made Acting Premier, a position that would naturally have gone to Deng.

To his supporters Zhou, and by extension Deng, rapidly became symbols of moderation against the Gang of Four. In early April the Chinese traditionally commemorate their dead at the **Qing Ming** festival and the Heroes Monument in Beijing's Tian'anmen Square was filled with wreathes in memory of Zhou, who was coming to represent rather more in death than he had in life. On 5 April radicals removed the wreaths and thousands of moderate supporters flooded into the square in protest; a riot broke out and many were attacked and arrested. The obvious scapegoat for what became known as the **Tian'anmen Incident** was Deng Xiaoping, and he was duly thrown out of office for a second time.

Mao Zedong was not publicly seen again. In July a catastrophic earthquake in the north killed approximately half a million people. In the Chinese system of myths a natural disaster always forshadowed the end of a dynasty. Mao died on 9 September 1976.

The fall of the Gang of Four and the rise of Deng Xiaoping

With Mao dead the differences between the left and right surfaced. Deprived of a figurehead, the Maoists quickly lost ground to the right amongst a population that could well remember the excesses of the last outburst of Maoism, the Cultural Revolution. Just a month after Mao's death Jiang Qing and the other members of the Gang of Four, **Weng Wenyuan**, **Wang Honqwen** and **Zhang Chunqiao** were arrested. Deng was able to return to the political scene for the third time and was granted a string of positions that included Vice Chairman of the Communist Party, Vice-Premier and Chief of Staff to the PLA. Hua Guofeng, Mao's chosen successor, was ousted a couple of years later. More moderates came into the running of the Party and the move away from Mao's policies was rapid: by 1980 criticism of Mao's actions and policies was open and his portraits and statues were coming down.

In 1981 the Gang of Four were brought to trial and though the verdict was a formality, the sentences were not, for they would be an indication to the people not only of the tenor of the new administration but also of how it saw the Cultural Revolution and Mao himself. If the death sentence were carried out, Mao's widow might easily become a martyr; if a death sentence were given and suspended the ability ever to execute counter-revolutionaries again would be highly doubtful. But the latter course was chosen and Jiang and Zhang Chunqiao were given 2 years to reform their ways – which they duly did.

Deng and the Moderates were careful. To denounce Mao would have caused a backlash among the people, so in 1981 the Central Committee issued a carefully worded resolution that offered a compromise. Mao was a great leader who made mistakes, especially the Cultural Revolution, 'but if we judge his activities as a whole, his contribution to the Revolution far outweighs his errors'. Previously Deng had shown himself to be no less illiberal than his predecessor. In 1978 anti-Maoist dissidents were allowed to display wall posters in Beijing and elsewhere, and some actually criticised Mao by name. Most supported the Tian'anmen demonstrations and Deng himself, but though Deng agreed with many of the criticisms he was firmly against such views being publicly aired, and after a year the wall posters were pulled down for good, with Deng promoting a successful campaign to remove the right to such activity from the Chinese constitution.

China in the 1980s

Under Deng, China has become unrecognisable from the days when western thought was automatically suspect and the Red Guard enforced ideological purity. Though the Maoist elements are still present, ticking away, say some, to explode when Deng is dead and gone, the new **Open Door** policies of Deng have brought about a massive westernisation, especially in the cities, where western clothes, western music, Japanese motorbikes and fast food are all the rage. Without the Open Door you almost certainly would not be reading this book, since doors have been opened for travellers too. Deng's policy to increase the country's trade with the west, combined with less emphasis on ideological Communism, have inevitably led to westernisation, particularly among those too young to remember the postwar years but old enough to have been affected by the Cultural Revolution.

In 1982 Deng orchestrated the removal of many of his opponents from positions in the country's regional bureaucracy in an attempt to prevent disruption of his policies. But the removal of opposition did not stifle it. Deng's entrepreneurial approach of opposition did not stifle it. Deng's entrepreneurial approach has come under increasing fire from those on the left, notably Central Committee member **Chen Yun**, and despite Deng's insistence that his policies can be justified in the works of Marx and Mao, the party's Maoist wing is understandably displeased. Most visible of the problems the Open Door policy has brought is the upsurge in party elitism and corruption, both of which flower under the cover of *guanxi* – the old-boy network. Even after the purge of 1982, Party officials enjoy better wages, better housing, better cars and their children better education, and with a growing acceptance of capitalist values this stratification of an elite cadre is getting worse. On the streets posters advertising hairspray and jeans have replaced those of Mao and the 'evil winds' from the west – prostitution, pornography, racketeering and the black market – are blowing stronger.

Corruption exists throughout the system and, seemingly, those at the top are best protected: in 1986 the Minister for Astronautics, who was discovered to have embezzled a cool $41 million, received only disciplinary warnings from the Party – evidence (if any was needed) of *guanxi* in operation.

The future

Whether the new government can pull off a balancing act between capitalism and commercial growth remains to be seen, but one of its most successful moments came with the negotiations with Britain for the return of the colony of **Hong Kong** scheduled for 1997. The talks revealed China as a responsible member of the international community and boosted the reputation of Deng (who boasts he hopes still to be Party Chairman when China is handed over) and General Secretary **Hu Yaobang** a flamboyant character intent on the Open Door policy and tipped as successor to Deng. Also up-and-coming is Vice-Premier **Li Peng**, by comparison youthful and rumoured to be the adopted son of Zhou Enlai. It's likely that the Party Congress of 1987 will see Deng reshuffling these men so that Hu and Premier **Zhao Ziyang** rise to the Central Advisory Committee, a body currently headed by Deng.

But neither of these men played an active role in the Revolution or have links with the military – a crucial fact in the struggle to protect reforms. The last years of Mao's life were dedicated to creating a system that would outlive him. It failed, and it remains to be seen if Deng can rally the right people to take his reforms, and China, into the 21C.

MONUMENTAL CHRONOLOGY

4800BC	First evidence of **human settlement**	**Banpo** in the Yellow River basin built Bronze Age town of **Eriltou** in Henan Excavations at **Yin** in Anyang have revealed rich and developed culture
21C–16C BC Xia Dynasty		
16C–11C BC Shang Dynasty		
11C–771BC Zhou Dynasty	The concept of the **Mandate from Heaven** introduced Kong Zi or **Confucius** (c500BC) teaches a philosophy of adherence to ritual and propriety	
770BC–476BC Spring and Autumn Period		
457BC–221BC Warring States		
221BC–207BC Qin Dynasty	First centralised empire founded by Emperor **Qin Shihuang**	The **Great Wall** 'completed' **Terracotta Army** guard Qin's tomb **Han Tombs** near Xi'an
206BC–220AD Han Dynasty	**Han Emperors** bring stability and great advances in trade **Confucianism** and **Buddhism** ascendant	
The Three Kingdoms 220–265 **Wei** 221–263 **Shu Han** 222–280 **Wu**	Influence of Buddhist **India** and **Central Asia** enlivens a Dark age.	
265–420 Jin Dynasty	Absorption of northern barbarians into Chinese culture	
420–581 Southern and Northern Dynasties	Rapid succession of shortlived dynasties brings disunity	Earliest **Longmen caves** near Luowang
581–618 Sui Dynasty	Centralisation and growth under **Wen Di**	Completion of **Da Xing Cheng** near Xi'an; extension and strengthening of **Great Wall**; digging of **Grand Canal**
618–907 Tang Dynasty	Arts and literature reach their most developed stage	**Great Buddha** at Leshan completed
907–960 Five Dynasties	Decline of culture and the northern defences	**Cliff sculptures** of Dazu
960–1271 Song Dynasties	Consolidation of the lesser kingdoms	
1271–1368 Yuan Dynasty	**Genghis Khan** invades. Under **Kublai Khan** trade with Europe develops **Marco Polo** opens trade with Venice	**Forbidden City** built
1368–1644 Ming Dynasty	Isolationist policies end contact with rest of world	

1644–1911 Qing Dynasty	**Manchus** gain control over China and extend its boundaries. Under **Jian Long** (1711–99) culture flourishes	**Potala Palace** in Lhasa rebuilt by 5th Dalai Lama **Summer Palace** in Beijing completed
Late 18C	**East India Company** monopolises trade with Britain	
1839–62	**Opium Wars**. As part of the surrender settlement, Hong Kong is ceded to Britain.	
1851–64	**Taiping rebellion**	
1861–1900	Conservative policies of Dowager Empress **Ci Xi** allow foreign powers to take control of China's industry	
1899	**Boxer rebellion**	
1911 Republic	End of Imperial China, **Sun Yatsen** becomes leader of the **Republic**	
1921	Chinese Communist Party founded in Beijing	**Peasant Movement Training Institute** built in Guangzhou
1927	**Chiang Kaishek** orders massacre of Communists in Beijing. **Mao Zedong** organises first peasant-worker army	
1932	Japan invades Manchuria	
1936–41	**United Front**	
1945	Surrender of Japan. Civil war between the Nationalist **Kuomintang** and the **People's Liberation Army**	
1949 Liberation	Chiang Kaishek flees to **Taiwan**. **People's Republic** of China is founded	
1950–53	China supports the North in the **Korean War**	Much **rebuilding** of cities throughout the 1950s
1956	The **Hundred Flowers** campaign unsuccessfully attempts liberalisations	
1958	Agricultural Reform in the shape of the **Great Leap Forward** fails. Widespread famines result	Land organised into **Communes**. Heavy **industrial plants** built in rural areas
1964	China explodes its first atomic weapon	
1966–8	Red Guards purge anti-Maoist elements in the **Cultural Revolution**	Much destruction of ideologically unsound art and architecture
1971	People's Republic replaces Taiwan at **United Nations**	
1972	**President Nixon** visits Beijing	

1976	The **Tian'anmen Incident** reveals public support for moderate **Deng Xiaoping**. **Mao Zedong dies**, and the **Gang of Four** are arrested shortly afterwards
1977	Deng Xiaoping rises to become **Party Chairman**
1981	**Trial** of the Gang of Four
1980	Beginning of the **Open Door** policy
1986	Agreement reached on **Hong Kong's** return to China in 1997

CHINESE BELIEFS: THREE TEACHINGS FLOW INTO ONE

For the traveller in modern China, there are few indications of the traditional beliefs which formed and defined the country's civilisation. Relics litter the countryside, yet they appear sadly incongruous amid the furious pace of 20C change all around them. Dilapidated Buddhist and Taoist temples are frequented only by old women whose beliefs have somehow survived 30 years of determined cultural transformation. The restored temples – now 'Cultural Relics' with photo booths, concession stands, special foreign tourist shops and endless throngs of young Chinese on outings – are garish and evoke few mysteries. All old beliefs are derided as superstition, and the oldest and most firmly rooted of them all, **Confucianism**, has been constantly criticised and repudiated for nearly a century. One of the most astonishing – and for any student of Chinese culture the most saddening – aspects of modern China is the degree to which, on the surface at least, the Communist regime has succeeded in eradicating the ancient ('feudal') beliefs and replaced them with a new dogma.

While this is certainly disappointing for a traveller seeking **the Tao** (the Way) in China, it is not necessarily right to assume that the neglect of the outward forms indicates a corresponding demise of traditional beliefs in the minds of the Chinese people. The resilience of the old ideas, and their ability to absorb new streams of thought and eventually to dominate them, has been proved countless times. In any event, the philosophies which have unified China and defined the very idea of 'Chinese' for well over 2000 years are not likely to be forgotten in a mere 35 years of Communism.

The by-product of the oldest continuous civilisation on earth, Chinese culture is actually comprised of many disparate and sometimes contradictory elements. But at the heart of it all lie intermingled: Confucianism, Taoism and Buddhism. The way in which a harmonious balance has been created between these three is expressed in the often-quoted maxim San Jiao Fa Yi – Three Teachings Flow into One.

Both Confucianism and Taoism are belief systems rooted in the Chinese soil, and they form as much a part of the Chinese collective unconscious as Aristotelian logic does in the west. All thought is shaped by them. **Buddhism**, though, came to China from India; brought along the Silk Road by itinerant monks and missionaries from about the 1C AD. As such, it was the first organised religion to penetrate China and enjoyed a glorious, if brief, period of ascendancy under the Tang in the 8C. Just as the seeming contradictions of Confucianism and Taoism had been accommodated not only within society but also within individuals, however, so Buddhism did not for long eclipse other beliefs. As it established itself, its tenets were gradually integrated into the existing structure of beliefs and in turn transformed by them, into something very different from what had originally come out of India.

Chinese philosophy is thus an amalgam: it is from this flexibility that comes its strength. China, the nation, may have been conquered and ruled by foreign powers, but her culture has never been overwhelmed. Instead, the barbarian conquerors have found themselves slowly but inexorably Sinicised. On this strength rested the Chinese confidence in the absolute superiority of their culture over any other. The Chinese word for China, Zhong Guo, translates into Middle Kingdom, and reflects the confidence that China was literally the centre of the world. As a Chinese scholar of the 19C said:

> If we take the westerner's knowledge of machinery and mathematics in order to protect the Way of our sage Kings . . . this Way will gradually spread to the eight bounds of the earth. This is called using the ways of China to change the barbarians.

Confucianism

The way of the sage kings was first expounded by an obscure and unsuccessful scholar of pre-Imperial China. Born in about 551BC, into a period of feuding kingdoms and social disharmony, the scholar Kong Zi (**Confucius**) preached adherence to ritual and propriety as the supreme answer to the inherent disorder of the natural world. During his lifetime he wandered from court to court attempting to teach their rulers the correct way to rule. He was largely ignored. In the centuries after his death, however, Confucianism – as reflected in the *Analects*, a collection of writings on his life and sayings compiled by disciples – became the most influential and fundamental of Chinese philosophies.

Never a religion in the sense we know it, Confucianism is rather a set of moral and social values designed to bring the ways of man and government into harmony with each other and with the Universe. Through proper training in the scholarly classics and rigid adherence to the rules of propriety, the superior man could attain a level of moral righteousness which would, in turn, assure a stable and righteous social order. As a political theory Confucianism called for the wisest sage, the one whose moral sense was most refined, to be ruler. With a good ruler, one who practised the virtuous ways of the ancestors and was exemplary in terms of the five **Confucian virtues** (benevolence, righteousness, propriety, wisdom and trustworthiness) the world and society would naturally be in order. Force, the ultimate sanction, would be unnecessary. As Confucius said:

> Just as the ruler genuinely desires the good, the people will be good. The virtue of the ruler may be compared to the wind and that of the common people to the grass. The grass under the force of the wind cannot but bend.

The Gods play no part in this structure – man is capable of perfection in his own right, given a superior ruler whose virtues would be mirrored in the behaviour of his subjects. Five **hierarchical relationships** define the basis of a well-ordered society – given proper performance of the duties of mutual responsibility and obedience, the power of the state becomes redundant. The five Confucian relationships outline a strict structure of duty and obedience to authority: ruler to ruled; son to father, younger brother to older, wife to husband and, the only equal relationship, friend to friend. The intention is to create rule by a moral elite: in practice adherence to the unbending hierarchy

of these relationships as well as to the precepts of 'filial piety' has justified arbitrary and totalitarian rule throughout Chinese history. The supreme virtue of the well cultivated man (and infinitely more so woman) was submission.

From the Han dynasty (206BC–AD220) onwards Confucianism became institutionalised as a **system of government** which was to prevail in China for 2000 years. With it, and the notion of the scholar-official as the ideal ruler, came the notorious Chinese bureaucracy. Men would study most of their lives in order to pass the Imperial examinations and attain a government commission. These examinations were rigid tests of the scholar's knowledge of the Confucian classics. Thus power in China was wielded through a bureaucracy steeped in the classics of rites and rituals written five hundred years before Christ.

The Confucian ideal ruler, of course, never emerged (the Emperor was not expected to sit the exams) and the scholar-officials were more often a class of corrupt bureaucrats and exploitative landlords than a paragon of virtue whose standards the commoners might hope to emulate. The chief virtue of Confucianism as a moral doctrine was its emphasis on the family as the centre of life and duty for the individual. With its demands for loyalty and obedience this did at least succeed in creating a remarkably stable society, if not the perfectly harmonious one at which it aimed. And intense family loyalty is still a characteristic of Chinese society today.

Taoism

The second of the three major teachings which form the roots of Chinese culture is **Taoism**. The Tao translates simply to mean the Way and, in its purest form, Taoism is the study and pursuit of this ineffable Way. The name is derived from the fundamental text, the *Daodejing* (*Tao Te Ching*) or 'The Way and its Power'. Authorship of this obscure and mystical text is traditionally attributed to a sage by the name of **Lao Ži**, living about the same time as Confucius. Legend has it that, at the end of his life, the old hermit Lao Zi was wandering westward: at the western gate he was stopped and the gatekeeper, impressed by his wisdom, asked the old man to write down his ideas. The book that resulted was the *Daodejing*.

The Tao is never really defined – indeed by its very nature it is indefinable. The first lines of the *Daodejing* read:

The Tao that can be told
is not the eternal Tao.
The name that can be named
is not the eternal name.

In essence, however, it is the Way of Nature, the underlying principle and source of all being. It is the bond which unites man and nature – an effortless flow through all life, yielding and passive, like water, yet inexhaustible. Its central principle is *Wu Wei*, which can crudely be translated as 'no action', though it is probably better defined as 'no action which runs contrary to nature'.

Taoism was originally the creed of the recluse. A second major text was a book of parables written by the ideal practitioner of The Way, **Zhuang Zi**. Like the master Lao Zi, Zhuang is a semi-mythical figure. Acknowledged in his lifetime as a great sage, he rejected all offers of high rank in favour of a life of solitary reflection. His writings – allegorical tales which have delighted Chinese readers for centuries – reveal humour as well as perception; in the famous butterfly parable Zhuang Zi examined the Chinese acceptance of reality's many faces:

Once upon a time Zhuang Zi dreamed he was a butterfly. A butterfly flying around and enjoying itself. It did not know it was Zhuang Zi. Suddenly he awoke, and veritably he was Zhuang Zi again. We do not know whether it was Zhuang Zi dreaming that he was a butterfly, or a butterfly dreaming he was Zhuang Zi.

As it became part of Chinese culture, Taoism offered a contrast to the stern propriety of Confucianism. In traditional China it was said that the perfect lifestyle was that of a man who was a Confucian during the day – a righteous and firm administrator, upholding the virtues of the gentleman/ruler – and a Taoist after the duties of the day had been fulfilled. The practice of Taoism affirmed the virtues of withdrawing from public duties and giving oneself up to a life of contemplation and meditation. If Confucianism preached duty to family and to society, Taoism championed the sublimity of withdrawal and non-committedness. In its affirmation of the irrational and natural sources of human being, it has provided Chinese culture with a balance to the rigid social mores of Confucianism. The art and literature of China has been greatly enriched by its notions of contemplation, detachment and freedom from social entanglement, and the Tao has become embedded in the Chinese soul as a doctrine of contented yielding to the inevitable forces of Nature.

Buddhism

The Tang dynasty (AD618–906) was a period of unprecedented openness for the Chinese court. It was now that Buddhism, originally imported from India through Central Asia around the 1C AD, gained acceptance and came for a time to be the dominant religion in China. In the 8C there were over 300,000 Buddhist monks in China, and it was a period which saw the creation of much of the country's great religious art – above all the cave shrines at Luoyang (Henan), Datong (Shanxi) and Dunhuang (Gansu), where thousands of carvings of the Buddha and paintings of holy figures attest to the powerful influence of Indian art and religion.

Gradually, though, Buddhism too was submerged into the native belief system. Buddhism as it came from India is a doctrine which teaches that life on earth is essentially one of suffering, and that this is an endless cycle in which people are born, grow old and die only to be born again in other bodies. The goal is to break out of this cycle by attaining nirvana: this is done by losing all desire for things of the world, to withdraw completely from an 'illusory world' and find 'ultimate truth', to withdraw so completely that there is nothing left to be pulled back into another body. Instead the soul remains forever in a state of nirvana. This essentially selfish, individualistic doctrine had already been changed somewhat by the time it reached China. For the Mahayana school of Buddhism, perfection for one was not possible without perfection for all – thus those who had attained enlightenment would remain active in the world (as Bodhisattvas) to help others along the path. In time Bodhisattvas came to be ascribed miraculous powers, and were prayed to as if they were Gods. The mainstream of Chinese Buddhism came to be more about appealing to

Bodhisattvas for aid than about attaining nirvana.

An entirely new sect of Buddhism also arose in China, largely through contact with Taoism. Known in China as *Chan*, in Japan as **Zen Buddhism**, it offered a less extreme path to enlightenment. For a Chan Buddhist it is not necessary to become a monk or a recluse in order to achieve nirvana – instead this ultimate state of being could be reached through a life in accord with and in contemplation of The Way.

Buddhism, essentially nihilist, could hardly be further from the strict practicality of the Confucian code. 'Life, death, prosperity and health are all questions which we can't solve,' Confucius wrote. Yet these are fundamental concerns of the Buddhist. The doctrines, however, survived in perfect harmony in China. So how did they do it?

When Jesuit missionaries first arrived in China in the 16C and 17C they were astounded and dismayed by the Chinese flexibility of belief. If 'Three Teachings flow into One' why not a fourth, or fifth? As one frustrated Jesuit put it: 'in China, the educated believe nothing and the uneducated believe everything.' For those versed in the classics of Confucianism, Taoism and Buddhism, the normal belief was a healthy and tolerant scepticism. For the great majority of illiterate peasants, however, popular religion offered a plethora of ghosts, spirits, gods and ancestors who ruled over a capricious nature and protected humanity. If Christian missionaries handed out rice, clearly Christ was a powerful figure to place alongside them. In popular Buddhism the hope was to reach the 'Pure Land', a kind of heaven for believers ruled over by a female deity known as the Mother Ruler. Popular Taoism shared this feminine deity, but its concerns were rather with the sorcerers, alchemists and martial arts aficionados who sought solutions to the riddle of immortality.

Modern China
One of the reasons why modern China appears to lack the outward manifestation of her ancient beliefs is that they are not really essential. You will see the traditions more clearly expressed in how the Chinese think and act than in the symbols and rituals of overt worship. They represent who the Chinese are as much as what they believe.

This century, confronted by the superior military and technical power of the west, the Chinese have striven to change this nature. The Imperial examinations were abolished at the turn of the century and, ever since, Chinese intellectuals have been searching for a modern yet essentially Chinese, philosophy appropriate to the 20C. The Cultural Revolution can be seen as the culmination of these efforts to repudiate the past. Hundreds of thousands of temples, ancestral halls and religious objects were defaced and destroyed. Monasteries which had preserved their seclusion for centuries were burnt to the ground and their monks imprisoned. The Classics – the 'residue of the reactionary feudal past' – were burned in huge celebratory bonfires. At the end of the Cultural Revolution, in 1974, a campaign was launched to 'criticise Lin Biao and Confucius', pairing the general with the sage to imply that both were equally reactionary in their opposition to the government.

Yet the very fact that Confucius could be held up as an object for criticism in 1974 reveals the tenacity of traditional beliefs. Now, more and more, they are accepted as an essential part of the cultural tradition which binds the Chinese people together. The older generation, though inspired by a lifetime of commitment to a Marxist revolution, are comforted and strengthened by their knowledge of the national heritage. The young are rediscovering the classics. As one young writer,* a member of the 'lost generation' of Cultural Revolution activists, put it:

> Tradition is an eternal present; to neglect it is to neglect ourselves. We should, in the course of creation and criticism, begin from an exploration of the intrinsic elements of tradition, absorb them into our poems, and then enrich that tradition with our creations. . . . The more of tradition we can lay claim to in this way, the more distinct will be our realization of our own creative and innovative mission, the greater will be our place in history.

*Yang Lian in *Shanhua*, trans. Ginger Li.

CHINESE ART

This very brief survey aims to reflect, and to help you to follow, what you are likely to see most of in Chinese provincial and city museums – and to an extent in situ. Many of the museums have a similar layout and similar contents – some of the exhibits being copies of key discoveries from other areas – but often there is little or no explanation for Europeans.

The earliest Chinese objects are from the Neolithic farmers of the **Yangshao** culture – well-made **pottery** vessels in red, brown and buff ware, painted in red, black, brown and white with geometrical designs. You'll notice that the decoration is usually from the shoulders of the pots upwards; this is because what has survived is mostly from graves and was designed to be seen from above when the pots were placed round the dead. From the same period there are decorated clay heads, perhaps for magic or ritual, and pendants and small ornaments of polished stone or jade, with designs which are sometimes semi-abstract – there's a simplified sitting bird in polished jade which is a very early example of the powerful Chinese tradition of animal sculpture. Rather later is the Neolithic **Longshan** pottery – black, very thin and fine, wheel-turned and often highly polished, with elegant sharply defined shapes.

The subsequent era, from some 1500 years BC, is dominated by **Shang and Zhou bronze vessels**, used for preparing and serving food and wine, and for ceremonies and sacrifices. There are many distinct shapes, each with its own name and specific usage; one of the most common is the *ding*, a three- or four-legged vessel which harks back to the Neolithic pots used for cooking over open fires. As you'll see from the museums, these bronzes have survived in great numbers. The **Shang** bronze industry seems to appear already fully developed with advanced techniques and designs – no sign of a primitive stage. Casting methods were highly sophisticated, using moulds and the lost wax process, while design was firm and assured and decoration often stylised and linear, using both geometric and animal motifs, and grinning masks of humans and fabulous beasts. There are some naturalistic animal forms

among the vessels too – fierce tigers, solid elephants and surly-looking rhinoceros. Other bronze finds include weapons, decorated horse harness and sets of bells used in ritual music. Later, under the **Zhou**, the style of the bronzes becomes more varied and rich: some animal vessels are fantastically shaped and extravagantly decorated; others are simplified natural forms; others again seem to be depicting not so much a fierce tiger, for example, as utter ferocity itself. You will also see from the Shang and Zhou small objects – ornaments, ritual pieces, jewellery-pendants – with highly simplified but vivid forms of tortoises, salamanders and flying birds. From the end of this period there are also painted clay funeral figures and a few carved wooden figures.

The Shang produced a few small sculptured human figures and animals in marble and works in stone begin to be found in great quantities in **Han dynasty** tombs. The decorated bricks and tiles, the bas reliefs, the terracotta figurines of acrobats, horsemen, ladies in waiting placed in the tombs to serve the dead, even the massive stone men and beasts set to guard the Spirit Way leading to the tomb, all are lifelike and reflect a concern with everyday activities and material possessions. The scale models of houses with people looking out of the windows and of farmyards with their animals have a spontaneous gaiety and vigour; some of the watchdogs are the most realistic of all. Smaller objects like tiny statuettes and jewellery were also carved, from ivory, jade and wood.

It was the advent of **Buddhism** which encouraged stone carving on a large scale in the round, with mallet and chisel. Religious sculpture was introduced from India and in the 4C caves at DATONG and the earlier of the caves at LONGMEN, near Luoyang, the Indian influence is most strongly felt in the stylised Buddhas and attendants, sometimes of huge size, which have an aloof grace and a rhythmic quality in their flowing robes – but also a smooth, bland and static quality. Not until the **Tang** do you get the full flowering of a native Chinese style, where the figures are rounder, with movement, and the positions, expressions and clothes are more natural and realistic. Some of the best examples are to be seen at DUNHUANG and the later caves at LONGMEN. The Song continued to carve religious figures and at Dazu in Sichuan you will find good examples of a highly decorative style which had broadened its subject matter to include animals, ordinary people and scenes of everyday life; the treatment is down to earth, individual, sometimes even comic. The Dazu carvings are very well preserved and you see them painted, as they were meant to be. In later years less statuary was produced until the Ming emperors indulged their taste for massive and impressive tomb sculptures; you can see the best of these at NANJING and BEIJING.

In **ceramics** the Chinese tradition is very old. From the Neolithic painted pottery described above onwards, China developed a high level of excellence, based on the availability of high quality materials. Her pre-eminence was recognised by the fact that for more than 400 years the English language has been calling the stuff you eat off 'china'. In some of the early wares you can see the influence of shapes derived from bronzes, but soon the rise of regional potteries using different materials, and the development of special types for different uses, led to an enormous variety of shapes, textures and colours. This was noticeable by the **Tang** when an increase in the production of pottery for daily use was partly stimulated by the spread of tea drinking and by the restriction of the use of copper and bronze to coinage. The Tang also saw major technical advances; the production of true porcelain was finally achieved and Tang potters became very skilled in the use of polychrome glazing. You can see evidence of this in the *San Cai* – three colour – statuettes of horses and camels, jugglers, traders, polo players, grooms, court ladies, which have come in great numbers from Imperial tombs, and which reflect in vivid, often humourous, detail and still-brilliant colours so many aspects of the life of the time. It was a cosmopolitan civilisation open to foreign influences and this is clearly seen in Tang art.

The **Song** witnessed a great refinement of ceramic techniques and of regional specialisation, many wares being named by the area which produced them. The keynote was simplicity and quiet elegance, both in colour and form. There was a preference for using a single pure colour and for incised wares looking like a damask cloth. In the museums you will see the famous green celadons, the thin white porcelain *Ding* ware and the pale grey-green *Ju* ware reserved for Imperial use. The Mongol **Yuan** dynasty, in the early 14C, enriched Chinese tradition with outside influences – notably the introduction of cobalt blue underglaze, early examples of the blue and white porcelain which was to become so famous. The **Ming** saw the flowering of great potteries under imperial patronage, especially *Jingdezhen*. Taste moved away from Song simplicity and returned to the liking for vivid colour which the Tang had displayed – deep red, yellow and orange glazes, with a developing taste for pictorial representation. From the 17C Chinese export wares flowed in great quantity and variety to the west to satisfy a growing demand for chinoiserie, and the efforts of the Chinese artists to follow what they saw as the tastes and techniques of the west produced a style of its own. The early **Qing** produced delicate enamel wares and famille rose and verte. So precise were the craftsmen that some porcelain includes the instructions for the pattern in the glaze.

You can visit several potteries such as JINGDEZHEN, FOSHAN and GONGXIAN near Luoyang, where you will see both early wares and modern trends. Five years ago they were turning out thousands of figurines of Mao or of Lu Xun sitting in his armchair; now the emphasis is on table lamp bases in the shape of archaic maidens in flowing robes playing the lute, or creased and dimpled Laughing Buddhas.

All the objects so far described were produced by nameless craftsmen, but with **painting and calligraphy** we enter the realm of the amateur whose name has survived and who was often scholar, official, poet or all three. It has been said that the four great treasures of Chinese painting are the brush, the ink, the inkstone and the paper or silk. The earliest brush found, from about 400BC, is made of animal hairs glued to a hollow bamboo tube. Ink was made from pine soot mixed with glue and hardened into a stick; this would be rubbed with water on an inkstone made of non-porous slate, carved and decorated. Silk was used for painting as early as the 3C BC and paper was invented by *Cai Lun* in AD106. The first known **painting on silk** was found in a **Han** tomb; records show that there was a great deal of such painting but in AD190 the vast Imperial collection was destroyed in a civil war – the soldiers used the silk to make tents and knapsacks. So all we know of Han painting is from decorated tiles, lacquer, painted pottery and a few painted tombs, enough to show a great sense of movement and energy. About AD400 there was a famous painter *Gu Kaizhi* and a scroll in ink and colour on silk attributed to him – *Admonitions of the Instructress to Court Ladies* – is in the British Museum; we know that the theory of painting was already being discussed, since the treatise 'The Six Principles of Painting' dates from about AD500.

The **Sui–Tang** period, with a powerful stable empire and a brilliant court, was exactly the place for painting to develop and a great tradition of figure painting grew up, especially of court subjects – portraits, pictures of the emperor receiving envoys, court ladies, of which several are to be seen in Beijing. Although only a few of these survived, the walls of Tang tombs such as those near XI'AN are rich in vivid frescoes which provide a realistic portrayal of court life. Wang Wei in the mid-8C was an early exponent of monochrome **landscape** painting, but the great flowering of landscape painting came with the **Song**. An Academy was set up under Imperial patronage and different schools of painting emerged which analysed the natural world with great concentration and intensity; their style has set a mark on Chinese landscape painting ever since. There was also lively **figure painting**. There's a famous 17-foot long horizontal scroll in Beijing which shows the Qing Ming River Festival with great liveliness. The last Emperor of the northern Song *Hui Zong* was himself a painter of some note, which indicates the status of painting in China at the time. The southern Song preferred a more intimate style and such subjects as flowers, birds and still lifes grew in popularity.

Under the **Mongols** there were many officials who found themselves unwanted or unwilling to serve the alien Yuan dynasty and who preferred to retire and paint. This produced the **'literati' school**, with many painters harking back to the styles of the 10C. One of the great masters was *Ni Can*. He, among many others, also devoted himself to the ink paintings of bamboo which became important at this time. In this school, of which there is much to be seen, the highest skills of technique and composition were applied to the simplest of subjects, as also with the paintings of plum flowers. Both of these continued to be employed by painters of the next three or more centuries. From the **Yuan** onwards a tremendous quantity of paintings have survived. Under the **Ming** dynasty there was a great interest in collecting the works of previous ages and a linked willingness by painters to be influenced by tradition. So you will see bamboo and plum blossom, and bird and flower paintings being brought to a high decorative pitch, as well as a number of schools of landscape painting firmly rooted in traditional techniques. The arrival of the Manchu **Qing** dynasty did not disrupt the continuity of Chinese painting, but the art became wide open to many influences. It included the Italian *Castiglione* (Lang Shi-ning in Chinese) who specialised in horses, dogs and flowers under Imperial patronage, the Four Wangs who re-interpreted Song and Yuan styles in an orthodox manner, and the individualists such as the Eight Eccentrics of Yangzhou and some Buddhist monks who objected to derivative art and sought a more distinctive approach to subject and style. But on the whole the weight of tradition was powerful enough to maintain the old approach.

Calligraphy is literally 'beautiful writing' and the use of the brush saw the development of handwriting of various styles crystallise into a high art form, valued on a par with painting. There are a number of different scripts; the *seal script* is the archaic form found on oracle bones; the *lishu* is the clerical style and was used in inscriptions on stone, while the *kaishu* is the regular style closest to the modern printed form and cao shu – cursive, *grass* or *running* script – is the most individual handwritten style. Emperors, poets and scholars over centuries have left examples of their calligraphy cut into stone at beauty spots, on mountains and in grottoes, tombs and temples all over China. You can see some early examples in the caves at LONGMEN. At one stage in the Tang calligraphy was so highly thought of that it was the yardstick for the selection of high officials.

Two other art forms should be mentioned which have been constantly in use in China since earliest times – jade and lacquer. In Chinese eyes **jade** is the most precious of stones, very hard, in white and shades of green or brown. It was used to make the earliest ritual objects, such as the flat disc *Pi*, symbol of Heaven, which was found in Shang and Zhou graves and later. It was also used as a mark of rank and for ornament; perhaps its most striking use was in the jade burial suits which you will see. **Lacquer** is also found as early as the Zhou. It is made from the sap of the lac tree; many layers were painted on a wood or cloth base which was then carved and inlaid with gold, silver or tortoiseshell, or often most delicately painted. There are numerous examples of painted lacquer boxes and baskets from the Han and, as with jade, the use of this material has continued ever since.

In looking at **Chinese museums** it should be remembered that over more than 2000 years an empire with a splendid court inevitably produced an incredible wealth of art objects. However, from the mid-19C onwards many of these were acquired – more or less legitimately – or looted, by westerners. Later, too, some of the great Imperial collections were removed by the Nationalists to Taiwan, where they are now in the National Palace Museum. On the other hand recent years have produced many great archaeological finds, from which are drawn many new treasures.

CHINESE ARCHITECTURE

After several weeks in China you may find yourself reflecting that – apart from regional variations depending on climate and local materials – one temple looks very much like another, the differences between a palace, a pavilion or a substantial private house are negligible and that there is little sign of historical development.

On the whole, you would be right. Remarkably little has survived of the buildings of the world's longest continuous civilisation. Early structures were mainly of wood and were vulnerable to flood, fire, earthquakes and enemies; Emperors – for reasons political or economic – might up-sticks and set up a new capital elsewhere, abandoning their earlier palaces to crumble to dust; and a new dynasty often made a clean sweep and built afresh, either elsewhere or over the ruins of its defeated predecessors. There are half a dozen different early capitals in and near Xi'an, and the passion for continuity and precedent ensured that many structures were rebuilt several times over and in the same style – a style which had developed by the Han and crystallised by the 10C.

Whether for a capital city, Imperial palace, ceremonial building or dwelling house, the position and **site** were all-important and were determined by *Feng Shui* – literally wind and water – a form of divining to assess those intangible forces which would ensure the building a favourable ambiance and shield it from evil influences. A single structure, a group of buildings or indeed a whole city, would be carefully orientated according to the points of the compass: southward-facing on a north–south axis, inside a walled enclosure with a screen or gate to deflect evil.

Excavations have uncovered the plans of Bronze Age town sites and Shang and Zhou dynasty capital cities and tombs, whilst from the huge building works of the Qin there is more substantial evidence: above ground, the Great Wall and Imperial palaces; below, tombs and, at Xi'an, a city for the dead Emperor and his guardian Terracotta Army. Well before the Han dynasty, then, there was an established pattern of **rectangular cities** – sometimes varied to fit in with

natural features – guarded by high outer walls with gates and towers in each side. Main thoroughfares on a grid pattern linked the main gates and within the city proper was a walled Imperial city and within that again an Imperial palace. In the remaining area were residential and commercial quarters. This remained the pattern and was echoed in temple and domestic architecture down the centuries, although timber was generally used for the less permanent living quarters, stone and brick being kept for tombs, bridges and ceremonial buildings.

The native Chinese building tradition – pagodas are part of the Buddhist tradition from India – also used a single basic **building structure**, varied only according to status. On a raised platform which could be earth, brick or stone according to the building's importance, wooden columns rested on stone bases; the heads of the columns were linked by beams running lengthways and across, to provide the structural framework, to give stability and to bear the roof. Beams of diminishing length, raised one above the other on short posts set on the beam below, created an interlocking structure which was often put together without a single nail and rose to the point of the roof where single posts at the centre supported the roof ridge.

This structure produced the characteristic **curved roof**, with its spreading upcurled eaves. The roofs, which in poorer houses or in very early times might have been thatch, could now be heavier ceramic tiles; cantilevered brackets allowed the curving eaves to extend well beyond the pillars; the eaves acquired an increasingly decorative value which was supplemented by the lines of carved animals and figures on the gable ends of the roof. Variety was supplied by colour from the paint used to protect the wood – red for the columns and walls, blue and green for the brackets and yellow, green and blue for the roof tiles. Imperial buildings might be distinguished by four-sided roofs, by higher platforms reached by wide staircases and by special yellow glazed tiles for the roofs. Inside the building the spaces between the columns were filled by screens providing different combinations of wall, door, latticework, which could be removed or changed to alter the spaces within.

Common threads also run through the arrangement of **groups of buildings**, in compounds. These are characterised by high outer walls, their entrance closed by solid doors and giving onto a courtyard further protected by a painted screen, to ward off evil influences. In case any of the evil influences should manage to get past the screen the first courtyard contains the servants' quarters; a secondary opening or a moon gate – so called from its shape – leads through to a courtyard beyond which contains the family living quarters. You can see good examples of this layout in the centre of Anyang and (on the grand scale) in Beijing's Forbidden City. The same principle, however, applies throughout central and northern China's traditional domestic and ceremonial architecture.

Buddhist temples, once adapted to China, followed the pattern, an entrance in their high compound wall leading to a succession of halls in a series of courtyards. The entrance is usually protected by two massive painted plaster guardians; the first hall dedicated to the Four Heavenly Kings of the Four Directions, with the Maitreya (laughing Buddha) in the centre flanked by Wei Tuo the God of Wisdom. The main hall will have a statue of *Sakyamuni* with several *Buddhas* and *Boddhisattvas* on either side; behind him and facing the other way will be Guanyin the Goddess of Mercy, riding the waves on mythical fish, a few *Arhats* or *Lohans* (Buddhist saints) may line the side walls but if there are a lot of them they will have a hall to themselves.

The earliest wooden **pagodas** were introduced from India but the square brick style harks back to indigenous watch towers. Most surviving pagodas are polygonal with a central stairway rising through an uneven number of storeys – anything from 3 to 17; many of them were built to house Buddhist relics. Buddhism also gave rise to the extraordinary **cave temples** and grottoes, best preserved in the north-west at Binglingsi and Mogao.

Taoist temples are very similar to Buddhist temples, being a series of halls dedicated to mythical and legendary figures such as the Yellow Emperor and the Eight Immortals, or to historical people who were canonised like Guan Yu and Zhu Geliang of the Three Kingdoms period.

In the towns and cities you will see various **more modern styles** of architecture reflecting the history of the last 150 years or so. From the mid-19C onwards, in Treaty Ports and their Concessions, **European** merchants, banks, shipping firms, missionaries built offices, warehouses, Customs Houses and churches which, often carved up for Chinese use, still give those places a distinctive look. Hankou, part of Wuhan, has a Customs House and whole streets of European buildings. Shanghai waterfront looks like any great Victorian seaport. Often there are hill resorts nearby which were also built for Europeans and look like it, as do coastal resorts like Qingdao and Yantai. European building continued on into the 1930s.

After Liberation, under the Republic, Chinese building developed the use of Chinese styles with modern materials. Sometimes this amounted to no more than a curl in the roof, but you can find, as in Chongqing, a large hotel built in the style of a Ming palace. During the 1950s the favourite style was Soviet 'brutal' – you can't tell a factory from a hotel – and since then a modern international style has developed, exemplified in high-rise building in Beijing and Shanghai and in concrete and glass hotels which might be in any city in the world. Recently, however, there has been the resurgence of an attempt to marry the traditional Chinese idiom with modern needs; in new satellite towns you can find housing being built inside compound walls in the form of a series of courtyards connected by moon gates. And now that private ownership and therefore private building are permitted, you begin to find alongside them two-storey houses being put up by well-to-do peasants.

BOOKS

General introductions

Various, *The Times Atlas of China* (Time Books, 1974). Find a library copy of this for a succinct summary of China's history, well illustrated with maps showing just how much her borders have expanded and shrunk through the centuries. Each province has a separate map and substantial introduction; but beware place names, for this book uses the old Wade-Giles romanisation.

Mark Elvin and Caroline Blunden, *A Cultural Atlas of China* (1984). Another invaluable reference tool and one you can dip into for up to date and authoritative summaries of history, religions and cultural development; plenty of good photographs.

Cyril Birch, ed., *Anthology of Chinese Literature from Earliest Times to the 14th Century* (Penguin Classics, 1967). This survey spans 3000 years of literature, embracing poetry, philosophy, drama, biography and prose fiction, with interesting variations of translation.

Modern history and social

David Bonavia, *The Chinese – A Portrait* (Penguin, 1982). A highly readable introduction to contemporary China, focusing as much on the human aspects as a balance to the socio-political trends. Recommended.

Roger Garside, *China after Mao – Coming Alive* (Andre Deutsch, 1981). Garside served at the British Embassy in Beijing from 1968–1970 and from 1976–1979. Here he describes the aftermath of the Cultural Revolution and the downfall of the 'Gang of Four'.

Fox Butterfield, *China – Alive in the Bitter Sea* (Hodder & Stoughton, 1982). With the death of Mao in 1976, the Dark ages of the Cultural Revolution came to a close; China showed a face of enlightenment and steady progress towards the achievement of the 'Four Modernisations'. Fox Butterfield, *New York Times* correspondent, digs beneath the gleaming surface to catalogue the imperfections. The result is a long list of flaws and shortcomings which severely destracts from what most wide-eyed travellers in China today see as an economic Miracle. The title comes from a Buddhist saying about survival amid a sea of suffering, which aptly describes the experience of many Chinese during and after the Cultural Revolution. A useful book as a counterbalance to official propaganda; though the Chinese customs tend to confiscate it.

John Fraser, *The Chinese – Portrait of a People* (Fontana, 1981). John Fraser, correspondent of the *Toronto Globe and Mail*, arrived in China in 1977, during the turbulent aftermath of the Cultural Revolution. During his two-year stay he travelled widely and became personally involved in the Democracy Movement. *The Chinese* covers the whole spectrum of China in turmoil, from international politics through cumbersome bureaucracy, human rights abuses, to the author's personal relationships with Chinese friends. This period is essential to an understanding of China today.

Travel

Marco Polo, *The Travels* (tr. Penguin, 1965). The substance of this version by Latham, chronicles the journeys to and from Cathay – but by page 85 he is still on the Silk Route. One chapter is a sycophantic encomium to the mighty Kublai Khan, another deals with a journey south from Peking to Amoy. The book is of no use whatever as an aid to understanding or enjoying modern China, but it is amusing and interesting in itself, full of jolly quotes. You have to work very hard with the glossary to find the equivalent of modern place names.

G. E. Morrison, *An Australian in China* (1895, Oxford Paperbacks, 1985). Morrison arrived in China in 1894 and travelled overland to Burma on foot, by mule, in a sedan chair and by riverboat – an extraordinary journey by someone who could not speak a word of the language. His trenchant observations and keen eye make this much more than just a travel book, and laid the foundations for his remarkable despatches to *The Times*.

John Turner, *Kwangtung – or Five years in South China* (1894, Oxford Paperbacks 1984). Another attempt by a missionary to explain China to himself and the rest of the world. This focuses on Southern China, in particular Canton, Macau and Hong Kong.

E. H. Wilson, *A Naturalist in Western China with Vasculum, Camera and Gun*

– being some account of 11 years travel, exploration and observation in remote parts of the Flowery Kingdom (1913, Cadogan Books 1986). During these expeditions in the early 1900s through Hubei, Sichuan, and across the Sino–Tibetan border, to collect seeds and plants for the botanical gardens at Kew, Wilson also amassed a storehouse of facts about natural history and the culture and customs of the various ethnic groups in this remote area.

Mildred Cable with Francesca French, *The Gobi Desert* (1942, Virago 1984). Mildred Cable and Francesca French were missionaries with the China Inland Mission in the early part of this century. They lived most of their lives travelling round the wilder regions of China, then retired to a cottage in Dorset where this book and others were written. 'The Gobi Desert' is a poetic description of their life and travels in Gansu and Xinjiang, without the sanctimonious and patronising tone adopted by some of their contemporary missionaries. Very highly recommended, as is their other book, 'Travels in Northwest China'.

Dymphna Cusack, *Chinese Women Speak* (1958, Century Travellers 1986). Another intrepid Australian writer, born 1902, who followed in Morrison's footsteps to China, where, in the 1930s she spent some 18 months travelling and talking to women of all classes and types, from peasants to Manchu Princesses. Her conversations explore the whole spectrum of Chinese life, from the sale of children to footbinding.

Denton Welch, *Maiden Voyage* (1943, Penguin 1983). Highly idiosyncratic account of life in Shanghai in the 1930s.

Somerset Maugham, *On a Chinese Screen* (1922, Oxford Paperbacks 1985). These are brief, sometimes humorous and often biting sketches of the European missionaries, diplomats and businessmen whom Maugham encountered in China between 1919 and 1921; worth reading for background detail.

Peter Fleming, *One's Company – a Journey to China* (1933, Penguin 1983). This slim volume is an amusing account of a journey through Russia and Manchuria to China. En route, Peter Fleming, brother to Ian and, according to his KGB file 'the Darling of the English Upper Classes', encounters a wild assortment of Chinese and Japanese officials and the puppet Emperor Henry Pu Yi himself.

Peter Fleming, *News from Tartary* (1936, Futura 1983). In 1935, with his equally reckless and unusual companion, Ella Maillart, Fleming travelled 3500 miles across the roof of the world to Kashmir. What he calls 'this undeservedly successful expedition' lasted seven months. Read also Ella Maillart's version of the journey – *Forbidden Journey*.

Vikram Seth, *From Heaven Lake – travels through Sinkiang and Tibet* (Sphere Abacus Paperback, 1983). A student for two years at Nanjing university, Seth set out in 1982 to return home to Delhi via Tibet and Nepal. This account of how he hitched his way through 4 provinces, Xinjiang, Gansu, Qinghai and Tibet, is in the best tradition of the early travel books.

Carl Crow, *A Handbook for China* (1933, Oxford Paperbacks 1984). This was the standard guidebook in the 1930s for the well-heeled globetrotters for whom the advent of the railways had opened up the interior of China. The chapters on hunting, fishing, brigands, pirates, rebellions and Pidgin English may be more nostalgic than they are relevant today, but the section on flora and fauna and the gazetteer entries are fascinating.

Pan Ling, *In Search of Old Shanghai.* **Barry Till**, *In Search of Old Nanjing.* (Joint Publishing Company Hong Kong, 1982). If you're planning to stay some time in either city, these two (modern) guides are entertaining companions.

TIBET

Heinrich Harrer, *Seven Years in Tibet* (1952, Penguin 1984). Delightful book by a German climber who joined the gentry of Tibet in their idyll and became a teacher to the Dalai Lama. Nothing heavy and profound, but fascinating and well written, although one feels that he failed to observe much of the life of the ordinary Tibetan people. Also read *Return to Tibet*, the author's return as a tourist in 1982, and reappraisal of the situation.

Israel Epstein, *Tibet Transformed* (New World Press, Beijing 1983). This book fills in the blanks in Harrer's account of life in Tibet. Israel Epstein – for years editor of China's Foreign Language Press – paints a grisly picture of life in Tibet before 1951; but, predictably enough, he fails to mention a word about the desecrations and injustices perpetrated against the Tibetan people after 'Liberation'. Written in the ghastly, turgid style so beloved of apologists, you can't read it, but it has a host of good pictures. But for sheer callous misrepresentation on the truth, it's a pale shadow of **Han Suyin's**, *Lhasa, the Open City*.

Peter Fleming, *Bayonets to Lhasa* (1947). Fleming's jolly adventure story about the British invasion of Tibet in 1904 – interesting as background.

History
MODERN CHINA
Edwin M. Moise, *Modern China – A History* (Longman, 1986). Probably the most useful and certainly the most up to date history of 20C China. Even-handed and non-academic with as much emphasis on people as on policy.

Agnes Smedley, *China Correspondent* (Pandora 1984). Agnes Smedley travelled in China in the 1930s as war correspondent for the Manchester Guardian. This book is an account of her time as a medic with the Red Army, when she got to know Mao Zedong and Zhou Enlai, and witnessed the emergence of the new China. Probably the best of many books on these events. Also worth looking out is Smedley's *The Great Road – the life and times of Chu Teh*.

Edgar Snow, *Red Star Over China* (1959, Pelican 1978). In 1936, after seven years teaching in China, this 30-year-old American journalist penetrated the Nationalist blockade to reach the 'red' stronghold in Yenan, where the 15-year-old Communist Party had made their base after the 'Long March' from the south. His interviews with Mao and with other leaders provided the west and the rest of China with the first full account of this fledgling movement. Its immediacy still makes it compulsive reading. Also read *Red China Today*, Snow's reappraisal of changing conditions in the 1960s.

Dick Wilson, *The Long March* (1971, Penguin 1977). A well researched account of this astonishing epic; important to an understanding of China today, and a powerful story of adventure and revolution in itself.

Harrison Salisbury, *The Long March* (Macmillan, 1985). A more comprehensive account by the American China-

expert, who retraced the route of the actual march in 1983. Access to previously undisclosed archives and interviews with survivors, from Hu Yaobang to the ferryman, throw new light on the March.

William Hinton, *Fanshen* (Picador, 1970). A documentary of revolution in a Chinese village, by a wealthy American farmer, philanthropist and 'Radical' who threw in his lot with the Chinese peasants during the remodelling of Chinese agriculture after Liberation. *Shenfan* (Picador, 1980) documents his return and re-appraisal.

Liang Heng and Judith Shapiro, *Son of the Revolution* (Fontana, 1983). Liang Heng grew up with the Cultural Revolution; here he documents those years from the point of view of an ordinary Chinese, caught in the cruelty, madness and euphoria. Many books have been written on the Cultural Revolution by foreign observers and experts, but this one gives a new angle on this extraordinary phenomenon.

Jonathan Spence, *The Gate of Heavenly Peace* (1981, Penguin 1982). The Gate of Heavenly Peace guards the Imperial palace in Beijing and is a symbol both of state authority, and of revolution against it. This is a narrative *tour de force* which traces the history of the 20C through the eyes of the men and women caught up in it – writers, revolutionaries, poets, politicians . . . The best book for getting to grips with China's complex modern history.

EARLIER
Witold Rodzinski, *The Walled Kingdom* (Flamingo, 1984). The best complete history of China, from Longshan Man to the 12th CCP Congress in 1982 – the whole lot compressed into 450 pages. A good readable overall view by a leading China historian; his view of history is unashamedly in sympathy with the Communists, as one would expect from a modern eastern bloc scholar.

Jack Chen, *The Sinkiang Story* (1975). A complete history of Xinjiang, from Chaos to Liberation – thoroughly researched, passionate and brilliant, if also a little partisan. Apply the blue pencil lightly and you have the very best available history of Xinjiang; don't go there without reading this book.

Peter Hopkirk, *Foreign Devils on the Silk Road* (OUP, 1980). The story of the machinations of the various international booty-hunters and archaeologists who operated in Eastern Turkestan and the Gobi Desert round the turn of the century. An Elgin Marbles type debate boils today over the rights of possession of the priceless works of early Buddhist art that were discovered under the shifting sands of the Taklamakan desert. Essential for an appreciation of China's north-west regions.

Peter Hopkirk, *Trespassers on the Roof of the World* (OUP, 1980). Around the turn of the century, Imperial Britain, with the help of a remarkable band of Pundits and Wallahs from the Indian Survey, was discreetly charting every nook of the most inaccessible part of the earth – the High Tibetan Plateau. Peter Hopkirk has researched his subject thoroughly and come up with a highly readable account of this fascinating backwater of history.

Jacques Gernet, *Daily life in China on the Eve of the Mongol Invasion 1250–1276* (1959, Allen & Unwin 1962). Based on a wide variety of Chinese sources, including local gazetteers, letters and anecdotes, this is a fascinating and detailed survey of southern China under the Song, focussing on the capital, Hangzhou, then the largest and richest city in the world. He also deals with the daily lives of a cross section of society from peasant to leisured gentry, covering everything from cookery to death.

Peter Fleming, *The Siege at Peking* (1959, Oxford Paperbacks 1983). An account of the events which led up to 20 June 1900, when the foreign legations in Beijing were attacked by the 'Boxers' and the Chinese Imperial troops. The siege, which lasted 55 days, led to a watershed in China's relations with the rest of the world.

BIOGRAPHIES
There is a lot to be said for reading about the life of one interesting individual rather than trying to tackle the monumental sweep of China's long history.

Jung Chang with Jon Halliday, *Madame Sun Yatsen* (Penguin, 1986). Soong Li was the American educated daughter of the famous Soong family; she was 22 in 1915, when she married Dr Sun Yatsen, leader of the new Republic. After his death, she remained a staunch opponent of Chiang Kai-shek,

although he was married to her sister. She survived the political snakes and ladders to become honorary president of the Communist party before her death in May 1981.

Jonathan Spence, *The Death of Woman Wang* (Penguin 1979). Against the backdrop of a provincial county in Shandong in the 17C, Spence focusses on the lives of real ordinary people; for example, an irascible farmer, his unhappy wife, set against the grim cycle of floods, crop failures, the attentions of bandits and rapacious tax-collectors. Carefully researched from archives including local magistrates' reports and Gazetteers.

Jonathan Spence, *Emperor of China, Self Portrait of Kang Xi* (Jonathan Cape, 1974). A magnificent portrait of the longest reigning and probably the greatest emperor of modern China. Spence has sifted through letters, confidential palace memoes and writings to reveal the workings of an extraordinary mind whose scientific curiosity, political acumen, patronage of the arts and enormous energy for travel and hunting make fascinating reading.

Marina Warner, *The Dragon Empress* (Weidenfeld, 1972). Exploration of the life of a very different character, that of Zi Xi – one of only two women rulers of China. Born in 1935, daughter of a minor mandarin, she became an imperial concubine, then schemed and plotted her way to her most powerful role as Dowager Empress from 1861 to 1908. Warner lays bare the complex personality of a ruthless woman whose conservatism, passion for power, vanity and greed had such an impact on events which culminated in the collapse of the Imperial ruling house and the founding of the Republic.

Hugh Trevor-Roper, *Hermit of Peking: the Hidden Life of Sir Edmund Backhouse* (Penguin, 1978). Drawn from the voluminous (and often obscene) memoirs of this distinguished scholar and eccentric, who died in 1944. Amongst his more outrageous claims was that of intimacy with the Dowager Empress.

Literature
As well as a handful of translations of some of the great classics of Chinese literature published in Britain and the US there are also a good many cheap editions published by the Foreign

Languages Press (FLP) in Beijing available in the foreign language sections of bookshops in China. These can be well worth buying for those long waits and even longer journeys after your own supply of books has run out.

FICTION

Arthur Waley, *Monkey, A Journey to the West* (Unwin, 1979). Translation of Wu Chengen's 16C rewrite of the legendary journey of the Monk Tripitaka and his companions, Monkey, Piggy and Sandy to India is based on the real-life pilgrim Xuan Zang who brought back cartloads of Buddhist scriptures to the Tang capital in the 7C. This fantastical tale has spawned a host of operas, paintings and children's toys through the centuries.

Cao Xueqin, *The Story of the Stone* (Penguin, 3 vols, 1973, 1977, 1980). Also known as *The Romance of the Red Chamber* or *A Dream of Red Mansions*, this great semi-autobiographical novel of manners was written around 1760 by a man whose family had been commissioners of Imperial Textiles in Nanjing for several generations. He charts both the glory and the decline of the Jia family through the everyday lives and the relationships between the members of this family and their servants. The characterisation and detail of this magnificent translation make it a joy to read.

Wu Qingzi, *The Scholars, tr, Yang Xianyi and Gladys Yang* (FLP, Beijing, 1973). A somewhat long-drawn-out but amusing chronicle of the gentry class, set loosely in 17C China, that takes the lid off the bureaucracy, corruption, the literati and the examination system – the ladder many tried to climb in their pursuit of social and material advancement.

Lu Xun, *Short Stories, Selected Stories* and *Old tales Retold* (FLP, 1970s). These are all translations by Gladys Yang and Yang Xianyi of Xun's semi-autobiographical stories, many about his childhood in Shaoxing.

Lao She, *Rickshaw Boy* (FLP, 1982). The author was driven to suicide during the Cultural Revolution but was later rehabilitated. The story is a haunting account of a young rickshaw puller in pre-1949 Beijing.

AUTOBIOGRAPHY

Ba Jin, *Family* (1931, Anchor 1972). Born in 1904 into a wealthy Chengdu family, Ba Jin attacks the old family feudal system, chronicles his anarchist phase from age 15 until 1949 and traces the strong influence worked on him by Russian writers like Turgenev.

Naisingoro Pu Yi, *From Emperor to Citizen* (FLP, Beijing, 1983). The autobiography of the young boy, born into the Qing Imperial family and chosen by the Japanese to become the puppet emperor of the state of Manchukuo in 1931. Soon to be a major film!

Han Suyin, *The Crippled Tree, A Mortal Flower* and *Birdless summer* (Panther, 1972). Passionate account of the making of modern China. Bertrand Russell said of it 'during the first of many hours I spent reading it I learnt more about China than I did in a whole year spent in that country'.

Nien Cheng, *Life and Death in Shanghai* (Grafton Books, 1986). Harrowing personal account of the effects of the Cultural Revolution on this British-educated Chinese woman, denounced as a class enemy in 1966.

Art & architecture

Jessica Rawson, *Ancient China – Art and Archaeology* (British Museum Publications Paperback 1980). This scholarly introduction to Chinese art from the deputy keeper of oriental antiquities at the BM puts Chinese art in its historical context; beginning in Neolithic times, it explores the technology and social organisation which shaped its development up to the Han dynasty.

Mary Tregear, *Chinese Art* (Thames & Hudson, 1980). Authoritative summary of the main strands in Chinese art from Neolithic times, through the Bronze Age and up to the 20C. Both clearly written and well illustrated.

Sickman & Soper, *The Art and Architecture of China* (Pelican History of Art Series, 1971). **Michael Sullivan**, *The Arts of China* (Thames & Hudson, 1977). Two more standard works which may help to make museums and temples in China more accessible.

Religion

Kenneth Chen, *Buddhism in China* (Princetown, 1973). Very helpful if you want to trace the origin of Buddhist thought in China, the development of its many different schools and the four-way traffic of influence between India, Tibet, Japan and China.

Arthur Waley, transl., *Three Ways of Thought in Ancient China* (Allen & Unwin, 1939). Translated extracts from the writings of three of the early philosophers – Zhuang Zi, Mencius and Han Feizi. A useful introduction.

Confucius, *The Analects* (Penguin, 1979), **Lao zi**, *Tao Te Ching* (Penguin, 1963), Mencius (Penguin, 1970). Good modern translations of these classic texts.

TRAVEL ONWARDS: THE TRANS-SIBERIAN EXPRESS

Because of the availability of cheap air tickets in Hong Kong, travel onwards from China can mean just about anywhere. Basically, get yourself down to Hong Kong and take your pick . . . Rather more exciting though – and a unique opportunity if you've never been – is to make a leisurely way back to the west via the Soviet Union on the Trans-Siberian Express, 8000 kilometres of Asia and Europe rolling past your window for a fraction of the cost of flying.

Finally completed in 1916 after nearly half a century of piecemeal construction and bureaucratic bickering, the Trans-Siberian railway is the longest continuous rail line in the world, the vision of numerous engineers inspired by the idea of conquering such vast and inhospitable expanses with modern technology. The journey takes you through seven time zones, four Soviet republics, across two major mountain ranges and four mighty rivers: the equivalent, very roughly, of travelling from Shanghai to Istanbul. The difference with the Trans-Siberian is that most of this immense distance is contained within the borders of one country, the Soviet Union.

The line traditionally runs from Vladivostok in the east, but because of its sensitivity as a naval base this has long been closed to foreign tourists and nowadays you can either travel from Khabaravosk in Russia itself, or from Beijing in China. From Beijing, on the Chinese train you cross two borders, into Mongolia, on the Russian train only one, but the journey takes you through the undefined lands of many races, from Chinese through Mongolians, Cossacks, Uzbecks, Bruyats, Uighurs and finally Russians. Gradually, the landscape changes, and the golden roofs of Beijing and mud dwellings of northern China become the yurts and grasslands of Mongolia, the tinsel towns of Siberia, and, eventually, the domes and spires of European Russia. Asian peasant agriculture slowly gives way to the heavy industrialisation of Soviet Russia, all giving the chance to gently disengage yourself from the East. Politically, too, the trip is revealing. In the 1950s the Chinese saw the Soviet Union as their socialist mentor, and up until the recent opening of China to western (capitalist) technology and expertise, the Soviet Union was China's sole model for modernisation and industrial development. Travelling from one enormous socialist nation to another, and comparing Russia to its one-time protégé, speaks volumes about modern socialism.

Practical details

You can pick up information on the Trans-Siberian before you leave Britain from *Intourist* (official tourist agency of the Soviet Union), who have offices in London at 292 Regent Street, W1 (01–631 1252) and in Manchester at 41 Deansgate M3 2BW (061–834 0230). In Beijing itself there are a number of things to consider before reserving your ticket and getting your visas: these are, briefly, whether to take the Russian or Chinese train; which class to travel; and which country to use as exit-point from the Soviet Union.

The **Chinese train** (#3) leaves Beijing each Wednesday at 7.40am, travels north through Mongolia and arrives in Moscow the following Monday at 4.40pm – a six-day trip. It's slightly cheaper than the Russian train and is said to have better food and cleaner compartments. The **Russian train** (#19) takes half a day longer, leaving Saturday at 18.07pm heading north through Manchuria and reaching Moscow the following Friday at 1.56pm but it does give ever-bubbling samovars and the complete experience of travelling through Russia with Russian attendants and Russian food. On the whole, though, there's not a huge amount to choose between the two, and it's really down to your own schedule which you decide to use. With both, some rides are better than others.

On both trains three **classes** are available. Third class, which most budget travellers choose, is perfectly comfortable, with 4-bunk compartments, sheets and blankets and a PA system which you can switch off (luxury after the din of Chinese hard seat class). A ticket from Beijing to Berlin costs around ¥650. For another ¥120 you can travel second class, though all that gives you is an extra frill on the seat covers and a location slightly closer to the dining car. First class, however, is a different story, truly a rolling reminder of a past era, with teak-panelled double cabins and a shared bathroom and shower that at about ¥800 (to Moscow) could be a worthwhile investment if you've just spent several weeks slumming it in Chinese dormitories.

Reservations can be made in advance at CITS in Beijing or any branch of CITS in a major Chinese city including Guangzhou, Shanghai, Kunming and Chengdu. You can't, however, pick up or pay for your ticket until you have all the necessary **visas** stamped in your passport – a process for which you should allow at least a week in Beijing.

Before the Soviet Embassy will give you a stamp you must already have a visa for the country you intend to leave Russia by. Also, if you intend to take the Chinese train you need a visa for Mongolia, which they will not issue unless you can show your Soviet visa. All this is further complicated by the uncoordinated opening hours of the various embassies and the fact that some of them are less than helpful. Give over a day for the Soviet Embassy alone: they're always crowded and aren't terribly efficient. Basically, it's best to do things in the following order: first apply for your visa for your country of exit, then pick up your Soviet visa (it takes about a week) and head off to the Mongolian Embassy to get your third and final visa. Then you can return to CITS, flash your fully stamped passport and collect your ticket.

Some details on visa requirements: for a Soviet Visa you need three photographs and the cost is ¥15 (some nationalities ¥36); a Mongolian visa costs $2 (US nationals $4), takes about 2 hours to get and you need one photo; for a Polish visa you need 2 photos and ¥15, and you have to wait about an hour; a Hungarian visa costs ¥15, takes two days and demands two photos; and for Romania and Finland you don't need a visa at all. Chinese camera stores and/or photographic studios, many centred on Wangfujing Lu next to the Peking Hotel, will take small black and white visa photos, develop them and have them back to you the same afternoon or next day. For addresses and opening hours of the embassies, see p. 87.

On the train, the **currency** demanded in the dining car changes as you pass from China through Mongolia (if you're on the Chinese train) to the Soviet Union. No Chinese money is accepted after you've crossed the border. There are facilities for changing Chinese FECs into Mongolian roubles on the border, and for changing currency into Russian roubles on the Russian border. When you leave the Soviet Union make sure you have your exchange certificates proving you have changed at least as much as you want to change back: there is a huge black market in currency exchange and this is one method of curbing it. As far as **food** goes, it's advisable, though not essential, to bring your own. Supplies do run low, and one group's party the night before may result in unavoidable temperance for the entire train for the rest of the trip. But, in spite of the rumours of diets of black bread and water, or only champagne and caviar, usually the Trans-Siberian dining cars are quite adequate. And there are kiosks in every train station that often sell a broad array of cheese, beer, pastries, bread and Siberian delicacies. Coffee and tea are worth bringing along, as the hot water supply is endless; Chinese 'convenient' noodles make a quick and filling lunch; and fresh fruit will help keep you healthy.

Normally a Soviet transit visa gives you 48 hours to organise your passage out of Moscow and reach your **country of exit**. The most popular route to the west – and much the quickest and cheapest – is through Poland to East Berlin, and from there to the neon and vitality of West Berlin (both of which are covered in the forthcoming Rough Guide to Berlin). Alternatives are Hungary or Romania (see the new Rough Guide to Eastern Europe) or Finland (also soon to be part of a new Rough Guide). You can book a ticket to all these countries in Beijing, though you always have to change trains in Moscow (cross town from Yaroslavsky to Belorusskaya Station) and book a new berth on the on-going connection. While in Moscow if you want to **stay overnight** the alternatives are, if you're broke, limited. Intourist hotel rates start at about $30 a night; if you can't afford that you can either sleep in the railway station (plastic bucket seats and marble floors) or, if you're discreet, curl up on the couches of an Intourist hotel lobby.

Finally, if you're using the Trans-Siberian as a springboard for further travel in the **SOVIET UNION**, be prepared to do a great deal more advance planning and spend a lot more money. On the train, stopovers are permitted in Novosibirsk, capital of Western Siberia, and Irkutsk on the shores of Lake Baikal. A regular tourist visa takes at least three weeks to get, and your application must include your itinerary in the Soviet Union. In processing your application, Intourist will book you into hotels in all the cities you wish to visit and reserve train and plane tickets for you. Prices are fixed – rates range from $30 to $80 – and you have to pay when you pick up your visa.

LANGUAGE

You don't need to worry about not speaking Chinese – most foreign visitors can't, relying instead on the prodigious enthusiasm of the Chinese for learning English. In every major town, and even places out of the way, you're likely to meet someone who speaks a little English and who'll be only too pleased to get in some practice – with an eagerness that can sometimes be overbearing. But sooner or later you're going to be stumped for an English speaker, and it's then that a simple knowledge of Chinese will prove indispensable. As with every language, if you make just a little effort, people will appreciate it and respond. A few phrases like 'Hello, How are you, Please, Thank you, I live in Birmingham, The Workers Of Britain unite with me and salute the Red Flag Tractor Production Brigade' and so on, will really pay off. What follows isn't intended to be anything like a definitive account of Chinese but a simple description of the language and a few handy phrases. If you're staying in China any amount of time you'd be well advised to buy a phrasebook and dictionary.

Chinese is perhaps the oldest continuous spoken language in the world. Before 1949 few Chinese spoke anything but their local dialect, of which there were eight major variants, all pretty well mutually unintelligible. The Communists, seeing this as an obstacle to effective administration, encouraged the use of **Mandarin** as a lingua franca. Today, Mandarin, *Putonghua* or 'common speech' will get you by in most parts of China. Mandarin is predominantly monosyllabic – made up of simple one-syllable units – which may seem rather limited since the language does not make use of the different consonantal groups like Gr, Str, Sl, that we use. Each monosyllable ends with either a vowel or with -n or -ng, obviously a considerable limitation. There are in fact 400 different monosyllable units; the shortage is made up by **tones**. Mandarin has four tones, a difficult concept for the speaker of a non-tonal language to master.

The **level tone**, used without varying the pitch *mā* (Mother)
The **rising tone** *má* (hemp)
The **falling tone** *mà* (to abuse)
The **falling and rising tone** *mǎ* (horse)

Although the tonal aspect of the language is not as daunting as it seems, it's easy to make ghastly mistakes or be met with absolute incomprehension. A good way of learning the tones is to count to ten:

yī, èr, sān, sì, wǔ, lìu, qī, bā, jǐu, shí

As you struggle with this, bear in mind that Cantonese, spoken in the South, Hong Kong and Chinese restaurants around the world, has no fewer than nine tones.

Traditionally Chinese is written in **ideographs**, which while difficult in the extreme to comprehend, impart much beauty and fascination to the language. Numbering around 50,000 in all there's no easy way of learning them other than by doing your best to memorise as many as possible. A vocabulary of 2000 or so is needed to read a simple newspaper; a standard vocabulary consists of 4–5000; Even educated Chinese still come across characters they're unable to fathom without a dictionary. Not surprisingly dictionaries themselves are a complex affair, for without an alphabetical order the ideographs are arranged in order of the number of brushstrokes – from a single dash to the word for *flute* which has 17 strokes. Understanding ideographs is a matter of looking and learning as you go: here's a few examples with ideas to help remember them.

man (two legs)	人	rén
big (a man with arms outstretched)	大	dà
heaven (above man)	天	tiān
tree (which it looks like)	木	mù
wood (many trees)	林	lín
east (sun rising through trees)	东	dōng

As part of the drive for mass literacy, the script has been simplified in the People's Republic. The traditional script still used in Hong Kong and Taiwan is more aesthetically pleasing, but harder again to decode.

Another innovation under the Communists has been the **Pinyin** method of transliteration which we've used throughout this book. Replacing a former system known as the **Wade-Giles**, it removes the confusion caused by the use of hyphens and apostrophes: thus *Teng Hsiao-p'ing* has become *Deng Xiaoping*, Pei-ching Beijing and so on.

Many signs in China now appear in both Pinyin and ideographs, so many Chinese can read and understand advanced textbooks without being able to speak a word of English. Remember, too, that only in recent years *have* people been encouraged to talk to foreigners. They've heard rumours and seen tantalising glimpses of life outside China on television: you'll be beset by an audience wherever you go (especially on trains, where there's no escape) and expected to draw back the curtain a little on the rest of the world. The phrases that follow will be a starting point . . .

USEFUL WORDS AND PHRASES

Hello/How are you ?	ní hǎo	你好
Goodbye	zàijiàn	再见
Please	qǐng	请
Thank you	Xièxiè	谢谢
Yes/It is	shì	是
No/It isn't	bùshì	不是
Very good	hěn hǎo	很好
Very bad	hěn bù hǎo	很不好
Too much	tài duō	太多
Too little	tài shǎo	太少
I am sorry/excuse me	dùi bù qǐ	对不起
I can't speak Chinese	wǒ bù hùi jiǎng zhōngwén	我 不 会 讲 中文
May I/Is it allowed	Kěyǐ bù kěyǐ ?	可以不可以
Please tell me	qǐng gàosù wǒ	请告诉我
Wait a bit	Děngyīděng	等一等
I am English	wǒ shì yīnggúo rén	我是英国人
American	měigúo rén	美国人
Australian	aòdàlìyǎ rén	澳大利亚人
French	fǎgúo rén	法国人
German	dēgúo rén	德国人
I am a teacher	wǒ shì jiàoshī	我是教师
student	xüēshēng	学生
businessman	shāngrén	商人
doctor	yīshēng	医生
traveller	lǚyóu zhě	旅游者

Have you got/Is there ?	ni yǒu méiyǒu 你有没有
matches	huǒchái 火柴
chopsticks	kuàizi 筷子
I want/would like	wǒ yào 我要
to see a play/a film	kàn xì jù/diànyǐng 看戏剧/电影
to buy postcards /	mǎi míngxìnpiàn / 买明信片/
cigarettes	xiāngyān 香烟
to go to x	dào x qǔ 到 x 去

FINDING YOUR WAY ABOUT

Where is?	zài nálǐ ？ 在哪里
Where is the lavatory?	cèsuǒ zài nálǐ 厕所在哪里
Where is CITS	zhōngguó guójì lǚxíngshè zài nálǐ ？ 中国国际旅行社在哪里
Where is CAAC	zhōngguó hángkōng gōngsi zài nálǐ ？ 中国航空公司在哪里
How do I get to the museum?	dào bowùguǎn zěnme zǒu ？ 到 博物馆 怎么 走
How do I get to the park?	dào gōngyuán zěnme zǒu ？ 到 公园 怎么 走
I am lost	wǒ míle lù 我迷了路
directions	fāng xiàng 方向
North	běi 北
South	nán 南
East	dōng 东
West	xī 西
map	dìtú 地图
kilometre	gōnlǐ 公里
street	jiē or lù 街，路
bridge	qiáo 桥
temple	miào or sì 庙，寺

TRAVEL

railway train	huǒchē 火车
station	zhàn 站
bus/coach	gōnggòng qìchē 公共汽车
long distance station	chángtú qìchēzhàn 长途汽车站
boat	chuán 船
dock	mǎtou 码头
airplane	fēijī 飞机
airport	fēijī chǎng 飞机场

Which route/number bus ?	năyĭ lù qì chē ? 哪一路汽车
Which train ?	năyĭ hào huŏchē ? 哪一号火车
To get on	shàng chē 上车
To get off	xià chē 下车
What time does the train/	huŏchē/gōng gòng qìchē /chuán 火车／公 共 汽车／船
bus/boat leave ?	jĭ diăn zhōng chū fā ? 几 点 钟 出 发
When does it arrive ?	shēnme shíhòu dàodá ? 什么 时候 到达
I want to buy a ticket	wŏ yào măi chēpiào 我要买车票
oneway	dān chéng 单程
return	lái húi 来回
soft seat	ruănzuò 软座
soft berth	rŭanwò 软卧
hard seat	yìngzuò 硬座
hard berth	yìngwò 硬卧
timetable	shíkèbiăo 时刻表
to hire	zū 租
a bicycle	zìxíngchē 自行车
to call/order	jiào 叫
a taxi	chūzū qìchē 出租汽车

CASH, COMMUNICATIONS

Where is the Public Security Bureau ?	gōng ān jŭ zài nálĭ ? 公 安 局 在 哪里
I wish to extend my visa	wŏ yào yáncháng wŏ dè qiān zhèng 我要延长我的签证
I want a permit to visit x	wŏ yào dào x qŭ lŭyoúde qiān zhèng 我要到x去旅游的签证
passport	hùzhào 护照
post office	yóuzhèng jŭ 邮政局
stamp	yóupiào 邮票
airmail letter	hángkōngxìn 航空信
postcard	míngxìnpiàn 明信片
I want to make a telephone call	wŏ yào dă yī gè diànhùa 我 要 打 一 个 电话
bank	yínháng 银行
change money	huànqián 换钱
foreign exchange certificates	wàihùi jüàn 外汇券

people's money	rénmínbì 人民币
dollar	yuán/kuài 元/块
	= 10 máo/jiǎo 毛/角
	= 100 fēn 分
How much?	duōshǎo qián 多少钱
too expensive	tài guì 太贵
the cheapest	zùi piányí 最便宜

NUMBERS

1 2 3 4 5	yī èr sān sì wǔ 一 二 三 四 五
6 7 8 9 10	lìu qī bā júi shí 六 七 八 九 十
20	èrshí 二十
300	sānbǎi 三百
4000	sìqiān 四千
50000	wǔwàn 五万
one day	yī tīan 一天
two days	liǎng tīan 两天
three weeks	sāngè xīngqī 三个星期
four months	sìgē yüè 四个月
5 years	wǔ nían 五年

Monday to Sunday is expressed by putting the numbers 1-6 after xīngqī

Wednesday	xīngqī sān 星期三
Sunday	xīngqī tiān 星期天

TIME

When?	shénme shíhòu? 什么时候
now	xiànzài 现在
today	jīntiān 今天
yesterday	zúotiān 昨天
tomorrow	míngtīan 明天
the day after	hòutīan 后天
morning	zǎochén 早晨
afternoon	xìawǔ 下午
evening	wǎnshàng 晚上
What time is it?	jí diǎnzhōng? 几点钟
9 o'clock	júi diǎnzhōng 九点钟
12.30 pm	shíèr diǎn bàn 十二点半

When does it open?

shénme shíhòu kāimén ?
什 么 时候 开门

close?

guānmén 关门

ACCOMMODATION

hotel

fàndiàn 饭店

guesthouse

bīnguǎn 宾馆

hostel

zhāodàisuǒ 招待所

single room

dānrén fáng 单人房

double room

shuāngrén fáng 双人房

dormitory bed

chuángwèi 床位

old wing/floor

lǎo lóu 老楼

airconditioned

yǒu lěngqì dē 有冷气的

with bath/shower

yǒu yùshì 有浴室

fan

diànfēng shàn 电风扇

mosquito coil

wēn xiāng 蚊香

mosquito net

wēn zhàng 蚊帐

KEY TO PRONUNCIATION

This is to help in saying place names and streets.
For a more detailed explanation try one of the teach yourself books.

q is pronounced ch as in *ch*eek

x is pronounced hs or sh as in the *xi* of *taxi*

c is pronounced ts as in *its*

zh is pronounced j as in job

z is pronounced dz as in *adze*

INDEX

Accommodation 17
Altai Mountain Valleys 479
Amoy *see* Xiamen
Anhui province 283–90
Anning 398
Anyang 179
Aomen *see* Macau
Aqsu 480

Badaling 73
Baidicheng 435
Baiyinhushao 494
Baiyun Shan 339
Banks 10
Banpo 150
Baodingshan 431
Baoguo Si 420
Baotou 495
Bei'an 135
Beidaihe 97
Beihai 385
BEIJING 38–90
  Accommodation 43
  Air travel 43, 86, 90
  Badaling 73
  Bikes 49, 87
  Boats 89
  Buses 48, 89
  Chang'an 55
  China Art Gallery 68
  Cinema 84
  CITS 42
  Embassies 58, 87
  Forbidden City 59
  Friendship Store 58
  Great Wall 72
  Hall of the People 51
  History 39
  Imperial Palace 59
  Jie Tai Si 76
  Listings 86
  Lugouqiao 77
  Mao Memorial 50
  Map 44
  Markets 52, 87
  Metro 48
  Military Museum 56
  Ming Tombs 74
  Minority Peoples 56
  Miyun 76
  Modern 41
  Nightlife 85
  Observatory 67
  Opera 84
  Parks 64
  Qianmen 51
  Qinlongqiao 73
  Restaurants 78
  Shops 88
  Sport 85
  Summer palaces 69
  Tan Zhe Si 76
  Taxis 49
  Temple of Heaven 53
  Theatre 84
  Tian'anmen Square 49
  Tiantan 53
  Trains 43, 88
  University 68
  Western Hills 70
  Zoo 67
Beishan 430
Bezeklik 474
Bikes 15
Binyang 384
Boats 15
Bureaucracy 9
Buses 6, 14, 15

Canton City *see* Guangzhou
Canton province *see* Guangdong
Changjiang *see* Yangzi River
Changsha 302
Changshou 434
Changzhou 230
Chengde 93
Chengdu 410
Chibi 298
Chishi 359
Chongqing 425
Conghua 240
Contraceptives 31
Costs 10
Cuiheng 340
Currency 11

Dabancheng 480
Dali 400
Dalian 128
Datong 100
Dazu 430
Dengfeng 172
Dingshan 228
Dongbei 125
Donghe 495
Drinks 21
Drugs 31
Dunhuang 450

Emei Shan 418
Entertainment 27

Fengdu 435
Flights 5, 16
Food 18
Foshan 342
Fujian province 354–64
Fulong 434
Fuzhou 363

Gansu province 444–57
Glossary of terms 32
Goachang 473
Golmud 465
Gong Xian 170
Grand Canal 214
Great Wall 72, 449
Guangdong province 323–53
Guangxi province 368–87
GUANGZHOU 325–29
    Arrival 325
    Boat trips 334
    Cultural park 337
    Ershatou island 335
    Guangxiao Si 336
    Hotels 327
    Huai Shang mosque 336
    Listings 337
    Liuhua park 337
    Map 328
    Mausoleum of 72 Martyrs 335
    Memorial Gardens 335
    Orchid gardens 337
    Peasant Movement Training
        Institute 336
    Qingping market 333
    Restaurants 331
    Shamian island 334
    Sun Yatsen Memorial Hall 335
    Temple of the 6 Banyan Trees 336
    Yanjiang Lu 333
    Yuexiu park 336
Guanshan 340
Guanxian 415
Guilin 369
Guiyang 389
Guizhou Province 388–90
Gulangyu 357
Guling 316
Gyanze 520

Hailar 497
Hainan Island 348–53
    Access 348
    Baoting 353
    Haikou 350
    Luhuitou 353
    Miao'an 350
    Qiongzhong 353
    Sanya 352
    Tianya Haijiao 353

Xincum 352
Xinlung 352
Hangzhou 256
Hankou 290
Hanyang 294
Harbin 132
Health care 11
Hebei province 91–9
Hefei 284
Henan Province 159–83
Hengshan 307
Henyang 308
Hitching 14
Hohhot 491
Holidays 29
HONG KONG 526–38
    Aberdeen 534
    Arrival 528
    Causeway Bay 534
    Central District 532
    Chek Lap Kok 528
    Cheung Chau 537
    Hong Kong Island 532
    Hotels 530
    Kowloon 535
    Lamma 538
    Lantau 537
    New Territories 536
    Nightlife 531
    Outlying islands 536
    Repulse Bay 534
    Restaurants 531
    Stanley 534
    Tap Mun 538
    Transport 529
    Tsimshatsui 535
    Victorial Peak 534
    Walled City 536
    Wanchai 534
    Western District 533
    Yaumatei 536
Hotels 17
Hua Qing 153
Hua Shan 157
Huaian 252
Huangshan 286
Hubei province 290–301
Huitengxile 494
Human province 301–11

Inner Mongolia 488–98

Jiangmen 340
Jiangsu province 214–55
Jiangxi province 311–20
Jiayuguan 449
Jie Tai Si 76
Jinan 107
Jingdezhen 318
Jinggangshan 314

Jingzhou 299
Jinhong 406
Jiuhuashan 289
Jiujiang 315

Kaifeng 175
Karakoram Highway 7, 486
Kasa 522
Kashgar 481
Kashi *see* Kashgar
Khunjerab Pass 487
Korla 480
Kucha 480
Kunming 350

Labro 449
Labuleng Si *see* Labro
Lake Dianchi 396
Lake Erhai 402
Language courses 30
Lanzhou 44
Laoshan 119
Leshan 422
Lhasa 511
Liancheng 449
Lianyungang 255
Lijiang (river) 377
Lijiang (town) 404
Linxian 182
Liuzhou 381
Longmen Caves 165
Lugouqiao 77
Luoyang 160
Lushan 316

MACAU 538
Maijishan 449
Manchuria *see* Dongbei
Maoling 156
Maps 9
Ming Tombs (Beijing) 74
Ming Tombs (Nanjing) 251
Mixian 171
Miyun 75
Mogao caves 452

Nanchang 312
Nanjing 241–252
Nanning 381
Nanshan grasslands 479
Ningbo 272
Ningxia Autonomous Region 457

Opening hours 25

Package tours 7
Peking *see* Beijing
Penglai 122
Phones 24

Photography 28
Pingfang 134
Post 23
Puqi 298
Putuoshan 277

Qianling 155
Qingcheng Shan 417
Qingdao 116
Qinghai lake 464
Qinghai province 248–67
Qinlongqiao 73
Qiqihar 134
Qixia 252
Quanzhou 361
Qufu 112
Qutan Si 463

Red Flag Canal 182

Sakya 521
Samye 523
Sanjiakou 481
Shaanxi province 141–59
Shalong Nature Reserve 134
Shandong province 106–23
SHANGHAI 187–213
    Arts and Crafts Institute 205
    Banks 212
    Boats 194
    Botanical Gardens 207
    Bund 197
    Buses 193, 194
    CITS 189
    Consulates 212
    Entertainment 210
    French Concession 205
    History 187
    Hotels 195
    Huangpu 200
    Jingan Temple 206
    Listings 212
    Longhua 207
    Lu Xun 208
    Map 190
    Museum of Art 203
    Nanjing Lu 210
    Nightlife 210
    Old City 202
    Orientation 189
    Planes 193, 212
    Restaurants 208
    Sun Yatsen Museum 205
    Temple of the Jade Buddha 207
    Trains 193
    Yu Garden 203
    Zoo 207
Shangrao 358
Shanhaiguan 99
Shantou 341

Shanxi Province 100–6
Shaolin 173
Shaoshan 306
Shaowu 359
Shaoxing 269
Shapim 401
Shashi 299
Shenyang 129
Shenzhen 340
Shijiazhuang 91
Shilin stone forest 399
Sichuan province 408–37
Silk Road 439
Simao 406
Songshan 171
Suzhou 216

Taersi Monastery 462
Tai'an 107
Taihu lake 226
Taishan 109
Taiyuan 104
Taklamakan desert 481
Tan Zhe Si 76
Tashkorgan 487
Taxis 16
Terracotta Army 152
Tianchi lake 477
Tianjin 90
Tibet 501
Tingri 522
Tourist Offices 8
Trains 6, 12
Turfan 470
Turpan *see* Turfan

Urumqi 475

Visas 7

Wanxian 435
Water 32
West Lake 261
Work 29
Wuchang 295
Wudalianchi 135
Wudang Shan 300
Wudangzhao 496
Wuhan 290
Wuhu 285
Wulantuge 494
Wunengqu 136
Wuxi 224
Wuyi Mountain Natural Reserve 358
Wuyigong 360
Wuzhou 380

Xi'an 141
Xiamen 354
Xiang Jiang *see* Yangzi River
Xiangfan 300
Xianggang *see* Hong Kong
Xianning 299
Xigar 521
Xigaze 519
Xindu 415
Xing Sha Wan 494
Xingcun 359
Xingzi County 318
Xining 459
**Xinjiang Autonomous
   Region** 467–88
Xinyang 183
Xiqiao Hills 340
Xishan 397
Xishuang Banna 406
Xizang *see* Tibet
Xuanggong Si 104
Xuzhou 252

Yan'an 158
Yangshuo 379
Yangzhou 236
Yangzi river 282, 283–320, 433
Yantai 119
Yellow River 138, 140–183
Yengi Hissar *see* Yingjishah
Yichang 299
Yichum 136
Yinchuan 458
Yingjishah 485
Yixing 228
Youtingpu 430
Yueyang 308
Yungang caves 102
Yunnan province 390–406
Yunyang 435

Zedang 522
Zhanjiang 346
Zhaoling 155
Zhaoqing 344
Zhejiang province 255–79
Zhengzhou 168
Zhenjiang 233
Zhong Yue 173
Zhongwei 457
Zhongxian 435
Zhuzhou 307
Zijin Shan 250

•

HELP US UPDATE

This is the first edition of **The Rough Guide to China**. It's taken over two years to put together and combines the travelling and research of around a dozen people. Throughout the book's preparation, we've had to constantly revise and update as the Chinese have liberalised policies towards independent travellers (most dramatically in the recent scrapping of permits for 'open' destinations) and, alongside, a tourists' and travellers' infrastructure has emerged.

Using the guide, you will inevitably find a lot of changes. Obviously, they're impossible to predict, however the trend towards easier and expanded travel in China looks set and it's almost certain that you'll find more rather than less in terms of routes, hotels and eating places, and visitable towns and sites.

We will be starting work on a **new edition** of the guide almost as soon as this one is published and as usual we're looking for your contributions. Any response – even a few notes scribbled on a postcard – is really helpful, and additional accounts of newly opened areas or towns invaluable. As usual, we'll acknowledge any letters we use and send a free copy of the next edition (or any other *Rough Guide* if you prefer) for the best.

Please write to: **The Rough Guides**
21 Ravensdon Street
London SE11 4AQ.

The essentials of independent travel...

If you want to travel at your own pace, seeing what you want to see and keeping to a budget, the Rough Guide series and the services of STA Travel are invaluable.

STA Travel works exclusively for the independent traveller. We offer the greatest selection of low-cost fares worldwide, and we can follow these up with tours, accommodation and insurance. In China we can pre-book all your travel and accommodation, giving you the opportunity to discover the country on your own without the practical problems of going it alone. Or you can take one of our recommended fully guided tours, designed for those who want more than the usual package.

So when you've read the book and want to go travelling, make sure your first call is at STA Travel.

TRAVEL OFFICES:
74 Old Brompton Road, SW7
117 Euston Road, NW1
25 Queens Road, Bristol
ULU, Malet Street, WC1
Queen Mary College, E1
Imperial College, SW7
London School of Economics, WC2
Kent University

Enquiries and Bookings
01-581-1022

Government Bonded under ATOL 822 in Association with SATAC Charterers Ltd.